THE EVERLASTING LIGHT

THE EVERLASTING LIGHT

THE LORD SHALL BE UNTO THEE AN EVERLASTING LIGHT, AND THY GOD THY GLORY *Isaiah 60:19*

The King James Version of the Bible Chronologically Condensed

---

by

ERMA WOOD CARLSON

SECOND PRINTING 1967

LIBRARY OF CONGRESS CATALOG CARD NUMBER: 66-6322

PRINTED IN THE UNITED STATES OF AMERICA BY

THE THOMAS TODD COMPANY, BOSTON

DEDICATION

To the friends and relatives who have given encouragement and inspiration, and invaluable assistance, and especially to my husband and parents, this book is gratefully and lovingly dedicated.

FOREWORD

"The Everlasting Light" is the King James Version of the Bible chronologically condensed, and designed to be enjoyed. It is composed of three parts. The first part includes all of the books of the Old Testament and is also entitled "The Everlasting Light." The second part, "The Light Shineth" is the life and works of Jesus the Christ, and is the four gospels, Matthew, Mark, Luke, and John, woven together into a unified whole. The third part is called "Children of Light" and includes the acts and writings of the apostles, or the rest of the books of the New Testament.

"The Bible is a book of writings accepted by Christians as inspired by God, and of divine authority," (Webster's New International Dictionary.) The Bible says that "God is Spirit", so anything of "Divine authority" must be spiritual. Paul says, "The things of the Spirit . . . are spiritually discerned." It is from this point of view that the Bible is approached in making the selections for this book.

"In the beginning God . . ." states the opening theme. And this theme, God, One Power and man's relationship to Him, is like a golden thread running throughout the Bible.

The object is to maintain the thread of the history, and bring out the continuity of the Bible while leaving out much material not immediately essential to the overall picture. It is hoped that this simplification will lead to an increased understanding of the Bible, and a greater desire to read the Bible itself. The selections are the words of the King James version, considered by many people as the most beautiful of all versions, and the finest example of the best in our language. All titles are taken from the Bible.

A List of References, which is also the Table of Contents,

begins on page 1337. This List shows all references selected, and the order in which they are combined. Using only parts of some verses, and the entire elimination of others is the method of simplification in this book. The letter " p " after a reference shows that only part of that verse is used. This is done for two reasons: (1) to eliminate redundant wording; and (2) by combining descriptive words and phrases from several books relating the same incident, to build up the whole picture and make the incident more complete than as related in any one book. This method is especially effective in combining the four gospels into a unified whole. And laws taken from Exodus, Leviticus, and Deuteronomy are combined under the Ten Commandments. Also since the Second Book of Samuel and the First Book of Chronicles cover the same period, these books are woven together. And the same method is used for the First and Second Books of Kings and the Second Book of Chronicles. The Prophets are included with the kings, or in the period in which they prophesied.

All changes made in the Bible text are shown in the List of References with a few exceptions. Changes which are not always indicated are as follows: (1) The antecedent of a pronoun may be substituted for the pronoun. (2) The tense of a verb might be changed to agree with the tense of other verbs in the same paragraph. (3) Some words may be changed such as " begat " to " was the father of ", and " seed " to " children ". And in the Gospels, "Esaias " is changed to " Isaiah ", and " Elias " to " Elijah ". (4) The Book of Nehemiah and part of the Book of Acts, which in the Bible are in first person, are here written in third person for the sake of clearness.

Since many people know the Psalms by number, they are arranged in the List of References by number, and then the group and title of each, and the page on which it will be found.

The Proverbs are arranged by subjects, and these subjects will be found in alphabetical order in the List of References with the page reference for each.

The List of References makes it possible to use any Bible Concordance with this book. However, it must be remembered that because of eliminations not all references are found in this List.

A Glossary giving definitions from Webster and the other sources mentioned in the Bibliography, and also Biblical names and terms, is included, beginning on page 1269. The Glossary is also a restricted Index.

The Old Testament

"Thou shalt have no other gods before Me."

IN THE BEGINNING GOD

GOD SAW EVERYTHING THAT HE HAD MADE, AND BEHOLD, IT WAS VERY GOOD

IN THE BEGINNING God created the heaven and the earth. And the earth was without form, and void; and darkness was upon the face of the deep. And the Spirit of God moved upon the face of the waters.

And God said, "Let there be light:" and there was light. And God saw the light, that it was good. And God divided the light from the darkness. And God called the light Day, and the darkness he called Night. And the evening and the morning were the first day.

And God said, "Let there be a firmament in the midst of the waters, and let it divide the waters from the waters." And God made the firmament, and divided the waters which were under the firmament from the waters which were above the firmament: and it was so. And God called the firmament Heaven. And the evening and the morning were the second day.

And God said, "Let the waters under the heaven be gathered together unto one place, and let the dry land appear:" and it was so. And God called the dry land Earth; and the gathering together of the waters called he Seas: and God saw that it was good. And God said, "Let the earth bring forth grass, the herb yielding seed, and the fruit-tree yielding fruit after his kind, whose seed is in itself, upon the earth:" and it was so. And the earth brought forth grass, and herb yielding seed after his kind, and the tree yielding fruit, whose seed was in itself, after his kind; and God saw that it was good. And the evening and the morning were the third day.

And God said, "Let there be lights in the firmament of the heaven, to divide the day from the night; and let them be for signs, and for seasons, and for days, and years. And let them be for lights in the firmament of the heaven to give light upon the earth;" and it was so. And God made two great lights, the greater light to rule the day, and the lesser light to rule the night; he made the stars also. And God set them in the firmament of the heaven to give light upon the earth, and to rule over the day, and over the night, and to divide the light from the darkness; and God saw that it was good. And the evening and the morning were the fourth day.

And God said, "Let the waters bring forth abundantly the moving creature that hath life, and fowl that may fly above the earth in the open firmament of heaven." And God created great whales, and every living creature that moveth, which the waters brought forth abundantly after their kind, and every winged fowl after his kind; and God saw that it was good. And God blessed them, saying, "Be fruitful and multiply, and fill the waters in the seas, and let fowl multiply in the earth." And the evening and the morning were the fifth day.

And God said, "Let the earth bring forth the living creature after his kind, cattle, and creeping thing, and beast of the earth after his kind;" and it was so. And God made the beast of the earth after his kind, and cattle after their kind, and everything that creepeth upon the earth after his kind; and God saw that it was good.

And God said, "Let us make man in our image, after our likeness; and let them have dominion over the fish of the sea, and over the fowl of the air, and over the cattle, and over all the earth, and over every creeping thing that creepeth upon the earth." So God created man in his own image, in the image of God created he him; male and female created he them. And God blessed them, and God said unto them, "Be fruitful, and multiply, and replenish the earth, and subdue it; and have dominion over the fish of the sea, and over the fowl of the air, and over every living thing that moveth upon the earth." And God said, "Behold, I have given you every herb bearing seed, which is upon the face of all the earth, and every tree, in the which is the fruit of a tree yielding seed; to you it shall be for meat. And to every beast of the earth, and to every fowl of the air, and to every thing that creepeth upon the earth, wherein there is life, I have given every green herb for meat;" and it was so. And God saw every thing that he had made: and behold, it was very good. And the evening and the morning were the sixth day. Thus the heavens and the earth were finished, and all the host of them.

And on the seventh day God ended his work which he had made; and he rested on the seventh day from all his work which he had made. And God blessed the seventh day, and sanctified it, because that in it he had rested from all his work which God created and made.

These are the generations of the heavens and of the earth when they were created, in the day that the Lord God made the earth and the heavens, and every plant of the field before it was in the earth, and every herb of the field before it grew.

BUT THERE WENT UP A MIST FROM THE EARTH

But there went up a mist from the earth, and watered the whole face of the ground. And the Lord God formed man of the dust of the ground, and breathed into his nostrils the breath of life; and man became a living soul.

And the Lord God planted a garden eastward in Eden; and there he put the man whom he had formed. And out of the ground made the Lord God to grow every tree that is pleasant to the sight, and good for food; the tree of life also in the midst of the garden, and the tree of knowledge of good and evil. And a river went out of Eden to water the garden, and from thence it parted, and became four rivers.

And the Lord God took the man, and put him into the garden of Eden, to dress it, and to keep it. And the Lord God commanded the man, saying, "Of every tree of the garden thou mayest freely eat; but of the tree of the knowledge of good and evil, thou shalt not eat of it, for in the day that thou eatest thereof thou shalt surely die."

And the Lord God said, "It is not good that the man should be alone; I will make him an help meet for him." And out of the ground the Lord God formed every beast of the field, and every fowl of the air, and brought them unto Adam to see what he would call them; and whatsoever Adam called every living creature, that was the name thereof. And Adam gave names to all cattle, and to the fowl of the air, and to every beast of the field; but for Adam there was not found an help meet for him.

And the Lord God caused a deep sleep to fall upon Adam, and he slept. And God took one of his ribs, and closed up the flesh instead thereof; and the rib which the Lord God had taken from man, made he a woman, and brought her unto the man.

And Adam said, "This is now bone of my bones, and flesh of my flesh; she shall be called Woman, because she was taken out of man." Therefore shall a man leave his father and his mother, and shall cleave unto his wife, and they shall be one flesh.

WHERE ART THOU?

Now the serpent was more subtil than any beast of the field which the Lord God had made; and he said unto the woman, "Yea, hath God said, 'Ye shall not eat of every tree of the garden?'"

And the woman said unto the serpent, "We may eat of the fruit of the trees of the garden; but of the fruit of the tree which is in the midst of the garden, God hath said, 'Ye shall not eat of it, neither shall ye touch it, lest ye die.'"

And the serpent said unto the woman, "Ye shall not surely die; for God doth know, that in the day ye eat thereof, then your eyes shall be opened, and ye shall be as gods, knowing good and evil."

And when the woman saw that the tree was good for food, and that it was pleasant to the eyes, and a tree to be desired to make one wise, she took of the fruit thereof, and did eat, and gave also unto her husband with her, and he did eat. And the eyes of them both were opened, and they knew that they were naked; and they sewed fig-leaves together, and made themselves aprons.

And they heard the voice of the Lord God walking in the garden in the cool of the day. And Adam and his wife hid themselves from the presence of the Lord God amongst the trees of the garden.

And the Lord God called unto Adam, and said unto him, "Where art thou?"

And Adam said, "I heard thy voice in the garden, and I was afraid, because I was naked, and I hid myself."

And God said, "Who told thee that thou wast naked? Hast thou eaten of the tree whereof I commanded thee, that thou shouldest not eat?"

And the man said, "The woman whom thou gavest to be with me, she gave me of the tree, and I did eat."

And the Lord God said unto the woman, "What is this that thou hast done?"

And the woman said, "The serpent beguiled me, and I did eat."

And the Lord God said unto the serpent, "Because thou hast done this, thou art cursed above all cattle, and above every beast of the field; upon thy belly shalt thou go, and dust shalt thou eat all the days of thy life. And I will put enmity between thee and the woman, and between thy seed and her seed; it shall bruise thy head, and thou shalt bruise his heel."

Unto the woman he said, "I will greatly multiply thy sorrow and thy conception; in sorrow thou shalt bring forth children; and thy desire shall be to thy husband, and he shall rule over thee."

And unto Adam he said, "Because thou hast hearkened unto the voice of thy wife, and hast eaten of the tree of which I commanded thee, saying, 'Thou shalt not eat of it,' cursed is the ground for thy sake; in sorrow shalt thou eat of it all the days of thy life; thorns also and thistles shall it bring forth to thee; and thou shalt eat the herb of the field; in the sweat of thy face shalt thou eat bread, till thou return unto the ground; for out of it wast thou taken; for dust thou art, and unto dust shalt thou return." Unto Adam also and to his wife did the Lord God make coats of skins, and clothed them.

And the Lord God said, "Behold, the man is become as one of us, to know good and evil." And now, lest he put forth his hand, and take also of the tree of life, and eat, and live for ever, therefore the Lord God sent him forth from the garden of Eden, to till the ground from whence he was taken. So he drove out the man; and he placed at the east of the garden of Eden Cherubim, and a flaming sword which turned every way, to keep the way of the tree of life.

AM I MY BROTHER'S KEEPER?

AND ADAM called his wife's name Eve, because she was the mother of all living. And Eve bare Cain, and said, "I have gotten a man from the Lord." And she again bare his brother Abel. And Abel was a keeper of sheep, but Cain was a tiller of the ground.

And in process of time it came to pass, that Cain brought of the fruit of the ground an offering unto the Lord. And Abel, he also brought of the firstlings of his flock, and of the fat thereof. And the Lord had respect unto Abel, and to his offering, but unto Cain, and to his offering, he had not respect. And Cain was very wroth, and his countenance fell.

And the Lord said unto Cain, "Why art thou wroth? and why is thy countenance fallen? If thou doest well, shalt thou not be accepted? And if thou doest not well, sin lieth at the door; and unto thee shall be his desire, and thou shalt rule over him."

And Cain talked with Abel his brother; and it came to pass when they were in the field, that Cain rose up against Abel his brother, and slew him.

And the Lord said unto Cain, "Where is Abel thy brother?"

And he said, "I know not; am I my brother's keeper?"

And God said, "What hast thou done? the voice of thy brother's blood crieth unto me from the ground. And now art thou cursed from the earth, which hath opened her mouth to receive thy brother's blood from thy hand. When thou tillest the ground, it shall not henceforth yield unto thee her strength. A fugitive and a vagabond shalt thou be in the earth."

And Cain said unto the Lord, "My punishment is greater than I can bear. Behold, thou hast driven me out this day from the face of the earth; and from thy face shall I be hid; and I shall be a fugitive and a vagabond in the earth; and it shall come to pass, that every one that findeth me shall slay me."

And the Lord said unto him, "Therefore whosoever slayeth Cain, vengeance shall be taken on him seven-fold." And the Lord set a mark upon Cain, lest any finding him should kill him.

And Cain went out from the presence of the Lord, and dwelt in the land of Nod, on the east of Eden.

And again Eve bare a son, and called his name Seth, "For God," said she, "hath appointed me another child instead of Abel, whom Cain slew."

And generations lived after Adam, and sons and daughters were born to them. And Jared was the father of Enoch. And Enoch was the father of Methuselah. And Enoch walked with God: and he was not, for God took him.

And Methuselah was the father of Lamech; and Lamech was the father of a son; and he called his son's name Noah.

BUILD THEE AN ARK

AND it came to pass, when men began to multiply on the face of the earth, and daughters were born unto them, that the sons of God saw the daughters of men that they were fair; and they took them wives of all which they chose. There were giants in the earth in those days.

And God saw that the wickedness of man was great in the earth, and that every imagination of the thoughts of his heart was only evil continually. And it repented the Lord that he had made man on the earth, and it grieved him at his heart.

And the Lord said, " My Spirit shall not always strive with man, for that he also is flesh. I will destroy man whom I have created from the face of the earth; both man and beast, and the creeping thing, and the fowls of the air; for it repenteth me that I have made them."

But Noah found grace in the eyes of the Lord. Noah was a just man, and perfect in his generations, and Noah walked with God.

And God looked upon the earth, and behold, it was corrupt: for all flesh had corrupted his way upon the earth. And God said unto Noah, " The end of all flesh is come before me; for the earth is filled with violence through them; and behold, I will destroy them with the earth. Make thee an ark of gopher-wood; rooms shalt thou make in the ark, and shalt pitch it within and without

with pitch. A window shalt thou make to the ark, and the door of the ark shalt thou set in the side thereof. With lower, second, and third stories shalt thou make it. And behold, I, even I, do bring a flood of waters upon the earth, to destroy all flesh; and everything that is in the earth shall die.

"But with thee will I establish my covenant; and thou shalt come into the ark, thou, and thy sons, and thy wife, and thy sons' wives with thee. And of every living thing of all flesh, two of every sort shalt thou bring into the ark, to keep them alive with thee; they shall be male and female. Of fowls after their kind, and of cattle after their kind, of every creeping thing of the earth after his kind; two of every sort shall come unto thee, to keep them alive. And take thou unto thee of all food that is eaten; and thou shalt gather it to thee; and it shall be for food for thee, and for them."

Thus did Noah; according to all that God commanded him, so did he.

And the Lord said unto Noah, "Come thou and all thy house into the ark; for thee have I seen righteous before me in this generation. For yet seven days, and I will cause it to rain upon the earth forty days and forty nights; and every living substance that I have made will I destroy from off the face of the earth."

And Noah did according unto all that the Lord commanded him. In the self-same day entered Noah, and Shem, and Ham, and Japheth, the sons of Noah, and Noah's wife, and the three wives of his sons with them into the ark; they, and every beast after his kind, and all the cattle after their kind, and every creeping thing that creepeth upon the earth after his kind, and every fowl after his kind, every bird of every sort. And they went in unto Noah into the ark, two and two of all flesh, wherein is the breath of life, as God commanded him; and the Lord shut him in.

And it came to pass, after seven days, were all the fountains of the great deep broken up, and the windows of heaven were opened. And the waters increased, and bare up the ark, and it was lifted up above the earth. And the waters prevailed, and were increased greatly upon the earth; and the ark went upon the face of the waters. And the waters prevailed exceedingly upon the earth; and all the high hills that were under the whole heaven were covered. Fifteen cubits upward did the waters prevail; and the mountains were covered. And the rain was upon the earth forty days and forty nights.

And every living substance was destroyed which was upon the face of the ground, both man, and cattle, and the creeping things, and the fowl of the heavens; they were destroyed from the earth. And Noah only remained alive, and they that were with him in the ark.

And God remembered Noah, and every living thing, and all the cattle that was with him in the ark; and God made a wind to pass over the earth, and the waters assuaged. The fountains also of the deep, and the windows of heaven were stopped, and the rain from heaven was restrained. And the waters returned from off the earth continually. And the ark rested upon the mountain of Ararat. And the waters decreased continually, until the tops of the mountains were seen.

And it came to pass, that Noah opened the window of the ark which he had made, and he sent forth a raven, which went forth to and fro, until the waters were dried up from off the earth. Also he sent forth a dove from him, to see if the waters were abated from off the face of the ground. But the dove found no rest for the sole of her foot, and she returned unto him into the ark; for the waters were on the face of the whole earth. Then Noah put forth his hand, and took her, and pulled her in unto him into the ark. And he stayed yet other seven days; and again he sent forth the dove out of the ark. And the dove came in to him in the evening, and lo, in her mouth was an olive-leaf plucked off. So Noah knew that the waters were abated from off the earth. And he stayed yet other seven days, and sent forth the dove, which returned not again unto him any more.

And it came to pass that Noah removed the covering of the ark, and looked, and behold, the waters were dried up from off the earth; the face of the ground was dry.

And God spake unto Noah, saying, "Go forth of the ark, thou and every living thing that is with thee of all flesh; that they may be fruitful, and multiply upon the earth."

And Noah went forth, and his sons, and his wife, and his sons' wives with him; every beast, every creeping thing, and every fowl, and whatsoever creepeth upon the earth, after their kinds, went forth of the ark. And Noah builded an altar unto the Lord, and took of every clean beast, and of every clean fowl, and offered burnt-offerings on the altar.

And the Lord said in his heart, "While the earth remaineth, seed time and harvest, and cold and heat, and summer and winter, and day and night, shall not cease."

And God blessed Noah and his sons, and said unto them, "Be fruitful and multiply and replenish the earth. And I, behold, I establish my covenant with you, and with your children after you, and with every living creature that is with you. I will establish my covenant with you; neither shall all flesh be cut off any more by the waters of a flood; neither shall there any more be a flood to destroy the earth. This is the token of the covenant which I make between me and you and every living creature for perpetual generations: I do set my bow in the cloud, and it shall be for a token of a covenant between me and the earth. And it shall come to pass, when I bring a cloud over the earth, that the bow shall be seen in the cloud, and I will remember my covenant, which is between me and you and every living creature, and the waters shall no more become a flood to destroy all flesh."

And the sons of Noah were Shem, Ham and Japheth. And by the families of the sons of Noah were the nations divided in the earth after the flood.

BABEL

AND the whole earth was of one language, and of one speech. And it came to pass, as they journeyed from the east, that they found a plain in the land of Shinar; and they dwelt there.

And they said one to another, " Go to, let us make brick, and burn them throughly." And they had brick for stone, and slime had they for mortar.

And they said, " Go to, let us build us a city, and a tower, whose top may reach unto heaven; and let us make us a name, lest we be scattered abroad upon the face of the whole earth."

And the Lord came down to see the city and the tower, which the children of men builded. And the Lord said, " Behold, the people is one, and they have all one language; and this they begin to do, and now nothing will be restrained from them, which they have imagined to do. Go to, let us go down, and there confound their language, that they may not understand one another's speech."

So the Lord scattered them abroad from thence upon the face of all the earth; and they left off to build the city. Therefore is the name of it called Babel, because the Lord did there confound the language of all the earth; and from thence did the Lord scatter them abroad upon the face of all the earth.

GET THEE OUT OF THY COUNTRY AND FROM THY KINDRED UNTO A LAND THAT I WILL SHOW THEE

NOW TERAH was the father of Abram, Nahor, and Haran. And Haran was the father of Lot. And Haran died before his father Terah in the land of his nativity, in Ur of the Chaldees. And Abram and Nahor took them wives. The name of Abram's wife was Sarai; and the name of Nahor's wife was Milcah.

Now the Lord said unto Abram, " Get thee out of thy country, and from thy kindred, and from thy father's house, unto a land that I will show thee. And I will make thee a great nation, and I will bless thee, and make thy name great; and thou shalt be a blessing."

So Abram departed as the Lord had spoken unto him. And Abram took Sarai his wife, and Lot, his brother's son, and all their substance that they had gathered, and they went forth to go into the land of Canaan, and into the land of Canaan they came. And the Lord appeared unto Abram, and said, " Unto thy seed will I give this land; " and there Abram builded an altar unto the Lord, and called upon the name of the Lord.

And Abram journeyed going toward the south, for there was a famine in the land, and Abram went down into Egypt to sojourn there; for the famine was very grievous in the land.

And it came to pass when Abram was come near to enter into Egypt that he said to Sarai, his wife, " Behold now, I know that thou art a fair woman to look upon. Therefore it shall come to pass when the Egyptians shall see thee, that they shall say, ' This is his wife; ' and they will kill me, but they will save thee alive. Say, I pray thee, that thou art my sister; that it may be well with me for thy sake; and I shall live because of thee."

And it came to pass, that when Abram was come into Egypt, that the Egyptians beheld Sarai that she was very fair. And the princes commended her before Pharaoh, and Sarai was taken into Pharaoh's house. And Pharaoh treated Abram well for her sake.

But the Lord plagued Pharaoh and his house with great plagues, and Pharaoh called Abram and said, " What is this that thou hast done unto me? Why didst thou not tell me that Sarai was thy wife? Why saidst thou, ' She is my sister? so I might have taken her to me to wife: now therefore behold thy wife, take her, and go thy way." And Pharaoh commanded his men, and they sent Abram away.

And Abram went up out of Egypt, he and his wife and all that he had, and Lot with him. And they went forth to go into the land of Canaan, and into the land of Canaan they came.

LET THERE BE NO STRIFE BETWEEN ME AND THEE

AND ABRAM was very rich in cattle, and in silver, and in gold. And Lot also which went with Abram had flocks, and herds, and tents. And the land was not able to bear them, that they might dwell together, for their substance was great, so that they could not dwell together. And there was strife between the herdmen of Abram's cattle and the herdmen of Lot's cattle.

And Abram said unto Lot, " Let there be no strife, I pray thee, between me and thee, and between my herdmen and thy herdmen; for we be brethren. Is not the whole land before thee? Separate thyself, I pray thee, from me; if thou wilt take the left hand, then I will go to the right; or if thou depart to the right hand, then I will go to the left."

And Lot lifted up his eyes, and beheld all the plain of Jordan, that it was well watered everywhere. Then Lot chose him all the plain of Jordan; and Lot journeyed east, and they separated themselves the one from the other. And Abram dwelled in the land of Canaan, and Lot dwelled in the cities of the plain, and pitched his tent toward Sodom.

And the Lord said unto Abram, after that Lot was separated from him, " Lift up now thine eyes, and look from the place where thou art northward, and southward, and eastward, and westward, for all the land which thou seest, to thee will I give it, and to thy seed for ever. And I will make thy seed as the dust of the earth; so that if a man can number the dust of the earth, then shall thy seed also be numbered. Arise, walk through the land in the length of it and in the breadth of it; for I will give it unto thee."

Then Abram built there an altar unto the Lord.

MELCHIZEDEK, PRIEST OF THE MOST HIGH GOD

AND IT came to pass that Chedorlaomer, king of Elam, and other kings that were with him made war, and they came to Kadesh and smote all of the country of the Amalekites and also the Amorites. And there went out the king of Sodom and the king of Gomorrah and other kings with them, and they did battle in the vale of Siddim. And the vale of Siddim was full of slime pits. And the kings of Sodom and Gomorrah fled and fell there, and they that remained fled to the mountains.

And Chedorlaomer and the kings with him took all of the goods of Sodom and Gomorrah, and all their victuals. And they also took Lot, Abram's brother's son who dwelt in Sodom, and all his goods, and they went their way.

And there came one that had escaped, and told Abram. And when Abram heard that Lot was taken captive, he armed his trained servants, born in his own house, three hundred and eighteen and pursued them unto Dan. And Abram smote them by night and pursued them unto Hobak which is on the left of Damascus. And he brought back all the goods, and also brought back Lot, and all the women and all the people.

And the king of Sodom went out to meet Abram after his return from the slaughter of Chedorlaomer and the kings that were with him.

And Melchizedek, king of Salem, brought forth bread and wine: He was the priest of the most high God. And he blessed Abram and said, "Blessed be Abram of the most high God, possessor of heaven and earth: and blessed be the most high God which hath delivered the enemy into thy hand." And Abram gave Melchizedek tithes of all.

And the king of Sodom said unto Abram, "Give me the people and take the goods to thyself."

And Abram said to the king of Sodom, "I have lifted up mine hand unto the Lord, the most high God, the possessor of heaven and earth, that I will not take a thread, even to a shoelatchet, and that I will not take anything that is thine, lest thou shouldest say, 'I have made Abram rich;' save only that which the young men have eaten, and the portion of the men which went with me; let them take their portion."

And Abram went his way.

THE SON OF THE BOND-WOMAN

Now Sarai, Abram's wife, bare him no children; and she had an handmaid, an Egyptian, whose name was Hagar. And Sarai, Abram's wife, took Hagar her maid the Egyptian, after Abram had dwelt ten years in the land of Canaan, and gave her to her husband Abram to be his wife. And Hagar conceived; and when she saw that she had conceived, her mistress was despised in her eyes.

And Sarai said unto Abram, "My wrong be upon thee; I have given my maid into thy bosom; and when she saw that she had conceived, I was despised in her eyes; the Lord judge between me and thee."

But Abram said unto Sarai, "Behold, thy maid is in thy hand; do to her as it pleaseth thee." And when Sarai dealt hardly with her, Hagar fled from her face.

And the Angel of the Lord found Hagar by a fountain of water in the wilderness. And he said, "Hagar, Sarai's maid, whence camest thou? and wither wilt thou go?"

And she said, "I flee from the face of my mistress, Sarai."

And the Angel of the Lord said unto her, "Return to thy mistress, and submit thyself under her hands. Behold, thou shalt bear a son, and shalt call his name Ishmael; because the Lord hath heard thy affliction. And he will be a wild man; his hand will be against every man, and every man's hand against him; and he shall dwell in the presence of all his brethren."

And Hagar said, "Thou God seest me!" for she said, "Have I here looked after him that seeth me."

And Hagar bare Abram a son; and Abram called his son's name, which Hagar bare, Ishmael.

I AM THY EXCEEDING GREAT REWARD

And when Abram was ninety years old and nine, the Lord appeared to Abram, and said unto him, "Fear not, Abram; I am thy shield, and thy exceeding great reward; I am the Almighty God; walk before me and be thou perfect; and I will make my covenant between me and thee, and will multiply thee exceedingly."

And Abram fell on his face; and God talked with him, saying, "As for me, behold, my covenant is with thee, and thou shalt be a father of many nations. Neither shall thy name any more be called Abram; but thy name shall be Abraham; for a father of many nations have I made thee."

And God brought him forth abroad, and said, "Look now toward heaven, and tell the stars, if thou be able to number them. So shall thy seed be." And Abraham believed in the Lord; and he counted it to him for righteousness.

And he said unto him, "I am the Lord that brought thee out of Ur of the Chaldees, to give thee this land to inherit it. And I will establish my covenant between me and thee, and thy seed after thee, in their generations, for an everlasting covenant; to be a God unto thee, and to thy seed after thee. And I will give unto thee, and to thy seed after thee, the land wherein thou art a stranger, all the land of Canaan, for an everlasting possession; and I will be their God."

And God said unto Abraham, "As for Sarai thy wife, thou shalt not call her name Sarai, but Sarah shall her name be. And I will bless her, and give thee a son also of her; yea, I will bless her, and she shall be a mother of nations; kings of people shall be of her."

Then Abraham fell upon his face, and laughed, and said in his heart, "Shall a child be born unto him that is an hundred years old? and shall Sarah, that is ninety years old bear?"

And Abraham said unto God, "O that Ishmael might live before thee!"

And God said, "Sarah thy wife shall bear thee a son indeed; and thou shalt call his name Isaac; and I will establish my covenant with him for an everlasting covenant, and with his seed after him. And as for Ishmael, I have heard thee; behold, I have blessed him, and will make him fruitful, and will multiply him exceedingly; he shall be the father of twelve princes, and I will make him a great nation. But my covenant will I establish with Isaac which Sarah shall bear unto thee at this set time in the next year."

And he left off talking with him, and God went up from Abraham.

THE CHILD OF PROMISE

AND ABRAHAM sat in the tent door in the heat of the day. And he lifted up his eyes and looked, and lo, three men stood by him. And when he saw them, he ran to meet them from the tent door, and bowed himself toward the ground, and said, "My Lord, if now I have found favour in thy sight, pass not away, I pray thee, from thy servant. Let a little water, I pray you, be fetched, and wash your feet, and rest yourselves under the tree. And I will fetch a morsel of bread, and comfort ye your hearts; after that ye shall pass on; for therefore are ye come to your servant."

And they said, "So do, as thou hast said."

And Abraham hastened into the tent unto Sarah, and said, "Make ready quickly three measures of fine meal, knead it, and make cakes upon the hearth."

And Abraham ran unto the herd, and fetched a calf tender and good, and gave it unto a young man; and he hasted to dress it. And he took butter, and milk, and the calf which he had dressed, and set it before them; and he stood by them under the tree, and they did eat.

And they said unto him, "Where is Sarah thy wife?"

And he said, "Behold, in the tent."

And he said, "I will certainly return unto thee according to the time of life; and lo, Sarah thy wife shall have a son."

And Sarah heard it in the tent door, which was behind him. Now Abraham and Sarah were old and well stricken in age. Therefore Sarah laughed within herself.

And the Lord said unto Abraham, "Wherefore did Sarah laugh, saying, 'Shall I of a surety bear a child, which am old?' Is any thing too hard for the Lord? At the time appointed I will return unto thee, according to the time of life, and Sarah shall have a son."

Then Sarah denied, saying, "I laughed not," for she was afraid.

And he said, "Nay, but thou didst laugh."

And the men rose up from thence, and looked toward Sodom; and Abraham went with them to bring them on the way.

WILT THOU NOT SPARE THE PLACE FOR THE RIGHTEOUS?

AND THE LORD SAID, "Shall I hide from Abraham that thing which I do, seeing that Abraham shall surely become a great and mighty nation, and all the nations of the earth shall be blessed in him? For I know him, that he will command his children and his household after him, and they shall keep the way of the Lord, to do justice and judgment; that the Lord may bring upon Abraham that which he hath spoken of him."

And the Lord said, "Because the cry of Sodom and Gomorrah is great, and because their sin is very grievous, I will go down now, and see whether they have done altogether according to the cry of it, which is come unto me; and if not, I will know." And the men turned their faces from thence, and went toward Sodom; but Abraham stood yet before the Lord.

And Abraham drew near, and said, "Wilt thou also destroy the righteous with the wicked? Peradventure there be fifty righteous within the city; wilt thou also destroy and not spare the place for the fifty righteous that are therein? That be far from thee to do after this manner, to slay the righteous with the wicked; and that the righteous should be as the wicked, that be far from thee. Shall not the Judge of all the earth do right?"

And the Lord said, "If I find in Sodom fifty righteous within the city, then I will spare all the place for their sakes."

And Abraham answered and said, "Behold now, I have taken

upon me (which am but dust and ashes) to speak unto the Lord, peradventure there shall lack five of the fifty righteous; wilt thou destroy all the city for lack of five?"

And the Lord said, "If I find there forty and five, I will not destroy it."

And Abraham spake unto him yet again, and said, "Peradventure there shall be forty found there?"

And the Lord said, "I will not do it for forty's sake."

And Abraham said unto him, "Oh, let not the Lord be angry, and I will speak: Peradventure there shall thirty be found there."

And he said, "I will not do it if I find thirty there."

And Abraham said, "Behold now, I have taken upon me to speak unto the Lord; Peradventure there shall be twenty found there."

And he said, "I will not destroy it for twenty's sake."

And Abraham said, "Oh, let not the Lord be angry, and I will speak yet but this once: Peradventure ten shall be found there."

And the Lord said, "I will not destroy it for ten's sake." And the Lord went his way, as soon as he had left communing with Abraham; and Abraham returned unto his place.

LOOK NOT BEHIND THEE

And there came two angels to Sodom at evening; and Lot sat in the gate of Sodom; and Lot seeing them, rose up to meet them; and he bowed himself with his face toward the ground; and he said, "Behold now, my lords, turn in I pray you, into your servant's house, and tarry all night, and wash your feet, and ye shall rise up early, and go on your ways."

And they said, "Nay; but we will abide in the street all night."

But Lot pressed upon them greatly; and they turned in unto him, and entered into his house; and he made them a feast, and did bake unleavened bread, and they did eat.

But before they lay down, the men of the city, even the men of Sodom, compassed the house round, both old and young, all the people from every quarter, and they called unto Lot, and said unto him, "Where are the men which came in to thee this night? Bring them out unto us, that we may know them."

And Lot went out at the door unto them, and shut the door after him, and said, "I pray you, brethren, do not so wickedly. Behold now, I pray you, unto these men do nothing, for therefore came they under the shadow of my roof."

And they said, "Stand back. This one fellow came in to sojourn, and he will needs be a judge; now will we deal worse with thee than with them." And they pressed sore upon Lot, and came near to break the door. But the men put forth their hand, and pulled Lot into the house to them, and shut to the door. And they smote the men that were at the door of the house with blindness, both small and great, so that they wearied themselves to find the door.

And the men said unto Lot, "Hast thou here any besides? sons-in-law, and thy sons, and thy daughters, and whatsoever thou hast in the city, bring them out of this place. For we will destroy this place, because the cry of them is waxen great before the face of the Lord; and the Lord hath sent us to destroy it."

And Lot went out, and spake unto his sons-in-law, which married his daughters, and said, "Up, get you out of this place; for the Lord will destroy this city;" but he seemed as one that mocked unto his sons-in-law.

And when the morning arose, then the angels hastened Lot, saying, "Arise, take thy wife, and thy two daughters which are here, lest thou be consumed in the iniquity of the city." And while he lingered, the angels laid hold upon his hand, and upon the hand of his wife, and upon the hand of his two daughters, the

Lord being merciful unto him, and they brought him forth, and set him without the city.

And it came to pass, when the angel had brought them forth abroad, that he said, " Escape for thy life; look not behind thee, neither stay thou in all the plain; escape to the mountain, lest thou be consumed."

And Lot said unto them, " Oh, not so, my Lord! behold now, thy servant hath found grace in thy sight, and thou hast magnified thy mercy, which thou hast showed unto me in saving my life; and I cannot escape to the mountain, lest some evil take me, and I die. Behold now, this city is near to flee unto, and it is a little one. Oh, let me escape thither! Is it not a little one? And my soul shall live."

And the angel said unto him, " See, I have accepted thee concerning this thing also, that I will not overthrow this city, for the which thou hast spoken. Haste thee, escape thither; for I cannot do any thing till thou be come thither." Therefore the name of the city was called Zoar.

The sun was risen upon the earth when Lot entered into Zoar. Then the Lord rained upon Sodom and upon Gomorrah brimstone and fire out of heaven; and he overthrew those cities, and all the plain, and all the inhabitants of the cities, and that which grew upon the ground. But Lot's wife looked back from behind him, and she became a pillar of salt.

And Abraham got up early in the morning, and he looked toward Sodom and Gomorrah, and toward all the land of the plain, and beheld, and, lo, the smoke of the country went up as the smoke of a furnace. And it came to pass, when God destroyed the cities of the plain, that God remembered Abraham, and sent Lot out of the midst of the overthrow, when He overthrew the cities in the which Lot dwelt.

And Lot went up out of Zoar, and dwelt in the mountain, and his two daughters with him.

THE BOND-WOMAN AND HER SON IN THE WILDERNESS

AND THE LORD did unto Sarah as he had spoken, for Sarah bare Abraham a son in his old age, at the set time of which God had spoken to him. And Abraham called the name of his son, that was born unto him, whom Sarah bare to him, Isaac. And Abraham was an hundred years old when his son Isaac was born unto him.

And the child grew and was weaned; and Abraham made a great feast the same day that Isaac was weaned. And Sarah saw Ishmael, the son of Hagar the Egyptian, which she had born unto Abraham, mocking.

Wherefore Sarah said unto Abraham, "Cast out this bond-woman and her son; for the son of this bond-woman shall not be heir with my son, even with Isaac." And the thing was very grievous in Abraham's sight because of his son.

And God said unto Abraham, "Let it not be grievous in thy sight, because of the lad, and because of thy bond-woman; in all that Sarah hath said unto thee, hearken unto her voice; for in Isaac shall thy seed be called. And also of Ishmael, the son of the bond-woman, will I make a nation, because he is thy seed."

And Abraham rose up early in the morning, and took bread, and a bottle of water, and gave it unto Hagar, putting it on her shoulder, and the child, and sent her away; and she departed, and wandered in the wilderness of Beer-sheba.

And the water was spent in the bottle, and Hagar cast Ishmael under one of the shrubs. And she went, and sat her down over against him, a good way off, as it were a bow-shot; for she said, "Let me not see the death of the child." And she sat over against him, and lifted up her voice, and wept.

And God heard the voice of the lad; and the angel of God called to Hagar out of heaven, and said unto her, "What aileth thee, Hagar? Fear not; for God hath heard the voice of the lad where he is. Arise, lift up the lad, and hold him in thine hand; for I will make him a great nation." And God opened her eyes, and she saw a well of water; and she went, and filled the bottle with water, and gave the lad drink.

And God was with Ishmael; and he grew, and dwelt in the wilderness, and became an archer. And he dwelt in the wilderness of Paran; and his mother took him a wife out of the land of Egypt.

GOD WILL PROVIDE HIMSELF A LAMB

AND IT CAME to pass after these things, that God did tempt Abraham, and said unto him, "Abraham."

And he said, "Behold, here I am."

And he said, "Take now thy son, thine only son Isaac, whom thou lovest, and get thee into the land of Moriah; and offer him there for a burnt-offering upon one of the mountains which I will tell thee of."

And Abraham rose up early in the morning, and saddled his ass, and took two of his young men with him, and Isaac his son, and clave the wood for the burnt-offering, and rose up, and went unto the place of which God had told him. Then on the third day Abraham lifted up his eyes, and saw the place afar off.

And Abraham said unto his young men, "Abide ye here with the ass; and I and the lad will go yonder and worship, and come again to you." And Abraham took the wood of the burnt-offering, and laid it upon Isaac his son; and he took fire in his hand, and a knife; and they went both of them together.

And Isaac spake unto Abraham his father, and said, "My father."

And he said, "Here am I, my son."

And Isaac said, "Behold the fire and the wood; but where is the lamb for a burnt-offering?"

And Abraham said, " My son, God will provide himself a lamb for a burnt-offering;" so they went both of them together.

And they came to the place which God had told him of; and Abraham built an altar there, and laid wood in order.

And the angel of the Lord called unto him out of heaven, and said, "Abraham, Abraham."

And he said, " Here am I."

And the angel said, " Lay not thine hand upon the lad, for now I know that thou fearest God, seeing thou hast not withheld thy son, thine only son from me."

And Abraham lifted up his eyes, and looked, and behold behind him a ram caught in a thicket by his horns; and Abraham went and took the ram, and offered him up for a burnt-offering in the stead of his son.

And the angel of the Lord called unto Abraham out of heaven the second time, and said, " By myself have I sworn, because thou hast done this thing, and hast not withheld thy son, thine only son, that in blessing I will bless thee, and in multiplying I will multiply thy seed as the stars of the heaven, and as the sand which is upon the sea shore; and thy seed shall possess the gate of his enemies; and in thy seed shall all the nations of the earth be blessed; because thou hast obeyed my voice."

So Abraham returned unto his young men, and they rose up and went together to Beer-sheba; and Abraham dwelt at Beer-sheba.

And it came to pass after these things, that Sarah died. Sarah was an hundred and seven and twenty years old. And Abraham came to mourn for Sarah, and to weep for her. And Abraham buried Sarah his wife in the cave of the field of Machpelah, in the land of Canaan.

THE LORD SHALL SEND HIS ANGEL BEFORE THEE

And Abraham was old, and well stricken in age; and the Lord had blessed Abraham in all things. And Abraham said unto his eldest servant of his house, that ruled over all that he had, "Put, I pray thee, thy hand under my thigh, and I will make thee swear by the Lord, the God of heaven, and the God of the earth, that thou shalt not take a wife unto my son of the daughters of the Canaanites, among whom I dwell. But thou shalt go unto my country, and to my kindred, and take a wife unto my son Isaac."

And the servant said unto him, "Peradventure the woman will not be willing to follow me unto this land; must I needs bring thy son again unto the land from whence thou camest?"

And Abraham said unto him, "Beware thou, that thou bring not my son thither again. The Lord God of heaven, which took me from my father's house, and that sware unto me, saying, 'Unto thy seed will I give this land,' He shall send His angel before thee, and thou shalt take a wife unto my son from thence. And if the woman will not be willing to follow thee, then thou shalt be clear from this my oath; only bring not my son thither again."

And the servant put his hand under the thigh of Abraham, his master, and sware to him concerning that matter. And the servant took ten camels, of the camels of his master, for all the goods of his master were in his hand, and he arose, and went to Mesopotamia, unto the city of Nahor.

And he made his camels to kneel down without the city by a well of water at the time of the evening, even the time that women go out to draw water. And he said, "O Lord God of my master Abraham, I pray thee, send me good speed this day, and show kindness unto my master Abraham. Behold, I stand here by the well of water; and the daughters of the men of the city come out to draw water. Let it come to pass, that the damsel to whom I shall say, 'Let down thy pitcher, I pray thee, that I may drink,' and she shall say, 'Drink, and I will give thy camels drink also,' let the same be she that thou hast appointed for thy servant Isaac. And thereby shall I know that thou hast shown kindness unto my master."

And it came to pass, before he had done speaking, that behold, Rebekah came out, who was born to Bethuel, son of Milcah, the wife of Nahor, Abraham's brother, with her pitcher upon her shoulder. And the damsel was very fair to look upon; and she went down to the well, and filled her pitcher, and came up.

And the servant ran to meet her, and said, "Let me, I pray thee, drink a little water of thy pitcher."

And she said, "Drink, my lord;" and she hasted, and let down her pitcher upon her hand, and gave him drink. And when she had done giving him drink, she said, "I will draw water for thy camels also, until they have done drinking." And she hasted, and emptied her pitcher into the trough, and ran again unto the well to draw water, and drew for all his camels.

And the man wondering at her held his peace, to wit whether the Lord had made his journey prosperous or not. And it came to pass, as the camels had done drinking, that the man took a golden ear-ring of half shekel weight, and two bracelets for her hands of ten shekels weight of gold, and said unto her, "Whose daughter art thou? tell me, I pray thee, is there room in thy father's house for us to lodge in?"

And she said unto him, "I am the daughter of Bethuel the son of Milcah, which she bare unto Nahor. We have both straw and provender enough, and room to lodge in."

And the man bowed down his head, and worshipped the Lord, and he said, "Blessed be the Lord God of my master Abraham, who hath not left destitute my master of his mercy and his truth: I being in the way, the Lord led me to the house of my master's brethren."

And the damsel ran, and told them of her mother's house these things. And Rebekah had a brother, and his name was Laban. And it came to pass, when he saw the ear-ring and bracelets upon his sister's hands, and when he heard the words of Rebekah his sister, saying, "Thus spake the man unto me," that he ran out unto the man, and, behold, he stood by the camels at the well.

And Laban said, "Come in, thou blessed of the Lord; wherefore standest thou without? for I have prepared the house, and room for the camels." And the man came into the house. And Laban ungirded his camels, and gave straw and provender for the camels, and water to wash the man's feet, and the men's feet that were with him.

And there was set meat before him to eat, but the man said, "I will not eat, until I have told mine errand."

And Laban said, "Speak on."

And he said, "I am Abraham's servant. And the Lord hath blessed my master greatly; and he hath given him flocks, and herds, and silver, and gold, and men-servants, and maid-servants, and camels, and asses; and he is become great. And Sarah my master's wife bare a son to my master when she was old; and unto him hath he given all that he hath. And my master made me swear, saying, 'Thou shalt not take a wife to my son of the daughters of the Canaanites, in whose land I dwell, but thou shalt go unto my father's house, and to my kindred, and take a wife unto my son. The Lord, before whom I walk, will send his angel with thee, and prosper thy way; and thou shalt take a wife for my son of my kindred. And when thou comest to my kindred, if they give not thee one, thou shalt be clear from my oath.'

"And I came this day unto the well, and said, 'O Lord God of my master Abraham, if now thou do prosper my way which I go: behold, I stand by the well of water; and it shall come to pass, that when the virgin cometh forth to draw water, and I say to her, 'Give me, I pray thee, a little water of thy pitcher to drink,' and she say to me, 'Both drink thou, and I will also draw for thy camels,' let the same be the woman whom the Lord hath appointed out for my master's son.' And before I had done speaking in mine heart, behold, Rebekah came forth with her pitcher on her shoulder, and she went down unto the well, and drew water. And I said unto her, 'Let me drink, I pray thee.' And she made haste, and let down her pitcher from her shoulder, and said, 'Drink, and I will give thy camels drink also;' so I drank, and she made the camels drink also. And I put the ear-ring upon her face, and the bracelets upon her hands; and I bowed down my head, and worshipped the Lord; and blessed the Lord God of my master Abraham, which had led me in the right way to take my master's brother's daughter unto his son. And now if ye will deal kindly and truly with my master, tell me; and if not, tell me; that I may turn to the right hand, or to the left."

Then Laban and Bethuel answered and said, "The thing proceedeth from the Lord: we cannot speak unto thee bad or good. Behold, Rebekah is before thee, take her, and go, and let her be thy master's son's wife, as the Lord hath spoken."

And it came to pass, that, when Abraham's servant heard their words, he worshipped the Lord bowing himself to the earth. And he brought forth jewels of silver, and jewels of gold, and raiment, and gave them to Rebekah; he gave also to her brother and to her mother precious things.

And they did eat and drink, he and the men that were with him, and tarried all night. And they rose up in the morning, and he said, "Send me away unto my master."

And her brother and her mother said, "Let the damsel abide with us a few days, at the least ten, after that she shall go."

And he said unto them, "Hinder me not, seeing the Lord hath prospered my way; send me away, that I may go to my master."

And they said, "We will call the damsel, and enquire at her mouth." And they called Rebekah, and said unto her, "Wilt thou go with this man?"

And she said, "I will go."

And they blessed Rebekah; and they sent away Rebekah their sister, and her nurse. And Rebekah arose, and her damsels, and they rode upon the camels, and followed Abraham's servant, and his men.

And Isaac went out to meditate in the field at the eventide. And he lifted up his eyes, and saw, and, behold the camels were coming. And Rebekah lifted up her eyes, and when she saw Isaac, she lighted off the camel, for she said unto the servant, " What man is this that walketh in the field to meet us? "

And the servant said, " It is my master; " therefore she took a vail and covered herself.

And the servant told Isaac all things that he had done. And Isaac brought her into his mother Sarah's tent, and took Rebekah, and she became his wife, and he loved her. And Isaac was comforted after his mother's death.

And these are the days of the years of Abraham's life which he lived, an hundred threescore and fifteen years. Then Abraham died in a good old age, an old man, and full of years; and was gathered to his people. And his sons Isaac and Ishmael buried him in the cave of Machpelah; there was Abraham buried, and Sarah his wife.

TWO NATIONS, AND TWO MANNER OF PEOPLE

And Isaac was forty years old when he took Rebekah to wife. And Isaac entreated the Lord for his wife, because she was barren: and the Lord was entreated of him, and Rebekah his wife conceived.

And the children struggled together within her; and she said, "If it be so, why am I thus?" And she went to inquire of the Lord.

And the Lord said unto her, "Two nations, and two manner of people shalt thou bear; and the one people shall be stronger than the other people; and the elder shall serve the younger."

And behold, Rebekah bare twins. And the first was red all over like an hairy garment; and they called his name Esau. And after that came his brother, and his name was called Jacob. And Isaac was threescore years old when she bare them.

And Isaac waxed great, and went forward and grew until he became very great: for he had possession of herds, and great store of servants.

WHAT PROFIT SHALL THIS BIRTHRIGHT DO ME?

And the boys grew; and Esau was a cunning hunter, a man of the field; and Jacob was a plain man, dwelling in tents. And Isaac loved Esau, because he did eat of his venison; but Rebekah loved Jacob.

And Jacob sod pottage. And Esau came from the field, and he was faint. And Esau said to Jacob, "Feed me, I pray thee, with that same red pottage, for I am faint."

And Jacob said, "Sell me this day thy birthright."

And Esau said, "Behold, I am at the point to die; and what profit shall this birthright do to me?"

And Jacob said, "Swear to me this day;" and he sware unto him; and he sold his birthright unto Jacob. Then Jacob gave Esau bread and pottage of lentiles; and he did eat and drink, and rose up, and went his way. Thus Esau despised his birthright.

BLESS ME, EVEN ME ALSO, O MY FATHER!

AND IT CAME TO PASS, that when Isaac was old, and his eyes were dim, so that he could not see, he called Esau his eldest son, and said unto him, "My son."

And Esau said unto him, "Behold, here am I."

And Isaac said, "Behold now, I am old; I know not the day of my death. Now therefore take, I pray thee, thy weapons, thy quiver and thy bow, and go out to the field, and take me some venison; and make me savoury meat, such as I love, and bring it to me, that I may eat; that my soul may bless thee before I die." And Esau went to the field to hunt for venison, and to bring it.

And Rebekah heard when Isaac spake to Esau. And Rebekah spake unto Jacob, saying, "Behold, I heard thy father speak unto Esau thy brother, saying, 'Bring me venison, and make me savoury meat, that I may eat, and bless thee before the Lord before my death.' Now therefore, my son, obey my voice according to that which I command thee. Go now to the flock, and fetch me from thence two good kids of the goats; and I will make them savoury meat for thy father, such as he loveth. And thou shalt bring it to thy father, that he may eat, and that he may bless thee before his death."

And Jacob said to Rebekah his mother, "Behold, Esau my brother is a hairy man, and I am a smooth man. My father peradventure will feel me, and I shall seem to him as a deceiver; and I shall bring a curse upon me, and not a blessing."

And his mother said unto him, " Upon me be thy curse, my son; only obey my voice, and go fetch me them."

And he went, and fetched, and brought them to his mother; and his mother made savoury meat, such as his father loved. And Rebekah took goodly raiment of her eldest son, Esau, which were with her in the house, and put them upon Jacob her younger son. And she put the skins of the kids of the goats upon his hands, and upon the smooth of his neck. And she gave the savoury meat and the bread, which she had prepared, into the hand of her son Jacob.

And he came unto his father, and said, " My father."

And Isaac said, " Here am I; who art thou, my son? "

And Jacob said unto his father, " I am Esau thy first-born; I have done according as thou badest me. Arise, I pray thee, sit and eat of my venison, that thy soul may bless me."

And Isaac said unto his son, " How is it that thou hast found it so quickly, my son? "

And he said, " Because the Lord thy God brought it to me."

And Isaac said unto Jacob, " Come near, I pray thee, that I may feel thee, my son, whether thou be my very son Esau or not." And Jacob went near unto Isaac his father; and he felt him, and said, " The voice is Jacob's voice, but the hands are the hands of Esau." And he discerned him not, because his hands were hairy, as his brother Esau's hands. And he said, " Art thou my very son Esau? "

And Jacob said, " I am."

And Isaac said, " Bring it near to me, and I will eat of my son's venison, that my soul may bless thee." And he brought it near to him, and Isaac did eat; and he brought him wine, and he drank.

And Isaac said unto him, " Come near now, and kiss me, my son." And he came near, and kissed him. And Isaac smelled the smell of his raiment, and blessed him, and said, " See, the smell of my son is as the smell of a field which the Lord hath blessed.

Therefore God give thee of the dew of heaven, and the fatness of the earth, and plenty of corn and wine. Let people serve thee, and nations bow down to thee; be lord over thy brethren, and let thy mother's sons bow down to thee; cursed be every one that curseth thee, and blessed be he that blesseth thee."

And it came to pass, as soon as Isaac had made an end of blessing Jacob, and Jacob was yet scarce gone out from the presence of Isaac his father, that Esau his brother came in from his hunting. And he also had made savoury meat, and brought it unto his father, and said unto his father, "Let my father arise, and eat of his son's vension, that thy soul may bless me."

And Isaac said unto him, "Who art thou?"

And he said, "I am thy son, thy first-born Esau."

And Isaac trembled very exceedingly, and said, "Who? Where is he that hath taken venison, and brought it me, and I have eaten of all before thou camest, and have blessed him? Yea, and he shall be blessed."

And when Esau heard the words of his father, he cried with a great and exceeding bitter cry, and said unto his father, "Bless me, even me also, O my father!"

And Isaac said, "Thy brother came with subtilty, and hath taken away thy blessing."

And Esau said, "Is not he rightly named Jacob? for he hath supplanted me these two times: he took away my birth-right; and, behold, now he hath taken away my blessing." And he said, "Hast thou not reserved a blessing for me?"

And Isaac said unto Esau, "Behold, I have made him thy lord, and all his brethren have I given to him for servants; and with corn and wine have I sustained him; and what shall I do now unto thee, my son?"

And Esau said, "Hast thou but one blessing, my father? Bless me, even me also, O my father!" And Esau lifted up his voice and wept.

And Isaac said unto him, "Behold, thy dwelling shall be the

fatness of the earth, and of the dew of heaven from above. And by thy sword shalt thou live, and shalt serve thy brother; and it shall come to pass when thou shalt have the dominion, that thou shalt break his yoke from off thy neck."

And Esau hated Jacob because of the blessing wherewith his father blessed him.

GOD IS IN THIS PLACE, AND I KNEW IT NOT

And Esau said in his heart, "The days of mourning for my father are at hand; then will I slay my brother Jacob."

And these words of Esau were told to Rebekah, and she sent and called Jacob her younger son, and said unto him, "Behold, thy brother Esau, as touching thee, doth comfort himself, purposing to kill thee. Now therefore, my son, obey my voice; and arise, flee to Laban my brother to Haran, and tarry with him a few days, until thy brother's anger turn away from thee, and he forget that which thou hast done to him; then I will send, and fetch thee from thence."

And Rebekah said to Isaac, "I am weary of my life because of the daughters of Heth; if Jacob take a wife of the daughters of Heth, such as these which are of the daughters of the land, what good shall my life do me?"

And Isaac called Jacob, and blessed him, and said unto him, "Thou shalt not take a wife of the daughters of Canaan. Arise, go to the house of Bethuel thy mother's father; and take thee a wife from thence of the daughters of Laban thy mother's brother. And God Almighty bless thee, and make thee fruitful, and multiply thee, and give the blessing of Abraham to thee, and to thy seed with thee; that thou mayest inherit the land wherein thou art a stranger, which God gave unto Abraham."

And Isaac sent away Jacob. And Jacob went out from Beer-sheba, and went toward Haran. And he lighted upon a certain place, and tarried there all night, because the sun was set. And he took of the stones of that place, and put them for his pillows, and lay down in that place to sleep.

And he dreamed, and behold a ladder set up on the earth, and the top of it reached to heaven; and behold the angels of God ascending and descending on it. And behold, the Lord stood above it and said,

"I am the Lord God of Abraham thy father, and the God of Isaac; the land whereon thou liest, to thee will I give it, and to thy seed; and thy seed shall be as the dust of the earth, and thou shalt spread abroad to the west, and to the east, and to the north, and to the south; and in thee and in thy seed shall all the families of the earth be blessed. And behold, I am with thee, and will keep thee in all places whither thou goest, and will bring thee again into this land; for I will not leave thee, until I have done that which I have spoken to thee of."

And Jacob awaked out of his sleep, and he said, "Surely, the Lord is in this place, and I knew it not." And he was afraid and said, "How dreadful is this place! this is none other but the house of God, and this is the gate of heaven."

And Jacob rose up early in the morning, and took the stone that he had put for his pillows, and set it up for a pillar, and poured oil upon the top of it. And he called the name of that place Beth-el.

And Jacob vowed a vow, saying, "If God will be with me, and will keep me in this way that I go, and will give me bread to eat, and raiment to put on, so that I come again to my father's house in peace, then shall the Lord be my God; and this stone, which I have set for a pillar, shall be God's house; and of all that thou shalt give me I will surely give the tenth unto thee."

Then Jacob went on his journey.

I WILL SERVE THEE SEVEN YEARS FOR RACHEL

Then Jacob came into the land of the people of the east. And he looked, and behold a well in the field, and lo, there were three flocks of sheep lying by it; for out of that well they watered the flocks; and a great stone was upon the well's mouth. And thither were all the flocks gathered; and they rolled the stone from the well's mouth, and watered the sheep, and put the stone again upon the well's mouth in his place.

And Jacob said unto them, "My brethren, whence be ye?"

And they said, "Of Haran are we."

And he said, "Know ye Laban the son of Nahor?"

And they said, "We know him."

And Jacob said unto them, "Is he well?"

And they said, "He is well. And behold, Rachel his daughter cometh with the sheep." And while he yet spake, Rachel came with her father's sheep, for she kept them.

And it came to pass, when Jacob saw Rachel the daughter of Laban his mother's brother, that Jacob went near, and rolled the stone from the well's mouth, and watered the flock of Laban. And Jacob kissed Rachel, and lifted up his voice, and wept. And Jacob told Rachel that he was Rebekah's son. And Rachel ran and told her father.

And it came to pass, when Laban heard the tidings of Jacob his sister's son, that he ran to meet him, and embraced him, and kissed him, and brought him to his house. And Laban said to him, "Surely thou art my bone and my flesh." And Jacob abode with him the space of a month.

And Laban said unto Jacob, "Because thou art my brother, shouldst thou therefore serve me for nought? tell me, what shall thy wages be?"

And Laban had two daughters: the name of the elder was Leah, and the name of the younger was Rachel. Leah was tender-eyed; but Rachel was beautiful and well-favoured. And

Jacob loved Rachel; and said, "I will serve thee seven years for Rachel thy younger daughter."

And Laban said, "It is better that I give her to thee, than that I should give her to another man; abide with me."

And Jacob served seven years for Rachel; and they seemed unto him but a few days, for the love he had to her. And Jacob said unto Laban, "Give me my wife, for my days are fulfilled."

And Laban gathered together all the men of the place, and made a feast. And it came to pass in the evening, that he took Leah his daughter, and brought her to Jacob.

And Jacob said to Laban, "What is this thou hast done unto me? did not I serve with thee for Rachel? wherefore then hast thou beguiled me?"

And Laban said, "It must not be so done in our country, to give the younger before the first-born. Fulfil her week, and we will give thee Rachel also for the service which thou shalt serve with me yet seven other years."

And Jacob did so, and fulfilled Leah's week; and Laban gave him Rachel his daughter to wife also. And Jacob loved Rachel more than Leah, and served with Laban yet seven other years.

And Leah bare a son, and she called his name Reuben; for she said, "Surely the Lord hath looked upon my affliction; now therefore my husband will love me." And she again bare a son, and said, "Because the Lord hath heard that I was hated, he hath therefore given me this son also;" and she called his name Simeon. And after that there were born unto Jacob, Levi, Judah, Dan, Naphtali, Gad, Asher, Issachar, Zebulum, and a daughter Dinah.

But Rachel was barren. And when Rachel saw that she bare Jacob no children, she envied her sister, and said unto Jacob, "Give me children, or else I die." And God remembered Rachel, and God hearkened to her, and she conceived, and bare a son. And she called his name Joseph.

THE LORD WATCH BETWEEN ME AND THEE

AND IT CAME TO PASS, when Rachel had born Joseph, that Jacob said unto Laban, " Send me away, that I may go unto mine own place, and to my country. Give me my wives and my children, for whom I have served thee, and let me go, for thou knowest the service which I have done thee."

And Laban said unto him, " I pray thee, if I have found favour in thine eyes, tarry; for I have learned by experience that the Lord hath blessed me for thy sake. Appoint me thy wages, and I will give it."

And Jacob said, "Thou knowest how I have served thee; for it was little which thou hadst before I came, and it is now increased unto a multitude; and the Lord hath blessed thee since my coming. And now, when shall I provide for mine own house also? "

And Laban said, " What shall I give thee? "

And Jacob said, "Thou shalt not give me any thing; if thou wilt do this thing for me, I will again feed and keep thy flock. I will pass through all thy flock today, removing from thence all the speckled and spotted cattle, and all the brown cattle among the sheep, and the spotted and speckled among the goats; of such shall be my hire. Every one that is not speckled and spotted among the goats, and brown among the sheep, that shall be counted stolen with me."

And Laban said, "Behold, I would it might be according to thy word." And he removed that day the he-goats that were ring-streaked and spotted, and all the she-goats that were speckled and spotted, and every one that had some white in it, and all the brown among the sheep, and gave them into the hand of his sons. And he set three days journey betwixt himself and Jacob.

And Jacob fed the rest of Laban's flocks. And Jacob took him rods of green poplar, and of the hazel and chestnut-tree, and pilled white streaks in them, and made the white appear which was in the rods. And he set the rods which he had pilled before the flocks in the gutters in the watering-troughs when the flocks came to drink. And the flocks conceived before the rods, and brought forth cattle ring-streaked, speckled, and spotted. And when the stronger cattle did conceive, Jacob laid the rods before the eyes of the cattle in the gutters. But when the cattle were feeble, he put them not in; so the feebler were Laban's and the stronger Jacob's. And Jacob did separate the lambs, and he put his own flocks by themselves, and put them not unto Laban's cattle. And Jacob increased exceedingly, and had much cattle, and maid-servants, and men-servants, and camels, and asses.

And Jacob heard the words of Laban's sons, saying, "Jacob hath taken away all that was our father's; and of that which was our father's hath he gotten all this glory." And Jacob beheld the countenance of Laban, and, behold, it was not toward him as before.

And the Lord said unto Jacob, "Return unto the land of thy fathers, and to thy kindred; and I will be with thee."

And Jacob sent and called Rachel and Leah to the field unto his flock, and said unto them, "I see your father's countenance, that it is not toward me as before; but the God of my father hath been with me. And ye know that with all my power I have served your father. And your father hath deceived me, and changed my wages ten times; but God suffered him not to hurt me. If he said thus, 'The speckled shall be thy wages;' then all the cattle bare speckled; and if he said thus, 'The ring-streaked shall be thy hire;' then bare all the cattle ring-streaked. Thus God hath taken away the cattle of your father, and given them to me. And the angel of God spake unto me in a dream, saying, 'Jacob, arise, get thee out from this land, and return unto the land of thy kindred.'"

And Rachel and Leah answered, and said unto him, "Is there yet any portion or inheritance for us in our father's house? Are we not counted of him strangers? for he hath sold us, and hath quite devoured also our money. For all the riches which God hath taken from our father, that is ours, and our children's; now then, whatsoever God hath said unto thee, do."

Then Jacob rose up, and set his sons and his wives upon camels; and he carried away all his cattle, and all his goods which he had gotten, for to go to Isaac his father in the land of Canaan. And Jacob stole away unawares to Laban, in that he told him not that he fled. So Jacob fled with all that he had.

And it was told Laban on the third day, that Jacob fled. And he took his brethren with him, and pursued after him seven days journey. And God came to Laban in a dream by night, and said unto him, "Take heed that thou speak not to Jacob either good or bad."

Then Laban overtook Jacob. And Laban said to Jacob, "What hast thou done, that thou hast stolen away unawares to me, and carried away my daughters, as captives taken with the sword? Wherefore didst thou flee away secretly, and steal away from me, and didst not tell me, that I might have sent thee away with mirth, and with songs, with tabret, and with harp? And hast not suffered me to kiss my sons and my daughters? thou hast now done foolishly in so doing. It is in the power of my hand to do you hurt; but the God of your fathers spake unto me yesterday night, saying, 'Take thou heed that thou speak not to Jacob either good or bad.' And now, though thou wouldest needs be gone, because thou sore longedst after thy father's house, yet wherefore hast thou stolen my gods?" Now Rachel had stolen the images that were her father's, but Jacob knew not that Rachel had stolen them.

And Jacob answered and said to Laban, "I was afraid; for I said, peradventure thou wouldest take by force thy daughters from me. With whomsoever thou findest thy gods, let him not live."

And Laban went into Jacob's tent, and into Leah's tent, and into the two maid-servants' tents; but he found them not. Then went he out of Leah's tent, and entered into Rachel's tent. Now Rachel had taken the images, and put them in the camel's furniture, and sat upon them. And she said to her father, "Let it not displease my lord that I cannot rise up before thee." And Laban searched all the tent, but found them not.

And Jacob was wroth, and said to Laban, "What is my trespass? what is my sin, that thou hast so hotly pursued after me? Whereas thou hast searched all my stuff, what hast thou found of all thy household stuff? set it here before my brethren and thy brethren, that they may judge betwixt us both. This twenty years have I been with thee: I served thee fourteen years for thy two daughters, and six years for thy cattle; and thou hast changed my wages ten times. Except the God of my father had been with me, surely thou hadst sent me away now empty. God hath seen mine affliction and the labour of my hands, and rebuked thee yesternight."

And Laban answered and said unto Jacob, "These daughters are my daughters, and these children are my children, and these cattle are my cattle, and all that thou seest is mine; and what can I do this day unto these my daughters, or unto their children which they have born? Now therefore come thou, let us make a covenant, I and thou; and let it be for a witness between me and thee."

And Jacob took a stone, and set it up for a pillar. And Jacob said unto his brethren, "Gather stones;" and they took stones and made an heap; and they did eat there upon the heap.

And Laban said, "This heap is a witness between me and thee this day. The Lord watch between me and thee, when we are absent one from another. This heap be witness, and this pillar be witness, that I will not pass over this heap to thee, and that thou shalt not pass over this heap and this pillar unto me for harm. The God of Abraham judge betwixt us."

Then Jacob offered sacrifice upon the mount, and called his brethren to eat bread; and they did eat bread, and tarried all night in the mount. And early in the morning Laban rose up, and kissed his sons and his daughters, and blessed them, and Laban departed, and returned unto his place.

I WILL NOT LET THEE GO, EXCEPT THOU BLESS ME

And Jacob went on his way. And he sent messengers before him to Esau, his brother, unto the land of Seir, the country of Edom. And he commanded them saying, "Thus shall ye speak unto my lord Esau; 'Thy servant Jacob saith thus: "I have sojourned with Laban, and stayed there until now. And I have oxen, and asses, flocks, and men-servants, and women-servants. And I have sent to tell my lord, that I may find grace in thy sight." ' "

And the messengers returned to Jacob, saying, "We came to thy brother Esau, and also he cometh to meet thee, and four hundred men with him."

Then Jacob was greatly afraid, and distressed; and he divided the people that were with him, and the flocks, and herds, and the camels, into two bands, and said, "If Esau come to the one company, and smite it, then the other company which is left shall escape."

And Jacob said, "O God of my father Abraham, and God of my father Isaac, the Lord which saidst unto me, 'Return unto thy country, and to thy kindred, and I will deal well with thee;' I am not worthy of the least of all the mercies, and of all the truth which thou hast showed unto thy servant. Deliver me, I pray thee, from the hand of my brother, from the hand of Esau, for I fear him lest he will come and smite me, and the mother with the children. And thou saidst, 'I will surely do thee good, and make thy seed as the sand of the sea, which cannot be numbered for multitude.' "

And Jacob lodged there that same night; and took of that which came to his hand a present for Esau his brother: two hundred and twenty goats, two hundred and twenty sheep, thirty milk camels with their colts, fifty cattle, thirty asses. And he delivered them into the hand of his servants, every drove by themselves; and said unto his servants, " Pass before me, and put a space betwixt drove and drove." And he commanded the foremost, saying, " When Esau my brother meeteth thee, and asketh thee saying, ' Whose art thou? and whither goest thou? and whose are these before thee? ' Then thou shalt say, ' They be thy servant Jacob's; it is a present sent unto my lord Esau; and behold, also he is behind us.' " And so commanded Jacob the second, and the third, and all that followed the droves; for he said, " I will appease Esau with the present that goeth before me, and afterward I will see his face; peradventure he will accept of me." So went the present over before him. And Jacob took his wives and his eleven sons, and sent them over the brook, and sent over all that he had.

And Jacob was left alone; and there wrestled a man with him, until the breaking of the day. And when he saw that he prevailed not against him, he touched the hollow of his thigh; and the hollow of Jacob's thigh was out of joint, as he wrestled with him.

And he said, " Let me go, for the day breaketh."

And Jacob said, " I will not let thee go, except thou bless me."

And he said unto him, " What is thy name? "

And he said, " Jacob."

And he said, " Thy name shall be called no more Jacob, but Israel: for as a prince hast thou power with God, and with men, and hast prevailed."

And Jacob asked him, and said, " Tell me, I pray thee, thy name."

And he said, " Wherefore is it that thou dost ask after my name? " And he blessed him there.

And Jacob called the name of the place Peniel: "For I have seen God face to face, and my life is preserved."

And as Jacob passed over, the sun rose upon him.

I SAW THY FACE, AS THOUGH IT WERE THE FACE OF GOD

And Jacob lifted up his eyes, and looked, and, behold, Esau came, and with him four hundred men. And Jacob divided the children unto Leah, and unto Rachel, and unto the two handmaids. And he passed over before them, and bowed himself to the ground seven times, until he came near to his brother.

And Esau ran to meet him, and embraced him, and fell on his neck, and kissed him; and they wept. And Esau lifted up his eyes, and saw the women and the children, and said, "Who are those with thee?"

And Jacob said, "The children which God hath graciously given thy servant." And Leah with her children came near, and bowed themselves; and after came Joseph near and Rachel, and they bowed themselves.

And Esau said, "What meanest thou by all this drove which I met?"

And Jacob said, "These are to find grace in the sight of my lord."

And Esau said, "I have enough, my brother; keep that thou hast unto thyself."

And Jacob said, "Nay, I pray thee, if now I have found grace in thy sight, then receive my present at my hand; for therefore I have seen thy face, as though I had seen the face of God, and thou wast pleased with me. Take, I pray thee, my blessing that is brought to thee; because God hath dealt graciously with me, and because I have enough;" and he urged him, and he took it.

So Esau returned that day on his way unto Seir. And Jacob journeyed to Succoth, and built him an house, and made booths for his cattle.

And Rachel bare Jacob another son. And it came to pass, as her soul was in departing, for she died, that she called his name Ben-oni; but his father called him Benjamin. And Rachel died and was buried; and Jacob set a pillar upon her grave.

And Jacob came unto Isaac, his father. And the days of Isaac were an hundred and fourscore years. And Isaac died, and was gathered unto his people, being old and full of days; and his sons Esau and Jacob buried him.

HEAR THIS DREAM WHICH I HAVE DREAMED

AND JACOB dwelt in the land of Canaan. And Joseph, being seventeen years old, fed the flock with his brethren. Now Jacob loved Joseph more than all his children, because he was the son of his old age, and he made him a coat of many colours. And when his brethren saw that their father loved Joseph more than all his brethren, they hated him, and could not speak peaceably unto him.

And Joseph dreamed a dream, and he told it his brethren, and they hated him yet the more. And he said, "Hear, I pray you, this dream which I have dreamed. Behold, we were binding sheaves in the field, and lo, my sheaf arose, and stood upright; and behold, your sheaves stood round about, and made obeisance to my sheaf."

And his brethren said to him, "Shalt thou indeed reign over us? or shalt thou indeed have dominion over us?" And they hated him yet the more for his dreams, and for his words.

And Joseph dreamed yet another dream, and told it his brethren, and said, "Behold, I have dreamed a dream more. Behold, the sun and the moon and the eleven stars made obeisance to me."

And he told it to his father, and to his brethren, and his father rebuked him, and said to him, "What is this dream that thou hast dreamed? Shall I and thy mother and thy brethren indeed come to bow down ourselves to thee to the earth?" And his brethren envied him, but his father observed the saying.

And his brethren went to feed their father's flock in Shechem. And Jacob said unto Joseph, "Do not thy brethren feed the flock in Shechem? Go, I pray thee, see whether it be well with thy brethren, and well with the flocks, and bring me word again."

And Joseph went after his brethren, and found them. And when they saw him afar off, even before he came near unto them, they said one to another, "Behold, this dreamer cometh. Come now therefore, and let us slay him, and cast him into some pit, and we will say, 'Some evil beast hath devoured him,' and we shall see what will become of his dreams."

And Reuben heard it, and said, "Let us not kill him. Shed no blood, but cast him into this pit that is in the wilderness, and lay no hand upon him," that Reuben might rid him out of their hands to deliver him to his father again.

And it came to pass, when Joseph was come unto his brethren, that they stript Joseph out of his coat, his coat of many colours that was on him. And they took him, and cast him into a pit; and the pit was empty, there was no water in it. And they sat down to eat bread. And they lifted up their eyes and looked, and behold, a company of Ishmaelites came with their camels bearing spicery, and balm, and myrrh, going to carry it down to Egypt.

And Judah said unto his brethren, "What profit is it if we slay our brother, and conceal his blood? Come, and let us sell him to the Ishmaelites and let not our hand be upon him, for he is our brother and our flesh." And his brethren were content. And they drew and lifted up Joseph out of the pit, and sold Joseph to the Ishmaelites for twenty pieces of silver.

And Reuben returned unto the pit, and behold, Joseph was not in the pit, and he rent his clothes. And he returned unto his brethren, and said, "The child is not, and I, whither shall I go?"

And they took Joseph's coat, and killed a kid of the goats, and dipped the coat in the blood, and brought the coat of many colours to their father, and said, "This have we found; know now whether it be thy son's coat or no."

And Jacob knew it, and said, "It is my son's coat. An evil beast hath devoured him. Joseph is without doubt rent in pieces." And Jacob rent his clothes, and put sackcloth upon his loins, and mourned for his son many days. And all his sons and all his daughters rose up to comfort him, but he refused to be comforted, and he said, "For I will go down into the grave unto my son mourning." Thus his father wept for him.

DO NOT INTERPRETATIONS BELONG TO GOD?

And Joseph was brought down to Egypt; and Potiphar, an officer of Pharaoh, captain of the guard, an Egyptian, bought him of the hands of the Ishmaelites.

And the Lord was with Joseph; and his master saw that the Lord was with him, and that the Lord made all that he did to prosper in his hand. And Joseph found grace in his sight, and served him. And Potiphar made him overseer over his house, and all that he had he put into his hand. And it came to pass, from the time he made Joseph overseer in his house, and over all that he had, that the Lord blessed the Egyptian's house for Joseph's sake; and the blessing of the Lord was upon all that he had in the house, and in the field. And he left all that he had in Joseph's hand; and he knew not aught he had, save the bread which he did eat.

And Joseph was a goodly person, and well-favoured. And it came to pass after these things, that his master's wife cast her eyes upon Joseph; and she said, "Lie with me."

But he refused, and said unto his master's wife, "Behold, my master hath committed all that he hath to my hand. There is none greater in this house than I; neither hath he kept back any thing from me, but thee, because thou art his wife; how then can I do this great wickedness, and sin against God?"

And it came to pass, as she spake to Joseph day by day, that he hearkened not unto her to be with her. And it came to pass about this time, that Joseph went into the house, and there was none of the men of the house within, and she caught him by his garment, saying, "Lie with me," and he left his garment in her hand, and fled, and got him out.

And she laid up his garment by her, until his lord came home. And she spake unto him, saying, "The Hebrew servant, which thou hast brought unto us, came in unto me to mock me; and it came to pass, as I lifted up my voice and cried, that he left his garment with me, and fled out."

And when Potiphar heard the words of his wife, his wrath was kindled. And he took Joseph and put him into the prison, a place where the king's prisoners were bound.

And Joseph was there in the prison; but the Lord was with him, and showed him mercy, and gave him favour in the sight of the keeper of the prison. And the keeper of the prison committed to Joseph's hand all the prisoners that were in the prison. And the Lord was with Joseph; and that which he did, the Lord made it to prosper.

And it came to pass after these things, that Pharaoh was wroth against the chief of the butlers, and against the chief of the bakers. And he put them into the prison where Joseph was bound. And the captain of the guard charged Joseph with them, and he served them.

And they dreamed a dream both of them. And Joseph came in unto them in the morning, and looked upon them, and behold, they were sad. And he asked them, saying, "Wherefore look ye so sadly today?"

And they said unto him, "We have dreamed a dream, and there is no interpreter of it."

And Joseph said unto them, "Do not interpretations belong to God? tell me them, I pray you."

And the chief butler told his dream to Joseph and said to him, "In my dream, behold, a vine was before me; and in the vine were three branches; and it was as though it budded, and her blossoms shot forth; and the clusters thereof brought forth ripe grapes. And Pharaoh's cup was in my hand, and I took the grapes, and pressed them into Pharaoh's cup, and I gave the cup into Pharaoh's hand."

And Joseph said unto him, "This is the interpretation of it: The three branches are three days; within three days shall Pharaoh lift up thy head, and restore thee unto thy place; and thou shalt deliver Pharaoh's cup into his hand, after the former manner when thou wast his butler. But think on me when it shall be well with thee, and show kindness, I pray thee, unto me, and make mention of me unto Pharaoh, and bring me out of this house. For indeed I was stolen away out of the land of the Hebrews; and here also have I done nothing that they should put me into the dungeon."

When the chief baker saw that the interpretation was good, he said unto Joseph, "I also was in my dream, and, behold, I had three white baskets on my head; and in the uppermost basket there was of all manner of bake-meats for Pharaoh; and the birds did eat them out of the basket upon my head."

And Joseph answered, and said, "This is the interpretation thereof: The three baskets are three days; yet within three days shall Pharaoh lift up thy head from off thee, and shall hang thee on a tree; and the birds shall eat thy flesh from off thee."

And it came to pass the third day, which was Pharaoh's birthday, that he made a feast unto all his servants; and he lifted up the head of the chief butler and of the chief baker among his servants. And he restored the chief butler unto his butlership again; and he gave the cup into Pharaoh's hand. But he hanged the chief baker, as Joseph had interpreted to them. Yet did not the chief butler remember Joseph, but forgot him.

GOD SHALL GIVE PHARAOH AN ANSWER OF PEACE

AND IT CAME TO PASS, at the end of two full years, that Pharaoh dreamed: and, behold, he stood by the river. And, behold, there came up out of the river seven well-favoured kine and fat-fleshed; and they fed in a meadow. And, behold, seven other kine came up after them out of the river, ill-favoured and lean-fleshed; and stood by the other kine upon the brink of the river. And the ill-favoured and lean-fleshed kine did eat up the seven well-favoured and fat kine. So Pharaoh awoke.

And he slept and dreamed the second time: and, behold, seven ears of corn came up upon one stalk, rank and good. And, behold, seven thin ears and blasted with the east wind sprung up after them. And the seven thin ears devoured the seven rank and full ears. And Pharaoh awoke, and, behold, it was a dream.

And it came to pass in the morning, that his spirit was troubled; and he sent and called for all the magicians of Egypt, and all the wise men thereof; and Pharaoh told them his dream; but there was none that could interpret them unto Pharaoh.

Then spake the chief butler unto Pharaoh, saying, "I do remember my faults this day. When Pharaoh was wroth with his servants, and put me in prison in the captain of the guard's house, both me and the chief baker, we dreamed a dream in one night, I and he. And there was there with us a young man, an Hebrew, servant to the captain of the guard, and we told him, and he interpreted to us our dreams. And it came to pass, as he interpreted to us, so it was: me he restored unto mine office, and him he hanged."

Then Pharaoh sent and called Joseph, and they brought him hastily out of the dungeon; and he shaved himself, and changed his raiment, and came in unto Pharaoh. And Pharaoh said unto Joseph, "I have dreamed a dream, and there is none that can interpret it; and I have heard say of thee, that thou canst understand a dream to interpret it."

And Joseph answered Pharaoh, saying, "It is not in me: God shall give Pharaoh an answer of peace."

And Pharaoh said unto Joseph, "In my dream, behold, I stood upon the bank of the river: and, behold, there came up out of the river seven kine, fat-fleshed, and well-favoured; and they fed in a meadow. And, behold, seven other kine came up after them, poor, and very ill-favoured, and lean fleshed, such as I never saw in all the land of Egypt for badness. And the lean and ill-favoured kine did eat up the first seven fat kine; and when they had eaten them up, it could not be known that they had eaten them; but they were still ill-favoured, as at the beginning. So I awoke. And I saw in my dream, and, behold, seven ears came up in one stalk, full and good. And, behold, seven ears, withered, thin, and blasted with the east wind, sprung up after them; and the thin ears devoured the seven good ears. And I told this unto the magicians; but there was none that could declare it to me."

And Joseph said unto Pharaoh, "The dream of Pharaoh is one: God hath showed Pharaoh what he is about to do. The seven good kine are seven years; and the seven good ears are seven years; the dream is one. And the seven thin and ill-favoured kine that came up after them are seven years; and the seven empty ears blasted with the east wind shall be seven years of famine. What God is about to do He showeth unto Pharaoh. Behold, there come seven years of great plenty throughout all the land of Egypt; and there shall arise after them seven years of famine; and all the plenty shall be forgotten in the land of Egypt; and the famine shall consume the land; and the plenty shall not be known in the land by reason of that famine following; for it shall be very grievous. And for that the dream was doubled unto

Pharaoh twice; it is because the thing is established by God, and God will shortly bring it to pass. Now therefore let Pharaoh look out a man discreet and wise, and set him over the land of Egypt. Let Pharaoh do this, and let him appoint officers over the land, and take up the fifth part of the land of Egypt in the seven plenteous years. And let them gather all the food of those good years that come, and lay up corn under the hand of Pharaoh, and let them keep food in the cities. And that food shall be for store to the land against the seven years of famine, which shall be in the land of Egypt; that the land perish not through the famine."

And the thing was good in the eyes of Pharaoh, and in the eyes of all his servants. And Pharaoh said unto his servants, "Can we find such a one as this is, a man in whom the spirit of God is?" And Pharaoh said unto Joseph, "Forasmuch as God hath showed thee all this, there is none so discreet and wise as thou art. Thou shalt be over my house, and according unto thy word shall all my people be ruled; only in the throne will I be greater than thou."

And Pharaoh said unto Joseph, "See, I have set thee over all the land of Egypt." And Pharaoh took off his ring from his hand, and put it upon Joseph's hand, and arrayed him in vestures of fine linen, and put a gold chain about his neck. And he made him to ride in the second chariot which he had; and they cried before him, "Bow the knee;" and he made him ruler over all the land of Egypt. And Pharaoh gave Joseph to wife Asenath the daughter of Potipherah priest of On.

And Joseph was thirty years old when he stood before Pharaoh king of Egypt. And Joseph went out from the presence of Pharaoh, and went throughout all the land of Egypt. And in the seven plenteous years the earth brought forth by handfuls. And he gathered up all the food of the seven years, which were in the land of Egypt, and laid up the food in the cities; the food of the field which was round about every city, laid he up in the same.

And Joseph gathered corn as the sand of the sea, very much, until he left numbering; for it was without number.

And unto Joseph were born two sons before the years of famine came; which Asenath bare unto him. And Joseph called the name of the first-born Manasseh: "For God," said he, "hath made me forget all my toil, and all my father's house." And the name of the second called he Ephraim: "For God hath caused me to be fruitful in the land of my affliction."

And the seven years of plenteousness, that was in the land of Egypt, were ended. And the seven years of dearth began to come, according as Joseph had said; and the dearth was in all lands; but in all the land of Egypt there was bread. And when all the land of Egypt was famished, the people cried to Pharaoh for bread; and Pharaoh said unto all the Egyptians, "Go unto Joseph; what he saith to you do." And the famine was over all the face of the earth; and Joseph opened all the storehouses, and sold unto the Egyptians; and the famine waxed sore in the land of Egypt. And all countries came into Egypt to Joseph for to buy corn; because that the famine was so sore in all lands.

GOD DID SEND ME BEFORE YOU TO PRESERVE LIFE

Now when Jacob saw that there was corn in Egypt, he said unto his sons, "Why do ye look one upon another? Behold, I have heard that there is corn in Egypt; get you down thither, and buy for us from thence, that we may live, and not die." And Joseph's ten brethren went down to buy corn in Egypt. But Benjamin, Joseph's brother, Jacob sent not with his brethren, for he said, "Lest peradventure mischief befall him."

And the sons of Israel came to buy corn among those that came, for the famine was in the land of Canaan. And Joseph's brethren came, and bowed down themselves before him with their faces to the earth. And Joseph saw his brethren, and he knew them, but they knew not him, and he made himself strange unto them, and spake roughly unto them, and he said, " Whence come ye? "

And they said, " From the land of Canaan to buy food."

And Joseph remembered the dreams which he dreamed of them, and said unto them, " Ye are spies; to see the nakedness of the land ye are come."

And they said unto him, " Nay, my lord, but to buy food are thy servants come. We are all one man's sons; we are true men; thy servants are no spies."

And Joseph said, " Nay, but to see the nakedness of the land ye are come."

And they said, " Thy servants are twelve brethren, the sons of one man in the land of Canaan; and behold, the youngest is this day with our father, and one is not."

And Joseph said unto them, " That is it that I spake unto you, ye are spies. Hereby ye shall be proved: by the life of Pharaoh ye shall not go forth hence, except your youngest brother come hither. Send one of you, and let him fetch your brother, and ye shall be kept in prison, that your words may be proved, whether there be any truth in you, or else, by the life of Pharaoh, surely ye are spies." And he put them all together into prison three days.

And Joseph said unto them the third day, " This do, and live; for I fear God: if ye be true men, let one of your brethren be bound in prison; go ye, carry corn for the famine of your houses; but bring your youngest brother unto me, so shall your words be verified, and ye shall not die."

And they said one to another, " We are verily guilty concerning our brother Joseph, in that we saw the anguish of his soul, when he besought us, and we would not hear, therefore is this distress come upon us."

And Reuben answered them, " Spake I not unto you, saying,

'Do not sin against the child;' and ye would not hear? therefore, behold, also his blood is required."

And they knew not that Joseph understood them, for he spake unto them by an interpreter. And he turned himself about from them, and wept; and returned to them again, and communed with them, and took from them Simeon, and bound him before their eyes.

And Joseph commanded the steward of his house to fill their sacks with corn, and to restore every man's money into his sack, and to give them provision for the way, and thus did he. And they laded their asses with the corn, and departed thence. And as one of them opened his sack to give his ass provender in the inn, he espied his money, for, behold, it was in his sack's mouth.

And he said unto his brethren, "My money is restored, and, lo, it is even in my sack;" and their heart failed them, and they were afraid, saying one to another, "What is this that God hath done unto us?"

And they came unto Jacob their father unto the land of Canaan, and told him all that befell unto them, saying, "The man who is the lord of the land, spake roughly to us, and took us for spies of the country. And we said unto him, 'We are true men; we are no spies; we be twelve brethren, sons of our father, one is not, and the youngest is this day with our father in the land of Canaan.' And the man, the lord of the country, said unto us, 'Hereby shall I know that ye are true men: leave one of your brethren here with me, and take food for the famine of your households, and be gone; and bring your youngest brother unto me, then shall I know that ye are no spies, but that ye are true men; so will I deliver you your brother, and ye shall traffick in the land.'"

And it came to pass as they emptied their sacks, that, behold, every man's bundle of money was in his sack, and when both they and their father saw the bundles of money, they were afraid. And Jacob their father said unto them, "Me have ye bereaved of my children: Joseph is not, and Simeon is not, and ye will take Benjamin away; all these things are against me."

And Reuben spake unto his father, saying, "Deliver Benjamin into my hand, and I will bring him to thee again; slay my two sons, if I bring him not to thee."

And Jacob said, "My son shall not go down with you; for his brother is dead, and he is left alone; if mischief befall him by the way in the which ye go, then shall ye bring down my gray hairs with sorrow to the grave."

And the famine was sore in the land. And it came to pass when they had eaten up the corn which they had brought out of Egypt, their father said unto them, "Go again, buy us a little food."

And Judah spake unto him, saying, "The man did solemnly protest unto us, saying, 'Ye shall not see my face, except your brother be with you.' If thou wilt send our brother with us, we will go down and buy thee food, but if thou wilt not send him, we will not go down."

And Jacob said, "Wherefore dealt ye so ill with me, as to tell the man whether ye had yet a brother?"

And they said, "The man asked us straitly of our state, and of our kindred, saying, 'Is your father yet alive? have ye another brother?' and we told him; could we certainly know that he would say, 'Bring your brother down?'"

And Judah said unto his father, "Send the lad with me, and we will arise and go, that we may live, and not die, both we, and thou, and also our little ones. I will be surety for him, of my hand shalt thou require him: if I bring him not unto thee, and set him before thee, then let me bear the blame for ever."

And their father Israel said unto them, "If it must be so now, do this: take of the best fruits in the land in your vessels, and carry down the man a present, a little balm, and a little honey, spices, and myrrh, nuts, and almonds; and take double money in your hand; and the money that was brought again in the mouth of your sacks, carry it again in your hand, peradventure it was an oversight; take also your brother, and arise, go again unto the man. And God Almighty give you mercy before the man, that he may send away your other brother, and Benjamin. If I be bereaved of my children, I am bereaved."

And the men took that present, and they took double money in their hand, and Benjamin, and rose up, and went down to Egypt, and stood before Joseph. And when Joseph saw Benjamin with them, he said to the ruler of his house, "Bring these men home, and make ready, for these men shall dine with me at noon." And he did as Joseph bade, and brought the men into Joseph's house.

And the men were afraid, because they were brought into Joseph's house, and they said, "Because of the money that was returned in our sacks at the first time, are we brought in, that he may seek occasion against us, and fall upon us, and take us for bondmen, and our asses."

And they came near to the steward of Joseph's house, and they communed with him at the door of the house, and said, "O sir, we came indeed down at the first time to buy food, and it came to pass, when we came to the inn, that we opened our sacks, and, behold, every man's money was in the mouth of his sack, our money in full weight, and we have brought it again in our hand. And other money have we brought down in our hands to buy food; we cannot tell who put our money in our sacks."

And he said, "Peace be to you, fear not: your God, and the God of your father, hath given you treasure in your sacks; I had your money." And he brought Simeon out unto them. And he brought them into Joseph's house, and gave them water, and they washed their feet, and he gave their asses provender. And they made ready the present against Joseph came at noon, for they heard that they should eat bread there.

And when Joseph came home, they brought him the present

which was in their hand, and bowed themselves to him to the earth. And he asked them of their welfare, and said, " Is your father well, the old man of whom ye spake? Is he yet alive? "

And they answered, "Thy servant our father is in good health, he is yet alive." And they bowed down their heads, and made obeisance.

And Joseph lifted up his eyes, and saw his brother Benjamin, his mother's son, and said, "Is this your younger brother, of whom ye spake unto me? " And he said, " God be gracious unto thee, my son." And Joseph made haste, for he did yearn upon his brother, and he sought where to weep; and he entered into his chamber, and wept there. And he washed his face, and went out, and refrained himself, and said, " Set on bread."

And they sat before him, the first-born according to his birthright, and the youngest according to his youth, and the men marvelled one at another. And Joseph took and sent messes unto them from before him, but Benjamin's mess was five times as much as any of theirs. And they drank, and were merry with him.

And Joseph commanded the steward of his house, saying, " Fill the men's sacks with food, as much as they can carry, and put every man's money in his sack's mouth. And put my cup, the silver cup, in the sack of the youngest, and his corn-money." And he did according to the word that Joseph had spoken.

As soon as the morning was light, the men were sent away, they, and their asses. And when they were gone out of the city, and not yet far off, Joseph said unto his steward, " Up, follow after the men; and when thou dost overtake them, say unto them, ' Wherefore have ye rewarded evil for good? Have ye not taken the cup from which my lord drinketh? ' " And the steward overtook them, and he spake unto them these same words.

And they said unto him, "Wherefore saith my lord these words? God forbid that thy servants should do according to this thing. Behold, the money which we found in our sacks' mouths, we brought again unto thee out of the land of Canaan; how then should we steal out of thy lord's house silver or gold? With whomsoever of thy servants it be found both let him die, and we also will be my lord's bond-men."

And he said, "He with whom it is found shall be my servant, and ye shall be blameless."

Then they speedily took down every man his sack to the ground, and opened every man his sack. And he searched, and began at the eldest, and left at the youngest; and the cup was found in Benjamin's sack. Then they rent their clothes, and laded every man his ass, and returned to the city. And Judah and his brethren came to Joseph's house, for he was yet there, and they fell before him on the ground.

And Joseph said unto them, "What deed is this that ye have done?"

And Judah said, "What shall we say unto my lord? what shall we speak? or how shall we clear ourselves? God hath found out the iniquity of thy servants; behold we are my lord's servants, both we, and he also with whom the cup is found."

And Joseph said, "God forbid that I should do so; but the man in whose hand the cup is found, he shall be my servant, and as for you, get you up in peace unto your father."

Then Judah came near unto him, and said, "O my lord, let thy servant, I pray thee, speak a word in my lord's ears, and let not thine anger burn against thy servant, for thou art even as Pharaoh. My lord asked his servants, saying, 'Have ye a father, or a brother?' And we said unto my lord, 'We have a father, an old man, and a child of his old age, a little one, and his brother is dead, and he alone is left of his mother, and his father loveth him.' And thou saidst unto thy servants, 'Bring him down unto me, that I may set mine eyes upon him.' And we said unto my lord, 'The lad cannot leave his father, for if he should leave his father, his father would die.' And thou saidst unto thy servants, 'Except your youngest brother come down with you, ye shall see my face no more.' And it came to pass, when we came unto my father, we told him the words of my lord. And our father said, 'If ye take this son also from me, and mischief befall him, ye shall bring down my gray hairs with sorrow to the grave.' And thy servant became surety for the lad, saying, 'If I bring him not unto thee, then I shall bear the blame to my father for ever.' Now therefore when I come to thy servant my father, and the lad be not with us, seeing that his life is bound up in the lad's life, it shall come to pass, when he seeth that the lad is not with us, that he will die; and thy servants shall bring down the gray hairs of our father with sorrow to the grave. Now therefore, I pray thee, let thy servant abide instead of the lad a bondman to my lord, and let the lad go up with his brethren. For how shall I go up to my father, and the lad be not with me? lest peradventure I see the evil that shall come on my father."

Then Joseph could not refrain himself before all them that stood by him; and he cried, "Cause every man to go out from me;" and there stood no man with him, while Joseph made himself known unto his brethren. And he wept aloud. And he said unto his brethren, "I am Joseph; doth my father yet live?" And his brethren could not answer him, for they were troubled at his presence.

And Joseph said unto his brethren, "Come near to me, I pray you," and they came near, and he said, "I am Joseph your brother, whom ye sold into Egypt. Now therefore be not grieved, nor angry with yourselves, that ye sold me hither, for God did send me before you to preserve life. For these two years hath the famine been in the land; and yet there are five years, in the which there shall neither be earing nor harvest. And God sent me before you, to preserve you a posterity in the earth, and to save your lives by a great deliverance. So now it was not you that sent me hither, but God; and he hath made me lord of all Pharaoh's house, and a ruler throughout all the land of Egypt. Haste ye, and go up to my father, and say unto him, thus saith thy son Joseph, ‘ God hath made me lord of all Egypt; come down unto me, tarry not. And thou shalt dwell in the land of Goshen, and thou shalt be near unto me, thou, and thy children, and thy children's children, and thy flocks, and thy herds, and all that thou hast; and I will nourish thee, for yet there are five years of famine, lest thou, and thy household come to poverty.' And ye shall tell my father of all my glory in Egypt, and of all that ye have seen; and ye shall haste, and bring down my father hither." And he fell upon his brother Benjamin's neck, and wept; and Benjamin wept upon his neck. Moreover he kissed all his brethren, and wept upon them; and after that his brethren talked with him.

And the fame thereof was heard in Pharaoh's house, saying, " Joseph's brethren are come; " and it pleased Pharaoh well, and his servants.

And Pharaoh said unto Joseph, " Say unto thy brethren, ‘ This do ye; lade your beasts, and go, get you unto the land of Canaan; and take your father, and your households, and come unto me; and I will give you the good of the land of Egypt, and ye shall eat the fat of the land. Take you wagons out of the land of Egypt for your little ones, and for your wives, and bring your father, and come.' "

And the children of Israel did so; and Joseph gave them wagons, and gave them provision for the way. To all of them he gave each man changes of raiment; but to Benjamin he gave three hundred pieces of silver, and five changes of raiment. And to his father he sent ten asses laden with the good things of Egypt, and ten asses laden with corn and bread and meat for his father by the way.

So he sent his brethren away, and they departed. And they went up out of Egypt, and came into the land of Canaan unto Jacob their father, and told him, saying, " Joseph is yet alive, and he is governor over all the land of Egypt." And Jacob's heart fainted, for he believed them not.

And they told him all the words of Joseph, which he had said unto them; and when Jacob saw the wagons which Joseph had sent to carry him, the spirit of Jacob their father revived. And he said, " It is enough; Joseph my son is yet alive; I will go and see him before I die."

I AM WITH THEE IN ALL PLACES

AND ISRAEL offered sacrifices unto the God of his father, Isaac. And God spake unto Israel in the visions of the night, and said, " Jacob, Jacob! "

And Jacob said, " Here am I."

And God said, " I am God, the God of thy father; fear not to go down into Egypt; for I will there make of thee a great nation; I will go down with thee into Egypt; and I will also surely bring thee up again."

And Jacob rose up from Beer-sheba; and the sons of Israel carried Jacob their father, and their little ones, and their wives, in the wagons which Pharaoh had sent to carry him. And they took their cattle, and their goods, which they had gotten in the land of Canaan, and came into Egypt, Jacob, and all his children with him.

And Jacob sent Judah before him unto Joseph, to direct his face unto Goshen; and they came into the land of Goshen. And Joseph made ready his chariot, and went up to meet Israel his father, to Goshen, and presented himself unto him; and he fell on his neck, and wept on his neck a good while. And Israel said unto Joseph, "Now let me die, since I have seen thy face, because thou art yet alive."

Then Joseph came and told Pharaoh, and said, " My father and my brethren, and their flocks, and their herds, and all that they have, are come out of the land of Canaan; and, behold, they are in the land of Goshen."

And Pharaoh spake unto Joseph, saying, "Thy father and thy brethren are come unto thee: the land of Egypt is before thee; in the best of the land make thy father and brethren to dwell; in the land of Goshen let them dwell; and if thou knowest any men of activity among them, then make them rulers over my cattle."

And Joseph brought in Jacob his father, and set him before Pharaoh; and Jacob blessed Pharaoh. And Pharaoh said unto Jacob, "How old art thou?"

And Jacob said unto Pharaoh, "The days of the years of my pilgrimage are an hundred and thirty years; few and evil have the days of my life been, and have not attained unto the days of the years of my fathers in their pilgrimage." And Jacob blessed Pharaoh, and went out from before Pharaoh.

And Joseph placed his father and his brethren, and gave them a possession in the land of Egypt, in the best of the land, as Pharaoh had commanded. And Joseph nourished his father, and his brethren, and all his father's household, with bread according to their families. And Israel dwelt in the land of Egypt, in the country of Goshen; and they had possessions therein, and grew, and multiplied exceedingly.

And Jacob lived in the land of Egypt seventeen years; so the whole age of Jacob was an hundred forty and seven years. And the time drew nigh that Israel must die; and he called his son Joseph, and said unto him, "If now I have found grace in thy sight, put, I pray thee, thy hand under my thigh, and deal kindly and truly with me; bury me not, I pray thee, in Egypt; but I will lie with my fathers, and thou shalt carry me out of Egypt, and bury me in their burying place."

And Joseph said, "I will do as thou hast said."

And Jacob said, "Swear unto me;" and he sware unto him. And Israel bowed himself upon the bed's head.

And Israel beheld Joseph's sons, and said, "Who are these?"

And Joseph said unto his father, "They are my sons, whom God hath given me in this place."

And Jacob said, " Bring them, I pray thee, unto me, and I will bless them." Now the eyes of Israel were dim for age, so that he could not see, so Joseph brought them near unto him, and he kissed them, and embraced them. And Israel said unto Joseph, " I had not thought to see thy face, and lo, God hath showed me also thy children."

And Israel stretched out his right hand, and laid it upon Ephraim's head, who was the younger, and his left hand upon Manasseh's head, guiding his hands wittingly; for Manasseh was the first-born. And Joseph said unto his father, " Not so, my father, for this is the first-born; put thy right hand upon his head."

And his father refused, and said, " I know it, my son, I know it; he also shall become a people, and he also shall be great; but truly his younger brother shall be greater than he, and his seed shall become a multitude of nations." And he blessed them that day, saying, " God, before whom my fathers Abraham and Isaac did walk, the God which fed me all my life long unto this day, the Angel which redeemed me from all evil, bless the lads; and let my name be named on them, and the name of my fathers Abraham and Isaac; and let them grow into a multitude in the midst of the earth."

And Israel said unto Joseph, " Behold, I die; but God shall be with you, and bring you again unto the land of your fathers."

And Jacob called unto his sons, and said, " Gather yourselves together! Gather yourselves together, and hear, ye sons of Jacob; and hearken unto Israel your father." These are the twelve tribes of Israel: Reuben, Simeon, Levi, Judah, Zebulun, Issachar, Dan, Gad, Asher, Naphtali, Joseph, and Benjamin; and their father spake unto them, and blessed them; every one according to his blessing, he blessed them. And he charged them, and said, " I am to be gathered unto my people; bury me with my fathers in the cave that is in the field of Machpelah, in the land of Canaan. There they buried Abraham and Sarah; there they buried Isaac and Rebekah; and there I buried Leah." And when Jacob had made an end of commanding his sons, he gathered up his feet into the bed, and was gathered unto his people.

And Joseph fell upon his father's face, and wept upon him, and kissed him. And when the days of his mourning were past, Joseph went up to bury his father; and with him went up all the servants of Pharaoh, the elders of his house, and all the elders of the land of Egypt, and all the house of Joseph, and his brethren, and his father's house; only their little ones, and their flocks, and their herds, they left in the land of Goshen. And there went up with him both chariots and horsemen; and it was a very great company. And Jacob's sons did unto him according as he commanded them, for his sons carried him into the land of Canaan, and buried him in the cave of the field of Machpelah. And Joseph returned into Egypt, he and his brethren, and all that went up with him, after he had buried his father.

And when Joseph's brethren saw that their father was dead, they said, "Joseph will peradventure hate us, and will certainly requite us all the evil which we did unto him." And they sent a messenger unto Joseph, saying, "Thy father did command before he died, saying, 'So shall ye say unto Joseph, "Forgive, I pray thee now, the trespass of thy brethren, and their sin; for they did unto thee evil;" and now, we pray thee, forgive the trespass of the servants of the God of thy father.' "

And Joseph wept when they spake unto him. And his brethren went and fell down before his face; and they said, "Behold, we be thy servants."

And Joseph said unto them, "Fear not; for am I in the place of God? But as for you, ye thought evil against me; but God meant it unto good, to bring to pass, as it is this day, to save much people alive. Now therefore fear ye not; I will nourish you, and your little ones." And he comforted them, and spake kindly unto them.

And Joseph dwelt in Egypt, he, and his father's house; and

Joseph lived an hundred and ten years. And Joseph died, and all his brethren, and all that generation. And the children of Israel were fruitful, and increased abundantly, and multiplied, and waxed exceeding mighty; and the land was filled with them.

" I will redeem you with a stretched out arm."

EXODUS

AND SHE CALLED HIS NAME MOSES

Now there arose up a new king over Egypt, which knew not Joseph. And he said unto his people, "Behold, the people of the children of Israel are more and mightier than we. Come on, let us deal wisely with them; lest they multiply, and it come to pass, that, when there falleth out any war, they join also unto our enemies, and fight against us, and so get them up out of the land."

Therefore they did set over them task-masters, to afflict them with their burdens. And they built for Pharaoh treasure-cities, Pithom, and Raamses. But the more they afflicted them, the more they multiplied and grew. And the Egyptians were grieved because of the children of Israel. And the Egyptians made the children of Israel to serve with rigour. And they made their lives bitter with hard bondage, in mortar, and in brick, and in all manner of service in the field; all their service wherein they made them serve was with rigour.

And Pharaoh charged all his people saying, "Every son that is born to the Hebrew women, ye shall cast into the river, and every daughter ye shall save alive."

And there went a man of the house of Levi, and took to wife a daughter of Levi. And the woman conceived and bare a son; and when she saw him that he was a goodly child, she hid him three months. And when she could no longer hide him, she took for him an ark of bulrushes, and daubed it with slime and with pitch, and put the child therein; and she laid it on the flags by the river's brink. And his sister stood afar off, to wit what would be done to him.

And the daughter of Pharaoh came down to wash herself at the river; and her maidens walked along by the river's side; and when she saw the ark among the flags, she sent her maid to fetch it. And when she had opened it, she saw the child; and behold, the babe wept. And she had compassion on him, and said, " This is one of the Hebrews' children."

Then said his sister to Pharaoh's daughter, " Shall I go, and call to thee a nurse of the Hebrew women, that she may nurse the child for thee? "

And Pharaoh's daughter said to her, " Go." And the maid went and called the child's mother. And Pharaoh's daughter said unto her, " Take this child away and nurse it for me, and I will give thee thy wages." And the woman took the child and nursed it.

And the child grew, and she brought him unto Pharaoh's daughter, and he became her son. And she called his name Moses: and she said, " Because I drew him out of the water."

MOSES LOOKED ON THE BURDENS OF HIS BRETHREN

AND IT CAME TO PASS in those days, when Moses was grown, that he went out unto his brethren, and looked on their burdens; and he spied an Egyptian smiting an Hebrew, one of his brethren. And he looked this way and that way, and when he saw that there was no man, he slew the Egyptian, and hid him in the sand.

And when Moses went out the second day, behold, two men of the Hebrews strove together; and he said to him that did the wrong, " Wherefore smitest thou thy fellow? "

And he said, " Who made thee a prince and a judge over us? intendest thou to kill me, as thou killedst the Egyptian? "

And Moses feared, and said, " Surely this thing is known."

Now when Pharaoh heard this thing, he sought to slay Moses. But Moses fled from the face of Pharaoh, and dwelt in the land of Midian; and he sat down by a well. Now the priest of Midian had seven daughters; and they came and drew water, and filled the troughs to water their father's flock. And the shepherds came and drove them away; but Moses stood up and helped them, and watered their flock.

And when they came to Jethro their father, he said, " How is it that ye are come so soon today? "

And they said, " An Egyptian delivered us out of the hand of the shepherds, and also drew water enough for us, and watered the flock."

And Jethro said unto his daughters, " And where is he? why is it that ye have left the man? call him, that he may eat bread."

And Moses was content to dwell with Jethro; and he gave Moses, Zipporah his daughter. And she bare him a son, and he called his name Gershom; for he said, " I have been a stranger in a strange land."

I AM

AND IT CAME TO PASS, in process of time, that the king of Egypt died; and the children of Israel sighed by reason of the bondage, and they cried; and their cry came unto God, by reason of the bondage. And God heard their groaning, and God remembered his covenant with Abraham, with Isaac, and with Jacob.

Now Moses kept the flock of Jethro his father-in-law, the priest of Midian; and he led the flock to the back side of the desert, and came to the mountain of God, even to Horeb. And the Angel of the Lord appeared unto him in a flame of fire out of the midst of a bush; and he looked, and, behold, the bush burned with fire, and the bush was not consumed. And Moses said, " I will now turn aside, and see this great sight, why the bush is not burnt."

And when the Lord saw that he turned aside to see, God called unto him out of the midst of the bush, and said, " Moses, Moses! "

And he said, " Here am I."

And God said, " Draw nigh hither; put off thy shoes from off thy feet; for the place whereon thou standest is holy ground. I am the God of thy father, the God of Abraham, the God of Isaac, and the God of Jacob." And Moses hid his face: for he was afraid to look upon God.

And the Lord said, " I have surely seen the affliction of my people which are in Egypt, and have heard their cry by reason of their taskmasters; for I know their sorrows; and I am come down to deliver them out of the hand of the Egyptians, and to bring them up out of that land, unto a good land, and a large, unto a land flowing with milk and honey; unto the place of the Canaanites, and the Hittites, and the Amorites, and the Perizzites, and the Hivites, and the Jebusites. Now therefore, behold, the cry of the children of Israel is come unto me; and I have also seen the oppression wherewith the Egyptians oppress them. Come now, therefore, and I will send thee unto Pharaoh, that thou mayest bring forth my people, the children of Israel, out of Egypt."

And Moses said unto God, "Who am I, that I should go unto Pharaoh, and that I should bring forth the children of Israel out of Egypt?"

And God said, "Certainly I will be with thee; and this shall be a token unto thee, that I have sent thee; when thou hast brought forth the people out of Egypt, ye shall serve God upon this mountain."

And Moses said unto God, "Behold, when I come unto the children of Israel, and shall say unto them, 'The God of your fathers hath sent me unto you;' and they shall say to me, 'What is his name?' what shall I say unto them?"

And God said unto Moses, "I AM THAT I AM: Thus shalt thou say unto the children of Israel, 'I AM hath sent me unto you;' this is my name for ever, and this is my memorial unto all generations. Go, and gather the elders of Israel together, and say unto them, 'The Lord God of your fathers, the God of Abraham, of Isaac, and of Jacob, appeared unto me, saying, "I have surely visited you, and seen that which is done to you in Egypt; and I will bring you up out of the affliction of Egypt, unto a land flowing with milk and honey.'" And they shall hearken to thy voice; and thou shalt come, thou and the elders of Israel, unto the king of Egypt, and ye shall say unto him, 'The Lord God of the Hebrews hath met with us; and now let us go, we beseech thee, three days' journey into the wilderness, that we may sacrifice to the Lord our God.' And I am sure that the king of Egypt will not let you go, no, not by a mighty hand. And I will stretch out my hand, and smite Egypt with all my wonders which I will do in the midst thereof; and after that he will let you go."

And Moses said, "But, behold, they will not believe me, nor

hearken unto my voice; for they will say, 'The Lord hath not appeared unto thee.'"

And the Lord said, "What is that in thine hand?"

And he said, "A rod."

And the Lord said, "Cast it on the ground." And he cast it on the ground, and it became a serpent; and Moses fled from before it.

And the Lord said unto Moses, "Put forth thine hand, and take it by the tail." And he put forth his hand, and caught it, and it became a rod in his hand.

And the Lord said unto him, "Put now thine hand into thy bosom." And he put his hand into his bosom; and when he took it out, behold, his hand was leprous as snow.

And the Lord said, "Put thine hand into thy bosom again." And he put his hand into his bosom again, and plucked it out of his bosom, and, behold, it was turned again as his other flesh.

"And it shall come to pass, if they will not believe thee, neither hearken to the voice of the first sign, that they will believe the voice of the latter sign. And it shall come to pass, if they will not believe also these two signs, neither hearken unto thy voice, that thou shalt take of the water of the river, and pour it upon the dry land; and the water which thou takest out of the river shall become blood upon the dry land."

And Moses said unto the Lord, "O my Lord, I am not eloquent, neither heretofore, nor since thou hast spoken unto thy servant; but I am slow of speech, and of a slow tongue."

And the Lord said unto him, "Who hath made man's mouth? or who maketh the dumb, or deaf, or the seeing, or the blind? have not I the Lord? Now therefore go, and I will be with thy mouth, and teach thee what thou shalt say."

And Moses said, "O my Lord, send, I pray thee, by the hand of him whom thou wilt send."

And the anger of the Lord was kindled against Moses, and he said, "Is not Aaron the Levite thy brother? I know that he can speak well. And also, behold, he cometh forth to meet thee; and when he seeth thee, he will be glad in his heart. And thou shalt speak unto him, and put words in his mouth; and I will be with thy mouth, and with his mouth, and will teach you what ye shall do. And he shall be thy spokesman unto the people; and he shall be, even he shall be to thee instead of a mouth, and thou shalt be to him instead of God. And thou shalt take this rod in thine hand, wherewith thou shalt do signs."

And Moses went, and returned to Jethro his father-in-law, and said unto him, "Let me go, I pray thee, and return unto my brethren which are in Egypt, and see whether they be yet alive."

And Jethro said to Moses, "Go in peace." And Moses took his wife, and his sons, and set them upon an ass, and he returned to the land of Egypt. And Moses took the rod of God in his hand.

And the Lord said to Aaron, "Go into the wilderness to meet Moses." And Aaron went, and met him in the mount of God, and kissed him. And Moses told Aaron all the words of the Lord who had sent him, and all the signs which he had commanded him.

And Moses and Aaron went, and gathered together all the elders of the children of Israel. And Aaron spake all the words which the Lord had spoken unto Moses, and did the signs in the sight of the people. And the people believed; and when they heard that the Lord had visited the children of Israel, and that he had looked upon their affliction, then they bowed their heads and worshipped.

WHO IS THE LORD THAT I SHOULD OBEY HIS VOICE?

AND AFTERWARD Moses and Aaron went in, and told Pharaoh, " Thus saith the Lord God of Israel, ' Let my people go, that they may hold a feast unto me in the wilderness.' "

And Pharaoh said, " Who is the Lord, that I should obey his voice to let Israel go? I know not the Lord, neither will I let Israel go."

And they said, " The God of the Hebrews hath met with us; let us go, we pray thee, three days' journey into the desert, and sacrifice unto the Lord our God; lest he fall upon us with pestilence, or with the sword."

And the king of Egypt said unto them, " Wherefore do ye, Moses and Aaron, let the people from their works? get you unto your burdens. Behold, the people of the land now are many, and ye make them rest from their burdens."

And Pharaoh commanded the same day the taskmasters of the people, and their officers, saying, " Ye shall no more give the people straw to make brick, as heretofore: let them go and gather straw for themselves. And the tale of the bricks which they did make heretofore, ye shall lay upon them; ye shall not diminish aught thereof; for they be idle; therefore they cry, saying, 'Let us go and sacrifice to our God.' Let more work be laid upon the men, that they may labour therein; and let them not regard vain words."

And the taskmasters of the people went out, and their officers, and they spake to the people, saying, " Thus saith Pharaoh, ' I will not give you straw. Go ye, get you straw where you can find it; yet not aught of your work shall be diminished.' "

So the people were scattered abroad throughout all the land of Egypt, to gather stubble instead of straw. And the taskmasters hasted them, saying, " Fulfil your works, your daily tasks, as when there was straw." And the officers of the children of Israel, which Pharaoh's taskmasters had set over them, were beaten, and demanded, "Wherefore have ye not fulfilled your task in making brick, both yesterday and today as heretofore?"

Then the officers of the children of Israel came and cried unto Pharaoh, saying, "Wherefore dealest thou thus with thy servants? There is no straw given unto thy servants, and they say to us, 'Make brick;' and behold, thy servants are beaten, but the fault is in thine own people."

But Pharaoh said, "Ye are idle, ye are idle; therefore ye say, 'Let us go, and do sacrifice to the Lord.' Go therefore now, and work; for there shall no straw be given you, yet shall ye deliver the tale of bricks."

And the officers of the children of Israel did see that they were in evil case, after it was said, "Ye shall not diminish aught from your bricks of your daily task." And they met Moses and Aaron, who stood in the way, as they came forth from Pharaoh; and they said unto them, "The Lord look upon you, and judge; because ye have made our savour to be abhorred in the eyes of Pharaoh, and in the eyes of his servants, to put a sword in their hand to slay us."

And Moses returned unto the Lord, and said, "Lord, wherefore hast thou so evil-entreated this people? why is it that thou hast sent me? For since I came to Pharaoh to speak in thy name, he hath done evil to this people; neither hast thou delivered thy people at all."

And God spake unto Moses, and said unto him, "I am the Lord: and I appeared unto Abraham, unto Isaac, and unto Jacob, by the name of God Almighty, but by my name JEHOVAH was I not known to them. And I have also established my covenant with them, to give them the land of Canaan, the land of their pilgrimage, wherein they were strangers. And I have also heard the groaning of the children of Israel, whom the Egyptians keep in bondage; and I have remembered my covenant. Wherefore say unto the children of Israel, 'I am the Lord, and

I will bring you out from under the burdens of the Egyptians, and I will rid you out of their bondage, and I will redeem you with a stretched-out arm, and with great judgments; and I will take you to me for a people, and I will be to you a God; and ye shall know that I am the Lord your God, which bringeth you out from under the burdens of the Egyptians. And I will bring you in unto the land, concerning the which I did swear to give it to Abraham, to Isaac, and to Jacob; and I will give it you for an heritage; I am the Lord.' "

And Moses spake so unto the children of Israel; but they hearkened not unto Moses, for anguish of spirit, and for cruel bondage.

And the Lord spake unto Moses, saying, "Go in, speak unto Pharaoh king of Egypt, that he let the children of Israel go out of his land."

And Moses spake before the Lord, saying, "Behold, the children of Israel have not hearkened unto me; how then shall Pharaoh hear me? "

And the Lord said unto Moses, "Thou shalt speak all that I command thee; and Aaron thy brother shall speak unto Pharaoh, that he send the children of Israel out of his land. And I will multiply my signs and my wonders in the land of Egypt. And the Egyptians shall know that I am the Lord, when I stretch forth mine hand upon Egypt, and bring out the children of Israel from among them. When Pharaoh shall speak unto you, saying, 'Show a miracle for you; ' then thou shalt say unto Aaron, 'Take thy rod, and cast it before Pharaoh,' and it shall become a serpent."

And Moses and Aaron went in unto Pharaoh, and they did so as the Lord had commanded; and Aaron cast down his rod before Pharaoh, and before his servants, and it became a serpent. Then Pharaoh also called the wise men, and the sorcerers; now the magicians of Egypt, they also did in like manner with their enchantments. For they cast down every man his rod, and they became serpents; but Aaron's rod swallowed up their rods. And Pharaoh hearkened not unto them, as the Lord had said.

BLOOD

And the Lord said unto Moses, "Pharaoh's heart is hardened, he refuseth to let the people go. Get thee unto Pharaoh in the morning; lo, he goeth out unto the water, and thou shalt stand by the river's brink against he come; and the rod which was turned to a serpent shalt thou take in thine hand. And thou shalt say unto him, 'The Lord God of the Hebrews hath sent me unto thee, saying, "Let my people go, that they may serve me in the wilderness;" behold, hitherto thou wouldest not hear. Thus saith the Lord, "In this thou shalt know that I am the Lord; behold, I will smite with the rod that is in my hand upon the waters which are in the river, and they shall be turned to blood. And the fish that is in the river shall die, and the river shall stink; and the Egyptians shall loathe to drink of the water of the river."'"

And Moses and Aaron did so, as the Lord commanded; and Aaron lifted up the rod and smote the waters that were in the river, in the sight of Pharaoh, and in the sight of his servants; and all the waters that were in the river were turned into blood. And the fish that were in the river died; and the river stank, and the Egyptians could not drink of the water of the river; and there was blood throughout all the land of Egypt. And the magicians of Egypt did so with their enchantments; and Pharaoh's heart was hardened, neither did he hearken unto them; as the Lord had said. And Pharaoh turned and went into his house, neither did he set his heart to this also. And all the Egyptians digged round about the river for water to drink; for they could not drink of the water of the river. And seven days were fulfilled after that the Lord had smitten the river.

FROGS

And the Lord spake unto Moses, " Go unto Pharaoh, and say unto him, 'Thus saith the Lord, " Let my people go that they may serve me. And if thou refuse to let them go, behold, I will smite all thy borders with frogs; and the river shall bring forth frogs abundantly, which shall go up and come into thine house and into thy bed-chamber, and upon thy bed, and into the house of thy servants, and upon thy people, and into thine ovens, and into thy kneading-troughs; and the frogs shall come up both on thee, and upon thy people, and upon all thy servants." ' "

And the Lord spake unto Moses, " Say unto Aaron, ' Stretch forth thine hand with thy rod over the streams, over the rivers, and over the ponds, and cause frogs to come up upon the land of Egypt.' " And Aaron stretched out his hand over the waters of Egypt; and the frogs came up, and covered the land of Egypt. And the magicians did so with their enchantments, and brought up frogs upon the land of Egypt.

Then Pharaoh called for Moses and Aaron, and said, " Entreat the Lord that he may take away the frogs from me, and from my people; and I will let the people go, that they may do sacrifice unto the Lord."

And Moses said unto Pharaoh, " When shall I entreat for thee and for thy servants, and for thy people, to destroy the frogs from thee, and thy houses, that they may remain in the river only? "

And Pharaoh said, " Tomorrow."

And Moses said, " Be it according to thy word: that thou mayest know that there is none like unto the Lord our God. And the frogs shall depart from thee, and from thy houses, and from thy servants, and from thy people; they shall remain in the river only."

And Moses and Aaron went out from Pharaoh; and Moses cried unto the Lord, because of the frogs which he had brought against Pharaoh. And the Lord did according to the word of Moses; and the frogs died out of the houses, out of the villages, and out of the fields. And they gathered them together upon heaps; and the land stank. But when Pharaoh saw that there was respite, he hardened his heart, and hearkened not unto them.

LICE

And the Lord said unto Moses, "Say unto Aaron, 'Stretch out thy rod, and smite the dust of the land, that it may become lice throughout all the land of Egypt.'" And they did so; for Aaron stretched out his hand with his rod, and smote the dust of the earth, and it became lice in man and in beast; all the dust of the land became lice throughout all the land of Egypt.

And the magicians did so with their enchantments to bring forth lice, but they could not; so there were lice upon man, and upon beast. Then the magicians said unto Pharaoh, "This is the finger of God;" and Pharaoh's heart was hardened, and he hearkened not unto them.

SWARMS OF FLIES

And the Lord said unto Moses, "Rise up early in the morning, and stand before Pharaoh; lo, he cometh forth to the water; and say unto him, 'Thus saith the Lord, "Let my people go, that they may serve me. Else if thou wilt not let my people go, behold, I will send swarms of flies upon thee, and upon thy servants, and upon thy people, and into thy houses; and the houses of the Egyptians shall be full of swarms of flies, and also the ground whereon they are. And I will sever in that day the land of Goshen, in which my people dwell, that no swarms of flies shall be there; to the end thou mayest know that I am the Lord in the midst of the earth. And I will put a division between my people and thy people; tomorrow shall this sign be."'" And the Lord did so: and there came a grievous swarm of flies into the house of Pharaoh, and into his servants' houses, and into all the land of Egypt; the land was corrupted by reason of the swarms of flies.

And Pharaoh called for Moses, and for Aaron, and said, " Go ye, sacrifice to your God in the land."

And Moses said, " It is not meet so to do; for we shall sacrifice the abomination of the Egyptians to the Lord our God; lo, shall we sacrifice the abomination of the Egyptians before their eyes, and will they not stone us? We will go three days' journey into the wilderness, and sacrifice to the Lord our God, as he shall command us."

And Pharaoh said, " I will let you go, that ye may sacrifice to the Lord your God in the wilderness; only ye shall not go very far away; entreat for me."

And Moses said, " Behold, I go out from thee, and I will entreat the Lord that the swarms of flies may depart from Pharaoh, from his servants, and from his people, to-morrow; but let not Pharaoh deal deceitfully any more in not letting the people go to sacrifice to the Lord."

And Moses went out from Pharaoh, and entreated the Lord: and the Lord did according to the word of Moses, and he removed the swarms of flies; there remained not one. And Pharaoh hardened his heart at this time also, neither would he let the people go.

THE CATTLE OF EGYPT DIED

Then the Lord said unto Moses, " Go in unto Pharaoh, and tell him, 'Thus saith the Lord God of the Hebrews, " Let my people go, that they may serve me. For if thou refuse to let them go, and wilt hold them still, behold, the hand of the Lord is upon thy cattle which is in the field, upon the horses, upon the asses, upon the camels, upon the oxen, and upon the sheep: there shall be a very grievous murrain. And the Lord shall sever between the cattle of Israel, and the cattle of Egypt; and there shall nothing die of all that is the children's of Israel. Tomorrow the Lord shall do this thing in the land." ' "

And the Lord did that thing on the morrow, and all the cattle of Egypt died; but of the cattle of the children of Israel died not one. And Pharaoh sent, and behold, there was not one of the cattle of the Israelites dead. And the heart of Pharaoh was hardened, and he did not let the people go.

BOILS

And the Lord said unto Moses and unto Aaron, " Take to you handfuls of ashes of the furnace, and let Moses sprinkle it toward the heaven in the sight of Pharaoh. And it shall become small dust in all the land of Egypt, and shall be a boil breaking forth with blains upon man, and upon beast, throughout all the land of Egypt."

And they took ashes of the furnace, and stood before Pharaoh; and Moses sprinkled it up toward heaven; and it became a boil breaking forth with blains upon man, and upon beast. And the magicians could not stand before Moses, because of the boils; for the boil was upon the magicians, and upon all the Egyptians. And Pharaoh hearkened not unto them; as the Lord had spoken unto Moses.

HAIL

And the Lord said unto Moses, " Rise up early in the morning, and stand before Pharaoh, and say unto him, ' Thus saith the Lord God of the Hebrews, " Let my people go, that they may serve me. As yet exaltest thou thyself against my people, that thou wilt not let them go? Behold, tomorrow about this time I will cause it to rain a very grievous hail, such as hath not been in Egypt since the foundation thereof even until now. Send therefore now, and gather thy cattle, and all that thou hast in the field: for upon every man and beast which shall be found in the field, and shall not be brought home, the hail shall come down upon them, and they shall die.' ' "

He that feared the word of the Lord among the servants of Pharaoh made his servants and his cattle flee into the houses: and he that regarded not the word of the Lord left his servants and his cattle in the field.

And Moses stretched forth his rod toward heaven, and the Lord sent thunder and hail, and the fire ran along upon the ground; and the Lord rained hail upon the land of Egypt. So there was hail, and fire mingled with the hail, very grievous, such as there was none like it in all the land of Egypt since it became a nation. And the hail smote throughout all the land of Egypt all that was in the field, both man and beast, and the hail smote every herb of the field and brake every tree of the field. Only in the land of Goshen, where the children of Israel were, was there no hail.

And Pharaoh sent and called for Moses and Aaron, and said unto them, "I have sinned this time; the Lord is righteous, and I and my people are wicked. Entreat the Lord, for it is enough, that there be no more mighty thunderings and hail; and I will let you go, and ye shall stay no longer."

And Moses said unto him, "As soon as I am gone out of the city, I will spread abroad my hands unto the Lord; and the thunder shall cease, neither shall there be any more hail; that thou mayest know how that the earth is the Lord's." And Moses went out of the city from Pharaoh, and spread abroad his hands unto the Lord; and the thunders and hail ceased, and the rain was not poured upon the earth.

And when Pharaoh saw that the rain and the hail and the thunder were ceased, he sinned yet more, and hardened his heart, he and his servants. And the heart of Pharaoh was hardened, neither would he let the children of Israel go; as the Lord had spoken unto Moses.

LOCUSTS

And Moses and Aaron came in unto Pharaoh, and said unto him, " Thus saith the Lord God of the Hebrews, ' How long wilt thou refuse to humble thyself before me? Let my people go, that they may serve me. Else, if thou refuse to let my people go, behold, tomorrow will I bring the locusts into thy coast. And they shall cover the face of the earth, that one cannot be able to see the earth; and they shall eat the residue of that which is escaped, which remaineth unto you from the hail, and shall eat every tree which groweth for you out of the field; and they shall fill thy houses, and the houses of all the Egyptians; which neither thy fathers, nor thy fathers' fathers have seen, since the day that they were upon the earth unto this day.' " And he turned and went out from Pharaoh.

And Pharaoh's servants said unto him, " How long shall this man be a snare unto us? Let the men go, that they may serve the Lord their God; knowest thou not yet that Egypt is destroyed? "

And Moses and Aaron were brought again unto Pharaoh; and he said unto them, " Go, serve the Lord your God; but who are they that shall go? "

And Moses said, " We will go with our young and with our old, with our sons and with our daughters, with our flocks and with our herds will we go; for we must hold a feast unto the Lord."

And Pharaoh said unto them, " Not so; go now ye that are men, and serve the Lord; for that ye did desire." And they were driven out from Pharaoh's presence.

And the Lord said unto Moses, " Stretch out thine hand over the land of Egypt for the locusts, that they may come up upon the land of Egypt." And Moses stretched forth his rod over the land of Egypt, and the Lord brought an east wind upon the land all that day, and all that night; and when it was morning, the east wind brought the locusts. And the locusts went up over all the land of Egypt; very grievous were they; for they covered the face of the whole earth, so that the land was darkened; and they did eat every herb of the land, and all the fruit of the trees which the hail had left; and there remained not any green thing in the trees, or in the herbs of the field, through all the land of Egypt.

Then Pharaoh called for Moses and Aaron in haste; and he said, " I have sinned against the Lord your God, and against you. Now therefore forgive, I pray thee, my sin only this once, and entreat the Lord your God that he may take away from me this death only."

And Moses went out from Pharaoh, and entreated the Lord. And the Lord turned a mighty strong west wind which took away the locusts, and cast them into the Red sea; there remained not one locust in all the coasts of Egypt. But Pharaoh would not let the children of Israel go.

DARKNESS

And the Lord said unto Moses, " Stretch out thine hand toward heaven, that there may be darkness over the land of Egypt, even darkness which may be felt." And Moses stretched forth his hand toward heaven: and there was a thick darkness in all the land of Egypt three days; they saw not one another, neither rose any from his place for three days. But all the children of Israel had lights in their dwellings.

And Pharaoh called unto Moses, and said, " Go ye, serve the Lord: only let your flocks and your herds be stayed; let your little ones also go with you."

And Moses said, " Our cattle also shall go with us; there shall not an hoof be left behind; for thereof must we take to serve the Lord our God."

And Pharaoh said unto him, "Get thee from me, take heed to thyself, see my face no more: for in that day thou seest my face thou shalt die."

And Moses said, "Thou hast spoken well, I will see thy face again no more. But there shall be a great cry throughout all the land of Egypt, such as there was none like it, nor shall be like it any more. But against any of the children of Israel shall not a dog move his tongue, against man or beast; that ye may know how that the Lord doth put a difference between the Egyptians and Israel. And all these thy servants shall come down unto me, and bow themselves unto me, saying, 'Get thee out, and all the people shall follow thee;' and after that I will go out." And Moses went out from Pharaoh in a great anger.

DEATH

And the Lord said unto Moses, "Yet will I bring one plague more upon Pharaoh, and upon Egypt; afterwards he will let you go hence: when he shall let you go, he shall surely thrust you out hence altogether. Speak now in the ears of the people, and let every man borrow of his neighbour, and every woman of her neighbour, jewels of silver, and jewels of gold." And the Lord gave the people favour in the sight of the Egyptians. Moreover, the man Moses was very great in the land of Egypt, in the sight of Pharaoh's servants, and in the sight of the people.

And the Lord spake unto Moses and Aaron in the land of Egypt, saying, "This month shall be unto you the beginning of months; it shall be the first month of the year to you. Speak ye unto all the congregation of Israel, saying, 'In the tenth day of this month they shall take to them every man a lamb according to the house of their fathers, a lamb for an house. Your lamb shall be without blemish, a male of the first year; ye shall take it out from the sheep or from the goats; and ye shall keep it up until the fourteenth day of the same month; and the whole assembly of the congregation of Israel shall kill it in the evening. And they shall take of the blood, and strike it on the two side-posts, and on the upper door-post of the houses, wherein they shall eat it. And they shall eat the flesh in that night, roast with fire, and unleavened bread; and with bitter herbs they shall eat it. And ye shall let nothing of it remain until the morning; and that which remaineth of it until the morning ye shall burn with fire. And thus shall ye eat it; with your loins girded, your shoes on your feet, and your staff in your hand; and ye shall eat it in haste; it is the Lord's passover. For I will pass through the land of Egypt this night, and will smite all the first-born in the land of Egypt, both man and beast; and against all the gods of Egypt I will execute judgment: I am the Lord. And the blood shall be to you for a token upon the houses where ye are: and when I see the blood, I will pass over you, and the plague shall not be upon you to destroy you, when I smite the land of Egypt. And this day shall be unto you for a memorial; and ye shall keep it a feast to the Lord throughout your generations: ye shall keep it a feast by an ordinance for ever. And ye shall observe the feast of unleavened bread; for in this self-same day have I brought your armies out of the land of Egypt; therefore shall ye observe this day in your generations by an ordinance for ever.' "

Then Moses called for all the elders of Israel, and said unto them, " Draw out, and take you a lamb, according to your families, and kill the passover. And ye shall take a bunch of Hyssop, and dip it in the blood that is in the basin, and strike the lintel and the two side-posts with the blood that is in the basin; and none of you shall go out at the door of his house until the morning. For the Lord will pass through to smite the Egyptians; and when he seeth the blood upon the lintel, and on the side-posts, the Lord will pass over the door, and will not suffer the destroyer to come in unto your houses to smite you. And ye shall observe this thing for an ordinance to thee and to thy sons for ever. And it shall come to pass, when ye be come to the land which the Lord will give you, according as he hath promised, that ye shall keep this service. And when your children shall say unto you, 'What mean ye by this service?' That ye shall say, 'It is the sacrifice of the Lord's passover, who passed over the houses of the children of Israel in Egypt, when he smote the Egyptians, and delivered our houses.'" And the people bowed the head and worshipped. And the children of Israel went away, and did as the Lord had commanded Moses and Aaron, so did they.

And it came to pass, that at midnight the Lord smote all the first-born in the land of Egypt, from the first-born of Pharaoh that sat on his throne, unto the first-born of the captive that was in the dungeon; and all the first-born of cattle. And Pharaoh rose up in the night, he, and all his servants, and all the Egyptians; and there was a great cry in Egypt; for there was not a house where there was not one dead.

And Pharaoh called for Moses and Aaron by night, and said, "Rise up, and get you forth from among my people, both ye and the children of Israel; and go, serve the Lord, as ye have said. Also take your flocks and your herds, as ye have said, and be gone; and bless me also."

And the Egyptians were urgent upon the people, that they might send them out of the land in haste; for they said, "We be all dead men." And the children of Israel did according to the word of Moses: and they borrowed of the Egyptians jewels of silver, and jewels of gold, and raiment. And the Egyptians lent unto them such things as they required.

Now the sojourning of the children of Israel in Egypt was four hundred and thirty years. And it came to pass at the end of four hundred and thirty years, even the selfsame day that all the children of Israel went out from the land of Egypt. And the children of Israel journeyed about six hundred thousand on foot, a mixed multitude, and with them, flocks, and herds, and even very much cattle.

And God led the people through the way of the wilderness of the Red Sea. And the Lord went before them by day in a pillar of a cloud, to lead them the way, and by night in a pillar of fire, to give them light; to go by day and by night. And the Lord spake unto Moses, saying, " Speak unto the children of Israel, that they turn and encamp by the sea." And they did so.

GO FORWARD

And it was told the king of Egypt that the people fled: and the heart of Pharaoh and of his servants was turned against the people, and they said, " Why have we done this, that we have let Israel go from serving us? " And Pharaoh made ready his chariot, and took his people with him: and he took six hundred chosen chariots, and all the chariots of Egypt, and captains over every one of them. And he pursued after the children of Israel. And his army overtook them encamping by the sea.

And when Pharaoh drew nigh, the children of Israel lifted up their eyes, and behold, the Egyptians marched after them; and they were sore afraid: and the children of Israel cried out unto the Lord. And they said unto Moses, " Because there were no graves in Egypt, hast thou taken us away to die in the wilderness? Wherefore hast thou dealt thus with us, to carry us forth out of Egypt? Is not this the word that we did tell thee in Egypt, saying, ' Let us alone, that we may serve the Egyptians? ' For it had been better for us to serve the Egyptians, than that we should die in the wilderness."

And Moses said unto the people, " Fear ye not, stand still, and see the salvation of the Lord, which he will show to you today: for the Egyptians whom ye have seen today, ye shall see them again no more for ever. The Lord shall fight for you, and ye shall hold your peace."

And the Lord said unto Moses, "Wherefore criest thou unto me? Speak unto the children of Israel, that they go forward: but lift thou up thy rod, and stretch out thine hand over the sea, and divide it: and the children of Israel shall go on dry ground through the midst of the sea."

And the angel of God which went before the camp of Israel, removed, and went behind them; and the pillar of the cloud went from before their face, and stood behind them: and it came between the camp of the Egyptians and the camp of Israel; and it was a cloud and darkness to them, but it gave light by night to these: so that the one came not near the other all the night.

And Moses stretched out his hand over the sea; and the Lord caused the sea to go back by a strong east wind all that night, and made the sea dry land, and the waters were divided. And the children of Israel went into the midst of the sea upon the dry ground: and the waters were a wall unto them on their right hand, and on their left. And the Egyptians pursued, and went in after them, to the midst of the sea, even all Pharaoh's horses, his chariots, and his horsemen.

And the Lord said unto Moses, "Stretch out thine hand over the sea, that the waters may come again upon the Egyptians, upon their chariots, and upon their horsemen." And Moses stretched forth his hand over the sea, and the sea returned to his strength when the morning appeared; and the Egyptians fled against it; and the Lord overthrew the Egyptians in the midst of the sea. And the waters returned, and covered the chariots, and the horsemen, and all the host of Pharaoh that came into the sea: there remained not so much as one of them.

But the children of Israel walked upon dry land in the midst of the sea; and the waters were a wall unto them on their right hand, and on their left. Thus the Lord saved Israel that day out of the hand of the Egyptians: and Israel saw the Egyptians dead upon the sea-shore. And Israel saw that great work which the

Lord did upon the Egyptians: and the people feared the Lord, and believed the Lord, and his servant Moses.

Then sang Moses and the children of Israel this song unto the Lord:

"The Lord is my strength and song,
And he is become my salvation:
He is my God, and I will prepare him an habitation;
My father's God, and I will exalt him.

The enemy said:
'I will pursue,
I will overtake,
I will divide the spoil;
My lust shall be satisfied upon them;
I will draw my sword,
My hand shall destroy them.'

Thou didst blow with thy wind,
The sea covered them;
They sank as lead in the mighty waters.

Who is like unto thee, O Lord, among the gods?
Who is like thee, glorious in holiness,
Fearful in praises, doing wonders?
Thou in thy mercy hast led forth the people which thou hast redeemed,
Thou hast guided them in thy strength unto thy holy habitation.

Thou shalt bring them in, and plant them in the mountain of thine inheritance,
In the place, O Lord, which thou hast made for thee to dwell in,
In the Sanctuary, O Lord, which thy hands have established.

The Lord shall reign for ever and ever."

And Miriam the prophetess, the sister of Aaron, took a timbrel in her hand; and all the women went out after her, with timbrels, and with dances. And Miriam answered them,

" Sing ye to the Lord, for he hath triumphed gloriously;
The horse and his rider hath he thrown into the sea."

So Moses brought Israel from the Red Sea, and they went out into the wilderness of Shur; and they went three days in the wilderness, and found no water. And when they came to Marah, they could not drink of the waters of Marah, for they were bitter. And the people murmured against Moses, saying, " What shall we drink? "

And Moses cried unto the Lord; and the Lord showed him a tree, which when he had cast into the waters, the waters were made sweet. There he made for them a statute and an ordinance, and there he proved them, and said, " If thou wilt diligently hearken to the voice of the Lord thy God, and wilt do that which is right in his sight, and wilt give ear to his commandments, and keep all his statutes, I will put none of these diseases upon thee, which I have brought upon the Egyptians: for I am the Lord that healeth thee."

And they came to Elim, where were twelve wells of water, and threescore and ten palm-trees; and they encamped there by the waters.

THE BREAD WHICH THE LORD HATH GIVEN

And they took their journey from Elim, and all the congregation of the children of Israel came unto the wilderness of Sin, which is between Elim and Sinai, on the fifteenth day of the second month after their departing out of the land of Egypt. And the whole congregation of the children of Israel murmured against Moses and Aaron in the wilderness: and they said unto them, "Would to God we had died by the hand of the Lord in the land of Egypt, when we sat by the flesh-pots, and when we did eat bread to the full: for ye have brought us forth into this wilderness, to kill this whole assembly with hunger."

Then said the Lord unto Moses, "Behold, I will rain bread from heaven for you; and the people shall go out and gather a certain rate every day, that I may prove them, whether they will walk in my law, or no. And it shall come to pass, that on the sixth day they shall prepare that which they bring in; and it shall be twice as much as they gather daily."

And Moses and Aaron said unto all the children of Israel, "At even, then ye shall know that the Lord hath brought you out from the land of Egypt: and in the morning, then ye shall see the glory of the Lord: this shall be when the Lord shall give you in the evening flesh to eat, and in the morning bread to the full; for the Lord heareth your murmurings which ye murmur against him: for what are we, that ye murmur against us? your murmurings are not against us, but against the Lord."

And it came to pass, as Aaron spake unto the whole congregation of the children of Israel, that they looked toward the wilderness, and behold, the glory of the Lord appeared in the cloud, and the Lord spake unto Moses, saying, "I have heard the murmurings of the children of Israel; speak unto them saying, 'At even ye shall eat flesh, and in the morning ye shall be filled with bread: and ye shall know that I am the Lord your God.' "

And it came to pass, that at even the quails came up, and covered the camp: and in the morning the dew lay round about the host. And when the dew that lay was gone up, behold, upon the face of the wilderness there lay a small round thing, as small as the hoar frost on the ground. And when the children of Israel saw it, they said one to another, "It is manna:" for they wist not what it was.

And Moses said unto them, "This is the bread which the Lord hath given you to eat. This is the thing which the Lord hath commanded, 'Gather of it every man according to his eating: an omer for every man according to the number of your persons, take ye every man for them which are in his tents.'" And the children of Israel did so, and gathered, some more, some less. And when they did mete it with an omer, he that gathered much had nothing over, and he that gathered little had no lack: they gathered every man according to his eating. And it was like white coriander seed. And the people gathered it, and ground it in mills, or beat it in a mortar, and baked it in pans, and made cakes of it. And the taste of it was like wafers made with honey.

And Moses said, "Let no man leave of it till the morning." Notwithstanding, they hearkened not unto Moses; but some of them left of it until the morning, and it bred worms, and stank: and Moses was wroth with them. And they gathered it every morning, every man according to his eating; and when the sun waxed hot it melted.

And it came to pass, that on the sixth day they gathered twice as much bread, two omers for one man: and all the rulers of the congregation came and told Moses. And he said unto them, "This is that which the Lord hath said, 'Tomorrow is the rest of the holy sabbath unto the Lord: bake that which ye will bake today, and seethe that ye will seethe; and that which remaineth over, lay up for you to be kept until the morning.'"

And they laid it up till the morning, as Moses bade: and it did not stink, neither was there any worm therein.

And Moses said, "Eat that today; for today is a sabbath unto the Lord; today ye shall not find it in the field. Six days ye shall gather it; but on the seventh day, which is the sabbath, in it there shall be none." And it came to pass, that there went out some of the people on the seventh day for to gather, and they found none.

And the Lord said unto Moses, "How long refuse ye to keep my commandments and my laws? See, for that the Lord hath given you the sabbath, therefore he giveth you on the sixth day the bread of two days: abide ye every man in his place, let no man go out of his place on the seventh day." So the people rested on the seventh day.

And the children of Israel did eat manna forty years, until they came to a land inhabited: they did eat manna, until they came unto the borders of the land of Canaan.

IS THE LORD AMONG US, OR NOT?

AND ALL the congregation of the children of Israel journeyed from the wilderness of Sin, according to the commandment of the Lord, and pitched in Rephidim: and there was no water for the people to drink. Wherefore the people did chide with Moses, and said, "Give us water that we may drink."

And Moses said unto them, "Why chide ye with me? wherefore do ye tempt the Lord?"

And the people thirsted there for water; and the people murmured against Moses, and said, "Wherefore is this that thou hast brought us up out of Egypt to kill us and our children and our cattle with thirst?"

And Moses cried unto the Lord, saying, " What shall I do unto this people? they be almost ready to stone me."

And the Lord said unto Moses, " Go on before the people, and take with thee of the elders of Israel: and thy rod, wherewith thou smotest the river, take in thine hand, and go. Behold, I will stand before thee there upon the rock in Horeb; and thou shalt smite the rock, and there shall come water out of it, that the people may drink."

And Moses did so in the sight of the elders of Israel. And he called the name of the place Massah, and Meribah, because of the chiding of the children of Israel, and because they tempted the Lord, saying, " Is the Lord among us, or not? "

Then came Amalek, and fought with Israel in Rephidim. And Moses said unto Joshua, " Choose us out men, and go out, fight with Amalek: tomorrow I will stand on the top of the hill with the rod of God in mine hand."

So Joshua did as Moses had said to him, and fought with Amalek: and Moses, Aaron, and Hur, went up to the top of the hill. And it came to pass, when Moses held up his hand, that Israel prevailed: and when he let down his hand, Amalek prevailed. But Moses' hands were heavy; and they took a stone, and put it under him, and he sat thereon: and Aaron and Hur stayed up his hands, the one on the one side, and the other on the other side; and his hands were steady until the going down of the sun. And Joshua discomfited Amalek and his people with the edge of the sword. And Moses built an altar, and called the name of it Jehovah-nissi.

THE LAW

" The commandment is a lamp,
And the law is light."

I MAKE THEM KNOW THE STATUTES AND LAWS OF GOD

When Jethro the priest of Midian, Moses' father-in-law, heard of all that God had done for Moses, and for Israel his people, and that the Lord had brought Israel out of Egypt, then Jethro took Zipporah, Moses' wife, for Moses had sent her back, and her two sons, and came unto Moses into the wilderness, where he encamped at the mount of God. And he said unto Moses, "I thy father-in-law Jethro am come unto thee, and thy wife, and her two sons with her."

And Moses went out to meet his father-in-law, and did obeisance, and kissed him: and they asked each other of their welfare; and they came into the tent. And Moses told his father-in-law all that the Lord had done unto Pharaoh, and to the Egyptians for Israel's sake, and all the travail that had come upon them by the way, and how the Lord delivered them.

And Jethro rejoiced for all the goodness which the Lord had done to Israel, whom he had delivered out of the hand of the Egyptians. And Jethro said, "Blessed be the Lord, who hath delivered you out of the hand of the Egyptians, and out of the hand of Pharaoh, who hath delivered the people from under the hand of the Egyptians. Now I know that the Lord is greater than all gods: for in the thing wherein they dealt proudly, he was above them." And Jethro took a burnt offering and sacrifices for God: and Aaron came, and all the elders of Israel to eat bread with Moses' father-in-law, before God.

And it came to pass on the morrow, that Moses sat to judge the people: and the people stood by Moses from the morning unto the evening. And when Moses' father-in-law saw all that he did to the people, he said, "What is this thing that thou doest to the people? Why sittest thou thyself alone, and all the people stand by thee from morning unto even?"

And Moses said unto his father-in-law, “Because the people come unto me to inquire of God: when they have a matter, they come unto me, and I judge between one and another, and I do make them know the statutes of God, and his laws.”

And Moses' father-in-law said unto him, “The thing that thou doest is not good. Thou wilt surely wear away, both thou, and this people that is with thee: for this thing is too heavy for thee; thou art not able to perform it thyself alone. Hearken now unto my voice, I will give thee counsel, and God shall be with thee: Be thou for the people God-ward, that thou mayest bring the causes unto God: and thou shalt teach them ordinances and laws, and shalt show them the way wherein they must walk, and the work that they must do. Moreover, thou shalt provide out of all the people, able men, such as fear God, men of truth, hating covetousness; and place such over them to be rulers of thousands, and rulers of hundreds, rulers of fifties, and rulers of tens: and let them judge the people at all seasons. And it shall be, that every great matter they shall bring unto thee, but every small matter they shall judge; so shall it be easier for thyself, and they shall bear the burden with thee. If thou shalt do this thing, and God command thee so, then thou shalt be able to endure, and all this people shall also go to their place in peace.”

So Moses hearkened to the voice of his father-in-law, and did all that he had said. And Moses chose able men out of all Israel, and made them heads over the people, rulers of thousands, rulers of hundreds, rulers of fifties, and rulers of tens. And they judged the people at all seasons: the hard causes they brought unto Moses, but every small matter they judged themselves.

And Moses let his father-in-law depart: and he went his way into his own land.

THE TEN COMMANDMENTS

IN THE THIRD MONTH, after the children of Israel were gone forth out of the land of Egypt, they came into the wilderness of Sinai, and there Israel camped before the mount.

And Moses went up unto God, and the Lord called unto him out of the mountain, saying, "Thus shalt thou say to the house of Jacob, 'Ye have seen what I did unto the Egyptians, and how I bare you on eagles' wings, and brought you unto myself. Now therefore, if ye will obey my voice indeed, and keep my covenant, then ye shall be a peculiar treasure unto me above all people: for all the earth is mine; and ye shall be unto me a holy nation.' These are the words which thou shalt speak unto the children of Israel."

And Moses came and called for the elders of the people, and laid before their faces all these words which the Lord commanded him. And all the people answered together, and said, "All that the Lord hath spoken we will do." And Moses returned the words of the people unto the Lord.

And the Lord said unto Moses, "Lo, I come unto thee in a thick cloud, that the people may hear when I speak with thee, and believe thee for ever. Go unto the people, and sanctify them today and tomorrow, and let them wash their clothes, and be ready against the third day; for the third day I will come down in the sight of all the people upon mount Sinai."

And Moses went down from the mount unto the people, and sanctified the people; and they washed their clothes. And he said unto the people, "Be ready against the third day."

And it came to pass on the third day in the morning, that there were thunders and lightnings, and a thick cloud upon the mount, and the voice of the trumpet exceeding loud; so that all the people that were in the camp trembled. And Moses brought forth the people out of the camp to meet with God; and they stood at the nether part of the mount. And mount Sinai was altogether on a smoke, because the Lord descended upon it in fire: and the smoke thereof ascended as the smoke of a furnace, and the whole mount quaked greatly. And when the voice of the trumpet sounded long, and waxed louder and louder, Moses spake, and God answered him by a voice. And the Lord came down upon mount Sinai, on the top of the mount.

And God spake all these words, saying, "I am the Lord thy God, which have brought thee out of the land of Egypt, out of the house of bondage:

I

"Thou shalt have no other gods before me.

II

"Thou shalt not make unto thee any graven image, or any likeness of anything that is in heaven above, or that is in the earth beneath, or that is in the water under the earth: thou shalt not bow down thyself to them, nor serve them: for I the Lord thy God am a jealous God, visiting the iniquity of the fathers upon the children unto the third and fourth generation of them that hate me; and showing mercy unto thousands of them that love me, and keep my commandments.

III

"Thou shalt not take the name of the Lord thy God in vain: for the Lord will not hold him guiltless that taketh his name in vain.

IV

"Remember the sabbath day to keep it holy. Six days shalt thou labour, and do all thy work: but the seventh day is the sabbath of the Lord thy God: in it thou shalt not do any work, thou, nor thy son, nor thy daughter, thy man-servant, nor thy maid-servant, nor thy cattle, nor thy stranger that is within thy gates: for in six days the Lord made heaven and earth, the sea and all that in them is, and rested the seventh day: wherefore the Lord blessed the sabbath day and hallowed it.

V

"Honour thy father and thy mother; that thy days may be long upon the land which the Lord thy God giveth thee.

VI

"Thou shalt not kill.

VII

"Thou shalt not commit adultery.

VIII

"Thou shalt not steal.

IX

"Thou shalt not bear false witness against thy neighbour.

X

"Thou shalt not covet thy neighbour's house, thou shalt not covet thy neighbour's wife, nor his man-servant, nor his maid-servant, nor his ox, nor his ass, nor anything that is thy neighbour's."

And all the people saw the thunderings, and the lightnings, and the noise of the trumpet, and the mountain smoking. And when the people saw it, they removed, and stood afar off. And they said unto Moses, "Speak thou with us, and we will hear: but let not God speak with us, lest we die."

And Moses said unto the people, "Fear not: for God is come to prove you, and that his fear may be before your faces, that ye sin not." And the people stood afar off, and Moses drew near unto the thick darkness where God was.

And the Lord said unto Moses, "Thus thou shalt say unto the children of Israel: 'Ye have seen that I have talked with you from heaven. Ye shall not make gods of silver, neither shall ye make unto you gods of gold. An altar of earth thou shalt make unto me, and shalt sacrifice thereon thy burnt offerings, and thy peace offerings, thy sheep, and thine oxen. In all places where I record my name I will come unto thee, and I will bless thee. Behold, I send an Angel before thee, to keep thee in the way, and to bring thee into the place which I have prepared. And ye shall serve the Lord your God, and he shall bless thy bread, and thy water, and will take sickness away from the midst of thee. I will send my fear before thee, for I will deliver the inhabitants of the land into your hand; and thou shalt drive them out before thee. Thou shalt make no covenant with them, nor with their gods. They shall not dwell in thy land, lest they make thee sin against me. Thou shalt not bow down to their gods, nor serve them, nor do after their works: but thou shalt utterly overthrow them, and quite break down their images. For if thou serve their gods, it will surely be a snare unto thee."

And Moses came and told the people all the words of the Lord, and all the judgments: and all the people answered with one voice, and said, "All the words which the Lord hath said will we do."

And Moses wrote all the words of the Lord, and rose up early in the morning, and builded an altar under the hill, and twelve pillars according to the twelve tribes of Israel. And he sent young men of the children of Israel, which offered burnt-offerings, and sacrificed peace-offerings of oxen unto the Lord. And he took the book of the covenant, and read in the audience of the people. And they said, " All that the Lord hath said will we do, and be obedient."

And the Lord said unto Moses, " Come up to me into the mount, and be there; and I will give thee tables of stone, and a law, and commandments which I have written; that thou mayest teach them."

And Moses rose up, and his minister Joshua, and he said unto the elders, " Tarry ye here for us, until we come again unto you. And behold, Aaron and Hur are with you; if any man have any matters to do, let him come unto them."

And Moses went up into the mount, and a cloud covered the mount. And the glory of the Lord abode upon mount Sinai, and the cloud covered it six days: and the seventh day God called unto Moses out of the midst of the cloud. And the sight of the glory of the Lord was like devouring fire on the top of the mount in the eyes of the children of Israel. And Moses went into the midst of the cloud, and got him up into the mount.

THE LAW IS HOLY, AND THE COMMANDMENT IS HOLY, AND JUST, AND GOOD

AND MOSES was in the mount forty days and forty nights, and the Lord spake unto Moses, saying, "Speak unto all the congregation of the children of Israel, and say unto them: Ye shall be holy for I the Lord your God am holy. I Am the Lord that brought you up out of the land of Egypt to be your God. Ye shall therefore be holy for I am holy. Ye shall keep all my statutes and all my judgments, and do them. I am the Lord your God which have separated you from other people, that ye should be mine. Ye shall therefore sanctify yourselves, and ye shall be holy, for I am holy."

"AND THOU SHALT LOVE THE LORD THY GOD WITH ALL THINE HEART, AND WITH ALL THY SOUL, AND WITH ALL THY MIGHT."

I

"*Thou shalt have no other gods before me.* Thou shalt not go aside from any of the words which I command thee this day, to the right hand or to the left, to go after other gods to serve them. If there arise among you a prophet, or a dreamer of dreams, and giveth thee a sign or a wonder, and the sign or the wonder come to pass whereof he spake unto thee, saying, 'Let us go after other gods, which thou hast not known, and let us serve them;' thou shalt not hearken unto the words of that prophet, or that dreamer of dreams: for the Lord your God proveth you, to know whether ye love the Lord your God with all your heart, and with all your soul. And if thy brother, the son of thy mother, or thy son, or thy daughter, or the wife of thy bosom, or thy friend, which is as thine own soul, entice thee secretly, saying, 'Let us go and serve other gods, which thou hast not known,' thou shalt not consent unto him, or hearken unto him. Ye shall walk after the Lord your God, and fear him, and keep his commandments, and obey his voice, and ye shall serve him, and cleave unto him. In all things that I have said unto you, be circumspect: and make no mention of the name of other gods, neither let it be heard out of thy mouth.

II

"*Thou shalt not make unto thee any graven image.* Turn ye not unto idols, nor make to yourselves molten gods: I am the Lord your God. Ye shall make you no idols nor graven image, neither rear you up a standing image, neither shall ye set up an image of stone in your land to bow down unto it: for I am the Lord your God. Take ye therefore good heed unto yourselves, lest ye corrupt yourselves, and make you a graven image, the similitude of any figure, the likeness of male or female, the likeness of any beast that is on the earth, the likeness of any winged fowl that flieth in the air, the likeness of any thing that creepeth upon the ground, the likeness of any fish that is in the waters beneath the earth; and lest thou lift up thine eyes unto heaven, and when thou seest the sun, and the moon, and the stars, even all the host of heaven shouldest be driven to worship them, and serve them. Take heed unto yourselves, lest ye forget the covenant of the Lord your God, which he made with you, and make a graven image, or the likeness of any thing which the Lord thy God hath forbidden thee. For the Lord thy God is a consuming fire, even a jealous God, visiting the iniquity of the fathers upon the children unto the third and fourth generation of them that hate me, and showing mercy unto thousands of them that love me and keep my commandments.

III

"*Thou shalt not take the name of the Lord thy God in vain.* Profane not my holy name; but I will be hallowed among the children of Israel: I am the Lord which hallow you. The Lord will not hold him guiltless that taketh his name in vain.

IV

"*Remember the Sabbath day to keep it holy.* Verily my sabbaths ye shall keep: for it is a sign between me and you throughout your generations, that ye may know that I am the Lord that doth sanctify you. Wherefore the children of Israel shall keep the sabbath for a perpetual covenant. It is a sign between me and the children of Israel for ever: for in six days the Lord made heaven and earth, and on the seventh day he rested and was refreshed. Ye shall keep the sabbath therefore: for it is holy unto you.

"Keep the sabbath day and sanctify it, as the Lord thy God hath commanded thee. Six days may work be done, but the seventh is the sabbath of rest, holy to the Lord. On the seventh day thou shalt rest, that thine ox and thine ass may rest, and the son of thy handmaid, and the stranger, may be refreshed.

"And when ye come into the land which I give you, then shall the land keep a sabbath unto the Lord. Six years thou shalt prune thy vineyard, and gather in the fruit thereof; but in the seventh year shall be a sabbath of rest unto the land, a sabbath for the Lord: thou shalt neither sow thy field, nor prune thy vineyard. That which groweth of its own accord of thy harvest, thou shalt not reap, neither gather the grapes of thy vine undressed: for it is a year of rest unto the land. And if ye shall say, 'What shall we eat the seventh year? behold, we shall not sow nor gather in our increase;' then I will command my blessing upon you in the sixth year, and it shall bring forth fruit for three years. And ye shall sow the eighth year, and eat yet of old fruit until the ninth year; until her fruits come in ye shall eat of the old store.

"At the end of every seven years thou shalt make a release. And this is the manner of the release: Every creditor that lendeth aught unto his neighbour shall release it; he shall not exact it of his neighbour, or of his brother; because it is called the Lord's release. That which is thine with thy brother, thine hand shall release. And if thy brother, an Hebrew man, or an Hebrew woman, be sold unto thee, and serve thee six years, then in the seventh year thou shalt let him go free from thee. And when thou sendest him out free from thee, thou shalt not let him go away empty: Thou shalt furnish him liberally out of thy flock, and out of thy floor, and out of thy wine-press: of that wherewith the Lord thy God hath blessed thee thou shalt give unto him. And thou shalt remember that thou wast a bond-man in the land of Egypt, and the Lord thy God redeemed thee; therefore I command thee this thing today. It shall not seem hard unto thee, when thou sendest him away free: for he hath been worth a double hired servant to thee, in serving thee six years; and the Lord thy God shall bless thee in all that thou doest.

"And thou shalt number seven sabbaths of years unto thee, seven times seven years; and the space of the seven sabbaths of years shall be unto thee forty and nine years. Then shalt thou cause the trumpet of the jubilee to sound. In the day of atonement shall ye make the trumpet sound throughout all your land. And ye shall hallow the fiftieth year, and proclaim liberty throughout all the land unto all the inhabitants thereof: it shall be a jubilee unto you; and ye shall return every man unto his possession, and ye shall return every man unto his family. A jubilee shall that fiftieth year be unto you: ye shall not sow, neither reap that which groweth of itself, nor gather the grapes of thy vine. For it is the jubilee; it shall be holy unto you. And if thou sell aught unto thy neighbour, or buyest aught of thy neighbour's hand, ye shall not oppress one another; but thou shalt fear thy God: for I am the Lord your God. Wherefore ye shall do my statutes, and keep my judgments, and do them; and ye shall dwell in the land in safety. And the land shall yield her fruit, and ye shall eat your fill, and dwell therein in safety.

"Ye shall keep my sabbaths, and reverence my sanctuary: I am the Lord.

V

"*Honour thy Father and thy Mother.* Honour thy Father and thy Mother as the Lord thy God hath commanded thee, that thy days may be prolonged, and that it may go well with thee in the land which the Lord thy God giveth thee.

VI

"*Thou shalt not kill.* He that killeth any man shall surely be put to death. And he that killeth a beast shall make it good; beast for beast. And if a man cause a blemish in his neighbor, as he hath done, so shall it be done unto him: breach for breach, eye for eye, tooth for tooth; as he hath caused a blemish in a man, so shall it be done to him again. The innocent and the righteous slay thou not; for I will not justify the wicked. The fathers shall not be put to death for the children, neither shall the children be put to death for the fathers.

"Ye shall have one manner of law, as well for the stranger as for one of your own country. Thou shalt not oppress the stranger. And if a stranger sojourn with thee in your land, ye shall not vex him. But the stranger that dwelleth with you, shall be unto you as one born among you, and thou shalt love him as thyself.

"Thou shalt not oppress an hired servant that is poor and needy whether he be of thy brethren or the stranger that is in thy land. If there be among you a poor man of one of thy brethren within thy gates, thou shalt not harden thy heart, nor shut thine hand from thy poor brother, but thou shalt open thine hand wide unto him, and shalt surely lend him sufficient for his need, in that which he wanteth. And if thy brother be waxen poor, and fallen into decay with thee, then thou shalt relieve him, yea though he be a stranger or a sojourner. Take thou no usury of him, or increase; but fear thy God that thy brother may live with thee. And thine heart shall not be grieved when thou givest him, because that for this thing the Lord shall bless thee in all thy works, and in all that thou puttest thine hand unto. For the poor shall never cease out of the land: therefore, I command thee, saying, thou shalt open thine hand wide unto thy brother, to thy poor, and to thy needy in the land. And when ye reap the harvest of your land, thou shalt not wholly reap the corners of thy field, neither shalt thou gather the gleanings of thy harvest; it shall be for the stranger, for the fatherless, and for the widow; that the Lord thy God may bless thee in all the works of thy hands.

"Thou shalt not hate thy brother in thine heart; thou shalt in any wise rebuke thy neighbour, and not suffer sin upon him. Thou shalt not avenge, nor bear any grudge against the children of thy people, but thou shalt love thy neighbour as thyself; I am the Lord.

VII

"*Thou shalt not commit adultery*. He that committeth adultery, the adulterer and the adulteress shall surely be put to death; they have wrought confusion; it is a wicked and an unclean thing, and they shall be cut off in the sight of their people. Thou shalt not let thy cattle gender with a diverse kind; thou shalt not sow thy field with mingled seed: it is confusion. Defile not ye yourselves in any of these things.

"Regard not them that have familiar spirits, neither seek after wizards to be defiled by them. The soul that turneth after such as have familiar spirits, and after wizards to go a whoring after them, I will even set my face against that soul, and will cut him off from among his people. There shall not be found among you any one that maketh his son or his daughter pass through the fire, or that useth divination, or an observer of times, or an enchanter, or a witch, or a charmer, or a consulter with familiar spirits, or a wizard, or a necromancer. For all of these things are an abomination unto the Lord; for in all these the nations are defiled which I cast out before you. And the land is defiled: therefore I do visit the iniquity thereof upon it, and the land itself vomiteth out her inhabitants. Ye shall therefore keep my statutes and my judgments, and shall not commit any of these abominations that the land spue you not out also, as it spued out the nations that were before you. Therefore shall ye keep mine ordinance, that ye commit not any of these abominable customs, and that ye defile not yourselves. Thou shalt be perfect with the Lord thy God. Sanctify yourselves therefore, and be ye holy: for I am the Lord your God.

VIII

"*Thou shalt not steal.* Ye shall not steal, neither deal falsely, neither lie one to another. Thou shalt not defraud thy neighbour, neither rob him. Thou shalt not see thy brother's ox or his sheep go astray and hide thyself from them; thou shalt in any case bring them again unto thy brother. And with all lost things of thy brother's which he hath lost, and thou hast found, shalt thou do likewise; thou mayest not hide thyself. Thou shalt not see thy brother's ass or his ox fall down by the way, and hide thyself from them: thou shalt surely help him lift them up again.

"Ye shall do no unrighteousness in judgment, in mete-yard, in weight, or in measure. Just balances, just weights, a just epha, and a just bin shall ye have.

"Judges and officers shalt thou make thee in thy gates, which the Lord thy God giveth thee throughout thy tribes: and they shall judge the people with just judgment. Thou shalt not wrest judgment; thou shalt not respect persons, neither take a gift: for a gift doth blind the eyes of the wise, and pervert the words of the righteous. If there be a controversy between men, and they come unto judgment, that the judges may judge them, then they shall justify the righteous and condemn the wicked. Ye shall not respect persons in judgment; but ye shall hear the small as well as the great; ye shall not be afraid of the face of a man, for the judgment is God's. That which is altogether just shalt thou follow, that thou mayest live, and inherit the land which the Lord thy God giveth thee.

IX

"*Thou shalt not bear false witness.* Thou shalt not raise a false report. Neither shalt thou bear false witness against thy neighbour. Put not thine hand with the wicked to be an unrighteous witness. Thou shalt not follow a multitude to do evil; neither shalt thou speak in a cause to decline after many to wrest judgment.

"If a false witness shall rise up against any man to testify against him that which is wrong, then both the men between whom the controversy is, shall stand before the Lord, before the priests and the judges, and the judges shall make diligent inquisition; and behold, if the witness be a false witness, and hath testified falsely against his brother, then shall ye do unto him, as he had thought to have done unto his brother; so shalt thou put the evil away from among you. And those which remain shall hear, and fear, and shall henceforth commit no more any such evil among you.

"Thou shalt not go up and down as a tale bearer, among thy people. Keep thee far from a false matter. For thy God is a God of Truth, and without inquity, just and right is he.

X

"*Thou shalt not covet.* Thou shalt not covet thy neighbour's house; neither shalt thou desire thy neighbour's wife; neither shalt thou covet thy neighbour's field, or his man-servant, or his maid-servant, his ox, or his ass, or anything that is thy neighbour's. Because the Lord thy God shall bless thee in all thine increase, and in all the works of thine hands, therefore thou shalt surely rejoice. Thou shalt love thy neighbour as thyself.

"If ye walk in my statutes and keep my commandments, and do them, then I will give you rain in due season, and the land shall yield her increase, and the trees of the field shall yield their fruit: and your threshing shall reach unto the vintage, and the vintage shall reach unto the sowing time; and ye shall eat your bread to the full, and dwell in your land safely. And ye shall eat old store, and bring forth the old because of the new. And I will take sickness away from the midst of thee.

"And I will give peace in the land, and ye shall lie down, and none shall make you afraid: and I will rid evil beasts out of the land, neither shall the sword go through your land.

"And I will set my tabernacle among you. And I will walk among you, and will be your God, and ye shall be my people. Ye shall be holy, for I the Lord your God am holy."

These are the commandments which the Lord commanded Moses for the children of Israel in mount Sinai. And Moses was in the mount forty days and forty nights. And God gave unto Moses, when he had made an end of communing with him, upon mount Sinai, two tables of testimony, tables of stone, written with the finger of God.

WHO IS ON THE LORD'S SIDE?

AND WHEN THE PEOPLE saw that Moses delayed to come down out of the mount, the people gathered themselves together unto Aaron, and said unto him, "Up, make us gods, which shall go before us; as for this Moses, the man that brought us up out of the land of Egypt, we wot not what is become of him."

And Aaron said unto them, "Break off the golden ear-rings, which are in the ears of your wives, of your sons, and of your daughters, and bring them unto me."

And all the people brake off the golden ear-rings which were in their ears, and brought them unto Aaron. And he received them at their hand, and fashioned it with a graving tool, after it was molten, and made a golden calf.

And they said, "These be thy gods, O Israel, which brought thee up out of the land of Egypt."

And Aaron built an altar before it, and made proclamation and said, "Tomorrow is a feast day."

And they rose up early on the morrow, and offered burnt offerings, and brought peace offerings; and the people sat down to eat and drink, and rose up to play.

And the Lord said unto Moses, "Go, get thee down; for thy people which thou broughtest out of the land of Egypt, have corrupted themselves. They have turned aside quickly out of the way which I commanded them; they have made them a molten calf, and have worshipped it, and have sacrificed thereunto, and said, 'These be thy gods, O Israel, which have brought thee up out of the land of Egypt.'"

And Moses turned, and went down from the mount, and the two tables of the testimony were in his hand: the tables were written on both their sides; on the one side, and on the other were they written. And the tables were the work of God, and the writing was the writing of God, graven upon the tables.

And it came to pass, as soon as Moses came nigh unto the camp, that he saw the calf, and the dancing; and Moses' anger waxed hot, and he cast the tables out of his hands, and brake them beneath the mount. And he took the calf which they had made, and burnt it in the fire, and ground it to powder, and strewed it upon the water, and made the children of Israel drink it.

And Moses said unto Aaron, "What did this people unto thee, that thou hast brought so great a sin upon them?"

And Aaron said, "Let not the anger of my lord wax hot: thou knowest the people, that they are set on mischief. For they said unto me, 'Make us gods which shall go before us: for, as for this Moses, the man that brought us up out of the land of Egypt, we wot not what is become of him.' And I said unto them, 'Whosoever hath any gold, let them break it off.' So they gave it me; then I cast it into the fire, and there came out this calf."

Then Moses stood in the gate of the camp, and said, "Who is on the Lord's side? Let him come unto me."

And he said unto them, "Consecrate yourselves today to the Lord, even every man that he may bestow upon you a blessing this day."

And it came to pass on the morrow, that Moses said unto the people, "Ye have sinned a great sin: and now I will go up unto the Lord: peradventure I shall make an atonement for your sin."

And Moses returned unto the Lord and said, "Oh, this people have sinned a great sin, and have made them gods of gold. Yet now, if thou wilt, forgive their sin: and if not, blot me I pray thee, out of thy book which thou hast written."

And the Lord said unto Moses, "Whosoever hath sinned against me, him will I blot out of my book. Therefore, depart and go up hence, thou, and the people which thou hast brought up out of the land of Egypt, unto the land which I sware unto Abraham, to Isaac, and to Jacob, saying, 'Unto thy seed will I give it.' And I will send an angel before thee, unto a land flowing with milk and honey. Now go, lead the people unto the place of which I have spoken unto thee. Behold, mine angel shall go before thee. But say unto the children of Israel, 'Ye are a stiff-necked people: therefore now put off thy ornaments from thee, that I may know what to do unto thee, lest I consume thee in the way.'"

And when the children of Israel heard these tidings, they mourned, and stripped themselves of their ornaments.

And Moses took the tabernacle, and pitched it without the camp afar off from the camp, and called it the Tabernacle of the Congregation. And it came to pass, that every one which sought the Lord, went out unto the Tabernacle of the Congregation, which was without the camp.

And when Moses went out unto the Tabernacle, all the people rose up, and stood every man at his tent-door, and looked after Moses, until he was gone into the Tabernacle. And it came to pass as Moses entered into the Tabernacle, the cloudy pillar descended, and stood at the door of the Tabernacle, and the Lord talked with Moses.

And all the people saw the cloudy pillar stand at the Tabernacle-door; and all the people rose up and worshipped, every man in his tent-door.

And the Lord said unto Moses, "Hew thee two tables of stone like unto the first: and I will write upon these tables the words that were in the first tables which thou breakest. And be ready in the morning, and come up in the morning unto mount Sinai, and present thyself there to me, in the top of the mount. And no man shall come up with thee, neither let any man be seen throughout all the mount; neither let the flocks nor herds feed before that mount."

MOSES' FACE SHOWN

MOSES hewed two tables of stone, like unto the first; and Moses rose up early in the morning, and went up unto Mount Sinai, as the Lord had commanded him, and took in his hand the two tables of stone.

And the Lord descended in the cloud, and stood with him there, and proclaimed the name of the Lord. And the Lord passed by before him, and proclaimed, "The Lord, the Lord God, merciful and gracious, long-suffering, and abundant in goodness and truth, keeping mercy for thousands, forgiving iniquity and transgression and sin." And Moses made haste and bowed his head toward the earth and worshipped.

And the Lord spake unto Moses face to face, as a man speaketh unto his friend.

And Moses said, "If now I have found grace in thy sight, O Lord, let my Lord, I pray thee, go among us (for it is a stiff-necked people), and pardon our iniquity and sin, and take us for thine inheritance. See, thou sayest unto me, 'Bring up this people:' and thou hast not let me know whom thou wilt send with me. Yet thou hast said, 'I know thee by name, and thou hast found grace in my sight.' Now therefore, I pray thee, if I have found grace in thy sight, show me now thy way, that I may know thee, that I may find grace in thy sight: and consider that this nation is thy people."

And the Lord said, "My presence shall go with thee, and I will give thee rest."

And Moses said, "I beseech thee, show me thy glory."

And the Lord said, "I will make all my goodness pass before thee; and I will proclaim the name of the Lord before thee. Behold, thou shalt stand upon a rock: and it shall come to pass while my glory passeth by, that I will put thee in a cleft of the rock; and I will cover thee with my hand while I pass by."

And Moses made haste, and bowed his head toward the earth, and worshipped.

And the Lord said unto Moses, "Write thou these words: for after the tenor of these words I have made a covenant with thee, and with Israel." And Moses was there with the Lord forty days and forty nights; he did neither eat bread nor drink water. And he wrote upon the tables the words of the covenant, the ten commandments.

And it came to pass when Moses came down from mount Sinai, with the two tables of testimony in his hand, that Moses wist not that the skin of his face shone while he talked with God.

And when Aaron, and all the children of Israel saw Moses, behold, the skin of his face shone; and they were afraid to come nigh him. And Moses called unto them; and Aaron and all the rulers of the congregation returned unto him. And Moses put a veil upon his face. And afterward all the children of Israel returned unto him. And Moses talked with them, and gave them in commandment all that the Lord had spoken with him in mount Sinai. And till Moses had done speaking with them, he kept a veil on his face, for the children of Israel saw the face of Moses, that the skin of Moses' face shone.

MAKE ME A SANCTUARY

AND THE LORD spake unto Moses, saying, "Speak unto the children of Israel that they bring me an offering; of every man that giveth it willingly with his heart, ye shall take my offering. And let them make me a sanctuary, that I may dwell among them. According to all that I show thee, after the pattern of the tabernacle, and the pattern of all the instruments thereof, even so shall ye make it.

"They shall make an ark of shittim wood, and shall overlay it with pure gold, within and without, and shall make upon it a crown of gold round about. And they shall cast four rings of gold for it, and put them in the four corners thereof; and shall make staves of shittim wood, and overlay them with gold, and put the staves into the rings by the side of the Ark, that the Ark may be borne with them. And thou shalt put into the Ark the testimony, the two tables of stone, the Ten Commandments written with the finger of God.

"And thou shalt make a mercy seat of pure gold, and make two cherubims of gold in the two ends of the mercy seat. And the cherubims shall stretch forth their wings on high, covering the mercy seat with their wings, and their faces shall look one to another. And thou shalt put the mercy seat above upon the Ark. And there I will meet with thee, and commune with thee from above the mercy seat, between the two cherubims, of all things which I will give thee in commandment unto the children of Israel.

"And thou shalt make a veil of blue, and purple, and scarlet, and fine twined linen, and thou shalt hang it upon four pillars of shittim wood overlaid with gold, that thou mayest bring in thither within the veil, the Ark of the testimony: and the veil shall divide between the holy place and the most holy place. And thou shalt put the Ark of the testimony in the most holy place within the veil.

"And thou shalt make the tabernacle with ten curtains of fine twined linen, and blue, and purple, and scarlet; with cherubims of cunning work shalt thou make them. And thou shalt make the court of the tabernacle with the pillars thereof and the hangings thereof. The length of the court shall be an hundred cubits, and the breadth fifty, and the hangings shall be of fine twined linen, blue, and purple and scarlet, wrought with needle work. All the pillars round about the court shall be filleted with silver.

"And thou shalt make a table of shittim wood, and overlay it with pure gold, and make for it four rings of gold, and put the rings in the four corners, and make staves of shittim wood and overlay them with gold, that the table may be borne with them. And thou shalt make the dishes, and spoons, and bowls thereof of pure gold. And thou shalt set upon the table shewbread before me always.

"And thou shalt make a candlestick of pure gold; and six branches shall come out of the sides of it. All of it shall be one beaten work of pure gold. And thou shalt make the seven lamps thereof, and they shall light the lamps. And the children of Israel shall bring pure olive oil beaten for the light, to cause the lamp to burn always. And thou shalt set the table in the tabernacle outside the veil, and the candlestick on the other side of the tabernacle.

"And thou shalt make an altar to burn incense upon: of shittim wood shalt thou make it; foursquare shall it be, and make the horns of it upon the four corners. And thou shalt overlay it with pure gold, and thou shalt make a crown of gold upon it round about, and the two golden rings under the crown upon the two sides of it, and they shall be places for the staves to bear it withal. And thou shalt make the staves of shittim wood and overlay them with gold. And the altar thou shalt put before the veil.

"And take unto thee Aaron thy brother, and his sons, that he may minister unto Me in the priest's office; and thou shalt make holy garments for Aaron for glory and for beauty. And Aaron shall bear the names of the children of Israel in the breastplate of judgment upon his heart, when he goeth in unto the holy place, for a memorial before the Lord continually. And thou shalt put in the breastplate of judgment the Urim and the Thummin; and they shall be upon Aaron's heart when he goeth in before the Lord, continually.

"And thou shalt make an oil of holy ointment; and it shall be a holy anointing oil. And thou shalt anoint Aaron and his sons, and consecrate them, that they may minister unto Me in the priest's office. And thou shalt say unto the children of Israel,

'This is an holy anointing oil unto Me, and it shall be holy unto you.'

"And Aaron shall burn incense upon the altar every morning when he dresseth the lamps. And when he lighteth the lamps at even he shall burn incense upon the altar: a perpetual incense before the Lord throughout your generations.

"And Aaron shall make an atonement upon the horns of the altar once a year with the blood of the sin offering: once in the year shall he make atonement; it is most holy unto the Lord.

"And thou shalt make an altar of shittim wood; the altar shall be foursquare. And thou shalt make horns upon the four corners thereof. And thou shalt overlay it with brass. And thou shalt make staves for the altar, and the staves shall be overlaid with brass, and shall be put in rings of brass on the sides of the altar to bear it.

"And thou shalt make pans to receive the ashes, and shovels and basons and fleshhooks, and firepans; all the vessels thereof shall be of brass.

"And thou shalt set the altar within the door of the tabernacle of the congregation. And Aaron and his sons shall offer every day a bullock for a sin offering for atonement. And they shall cleanse the altar when they have made an atonement, and they shall anoint it, to sanctify it. Seven days shall they make an atonement.

"And they shall offer two lambs of the first year, day by day continually. One lamb in the morning, and the other lamb they shall offer in the evening, an offering made by fire unto the Lord. This shall be a continual burnt offering throughout your generations, at the door of the tabernacle of the congregation before the Lord, where I will meet you.

"I will dwell among the children of Israel, and will be their God. And they shall know that I AM the Lord their God that brought them forth out of the land of Egypt. I AM the Lord.

"And thou shalt make a laver of brass, and shall put it between the tabernacle of the congregation and the altar; and thou shalt put water therein. And Aaron and his sons shall wash their hands and their feet when they go into the tabernacle of the congregation, or when they come near to the altar to minister, or to burn offering made by fire unto the Lord. They shall wash their hands and their feet that they die not.

"See that thou make all things according to the pattern showed to thee; after the pattern of the tabernacle, and the pattern of all the instruments thereof, even so shall ye make it."

And Moses gathered all of the congregation of the children of Israel together, and said unto them, "Take ye from among you an offering unto the Lord. Whosoever is of a willing heart let him bring an offering for all of the work of the sanctuary, and to make all that the Lord hath commanded." And all of the congregation of the children of Israel departed from the presence of Moses.

And they came, both men and women, as many as were willing-hearted and brought bracelets and ear-rings, and rings, and tablets, all jewels of gold. And every man offered an offering of gold unto the Lord. And every one did offer an offering of silver and brass, and of shittim wood for the work of the service. And all the women that were wise-hearted did spin with their hands, and brought that which they had spun, both of blue, and of purple, and of scarlet, and of fine linen. And the rulers brought onyx-stones, and stones to be set for the ephod, and for the breastplate; and spice, and anointing oil, and sweet incense, and pure olive-oil beaten for the light, to cause the lamp to burn always. The children of Israel brought a willing offering unto the Lord, for all manner of work which the Lord had commanded to be made by the hand of Moses.

And Moses called every man in whose heart the Lord had put wisdom, to come unto the work to do it. And they received of Moses all the offering which the children of Israel had brought for the work of the service of the sanctuary. And the people brought yet unto Moses free-offerings every morning. And all the wise men that wrought all the work of the sanctuary, came from the work which they made, and spake unto Moses, saying, " The people bring much more than enough for the service of the work which the Lord commanded to make."

And Moses gave commandment throughout the camp, saying, " Let neither man nor woman make any more work for the offering of the sanctuary." So the people were restrained from bringing. For the stuff they had was sufficient for all the work to make it, and too much.

Thus was all the work of the tabernacle finished according to all that the Lord had commanded Moses. And they brought the tabernacle unto Moses. And Moses did look upon all the work, and behold, they had done it as the Lord had commanded, and Moses blessed them.

And the Lord spake unto Moses, saying, " Thou shalt bring Aaron and his sons unto the door of the tabernacle, and wash them with water. And put upon Aaron the holy garments, and anoint him, and sanctify him, that he may minister unto me in the priest's office. And bring his sons, and clothe them with coats, and anoint them, that they may minister unto me in the priest's office: for the anointing shall surely be an everlasting priesthood throughout their generations. And speak unto Aaron, and unto his sons, saying, 'On this wise ye shall bless the children of Israel, saying unto them:

" The Lord bless thee, and keep thee:
The Lord make his face shine upon thee,
And be gracious into thee:
The Lord lift up his countenance upon thee,
And give thee peace." '

And they shall put my name upon the children of Israel, and I will bless them."

Thus did Moses; according to all that the Lord commanded him, so did he. So Moses finished the work. Then a cloud covered the tent of the congregation, and the glory of the Lord filled the tabernacle.

So it was always: the cloud covered it by day, and the appearance of fire by night. And when the cloud was taken up from the tabernacle, then after that the children of Israel journeyed: and in the place where the cloud abode, there the children of Israel pitched their tents. At the commandment of the Lord they journeyed, and at the commandment of the Lord they pitched their tents. For the cloud of the Lord was upon the tabernacle by day, and fire was on it by night, in the sight of all the house of Israel, throughout all their journeys.

NUMBERS

AND THE LORD spake unto Moses in the wilderness of Sinai, in the second year after they were come out of the land of Egypt, saying:

"Take ye the sum of all the congregation of the children of Israel, by the house of their fathers, every male from twenty years old and upward; all that are able to go forth to war in Israel. Thou and Aaron shall number them by their armies. And with you there shall be a man of every tribe, princes of the tribes of their fathers, and the renowned of the congregation."

And Moses and Aaron assembled all the congregation together. And as the Lord commanded Moses, so Moses and Aaron and the twelve princes of Israel, numbered the children of Israel by the house of their fathers according to the names thereof: the children of Reuben, the children of Simeon, of Gad, of Judah, of Issachar, of Zebulum, of Joseph, of Benjamin, of Dan, of Asher, of Naphtali. And they numbered them every male from twenty years old and upward; all that were able to go forth to war in Israel. And all that were numbered were six hundred three thousand five hundred and fifty.

But the Levites, after the tribe of their fathers, were not numbered among them. For the Lord had spoken unto Moses, saying, "Thou shalt not number the tribe of Levi. But thou shalt appoint the Levites over the tabernacle of testimony, and over all things that belong to it: they shall bear the tabernacle, and they shall minister unto it, and shall encamp round about the tabernacle. And when the tabernacle setteth forward, the Levites shall take it down; and when the tabernacle is to be pitched, the Levites shall set it up.

"And the children of Israel shall pitch their tents every man by his own standard, with the ensign of their father's house far off from the tabernacle. But the Levites shall pitch round about the tabernacle of testimony, and shall keep the charge of the tabernacle.

"And when thou comest into the land which the Lord thy God giveth thee, all the tribe of Levi shall have no part nor inheritance with Israel: the Lord is their inheritance. And this shall be their due from the people, the first fruits of thy corn, of thy wine, and thine oil, and the first of the fleece of thy sheep. For the Lord thy God hath chosen him out of all thy tribes, to stand to minister in the name of the Lord, him and his sons forever."

And the children of Israel did according to all that the Lord commanded Moses, so did they.

THOU SHALT SEE MY WORD COME TO PASS

And it came to pass in the second year, that the cloud was taken up from off the tabernacle of the testimony. And the children of Israel took their journey out of the wilderness of Sinai; and the ark of the covenant of the Lord went before them to search out a resting place for them; and the cloud rested in the wilderness of Paran.

And the children of Israel wept, and said, "Who shall give us flesh to eat? We remember the fish which we did eat in Egypt freely; the cucumbers, and the melons, and the leeks, and the onions, and the garlic. But now our soul is dried away; there is nothing at all, besides this manna, before our eyes."

The manna was as coriander-seed. And the people went about, and gathered it, and ground it in mills, or beat it in a mortar, and baked it in pans, and made cakes of it: and the taste of it was as the taste of fresh oil. And when the dew fell upon the camp in the night, the manna fell upon it.

Then Moses heard the people weep throughout their families, every man in the door of his tent. And Moses was displeased.

And Moses said unto the Lord, "Wherefore hast thou afflicted thy servant? and wherefore have I not found favour in thy sight, that thou layest the burden of all this people upon me? and that thou shouldest say unto me, 'Carry them in thy bosom, as a father beareth the nursing child, unto the land which thou swarest unto their fathers'? Whence should I have flesh to give unto all this people? for they weep unto me, saying, 'Give us flesh, that we may eat.' I am not able to bear this people alone, because it is too heavy for me."

And the Lord said unto Moses, "Gather unto me seventy men of the elders of Israel, whom thou knowest to be the elders of the people, and officers over them; and bring them unto the tabernacle of the congregation, that they may stand there with thee. And I will come down and talk with thee there; and I will take of the spirit which is upon thee, and will put it upon them: and they shall bear the burden of the people with thee, that thou bear it not thyself alone.

"And say thou unto the people, 'Sanctify yourselves against tomorrow, and ye shall eat flesh: for ye have wept in the ears of the Lord, saying, "Who shall give us flesh to eat? for it was well with us in Egypt:" therefore the Lord will give you flesh, and ye shall eat. Ye shall not eat one day, nor two days, nor five days, neither ten days, nor twenty days; but even a whole month, until it be loathsome unto you: Because that ye have despised the Lord which is among you, and have wept before him saying, "Why came we forth out of Egypt?" ' "

And Moses said, "The people among whom I am, are six hundred thousand footmen; and thou hast said, 'I will give them flesh, that they may eat a whole month.' Shall the flocks and the herds be slain for them, to suffice them? or shall all the fish of the sea be gathered together for them, to suffice them?"

And the Lord said unto Moses, "Is the Lord's hand waxed short? Thou shalt see now whether my word shall come to pass unto thee, or not."

And Moses went out, and told the people the words of the Lord, and gathered the seventy men of the elders of the people, and set them round about the tabernacle. And the Lord came down in a cloud, and spake unto him, and took of the spirit that was upon Moses, and gave it unto the seventy elders. And it came to pass, that when the spirit rested upon them, they prophesied, and did not cease.

And Joshua the son of Nun, the servant of Moses, said, "My Lord Moses, forbid them."

And Moses said unto him, "Enviest thou for my sake? Would God that all the Lord's people were prophets, and that the Lord would put his Spirit upon them!" And Moses went into the camp, he and the elders of Israel.

And there went forth a wind from the Lord, and brought

quails from the sea, and let them fall by the camp, as it were a day's journey on this side, and a day's journey on the other side, round about the camp, two cubits high upon the face of the earth. And the people stood up all that day, and all that night, and all the next day, and they gathered the quails. He that gathered least, gathered ten homers; and they spread them all abroad for themselves round about the camp.

MY SERVANT MOSES IS FAITHFUL IN ALL MY HOUSE

AND MIRIAM and Aaron spake against Moses; and they said, " Hath the Lord indeed spoken only by Moses? Hath he not spoken also by us? "

And the Lord heard it. (Now the man Moses was very meek, above all the men which were upon the face of the earth.) And the Lord spake suddenly unto Moses, and unto Aaron, and unto Miriam, " Come out ye three unto the tabernacle of the congregation." And they three came out.

And the Lord came down in the pillar of the cloud, and stood in the door of the tabernacle, and called Aaron and Miriam: and they both came forth. And he said, " Hear now my words: If there be a prophet among you, I the Lord will make myself known unto him in a vision, and will speak unto him in a dream. My servant Moses is not so, who is faithful in all mine house. With him will I speak mouth to mouth, even apparently, and not in dark speeches; and the similitude of the Lord shall he behold: wherefore then were ye not afraid to speak against my servant Moses? " And the anger of the Lord was kindled against them; and he departed.

And the cloud departed from off the tabernacle; and behold Miriam became leprous, white as snow: and Aaron looked upon Miriam, and behold, she was leprous. And Aaron said unto

Moses, " Alas, my lord, I beseech thee, lay not the sin upon us, wherein we have done foolishly, and wherein we have sinned. Let her not be as one dead, or whom the flesh is half consumed."

And Moses cried unto the Lord, saying, " Heal her now, O God, I beseech thee."

And the Lord said unto Moses, " Should she not be ashamed? Let her be shut out from the camp seven days, and after that let her be received in again."

And Miriam was shut out from the camp seven days: and the people journeyed not till Miriam was brought in again.

WE WERE IN OUR OWN SIGHT AS GRASSHOPPERS

AND THE LORD spake unto Moses, saying, " Send thou men, that they may search the land of Canaan, which I give unto the children of Israel: of every tribe shall ye send a man, every one a ruler among them."

And Moses sent men who were heads of the children of Israel to spy out the land of Canaan, and he said unto them, " Get you up this way southward, and go up into the mountain. And see the land, what it is; and the people that dwelleth therein, whether they be strong or weak, few or many; and what the land is that they dwell in, whether it be good or bad; and what cities they dwell in, whether in tents, or in strong holds; and what the land is, whether it be fat or lean, whether there be wood therein, or not. And be ye of good courage, and bring of the fruits of the land." Now the time was the time of the first ripe grapes.

So the men went up, and searched the land from the wilderness of Zin unto Rehob. And they ascended by the south, and came unto Hebron, where the children of Anak were. And they came unto a brook, and cut down from thence a branch with one cluster of grapes, and they bare it between two upon a staff; and they brought of the pomegranates, and of the figs. And they returned from searching the land after forty days.

And they came to Moses, and to Aaron, and to all the congregation of the children of Israel, and brought back word unto them, and showed them the fruit of the land. And they said, "We came unto the land whither thou sent us, and surely it floweth with milk and honey; and this is the fruit of it. Nevertheless, the people be strong that dwell in the land, and the cities are walled, and very great: and moreover, we saw the children of Anak there. The Amalekites dwell in the land of the south: and the Hittites, and the Jebusites, and the Amorites, dwell in the mountains; and the Canaanites dwell by the sea, and by the coast of Jordan."

And Caleb stilled the people before Moses, and said, "Let us go up at once, and possess it; for we are well able to overcome it."

But the men that went up with him said, "We be not able to go up against the people; for they are stronger than we." And they brought up an evil report of the land which they had searched, saying, "The land through which we have gone to search it, is a land that eateth up the inhabitants thereof; and all the people that we saw in it are men of great stature. And there we saw the giants, the sons of Anak, which come of the giants: and we were in our own sight as grasshoppers, and so we were in their sight."

And all the congregation lifted up their voice and cried; and the people wept that night. And all the children of Israel murmured against Moses and against Aaron, and said unto them: "Would God that we had died in the land of Egypt! or would God we had died in this wilderness! Wherefore hath the Lord brought us unto this land, to fall by the sword, that our wives and our children should be a prey? were it not better for us to return into Egypt?" And they said one to another, "Let us make a captain, and let us return into Egypt."

And Moses said, " Dread not, neither be afraid of them. The Lord your God which goeth before you, he shall fight for you, according to all that he did for you in Egypt, and in the wilderness."

And Joshua and Caleb, which were of them that searched the land, rent their clothes; and they spake unto all the children of Israel, "The land which we passed through to search it, is an exceeding good land. If the Lord delight in us, then he will bring us into this land and give it us; a land which floweth with milk and honey. Only rebel not ye against the Lord, neither fear ye the people of the land; for their defense is departed from them, and the Lord is with us: fear them not." But all the congregation bade stone them with stones.

And the glory of the Lord appeared in the tabernacle of the congregation before all the children of Israel. And the Lord said unto Moses, " How long will this people provoke me? and how long will it be ere they believe me, for all the signs which I have showed among them? "

And Moses said unto the Lord, " Pardon, I beseech thee, the iniquity of this people according unto the greatness of thy mercy, and as thou hast forgiven this people, from Egypt even until now."

And the Lord said, " I have pardoned according to thy word: but as truly as I live, all the earth shall be filled with the glory of the Lord. Because all those men which have seen my glory, and my miracles, which I did in Egypt and in the wilderness, and have tempted me now these ten times, and have not hearkened to my voice, surely they shall not see the land which I sware unto their fathers, neither shall any of them that provoked me see it. But my servant Caleb, because he had another spirit with him, and hath followed me fully, him will I bring into the land whereinto he went; and his children shall possess it. Tomorrow turn you, and get you into the wilderness by way of the Red sea."

And the Lord spake unto Moses and unto Aaron, saying, " I

have heard the murmurings of the children of Israel, which they murmur against me. Say unto them, 'As truly as I live, as ye have spoken in mine ears, so will I do to you: Your carcasses shall fall in this wilderness, all of you from twenty years old and upward, which have murmured against me. Ye shall not come into the land concerning which I sware to make you dwell therein, save Caleb and Joshua. But your little ones, which ye said should be a prey, them will I bring in, and they shall know the land which ye have despised. But as for you, you shall fall in this wilderness. And your children shall wander in the wilderness forty years, after the number of the days in which ye searched the land, even forty days, each day for a year, ye bear your iniquities even forty years. I the Lord have said, I will surely do it unto all this evil congregation, that are gathered together against me.'"

And Moses told these sayings unto all the children of Israel: and the people mourned greatly. And they rose up early in the morning, and gat them up into the top of the mountain, saying, "Lo, we be here, and will go up unto the place which the Lord hath promised."

And Moses said, "Wherefore now do ye transgress the commandment of the Lord? but it shall not prosper. Go not up, that ye be not smitten before your enemies, for the Lord is not among you, and ye shall fall by the sword: because ye are turned away from the Lord, therefore the Lord will not be with you."

But they presumed to go up unto the hill-top: nevertheless the ark of the covenant of the Lord and Moses, departed not out of the camp.

Then the Amalekites came down, and the Canaanites which dwelt in that mountain, and smote them, and discomfited them, and chased them as bees do, and they returned and wept before the Lord.

THE LORD WILL SHOW WHOM HE HATH CHOSEN

Now Korah, of the tribe of Levi, and Dathan and Abiram of the tribe of Reuben, took men, and they rose up before Moses, with certain of the children of Israel, two hundred and fifty princes of the assembly, famous in the congregation, men of renown. And they gathered themselves together against Moses and against Aaron, and said unto them, "Ye take too much upon you, seeing all the congregation are holy, every one of them, and the Lord is among them: wherefore then lift ye up yourselves above the congregation of the Lord?"

And when Moses heard it he fell upon his face, and he spake unto Korah, and unto all his company, saying, "Even tomorrow the Lord will show who are his, and who is holy; and will cause him whom he hath chosen to come near unto him. This do: Take you censers, Korah, and all his company, and put fire therein, and put incense in them before the Lord tomorrow. And it shall be that the man whom the Lord doth choose, he shall be holy. Ye take too much upon you."

And Moses said unto Korah, "Hear, I pray you, ye sons of Levi: Seemeth it but a small thing unto you, that the God of Israel hath separated you from the congregation to bring you near unto himself to do the service of the tabernacle of the Lord, and to stand before the congregation to minister unto them? He hath brought thee near to him, and all thy brethren, the sons of Levi with thee, and seek ye the priesthood also? For which cause both thou and all thy company are gathered together against the Lord. And what is Aaron, that ye murmur against him?"

And Moses sent to call Dathan and Abiram, of the tribe of Reuben, who said, "We will not come up. Is it a small thing that thou hast brought us up out of a land that floweth with milk and honey, to kill us in the wilderness, except thou make thyself altogether a prince over us? Moreover, thou hast not brought us into a land that floweth with milk and honey, or given us inheritance of fields and vineyards. We will not come up."

And Moses was very wroth, and said unto the Lord, "Respect not thou their offering. I have not taken one ass from them, neither have I hurt one of them."

And Moses said unto Korah, "Be thou and all thy company before the Lord, thou, and they, and Aaron, tomorrow. And take every man his censer, and put incense in them, and bring ye before the Lord every man his censer, two hundred and fifty censers."

And they took every man his censer, and put fire in them, and laid incense thereon, and stood in the door of the tabernacle of the congregation with Moses and Aaron.

And Korah gathered all the congregation against them unto the door of the tabernacle of the congregation.

And the glory of the Lord appeared unto all the congregation. And the Lord spake unto Moses, saying, "Speak unto the congregation, saying, 'Separate yourselves from Korah, Dathan, and Abiram, that I may consume them in a moment.'"

And Moses rose up, and went unto Korah, Dathan and Abiram, and the elders of Israel followed him. And he spake unto the congregation, saying, "Depart, I pray you, from the tents of these wicked men, and touch nothing of theirs, lest ye be consumed in all their sins." So the people got them up from the tabernacle of Korah, Dathan, and Abiram, on every side.

And Korah, Dathan and Abiram came out, and stood in the door of their tents, and their wives, and their sons, and their little children.

And Moses said, "Hereby ye shall know that the Lord hath sent me to do all these works: for I have not done them of mine own mind. If these men die the common death of all men, then the Lord hath not sent me. But if the Lord make a new thing, and the earth open her mouth, and swallow them up, with all that appertain unto them, and they go down quick into the pit;

then ye shall understand that these men have provoked the Lord."

And it came to pass, as he made an end of speaking all these words, that the ground clave asunder that was under them: and the earth opened her mouth, and swallowed them up, and their houses, and all the men that followed Korah, and all their goods, and all that appertained to them, went down alive into the pit, and the earth closed upon them, and they perished from among the congregation. And there came out fire, and consumed the two hundred and fifty men that offered incense.

And all Israel that were round about them, fled at the cry of them, for they said, "Lest the earth swallow us up also." But on the morrow, all the congregation of the children of Israel murmured against Moses and against Aaron, saying, "Ye have killed the people of the Lord."

And it came to pass when the congregation was gathered against Moses and against Aaron, that they looked toward the tabernacle of the congregation, and behold, the cloud covered it, and the glory of the Lord appeared. And Moses and Aaron came before the tabernacle, and the Lord spake unto Moses, saying, "Get you up from among this congregation, that I may consume them as in a moment."

And Moses said unto Aaron, "Take a censer, and put fire therein from off the altar, and put on incense, and go quickly unto the congregation, and make an atonement for them: for there is wrath gone out from the Lord; the plague is begun."

And Aaron took as Moses commanded, and ran into the midst of the congregation; and behold, the plague was begun among the people; and he put on incense, and made an atonement for the people. And he stood between the dead and the living; and the plague was stayed.

Now they that died in the plague were fourteen thousand and seven hundred, beside them that died about the matter of Korah.

THE ROD OF AARON BUDDED AND BLOOMED

AND THE LORD spake unto Moses, saying, "Speak unto the children of Israel, and take of every one of them a rod according to the house of their fathers, twelve rods: write thou every man's name upon his rod. And thou shalt write Aaron's name upon the rod of Levi: for one rod shall be for the head of the house of their fathers. And thou shalt lay them up in the tabernacle of the congregation before the testimony, where I will meet with you. And it shall come to pass, that the man's rod whom I shall choose shall blossom: and I will make to cease from me the murmurings of the children of Israel, whereby they murmur against you."

And Moses spake unto the children of Israel, and every one of their princes gave him a rod, one for each prince, according to their father's houses, even twelve rods: and the rod of Aaron was among their rods. And Moses laid up the rods before the Lord in the tabernacle of witness.

And it came to pass, that on the morrow Moses went into the tabernacle of witness; and behold, the rod of Aaron for the house of Levi was budded, and brought forth buds, and bloomed blossoms, and yielded almonds. And Moses brought out all the rods from before the Lord unto all the children of Israel: and they looked, and took every man his rod.

And the Lord said unto Moses, "Bring Aaron's rod again before the testimony, to be kept for a token against the rebels; and thou shalt quite take away their murmurings from me."

And Moses did so: as the Lord commanded him, so did he.

SPEAK YE UNTO THE ROCK

THEN CAME the children of Israel, even the whole congregation, into the desert of Zin, and the people abode in Kadesh. And Miriam died there, and was buried there.

And there was no water for the congregation: and they gathered themselves together against Moses and against Aaron, and spake, saying, "Would God that we had died when our brethren died before the Lord! Why have ye brought up the congregation of the Lord into this wilderness, that we and our cattle should die there? And wherefore have ye made us to come up out of Egypt, to bring us unto this evil place? It is no place of seed, or of figs, or of vines, or of pomegranates; neither is there any water to drink."

And Moses and Aaron went from the presence of the assembly unto the door of the tabernacle of the congregation, and they fell upon their faces: and the glory of the Lord appeared unto them.

And the Lord spake unto Moses, saying, "Take the rod, and gather thou the assembly together, thou and Aaron thy brother, and speak ye unto the rock before their eyes; and it shall give forth water, and thou shalt bring forth to them water out of the rock: so thou shalt give the congregation and their beasts to drink."

And Moses took the rod from before the Lord, as he commanded him. And Moses and Aaron gathered the congregation together before the rock, and he said unto them, "Hear now, ye rebels; must we fetch you water out of this rock?" And Moses lifted up his hand, and with his rod he smote the rock twice: and the water came out abundantly, and the congregation drank, and their beasts also.

And the Lord spake unto Moses and Aaron, "Because ye believed me not, to sanctify me in the eyes of the children of

Israel, therefore ye shall not bring this congregation into the land which I have given them."

This is the water of Meribah; because the children of Israel strove with the Lord, and he was sanctified in them.

ALL THE CONGREGATION MOURNED FOR AARON

AND MOSES sent messengers from Kadesh unto the king of Edom, "Thus saith thy brother Israel, 'Thou knowest all the travail that hath befallen us: how our fathers went down into Egypt, and we have dwelt in Egypt a long time. And the Egyptians vexed us, and our fathers. And when we cried unto the Lord, he heard our voice, and sent an angel, and hath brought us forth out of Egypt. And behold, we are in Kadesh, a city in the uttermost of thy border. Let us pass, I pray thee, through thy country: we will not pass through the fields, or through the vineyards, neither will we drink of the water of the wells. We will go by the king's highway, we will not turn to the right hand nor to the left, until we have passed thy borders.' "

And Edom said unto him, "Thou shalt not pass by me, lest I come out against thee with the sword."

And the children of Israel said unto him, "We will go by the highway; and if I and my cattle drink of thy water, then I will pay for it. I will only, without doing anything else, go through on my feet."

And Edom refused to give Israel passage through his border; wherefore Israel turned away from him. And the children of Israel, even the whole congregation, journeyed from Kadesh, and came unto mount Hor.

And the Lord spake unto Moses and Aaron in mount Hor, by the coast of the land of Edom, saying, "Aaron shall be gathered unto his people, for he shall not enter into the land which I have given unto the children of Israel, because ye rebelled against my word at the water of Meribah. Take Aaron and Eleazar his son, and bring them up unto mount Hor. And strip Aaron of his garments, and put them upon Eleazar, his son. And Aaron shall be gathered unto his people, and shall die there."

And Moses did as the Lord commanded; and they went up unto mount Hor in the sight of all the congregation. And Moses stripped Aaron of his garments, and put them upon Eleazar his son. And Aaron died there in the top of the mount, in the fortieth year after the children of Israel were come out of the land of Egypt. And Aaron was an hundred and twenty and three years old when he died in mount Hor.

And Moses and Eleazar came down from the mount. And when all the congregation saw that Aaron was dead, they mourned for Aaron thirty days, even all the house of Israel.

MOSES MADE A SERPENT OF BRASS

AND THE CHILDREN of Israel journeyed from mount Hor by way of the Red Sea, to compass the land of Edom. And the soul of the people was much discouraged because of the way.

And the people spake against God, and against Moses, "Wherefore have ye brought us up out of Egypt to die in the wilderness? for there is no bread, neither is there any water; and our soul loatheth this light bread."

And the Lord sent fiery serpents among the people, and they bit the people; and much people of Israel died. Therefore the people came to Moses, and said, "We have sinned, for we have spoken against the Lord, and against thee; pray unto the Lord that he take away the serpents from us."

And Moses prayed for the people. And the Lord said unto Moses, "Make thee a fiery serpent, and set it upon a pole; and it shall come to pass, that every one that is bitten, when he looketh upon it, shall live."

And Moses made a serpent of brass, and put it upon a pole. And it came to pass, that if a serpent had bitten any man, when he beheld the serpent of brass, he lived.

WHAT THE LORD SAITH, THAT WILL I SPEAK

AND THE CHILDREN of Israel set forward, and journeyed toward the rising sun. And Israel sent messengers unto Sihon king of the Amorites, saying, "Let me pass through thy land: we will not turn into the fields, or into the vineyards; we will not drink of the waters of the well; but we will go along by the king's highway, until we be past thy borders."

And Sihon would not suffer Israel to pass through his border; but Sihon gathered his people together, and went out against Israel into the wilderness, and fought against Israel. And Israel smote him with the edge of the sword, and possessed his land, and took all the cities of the Amorites.

And the children of Israel turned and went up by the way of Bashan. And Og the king of Bashan went out against them, he, and all his people, to the battle.

And the Lord said unto Moses, "Fear him not; for I have delivered him into thy hand, and all his people, and his land; and thou shalt do to him as thou didst unto Sihon king of the Amorites." So they smote him, and his sons, and all his people, until there was none left alive, and they possessed his land.

And the children of Israel set forward, and pitched in the plains of Moab on this side Jordan by Jericho. And Balak, the son of Zippor, was king of Moab at that time. And Balak saw all that Israel had done to the Amorites, and was sore afraid of the people because they were many. And he said unto the elders of Midian, "Now shall this company lick up all that are round about us, as the ox licketh up the grass of the field."

Balak sent messengers therefore unto Balaam (a prophet of Baal) to call him, saying, " Behold, there is a people come out from Egypt. Behold, they cover the face of the earth, and they abide over against me. Come now therefore, I pray thee, curse me this people; for they are too mighty for me; peradventure I shall prevail, that we may smite them, and that I may drive them out of the land; for I wot that he whom thou blessest is blessed, and he whom thou cursest is cursed."

And the elders of Moab and the elders of Midian departed with the reward of divination in their hand; and they came unto Balaam, and spake unto him the words of Balak. And Balaam said unto them, " Lodge here this night, and I will bring you word again, as the Lord shall speak unto me." And the princes of Moab abode with Balaam.

And God came unto Balaam, and said, " Thou shalt not go with these men; thou shalt not curse the children of Israel, for they are blessed."

And Balaam rose up in the morning, and said unto the princes of Balak, " Get you into your land, for the Lord refuseth to give me leave to go with you."

And the princes of Moab rose up, and they went unto Balak, and said, " Balaam refuseth to come with us."

And Balak sent yet again princes, more, and more honourable than they. And they came to Balaam, and said to him, " Thus saith Balak the son of Zippor, 'Let nothing, I pray thee, hinder thee from coming unto me; for I will promote thee unto very great honour, and I will do whatsoever thou sayest unto me; come therefore, I pray thee, curse me this people.' "

And Balaam answered and said unto the servants of Balak, " If Balak would give me his house full of silver and gold, I cannot go beyond the word of the Lord my God, to do less or more. Now therefore, I pray you, tarry ye also here this night, that I may know what the Lord will say unto me more."

And God came unto Balaam at night, and said unto him,

"If the men come to call thee, rise up, and go with them; but yet the word which I shall say unto thee, that shalt thou do."

And Balaam rose up in the morning, and saddled his ass, and went with the princes of Moab. And the angel of the Lord stood in the way. Now Balaam was riding upon his ass, and his two servants were with him. And the ass saw the angel of the Lord standing in the way, and his sword drawn in his hand; and the ass turned aside out of the way, and went into the field. And Balaam smote the ass, to turn her into the way.

But the angel of the Lord stood in a path of the vineyard, a wall being on this side, and a wall on that side. And when the ass saw the angel of the Lord, she thrust herself unto the wall, and crushed Balaam's foot against the wall, and he smote her again. And the angel of the Lord went further, and stood in a narrow place where was no way to turn either to the right hand or to the left. And when the ass saw the angel of the Lord, she fell down under Balaam; and Balaam's anger was kindled, and he smote the ass with a staff.

And the Lord opened the mouth of the ass, and she said unto Balaam, "What have I done unto thee, that thou hast smitten me these three times?"

And Balaam said unto the ass, "Because thou hast mocked me. I would there were a sword in mine hand, for now would I kill thee."

And the ass said unto Balaam, "Am not I thine ass, upon which thou hast ridden ever since I was thine unto this day? was I ever wont to do so unto thee?"

And Balaam said, "Nay." Then the Lord opened the eyes of Balaam, and he saw the angel of the Lord standing in the way, and his sword drawn in his hand; and Balaam bowed down his head, and fell flat on his face.

And the angel of the Lord said unto him, "Wherefore hast thou smitten thine ass these three times? behold, I went out to withstand thee, because thy way is perverse before me. And the ass saw me, and turned from me these three times; unless she had turned from me, surely now also I had slain thee, and saved her alive."

And Balaam said unto the angel of the Lord, "I have sinned, for I knew not that thou stoodest in the way against me. Now therefore, if it displease thee, I will get me back again."

And the angel said unto Balaam, "Go with the men; but only the word that I shall speak unto thee, that thou shalt speak." So Balaam went with the princes of Balak.

And when Balak heard that Balaam was come, he went out to meet him unto a city of Moab, which is in the utmost coast. And Balak said unto Balaam, "Did I not earnestly send unto thee to call thee? wherefore camest thou not unto me? am I not able indeed to promote thee to honour?"

And Balaam said unto Balak, "Lo, I am come unto thee; have I any power at all to say anything? the word that God putteth in my mouth, that shall I speak."

And Balaam went with Balak. And on the morrow, Balak took Balaam up into the high places of Baal, that thence he might see the utmost part of the people. And Balaam said unto Balak, "Build me here seven altars, and prepare me here seven oxen and seven rams." And Balak did as Balaam had spoken; and they offered on every altar a bullock and a ram.

And Balaam said unto Balak, "Stand by thy burnt-offering, and I will go; peradventure the Lord will come to meet me; and whatsoever he showeth me I will tell thee." And he went to an high place.

And God met Balaam. And the Lord put a word in Balaam's mouth, and said, "Return unto Balak, and thus shalt thou speak." And Balaam returned. And lo, Balak stood by his burnt-sacrifice, he, and all the princes of Moab.

And Balaam took up his parable, and said, "Balak, the king of Moab, hath brought me out of the mountains of the east, saying, 'Come, curse me Jacob, and come, defy Israel.' How shall I curse, whom God hath not cursed? Or how shall I defy, whom the Lord hath not defied? For from the top of the rocks I see him, and from the hills I behold him: lo, the people shall dwell alone, and shall not be reckoned among the nations. Who can count the dust of Jacob, and number the fourth part of Israel? "

And Balak said unto Balaam, " What hast thou done unto me? I took thee to curse mine enemies, and behold, thou hast blessed them altogether."

And Balaam said, " Must I not take heed to speak that which the Lord hath put in my mouth? "

And Balak said unto him, " Come, I pray thee, with me unto another place, from whence thou mayest see them; thou shalt see but part of them, and shalt not see them all; and curse me them from thence."

And Balak brought him to the top of Pisgah, and built seven altars, and offered a bullock and a ram on every altar. And Balaam said unto Balak, " Stand here by thy burnt-offering, while I meet the Lord yonder."

And the Lord met Balaam, and put a word in his mouth, and said, " Go again unto Balak, and say thus."

And when Balaam came to him, behold, Balak stood by his burnt-offering, and the princes of Moab with him. And Balak said, " What hath the Lord spoken? "

And Balaam took up his parable, and said, " Rise up, Balak, and hear; hearken unto me, thou son of Zippor: God is not a man, that he should lie; neither the son of man, that he should repent; hath he said, and shall he not do it? or hath he spoken, and shall he not make it good? Behold, I have received commandment to bless: and he hath blessed, and I cannot reverse it. he hath not beheld iniquity in Jacob, neither hath he seen perverseness in Israel: the Lord his God is with him, and the shout of a king is among them. Surely there is no enchantment against Jacob, neither is there any divination against Israel.

And Balak said unto Balaam, "Neither curse them at all, nor bless them at all."

But Balaam answered, "Told not I thee, saying 'All that the Lord speaketh, that I must do'?"

And Balak said, "Come, I pray thee, I will bring thee unto another place; peradventure it will please God that thou mayest curse me them from thence."

And Balak brought Balaam unto the top of Peor. And Balaam said unto Balak, "Build me here seven altars, and prepare me here seven bullocks and seven rams." And Balak did as Balaam had said, and offered a bullock and a ram on every altar.

And when Balaam saw that it pleased the Lord to bless Israel, he went not as at other times, to seek for enchantments, but he set his face toward the wilderness. And Balaam lifted up his eyes, and he saw Israel abiding in his tents according to their tribes, and the Spirit of God came upon him. And he took up his parable, and said, "Balaam, the son of Beor, the man whose eyes are open, who heard the words of God, who saw the vision of the Almighty, but having his eyes open, hath said, 'How goodly are thy tents, O Jacob, and thy tabernacles, O Israel! As the valleys are they spread forth, as gardens by the river's side, as trees which the Lord hath planted, and as cedar trees beside the waters. His king shall be higher than Agog, and his kingdom shall be exalted. God brought him forth out of Egypt; he hath as it were the strength of an unicorn: he shall eat up the nations, and pierce them through with his arrows. Blessed is he that blesseth thee, and cursed is he that curseth thee.'"

And Balak's anger was kindled against Balaam, and he smote his hands together, and said unto Balaam, "I called thee to curse mine enemies, and behold, thou hast altogether blessed them these three times. Therefore now flee thou to thy place; I thought to promote thee unto great honour; but, lo, the Lord hath kept thee back from honour."

And Balaam said unto Balak, "If Balak would give me his

house full of silver and gold, I cannot go beyond the commandment of the Lord, to do either good or bad of mine own mind; but what the Lord saith, that will I speak. I shall see him, but not now; I shall behold him, but not nigh. There shall come a Star out of Jacob, and a Sceptre shall rise out of Israel. Out of Jacob shall come he that shall have dominion. And now, behold, I go unto my people."

And Balaam rose up, and went and returned to his place; and Balak also went his way.

And Israel abode in Shittim, and the people began to commit whoredom with the daughters of Moab, and to eat and bow down unto Baalpeor, their god.

And Moses said unto the judges of Israel, "Slay ye every one his men that were joined unto Baalpeor."

And, behold, one of the children of Israel came and brought unto his brethren a Midianitish woman in the sight of Moses, and in the sight of all the congregation, who were weeping before the door of the tabernacle.

And when Phinehas, the son of Eleazar, the priest, saw it, he rose up from among the congregation, and took a javelin in his hand, and thrust both of them through. So the plague was stayed from the children of Israel; those that died in the plague were twenty and four thousand.

And Moses sent them to war against the Midianites, a thousand of every tribe. And they slew the kings of Midian beside the rest of them that were slain. And Balaam also the son of Beor, they slew with the sword. And the children of Israel took all the women of Midian captives, and their little ones, and took spoil of all their cattle, and all their flocks, and all their goods. And they burnt all of the cities wherein they dwelt. And they brought the captives and the prey and the spoil unto Moses.

And Moses was wroth with the officers of the host. And Moses said unto them, "Have ye saved all of the women alive?

Behold, these caused the children of Israel, through the counsel of Balaam to commit trespass against the Lord. And there was a plague among the congregation of the Lord. Now therefore kill every woman that hath known man by lying with him. And do ye abide without the camp seven days whosoever hath killed any person, and purify both yourselves and your captives. And levy a tribute unto the Lord of the men of war which went out to battle."

And the officers which were over the host came near unto Moses, and they said unto him, "We have brought an oblation unto the Lord, of jewels of gold, chains and bracelets, rings, earrings and tablets to make an atonement for our souls before the Lord."

And Moses and Eleazar, the priest, took the gold of the captains and brought it into the tabernacle of the congregation for a memorial of the children of Israel before the Lord.

INHERITANCE LAW OF THE CHILDREN OF ISRAEL

AND IT CAME TO PASS that the Lord spake unto Moses, and unto Eleazar, the son of Aaron, saying, "Take the sum of all the congregation of the children of Israel, from twenty years old and upward, all that are able to go to war in Israel."

And Moses and Eleazar the priest, numbered the children of Israel in the plains of Moab by Jordan near Jericho. And they numbered six hundred thousand, and a thousand seven hundred and thirty. But among these there was not a man of them whom Moses and Aaron numbered, when they numbered the children of Israel in the wilderness of Sinai. For the Lord had said of them, "They shall surely die in the wilderness." And there was not a man left of them, save Caleb the son of Jephunneh, and Joshua the son of Nun.

And the Lord spake unto Moses, saying, "Unto these the land shall be divided for an inheritance according to the number of their names. To many thou shalt give more inheritance, and to few thou shalt give less inheritance: Notwithstanding the land shall be divided by lot. Every man's inheritance shall be in the place where his lot falleth; according to the tribes of their fathers they shall inherit, and according to lot shall the possession be divided."

Then came the daughters of Zelophehad, of the tribe of Joseph. And they stood before Moses, and before Eleazar the priest, and before the princes, and all the congregation, by the door of the tabernacle, saying, "Our father died in the wilderness, and had no sons. Why should the name of our father be done away from among his family, because he hath no son? Give us therefore a possession among the brethren of our father."

And Moses brought their cause before the Lord. And the Lord spake unto Moses, saying, "The daughters of Zelophehad speak right: thou shalt surely give them a possession among their father's brethren; and thou shalt cause the inheritance of their father to pass to them. And thou shalt speak unto the children of Israel, saying, 'If a man die and have no son, then ye shall cause his inheritance to pass unto his daughter, and it shall be unto the children of Israel a statute of judgment.'"

Now the children of Reuben and the children of Gad had a very great multitude of cattle, and when they saw the land of Jazer and the land of Gilead, that, behold, the place was a place for cattle, they came and spake unto Moses, and to Eleazar the priest, and unto the princes of the congregation, saying, "This country is a land for cattle, and thy servants have cattle. Wherefore, if we have found grace in thy sight, let this land be given unto thy servants for a possession, and bring us not over Jordan."

And Moses said unto them, "Shall your brethren go to war,

and shall ye sit here? Wherefore discourage ye the heart of the children of Israel from going over into the land which the Lord hath given them? Thus did your fathers when I sent them from Kadesh-barnea to see the land. For when they went up unto the valley of Eschol, and saw the land, they discouraged the heart of the children of Israel, that they should not go into the land which the Lord had given them. And the Lord's anger was kindled against Israel, and he made them wander in the wilderness forty years. And behold, ye are risen up in your fathers' stead, to augment yet the fierce anger of the Lord toward Israel. For if ye turn away from him, he will yet again leave them in the wilderness; and ye shall destroy all the people."

And they came near unto Moses, and said, "We will build sheep folds here for our cattle, and cities for our little ones. But we ourselves will go ready armed before the children of Israel, until we have brought them unto their place. We will not return unto our houses until the children of Israel have inherited every man his inheritance. For we will not inherit with them on yonder side of Jordan, because our inheritance is fallen to us on this side Jordan."

And Moses said unto them, "If ye will do this thing, if ye will go, all of you armed over Jordan before the Lord, until he hath driven out his enemies from before him, and the land be subdued before the Lord; then afterward ye shall return, and be guiltless before the Lord, and before Israel; this land shall be your possession. But if ye will not do so, behold, ye have sinned against the Lord: and be sure your sin will find you out."

And Moses gave unto the children of Gad, and the children of Reuben, and half the tribe of Manasseh, son of Joseph, the kingdom of Sihon king of the Amorites, and the kingdom of Og king of Bashan, the land, with the cities thereof, even the cities of the country round about.

A MAN IN WHOM IS THE SPIRIT

AND THE LORD said unto Moses, "Get thee up into mount Nebo, and see the land which I have given unto the children of Israel. And when thou hast seen it thou also shalt be gathered unto thy people, as Aaron thy brother was gathered. For ye rebelled against my commandment to sanctify me before the eyes of the congregation at the water of Meribah, in the wilderness of Zin."

And Moses spake unto the Lord saying, "O Lord God, thou hast begun to show thy servant thy greatness, and thy mighty hand; for what God is there in heaven or earth that can do according to thy works, and according to thy might? I pray thee, let me go over, and see the good land that is beyond Jordan, that goodly mountain, and Lebanon."

But the Lord said, "Get thee up into the top of Nebo, and lift up thine eyes westward, and southward, and eastward, and northward, and behold it with thine eyes. Let it suffice thee, for thou shalt not go over this Jordan. Speak no more unto me of this matter."

And Moses said unto the Lord, "Let the Lord set a man over the congregation, which may lead them out, and which may bring them in, that the congregation of the Lord be not as sheep which have no shepherd."

And the Lord said unto Moses, "Take thee Joshua, the son of Nun, a man in whom is the spirit, and lay thine hand upon him, and set him before Eleazar the priest, and before all the congregation, and put some of thine honor upon him, that all the congregation of the children of Israel may be obedient: and give him a charge in their sight; encourage him, and strengthen him, for he shall go over before his people, and he shall cause them to inherit the land which thou shalt see."

And Moses did as the Lord commanded him: and he took Joshua, and set him before Eleazar the priest, and before all the congregation; and he laid his hands upon him, and gave him a charge as the Lord commanded.

THOU SHALT BE PERFECT WITH THE LORD THY GOD

AND IT CAME TO PASS in the fortieth year, in the eleventh month, on the first day of the month, that Moses spake unto the children of Israel, all that the Lord had given him in commandment. These are the words which Moses spake on this side Jordan, in the land of Moab:

"Hear, O Israel! The Lord thy God hath multiplied you, and behold, ye are this day as the stars of heaven for multitude. And I have led you forty years in the wilderness: your clothes are not waxen old upon you, and thy shoe is not waxen old upon thy foot. For the Lord thy God hath blessed thee in all the works of thy hand: He knoweth thy walking through this great wilderness; these forty years the Lord hath been with thee; thou hast lacked nothing.

"Now therefore, hearken, O Israel, unto the statutes and unto the judgments which I teach you, for to do them, that ye may live, and go in and possess the land which the Lord God of your fathers giveth you.

"Behold, the Lord hath set the land before thee. Thou art to pass over Jordan, to go in to possess nations greater and mightier than thyself; cities great and fenced up to heaven; a people great and tall, of whom thou hast heard say, 'Who can stand before the children of Anak?' Understand therefore this day, that the Lord thy God is he which goeth over before thee; as a consuming fire he shall destroy them; so thou shalt drive them out quickly.

"And Joshua shall go before thee as the Lord hath said. For I am an hundred and twenty years old, and the Lord hath said unto me, 'Thou shalt not go over this Jordan.'"

And Moses called Joshua, and said unto him in the sight of all Israel, "Be strong and of good courage: for thou must go with this people unto the land which the Lord hath sworn unto their fathers to give them; thou shalt cause them to inherit it. And the Lord, he it is that doth go before thee; he will be with thee, he will not fail thee, neither forsake thee: fear not, neither be dismayed.

"The Lord hath given you this land to possess it: Ye shall pass over armed, all that are meet for war. And when thou goest forth against thine enemies, then keep thee from every wicked thing: for the Lord thy God walketh in the midst of thy camp, to deliver thee, and to give up thine enemies before thee; therefore shall thy camp be holy.

"And when thou goest out to battle against thine enemies, and seest horses, and chariots, and a people more than thou, be not afraid of them: for the Lord thy God is with thee, which brought thee up out of the land of Egypt. And it shall be when ye are come nigh unto the battle, that the priest shall approach and speak unto the people, and shall say unto them, 'Hear, O Israel, ye approach this day unto battle against your enemies: let not your hearts faint; fear not, and do not tremble, neither be ye terrified because of them; for the Lord your God is he that goeth with you to fight for you against your enemies, to save you.'

"And the officers shall speak unto the people, and they shall say, 'What man is there that is fearful and faint-hearted? let him go and return unto his house, lest his brethren's heart faint as well as his heart.'

"For if ye shall diligently keep all the commandments which I command you, to do them, to love the Lord your God, to walk in all his ways, and to cleave unto him, then will the

Lord drive out all these nations from before you, and ye shall possess greater nations and mightier than yourselves. Every place whereon the soles of your feet shall tread shall be yours: from the wilderness and Lebanon, from the river Euphrates, even unto the uttermost sea shall your coast be. There shall no man be able to stand before you: for the Lord your God shall lay the fear of you, and the dread of you upon all the land.

"Ye shall utterly destroy all the places, wherein the nations which ye shall possess served their gods, upon the high mountains, and upon the hills, and under every green tree. And ye shall overthrow their altars, and break their pillars, and burn their groves with fire; and ye shall hew down the graven images of their gods, and destroy the names of them out of that place.

"Be strong and of good courage, fear not nor be afraid of them: for the Lord is with thee; he will not fail thee nor forsake thee.

"When thou art come into the land which the Lord thy God giveth thee, and shall possess it, and shall dwell therein, speak not thou in thine heart, saying, 'For my righteousness the Lord hath brought me in to possess this land.' But for the wickedness of these nations the Lord doth drive them out, that he may perform the word which he sware unto thy fathers, Abraham, Isaac, and Jacob.

"And thou shalt remember all the way which the Lord thy God led thee these forty years in the wilderness, to humble thee, and to prove thee, to know what was in thine heart, whether thou wouldst keep his commandments, or no. And he humbled thee, and suffered thee to hunger, and fed thee with manna, which thou knewest not, neither did thy fathers know; that he might make thee know that man doth not live by bread only, but by every word that proceedeth out of the mouth of the Lord, doth man live. Thy raiment waxed not old upon thee, neither did thy foot swell these forty years.

"Thou shalt also consider in thine heart, that as a man

chasteneth his son, so the Lord thy God chasteneth thee. Therefore thou shalt keep the commandments of the Lord, to walk in his ways, and to fear him.

"For the Lord thy God bringeth thee into a good land, a land of brooks of water, of fountains, and depths that spring out of the valleys and hills; a land of wheat, and barley, and vines, and fig-trees, and pomegranates, a land of oil-olive, and honey; a land wherein thou shalt eat bread without scarceness, and thou shalt not lack anything in it; a land whose stones are iron, and out of whose hills thou mayest dig brass. When thou hast eaten and art full, then thou shalt bless the Lord for the good land which he hath given thee. And ye shall rejoice before the Lord your God.

"Beware that thou forget not the Lord thy God, lest when thou hast eaten and art full, and hast built goodly houses, and dwell therein; and when thine herds and thy flocks multiply, and thy silver and thy gold is multiplied, and all that thou hast is multiplied; then thy heart be lifted up, and thou forget the Lord, which brought thee forth out of the land of Egypt, from the house of bondage; who led thee through that great and terrible wilderness, and wherein were fiery serpents, and scorpions, and drought, where there was no water; who brought thee forth water out of the rock of flint; and say in thine heart, 'My power and the might of mine hand hath gotten me this wealth.' But thou shalt remember the Lord, for it is he that giveth thee power to get wealth.

"And it shall be, if thou do at all forget the Lord thy God, and walk after other gods, and serve them, and worship them, ye shall surely perish. And if thou wilt not hearken to the voice of the Lord, to observe all of his commandments, and his statutes which I command thee this day, the Lord shall bring a nation against thee from far, from the end of the earth, as swift as the eagle flieth, a nation whose tongue thou shalt not understand; a nation of fierce countenance, which shall not regard the person of the old, nor show favour to the young; and he shall besiege thee in all thy gates, until thy high fenced walls come down, wherein thou trusted, throughout all thy land. And in the siege, and in the straitness wherewith thine enemies shall distress thee, the man that is tender and delicate among you, his eye shall be evil toward his brother, and toward the wife of his bosom, and toward his children: and the tender and delicate woman among you, her eye shall be evil toward her husband, and toward her son, and toward her daughter, for want of all things in the siege and straitness wherein thine enemy shall distress thee in thy gates.

"And the Lord shall scatter thee among all people from one end of the earth even unto the other. And among these nations thou shalt find no ease, neither shall the sole of thy foot have rest: but thou shalt have a trembling heart, and failing eyes, and sorrow of mind. And thy life shall hang in doubt before thee; and thou shalt fear day and night, and shall have none assurance of thy life. In the morning thou shalt say, 'Would God it were evening!' and at even thou shalt say, 'Would God it were morning!' for the fear of thine heart wherewith thou shalt fear, and for the sight of thine eyes which thou shalt see. And there ye shall serve other gods, the work of men's hands, wood and stone, which neither see, nor hear, nor eat, nor smell.

"But if from thence thou shalt seek the Lord thy God, thou shalt find him, if thou seek him with all thine heart, and with all thy soul. When thou art in tribulation, and all these things are come upon thee, even in the latter days, if thou turn to the Lord thy God, and shalt be obedient unto his voice, thou shalt find him. For the Lord thy God is a merciful God; he will not forsake thee, neither destroy thee, nor forget the covenant of thy fathers, which he sware unto them.

"Now therefore hearken, O Israel! Behold, I have taught you statutes and judgments, as the Lord thy God commanded me.

Keep therefore and do them: for this is your wisdom and your understanding in the sight of the nations, which shall hear all these statutes, and say, 'Surely this great nation is a wise and understanding people.'

"For what nation is there so great, who hath God so nigh unto them, as the Lord our God is in all things that we call upon him for? And what nation is there so great, that hath statutes and judgments so righteous as this law which I set before you this day? Know therefore this day, and consider it in thine heart that the Lord he is God in heaven above, and upon the earth beneath: there is none else.

"Hear, O Israel! The Lord our God is one Lord: and thou shalt love the Lord thy God with all thine heart, and with all thy soul, and with all thy might. And these words shall be in thine heart; and thou shalt talk of them when thou sittest in thine house, and when thou walkest by the way, and when thou liest down, and when thou risest up. And thou shalt bind them for a sign upon thine hand, and they shall be as frontlets between thine eyes. And thou shalt do that which is right and good in the sight of the Lord. Thou shalt be perfect with the Lord thy God.

"The Lord did not set his love upon you, nor choose you, because you were more in number than any people; for ye were the fewest of all people: But because the Lord loved you, and because he would keep the oath which he had sworn unto your fathers. Wherefore, if ye hearken to these judgments, and keep and do them, the Lord will love thee and bless thee; he shall command his blessing upon thee in thy storehouse, and in all that thou settest thine hand unto; and he shall bless thee in the land which he giveth thee. Thou shalt be blessed above all people: and the Lord will take away from thee all sickness, and thou shalt be perfect with the Lord thy God.

"And the Lord will raise up unto thee a Prophet from the midst of thee, of thy brethren, like unto me; unto him ye shall hearken. For the Lord said unto me, 'I will raise them up a Prophet from among their brethren, like unto thee, and will put my words in his mouth; and he shall speak unto them all that I shall command him.'

"Ye stand this day all of you before the Lord your God; your captains of your tribes, your elders, and your officers, with all the men of Israel. Thou shalt hearken unto the voice of the Lord thy God, to keep his commandments and his statutes which are written in this book of the law, and turn unto the Lord thy God with all thine heart and with all thy soul.

"For this commandment which I command thee this day, it is not hidden from thee, neither is it far off. It is not in heaven, that thou shouldst say, 'Who shall go up for us to heaven, and bring it unto us, that we may hear it, and do it?' Neither is it beyond the sea, that thou shouldest say, 'Who shall go over the sea for us, and bring it unto us, that we may hear it, and do it?' But the word is very nigh unto thee, in thy mouth, and in thy heart, that thou mayest do it.

"See, I have set before thee this day life and good, and death and evil; in that I command thee this day to love the Lord thy God, to walk in his ways, and to keep his commandments, and his statutes, and his judgments, that thou mayest live; and the Lord thy God shall bless thee in the land whither thou goest to possess it.

"But if thine heart turn away, so that thou wilt not hear, but shall be drawn away, and worship other gods, and serve them, I denounce unto you this day, that ye shall surely perish, and that ye shall not prolong your days upon the land, whither thou passest over Jordan to possess it.

"I call heaven and earth to record this day against you, that I have set before you life and death, blessing and cursing; therefore choose life, that both thou and thy seed may live; that thou mayest love the Lord thy God, and that thou mayest obey his voice, and that thou mayest cleave unto him, for he is thy life, and the length of thy days."

And Moses spake in the ears of all the congregation of Israel the words of this song until they were ended:

"Give ear, O ye heavens, and I will speak;
And hear, O earth, the words of my mouth.
My doctrine shall drop as the rain,
My speech shall distil as the dew,
As the small rain upon the tender herb,
And as the showers upon the grass:
Because I will publish the name of the Lord:
Ascribe ye greatness unto our God.
He is the Rock, his work is perfect:
For all his ways are judgment:
A God of Truth and without iniquity,
Just and right is he.

"For the Lord's portion is his people;
Jacob is the lot of his inheritance.
He found him in a desert land,
In a waste howling wilderness;
He led him about, he instructed him,
He kept him as the apple of his eye.
As an eagle stirreth up her nest,
Fluttereth over her young,
Spreadeth abroad her wings,
Taketh them, beareth them on her wings,
So the Lord alone did lead him,
And there was no strange god with him.

"See now that I, even I, am he,
And there is no god with me,

And none can deliver out of my hand.
Rejoice, O ye nations, with his people;
For he will be merciful unto his land,
And to his people."

THE ETERNAL GOD IS THY REFUGE

And the Lord spake unto Moses that selfsame day, saying, "Get thee up into mount Nebo, which is in the land of Moab, that is over against Jericho; and behold the land of Canaan which I give unto the children of Israel for a possession; and be gathered unto thy people, as Aaron thy brother was gathered unto his people. Thou shalt see the land before thee which I give to the children of Israel."

And Moses the man of God blessed the children of Israel before his death. And he said:

"The eternal God is thy refuge,
And underneath are the everlasting arms:
He shall thrust out the enemy from before thee;
And shall say, 'Destroy them.'
Israel then shall dwell in safety alone,
Upon a land of corn and wine;
And his heavens shall drop down dew.
Happy art thou, O Israel!
Who is like unto thee,
O people, saved by the Lord,
The shield of thy help,
And who is the sword of thy excellency!
Thine enemies shall be found liars unto thee;
And thou shalt tread upon their high places."

And Moses went up from the plains of Moab, unto the mountain of Nebo that is over against Jericho. And the Lord showed him all the land of Gilead, unto Dan, and all Naphtali, and the land of Ephraim, and Manasseh, and all the land of Judah, unto the utmost sea, and the south, and the plain of the valley of Jericho, the city of palm-trees, unto Zoar.

And the Lord said unto him, " This is the land which I sware unto Abraham, unto Isaac, and unto Jacob, saying, ' I will give it unto thy seed.' I have caused thee to see it with thine eyes."

So Moses, the servant of the Lord, died there in the land of Moab, according to the word of the Lord, but no man knoweth of his sepulchre unto this day.

And Moses was an hundred and twenty years old when he died: his eye was not dim, nor his natural force abated. And the children of Israel wept for Moses in the plains of Moab. And there arose not a prophet since in Israel like unto Moses, whom the Lord knew face to face.

" All good things are come upon you
which the Lord your God promised you."

THE BOOK OF JOSHUA

JOSHUA SHALL GO BEFORE HIS PEOPLE

NOW AFTER THE DEATH of Moses, the servant of the Lord, it came to pass, that the Lord spake unto Joshua, the son of Nun, Moses' minister, saying:

" Moses, my servant, is dead; now therefore arise, go over this Jordan, thou, and all this people, unto the land which I do give to them, even to the children of Israel. Every place that the sole of your foot shall tread upon, that have I given unto you, as I said unto Moses. From the wilderness and this Lebanon even unto the great river, the river Euphrates, all the land of the Hittites, and unto the great sea toward the going down of the sun, shall be your coast. There shall not any man be able to stand before thee all the days of thy life; as I was with Moses, so I will be with thee; I will not fail thee, nor forsake thee. Be strong and of a good courage; for unto this people shalt thou divide for an inheritance the land, which I sware unto their fathers to give them. Only be thou strong and very courageous, that thou mayest observe to do according to all the law, which Moses my servant commanded thee; turn not from it to the right hand or to the left, that thou mayest prosper whithersoever thou goest.

" This book of the law shall not depart out of thy mouth; but thou shalt meditate therein day and night, that thou mayest observe to do according to all that is written therein; for then thou shalt make thy way prosperous, and then thou shalt have good success. Have not I commanded thee? Be strong and of a good courage; be not afraid, neither be thou dismayed; for the Lord thy God is with thee withersoever thou goest."

Then Joshua commanded the officers of the people, saying, " Pass through the host, and command the people, saying, ' Prepare you victuals; for within three days ye shall pass over this Jordan, to go in to possess the land, which the Lord your God giveth you to possess it.' "

And they answered Joshua, saying, "All that thou commandest us we will do, and whithersoever thou sendest us, we will go. According as we hearkened unto Moses in all things, so will we hearken unto thee; only the Lord thy God be with thee, as he was with Moses."

TWO MEN SENT TO JERICHO

AND JOSHUA sent out two men to spy secretly, saying, "Go view the land, even Jericho."

And they went, and came into an harlot's house, named Rahab, and lodged there. And the woman took the two men, and hid them.

And it was told the king of Jericho, saying, "Behold, there came men tonight of the children of Israel to search out the country."

And the king of Jericho sent unto Rahab, saying, "Bring forth the men which are entered into thine house; for they be come to search out all the country."

And the woman said thus, "There came men, but I wist not whence they were. And about the time of the shutting of the gate, when it was dark, the men went out; whither the men went I wot not; pursue after them quickly; for ye shall overtake them." And the men pursued after them the way to Jordan unto the fords.

But she had brought them up to the roof of the house, and hid them with the stalks of flax, which she had laid in order upon the roof. And before they were laid down, she came up upon the roof, and she said unto the men, "I know that the Lord hath given you the land, and that your terror is fallen upon us, and that all the inhabitants of the land faint because of you. For we have heard how the Lord dried up the water of the Red sea for you, when ye came out of Egypt; and what ye did unto the two kings of the Amorites, that were on the other side Jordan, whom ye utterly destroyed. And as soon as we had heard these things, our hearts did melt, neither did there remain any more courage in any man because of you; for the Lord your God, he is God in heaven above, and in the earth beneath.

"Now therefore, I pray you, swear unto me by the Lord, since I have shown you kindness, that ye will also show kindness unto my father's house, and that ye will save alive my father, and my mother, and my brethren, and my sisters, and all that they have, and deliver our lives from death."

And the men answered her, "If ye utter not this our business, it shall be, when the Lord hath given us the land, that we will deal kindly and truly with thee."

Then she let them down by a cord through the window; for her house was upon the town wall. And she said unto them, "Get you to the mountain, lest the pursuers meet you; and hide yourselves there three days, until the pursuers be returned; and afterward may ye go your way."

And the men said, "Behold, when we come into the land, thou shalt bind this line of scarlet thread in the window which thou didst let us down by; and thou shalt bring thy father, and thy mother, and thy brethren, and all thy father's household, home unto thee. And whosoever shall be with thee in the house, his blood shall be on our head, if any hand be upon him. And if thou utter this our business, then we will be quit of thine oath which thou hast made us to swear."

And she said, "According unto your words, so be it." And she sent them away, and they departed; and she bound the scarlet line in the window.

And the men came unto the mountain, and abode there three days, until the pursuers were returned; and the pursuers sought them throughout all the way, but found them not.

So the two men descended from the mountain, and passed over, and came to Joshua and told him all things that befell them.

And they said, "Truly the Lord hath delivered into our hands all the land; for even all the inhabitants of the country do faint because of us."

YE SHALL KNOW, THAT THE LIVING GOD IS AMONG YOU

And Joshua rose early in the morning, and came to Jordan, he and all the children of Israel, and lodged there before they passed over.

And it came to pass after three days that the Lord said unto Joshua, "This day will I begin to magnify thee in the sight of all Israel, that they may know that as I was with Moses, so will I be with thee."

And Joshua said unto the children of Israel, "Come hither and hear the words of the Lord your God. Hereby ye shall know that the living God is among you, and that he will without fail drive out from before you the Canaanites, and the Hittites, and the Hivites, and the Perizzites, and the Girgashites, and the Amorites and the Jebusites. Behold, the ark of the covenant of the Lord of all the earth passeth over before you into Jordan. And it shall come to pass, as soon as the soles of the feet of the priests that bear the ark of the Lord shall rest in the waters of Jordan, that the waters of Jordan shall be cut off from the waters that come down from above; and they shall stand upon an heap."

And it came to pass, when the people removed from their tents to pass over Jordan, and the priests bearing the ark of the covenant were come unto Jordan, and the feet of the priests were dipped in the brim of the water, (for Jordan overfloweth all his banks all the time of harvest), that the waters which came down from above stood, and rose upon an heap, and those that came down toward the sea of the plain, even the salt sea, failed and were cut off: and the people passed over right against Jericho.

And the priests that bare the ark of the covenant of the Lord stood firm on dry ground in the midst of Jordan, and all the Israelites passed over on dry ground, until all the people were passed clean over Jordan.

And it came to pass, when all the people were clean passed over Jordan, the Lord spake unto Joshua saying, "Take you twelve men out of the people, out of every tribe a man, and command ye them, saying, 'Take you hence out of the midst of Jordan, out of the place where the priests' feet stood firm, twelve stones, and ye shall carry them over with you, and leave them in the lodging place, where ye shall lodge this night.' "

Then Joshua called the twelve men, out of every tribe a man, and said unto them, "Pass over before the ark of the Lord your God, and take you up every man of you a stone upon his shoulder, according unto the number of the tribes of the children of Israel: that this may be a sign among you, that when your children ask their fathers in time to come, saying, 'What mean ye by these stones?' Then ye shall let your children know, saying, 'Israel came over this Jordan on dry land. For the Lord your God dried up the waters of Jordan from before you, until ye were passed over, as the Lord your God did to the Red sea, which he dried up from before us, until we were gone over. That all the people of the earth might know the hand of the Lord, that it is mighty; that ye might fear the Lord your God for ever. And these stones shall be for a memorial unto the children of Israel for ever.' "

And the children of Israel did so as Joshua commanded, and took up twelve stones out of the midst of Jordan, and carried them unto the place where they lodged, and laid them down there.

And Joshua set up twelve stones in the midst of Jordan, in the place where the feet of the priests which bare the ark stood; and they are there unto this day.

And the Lord spake unto Joshua, saying, "Command the priests that bear the ark, that they come up out of Jordan."

Joshua therefore commanded the priests, and it came to pass, when the priests were come up out of the midst of Jordan, and the soles of the priests' feet were lifted up unto dry land, that the waters of Jordan returned unto their place, and flowed over all his banks, as they did before.

And the children of Israel encamped in Gilgal, and kept the passover on the fourteenth day of the month at even in the plains of Jericho.

And they did eat of the old corn of the land on the morrow after the passover, unleavened cakes, and parched corn in the selfsame day.

And the manna ceased on the morrow after they had eaten of the old corn of the land; neither had the children of Israel manna any more; but they did eat of the fruit of the land of Canaan that year.

CAPTAIN OF THE HOST OF THE LORD

AND IT CAME TO PASS when Joshua was by Jericho, that he lifted up his eyes and looked, and, behold, there stood a man over against him with his sword drawn in his hand: and Joshua went unto him, and said unto him, "Art thou for us, or for our adversaries?"

And he said, "Nay; but as captain of the host of the Lord am I now come."

And Joshua fell on his face to the earth, and did worship, and said unto him, "What saith my lord unto his servant?"

And the captain of the Lord's host said unto Joshua, "Loose thy shoe from off thy foot; for the place whereon thou standest is holy."

And Joshua did so.

SHOUT! FOR THE LORD HATH GIVEN YOU THE CITY

Now Jericho was straitly shut up because of the children of Israel: none went out, and none came in.

And the Lord said unto Joshua, "See, I have given into thine hand Jericho, and the king thereof, and the mighty men of valour. And ye shall compass the city, all ye men of war, and go round about the city once. Thus shalt thou do six days. And seven priests shall bear before the ark seven trumpets of rams' horns: and the seventh day ye shall compass the city seven times, and the priests shall blow with the trumpets. And it shall come to pass, that when they make a long blast with the ram's horn, and when ye hear the sound of the trumpet, all the people shall shout with a great shout; and the wall of the city shall fall down flat, and the people shall ascend up every man straight before him."

And Joshua the son of Nun called the priests, and said unto them, "Take up the ark of the covenant, and let seven priests bear seven trumpets of rams' horns before the ark of the Lord."

And he said unto the people, "Pass on, and compass the city, and let him that is armed pass on before the ark of the Lord."

And it came to pass, when Joshua had spoken unto the people, that the seven priests bearing the seven trumpets of rams' horns passed on before the Lord, and blew with the trumpets: and the ark of the covenant of the Lord followed them. And the armed men went before the priests that blew with the trumpets, and the rereward came after the ark, the priests going on, and blowing with the trumpets.

And Joshua had commanded the people, saying, "Ye shall not shout, nor make any noise with your voice, neither shall any word proceed out of your mouth, until the day I bid you shout; then shall ye shout."

So the ark of the Lord compassed the city, going about it once; and they came into the camp, and lodged in the camp.

And Joshua rose early in the morning, and the priests took up the ark of the Lord. And the armed men went before them; but the rereward came after the ark of the Lord, the priests going on, and blowing with the trumpets. And the second day they compassed the city once, and returned into the camp: so did they six days.

And it came to pass on the seventh day, that they rose early about the dawning of the day, and compassed the city after the same manner: only on that day they compassed the city seven times.

And it came to pass at the seventh time, when the priests blew with the trumpets, Joshua said unto the people, "Shout! for the Lord hath given you the city. And the city shall be accursed, even it, and all that are therein: only Rahab the harlot shall live, she and all that are with her in the house, because she hid the messengers that we sent. And ye, in any wise keep yourselves from the accursed thing, lest ye take of the accursed thing, and make the camp of Israel a curse, and trouble it. But all of the silver, and gold, and vessels of brass and iron, are consecrated unto the Lord: they shall come into the treasury of the Lord."

So the people shouted when the priests blew with the trumpets: and it came to pass, when the people shouted with a great shout, that the wall fell down flat, so that the people went up into the city, every man straight before him, and they took the city.

And they utterly destroyed all that was in the city, both man and woman, young and old, and ox, and sheep, and ass, with the edge of the sword.

But Joshua had said unto the two men that had spied out the country, "Go into the harlot's house, and bring out thence the woman, and all that she hath, as ye sware unto her." And the young men that were spies went in, and brought out Rahab, and her father, and her mother, and her brethren, and all that she had; and they brought out all her kindred, and left them without the camp of Israel.

And they burnt the city with fire, and all that was therein: only the silver, and the gold, and the vessels of brass and of iron, they put into the treasury of the house of the Lord.

And Joshua saved Rahab, the harlot alive, and her father's household, and all that she had; because she hid the messengers which Joshua sent to spy out Jericho.

So the Lord was with Joshua; and his fame was noised throughout all the country.

GET UP!
WHEREFORE LIEST THOU UPON THY FACE?

But the children of Israel committed a trespass in the accursed thing: for Achan, the son of Carmi, of the tribe of Judah, took of the accursed thing; and the anger of the Lord was kindled against the children of Israel.

And Joshua sent men from Jericho to Ai, and spake unto them saying, "Go up and view the country." And the men went up and viewed Ai.

And they returned unto Joshua, and said unto him, "Let not all the people go up; but let about two or three thousand men go up and smite Ai; and make not all the people to labour thither; for they are but few."

So there went up thither of the people about three thousand men: and they fled before the men of Ai. And the men of Ai chased them from before the gate, and smote them in the going down: wherefore the hearts of the people melted, and became as water.

And Joshua rent his clothes, and fell to the earth upon his face before the ark of the Lord until the eventide, he and the elders of Israel, and put dust upon their heads.

And Joshua said, " Alas, O Lord God, wherefore hast thou at all brought this people over Jordan, to deliver us into the hand of the Amorites, to destroy us? would to God we had been content, and dwelt on the other side Jordan! O Lord, what shall I say when Israel turneth their backs before their enemies. For the Canaanites and all the inhabitants of the land shall hear of it, and shall environ us round, and cut off our name from the earth: and what wilt thou do unto thy great name? "

And the Lord said unto Joshua, "Get thee up; wherefore liest thou thus upon thy face? Israel hath sinned, and they have also transgressed my covenant which I commanded them: for they have even taken of the accursed thing, and have also stolen, and dissembled also, and they have put it even among their own stuff. Therefore the children of Israel could not stand before their enemies, but turned their backs before their enemies, because they were accursed: neither will I be with you any more, except ye destroy the accursed from among you.

" Up, sanctify the people, and say, 'Sanctify yourselves against tomorrow: for thus saith the Lord God of Israel, " There is an accursed thing in the midst of thee, O Israel: thou canst not stand before thine enemies until ye take away the accursed thing from among you. In the morning therefore ye shall be brought according to your tribes: and it shall be, that the tribe which the Lord taketh shall come according to the families thereof; and the family which the Lord shall take shall come by households; and the household which the Lord shall take shall come man by man. And it shall be, that he that is taken with the accursed thing shall be burnt with fire, he and all that he hath: because he hath transgressed the covenant of the Lord and because he hath wrought folly in Israel." ' "

So Joshua rose up early in the morning, and brought Israel

by their tribes; and the tribe of Judah was taken; and he brought the family of Judah, and he brought the family man by man; and Zabdi was taken; and he brought his household man by man; and Achan, the son of Carmi was taken.

And Joshua said unto Achan, "My son, give, I pray thee, glory to the Lord God of Israel, and make confession unto him; and tell me now what thou hast done; hide it not from me."

And Achan answered Joshua, and said, "Indeed I have sinned against the Lord God of Israel. When I saw among the spoils a goodly Babylonish garment, and two hundred shekels of silver, and a wedge of gold of fifty shekels weight, then I coveted them; and, behold, they are hid in the earth in the midst of my tent, and the silver under it."

So Joshua sent messengers, and they ran unto the tent; and, behold, it was hid in his tent, and the silver under it. And they took them out of the midst of the tent, and brought them unto Joshua, and unto all the children of Israel, and laid them out before the Lord.

And Joshua, and all Israel with him, took Achan the son of Carmi, and the silver, and the garment, and the wedge of gold, and his sons, and his daughters, and his oxen, and his asses, and his sheep, and his tent, and all that he had: and they brought them unto the valley of Achor. And all Israel stoned him with stones, and burned them with fire. And they raised over him a great heap of stones unto this day. Wherefore the name of that place was called, The Valley of Achor.

FEAR NOT, ARISE, GO UP TO AI

AND THE LORD said unto Joshua, "Fear not, neither be thou dismayed; take all the people of war with thee, and arise, go up to Ai; see, I have given into thy hand the king of Ai, and his people, and his city and his land. And thou shalt do to Ai and her king as thou didst unto Jericho and her king. Lay thee in ambush for the city behind it."

So Joshua arose, and all the people of war, to go up against Ai. And Joshua chose out thirty thousand mighty men of valour, and he commanded them saying, "Behold, ye shall lie in wait behind the city; go not very far from the city, but be ye all ready; and I, and all the people that are with me, will approach unto the city; and when they come out against us, we will flee before them, till we have drawn them from the city; for they will say, 'They flee before us.' Then ye shall rise from the ambush, and seize upon the city; for the Lord your God will deliver it into your hand. And it shall be, when ye have taken the city, that ye shall set the city on fire; according to the commandment of the Lord shall ye do. See, I have commanded you."

Joshua therefore sent them forth; and they went to lie in ambush on the west side of Ai: but Joshua lodged that night among the people.

And Joshua rose up early in the morning, and numbered the people, and went up, he and the elders of Israel, before the people to Ai. And all the people of war that were with him went up, and came before the city, and pitched on the north side of Ai; now there was a valley between them and Ai.

And it came to pass, when the king of Ai saw it, that they hasted and rose up early, and the men of the city went out against Israel to battle; but he wist not that there were liers in ambush behind the city.

And Joshua and all Israel made as if they were beaten before them; and they pursued after Joshua, and were drawn away from the city. And there was not a man left in Ai that went not out after Israel, and they left the city open, and pursued after Israel.

And the Lord said unto Joshua, "Stretch out the spear that is in thy hand toward Ai; for I will give it into thine hand." And Joshua stretched out the spear that he had in his hand toward the city. And the ambush arose quickly out of their place, and they ran as soon as he had stretched out his hand; and they entered into the city, and took it, and hasted and set the city on fire.

And when the men of Ai looked behind them, they saw, and behold, the smoke of the city ascended up to heaven, and they had no power to flee this way or that way.

And when Joshua and all Israel saw that the ambush had taken the city, and that the smoke of the city ascended, then they turned again, and slew the men of Ai, so that they let none of them remain or escape. And Joshua burnt Ai, and made it an heap for ever, even a desolation unto this day.

Then Joshua built an altar unto the Lord God of Israel; and they offered thereon burnt offerings unto the Lord, and sacrificed peace offerings. And he wrote there upon the stones a copy of the law of Moses, which he wrote in the presence of the children of Israel. And afterward he read all the words of the law, according to all that is written in the book of the law. There was not a word of all that Moses commanded, which Joshua read not before all the congregation of Israel.

GIBEON MADE PEACE WITH ISRAEL

AND WHEN the inhabitants of Gibeon heard what Joshua had done unto Jericho and to Ai, they did work wilily, and went and made as if they had been ambassadors, and took old sacks upon their asses, and wine bottles, old, and rent, and bound up; and old shoes upon their feet, and old garments upon them; and all the bread of their provision was dry and mouldy.

And they went to Joshua unto the camp at Gilgal, and said unto him, and to the men of Israel, "We be come from a far country; now therefore make ye a league with us."

And the men of Israel said unto them, "Peradventure ye dwell among us; and how shall we make a league with you?"

And they said unto Joshua, "We are thy servants."

And Joshua said unto them, "Who are ye? and from whence come ye?"

And they said unto him, "From a very far country thy servants are come because of the name of the Lord thy God; for we have heard of the fame of him, and all that he did in Egypt, and all that he did to the two kings of the Amorites, that were beyond Jordan. Wherefore our elders and all the inhabitants of our country spake to us, saying, 'Take victuals with you for the journey, and go to meet them, and say unto them, "We are your servants; therefore now make ye a league with us."' This our bread we took hot for our provision out of our houses on the day we came forth to go unto you; but now, behold, it is dry, and it is mouldy; and these bottles of wine, which we filled were new; and, behold, they be rent; and these our garments and our shoes are become old by reason of the very long journey."

And the men of Israel took their victuals, and asked not counsel at the mouth of the Lord. And Joshua made peace with them, and made a league with them, to let them live; and the princes of the congregation sware unto them.

And it came to pass at the end of three days after they had made a league with them, that they heard that they were their neighbours, and that they dwelt among them.

And the children of Israel smote them not, because the princes of the congregation had sworn unto them by the Lord God of Israel. And all the congregation murmured against the princes.

But all the princes said unto all the congregation, "We have sworn unto them by the Lord God of Israel: now therefore we may not touch them. This we will do to them; we will even let them live, lest wrath be upon us, because of the oath which we sware unto them. Let them live; but let them be hewers of wood and drawers of water unto all the congregation; as the princes had promised them."

And Joshua called for them, and he spake unto them, saying, "Wherefore have ye beguiled us, saying, 'We are very far from you;' when ye dwell among us? Now therefore ye shall none of ye be freed from being bondmen, and hewers of wood, and drawers of water for the house of my God."

And they answered Joshua, and said, "Because it was certainly told thy servants, how that the Lord thy God commanded his servant Moses to give you all the land, and to destroy all the inhabitants of the land from before you; therefore we were sore afraid of our lives because of you, and have done this thing. And now, behold, we are in thine hand; as it seemeth good and right unto thee to do unto us, do."

And so did he unto them, and delivered them out of the hand of the children of Israel that they slew them not. And Joshua made them that day hewers of wood and drawers of water for the congregation, and for the altar of the Lord.

THE SUN STOOD STILL IN THE MIDST OF HEAVEN

NOW IT CAME TO PASS, when the king of Jerusalem had heard how Joshua had taken Ai, and had utterly destroyed it, as he had done to Jericho and her king, and how the inhabitants of Gibeon had made peace with Israel, and were among them, that he feared greatly, because Gibeon was a great city, as one of the royal cities, and because it was greater than Ai, and all the men thereof were mighty.

Wherefore the king of Jerusalem sent unto the king of Hebron, and unto the king of Jarmuth, and unto the king of Lachish, and unto the king of Eglon, saying, "Come up unto me, and help me, that we may smite Gibeon; for it hath made peace with Joshua and with the children of Israel."

Therefore the five kings of the Amorites, the king of Jerusalem, the king of Hebron, the king of Jarmuth, the king of Lachish, and the king of Eglon, gathered themselves together, and went up, they and all their host, and encamped before Gibeon and made war against it.

And the men of Gibeon sent unto Joshua to the camp to Gilgal, saying, " Slack not thy hand from thy servants; come up to us quickly, and save us, and help us; for all the kings of the Amorites that dwell in the mountains are gathered together against us."

So Joshua ascended from Gilgal, he, and all the people of war with him, and all the mighty men of valour.

And the Lord said unto Joshua, "Fear them not; for I have delivered them into thine hand; there shall not a man of them stand before thee."

Joshua therefore came unto them suddenly, and the Lord discomfited them before Israel, and slew them with a great slaughter at Gibeon, and chased them along the way that goeth up to Beth-horon, and smote them.

And it came to pass as they fled from before Israel, and were going down to Beth-horon that the Lord cast down great stones from heaven upon them; and there were more which died with hailstones than they whom the children of Israel slew with the sword.

Then spake Joshua to the Lord in the day when the Lord delivered up the Amorites before the children of Israel, and he said in the sight of Israel,

" Sun, stand thou still upon Gibeon;
And thou, Moon, in the valley of Ajalon."
And the sun stood still,
And the moon stayed,
Until the people had avenged themselves
upon their enemies.

Is not this written in the book of Jasher? "So the sun stood still in the midst of heaven, and hasted not to go down about a whole day. And there was no day like that before it or after it, that the Lord hearkened unto the voice of a man; for the Lord fought for Israel."

And Joshua returned, and all Israel with him, unto the camp to Gilgal.

But these five kings fled, and hid themselves in a cave at Makkedah. And it was told Joshua, saying, "The five kings are found hid in a cave at Makkedah."

And Joshua said, "Roll great stones upon the mouth of the cave, and set men by it for to keep them. And stay ye not, but pursue after your enemies, and smite the hindmost of them; suffer them not to enter into their cities: for the Lord your God hath delivered them into your hand."

And it came to pass, when Joshua and the children of Israel had made an end of slaying them with a very great slaughter, till they were consumed, all the people returned to the camp at Makkedah in peace. No one moved his tongue against the children of Israel.

Then said Joshua, "Open the mouth of the cave, and bring out those five kings unto me out of the cave."

And they did so, and brought forth those five kings unto him out of the cave, the king of Jerusalem, the king of Hebron, the king of Jarmuth, the king of Lachish, and the king of Eglon. And it came to pass, when they brought out those kings unto Joshua, that Joshua called for the men of Israel, and said unto the captains of the men of war which went with him, "Come near, put your feet upon the necks of these kings." And they came near, and put their feet upon the necks of them.

And Joshua said unto them, "Fear not, nor be dismayed, be strong and of good courage: for thus shall the Lord do to all your enemies against whom ye fight."

And afterward Joshua smote them, and slew them, and hanged

them on five trees. And at the time of the going down of the sun, Joshua commanded, and they took them down off the trees, and cast them into the cave wherein they had been hid, and laid great stones in the cave's mouth.

So Joshua smote all the country of the hills, and of the south, and of the vale, and of the springs, and all their kings: he left none remaining, but utterly destroyed all that breathed, as the Lord God of Israel commanded. And all these kings and their land did Joshua take at one time, because the Lord God of Israel fought for Israel.

And Joshua returned, and all Israel with him, unto the camp to Gilgal.

SO JOSHUA TOOK THE WHOLE LAND

And it came to pass, when Jabin king of Hazor had heard those things, that he sent to the king of Madon, and to the king of Shimron, and to the king of Achshaph, and the kings that were on the north of the mountains, and of the plains south of Chinneroth, and in the valley, and in the borders of Dor on the west, and to the Canaanites on the east and on the west, and to the Amorite, and the Hittite, and the Perizzite, and the Jebusite in the mountains, and to the Hivite under Hermon in the land of Mizpeh. And they went out, they and all their hosts with them, much people, even as the sand that is upon the sea shore in multitude, with horses and chariots very many. And when all these kings were met together, they came and pitched together at the waters of Merom, to fight against Israel.

And the Lord said unto Joshua, "Be not afraid because of them: for tomorrow about this time will I deliver them up all slain before Israel: thou shalt kill their horses, and burn their chariots with fire."

So Joshua came, and all the people of war with him, against them by the waters of Merom suddenly; and they fell upon them. And the Lord delivered them into the hand of Israel, who smote them, and chased them unto great Zidon, and unto Misrephoth-maim, and unto the valley of Mizpeh eastward; and they smote them, until they left them none remaining. And Joshua did unto them as the Lord bade him: he killed their horses, and burnt their chariots with fire.

And all the cities of those kings, and all the kings of them did Joshua take, and smote them with the edge of the sword, and he utterly destroyed them, as Moses the servant of the Lord commanded. Joshua left nothing undone of all that the Lord commanded Moses.

So Joshua took all that land, the hills, and all the south country, and all the land of Goshen, and the valley, and the plain, and the mountain of Israel, and the valley of the same. And all their kings he took, and smote them, and slew them. Joshua made war a long time with all those kings. There was not a city that made peace with the children of Israel save the inhabitants of Gibeon: all other they took in battle.

So Joshua took the whole land, according to all that the Lord said unto Moses. And the land rested from war.

ALL GOOD WHICH THE LORD HAD SPOKEN CAME TO PASS

And the Lord gave unto Israel all the land which he sware to give unto their fathers; and they possessed it, and dwelt therein. And the Lord gave them rest round about. There stood not a man of all their enemies before them; the Lord delivered all their enemies into their hand. And the land was subdued before them.

And the whole congregation of the children of Israel assembled together at Shiloh, and set up the tabernacle of the congregation there.

And Joshua said unto the children of Israel, "Give out from among you three men for each tribe: and I will send them, and they shall rise, and go through the land, and describe it, and bring the description hither to me, that I may cast lots for you here before the Lord our God."

And the men went and passed through the land, and described it by cities in a book, and came again to Joshua. And Joshua cast lots for them in Shiloh before the Lord: and there Joshua divided the land unto the children of Israel according to their divisions By lot was their inheritance divided. As the Lord commanded Moses, so the children of Israel did, and they divided the land.

But unto the Levites he gave none inheritance among them, save cities to dwell in, and their suburbs for their cattle and for their substance, for the priesthood of the Lord is their inheritance.

Then Caleb the son of Jephunneh said unto Joshua, "Thou knowest the thing that the Lord said unto Moses, the man of God, concerning me and thee in Kadesh-barnea. Forty years old was I when Moses the servant of the Lord sent me from Kadesh-barnea to espy out the land; and I brought him word again as it was in mine heart. Nevertheless my brethren that went up with me made the heart of the people melt: but I wholly followed the Lord my God. And Moses sware on that day, saying, 'Surely the land whereon thy feet have trodden shall be thine inheritance, and thy children's for ever, because thou hast wholly followed the Lord thy God.'

"And now, behold, the Lord hath kept me alive, as he said, these forty and five years, even since the Lord spake this word unto Moses, while the children of Israel wandered in the wilderness: and now, lo, I am this day fourscore and five years old.

As yet I am as strong this day as I was in the day that Moses sent me: as my strength was then, even so is my strength now, for war, both to go out, and to come in. Now therefore give me this mountain, whereof the Lord spake in that day; for thou heardest in that day how the Anakims were there, and that the cities were great and fenced: if so be the Lord will be with me, then I shall be able to drive them out, as the Lord said."

And Joshua blessed him, and gave unto Caleb the son of Jephunneh Hebron for an inheritance. Hebron therefore became the inheritance of Caleb the son of Jephunneh because that he wholly followed the Lord God of Israel.

When they had made an end of dividing the land for inheritance by their coasts, the children of Israel gave an inheritance to Joshua the son of Nun. According to the word of the Lord they gave him the city which he asked, even Timmath-serah in mount Ephraim; and he built the city, and dwelt therein.

So they made an end of dividing the country.

And the Lord gave them rest round about, according to all that He sware unto their fathers. There failed not ought of any good thing which the Lord had spoken unto the house of Israel; all came to pass.

WE WILL SERVE THE LORD, FOR HE IS OUR GOD

AND IT CAME TO PASS a long time after that the Lord had given rest unto Israel from all their enemies round about, that Joshua waxed old and stricken in age.

And Joshua called for all Israel, and for their elders, and for their heads, and for their judges, and for their officers, and said unto them, "I am old and stricken in age; and ye have seen all that the Lord your God hath done unto all these nations because of you; for the Lord your God is he that hath fought for you. Behold, I have divided unto you by lot these nations that remain, to be an inheritance for your tribes, from Jordan, even unto the great sea westward.

"But take diligent heed to do the commandment and the law, which Moses the servant of the Lord charged you, to love the Lord your God, and to walk in all his ways, and to keep his commandments, and to cleave unto him, and to serve him with all your heart and with all your soul. For the Lord hath driven out from before you great nations and strong. Take good heed therefore unto yourselves, that ye love the Lord your God.

"Else if ye do in any wise go back, and cleave unto the remnant of these nations, even these that remain among you, and shall make marriages with them, know for a certainty that they shall be snares and traps unto you, and scourges in your sides, and thorns in your eyes, until ye perish from off this good land which the Lord your God hath given you.

"And behold, this day I am going the way of all the earth; and ye know in all your hearts and in all your souls, that not one thing hath failed of all the good things which the Lord your God spake concerning you; all are come to pass unto you, and not one thing hath failed thereof.

"Therefore it shall come to pass, that as all good things are come upon you, which the Lord your God promised you, so shall evil things, when ye have transgressed the covenant of the Lord your God, which he commanded you, and have gone and served other gods, and bowed yourselves to them; ye shall perish quickly from off the good land which he hath given unto you.

"I have given you a land for which ye did not labour, and cities which ye built not, and ye dwell in them; of the vineyards and olive yards which ye planted not do ye eat. Now therefore, fear the Lord and serve him in sincerity and in truth. Choose you this day whom ye will serve. As for me and my house, we will serve the Lord."

And the people answered and said, " God forbid that we should forsake the Lord, to serve other gods. For the Lord our God, he it is that brought us up and our fathers out of the land of Egypt, from the house of bondage, and which did those great signs in our sight, and preserved us in all the way wherein we went, and among all the people through whom we passed. And the Lord drave out from before us all the people, which dwelt in the land; therefore will we also serve the Lord; for he is our God."

And Joshua said unto the people, " Ye are witnesses against yourselves that ye have chosen you the Lord, to serve him."

And the people said, " We are witnesses. The Lord our God will we serve, and his voice will we obey."

And Joshua wrote these words in the book of the law of God, and took a great stone, and set it up there under an oak, that was by the sanctuary of the Lord.

And Joshua said unto all the people, "Behold, this stone shall be a witness unto us; for it hath heard all the words of the Lord which he spake unto us; it shall be therefore a witness unto you, lest ye deny your God."

So Joshua let the people depart every man unto his inheritance.

And it came to pass after these things, that Joshua the son of Nun, the servant of the Lord, died, being an hundred and ten years old. And they buried him in the border of his inheritance.

And Israel served the Lord all the days of Joshua.

" The Lord raised up Judges which delivered Israel out of the hand of those that spoiled them."

THE BOOK OF JUDGES

ISRAEL HATH NOT NOT HEARKENED UNTO MY VOICE

AND THE PEOPLE served the Lord all the days of Joshua, and all the days of the elders that outlived Joshua, who had seen all the great works of the Lord, that he did for Israel. And Joshua, the son of Nun, the servant of the Lord died. And also all that generation were gathered unto their fathers.

And there arose another generation after them which knew not the Lord, nor yet the works which he had done for Israel. And they forsook the Lord God of their fathers, which brought them out of the land of Egypt, and followed other gods: gods of the people that were round about them, and bowed themselves unto them.

And the anger of the Lord was hot against Israel, and he said, "Israel hath not hearkened unto my voice," and he delivered them into the hands of spoilers that spoiled them. Whithersoever they went out, the hand of the Lord was against them, and they were greatly distressed.

And Eglon the king of Moab went and smote Israel, and possessed the city of palm trees. So the children of Israel served Eglon, the king of Moab, eighteen years.

But when the children of Israel cried unto the Lord, he raised them up a deliverer, Ehud, a man lefthanded. And by him the children of Israel sent a present unto Eglon, the king of Moab. But Ehud made a dagger which had two edges, of a cubit length; and he did gird it under his raiment upon his right thigh.

And he brought the present unto Eglon, king of Moab. Eglon was a very fat man. And when Ehud made an end to offer the present, he sent away the people that bore the present. But he himself turned again, and said, "I have a secret errand unto thee, O king."

And Eglon said, "Keep silence." And all that stood by him went out from him.

And Ehud came unto him, he was sitting in a summer parlour which he had for himself alone, and Ehud said, "I have a message from God unto thee."

And Eglon arose out of his seat. And Ehud put forth his left hand, and took the dagger from his right thigh, and thrust it into Eglon's belly, and the fat closed upon the blade, so that he could not draw the dagger out. Then Ehud went forth through the porch, and shut the doors of the parlour upon him and locked them.

When Ehud was gone out, Eglon's servants came, and when they saw that, behold, the doors of the parlour were locked, they said, "Surely he covereth his feet in his summer chamber." And they tarried till they were ashamed; and, behold, he opened not the doors of the parlour; therefore they took a key, and opened them; and, behold, their lord was fallen down dead on the earth.

And Ehud escaped while they tarried, and passed beyond the quarries and escaped. And it came to pass, when he was come, that he blew a trumpet in the mountain of Ephraim, and the children of Israel went down with him from the mount, and he before them. And he said unto them, "Follow after me; for the Lord hath delivered your enemies the Moabites into your hand."

And they went down after him, and took the fords of Jordan toward Moab. And they slew of Moab about ten thousand men, all men of valour; there escaped not a man. So Moab was subdued that day under the hand of Israel. And the land had rest fourscore years.

DEBORAH JUDGED ISRAEL

AND THE CHILDREN of Israel again did evil in the sight of the Lord, when Ehud was dead. And the Lord sold them into the hand of Jabin king of Canaan, that reigned in Hazor; the captain of whose host was Sisera. And the children of Israel cried unto the Lord, for Sisera had nine hundred chariots of iron. And for twenty years Jabin mightily oppressed the children of Israel.

And Deborah, a prophetess, judged Israel at that time. And she dwelt under the palm tree of Deborah in mount Ephraim: and the children of Israel came up to her for judgment.

And she sent and called Barak, the son of Abinoam out of Kadesh-naphtali, and said unto him, "Hath not the Lord God of Israel commanded, saying, 'Go and draw toward mount Tabor, and take with thee ten thousand men. And I will draw unto thee to the river Kishon, Sisera, the captain of Jabin's army, with his chariots and his multitude; and I will deliver him into thine hand.'"

And Barak said unto her, "If thou wilt go with me, then I will go: but if thou wilt not go with me, then I will not go."

And Deborah said, "I will surely go with thee: notwithstanding the journey that thou takest shall not be for thine honour; for the Lord shall sell Sisera into the hand of a woman." And Deborah arose, and went with Barak to Kadesh.

And Barak went up with ten thousand men at his feet: and Deborah went up with him. And Sisera gathered together all his chariots, even nine hundred chariots of iron, and all the people that were with him.

And Deborah said unto Barak, "Up! for this is the day in which the Lord hath delivered Sisera into thine hand: is not the Lord gone out before thee?" So Barak went down from mount Tabor, and ten thousand men after him.

And the Lord discomfited Sisera, and all his chariots, and all his host with the edge of the sword before Barak; so that Sisera lighted down off his chariot, and fled away on his feet. But Barak pursued after the chariots, and after the host; and all the host of Sisera fell upon the edge of the sword, and there was not a man left.

Howbeit Sisera fled away on his feet to the tent of Jael, the wife of Heber the Kenite: for there was peace between Jabin the king of Hazor and the house of Heber the Kenite.

And Jael went out to meet Sisera, and said unto him, "Turn in, my lord, turn in to me; fear not." And when he had turned in unto her into the tent, she covered him with a mantle.

And he said unto her, "Give me, I pray thee, a little water to drink; for I am thirsty." And she opened a bottle of milk, and gave him drink, and covered him. Again he said unto her, "Stand in the door of the tent, and it shall be, when any man doth come and enquire of thee, and say, 'Is there any man here?' thou shalt say, 'No.' "

Then Jael, Heber's wife, took a nail of the tent, and took an hammer in her hand, and went softly unto Sisera, and smote the nail into his temples, and fastened it into the ground; for he was fast asleep and weary. So he died.

And, behold, as Barak pursued Sisera, Jael came out to meet him, and said unto him, "Come, and I will show thee the man whom thou seekest." And when he came into her tent, behold, Sisera lay dead, and the nail was in his temples.

So God subdued on that day Jabin the King of Canaan before the children of Israel. And the hand of the children of Israel prospered, and prevailed until they had destroyed Jabin king of Canaan.

Then sang Deborah and Barak, on that day, saying:

"Hear, O ye kings;
Give ear, O ye princes;
I, even I, will sing unto the Lord;
I will sing praise to the Lord God of Israel

The inhabitants of the villages ceased,
They ceased in Israel,
Until that I Deborah arose,
That I arose a mother in Israel.
Awake, awake, Deborah:
Awake, awake, utter a song:
Arise, Barak, and lead thy captivity captive.
O my soul, thou hast trodden down strength.

Blessed above women shall Jael the wife of Heber
the Kenite be,
Blessed shall she be above women in the tent.
He asked water, and she gave him milk;
She brought him butter in a lordly dish.
She put her hand to the nail,
And her right hand to the workmen's hammer;
And with the hammer she smote Sisera;
At her feet he bowed, he fell;
Where he bowed, there he fell down dead.

So let all thine enemies perish, O Lord:
But let them that love him
Be as the sun when he goeth forth in his might."

And the land had rest forty years.

GO IN THIS THY MIGHT AND THOU SHALT SAVE ISRAEL

And the children of Israel did evil in the sight of the Lord: and the Lord delivered them into the hand of Midian seven years. And the hand of Midian prevailed against Israel: and because of the Midianites the children of Israel made them the dens which are in the mountains, and caves, and strong holds.

And so it was, when Israel had sown, that the Midianites came up, and the Amalekites, and the children of the east, even they, came up against them. And they encamped against them, and destroyed the increase of the earth, and left no sustenance for Israel, neither sheep, nor ox, nor ass. For they came up with their cattle and their tents, and they came as grasshoppers for multitude; for both they and their camels were without number: and they entered into the land to destroy it.

And Israel was greatly impoverished because of the Midianites, and the children of Israel cried unto the Lord.

And it came to pass, when the children of Israel cried unto the Lord because of the Midianites, that the Lord sent a prophet unto them, who said, " Thus saith the Lord God of Israel, ' I brought you up from Egypt, and brought you forth out of the house of bondage; and I delivered you out of the hand of the Egyptians, and out of the hand of all that oppressed you, and drove them out from before you, and gave you their land. And I said unto you, " I am the Lord your God; fear not the gods of the Amorites, in whose land ye dwell." But ye have not obeyed my voice.' "

And there came an angel of the Lord, and sat under an oak that pertained unto Joash: and his son, Gideon, threshed wheat by the winepress, to hide it from the Midianites. And the Angel of the Lord appeared unto him, and said unto him, " The Lord is with thee, thou mighty man of valour."

And Gideon said unto him, " Oh my Lord, if the Lord be with us, why then is all this befallen us? and where be all the miracles, which our fathers told us of, saying, ' Did not the Lord bring us up from Egypt? ' but now the Lord hath forsaken us, and delivered us into the hands of the Midianites."

And the angel looked upon him, and said, " Go in this thy might, and thou shalt save Israel from the hand of the Midianites: have not I sent thee? "

And Gideon said unto the angel, " Oh my Lord, wherewith shall I save Israel? behold, my family is poor in Manasseh, and I am the least in my father's house."

And the angel said unto him, " Surely I will be with thee, and thou shalt smite the Midianites as one man."

And Gideon said, " If now I have found grace in thy sight, then show me a sign that thou talkest with me. Depart not hence, I pray thee, until I come unto thee, and bring forth my present, and set it before thee."

And the angel said, " I will tarry until thou come again."

And Gideon went in, and made ready a kid, and unleavened cakes of an ephah of flour; the flesh he put in a basket, and he put the broth in a pot, and brought it out unto him under the oak, and presented it.

And the angel of God said unto him, " Take the flesh and the unleavened cakes, and lay them upon this rock, and pour out the broth." And he did so.

Then the angel put forth the end of the staff that was in his hand, and touched the flesh and the unleavened cakes; and there rose up fire out of the rock, and consumed the flesh and the unleavened cakes. Then the angel of the Lord vanished.

And when Gideon perceived that he was an angel of the Lord, Gideon said, " Alas, O Lord God! for I have seen an angel of the Lord face to face."

And the Lord said unto him, " Peace be unto thee; fear not: thou shalt not die." And Gideon built an altar unto the Lord.

THE DEW AND THE FLEECE

And it came to pass the same night, that the Lord said unto Gideon, "Take thy father's young bullock, even the second bullock of seven years old, and throw down the altar of Baal that thy father hath, and cut down the grove that is by it, and build an altar unto the Lord thy God upon the top of this rock, in the ordered place, and take the second bullock, and offer a burnt sacrifice with the wood of the grove which thou shalt cut down."

Then Gideon took ten men of his servants, and did as the Lord had said unto him. And because he feared his father's household, and the men of the city, he could not do it by day, he did it by night.

And when the men of the city arose early in the morning, behold, the altar of Baal was cast down, and the grove was cut down that was by it, and the second bullock was offered upon the altar that was built. And they said one to another, "Who hath done this thing?" And when they enquired and asked, they said, "Gideon the son of Joash hath done this thing."

Then the men of the city said unto Joash, "Bring out thy son that he may die: because he hath cast down the altar of Baal, and because he hath cut down the grove that was by it."

And Joash said unto all that stood against him, "Will ye plead for Baal? will ye save him? he that will plead for Baal, let him be put to death whilst it is yet morning. If Baal be a god, let him plead for himself, because one hath cast down his altar." Therefore on that day he called Gideon, Jerubbaal, saying, "Let Baal plead against him, because he hath thrown down his altar."

Then all the Midianites and the Amalekites and the children of the east gathered together, and went over, and pitched in the valley of Jezreel.

But the Spirit of the Lord came upon Gideon, and he blew a trumpet: and Abiezer was gathered after him. And he sent messengers unto Asher, and unto Zebulun, and unto Naphtali, and they came up to meet them. And he sent messengers throughout all Manasseh, who also gathered after him.

And Gideon said unto God, "If thou wilt save Israel by mine hand, as thou hast said, behold, I will put a fleece of wool on the floor; and if the dew be on the fleece only, and it be dry upon all the earth beside, then shall I know that thou wilt save Israel by mine hand, as thou hast said."

And it was so: for he rose up early on the morrow, and thrust the fleece together, and wringed the dew out of the fleece, a bowl full of water.

And Gideon said unto God, "Let not thine anger be hot against me, and I will speak but this once: let me prove, I pray thee, but this once with the fleece; let now it be dry only upon the fleece, and upon all the ground let there be dew."

And God did so that night; for it was dry upon the fleece only, and there was dew on all the ground.

WHOEVER IS FEARFUL AND AFRAID, LET HIM RETURN

THEN JERUBBAAL, who is Gideon, and all the people that were with him rose up early, and pitched beside the well of Harod; so that the host of the Midianites were on the north side of them.

And the Lord said unto Gideon, "The people that are with thee are too many for me to give the Midianites into their hands, lest Israel vaunt themselves against me, saying, 'Mine own hand hath saved me.' Now therefore proclaim in the ears of the people, saying, 'Whoever is fearful and afraid, let him return and depart early from mount Gilead.'" And there returned of the people twenty and two thousand; and there remained ten thousand.

And the Lord said unto Gideon, "The people are yet too many; bring them down unto the water, and I will try them for thee there: and it shall be, that of whom I say unto thee, 'This shall go with thee'; the same shall go with thee; and of whomsoever I say unto thee, 'This shall not go with thee,' the same shall not go."

So Gideon brought down the people unto the water: and the Lord said unto him, "Every one that lappeth of the water with his tongue, as a dog lappeth, him shalt thou set by himself; likewise every one that boweth down upon his knees to drink."

And the number of them that lapped, putting their hand to their mouth, were three hundred men: but all the rest of the people bowed down upon their knees to drink water.

And the Lord said unto Gideon, "By the three hundred men that lapped will I save you, and deliver the Midianites into thine hand: and let all the other people go every man unto his place."

So the people took victuals in their hand, and their trumpets. And Gideon sent all the rest of Israel every man unto his tent, and retained those three hundred men.

I WILL NOT RULE OVER YOU, THE LORD SHALL RULE OVER YOU

And the host of Midian was beneath Gideon in the valley. And it came to pass the same night, that the Lord said unto Gideon, "Arise, get thee down unto the host; for I have delivered it into thine hand. But if thou fear to go down, go thou with Phurah thy servant down to the host; and thou shalt hear what they say; and afterward shall thine hands be strengthened to go down unto the host."

Then went Gideon down with Phurah his servant unto the outside of the armed men that were in the host. And the Midianites, and the Amalekites and all the children of the east lay along in the valley like grasshoppers for multitude; and their camels were without number, as the sand by the sea side for multitude.

And when Gideon was come, behold, there was a man that told a dream unto his fellow, and said, "Behold, I dreamed a dream, and lo, a cake of barley bread tumbled into the host of Midian, and came unto a tent, and smote it that it fell, and overturned it, that the tent lay along."

And his fellow answered and said, "This is nothing else save the sword of Gideon, the son of Joash, a man of Israel: for into his hand hath God delivered Midian, and all the host."

And it was so, when Gideon heard the telling of the dream, and the interpretation thereof, that he worshipped, and returned into the host of Israel, and said, "Arise; for the Lord hath delivered into your hand the host of Midian."

And he divided the three hundred men into three companies, and he put a trumpet in every man's hand, with empty pitchers, and lamps within the pitchers. And he said unto them, "Look on me, and do likewise; and, behold, when I come to the outside of the camp, it shall be that, as I do, so shall ye do. When I blow with a trumpet, I and all that are with me, then blow ye the trumpets also on every side of all the camp, and say, 'The sword of the Lord, and of Gideon.'"

So Gideon, and the hundred men that were with him came unto the outside of the camp in the beginning of the middle watch; and they had but newly set the watch: and they blew the trumpets, and brake the pitchers that were in their hands. And the three companies blew the trumpets, and brake the pitchers, and held the lamps in their left hands, and the trumpets in their right hands to blow withal; and they cried, "The sword of the Lord, and of Gideon." And they stood every man in his place round about the camp; and all the host ran, and cried, and fled. And the three hundred blew the trumpets. And the Lord set every man's sword against his fellow, even throughout all the host; and the host fled.

And the men of Israel gathered themselves together and pursued after the Midianites. And Gideon came to Jordan, and passed over, he and the three hundred men that were with him, faint, yet pursuing them. And Gideon went up by the way of them that dwelt in tents on the east, and smote the host, and took the two kings of Midian, Zebah and Zalmunna, and discomfited all the host. And Gideon arose and slew Zebah and Zalmunna, and took away the ornaments that were on their camels' necks.

And Gideon, the son of Joash, returned from battle before the sun was up. Then the men of Israel said unto Gideon, "Rule thou over us, both thou, and thy son, and thy son's son also; for thou hast delivered us from the hand of Midian."

And Gideon said unto them, "I will not rule over you, neither shall my son rule over you; the Lord shall rule over you."

Thus was Midian subdued before the children of Israel, so that they lifted up their heads no more. And the country was in quietness forty years in the days of Gideon.

And Gideon, the son of Joash, died in a good old age, and was buried in the sepulchre of Joash his father.

And it came to pass, as soon as Gideon was dead, that the children of Israel remembered not the Lord their God, who had delivered them out of the hands of all their enemies on every side. Neither showed they kindness to the house of Gideon, according to all the goodness which he had shown unto Israel.

BEHOLD, HIS DAUGHTER CAME OUT TO MEET HIM

THEN THE CHILDREN of Ammon were gathered together, and encamped in Gilead. And the children of Israel assembled themselves together. And the people and princes of Gilead said one to another, "What man is he that will begin to fight against the children of Ammon? he shall be head over all the inhabitants of Gilead."

Now Jephthah, the Gileadite, was a mighty man of valour, and he was the son of an harlot. Gilead was the father of Jephthah. And Gilead's wife bare him sons; and his wife's sons grew up, and they thrust out Jephthah, and said unto him, "Thou shalt not inherit in our father's house; for thou art the son of a strange woman." Then Jephthah fled from his brethren, and dwelt in the land of Tob.

And it came to pass, when the children of Ammon made war against Israel, the elders of Israel went to fetch Jephthah out of the land of Tob. And they said unto Jephthah, "Come, and be our captain, that we may fight with the children of Ammon."

And Jephthah said unto the elders of Gilead, "Did not ye hate me, and expel me out of my father's house? and why are ye come unto me now when ye are in distress?"

And the elders of Gilead said unto Jephthah, "We turn to thee now, that thou mayest go with us, and fight against the children of Ammon, and be our head over all the inhabitants of Gilead."

And Jephthah said unto the elders, "If ye bring me home again to fight against the children of Ammon, and the Lord deliver them before me, shall I be your head?"

And the elders said, "The Lord be witness between us, if we do not according to thy words."

Then Jephthah went with the elders of Gilead, and the people made him head and captain over them.

And Jephthah vowed a vow unto the Lord, and said, " If thou shalt without fail deliver the children of Ammon into mine hands, then it shall be that whatsoever cometh forth of the doors of my house to meet me when I return in peace shall surely be the Lord's, and I will offer it up for a burnt offering."

So Jephthah passed over unto the children of Ammon to fight against them; and the Lord delivered them into his hands. And he smote them with a very great slaughter. Thus the children of Ammon were subdued before the children of Israel.

And Jephthah came to Mizpeh unto his house, and, behold, his daughter came out to meet him with timbrels and with dances: and she was his only child; beside her he had neither son nor daughter. And it came to pass, when he saw her, that he rent his clothes, and said, " Alas! my daughter! thou hast brought me very low; for I have opened my mouth unto the Lord, and I cannot go back."

And she said unto him, " My father, if thou hast opened thy mouth unto the Lord, do to me according to that which hath proceeded out of thy mouth; forasmuch as the Lord hath taken vengeance for thee of thine enemies, even of the children of Ammon."

And she said unto her father, " Let this thing be done for me: let me alone two months, that I may go up and down upon the mountains, and bewail my virginity, I and my fellows."

And he said, " Go." And he sent her away for two months: and she went with her companions, and bewailed her virginity upon the mountains. And at the end of two months, she returned unto her father, who did with her according to his vow which he had vowed. And it was a custom in Israel that the daughters of Israel went yearly to lament the daughter of Jephthah four days in the year.

And Jephthah judged Israel six years. Then died Jephthah, the Gileadite, and was buried in one of the cities of Gilead.

SAMSON SHALL BEGIN TO DELIVER ISRAEL

And the children of Israel did evil again in the sight of the Lord; and the Lord delivered them into the hand of the Philistines forty years.

And there was a certain man of Zorah, of the family of the Danites, whose name was Manoah; and his wife was barren, and bare not.

And the angel of the Lord appeared unto the woman, and said unto her, "Behold, now thou shalt bear a son. Now therefore beware, I pray thee, and drink not wine nor strong drink, and eat not any unclean thing: for lo, thou shalt conceive, and bear a son; and no razor shall come on his head: for the child shall be a Nazarite unto God from the womb; and he shall begin to deliver Israel out of the hand of the Philistines."

Then the woman came and told her husband, saying, "A man of God came unto me, and his countenance was like the countenance of an angel of God. And he said unto me, 'Behold, thou shalt conceive, and bear a son; and the child shall be a Nazarite to God from the womb to the day of his death.'"

So Manoah took a kid with a meat offering, and offered it upon a rock unto the Lord.

And the woman bare a son, and called his name Samson: and the child grew, and the Lord blessed him.

And Samson went down to Timnath, and saw a woman in Timnath of the daughters of the Philistines. And he came up, and told his father and his mother, and said, "I have seen a woman in Timnath of the daughters of the Philistines; now therefore get her for me to wife."

Then his father and his mother said unto him, "Is there never a woman among the daughters of thy brethren, or among all my people, that thou goest to take a wife of the Philistines?"

But his father and his mother knew not that it was of the Lord; for at that time the Philistines had dominion over Israel.

And Samson said unto his father, "Get her for me; for she pleaseth me well."

Then went Samson down, to Timnath, and came to the vineyards: and behold, a young lion roared against him. And the Spirit of the Lord came mightily upon him, and he rent him as he would have rent a kid, and he had nothing in his hand. And he went down, and talked with the woman; and she pleased him well.

And after a time he returned to take her, and he turned aside to see the carcase of the lion; and behold, there was a swarm of bees and honey in the carcase of the lion. And he took thereof in his hands, and went on eating, and came to his father and mother, and he gave them, and they did eat; but he told them not that he had taken the honey out of the carcase of the lion.

So his father went down unto the woman; and Samson made there a feast; for so used the young men to do. And it came to pass, when they saw him, that they brought thirty companions to be with him.

And Samson said unto them, "I will now put forth a riddle unto you; if you can certainly declare it me within the seven days of the feast, and find it out, then I will give you thirty sheets and thirty changes of garments; but if ye cannot declare it me, then shall ye give me thirty sheets and thirty changes of garments."

And they said unto him, "Put forth thy riddle, that we may hear it."

And he said unto them,

"Out of the eater came forth meat,
And out of the strong came forth sweetness."

And they could not in three days expound the riddle. And it came to pass on the seventh day that they said unto Samson's wife, "Entice thy husband, that he may declare unto us the riddle, lest we burn thee and thy father's house with fire; have ye called us to take that we have? is it not so?"

And Samson's wife wept before him and said, "Thou dost but hate me, and lovest me not: thou hast put forth a riddle unto the children of my people, and hast not told it me."

And he said unto her, "Behold, I have not told it my father nor my mother, and shall I tell it thee?"

And she wept before him the seven days, while their feast lasted: and it came to pass on the seventh day, that he told her, because she lay sore upon him; and she told the riddle to the children of her people. And the men of the city said unto Samson on the seventh day before the sun went down,

"What is sweeter than honey?
And what is stronger than a lion?"

And Samson said unto them, "If ye had not threatened my wife, ye had not found out my riddle." And he went down to Ashkelon, and slew thirty men of them, and took their spoil, and gave change of garments unto them which expounded the riddle. And his anger was kindled, and he went up to his father's house. But Samson's wife was given to his companion, whom he had used as his friend.

But it came to pass within a while after, in the time of wheat harvest, that Samson visited his wife with a kid; and he said, "I will go in to my wife."

But her father would not suffer him to go in. And her father said, "I verily thought that thou hadst utterly hated her; therefore I gave her to thy companion; is not her younger sister fairer than she? take her, I pray thee, instead of her."

And Samson said concerning them, "Now shall I be more blameless than the Philistines, though I do them a displeasure."

And Samson went and caught three hundred foxes, and took firebrands, and turned tail to tail, and put a firebrand in the midst between two tails. And when he had set the brands on fire, he let them go into the standing corn of the Philistines, and burnt up both the shocks, and also the standing corn, with the vineyards and olives.

Then the Philistines said, " Who hath done this? "

And they answered, " Samson, the son in law of the Timnite, because he had taken his wife, and given her to his companion." And the Philistines came up, and burnt her and her father with fire.

And Samson said unto them, " Though ye have done this, yet will I be avenged of you, and after that I will cease." And he smote them hip and thigh with a great slaughter: and he went down and dwelt in the top of the rock Etam.

Then the Philistines went up, and pitched in Judah, and spread themselves in Lehi. And the men of Judah said, " Why are ye come up against us? "

And they answered, " To bind Samson are we come up, to do to him as he hath done to us."

Then three thousand men of Judah went to the top of the rock Etam, and said to Samson, " Knowest thou not that the Philistines are rulers over us? what is this that thou hast done unto us? "

And Samson said, " As they did unto me, so have I done unto them."

And they said unto him, " We are come down to bind thee, that we may deliver thee into the hand of the Philistines."

And Samson said, " Swear unto me that ye will not fall upon me yourselves."

And they spake, saying, " No; but we will bind thee fast, and deliver thee into their hand: but surely we will not kill thee." And they bound him with two new cords, and brought him up from the rock.

And when he came unto Lehi, the Philistines shouted against him: and the Spirit of the Lord came mightily upon him, and the cords that were upon his arms became as flax that was burnt with fire, and his bands loosed from off his hands. And he found a new jawbone of an ass, and put forth his hand, and took it and slew a thousand men therewith.

And Samson said,

"With the jawbone of an ass, heaps upon heaps,
With the jaw of an ass have I slain a thousand men."

And it came to pass, when he had made an end of speaking, that he cast away the jawbone out of his hand, and called that place Ramath-lehi. And he was sore athirst, and called on the Lord, and said, "Thou hast given this great deliverance into the hand of thy servant: and now shall I die for thirst?"

But God clave an hollow place that was in the jaw, and there came water thereout; and when he had drunk, his spirit came again, and he revived.

WHEREIN LIETH THY STRENGTH?

AND IT CAME TO PASS afterward, that Samson loved a woman in the valley of Sorek, whose name was Delilah.

And the lords of the Philistines came up unto her, and said, "Entice him, and see wherein his great strength lieth, and by what means we may prevail against him: that we may bind him to afflict him; and we will give thee every one of us eleven hundred pieces of silver."

And Delilah said to Samson, "Tell me, I pray thee, wherein thy great strength lieth, and wherewith thou mightest be bound to afflict thee."

And Samson said unto her, "If they bind me with seven green withs that were never dried, then shall I be weak and be as another man."

Then the lords of the Philistines brought up to her seven green withs that were never dried, and she bound him with them. Now there were men lying in wait, abiding with her in the chamber. And she said unto him, "The Philistines be upon thee, Samson." And he brake the withs, as a thread of tow is broken when it toucheth the fire. So his strength was not known.

And Delilah said unto Samson, "Behold, thou hast mocked me, and told me lies: now tell me, I pray thee, wherewith thou mightest be bound."

And he said unto her, "If they bind me fast with new ropes that never were occupied, then shall I be weak, and be as another man."

Delilah therefore took new ropes and bound him therewith, and said unto him, "The Philistines be upon thee, Samson." And there were liers in wait abiding in the chamber. And Samson brake the ropes from off his arms like a thread.

And Delilah said unto Samson, "Hitherto thou hast mocked me, and told me lies: tell me wherewith thou mightest be bound."

And he said, "If thou weavest the seven locks of my head with the web." And she fastened it with the pin, and said unto him, "The Philistines be upon thee, Samson." And he awaked out of his sleep, and went away with the pin of the beam, and with the web.

And she said unto him, "How canst thou say, 'I love thee,' when thine heart is not with me? thou hast mocked me these three times, and hast not told me wherein thy great strength lieth."

And it came to pass, when she pressed him daily with her words, and urged him, so that his soul was vexed unto death; that he told her all his heart, and said unto her, "There hath not come a razor upon mine head; for I have been a Nazarite unto God from my mother's womb: if I be shaven, then my strength will go from me, and I shall become weak, and be like any other man."

And when Delilah saw that he had told her all his heart,

she sent and called for the lords of the Philistines, saying, "Come up this once, for he hath showed me all his heart." Then the lords of the Philistines came up unto her, and brought money in their hand.

And Delilah made Samson sleep upon her knees; and she called for a man, and she caused him to shave off the seven locks of his head; and she began to afflict him, and his strength went from him. And she said, "The Philistines be upon thee, Samson."

And he awoke out of his sleep, and said, "I will go out as at other times before, and shake myself." And he wist not that the Lord was departed from him.

But the Philistines took him, and put out his eyes, and brought him down to Gaza, and bound him with fetters of brass; and he did grind in the prison house. Howbeit the hair of his head began to grow again after he was shaven.

Then the lords of the Philistines gathered them together for to offer a great sacrifice unto Dagon their god, and to rejoice: for they said, "Our god hath delivered Samson our enemy into our hand."

And the people praised their god; for they said, "Our god hath delivered into our hands our enemy, and the destroyer of our country, which slew many of us."

And it came to pass, when their hearts were merry, that they said, "Call for Samson, that he make us sport." And they called for Samson out of the prison house; and he made them sport: and they set him between the pillars.

And Samson said unto the lad that held him by the hand, "Suffer me that I may feel the pillars whereupon the house standeth, that I may lean upon them."

Now the house was full of men and women; and all the lords of the Philistines were there; and there were upon the roof about three thousand men and women, that beheld while Samson made sport.

And Samson called unto the Lord, and said, " O Lord God, remember me, I pray thee, and strengthen me, I pray thee, only this once, O God, that I may be at once avenged of the Philistines for my two eyes."

And Samson took hold of the two middle pillars upon which the house stood, and on which it was borne up, of the one with his right hand, and of the other with his left. And Samson said, " Let me die with the Philistines." And he bowed himself with all his might; and the house fell upon the lords, and upon all the people that were therein. So the dead which he slew at his death were more than they which he slew in his life.

Then his brethren and all the house of his father came down, and took him, and brought him up, and buried him in the burying place of Manoah his father.

Samson had judged Israel twenty years.

IN THOSE DAYS EVERY MAN DID THAT WHICH WAS RIGHT IN HIS OWN EYES

DAN

THERE WAS A MAN of mount Ephraim whose name was Micah. And he said unto his mother, "The eleven hundred shekels of silver that were taken from thee, about which thou cursedst and spakest in mine ears, behold, the silver is with me; I took it."

And when he had restored the eleven hundred shekels of silver to his mother, she said, "Blessed be thou of the Lord, my son. I had wholly dedicated the silver unto the Lord." And his mother took two hundred shekels of silver, and gave them to the founder who made thereof a graven image and a molten image; and they were in the house of Micah. And Micah made an ephod, and teraphim and consecrated one of his sons, who became his priest.

And there was a young man of Bethlehem-judah who was a Levite. And he departed out of Bethlehem-judah to sojourn where he could find a place. And he came to mount Ephraim to the house of Micah, as he journeyed.

And Micah said unto him, "Whence comest thou?"

And he said, "I am a Levite of Bethlehem-judah, and I go to sojourn where I may find a place."

And Micah said unto him, "Dwell with me, and be unto me a father and a priest, and I will give thee ten shekels of silver by the year, and a suit of apparel and thy victuals."

So the Levite went in and was content to dwell with him. And the young man was unto him as one of his sons. Then said Micah, "Now I know that the Lord will do me good, seeing I have a Levite as my priest."

In those days the tribe of Dan sought them an inheritance to dwell in, for unto that day their inheritance had not fallen unto them among the tribes of Israel.

And the children of Dan sent five men from their coasts, men of valour, from Zorah and from Eshtaol, to spy out the land and to search it. And they said unto them, " Go, search the land."

And when the men came to mount Ephraim, to the house of Micah, they lodged there. And they said unto the Levite, " Who brought thee thither? and what doest thou in this place? "

And he said, " Micah hath hired me to be his priest."

And they said unto him, " Ask counsel, we pray thee, of God, that we may know whether our way which we go shall be prosperous."

And the priest said unto them, " Go in peace: before the Lord is your way wherein ye go."

Then the five men departed, and came to Laish, and saw the people that were therein how they dwelt careless, after the manner of the Zidonians, quiet and secure, and had no business with any man. And they returned unto their brethren, and said, " Arise that we may go up against them: for we have seen the land, and behold, it is very good. Be not slothful to go, and to enter to possess the land. Ye shall come unto a people secure; and to a large land, for God hath given it into your hands; a place where there is no want of anything that is in the earth."

And there went of the family of Dan, six hundred men, appointed with weapons. And they passed from thence, and came to mount Ephraim, unto the house of Micah.

Then the five men said unto their brethren, " Do ye know that there is in these houses an ephod, and teraphim, and a graven image, and a molten image? Consider what ye have to do."

And the six hundred men with their weapons of war, of the children of Dan, stood by the entering of the gate. And the priest stood in the entering of the gate with the six hundred men. And the five men went into Micah's house, and fetched the carved image, the ephod, and the teraphim, and the molten image.

Then said the priest, " What do ye? "

And they said unto him, " Hold thy peace; lay thine hand upon thy mouth and go with us, and be to us a father and a priest; is it better for thee to be a priest unto the house of one man, or that thou be a priest unto a tribe and a family of Israel? "

And the priest's heart was glad, and he took the ephod, and the teraphim, and the graven image, and went in the midst of the people. So they departed.

And the men that were in the houses near to Micah's house were gathered together, and overtook the children of Dan. And the children of Dan said unto Micah, " What aileth thee, that thou comest with such a company? "

And Micah said, " Ye have taken away my gods which I made, and the priest, and ye are gone away; and ye say unto me, ' What aileth thee? ' "

And the children of Dan said unto him, " Let not thy voice be heard among us, lest angry fellows run upon thee, and thou lose thy life, with the lives of thy household." And they went their way.

And when Micah saw that they were too strong for him, he turned and went back into his house.

And the children of Dan took the things which Micah had made and the priest, and came unto Laish, unto a people that were quiet and secure; and they smote them with the edge of the sword, and burnt the city with fire.

And they built a city and dwelt therein; and they called the name of the city Dan. And they set up the graven image, and Jonathan and his sons were priests to the tribe of Dan.

BENJAMIN

There was a certain Levite sojourning on the side of mount Ephraim, who took to him a concubine out of Bethlehem-judah. And his concubine played the whore against him, and went away from him unto her father's house and was there four whole months.

And her husband arose, and went after her to speak friendly unto her, and to bring her again. And she brought him into her father's house. And when her father saw him, he rejoiced to meet him; and he abode there three days.

And the Levite rose up and departed and came to Jebus, which is now Jerusalem. And there were with him two asses saddled, and his concubine also was with him. And when they were by Jebus, the day was far spent. And the servant said unto his master, " Come I pray thee, and let us turn into this city of the Jebsuites and lodge in it."

And his master said, " We will not turn aside into the city of a stranger that is not of the children of Israel; we will pass over to Gibeah."

And they passed on and went their way; and the sun went down upon them when they were by Gibeah, which belongeth to Benjamin. And they turned aside to go in and lodge in Gibeah, and went in and sat down in the street, for there was no man that took them into his house to lodge.

And behold, there came an old man from his work in the field, at even. He was also of mount Ephraim, but abode in Gibeah, but the men of the place were Benjamites. And when he lifted up his eyes, he saw a wayfaring man in the street of the city. And the old man said, " Whither goest thou? and whence comest thou? "

And the Levite said, " We are passing from Bethlehem-judah to mount Ephraim, from whence I am; and I am going to the house of the Lord. And there is no man that receiveth me to house. Yet there is both straw and provender for our asses, and there is bread and wine for me and the handmaid, and the young man which is my servant: there is no want of anything."

And the old man said, "Peace be with thee; howsoever, let all thy wants be upon me; only lodge not in the street." So he brought him into his house, and gave provender unto the asses, and they washed their feet, and did eat and drink.

Now as they were making their hearts merry, behold, the men of the city beset the house round about, and beat at the door, and spake to the master of the house, the old man, saying, "Bring forth the man that came into thine house, that we may know him."

And the master of the house went out, and said unto them, "Nay my brethren! nay, I pray you, do not so wickedly; seeing that this man is come into mine house do not this folly."

But the men would not hearken, so the man took the concubine and brought her forth unto them. And they abused her all the night until the morning; and when the day began to spring, they let her go.

Then at the dawning of the day, she came and fell down at the door of the man's house where her master was. And he rose up in the morning and opened the door, and behold, his concubine was fallen down at the door of the house, and her hands were upon the threshold.

And he said unto her, "Up, and let us be going." But none answered. Then he rose up, and took her upon an ass unto his own place, to mount Ephraim.

And when he was come into his house, he sent messages into all the twelve tribes of Israel. And it was so, that all that heard it said, "There was no such deed done nor seen from the day that the children of Israel came up out of the land of Egypt until this day: consider it, take advice, and speak your minds."

Then all the children of Israel went out, and the congregation was gathered together as one man, from Dan to Beersheba, unto the Lord in Mizpeh. Then said the children of Israel, "Tell us, how was this wickedness?"

Then the Levite, the husband of the woman that was slain, said, "I and my concubine came into Gibeah that belongeth to Benjamin, to lodge. And the men of Gibeah rose up against me; and beset the house round about by night, and thought to have slain me; and my concubine have they forced that she is dead. And I sent messages throughout all the country of the inheritance of Israel; for the Benjamites have committed lewdness and folly in Israel. Behold, ye are all children of Israel; give here your advice and counsel."

And all the people arose as one man, saying, "We will not any of us go to his tent, neither will we any of us turn into his house. But now this shall be the thing which we will do to Gibeah; we will go up by lot against it, that we may do to Gibeah of Benjamin according to all the folly that they have wrought in Israel."

So all the men of Israel were gathered against the city as one man. And the tribes of Israel sent men through all the tribe of Benjamin, saying, "What wickedness is this that is done among you? Now therefore, deliver to us the wicked men which are in Gibeah, that we may put them to death, and put away the evil from Israel."

But the children of Benjamin would not hearken to the voice of their brethren, the children of Israel, but gathered themselves together out of the cities unto Gibeah, to go out to battle against the children of Israel.

And the children of Israel arose, and went up to the house of God, and asked counsel of God. And they arose in the morning, and came against Gibeah ten thousand chosen men out of all Israel. And the children of Benjamin went out against them. And the battle was sore. And the children of Israel destroyed the Benjamites that day. And the children of Benjamin saw that they were smitten, and they turned and fled toward the wilderness unto the rock Rimmon. And the men of Israel smote all that came to hand, and set on fire all the cities that they came to.

Now the men of Israel had sworn in Mizpeh, saying, " There shall not any of us give his daughter unto Benjamin to wife."

And the children of Israel grieved for Benjamin their brother, and said, " There is one tribe cut off from Israel this day. O Lord God of Israel, why is this come to pass in Israel, that there should be today one tribe lacking to Israel? " And they said, " How shall we do for wives for them that remain seeing we have sworn by the Lord that we will not give them of our daughters to be their wives, and the women are destroyed out of Benjamin?" And they said, " There must be an inheritance for them that be escaped of Benjamin, that a tribe be not destroyed out of Israel."

Then they said, " Behold, there is a feast of the Lord in Shiloh yearly in a place which is on the north side of Bethel, on the east side of the highway that goeth up from Bethel to Shechem."

Therefore they commanded the children of Benjamin, saying, " Go and lie in wait in the vineyards, and see, and, behold, if the daughters of Shiloh come out to dance in dances, then come ye out of the vineyards, and catch you every man his wife of the daughters of Shiloh, and go to the land of Benjamin. And it shall be, when their fathers or their brethren come unto us to complain, that we will say unto them, 'Be favourable unto them for our sakes: because we reserved not to each man his wife in the war: and ye did not give unto them at this time, that ye should be guilty! "

And the children of Benjamin did so, and took them wives, according to their number, of them that danced, whom they caught: and they went and returned unto their inheritance, and repaired the cities, and dwelt in them.

And the children of Israel departed thence, every man to his tribe and to his family, and every man to his inheritance.

In those days every man did that which was right in his own eyes.

“ Thou hast shown kindness.”

THE BOOK OF RUTH

RUTH

Now it came to pass in the days when the judges ruled, that there was a famine in the land. And a certain man of Bethlehem-judah went to sojourn in the country of Moab, he, and his wife, and his two sons. And the name of the man was Elimelech, and the name of his wife Naomi, and the name of his two sons Mahlon and Chilion. And they came into the country of Moab, and continued there.

And Elimelech, Naomi's husband, died; and she was left, and her two sons. And they took them wives of the women of Moab; and the name of the one was Orpah, and the name of the other Ruth: and they dwelled there about ten years. And Mahlon and Chilion died also both of them; and Naomi was left of her two sons and her husband.

Then she arose with her daughters-in-law, that she might return from the country of Moab: for she had heard how the Lord had visited his people in giving them bread. Wherefore she went forth out of the place where she was, and her two daughters-in-law with her; and they went on the way to return unto the land of Judah.

And Naomi said unto her two daughters-in-law, "Go, return each to her mother's house: the Lord deal kindly with you, as ye have dealt with the dead, and with me. The Lord grant you that ye may find rest, each of you in the house of her husband." Then she kissed them; and they lifted up their voice, and wept.

And they said unto her, "Surely we will return with thee unto thy people."

And Naomi said, "Turn again my daughters: why will ye go with me? Turn again, my daughters, go your way; for I am old, and it grieveth me much for your sakes that the hand of the Lord is gone out against me."

And they lifted up their voice, and wept again: and Orpah kissed her mother-in-law; but Ruth clave unto her.

And Naomi said, "Behold, thy sister-in-law is gone back unto her people, and unto her gods: return thou after thy sister-in-law."

And Ruth said, " Intreat me not to leave thee, or to return from following after thee: for whither thou goest, I will go; and where thou lodgest, I will lodge: thy people shall be my people, and thy God my God. Where thou diest, will I die, and there will I be buried: the Lord do so to me, and more also, if ought but death part thee and me." When Naomi saw that Ruth was stedfastly minded to go with her, then she left speaking with her.

So they went until they came to Bethlehem. And it came to pass, when they were come to Bethlehem, that all the city was moved about them, and they said, " Is this Naomi? "

And Naomi said unto them, " Call me not Naomi, call me Mara: for the Almighty hath dealt very bitterly with me. I went out full, and the Lord hath brought me home again empty: why then call ye me Naomi? "

So Naomi returned, and Ruth the Moabitess, her daughter-in-law, with her; and they came to Bethlehem in the beginning of barley harvest. And Naomi had a kinsman of her husband's, a mighty man of wealth, of the family of Elimelech; and his name was Boaz. And Ruth said unto Naomi, " Let me now go to the field, and glean ears of corn after him in whose sight I shall find grace."

And Naomi said unto her, " Go my daughter."

And Ruth went and gleaned in the field after the reapers; and her hap was to light on a part of the field belonging unto Boaz, who was of the kindred of Elimelech. And, behold, Boaz came from Bethlehem, and said unto the reapers, " The Lord be with you."

And they answered him, " The Lord bless thee."

Then said Boaz unto his servant that was set over the reapers, " Whose damsel is this? "

And the servant answered, " It is the damsel that came back with Naomi out of the country of Moab. And she said, 'I pray you, let me glean and gather after the reapers among the sheaves;' so she came, and hath continued even from the morning until now."

Then said Boaz unto Ruth, " Hearest thou, my daughter; go not to glean in another field, neither go from hence, but abide here fast by my maidens; let thine eyes be on the field that they do reap, and go thou after them; have I not charged the young men that they shall not touch thee? and when thou art athirst, go unto the vessels, and drink of that which the young men have drawn."

Then she fell on her face, and bowed herself to the ground, and said unto him, " Why have I found grace in thine eyes, that thou shouldest take knowledge of me, seeing I am a stranger? "

And Boaz said unto her, " It hath fully been shown me all that thou hast done unto thy mother-in-law since the death of thine husband; and how thou hast left thy father and thy mother, and the land of thy nativity, and art come unto a people which thou knewest not heretofore. The Lord recompense thy work, and a full reward be given thee of the Lord God of Israel, under whose wings thou art come to trust."

Then Ruth said, " Let me find favour in thy sight, my lord; for thou hast comforted me, and hast spoken friendly unto thine handmaid, though I be not like unto one of thine handmaidens."

And Boaz said, " At mealtime come thou thither, and eat of the bread, and dip thy morsel in the vinegar." And she sat beside the reapers; and he reached her parched corn, and she did eat, and was sufficed, and left.

And when Ruth was risen up to glean, Boaz commanded his young men, saying, " Let her glean even among the sheaves, and reproach her not; and let fall also some of the handfuls of purpose for her, and leave them, that she may glean them, and rebuke her not."

So Ruth gleaned in the field until even, and beat out that she had gleaned; and it was about an ephah of barley. And she took it up, and went into the city.

And her mother-in-law saw what she had gleaned, and said unto her, "Where hast thou gleaned today? and where wroughtest thou? blessed be he that did take knowledge of thee."

And Ruth said, "The man's name with whom I wrought today, is Boaz."

And Naomi said unto her daughter-in-law, "Blessed be he of the Lord, who hath not left off his kindness to the living and to the dead. The man is near of kin unto us, one of our next kinsmen."

And Ruth said, "He said unto me also, 'Thou shalt keep fast by my young men until they have ended all my harvest.' "

And Naomi said, "It is good, my daughter, that thou go out with his maidens, and that they meet thee not in any other field."

So Ruth kept fast by the maidens of Boaz to glean unto the end of barley harvest and of wheat harvest; and dwelt with her mother-in-law.

Then Naomi said unto her, "My daughter, shall I not seek rest for thee, that it may be well with thee? And now is not Boaz of our kindred, with whose maidens thou wast? Behold, he winnoweth barley tonight in the threshing floor. Wash thyself therefore, and anoint thee, and put thy raiment upon thee, and get thee down to the floor; but make not thyself known unto the man, until he shall have done eating and drinking. And it shall be, when he lieth down, that thou shalt mark the place where he shall lie, and thou shalt go in, and uncover his feet, and lay thee down; and he will tell thee what thou shalt do."

And Ruth said unto her, "All that thou sayest unto me I

will do." And she went down unto the floor, and did according to all that her mother-in-law bade her.

And when Boaz had eaten and drunk, and his heart was merry, he went to lie down at the end of the heap of corn; and she came softly, and uncovered his feet, and laid her down. And it came to pass at midnight, that the man was afraid, and turned himself; and, behold, a woman lay at his feet. And he said, "Who art thou?"

And she answered, "I am Ruth thine handmaid; spread therefore thy skirt over thine handmaid; for thou art a near kinsman."

And he said, "Blessed be thou of the Lord, my daughter; for thou hast shown more kindness in the latter end than at the beginning, inasmuch as thou followedst not young men, whether poor or rich. And now, my daughter, fear not; I will do to thee all that thou requirest; for all the city of my people doth know that thou art a virtuous woman. And now it is true that I am thy near kinsman; howbeit there is a kinsman nearer than I. Tarry this night, and it shall be in the morning, that if he will perform unto thee the part of a kinsman, well; let him do the kinsman's part; but if he will not do the part of a kinsman to thee, then will I do the part of a kinsman to thee, as the Lord liveth; lie down until the morning."

And she lay at his feet until the morning; and she rose up before one could know another. And he said, "Let it not be known that a woman came unto the floor." And he said, "Bring the veil that thou hast upon thee, and hold it." And when she held it, he measured six measures of barley, and laid it on her, and she went into the city.

And when she came to her mother-in-law, Naomi said, "Who art thou, my daughter?"

And Ruth told her all that the man had done to her. And she said, "These six measures of barley gave he me; for he said to me, 'Go not empty unto thy mother-in-law.'"

Then said Naomi, "Sit still, my daughter, until thou know

how the matter will fall: for the man will not rest, until he have finished the thing this day."

Then went Boaz up to the gate, and sat him down there; and, behold, the kinsman of whom Boaz spoke came by, unto whom he said, "Ho, such a one! turn aside, and sit down here." And he turned aside, and sat down. And Boaz took ten men of the elders of the city, and said, "Sit ye down here." And they sat down.

And Boaz said unto the kinsman, "Naomi, that is come again out of the country of Moab, selleth a parcel of land, which was our brother Elimelech's; and I thought to advertise thee, saying, 'Buy it before the inhabitants, and before the elders of my people.' If thou wilt redeem it, redeem it; but if thou wilt not redeem it, then tell me, that I may know; for there is none to redeem it beside thee, and I am after thee."

And the man said, "I will redeem it."

Then said Boaz, "What day thou buyest the field of the hand of Naomi, thou must buy it also of Ruth the Moabitess, the wife of the dead, to raise up the name of the dead upon his inheritance."

And the kinsman said, "I cannot redeem it for myself, lest I mar mine own inheritance; redeem thou my right to thyself; for I cannot redeem it."

Now this was the manner in former time in Israel concerning redeeming and concerning changing, for to confirm all things: a man plucked off his shoe, and gave it to his neighbour; and this was a testimony in Israel. Therefore the kinsman said unto Boaz, "Buy it for thee." So he drew off his shoe.

And Boaz said unto the elders, and unto all the people, "Ye are witnesses this day, that I have bought all that was Elimelech's, and all that was Chilion's and Mahlon's, of the hand of Naomi. Moreover Ruth the Moabitess, the wife of Mahlon, have I purchased to be my wife, to raise up the name of the dead upon his inheritance, that the name of the dead be not cut off from among his brethren, and from the gate of his place; ye are witnesses this day."

And all the people that were in the gate, and the elders, said, "We are witnesses. The Lord make the woman that is come into thine house like Rachel and like Leah, which two did build the house of Israel."

So Boaz took Ruth, and she was his wife; and she bore a son.

And the women said unto Naomi, "Blessed be the Lord, which hath not left thee this day without a kinsman, that his name may be famous in Israel. And he shall be unto thee a restorer of thy life, and a nourisher of thine old age; for thy daughter-in-law which loveth thee, which is better to thee than seven sons, hath born him."

And Naomi took the child, and laid it in her bosom, and became nurse unto it. And the women her neighbours gave it a name, saying, "There is a son born to Naomi;" and they called his name Obed.

And Obed was the father of Jesse, and Jesse was the father of David.

" Behold, to obey is better than sacrifice,
And to hearken than the fat of rams."

THE FIRST BOOK OF SAMUEL

FOR THIS CHILD I PRAYED

Now there was a certain man of mount Ephraim, and his name was Elkanah. And he had two wives; the name of the one was Hannah, and the name of the other Peninnah. And Peninnah had children, but Hannah had no children.

And Elkanah went up out of his city yearly to worship and to sacrifice unto the Lord of hosts in Shiloh. And when the time was that he offered, he gave to Peninnah his wife, and to all her sons and her daughters, portions; but unto Hannah he gave a worthy portion, for he loved Hannah. And he did so year by year.

But Hannah had no children, and Peninnah provoked her sore for to make her fret because she had no children; therefore she wept, and did not eat.

Then said Elkanah her husband to her, "Hannah, why weepest thou? and why eatest thou not? am not I better to thee than ten sons?"

So Hannah rose up, after they had eaten in Shiloh. And she was in bitterness of soul, and prayed unto the Lord, and wept sore. And she vowed a vow, and said, "O Lord of hosts, if thou wilt indeed look on the affliction of thine handmaid, and remember me, and not forget thine handmaid, but wilt give unto thine handmaid a man child, then I will give him unto the Lord all the days of his life, and there shall no razor come upon his head."

Now Eli, the priest, sat upon a seat by a post of the temple of the Lord. And it came to pass as Hannah continued praying before the Lord, that Eli marked her mouth. Now Hannah spake in her heart, only her lips moved but her voice was not heard: therefore Eli thought she had been drunken. And Eli said unto her, " How long wilt thou be drunken? put away thy wine from thee."

And Hannah answered and said, " No, my lord, I am a woman of sorrowful spirit. I have drunk neither wine nor strong drink, but have poured out my soul before the Lord. Count not thine handmaid for a daughter of Belial: for out of the abundance of my complaint and grief have I spoken hitherto."

Then Eli said, " Go in peace: and the God of Israel grant thee thy petition that thou hast asked of him."

And she said, " Let thine handmaid find grace in thy sight." So she went her way, and did eat, and her countenance was no more sad. And they rose up in the morning early, and worshipped before the Lord, and returned, and came to their house to Ramah.

And the Lord remembered Hannah: wherefore it came to pass that she bare a son, and called his name Samuel, saying, " Because I have asked him of the Lord."

And Elkanah, and all his house, went up to offer unto the Lord the yearly sacrifice, and his vow. But Hannah went not up: for she said unto her husband, "I will not go up until the child be weaned, and then I will bring him, that he may appear before the Lord, and there abide for ever."

And Elkanah said, "Do what seemeth thee good; tarry until thou have weaned him; only the Lord establish his word."

So Hannah abode. And when she had weaned Samuel, she took him up with her, with three bullocks, and one ephah of flour, and a bottle of wine, and brought him unto the house of the Lord in Shiloh.

And the child was young. And they brought the child to Eli. And she said, " Oh my lord, as thy soul liveth, my lord, I am the woman that stood by thee here, praying unto the Lord. For this child I prayed: and the Lord hath given me my petition which I asked of him. Therefore also I have lent him to the Lord; as long as he liveth, he shall be lent to the Lord."

And Hannah prayed, and said:

"My heart rejoiceth in the Lord,
Mine horn is exalted in the Lord;
There is none holy as the Lord
For there is none beside thee;
Neither is there any rock like our God.
Talk no more so exceeding proudly;
Let not arrogancy come out of your mouth;
For the Lord is a God of knowledge,
And by him actions are weighed."

And Elkanah went to Ramah to his house. And the child, Samuel, did minister unto the Lord before Eli the priest.

ELI HEARD ALL THAT HIS SONS DID

AND THE TWO SONS of Eli, Hophni and Phinehas, the priests of the Lord, were there. Now the sons of Eli were sons of Belial; they knew not the Lord. Wherefore the sin of the young men was very great before the Lord.

Now Eli was very old, and heard all that his sons did unto all Israel, and he said unto them, "Why do ye such things? For I hear of your evil dealings by all this people. Nay, my sons, for it is no good report that I hear; ye make the Lord's people to transgress. If one man sin against another, the judge shall judge him; but if a man sin against the Lord, who shall intreat for him?"

Notwithstanding they hearkened not unto the voice of their father.

And there came a man of God unto Eli, and said unto him, "The Lord God of Israel saith, 'I said indeed that thy house, and the house of thy father, should walk before me forever;' but now the Lord saith, 'Be it far from me; for them that honour me, I will honour, and they that despise me shall be lightly esteemed. Behold, the days come, that all the increase of thine house shall die in the flower of their age. And this shall be a sign unto thee, that shall come upon thy two sons, on Hophni and Phinehas; in one day they shall die both of them. And I will raise me up a faithful priest, that shall do according to that which is in mine heart and in my mind: and I will build him a sure house; and he shall walk before mine anointed for ever.'"

SPEAK, LORD, FOR THY SERVANT HEARETH

AND THE CHILD Samuel grew on, and was in favour both with the Lord and also with men. And Samuel ministered before the Lord, being a child, girded with a linen ephod. Moreover his mother made him a little coat, and brought it to him from year to year, when she came up with her husband to offer the yearly sacrifice.

And Eli blessed Elkanah and his wife, and said, "The Lord give thee children for the loan which is lent to the Lord." And they went unto their own home. And the Lord blessed Hannah, and she bare three sons and two daughters.

And the child Samuel grew before the Lord, and ministered unto the Lord before Eli. And the word of the Lord was precious in those days; there was no open vision.

And it came to pass at that time, when Eli was laid down in his place, and his eyes began to wax dim that he could not see, and ere the lamp of God went out in the temple of the Lord, where the ark of God was, and Samuel was laid down to sleep, that the Lord called Samuel, and he answered, "Here am I."

And Samuel ran to Eli, and said, "Here am I; for thou calledst me."

And Eli said, "I called not; lie down again." And Samuel went and lay down.

And the Lord called yet again, "Samuel."

And Samuel arose and went to Eli, and said, "Here am I; for thou didst call me."

And he answered, "I called not, my son, lie down again."

Now Samuel did not yet know the Lord, neither was the word of the Lord revealed unto him. And the Lord called Samuel again the third time. And he arose and went to Eli, and said, "Here am I; for thou didst call me."

And Eli perceived that the Lord had called the child, therefore Eli said unto Samuel, "Go, lie down; and it shall be, if he call thee, that thou shalt say, 'Speak, Lord, for thy servant heareth.'" So Samuel went and lay down in his place.

And the Lord came, and stood, and called as at other times, "Samuel, Samuel."

Then Samuel answered, "Speak, for thy servant heareth."

And the Lord said to Samuel, "Behold, I will perform against Eli all things which I have spoken concerning his house. For I have told him that I will judge his house for ever for the iniquity which he knoweth; because his sons made themselves vile, and he restrained them not. And therefore I have sworn unto the house of Eli, that the iniquity of Eli's house shall not be purged with sacrifice nor offering for ever."

And Samuel lay until morning, and opened the doors of the house of the Lord. And Samuel feared to show Eli the vision.

Then Eli called Samuel and said, "Samuel, my son."

And he answered, "Here am I."

And Eli said, "What is the thing that the Lord said unto

thee? I pray thee hide it not from me. God do so to thee, and more also, if thou hide any thing from me of all the things that he said unto thee."

And Samuel told him every whit, and hid nothing from him. And Eli said, "It is the Lord; let him do what seemeth him good."

And Samuel grew, and the Lord was with him. And the Lord revealed himself to Samuel in Shiloh by the word of the Lord. And the word of Samuel came to all Israel, and all Israel from Dan even to Beersheba knew that Samuel was established to be a prophet of the Lord.

AND THE ARK OF GOD WAS TAKEN

Now Isreal went out against the Philistines to battle. And the Philistines put themselves in array against Israel; and when they joined battle, Israel was smitten before the Philistines. And the elders of Israel said, "Wherefore hath the Lord smitten us today before the Philistines? Let us fetch the ark of the covenant of the Lord out of Shiloh unto us, that when it cometh among us, it may save us out of the hand of our enemies."

So the people sent to Shiloh, that they might bring from thence the ark of the covenant of the Lord of hosts, which dwelleth between the cherubims. And the two sons of Eli, Hophni and Phinehas, were there with the ark. And when the ark of the covenant of the Lord came into the camp, all Israel shouted with a great shout, so that the earth rang again.

And when the Philistines heard the noise of the shout, they said, "What meaneth the noise of this great shout in the camp of the Hebrews?" And they understood that the ark of the Lord was come into the camp. And the Philistines were afraid, for they said, "God is come into the camp. Woe unto us! for there hath not been such a thing heretofore. Woe unto us! who shall deliver us out of the hand of these mighty Gods? these are the Gods that smote the Egyptians with all the plagues in the wilderness. Be strong, and quit yourselves like men, O ye Philistines, that ye be not servants unto the Hebrews, as they have been to you; quit yourselves like men, and fight."

And the Philistines fought, and Israel was smitten, and they fled every man into his tent; and there was a very great slaughter; for there fell of Israel thirty thousand footmen. And the ark of God was taken; and the two sons of Eli, Hophni and Phinehas, were slain.

And there ran a man of Benjamin out of the army, and came to Shiloh the same day with his clothes rent, and with earth upon his head. And when he came, lo, Eli sat upon a seat by the wayside watching; for his heart trembled for the ark of God. And when the man came into the city, and told it, all the city cried out.

And when Eli heard the noise of the crying, he said, "What meaneth the noise of this tumult?" Now Eli was ninety and eight years old; and his eyes were dim, that he could not see.

And the man said unto Eli, "I am he that came out of the army, and I fled today out of the army."

And Eli said, "What is there done, my son?"

And the messenger answered and said, "Israel is fled before the Philistines, and there hath been also a great slaughter among the people, and thy two sons also, Hophni and Phinehas, are dead, and the ark of God is taken."

And it came to pass, when he made mention of the ark of God, that Eli fell from off the seat backward by the side of the gate, and his neck brake, and he died; for he was an old man, and heavy. And he had judged Israel forty years.

SEND AWAY THE ARK OF THE GOD OF ISRAEL

AND THE PHILISTINES took the ark of God, and brought it from Eben-ezer unto Ashdod. And they brought it into the house of Dagon their god, and set it by Dagon. And when they of Ashdod arose early on the morrow, behold, Dagon was fallen upon his face to the earth before the ark of the Lord. And they took Dagon, and set him in his place again.

And when they arose early on the morrow morning, behold, Dagon was fallen upon his face to the ground before the ark of the Lord; and the head of Dagon and both the palms of his hands were cut off upon the threshold; only the stump of Dagon was left to him.

And the hand of the Lord was heavy upon them of Ashdod, and he smote them with emerods. And when the men of Ashdod saw that it was so, they said, "The ark of the God of Israel shall not abide with us; for his hand is sore upon us, and upon Dagon our god." They sent therefore and gathered all the lords of the Philistines unto them, and said, "What shall we do with the ark of the God of Israel?"

And they answered, "Let the ark of the God of Israel be carried about unto Gath." And they carried the ark of God thither.

And it was so, that after they had carried it about, the hand of the Lord was against the city with a very great destruction: and he smote the men of the city, both small and great, and they had emerods in their secret parts. Therefore they sent the ark of God to Ekron.

And it came to pass, as the ark of God came to Ekron, that the Ekronites cried out, saying, "They have brought the ark of the God of Israel to us, to slay us and our people." So they sent and gathered together all the lords of the Philistines and said, "Send away the ark of the God of Israel, and let it go again to his own place, that it slay us not, and our people;" for there was a deadly destruction throughout all the city. And the cry of the city went up to heaven.

And the ark of the Lord was in the country of the Philistines seven months. And the Philistines called for the priests and the diviners, saying, "What shall we do to the ark of the Lord? Tell us wherewith we shall send it to his place."

And they said, "If ye send away the ark of the God of Israel, send it not empty; but in any wise return him a trespass offering; then ye shall be healed."

Then said they, "What shall be the trespass offering which we shall return to him?"

They answered, "Five golden emerods, and five golden mice, according to the number of the lords of the Philistines: for one plague was on you all, and on your lords. Wherefore ye shall make images of your emerods, and images of your mice that mar the land; and ye shall give glory unto the God of Israel; peradventure he will lighten his hand from off you, and from off your gods, and from off your land.

"Now therefore make a new cart, and take two milk kine on which there hath come no yoke, and tie the kine to the cart, and bring their calves home from them. And take the ark of the Lord, and lay it upon the cart; and put the jewels of gold, which ye return for a trespass offering, in a coffer by the side thereof; and send it away that it may go. And see, if it goeth up by the way of his own coast to Bethshemesh, then he hath done us this great evil: but if not, then we shall know that it is not his hand that smote us; it was a chance that happened to us."

And the men did so; and took two milk kine, and tied them to the cart, and shut up their calves at home. And they laid the ark of the Lord upon the cart, and the coffer with the mice of gold and the images of their emerods.

And the kine took the straight way to the way of Bethshemesh, and went along the highway, lowing as they went, and turned not aside to the right hand or to the left; and the lords of the Philistines went after them unto the border of Bethshemesh.

And they of Bethshemesh were reaping their wheat harvest in the valley: and they lifted up their eyes and saw the ark, and rejoiced to see it. And the cart came into the field, and stood there, where there was a great stone. And the Levites took down the ark of the Lord, and the coffer that was with it, wherein the jewels of gold were, and put them on the great stone; and they offered burnt-offerings and sacrificed sacrifices the same day unto the Lord.

And they sent messengers, saying, "The Philistines have brought again the ark of the Lord. Come ye down, and fetch it up to you."

And when the five lords of the Philistines had seen it, they returned to Ekron the same day.

HITHERTO HATH THE LORD HELPED US

And Samuel spake unto all the house of Israel, saying, "If ye do return unto the Lord with all your hearts, then put away the strange gods from among you, and prepare your hearts unto the Lord, and serve him only; and he will deliver you out of the hand of the Philistines." And the children of Israel did put away Baalim and Ashtaroth, and served the Lord only.

And Samuel said, "Gather all Israel to Mizpeh, and I will pray for you unto the Lord." And they gathered together to Mizpeh, and drew water, and poured it out before the Lord, and fasted on that day, and said there, "We have sinned against the Lord." And Samuel judged the children of Israel in Mizpeh.

And when the Philistines heard that the children of Israel were gathered together in Mizpeh, the lords of the Philistines went up against Israel.

And when the children of Israel heard it, they were afraid of the Philistines, and said to Samuel, "Cease not to cry unto the Lord our God for us, that he will save us out of the hand of the Philistines."

And Samuel took a lamb, and offered it for a burnt-offering unto the Lord: and Samuel cried unto the Lord for Israel; and the Lord heard him.

And as Samuel was offering up the burnt-offering, the Philistines drew near to battle against Israel: but the Lord thundered with a great thunder on that day upon the Philistines, and discomfited them; and they were smitten before Israel. And the men of Israel went out of Mizpeh, and pursued the Philistines, and smote them.

Then Samuel took a stone, and set it between Mizpeh and Shen, saying, "Hitherto hath the Lord helped us."

So the Philistines were subdued, and they came no more into the coast of Israel: and the hand of the Lord was against the Philistines all the days of Samuel. And the cities which the Philistines had taken from Israel were restored to Israel, from Ekron even unto Gath; and the coasts thereof did Israel deliver out of the hands of the Philistines. And there was peace between Israel and the Amorites.

And Samuel judged Israel all the days of his life. And he went from year to year in circuit to Bethel, and Gilgal, and Mizpeh, and judged Israel in all those places. And his return was to Ramah; for there was his house; and there he judged Israel; and there he built an altar unto the Lord.

GIVE US A KING, THAT WE MAY BE LIKE ALL THE NATIONS

And it came to pass, when Samuel was old, that he made his sons judges over Israel. And his sons walked not in his ways, but turned aside after lucre, and took bribes, and perverted judgment.

Then all the elders of Israel gathered themselves together, and came to Samuel unto Ramah, and said unto him, "Behold, thou art old, and thy sons walk not in thy ways: now make us a king to judge us like all the nations."

But the thing displeased Samuel, when they said, "Give us a king to judge us." And Samuel prayed unto the Lord.

And the Lord said unto Samuel, "Hearken unto the voice of the People in all that they say unto thee: for they have not rejected thee, but they have rejected me, that I should not reign over them. According to all the works which they have done since the day that I brought them up out of Egypt even unto this day, wherewith they have forsaken me, and served other gods, so do they also unto thee. Now therefore hearken unto their voice: howbeit yet protest solemnly unto them, and show them the manner of the king that shall reign over them."

And Samuel told all the words of the Lord unto the people that asked of him a king. And he said, "This will be the manner of the king that shall reign over you: He will take your sons, and appoint them for himself, for his chariots, and to be his horsemen; and some shall run before his chariots. And he will appoint him captains over thousands, and captains over fifties; and will set them to ear his ground, and to reap his harvest, and to make his instruments of war, and instruments of his chariots.

"And he will take your daughters to be confectionaries, and to be cooks, and to be bakers. And he will take your fields, and your vineyards, and your olive-yards, even the best of them, and give them to his servants. And he will take the tenth of your seed, and of your vineyards, and give to his officers, and to his servants. And he will take your men-servants, and your maidservants, and your goodliest young men, and your asses, and put them to his work. He will take the tenth of your sheep; and ye shall be his servants.

"And ye shall cry out in that day because of your king which ye shall have chosen you; and the Lord will not hear you in that day."

Nevertheless the people refused to obey the voice of Samuel; and they said, "Nay; but we will have a king over us; that we also may be like all the nations; and that our king may judge us, and go out before us, and fight our battles."

And Samuel heard all the words of the people, and he rehearsed them in the ears of the Lord. And the Lord said to Samuel, "Hearken unto their voice, and make them a king."

And Samuel said unto the men of Israel, "Go ye every man unto his city."

BEHOLD THE KING WHOM YE HAVE CHOSEN

NOW THERE WAS A MAN of Benjamin whose name was Kish, a mighty man of power. And he had a son, whose name was Saul, a choice young man, and a goodly: and there was not among the children of Israel a goodlier person than he: from his shoulders and upward he was higher than any of the people.

And the asses of Kish, Saul's father, were lost. And Kish said to Saul his son, "Take now one of the servants with thee, and arise, go seek the asses."

And Saul passed through mount Ephraim, and passed through the land of Shalisha, but found them not; then they passed through the land of Shalim, and there they were not; and he passed through the land of the Benjamites, but they found them not. And when they were come to the land of Zuph, Saul said to his servant that was with him, "Come, and let us return; lest my father leave caring for the asses, and take thought for us."

And the servant said unto him, "Behold now, there is in this city a man of God, and he is an honourable man; all that he saith cometh surely to pass: now let us go thither; peradventure he can show us our way that we should go."

Then said Saul to his servant, "But behold, if we go what shall we bring the man? for the bread is spent in our vessels, and there is not a present to bring to the man of God: what have we?"

And the servant answered Saul again, and said, "Behold, I have here at hand the fourth part of a shekel of silver: that will I give to the man of God, to tell us our way."

(Beforetime in Israel, when a man went to inquire of God, thus he spake, "Come, and let us go to the seer:" for he that is now called a Prophet was before time called a Seer.)

Then said Saul to his servant, "Well said; come, let us go:" so they went unto the city where the man of God was. And as they went up the hill to the city, they found young maidens going out to draw water, and said unto them, "Is the Seer here?"

And they answered them, "He is; behold, he is before you: make haste now, for he came today to the city; for there is a sacrifice of the people today in the high place. As soon as ye be come into the city, ye shall straightway find him, before ye go up to the high place to eat: for the people will not eat until he come, because he doth bless the sacrifice; and afterwards they eat that be bidden. Now therefore get you up; for about this time ye shall find him."

And they went up into the city: and when they were come into the city, behold, Samuel came out for to go up to the high place.

Now the Lord had told Samuel in his ear a day before Saul came, saying, "Tomorrow about this time, I will send thee a man out of the land of Benjamin, and thou shalt anoint him to be captain over my People Israel, that he may save my people out of the hand of the Philistines: for I have looked upon my people, because their cry is come unto me."

And when Samuel saw Saul, the Lord said unto him, "Behold the man whom I spake to thee of! this same shall reign over my people."

Then Saul drew near to Samuel in the gate, and said, "Tell me, I pray thee, where the Seer's house is."

And Samuel answered Saul, "I am the Seer: go up before me unto the high place; for ye shall eat with me today, and tomorrow I will let thee go, and will tell thee all that is in thy heart. And as for thine asses that were lost three days ago, set not thy mind on them, for they are found. And on whom is all the desire of Israel? Is it not on thee, and on all thy father's house?"

And Saul said, "Am not I a Benjamite, of the smallest of the tribes of Israel? and my family the least of all the families of the tribe of Benjamin? wherefore then speakest thou so to me?"

And Samuel took Saul, and his servant, and brought them into the parlour, and made them sit in the chiefest place among them that were bidden, which were about thirty persons.

So Saul did eat with Samuel that day. And when they were come down from the high place into the city, Samuel said to Saul, "Bid the servant pass on before us, but stand thou still a while, that I may show thee the word of God." And the servant passed on.

Then Samuel took a vial of oil, and poured it upon Saul's head, and kissed him, and said, "The Lord hath anointed thee to be captain over his inheritance. When thou art departed from me today, then thou shalt find two men by Rachel's sepulchre in the border of Benjamin at Zelzah; and they will say unto thee, 'The asses which thou wentest to seek are found: and lo, thy father hath left the care of the asses, and sorroweth for you.' Then thou shalt go on forward from thence, and thou shalt come to the plain of Tabor, and there shall meet thee three men going up to God to Bethel, one carrying three kids, and another carrying three loaves of bread, and another carrying a bottle of wine: And they shall salute thee, and give thee two loaves of bread; which thou shalt receive of their hands. After that thou shalt meet a company of prophets coming down from the high place with a psaltery, and a tabret, and a pipe, and a harp before them; and they shall prophesy. And the Spirit of the Lord will come upon thee, and thou shalt prophesy with them, and shalt be turned into another man."

And it was so, that when Saul had turned his back to go from Samuel, God gave him another heart: and all those signs came to pass that day.

And Samuel called the people together unto the Lord to Mizpeh; and said unto the children of Israel, "Ye have this day rejected your God, who himself saved you out of all your adversities and your tribulations; and ye have said unto him, 'Nay, but set a king over us.' Now therefore present yourselves before the Lord by your tribes, and by your thousands."

And when Samuel had caused all the tribes of Israel to come near, the tribe of Benjamin was taken. When he had caused the tribe of Benjamin to come near by their families, the family of Matri was taken, and Saul, the son of Kish was taken; and when they sought him, he could not be found. And they ran and fetched him thence; and when he stood among the people, he was higher than any of the people from his shoulders and upward.

And Samuel said to all the people, "See ye him whom the Lord hath chosen, that there is none like him among all the people?"

And all the people shouted, and said, "God save the king."

Then Samuel told the people the manner of the kingdom, and wrote it in a book, and laid it up before the Lord. Then said Samuel to the people, "Come, let us go to Gilgal, and renew the kingdom there."

And all the people went to Gilgal; and there they made Saul king before the Lord; and there they sacrificed peace offerings before the Lord; and there Saul and all the men of Israel rejoiced greatly.

And Samuel said unto all Israel, "Behold, I have hearkened unto your voice in all that ye said unto me, and have made a king over you. And now, behold, the king walketh before you: and I am old and gray-headed; and behold, I have walked before you from my childhood unto this day. Behold, here I am: witness against me before the Lord, and before his anointed; whose ox have I taken? or whose ass have I taken? or whom have I defrauded: whom have I oppressed? or of whose hand have I received any bribe to blind mine eyes therewith? and I will restore it you."

And they said, "Thou hast not defrauded us, nor oppressed us, neither hast thou taken aught of any man's hand."

And he said unto them, "The Lord is witness against you, and his anointed is witness this day that ye have not found aught in mine hand."

And they answered, "He is witness."

And Samuel said unto the people, "Now therefore stand still, that I may reason with you before the Lord. When ye saw that Nahash the king of the children of Ammon came against you, ye said unto me, 'Nay; but a king shall reign over us:' when the Lord your God was your king. Now therefore, behold the king whom ye have chosen, and whom ye have desired! and behold the Lord hath set a king over you. If ye will fear the Lord, and serve him, and obey his voice, and not rebel against the commandment of the Lord then shall both ye, and also the king that reigneth over you, continue following the Lord your God. But if ye will not obey the voice of the Lord, but rebel against the commandments of the Lord, then shall the hand of the Lord be against you, as it was against your fathers.

"Now therefore stand and see this great thing, which the Lord will do before your eyes. Is it not wheat harvest today? I will call unto the Lord, and he shall send thunder and rain; that ye may perceive and see that your wickedness is great, which ye have done in the sight of the Lord in asking you a king."

So Samuel called unto the Lord; and the Lord sent thunder and rain that day: and all the people greatly feared the Lord and Samuel. And all the people said unto Samuel, "Pray for thy servants unto the Lord thy God, that we die not: for we have added unto all our sins this evil, to ask us a king."

And Samuel said, "Fear not: turn not aside from following the Lord, for then should ye go after vain things, which cannot profit nor deliver; for they are vain, but serve the Lord with all your heart. For the Lord will not forsake his people for his great name's sake: because it hath pleased the Lord to make you his people. Moreover as for me, God forbid that I should cease to pray for you: but I will teach you the good and the right way: only fear the Lord, and serve him in truth with all your heart: for consider how great things he hath done for you."

So Saul took the kingdom over Israel, and fought against all his enemies on every side. And whithersoever he turned himself, he vexed them. And he gathered an host, and delivered Israel out of the hands of them that spoiled them. And there was sore war against the Philistines all the days of Saul; and when Saul saw any strong man, or any valiant man, he took him unto him.

BEHOLD, TO OBEY IS BETTER THAN SACRIFICE AND TO HEARKEN THAN THE FAT OF RAMS

SAUL REIGNED one year; and when he had reigned two years over Israel, Samuel said unto Saul, "The Lord sent me to anoint thee to be king over his people, over Israel; now therefore hearken thou unto the voice of the words of the Lord. Thus saith the Lord of hosts: 'I remember that which Amalek did to Israel, how he laid wait for him in the way, when he came up from Egypt. Now go and smite Amalek, and utterly destroy all that they have, and spare them not; but slay both man and woman, infant and suckling, ox and sheep, camel and ass.' "

And Saul gathered the people together, and numbered them in Telaim, two hundred thousand footmen, and ten thousand men of Judah.

And Saul came to a city of Amalek, and laid wait in the valley. And Saul smote the Amalekites. And he took Agag the king of the Amalekites alive, and utterly destroyed all the people with the edge of the sword. But Saul and the people spared Agag, and the best of the sheep, and of the oxen, and of the fatlings, and the lambs, and all that was good, and would not utterly destroy them; but everything that was vile and refuse, that they destroyed utterly.

Then came the word of the Lord unto Samuel, saying, "It repenteth me that I have set up Saul to be king: for he is turned back from following me, and hath not performed my commandments." And it grieved Samuel; and he cried unto the Lord all night.

And Samuel rose early to meet Saul in the morning. And Samuel came to Saul: and Saul said unto him, " Blessed be thou of the Lord: I have performed the commandment of the Lord."

And Samuel said, " What meaneth then this bleating of the sheep in mine ears, and the lowing of the oxen which I hear? "

And Saul said, " They have brought them from the Amalekites: for the people spared the best of the sheep and of the oxen, to sacrifice unto the Lord thy God; and the rest we have utterly destroyed."

Then Samuel said unto Saul, " Stay, and I will tell thee what the Lord hath said to me this night."

And Saul said, " Say on."

And Samuel said, " When thou wast little in thine own sight, wast thou not made the head of the tribes of Israel, and the Lord anointed thee king over Israel? And the Lord sent thee on a journey, and said, 'Go and utterly destroy the sinners, the Amalekites, and fight against them until they be consumed.' Wherefore then didst thou not obey the voice of the Lord, but didst fly upon the spoil, and didst evil in the sight of the Lord?"

And Saul said unto Samuel, " Yea, I have obeyed the voice of the Lord, and have gone the way which the Lord sent me, and have brought Agag the king of Amalek, and have utterly destroyed the Amalekites. But the people took of the spoil, sheep and oxen, the chief of the things, which should have been utterly destroyed, to sacrifice unto the Lord thy God in Gilgal."

And Samuel said, " Hath the Lord as great delight in burnt-offerings and sacrifices, as in obeying the voice of the Lord? Behold, to obey is better than sacrifice, and to hearken than the fat of rams. For rebellion is as the sin of witchcraft, and stubbornness is as iniquity and idolatry. Because thou hast rejected the word of the Lord, he hath also rejected thee from being king. The Lord thy God would have established thy kingdom upon Israel for ever. But now thy kingdom shall not continue: the Lord hath sought him a man after his own heart, and the Lord hath commanded him to be captain over his people, because thou hast not kept that which the Lord commanded thee."

And Saul said unto Samuel, "I have sinned: for I have transgressed the commandment of the Lord, and thy words: because I feared the people, and obeyed their voice. Now therefore, I pray thee, pardon my sin, and turn again with me, that I may worship the Lord."

And Samuel said unto Saul, "I will not return with thee: for thou hast rejected the word of the Lord, and the Lord hath rejected thee from being king over Israel."

And as Samuel turned about to go away, he laid hold upon the skirt of Saul's mantle, and it rent. And Samuel said unto him, "The Lord hath rent the kingdom of Israel from thee this day, and hath given it to a neighbour of thine that is better than thou."

Then Samuel went to Ramah; and Saul went up to his house to Gibeah of Saul. And Samuel came no more to see Saul until the day of his death.

THE LORD SEETH NOT AS MAN SEETH

AND THE LORD said unto Samuel, "How long wilt thou mourn for Saul, seeing I have rejected him from reigning over Israel? fill thy horn with oil, and go, I will send thee to Jesse the Bethlehemite: for I have provided me a king among his sons."

And Samuel said, "How can I go? if Saul hear it, he will kill me."

And the Lord said, "Take an heifer with thee, and say, 'I am come to sacrifice to the Lord.' And call Jesse to the sacrifice, and I will show thee what thou shalt do: and thou shalt anoint unto me him whom I name unto thee."

And Samuel did that which the Lord spake, and came to Bethlehem. And the elders of the town trembled at his coming, and said, "Comest thou peaceably?"

And Samuel said, "Peaceably: I am come to sacrifice unto the Lord: sanctify yourselves, and come with me to the sacrifice."

And he sanctified Jesse and his sons, and called them to the sacrifice. And it came to pass when they were come, that he looked on Eliab, and said, "Surely the Lord's anointed is before him."

But the Lord said unto Samuel, "Look not on his countenance, or on the height of his stature; because I have refused him: for the Lord seeth not as man seeth; for man looketh on the outward appearance, but the Lord looketh on the heart."

Then Jesse called Abinadab, and made him pass before Samuel. And he said, "Neither hath the Lord chosen this." Then Jesse made Shammah to pass by. And he said, "Neither hath the Lord chosen this." Again Jesse made seven of his sons to pass before Samuel: and Samuel said unto Jesse, "The Lord hath not chosen these." And Samuel said unto Jesse, "Are here all thy children? "

And Jesse said, "There remaineth yet the youngest, and behold, he keepeth the sheep."

And Samuel said unto Jesse, "Send and fetch him: for we will not sit down till he come hither."

And Jesse sent, and brought David in. Now he was ruddy, and withal of a beautiful countenance, and goodly to look to. And the Lord said, "Arise, anoint him: for this is he."

Then Samuel took the horn of oil, and anointed him in the midst of his brethren: and the Spirit of the Lord came upon David from that day forward.

So Samuel rose up, and went to Ramah.

DAVID TOOK AN HARP, AND PLAYED AND SAUL WAS REFRESHED

But the Spirit of the Lord departed from Saul, and an evil spirit troubled him. And Saul's servants said unto him, "Behold now, an evil spirit troubleth thee. Let our lord now command thy servants, which are before thee, to seek out a man who is a cunning player on an harp: and it shall come to pass, when the evil spirit is upon thee, that he shall play with his hand, and thou shalt be well."

And Saul said unto his servants, "Provide me now a man that can play well, and bring him to me."

Then answered one of the servants and said, "Behold, I have seen a son of Jesse the Bethlehemite, that is cunning in playing, and a mighty valiant man, and a man of war, and prudent in matters, and a comely person, and the Lord is with him."

Wherefore Saul sent messengers unto Jesse, and said, "Send me David thy son, which is with the sheep."

And Jesse took an ass laden with bread, and a bottle of wine, and a kid, and sent them by David his son, unto Saul. And David came to Saul, and stood before him: and Saul loved him greatly; and David became his armour-bearer.

And Saul sent to Jesse, saying, "Let David, I pray thee, stand before me; for he hath found favour in my sight."

And it came to pass, when the evil spirit was upon Saul, that David took an harp, and played with his hand:

"The Lord is my shepherd; I shall not want.
He maketh me to lie down in green pastures;
He leadeth me beside the still waters.
He restoreth my soul;
He leadeth me in the paths of righteousness for
his name's sake.
Yea, though I walk through the valley of the
shadow of death,
I will fear no evil: for thou art with me;
Thy rod and thy staff they comfort me.
Thou preparest a table before me in the presence
of mine enemies:
Thou anointest my head with oil; my cup runneth over.
Surely goodness and mercy shall follow me all
the days of my life,
And I will dwell in the house of the Lord for ever."

So Saul was refreshed, and was well, and the evil spirit departed from him.

THE LORD SAVETH NOT WITH SWORD AND SPEAR

Now the Philistines gathered together their armies to battle. And Saul and the men of Israel were gathered together, and pitched by the valley of Elah, and set the battle in array against the Philistines. And the Philistines stood on a mountain on the one side, and Israel stood on a mountain on the other side; and there was a valley between them.

And there went out a champion out of the camp of the Philistines, named Goliath, of Gath, whose height was six cubits and a span. And he had an helmet of brass upon his head, and he was armed with a coat of mail; and the weight of the coat was five thousand shekels of brass. And he had greaves of brass upon his legs, and a target of brass between his shoulders. And the staff of his spear was like a weaver's beam; and his spear's head weighed six hundred shekels of iron; and one bearing a shield went before him.

And he stood and cried unto the armies of Israel, and said unto them, "Why are ye come out to set your battle in array? Am not I a Philistine, and ye servants to Saul? Choose you a man for you, and let him come down to me. If he be able to fight with me, and to kill me, then will we be your servants; but if I prevail against him, and kill him, then shall ye be our servants, and serve us." And the Philistine said, "I defy the armies of Israel this day; give me a man that we may fight together."

When Saul and all Israel heard those words of the Philistine, they were dismayed, and greatly afraid. And the Philistine drew near morning and evening, and presented himself forty days.

Now David was the son of Jesse; and Jesse had eight sons. And David was the youngest; and the three eldest followed Saul. But David had returned from Saul to feed his father's sheep at Bethlehem.

And Jesse said unto David his son, "Take now for thy brethren an ephah of this parched corn, and these ten loaves, and run to the camp to thy brethren. And carry these ten cheeses unto the captain of their thousand, and look how thy brethren fare and take their pledge."

And David rose up early in the morning, and left the sheep with a keeper, and took, and went, as Jesse had commanded him; and he came to the trench as the host was going forth to the fight, and shouted for the battle. For Israel and the Philistines had put the battle in array, army against army. And David left his carriage in the hand of the keeper of the carriages, and ran into the army, and came and saluted his brethren. And as he talked with them, behold, there came up the champion, the Philistine of Gath, Goliath by name, out of the armies of the Philistines, and spake according to the same words; and David heard them.

And all the men of Israel, when they saw the man, fled from him, and were sore afraid. And the men of Israel said, "Have ye seen this man that is come up? surely to defy Israel is he come up."

And David spoke to the men that stood by him saying, "What shall be done to the man that killeth this Philistine and taketh away the reproach from Israel? for who is this Philistine, that he should defy the armies of the living God!"

And the people answered him, saying, "The man who killeth Goliath, the king will enrich him with great riches, and will give him his daughter, and make his father's house free in Israel."

And Eliab, David's eldest brother heard when he spoke unto the men; and Eliab's anger was kindled against David, and he said, "Why camest thou down hither? and with whom hast thou left those few sheep in the wilderness? I know thy pride, and the naughtiness of thine heart; for thou art come down that thou mightest see the battle."

And David said, "What have I now done? Is there not a

cause?" And he turned from him toward another and said, "Who is this Philistine, that he should defy the armies of the living God?"

And the words which David spoke were rehearsed before Saul; and Saul sent for him. And David said to Saul, "Let no man's heart fail because of Goliath; thy servant will go and fight with this Philistine."

And Saul said to David, "Thou art not able to go against this Philistine to fight with him; for thou art but a youth, and he a man of war from his youth."

And David said unto Saul, "Thy servant kept his father's sheep, and there came a lion, and a bear, and took a lamb out of the flock; and I went out after him, and smote him, and delivered it out of his mouth; and when he arose against me, I caught him by his beard, and smote him and slew him. Thy servant slew both the lion and the bear; and this Philistine shall be as one of them, seeing he hath defied the armies of the living God."

David said moreover, "The Lord that delivered me out of the paw of the lion, and out of the paw of the bear, he will deliver me out of the hand of this Philistine."

And Saul said unto David, "Go, and the Lord be with thee."

And Saul armed David with his armour, and he put a helmet of brass upon his head; also he armed him with a coat of mail. And David girded his sword upon his armour, and he assayed to go; for he had not proved it. And David said unto Saul, "I cannot go with these; for I have not proved them."

And David put them off him. And he took his staff in his hand, and chose him five smooth stones out of the brook, and put them in a shepherd's bag which he had, even in a scrip; and his sling was in his hand; and he drew near to the Philistine.

And the Philistine came on and drew near unto David; and the man that bore the shield went before him. And when the Philistine looked about, and saw David, he disdained him; for he was but a youth, and ruddy, and of a fair countenance. And the Philistine said unto David, "Am I a dog, that thou comest to me with staves? "

And the Philistine cursed David by his gods. And the Philistine said to David, "Come to me, and I will give thy flesh unto the fowls of the air, and to the beasts of the field."

Then said David to the Philistine, "Thou comest to me with a sword, and with a spear, and with a shield; but I come to thee in the name of the Lord of hosts, the God of the armies of Israel, whom thou hast defied. This day will the Lord deliver thee into mine hand; and I will smite thee, and take thine head from thee; and I will give the carcasses of the host of the Philistines this day unto the fowls of the air, and to the wild beasts of the earth: that all the earth may know that there is a God in Israel. And all this assembly shall know that the Lord saveth, not with sword and spear; for the battle is the Lord's, and he will give you into our hands."

And it came to pass, when the Philistine arose, and came and drew nigh to meet David, that David hasted, and ran toward the army to meet the Philistine. And David put his hand in his bag, and took thence a stone, and slang it, and smote the Philistine in his forehead, that the stone sunk into his forehead; and he fell upon his face to the earth.

So David prevailed over the Philistine with a sling and with a stone, and smote the Philistine, and slew him; but there was no sword in the hand of David. Therefore David ran and stood upon the Philistine, and took his sword, and drew it out of the sheath thereof, and cut off his head therewith.

And when the Philistines saw their champion was dead, they fled. And the men of Israel and of Judah arose, and shouted, and pursued the Philistines, until thou come to the valley, and to the gates of Ekron.

And the children of Israel returned from chasing after the Philistines.

JONATHAN LOVED DAVID AS HIS OWN SOUL

AND AS DAVID returned from the slaughter of the Philistine, Abner, the captain of the host, took him, and brought him before Saul. And Saul took him that day, and would let him go no more home to his father's house.

Now the sons of Saul were Jonathan, and Ishui, and Melchishua; and the names of his two daughters were these; the name of the firstborn Merab, and the name of the younger Michal.

And it came to pass, that the soul of Jonathan was knit with the soul of David, and Jonathan loved him as his own soul. Then Jonathan and David made a covenant, because he loved him as his own soul. And Jonathan stripped himself of the robe that was upon him, and gave it to David, and his garments, even to his sword, and to his bow, and to his girdle.

And David went out whithersoever Saul sent him, and behaved himself wisely. And Saul set him over the men of war, and he was accepted in the sight of all the people, and also in the sight of Saul's servants.

And it came to pass, when David was returned from the slaughter of the Philistine, that the women came out of all the cities of Israel, singing and dancing, to meet king Saul, with tabrets, with joy, and with instruments of music. And the women answered one another as they played, and said,

"Saul hath slain his thousands,
And David his ten thousands."

And Saul was very wroth, and the saying displeased him; and he said, "They have ascribed unto David ten thousands, and to me they have ascribed but thousands: and what can he have more but the kingdom?" And Saul eyed David from that day and forward.

And it came to pass on the morrow, that the evil spirit came upon Saul. And David played with his hand as at other times. And there was a javelin in Saul's hand. And Saul cast the javelin; for he said, I will smite David even to the wall with it. And David avoided out of his presence twice.

And Saul was afraid of David, because the Lord was with him, and was departed from Saul. Therefore Saul removed David from him, and made him his captain over a thousand. And David went out and came in before the people. And David behaved himself wisely in all his ways; and the Lord was with him. Wherefore when Saul saw that he behaved himself very wisely, he was afraid of him. But all Israel and Judah loved David, because he went out and came in before them.

And Saul said to David, " Behold, my elder daughter Merab, her will I give thee to wife: only be thou valiant for me and fight the Lord's battles." (For said Saul, " Let not mine hand be upon him, but let the hand of the Philistines be upon him.")

And David said unto Saul, " Who am I? and what is my life, or my father's family in Israel, that I should be son-in-law to the king? "

But it came to pass at the time when Merab, Saul's daughter, should have been given to David, that she was given unto Adriel.

And Michal, Saul's daughter, loved David: and they told Saul, and the thing pleased him. And Saul said, "I will give him her, that she may be a snare to him, and that the hand of the Philistines may be against him." And Saul commanded his servants, saying, " Commune with David secretly, and say, " ' Behold, the king hath delight in thee, and all his servants love thee: now therefore be the king's son-in-law.' "

And Saul's servants spake those words in the ears of David. And David said, " Seemeth it to you a light thing to be a king's son-in-law, seeing that I am a poor man, and lightly esteemed? "

And the servants of Saul told him, saying, " On this manner spake David."

And Saul said, "Thus shall ye say to David, 'The king desireth not any dowry, but an hundred Philistines, to be avenged of the king's enemies.'" But Saul thought to make David fall by the hand of the Philistines.

And when the servants told David these words, it pleased David well to be the king's son-in-law. Wherefore, David arose and went, he and his men, and slew the Philistines, two hundred men. And Saul gave him Michal, his daughter, to wife.

And Saul saw and knew that the Lord was with David, and that Michal, Saul's daughter, loved him. And Saul was yet the more afraid of David; and Saul became David's enemy continually.

And Saul spake to Jonathan his son, and to all his servants, that they should kill David. But Jonathan delighted much in David. And Jonathan told David, saying, "Saul, my father, seeketh to kill thee: now therefore, I pray thee, take heed to thyself until the morning, and abide in a secret place, and hide thyself. And I will go out and stand beside my father in the field where thou art, and I will commune with my father of thee; and what I see, that I will tell thee."

And Jonathan spake good of David unto Saul, his father, and said unto him, "Let not the king sin against his servant, against David; because he hath not sinned against thee, and because his works have been to thee-ward very good. For he did put his life in his hand, and slew the Philistine, and the Lord wrought a great salvation for all Israel: thou sawest it and didst rejoice: wherefore then wilt thou sin against innocent blood, to slay David without a cause?"

And Saul hearkened unto the voice of Jonathan: and Saul sware, "As the Lord liveth, he shall not be slain."

And Jonathan called David, and showed him all those things. And Jonathan brought David to Saul, and he was in his presence, as in times past.

And there was war again: and David went out, and fought

with the Philistines, and slew them with a great slaughter; and they fled from him.

And the evil spirit was upon Saul as he sat in his house with his javelin in his hand: and David played with his hand. And Saul sought to smite David even to the wall with the javelin. But David slipped away out of Saul's presence, and Saul smote the javelin into the wall: and David fled, and escaped that night.

And Saul sent messengers unto David's house, to watch him, and to slay him in the morning. And Michal, David's wife, told David saying, "If thou save not thy life tonight, tomorrow thou shalt be slain." So Michal let David down through a window: and he went, and fled, and escaped. And Michal took an image, and laid it in the bed, and put a pillow of goat's hair for his bolster, and covered it with a cloth. And when Saul sent messengers to take David, she said, "He is sick."

And Saul sent the messengers again to see David, saying, "Bring him up to me in the bed, that I may slay him." And when the messengers were come in, behold, there was an image in the bed, with a pillow of goat's hair for his bolster.

And Saul said unto Michal, "Why hast thou deceived me so, and sent away mine enemy, that he is escaped?"

And Michal answered Saul, "He said unto me, 'Let me go; why should I kill thee?'"

So David fled, and escaped, and came to Samuel in Ramah, and told him all that Saul had done to him. And he and Samuel went and dwelt in Naioth.

And David fled from Naioth in Ramah, and came and said before Jonathan, "What have I done? what is mine iniquity? and what is my sin before thy father, that he seeketh my life?"

And Jonathan said unto him, "God forbid; thou shalt not die: behold, my father will do nothing either great or small, but that he will show it me: and why should my father hide this thing from me? it is not so."

And David sware moreover, and said, "Thy father certainly

knoweth that I have found grace in thine eyes; and he saith, 'Let not Jonathan know this, lest he be grieved;' but truly as the Lord liveth, and as thy soul liveth, there is but a step between me and death."

Then said Jonathan, "Whatsoever thy soul desireth, I will even do it for thee."

And David said, "Behold, tomorrow is the new moon, and I should not fail to sit with the king at meat: but let me go, that I may hide myself in the field unto the third day at even. If thy father at all miss me, then say, 'David earnestly asked leave of me, that he might run to Bethlehem his city: for there is a yearly sacrifice there for all the family.' If he say thus, 'It is well:' thy servant shall have peace: but if he be very wroth, then be sure that evil is determined by him. Therefore thou shalt deal kindly with thy servant; for thou hast brought thy servant into a covenant of the Lord with thee: notwithstanding, if there be in me iniquity, slay me thyself; for why shouldst thou bring me to thy father?"

And Jonathan said, "Far be it from thee: for if I knew certainly that evil were determined by my father to come upon thee, then would not I tell it thee?"

Then said David, "Who shall tell me if thy father answer thee roughly?"

And Jonathan said, "Come, and let us go out into the field." And they went out both of them into the field. And Jonathan said, "O Lord God of Israel, when I have sounded my father about tomorrow any time, or the third day, and behold, if there be good toward David, and I then send not unto thee, and show it thee, the Lord do so and much more to Jonathan: but if it please my father to do thee evil, then I will show it thee, and send thee away, that thou mayest go in peace: and the Lord be with thee, as he hath been with my father. And thou shalt not only while I live show me the kindness of the Lord, but thou shalt not cut off thy kindness from my house forever."

So Jonathan made a covenant with the house of David. And Jonathan caused David to swear again, because he loved him. Then Jonathan said to David, "Tomorrow is the new moon: and thou shalt be missed, because thy seat will be empty. And when thou hast stayed three days then thou shalt go down quickly, and come to the place where thou didst hide thyself when the business was in hand, and shalt remain by the stone Ezel. And I will shoot three arrows on the side thereof, as though I shot at a mark. And behold, I will send a lad, saying, 'Go, find out the arrows.' If I expressly say unto the lad, 'Behold, the arrows are on this side of thee, take them;' then come thou: for there is peace to thee, and no hurt, as the Lord liveth. But if I say thus unto the young man, 'Behold, the arrows are beyond thee;' go thy way: for the Lord hath sent thee away. And touching the matter which thou and I have spoken of, behold, the Lord be between thee and me for ever." So David hid himself in the field.

And when the new moon was come, the king sat him down to eat meat. And the king sat upon his seat, as at other times, even upon a seat by the wall: and Jonathan arose, and Abner sat by Saul's side, and David's place was empty. Nevertheless Saul spake not any thing that day: for he thought, "Something hath befallen him."

And it came to pass on the morrow, which was the second day of the month, that David's place was empty. And Saul said unto Jonathan, "Wherefore cometh not the son of Jesse to meat, neither yesterday, nor today?"

And Jonathan answered Saul, "David earnestly asked leave of me to go to Bethlehem: and he said, 'Let me go, I pray thee; for our family hath a sacrifice in the city; and my brother hath commanded me to be there: and now, if I have found favour in thine eyes, let me get away, I pray thee, and see my brethren.' Therefore he cometh not unto the king's table."

Then Saul's anger was kindled against Jonathan, and he said

unto him, "Thou son of the perverse rebellious woman, do not I know that thou hast chosen the son of Jesse to thine own confusion? For as long as the son of Jesse liveth upon the ground, thou shalt not be established, nor thy kingdom. Wherefore now send and fetch him unto me, for he shall surely die."

And Jonathan answered Saul his father, and said unto him, "Wherefore shall he be slain? what hath he done?"

And Saul cast a javelin at him to smite him whereby Jonathan knew that it was determined of his father to slay David. So Jonathan arose from the table in fierce anger, and did eat no meat the second day of the month for he was grieved for David, because his father had done him shame.

And it came to pass in the morning, that Jonathan went out into the field at the time appointed with David, and a little lad with him. And he said unto his lad, "Run, find out now the arrows which I shoot." And as the lad ran, he shot an arrow beyond him. And when the lad was come to the place of the arrow, Jonathan cried after the lad, "Is not the arrow beyond thee? Make speed, haste, stay not." And Jonathan's lad gathered up the arrows, and came to his master. But the lad knew not anything: only Jonathan and David knew the matter. And Jonathan gave his artillery unto his lad, and said unto him, "Go carry them to the city."

And as soon as the lad was gone, David arose out of a place toward the south, and fell on his face to the ground, and bowed himself three times: and they kissed one another, and wept one with another.

And Jonathan said to David, "Go in peace, forasmuch as we have sworn both of us in the name of the Lord, saying, 'The Lord be between me and thee, and between my seed and thy seed for ever.'"

And David arose and departed: and Jonathan went into the city.

THOU HAST REWARDED ME GOOD FOR EVIL

THEN DAVID came to Nob to Ahimelech the priest: and Ahimelech was afraid at the meeting of David, and said unto him, "Why art thou alone, and no man with thee?"

And David said unto Ahimelech the priest, "The king hath commanded me a business, and hath said unto me, 'Let no man know any thing of the business whereabout I send thee, and what I have commanded thee;' and I have appointed my servants to such a place. Now therefore what is under thine hand? give me five loaves of bread in mine hand, or what there is present."

And the priest answered David, "There is no common bread under mine hand, but there is hallowed bread." So the priest gave him hallowed bread: for there was no bread there but the shew-bread, that was taken from before the Lord.

And David said unto Ahimelech, "And is there not here under thine hand spear or sword? for I have neither brought my sword nor any weapons with me, because the king's business required haste."

And the priest said, "The sword of Goliath the Philistine, whom thou slewest in the valley of Elah, behold, it is here wrapped in a cloth behind the ephod: if thou wilt take that, take it: for there is no other save that here."

And David said, "There is none like that; give it me."

David therefore departed thence, and escaped to the cave Adullam: and when his brethren and all his father's house heard it, they went down to him. And every one that was in distress, and every one that was in debt, and every one that was discontented, gathered themselves unto him; and he became a captain over them: and there were with him about four hundred men.

And David went thence to Mizpeh of Moab: and he said unto the king of Moab, "Let my father and my mother, I pray thee, come forth, and be with you, till I know what God will do for me." And he brought them before the king of Moab: and they dwelt with him all the while that David was in the hold.

Now Saul abode in Gibeah under a tree in Ramah, having his spear in his hand, and all his servants were standing about him.

And David abode in the wilderness in strong holds, and remained in a mountain in the wilderness of Ziph. And Saul sought him every day, but God delivered him not into his hand. And David saw that Saul was come out to seek his life; and David was in the wilderness of Ziph in a wood.

And Jonathan, Saul's son, arose, and went to David into the wood. And he said unto David, "Fear not: for the hand of Saul my father shall not find thee; and thou shalt be king over Israel, and I shall be next unto thee; and that also Saul my father knoweth." And they two made a covenant before the Lord: and David abode in the wood, and Jonathan went to his house.

Then Saul took three thousand chosen men out of all Israel, and went to seek David and his men upon the rocks of the wild goats. And he came to the sheep-cotes by the way, where was a cave, and Saul went in to cover his feet.

Now David and his men were in the sides of the cave, and the men of David said unto him, "Behold the day of which the Lord said unto thee, 'Behold, I will deliver thine enemy into thine hand, that thou mayest do to him as it shall seem good unto thee.'"

Then David arose and cut off the skirt of Saul's robe privily. And it came to pass, that David's heart smote him, because he had cut off Saul's skirt. And he said unto his men, "The Lord forbid that I should do this thing unto my master, the Lord's anointed, to stretch forth mine hand against him, seeing he is the anointed of the Lord." So David stayed his servants with these words, and suffered them not to rise against Saul.

And Saul rose up out of the cave, and went on his way. And David also arose, and went out of the cave, and cried after Saul, saying, "My lord the king." And when Saul looked behind him, David stooped with his face to the earth, and bowed himself.

And David said to Saul, "Wherefore hearest thou men's words, saying, 'Behold, David seeketh thy hurt?' Behold, this day thine eyes have seen how that the Lord had delivered thee into mine hand in the cave: and some bade me kill thee; but mine eye spared thee; and I said, 'I will not put forth mine hand against my lord; for he is the Lord's anointed.' Moreover, my father, see, yea, see the skirt of thy robe in my hand? for in that I cut off the skirt of thy robe, and killed thee not, know thou and see that there is neither evil nor transgression in mine hand, and I have not sinned against thee; yet thou huntest my soul to take it. The Lord judge between me and thee, and the Lord avenge me of thee: but mine hand shall not be upon thee. As the proverb of the ancients saith,

'Wickedness proceedeth from the wicked:
But mine hand shall not be upon thee.'

"After whom is the king of Israel come out? after whom dost thou pursue? after a dead dog, after a flea. The Lord therefore be judge, and judge between me and thee, and see, and plead my cause, and deliver me out of thine hand."

And it came to pass when David had made an end of speaking these words unto Saul, that Saul said, "Is this thy voice, my son David?" And Saul lifted up his voice, and wept.

And Saul said to David, "Thou art more righteous than I: for thou hast rewarded me good, whereas I have rewarded thee evil. And thou hast showed this day how that thou hast dealt well with me; forasmuch as when the Lord had delivered me into thine hand, thou killedst me not. For if a man find his enemy, will he let him go well away? wherefore the Lord reward thee good, for that thou hast done unto me this day.

And now, behold, I know well that thou shalt surely be king, and that the kingdom of Israel shall be established in thine hand. Swear now therefore unto me by the Lord, that thou wilt not cut off my seed after me, and that thou wilt not destroy my name out of my father's house."

And David sware unto Saul. And Saul went home; but David and his men got them up unto the hold.

THY ADVICE HATH KEPT ME FROM AVENGING MYSELF

And Samuel died: and all the Israelites were gathered together, and lamented him, and buried him in his house at Ramah. And David arose, and went down to the wilderness of Paran.

And there was a man in Maon, whose possessions were in Carmel; and the man was very great, and he had three thousand sheep, and a thousand goats; and he was shearing his sheep in Carmel. Now the name of the man was Nabal; and the name of his wife Abigail; and she was a woman of good understanding, and of a beautiful countenance; but the man was churlish and evil in his doings.

And David heard in the wilderness that Nabal did shear his sheep. And David sent out ten young men, and David said unto the young men, "Get you up to Carmel, and go to Nabal, and greet him in my name; and thus shall ye say to him that liveth in prosperity, 'Peace be both to thee, and peace be to thine house, and peace be unto all that thou hast. And now I have heard that thou hast shearers; now thy shepherds which were with us we hurt them not, neither was there ought missing unto them, all the while they were in Carmel. Ask thy young men, and they will show thee. Wherefore let our young men find favour in thine eyes: for we come in a good day; give, I pray thee, whatsoever cometh to thine hand unto thy servants, and thy son David.' "

And when David's young men came, they spake to Nabal according to all those words in the name of David, and ceased.

And Nabal answered David's servants, and said, "Who is David? and who is the son of Jesse? there be many servants nowadays that break away every man from his master. Shall I then take my bread, and my water, and my flesh that I have killed for my shearers, and give it unto men, whom I know not whence they be? "

So David's young men turned their way, and went again, and came and told him all those sayings. And David said, "Surely in vain have I kept all that this fellow hath in the wilderness, so that nothing was missed of all that pertained unto him; and he hath requited me evil for good."

And David said unto his men, "Gird ye on every man his sword." And they girded on every man his sword; and David also girded on his sword; and there went up after David about four hundred men; and two hundred abode by the stuff.

But one of the young men told Abigail, Nabal's wife, saying, "Behold, David sent messengers out of the wilderness to salute our master; and he railed on them. But the men were very good unto us, and we were not hurt, neither missed we anything, as long as we were conversant with them, when we were in the fields; they were a wall unto us both by night and day, all the while we were with them keeping the sheep. Now therefore know and consider what thou wilt do; for evil is determined against our master, and against all his household; for he is such a son of Belial, that a man cannot speak to him."

Then Abigail made haste, and took two hundred loaves, and two bottles of wine, and five sheep ready dressed, and five measures of parched corn, and an hundred clusters of raisins, and two hundred cakes of figs, and laid them on asses. And she said unto her servants, "Go on before me; behold, I come after you." But she told not her husband Nabal.

And it was so, as she rode on the ass that she came down by the covert of the hill, and, behold, David and his men came down against her; and she met them. And when Abigail saw David, she hasted, and lighted off the ass, and fell before David on her face, and bowed herself to the ground.

And she said, "My lord, I pray thee, hear the words of thine handmaid. Let not my lord, I pray thee, regard this man of Belial, even Nabal: for as his name is, so is he; Nabal is his name, and folly is with him; but I thine handmaid saw not the young men of my lord, whom thou didst send. Now therefore, my lord, as the Lord liveth, and as thy soul liveth, the Lord hath withholden thee from coming to shed blood, and from avenging thyself with thine own hand. And now this blessing which thine handmaid hath brought unto my lord, let it even be given unto the young men that follow my lord. I pray thee, forgive the trespass of thine handmaid; for the Lord will certainly make my lord a sure house; and evil hath not been found in thee all thy days. And it shall come to pass, when the Lord shall have done to my lord according to all the good that he hath spoken concerning thee, and shall have appointed thee ruler over Israel, that this shall be no grief unto thee, nor offense of heart, either that thou hast shed blood causeless, or that my lord hath avenged himself; but when the Lord shall have dealt well with my lord, then remember thine handmaid."

And David said to Abigail, "Blessed be the Lord God of Israel, which sent thee this day to meet me; and blessed be thy advice, and blessed be thou, which hast kept me this day from coming to shed blood, and from avenging myself with mine own hand."

So David received of her hand that which she had brought

him, and said unto her, "Go up in peace to thine house; see, I hearkened to thy voice, and have accepted thy person."

And Abigail came to Nabal; and behold, he held a feast in his house, like the feast of a king; and Nabal's heart was merry within him, for he was very drunken; wherefore she told him nothing, less or more, until the morning light. But it came to pass in the morning, when the wine was gone out of Nabal, and his wife had told him these things that his heart died within him, and he became as a stone. And about ten days after, he died.

And when David heard that Nabal was dead, he said, "Blessed be the Lord, that hath kept his servant from evil; for the Lord hath returned the wickedness of Nabal upon his own head."

And David sent and communed with Abigail, to take her to him to wife. And when the servants of David were come to Abigail to Carmel, they spake unto her, saying, "David sent us unto thee, to take thee to him to wife."

And she arose, and bowed herself on her face to the earth. And Abigail hasted, and arose, and rode upon an ass, with five damsels of hers that went after her; and she went after the messengers of David, and became his wife.

David also took Ahinoam of Jezreel; and they were also both of them his wives. But Saul had given Michal, his daughter, David's wife, to Phalti the son of Laish, which was of Gallim.

THE LORD DELIVERED THEE INTO MINE HAND

AND THE ZIPHITES came unto Saul saying, "Doth not David hide himself in the hill of Hachilah?" Then Saul arose, and went down to the wilderness of Ziph, having three thousand chosen men of Israel with him, to seek David in the wilderness of Ziph. And Saul pitched in the hill of Hachilah.

But David abode in the wilderness, and he saw that Saul came after him into the wilderness. David therefore sent out spies, and understood that Saul was come in very deed. And David arose and came to the place where Saul had pitched: and David beheld the place where Saul lay, and Abner the son of Ner, the captain of the host. And Saul lay in the trench, and the people pitched round about him.

Then David said, " Who will go down with me to Saul to the camp? "

And Abishai said, " I will go down with thee."

So David and Abishai came to the people by night: and behold, Saul lay sleeping within the trench, and his spear stuck in the ground at his bolster. But Abner and the people lay round about him.

Then said Abishai to David, " God hath delivered thine enemy into thine hand this day: now therefore let me smite him, I pray thee, with the spear, even to the earth at once, and I will not smite him the second time."

And David said to Abishai, "Destroy him not: for who can stretch forth his hand against the Lord's anointed, and be guiltless? As the Lord liveth, the Lord shall smite him; or his day shall come to die; or he shall descend into battle, and perish. The Lord forbid that I should stretch forth mine hand against the Lord's anointed: but, I pray thee, take thou now the spear that is at his bolster, and the cruse of water, and let us go."

So David took the spear and the cruse of water from Saul's bolster; and they got them away, and no man saw it, nor knew it, neither awaked: for they were all asleep; because a deep sleep from the Lord was fallen upon them. Then David went over to the other side, and stood on the top of an hill afar off; a great space being between them.

And David cried to the people, and to Abner the son of Ner, saying, " Answerest thou not, Abner? "

Then Abner answered and said, "Who criest to the king? "

And David said to Abner, " Art not thou a valiant man? and who is like to thee in Israel? Wherefore then hast thou not kept thy lord the king? for there came one of the people in to destroy the king thy lord. This thing is not good that thou hast done. As the Lord liveth, ye are worthy to die, because ye have not kept your master the Lord's anointed. And now see where the king's spear is, and the cruse of water that was at his bolster."

And Saul knew David's voice, and said, "Is this thy voice, my son David? "

And David said, " It is my voice, my lord, O king. Wherefore doth my lord thus pursue after his servant? for what have I done? or what evil is in mine hand? Now therefore, I pray thee, let my lord the king hear the words of his servant. Let not my blood fall to the earth before the face of the Lord: for the king of Israel is come out to seek a flea, as when one doth hunt a partridge in the mountains."

Then said Saul, "I have sinned: return, my son David: for I will no more do thee harm, because my soul was precious in thine eyes this day: behold, I have played the fool, and have erred exceedingly."

And David answered, " Behold the king's spear! let one of the young men come and fetch it. The Lord render to every man his righteousness and his faithfulness: for the Lord delivered thee into my hand today, but I would not stretch forth mine hand against the Lord's anointed. And behold, as thy life was much set by this day in mine eyes so let my life be much set by in the eyes of the Lord, and let him deliver me out of all tribulation."

Then Saul said to David, "Blessed be thou, my son David: thou shalt both do great things, and also shalt still prevail."

So David went on his way, and Saul returned to his place. And David said in his heart, " I shall now perish one day by the hand of Saul: there is nothing better for me than that I should speedily escape into the land of the Philistines; and Saul shall despair of me, to seek me any more in any coast of Israel."

And David arose, and he passed over with the six hundred men that were with him unto Achish, the king of Gath. And David dwelt with Achish at Gath, he and his men, every man with his household, even David with his two wives, Ahinoam the Jezreelitess, and Abigail the Carmelitess, Nabal's wife.

And David said unto Achish, "If I have now found grace in thine eyes, let them give me a place in some town in the country, that I may dwell there: for why should thy servant dwell in the royal city with thee?" Then Achish gave him Ziklag that day: wherefore Ziklag pertaineth unto Judah unto this day.

And it was told Saul that David was fled to Gath: and he sought no more again for him.

And David, the servant of the Lord, spake the words of this song in the day that the Lord delivered him from the hand of Saul:

"I will love thee, O Lord, my strength.
The Lord is my rock, and my fortress, and my deliverer;
My God, my strength, in whom I will trust;
My buckler, and the horn of my salvation, and my high tower.
I will call upon the Lord, who is worthy to be praised:
So shall I be saved from mine enemies.
The Lord rewarded me according to my righteousness;
According to the cleanness of my hands hath he recompensed me.
For I have kept the ways of the Lord,
And have not wickedly departed from my God.
For all his judgments were before me,
And I did not put away his statutes from me.
Therefore hath the Lord recompensed me according to my righteousness,
According to the cleanness of my hands in his eyesight.

With the merciful thou wilt shew thyself merciful;
With an upright man thou wilt shew thyself upright;
With the pure thou wilt shew thyself pure;
And with the froward thou wilt shew thyself froward.
For thou wilt light my candle:
The Lord my God will enlighten my darkness.

As for God, his way is perfect:
The word of the Lord is tried:
He is a buckler to all those that trust in him.
For who is God save the Lord:
Or who is a rock save our God?
It is God that girdeth me with strength,
And maketh my way perfect."

A WOMAN AT ENDOR THAT HATH A FAMILIAR SPIRIT

Now Samuel was dead, and all Israel had lamented him, and buried him in Ramah, even in his own city. And Saul had put away those that had familiar spirits, and the wizards, out of the land.

And the Philistines gathered themselves together, and came and pitched in Shunem; and Saul gathered all Israel together, and they pitched in Gilboa. And when Saul saw the host of the Philistines, he was afraid, and his heart greatly trembled. And when Saul enquired of the Lord, the Lord answered him not, neither by dreams, nor by Urim, nor by prophets.

Then said Saul unto his servants, "Seek me a woman that hath a familiar spirit, that I may go to her, and enquire of her."

And his servant said to him, "Behold, there is a woman that hath a familiar spirit at Endor."

And Saul disguised himself, and put on other raiment, and he went, and two men with him, and they came to the woman by night. And Saul said, "I pray thee, divine unto me by the familiar spirit, and bring me him up, whom I shall name unto thee."

And the woman said unto him, "Behold, thou knowest what Saul hath done, how he hath cut off those that have familiar spirits, and the wizards, out of the land; wherefore then layest thou a snare for my life, to cause me to die?"

And Saul sware to her by the Lord, saying, "As the Lord liveth, there shall no punishment happen to thee for this thing."

Then said the woman, "Whom shall I bring up unto thee?"

And Saul said, "Bring me up Samuel."

And when the woman saw Samuel, she cried with a loud voice; and the woman spoke to Saul, saying, "Why hast thou deceived me? for thou art Saul."

And the king said unto her, "Be not afraid; for what sawest thou?"

And the woman said unto Saul, "I saw gods ascending out of the earth."

And he said unto her, "What form is he of?"

And she said, "An old man cometh up; and he is covered with a mantle."

And Saul perceived that it was Samuel, and he stooped with his face to the ground, and bowed himself.

And Samuel said to Saul, "Why hast thou disquieted me to bring me up?"

And Saul answered, "I am sore distressed; for the Philistines make war against me, and God is departed from me, and answereth me no more, neither by prophets, nor by dreams; therefore I have called thee, that thou mayest make known unto me what I shall do."

Then said Samuel, "Wherefore then dost thou ask of me,

seeing the Lord is departed from thee, for the Lord hath rent the kingdom out of thine hand, and given it to thy neighbour, even to David: because thou obeyedst not the voice of the Lord. Moreover the Lord will also deliver Israel with thee into the hand of the Philistines: and tomorrow shalt thou and thy sons be with me: the Lord also shall deliver the host of Israel into the hand of the Philistines."

Then Saul fell on the earth, and was sore afraid, because of the words of Samuel: and there was no strength in him; for he had eaten no bread all the day, nor all the night.

And the woman came unto Saul, and saw that he was sore troubled, and said unto him, "Behold, thine handmaid hath obeyed thy voice, and I have put my life in my hand, and have hearkened unto thy words which thou spokest unto me. Now therefore, I pray thee, hearken thou also unto the voice of thine handmaid, and let me set a morsel of bread before thee; and eat, that thou mayest have strength, when thou goest on thy way."

But Saul refused, and said, "I will not eat."

But his servants, together with the woman, compelled him; and he hearkened unto their voice. So he arose from the earth, and sat upon the bed. And the woman had a fat calf in the house; and she hastened, and killed it, and took flour, and kneaded it, and did bake unleavened bread thereof; and she brought it before Saul, and before his servants; and they did eat. Then they rose up and went away that night.

BUT DAVID ENCOURAGED HIMSELF IN THE LORD HIS GOD

Now the Philistines gathered together all their armies to Aphek; and the Israelites pitched by a fountain which is in Jezreel. And the lords of the Philistines passed on by hundreds, and by thousands; but David and his men passed on in the rearward with Achish.

Then said the princes of the Philistines, "What do these Hebrews here?"

And Achish said unto the princes of the Philistines, "Is not this David, the servant of Saul the king of Israel, which hath been with me these days, or these years, and I have found no fault in him since he fell unto me unto this day?"

And the princes of the Philistines were wroth with him, and said unto him, "Make this fellow return, that he may go again to his place which thou hast appointed him, and let him not go down with us to battle, lest in the battle he be an adversary to us: for wherewith should he reconcile himself unto his master? should it not be with the heads of these men? Is not this David, of whom they sang one to another in dances, saying,

"'Saul slew his thousands,
And David his ten thousands?'"

Then Achish called David, and said unto him, "Surely, as the Lord liveth, thou hast been upright, and thy going out and thy coming in with me in the host is good in my sight; for I have not found evil in thee since the day of thy coming unto me unto this day; nevertheless the lords favour thee not. Wherefore now return, and go in peace, that thou displease not the lords of the Philistines."

And David said unto Achish, "But what have I done? and what hast thou found in thy servant so long as I have been with thee unto this day, that I may not go fight against the enemies of my lord the king? "

And Achish answered and said to David, " I know that thou art good in my sight, as an angel of God; notwithstanding the princes of the Philistines have said, ' He shall not go up with us to the battle.' Wherefore now rise up early in the morning with thy master's servants that are come with thee; and as soon as ye be up early in the morning, and have light, depart."

So David and his men rose up early to depart in the morning, to return into the land of the Philistines. And the Philistines went up to Jezreel.

And it came to pass, when David and his men were come to Ziklag on the third day, that the Amalekites had invaded the south, and smitten Ziklag, and burned it with fire, and had taken captives all that were therein; they slew not any, either great or small, but carried them away, and went on their way.

So David and his men came to the city, and behold, it was burned with fire; and their wives, and their sons, and their daughters, were taken captives. Then David and the people that were with him lifted up their voice and wept, until they had no more power to weep.

And David's two wives were taken captives, Ahinoam, and Abigail. And David was greatly distressed: for the people spake of stoning him, because the soul of all the people was grieved, every man for his sons, and for his daughters. But David encouraged himself in the Lord his God.

And David said to Abiathar the priest, " I pray thee bring me hither the ephod." And Abiathar brought thither the ephod to David.

And David inquired of the Lord, saying, " Shall I pursue after this troop? shall I overtake them? "

And the Lord answered him, " Pursue: for thou shalt surely overtake them, and without fail recover all."

So David went and pursued, he and four hundred men: for

two hundred abode behind, which were so faint that they could not go over the brook Besor.

And they found an Egyptian in the field, and brought him to David, and gave him bread, and he did eat; and they made him drink water; and they gave him a piece of a cake of figs, and two clusters of raisins. And when he had eaten, his spirit came again to him: for he had eaten no bread, nor drunk any water, three days and three nights.

And David said unto him, " To whom belongest thou? and whence art thou? "

And he said, " I am a young man of Egypt, servant to an Amalekite; and my master left me, because three days agone I fell sick. We made an invasion upon the south, and upon the coast which belongeth to Judah, and we burned Ziklag with fire."

And David said to him, " Canst thou bring me down to this company? "

And he said, "Swear unto me by God, that thou wilt neither kill me, nor deliver me into the hands of my master, and I will bring thee down to this company."

And when he had brought them down, behold, they were spread abroad upon all the earth, eating and drinking, and dancing, because of all the great spoil that they had taken out of the land of the Philistines, and out of the land of Judah.

And David smote them from the twilight even unto the evening of the next day: and there escaped not a man of them, save four hundred young men, which rode upon camels, and fled.

And David recovered all that the Amalekites had carried away. And David rescued his two wives. And there was nothing lacking to them, neither small nor great, neither sons nor daughters, neither spoil, nor any thing that they had taken to them: David recovered all. And David took all the flocks and herds which they drove before the other cattle.

And David came to the two hundred men which were so faint that they could not follow David, and they went forth to meet David, and to meet the people that were with him. And when David came near to the people, he saluted them.

Then answered the wicked men of those that went with David, and said, "Because they went not with us, we will not give them aught of the spoil that we have recovered, save to every man his wife and his children, that they may lead them away, and depart."

Then said David, "Ye shall not do so, my brethren, with that which the Lord hath given us, who hath preserved us, and delivered the company that came against us into our hand. For who will hearken unto you in this matter? but as his part is that goeth down to the battle, so shall his part be that tarrieth by the stuff: they shall part alike."

And it was so from that day forward, that he made it a statute and an ordinance for Israel unto this day. And when David came to Ziklag, he sent of the spoil unto the elders of Judah, even to his friends, saying, "Behold, a present for you, of the spoil of the enemies of the Lord.

"The Lord liveth; and blessed be my Rock;
And let the God of my salvation be exalted.
It is God that avengeth me,
And subdueth the people under me.
He delivereth me from mine enemies:
Yea, thou liftest me up above those that rise up
against me:
Thou hast delivered me from the violent man.
Therefore will I give thanks unto thee, O Lord,
among the heathen,
And sing praises unto thy name."

THE BATTLE WENT SORE AGAINST SAUL

Now the Philistines fought against Israel: and the men of Israel fled from before the Philistines, and fell down slain in mount Gilboa. And the Philistines followed hard upon Saul and upon his sons. And the Philistines slew Jonathan, and Abinadab, and Melchishua, Saul's sons.

And the battle went sore against Saul, and the archers hit him; and he was sore wounded of the archers. Then said Saul unto his armour-bearer, "Draw thy sword, and thrust me through therewith; lest these Philistines come and thrust me through, and abuse me."

But the armour-bearer would not: for he was sore afraid. Therefore Saul took a sword, and fell upon it. And when his armour-bearer saw that Saul was dead, he fell likewise upon his sword, and died with him.

So Saul died, and his three sons, and his armour-bearer, and all his men, that same day together. And when the men of Israel that were on the other side of the valley, and they that were on the other side Jordan saw that the men of Israel fled, and that Saul and his sons were dead, they forsook the cities, and fled; and the Philistines came and dwelt in them.

And it came to pass on the morrow, when the Philistines came to strip the slain, that they found Saul and his three sons fallen in mount Gilboa. And they cut off his head, and stripped off his armour, and sent into the land of the Philistines round about, to publish it in the house of their idols, and among the people. And they put his armour in the house of Ashtaroth: and they fastened his body to the wall of Beth-shan.

And when the inhabitants of Jabesh-gilead heard of that which the Philistines had done to Saul, all the valient men arose, and went all night, and took the body of Saul, and the bodies of his sons from the wall of Beth-shan, and came to Jabesh, and burnt them there. And they took their bones, and buried them under a tree at Jabesh, and fasted seven days.

So Saul died for his transgression which he committed against the Lord, even against the word of the Lord, which he kept not, and also for asking counsel of one that had a familiar spirit, to inquire of it, and inquired not of the Lord. Therefore the Lord turned the kingdom unto David the son of Jesse.

HOW ARE THE MIGHTY FALLEN!

NOW IT CAME TO PASS when David was returned from the slaughter of the Amalekites, and David had abode two days in Ziklag, it came to pass on the third day, that behold, a man came out of the camp from Saul with his clothes rent, and earth upon his head. And when he came to David, he fell to the earth, and did obeisance.

And David said unto him, "From whence comest thou?"

And he said, "Out of the camp of Israel am I escaped."

And David said, "How went the matter? I pray thee, tell me."

And he answered, "The people are fled from the battle, and many of the people also are fallen and dead. And Saul and Jonathan his son are dead also."

And David said, "How knowest thou that Saul and Jonathan his son be dead?"

And the young man said, "As I happened by chance upon mount Gilboa, behold, Saul leaned upon his spear; and lo, the chariots and horsemen followed hard after him. And when he looked behind him, he saw me, and called unto me, and I answered, 'Here am I;' and he said unto me, 'Who art thou?' and

I answered him, 'I am an Amalekite.' He said unto me again, 'Stand, I pray thee, upon me, and slay me: for anguish is come upon me, because my life is yet whole in me.' So I stood upon him, and slew him, because I was sure he could not live after that he was fallen. And I took the crown that was upon his head, and the bracelet that was on his arm, and have brought them hither unto my lord."

Then David took hold on his clothes, and rent them; and likewise all the men that were with him. And they mourned and wept, and fasted until even, for Saul, and for Jonathan, his son, and for the people of the Lord, and for the house of Israel; because they were fallen by the sword.

And David said unto the young man that told him, "Whence art thou?"

And he answered, "I am the son of a stranger, an Amalekite."

And David said unto him, "How wast thou not afraid to stretch forth thine hand to destroy the Lord's anointed? Thy blood be upon thy head; for thy mouth hath testified against thee, saying, 'I have slain the Lord's anointed.'"

And David called one of the young men, and said, "Go near, and fall upon him." And he smote him that he died.

And David lamented with this lamentation over Saul, and over Jonathan his son:

"The beauty of Israel is slain upon thy high places:
How are the mighty fallen!
Tell it not in Gath, publish it not in the streets
of Askelon;
Lest the daughters of the Philistines rejoice.

"Ye mountains of Gilboa, let there be no dew,
Neither let there be rain upon you, nor fields of
offerings:
For the shield of the mighty is vilely cast away,

The shield of Saul, as though he had not been
anointed with oil.

"Saul and Jonathan were lovely and pleasant in their lives,
And in their death they were not divided:
They were swifter than eagles, they were stronger
than lions.
How are the mighty fallen in the midst of the battle!

"O Jonathan, thou wast slain in thine high places.
I am distressed for thee, my brother Jonathan:
Very pleasant hast thou been unto me:
Thy love to me was wonderful, passing the love of
women.

"How are the mighty fallen, and the weapons of war
perished!"

" Thy gentleness hath made me great."

THE SECOND BOOK OF SAMUEL

THE FIRST BOOK OF CHRONICLES

THEY ANOINTED DAVID KING OVER JUDAH

AND IT CAME TO PASS after the death of Saul, that David inquired of the Lord, saying, "Shall I go up into any of the cities of Judah?"

And the Lord said unto him, "Go up."

And David said, "Whither shall I go up?"

And He said, "Unto Hebron."

So David went up thither, and his two wives also, Ahinoam, and Abigail, and his men that were with him did David bring up, every man with his household: and they dwelt in the cities of Hebron.

And the men of Judah came, and there they anointed David king over the house of Judah. And they told David, saying, "The men of Jabesh-gilead were they that buried Saul."

And David sent messengers unto the men of Jabesh-gilead, and said unto them, "Blessed be ye of the Lord, that ye have shown this kindness unto your lord, even unto Saul, and have buried him. And now the Lord show kindness and truth unto you: and I also will requite you this kindness, because ye have done this thing. Therefore let your hands be strengthened, and be ye valiant: for your master Saul is dead, and also the house of Judah have anointed me king over them."

But Abner, the son of Ner, captain of Saul's host, took Ish-bosheth, the son of Saul, and made him king over the Ashurites, and over Jezreel, and over Ephraim, and over Benjamin, and over all Israel. Ish-bosheth, Saul's son was forty years old when he began to reign over Israel, and reigned two years. But the house of Judah followed David.

AND DAVID LAMENTED OVER ABNER

NOW THERE was long war between the house of Saul and the house of David: but David waxed stronger and stronger, and the house of Saul waxed weaker and weaker.

And it came to pass, while there was war between the house of Saul and the house of David, that Abner made himself strong for the house of Saul. And Saul had a concubine, whose name was Rizpah. And Ish-bosheth said to Abner, "Wherefore hast thou taken my father's concubine?"

Then was Abner very wroth for the words of Ish-bosheth, and said, "I do show kindness unto the house of Saul thy father, and against the house of Judah, and have not delivered thee into the hands of David. Am I a dog's head, that thou chargest me today with a fault against this woman? God do so to Abner, and more also, except I do translate the kingdom from the house of Saul and set up the throne of David over Israel, and over Judah from Dan to Beersheba."

And Ish-bosheth could not answer Abner a word because he feared him.

And Abner sent messengers to David on his behalf, saying, "Make thy league with me, and behold, my hand shall be with thee, to bring about all Israel unto thee."

And David said, "Well, I will make a league with thee: but one thing I require of thee, that is, thou shalt not see my face, except thou first bring Michal, Saul's daughter, when thou comest to see my face."

And David sent messengers to Ish-bosheth, Saul's son, saying, "Deliver me my wife Michal, which I espoused to me for an hundred Philistines."

And Ish-bosheth sent, and took her from her husband, even from Phaltiel the son of Laish. And her husband went with her along, weeping behind her. Then said Abner unto him, "Go, return." And he returned.

And Abner had communication with the elders of Israel, saying, "Ye sought for David in times past to be king over you: now then do it; for the Lord hath spoken of David, saying, 'By the hand of my servant David, I will save my people Israel out of the hand of the Philistines, and out of the hand of all their enemies.' "

And Abner also spake in the ears of Benjamin; and Abner went also to speak in the ears of David in Hebron all that seemed good to Israel, and that seemed good to the whole house of Benjamin.

So Abner came to David to Hebron, and twenty men with him; and David made Abner, and the men that were with him a feast. And Abner said unto David, "I will arise and go, and will gather all Israel unto my lord the king, that they may make a league with thee, and that thou mayest reign over all that thine heart desireth." And David sent Abner away in peace.

And behold, the servants of David and Joab came from pursuing a troop, and brought in a great spoil with them. When Joab and all the host were come, they told Joab, saying, "Abner the son of Ner came to the king, and he hath sent him away, and he is gone in peace."

Then Joab came to the king, and said, "What hast thou done? behold, Abner came unto thee; why is it that thou hast sent him away, and he is quite gone? Thou knowest Abner, that he came to deceive thee, and to know thy going out and thy coming in, and to know all that thou doest."

And when Joab was come out from David, he sent messengers after Abner, which brought him again (but David knew it not). And when Abner was returned to Hebron, Joab took him aside in the gate to speak with him quietly, and smote him there under the fifth rib that he died. So Joab slew Abner because he had slain his brother Asahel at Gibeon in the battle.

And when David heard it, he said, "I and my kingdom are guiltless before the Lord for ever from the blood of Abner the son of Ner. Let it rest on the head of Joab, and on all his father's house."

And David said to Joab, and to all the people that were with him, "Rend your clothes, and gird you with sackcloth, and mourn before Abner." And the king himself followed the bier.

And they buried Abner in Hebron: and the king lifted up his voice and wept at the grave of Abner; and all the people wept.

And when all the people came to cause David to eat meat while it was yet day, David sware saying, "So do God to me, and more also, if I taste bread or aught else, till the sun be down."

And all the people took notice of it, and it pleased them: as whatsoever the king did pleased all the people. For the people and all Israel understood that day that it was not of the king to slay Abner.

And the king said unto his servants, "Know ye not that there is a prince and a great man fallen this day in Israel? The Lord shall reward the doer of evil according to his wickedness."

And when Saul's son, Ish-bosheth, heard that Abner was dead in Hebron, his hands were feeble, and all the Israelites were troubled.

And Ish-bosheth had two men that were captains of bands: the name of the one was Baanah, and the name of the other Rechab. And Rechab and Baanah, went, and came about the heat of the day to the house of Ish-bosheth, who lay on a bed at noon, in his bed-chamber, and they smote him, and slew him, and beheaded him, and took his head, and gat them away through the plain all night.

And they brought the head of Ish-bosheth unto David to Hebron, and said to the king, "Behold the head of Ish-bosheth the son of Saul thine enemy, which sought thy life; and the Lord hath avenged my lord the king this day of Saul and of his seed."

And David answered Rechab and Baanah and said unto them,

"As the Lord liveth, who hath redeemed my soul out of all adversity, when one told me, saying, 'Behold, Saul is dead,' thinking to have brought good tidings, and that I would have given him a reward, I took hold of him and slew him in Ziklag. How much more, when wicked men have slain a righteous person in his own house upon his bed! Shall I not therefore now require his blood of your hand, and take you away from the earth?"

And David commanded his young men, and they slew them. But they took the head of Ish-bosheth and buried it in the sepulchre of Abner in Hebron.

THOU SHALT BE RULER OVER MY PEOPLE ISRAEL

THEN CAME all the tribes of Israel to David unto Hebron, and spake, saying, "Behold, we are thy bone and thy flesh. And moreover in time past, even when Saul was king, thou wast he that leddest out and broughtest in, Israel: and the Lord thy God said unto thee, 'Thou shalt feed my people Israel, and thou shalt be ruler over my people Israel.'"

Therefore came all the elders of Israel to Hebron, and David made a covenant with them in Hebron before the Lord; and they anointed David king over Israel, according to the word of the Lord by Samuel.

And there came the children of Benjamin unto David. And David went out to meet them, and said unto them, "If ye be come peaceably unto me to help me, mine heart shall be knit unto you: but if ye be come to betray me to mine enemies, seeing there is no wrong in mine hands, the God of our fathers look thereon, and rebuke it."

Then the spirit came upon Amasai, who was chief of the captains, and he said, "Thine are we, David, and on thy side, thou son of Jesse: peace, peace be unto thee, and peace be to thine helpers; for thy God helpeth thee." Then David received them, and made them captains of the band.

And all the men of war, that could keep rank, came with a perfect heart to Hebron, to make David king over all Israel: and all the rest also of Israel were of one heart to make David king.

Moreover, they that were nigh, brought bread on asses, and on camels, and on mules, and on oxen, and meat, meal, cakes of figs, and bunches of raisins, and wine, and oil, and oxen, and sheep abundantly. And there they were with David three days, eating and drinking; for their brethren had prepared for them. For there was joy in Israel.

And at that time, day by day they came to David to help him, until it was a great host, like the host of God. So David waxed greater and greater.

And David and all Israel went to Jerusalem where the Jebusites were the inhabitants of the land. And the Jebusites said to David, "Thou shalt not come hither."

Nevertheless, David took the strong hold of Zion. So David dwelt in Zion, and called it the city of David. And he built the city round about, and Joab repaired the rest of the city.

And David went on and grew great, and the Lord God of hosts was with him. And David said:

"Great is the Lord, and greatly to be praised
In the city of our God, in the mountain of his holiness.
Beautiful for situation, the joy of the whole earth
is mount Zion,
On the sides of the north, the city of the great King.
God is known in her palaces for a refuge.
Let mount Zion rejoice,
Let the daughters of Judah be glad, because of thy
judgments.

Walk about Zion, and go round about her:
Tell the towers thereof.
Mark ye well her bulwarks, consider her palaces;
That ye may tell it to the generation following.
For this God is our God for ever and ever.
Praise the Lord, O Jerusalem;
Praise thy God, O Zion."

THEY BROUGHT THE ARK OF GOD TO THE CITY OF DAVID

Now Hiram king of Tyre sent messengers to David, and timbers of cedars, with masons and carpenters, to build him an house. And David perceived that the Lord had confirmed him king over Israel, for his kingdom was lifted up on high, because of his people Israel. And the fame of David went out into all lands; and the Lord brought the fear of him upon all nations.

And David gathered together all the chosen men of Israel, and consulted with the captains of thousands, and hundreds, and with every leader. And David said unto all the congregation of Israel, "If it seem good unto you, and that it be of the Lord our God, let us bring again the ark of our God to us: for we inquired not at it in the days of Saul."

And all the congregation said that they would do so: for the thing was right in the eyes of all the people. And David went up, and all Israel to Kirjath-jearim, which belongeth to Judah, to bring up thence the ark of God the Lord, that dwelleth between the cherubims.

And they set the ark of God upon a new cart, and brought it out of the house of Abinadab that was at Gibeah. And Uzzah and Ahio the sons of Abinadab drove the new cart. And when they came to Nachon's threshing-floor, Uzzah put forth his hand to the ark of God, and took hold of it: for the oxen shook it.

And the anger of the Lord was kindled against Uzzah, and God smote him there for his error; and there he died by the ark of God.

And David was afraid of the Lord that day, and said, "How shall the ark of the Lord come to me?" So David would not remove the ark of the Lord into the city of David; but carried it into the house of Obed-edom.

And the ark of God remained with the family of Obed-edom in his house three months. And the Lord blessed the house of Obed-edom, and all that he had.

And David prepared a place for the ark of God in the city of David, and pitched for it a tent. Then David said, "None ought to carry the ark of God but the Levites: for them hath the Lord chosen to carry the ark of God, and to minister unto Him for ever."

And David gathered all Israel together to Jerusalem, to bring up the ark of the Lord unto his place, which he had prepared for it.

And David called for the priests, and for the Levites, and said unto them, "Ye are the chief of the fathers of the Levites: sanctify yourselves, that ye may bring up the ark of the Lord God of Israel unto the place that I have prepared for it. For because ye did it not at the first, the Lord our God made a breach upon us, for that we sought him not after the due order."

So the priests and the Levites sanctified themselves to bring up the ark of the Lord. And the children of the Levites bare the ark of God upon their shoulders with the staves thereon as Moses commanded, according to the word of the Lord.

So David and the elders of Israel, and the captains over

thousands, brought up the ark of the covenant of the Lord out of the house of Obed-edom with joy.

And David was clothed with a robe of fine linen, and also had upon him an ephod of linen. And David danced before the Lord with all his might.

And as the ark of the Lord came into the city of David, Michal, Saul's daughter, looked through a window, and saw king David leaping and dancing before the Lord; and she despised him in her heart. Therefore Michal had no child unto the day of her death.

And they brought in the ark of the Lord, and set it in his place, in the midst of the tabernacle that David had pitched for it: and David offered burnt-offerings, and peace-offerings before the Lord.

And when David had made an end of offering the burnt-offerings and the peace-offerings, he blessed the people in the name of the Lord. And he dealt to every one of Israel, both man and woman, to every one a loaf of bread, and a good piece of flesh, and a flagon of wine.

And he appointed certain of the Levites to minister before the ark of the Lord, and to record, and to thank and praise the Lord God of Israel.

Then on that day David delivered first this psalm, to thank the Lord, into the hand of Asaph and his brethren:

Give thanks unto the Lord, call upon his name,
Make known his deeds among the people.
Sing unto him, sing psalms unto him,
Talk ye of all his wondrous works.
Glory ye in his holy name:
Let the heart of them rejoice that seek the Lord.
Seek the Lord and his strength,
Seek his face continually.
Remember his marvellous works that he hath done,
His wonders, and the judgments of his mouth.

Sing unto the Lord, all the earth;
Show forth from day to day his salvation.
For great is the Lord, and greatly to be praised.
Glory and honour are in his presence;
Strength and gladness are in his place.
Give unto the Lord, ye kindreds of the people,
Give unto the Lord glory and strength.
Give unto the Lord the glory due unto his name:
Bring an offering, and come before him:
Worship the Lord in the beauty of holiness.
Let the heavens be glad, and let the earth rejoice:
And let men say among the nations, The Lord reigneth.

And all the people said, "Amen," and praised the Lord.

So David left there before the ark of the covenant of the Lord, Asaph and his brethren, to minister before the ark continually, as every day's work required: to offer burnt-offerings unto the Lord upon the altar continually, morning and evening, and to do according to all that is written in the law of the Lord, which he commanded Israel.

THY KINGDOM SHALL BE ESTABLISHED FOREVER

AND DAVID made him houses in the city of David; and took him wives and concubines; and there were sons and daughters born to David.

And it came to pass as David sat in his house, that he said to Nathan the prophet, "Lo, I dwell in an house of cedars, but the ark of the covenant of the Lord remaineth under curtains."

And Nathan said to the king, "Go, do all that is in thine heart: for the Lord is with thee."

And it came to pass the same night, that the word of God came to Nathan, saying, " Go and tell David my servant, 'Thus saith the Lord, Thou shalt not build me an house to dwell in. For I have not dwelt in any house since the time that I brought up the children of Israel out of Egypt, even to this day, but have walked in a tent and in a tabernacle. Now therefore, I took thee from the sheep-cote, from following the sheep, to be ruler over my people, over Israel. And I was with thee whithersoever thou wentest, and have cut off all thine enemies out of thy sight, and have made thee a great name, like unto the name of the great men that are in the earth.

" 'And it shall come to pass, when thy days be expired that thou must go to be with thy fathers, that I will raise up thy seed after thee, which shall be of thy sons; and I will establish his kingdom. He shall build me an house, and I will not take my mercy away from him, but I will settle him in mine house and in my kingdom for ever. Thy throne shall be established for ever.' "

According to all these words, and according to all this vision, so did Nathan speak unto David.

And David the king came and sat before the Lord, and said, " Who am I, O Lord God, and what is mine house, that thou hast brought me hitherto? O Lord, for thy servant's sake, and according to thine own heart, hast thou done all this greatness, in making known all these great things. O Lord, there is none like thee, neither is there any God besides thee; for thy words be true, and thou hast promised this goodness unto thy servant."

DAVID DEDICATED UNTO THE LORD THE SILVER AND GOLD

When the Philistines heard that David was anointed king over all Israel, all the Philistines went up to seek David. And David heard of it and went out against them. And the Philistines came and spread themselves in the valley of Rephaim.

And David inquired of God, saying, "Shall I go up against the Philistines? and wilt thou deliver them into mine hand?"

And the Lord said unto him, "Go up; for I will deliver them into thine hand." So they came up, and David smote them there.

And the Philistines yet again spread themselves abroad in the valley. Therefore David inquired again of God.

And God said unto him, "Go not up after them; turn away from them, and come upon them over against the mulberry trees. And it shall be, when thou shalt hear a sound of going in the tops of the mulberry-trees, that then thou shalt go out to battle: for God is gone forth before thee, to smite the host of the Philistines."

David therefore did as God commanded him: and they smote the host of the Philistines from Gibeon even to Gazer, and subdued them, and took Gath and her towns out of the hand of the Philistines.

And he smote Moab; and the Moabites became David's servants and brought gifts.

And David smote Hadarezer king of Zoah, as he went to establish his dominion by the river Euphrates. And David took from him a thousand chariots, and seven thousand horsemen, and twenty thousand footmen.

And when the Syrians of Damascus came to help Hadarezer, king of Zoah, David slew of the Syrians two and twenty thousand men. Then David put garrisons in Syria-damascus; and the Syrians became David's servants, and brought gifts. Thus the Lord preserved David whithersoever he went.

And David took the shields of gold that were on the servants of Hadarezer, and brought them to Jerusalem. And from the cities of Hadarezer, he took exceeding much brass.

When Toi, king of Hamath heard that David had smitten all the host of Hadarezer, he sent Joram, his son, unto king David, to salute him and to bless him. And Joram brought with him vessels of silver, and vessels of gold, and vessels of brass.

And king David dedicated unto the Lord the silver and the gold that he brought from all these nations.

So David reigned over all Israel, and executed judgment and justice among all his people.

I SHOW THEE KINDNESS FOR JONATHAN'S SAKE

AND DAVID said, " Is there yet any that is left of the house of Saul, that I may show him kindness for Jonathan's sake? "

And there was of the house of Saul a servant whose name was Ziba. And when they had called him unto David, the king said unto him, " Art thou Ziba? "

And he said, " Thy servant is he."

And the king said, " Is there not yet any of the house of Saul, that I may show the kindness of God unto him? "

And Ziba said unto the king, " Jonathan hath yet a son, which is lame on his feet. He was five years old when the tidings came of Saul and Jonathan out of Jezreel, and his nurse took him up, and fled: and it came to pass, as she made haste to flee, that he fell, and became lame. And his name is Mephibosheth."

And the king said, "Where is he?"

And Ziba said unto the king, "Behold, he is in the house of Machir."

Then king David sent, and fetched him out of the house of Machir; and when he was come unto David, he fell on his face, and did reverence. And David said, "Mephibosheth."

And he answered, "Behold thy servant!"

And David said unto him, "Fear not: for I will surely show thee kindness for Jonathan thy father's sake, and will restore thee all the land of Saul thy father; and thou shalt eat bread at my table continually."

And Mephibosheth bowed himself, and said, "What is thy servant, that thou shouldest look upon such a dead dog as I am?"

Then the king called to Ziba, Saul's servant, and said unto him, "I have given unto thy master's son all that pertained to Saul, and to all his house. Thou therefore, and thy sons, and thy servants, shall till the land for him, and thou shalt bring in the fruits that thy master's son may have food to eat. But Mephibosheth shall eat bread alway at my table."

Then said Ziba unto the king, "According to all that my lord the king hath commanded his servant, so shall thy servant do." Now Ziba had fifteen sons and twenty servants. And all that dwelt in the house of Ziba were servants unto Mephibosheth.

So Mephibosheth dwelt in Jerusalem: for he did eat continually at the king's table.

DAVID SENT TO COMFORT HANUN

AND IT CAME TO PASS after this, that the king of the children of Ammon died, and Hanun his son reigned in his stead. Then said David, "I will show kindness unto Hanun the son of Nahash, as his father showed kindness unto me." And David sent to comfort him by the hand of his servants. And David's servants came into the land of the children of Ammon.

And the princes of the children of Ammon said unto Hanun their lord, "Thinkest thou that David doth honour thy father, that he hath sent comforters unto thee? hath not David rather sent his servants unto thee to search the city, and to spy it out, and to overthrow it?"

Wherefore Hanun took David's servants, and shaved off the one half of their beards, and cut off their garments in the middle, even to their buttocks, and sent them away.

When they told it unto David, he sent to meet them, because the men were greatly ashamed. And the king said, "Tarry at Jericho until your beards be grown, and then return."

And when the children of Ammon saw that they had made themselves odious to David, Hanun and the children of Ammon sent a thousand talents of silver to hire them chariots and horsemen out of Mesopotamia, and out of Syria, and out of Zobah. So they hired thirty and two thousand chariots, and the king of Maachah and his people, who came and pitched before Medaba. And the children of Ammon gathered themselves together from their cities, and came to battle.

And when David heard of it, he sent Joab, and all the host of the mighty men.

And the children of Ammon came out, and put the battle in array at the entering in of the gate: and the Syrians were by themselves in the field. When Joab saw that the front of the battle was against him before and behind, he chose of all the choice men of Israel, and put them in array against the Syrians: and the rest of the people he delivered into the hand of Abishai his brother, that he might put them in array against the children of Ammon.

And Joab said, "If the Syrians be too strong for me, then thou shalt help me: but if the children of Ammon be too strong for thee, then I will come and help thee. Be of good courage, and let us behave ourselves valiantly for our people, and for the cities of God: and let the Lord do that which is good in his sight."

So Joab and the people that were with him drew nigh before the Syrians unto the battle; and they fled before him. And when the children of Ammon saw that the Syrians were fled, they likewise fled before Abishai, and entered into the city. Then Joab came to Jerusalem.

And when the Syrians saw that they were put to the worse before Israel, they sent messengers, and drew forth the Syrians that were beyond the river: and Shophach the captain of the host of Hadarezer went before them.

And it was told David; and he gathered all Israel, and passed over Jordan, and came upon them, and set the battle in array against them.

And the Syrians fled before Israel. And when all the kings that were servants to Hadarezer saw that they were smitten before Israel, they made peace with Israel, and served them. So the Syrians feared to help the children of Ammon any more.

WHY HAST THOU DESPISED THE COMMANDMENT OF THE LORD?

And it came to pass, after the year was expired, at the time when kings go forth to battle, that David sent Joab, and his servants with him, and all Israel, and they destroyed the children of Ammon, and besieged Rabbah.

But David tarried still at Jerusalem. And it came to pass in an eventide, that David arose from off his bed, and walked upon the roof of the king's house: and from the roof he saw a woman washing herself; and the woman was very beautiful to look upon.

And David sent and inquired after the woman. And one said, "Is not this Bath-sheba the daughter of Eliam, the wife of Uriah the Hittite?"

And David sent messengers and took her: and she came in unto him, and he lay with her; and she returned unto her house. And the woman conceived, and sent and told David, and said, "I am with child."

And David sent to Joab, saying, "Send me Uriah the Hittite." And Joab sent Uriah to David. And when Uriah was come unto him, David demanded of him how Joab did, and how the people did, and how the war prospered. And David said to Uriah, "Go down to thy house, and wash thy feet."

And Uriah departed out of the king's house, and there followed him a mess of meat from the king. But Uriah slept at the door of the king's house with all the servants of his lord, and went not down to his house.

And they told David, saying, "Uriah went not down unto his house."

David said unto Uriah, "Camest thou not from thy journey? why then didst thou not go down unto thine house?"

And Uriah said unto David, " The ark, and Israel, and Judah, abide in tents; and my lord Joab, and the servants of my lord are encamped in the open fields; shall I then go into mine house, to eat and to drink, and to be with my wife? As thou livest, and as thy soul liveth, I will not do this thing."

And David said to Uriah, "Tarry here today also, and tomorrow I will let thee depart." So Uriah abode in Jerusalem that day and the morrow. And when David had called him, he did eat and drink before him; and he made him drunk: and at even he went out to lie on his bed with the servants of his lord, but went not down to his house.

And it came to pass in the morning, that David wrote a letter to Joab, and sent it by the hand of Uriah. And he wrote in the letter, saying, " Set ye Uriah in the forefront of the hottest battle, and retire ye from him, that he may be smitten, and die."

And it came to pass when Joab observed the city, that he assigned Uriah unto a place where he knew that valiant men were. And the men of the city went out, and fought with Joab: and there fell some of the people of the servants of David; and Uriah the Hittite died also.

Then Joab sent and told David all the things concerning the war; and charged the messenger, saying, "When thou hast made an end of telling the matters of the war unto the king, and if so be that the king's wrath arise, and he say unto thee, ' Wherefore approached ye so nigh unto the city when ye did fight? knew ye not that they would shoot from the wall? why went ye nigh the wall? ' then say thou, 'Thy servant Uriah the Hittite is dead also.' "

So the messenger went, and came and showed David all that Joab had sent him for. And the messenger said unto David, " Surely the men prevailed against us, and came out unto us into the field, and we were upon them even unto the entering of the gate. And the shooters shot from off the wall upon thy servants:

and some of the king's servants be dead, and thy servant Uriah the Hittite is dead also."

Then said David unto the messenger, "Thus shalt thou say unto Joab, 'Let not this thing displease thee, for the sword devoureth one as well as another: make thy battle more strong against the city, and overthrow it;' and encourage thou him."

And when the wife of Uriah heard that Uriah her husband was dead, she mourned for her husband. And when the mourning was past, David sent and fetched her to his house, and she became his wife, and bare him a son.

But the thing that David had done displeased the Lord. And the Lord sent Nathan unto David, and he came and said unto him, "There were two men in one city; the one rich, and the other poor. The rich man had exceeding many flocks and herds: but the poor man had nothing save one little ewe lamb, which he had bought and nourished up; and it grew up together with him, and with his children; it did eat of his own meat, and drank of his own cup, and lay in his bosom, and was unto him as a daughter.

"And there came a traveller unto the rich man, and he spared to take his own flock and of his own herd, to dress for the wayfaring man that was come unto him; but took the poor man's lamb, and dressed it for the man that was come to him."

And David's anger was greatly kindled against the man; and he said to Nathan, "As the Lord liveth, the man that hath done this thing shall surely die. And he shall restore the lamb four-fold, because he did this thing, and because he had no pity."

And Nathan said to David, "Thou art the man. Thus saith the Lord God of Israel, 'I anointed thee king over Israel, and I delivered thee out of the hand of Saul; and I gave thee thy master's house, and gave thee the house of Israel and of Judah; and if that had been too little, I would moreover have given unto thee such and such things. Wherefore hast thou despised the commandment of the Lord, to do evil in his sight? thou hast killed Uriah the Hittite with the sword, and hast taken his wife to be thy wife, and hast slain him with the sword of the children of Ammon.

" 'Now therefore the sword shall never depart from thine house; because thou hast despised Me, and hast taken the wife of Uriah the Hittite to be thy wife. Behold, I will raise up evil against thee out of thine own house, and I will take thy wives before thine eyes, and give them unto thy neighbor, and he shall lie with thy wives in the sight of this sun. For thou didst it secretly: but I will do this thing before all Israel, and before the sun.' "

And David said unto Nathan, "I have sinned against the Lord."

And Nathan said unto David, "The Lord hath put away thy sin; thou shalt not die. Howbeit, because by this deed thou hast given great occasion to the enemies of the Lord to blaspheme, the child that is born unto thee shall surely die." And Nathan departed unto his house.

And the child that Uriah's wife bare unto David was very sick. David therefore besought God for the child; and David fasted, and went in, and lay all night upon the earth. And the elders of his house arose, and went to him, to raise him up from the earth: but he would not, neither did he eat bread with them. And David mourned:

"O Lord, rebuke me not in thy wrath:
Neither chasten me in thy hot displeasure.
For thine arrows stick fast in me,
And thy hand presseth me sore.
There is no soundness in my flesh because of thine anger;
Neither is there any rest in my bones because of my sin.
For mine iniquities are gone over mine head:
As a heavy burden they are too heavy for me.
My wounds stink, and are corrupt because of my foolishness.
I am troubled; I am bowed down greatly;

I go mourning all the day long.
Lord, all my desire is before thee;
And my groaning is not hid from thee.
My heart panteth, my strength faileth me;
As for the light of mine eyes, it also is gone from me.
For I am ready to halt, and my sorrow is continually
before me.
For I will declare mine iniquity;
I will be sorry for my sin.
Forsake me not, O Lord:
O my God, be not far from me.
Make haste to help me, O Lord my salvation."

And it came to pass on the seventh day, that the child died. And the servants of David feared to tell him that the child was dead: for they said, "Behold, while the child was yet alive, we spake unto him, and he would not hearken unto our voices: how will he then vex himself, if we tell him that the child is dead?"

But when David saw that his servants whispered, David perceived that the child was dead: therefore David said unto his servants, "Is the child dead?"

And they said, "He is dead."

Then David arose from the earth, and washed, and anointed himself, and changed his apparel, and came into the house of the Lord and worshipped:

"Have mercy upon me, O God, according to thy loving-
kindness:
According unto the multitude of thy tender mercies
blot out my transgressions.
Wash me throughly from mine iniquity,
And cleanse me from my sin.
For I acknowledge my transgressions:
And my sin is ever before me.
Hide thy face from my sins,

And blot out all mine iniquities.
Create in me a clean heart, O God:
And renew a right spirit within me.
For thou desirest not sacrifice; else would I give it:
Thou delightest not in burnt-offering.
The sacrifices of God are a broken spirit:
A broken and a contrite heart, O God, thou wilt not
despise."

Then David came to his own house, and when he required, they set bread before him, and he did eat.

Then said his servants unto him, "What thing is this that thou hast done? thou didst fast and weep for the child while it was alive; but when the child was dead, thou didst rise and eat."

And he said, "While the child was yet alive, I fasted, and wept: for I said, 'Who can tell whether God will be gracious to me, that the child may live?' But now he is dead, wherefore should I fast? can I bring him back again? I shall go to him, but he shall not return to me."

And David comforted Bath-sheba his wife, and went in unto her: and she bare a son, and he called his name Solomon: and the Lord loved him.

And Joab fought against Rabbah of the children of Ammon, and took the royal city. And Joab sent messengers to David, and said, "I have fought against Rabbah, and have taken the city of waters. Now therefore gather the rest of the people together, and encamp against the city, and take it: lest I take the city, and it be called after my name."

And David gathered all the people together, and went to Rabbah, and fought against it, and took it. And he took their king's crown from off his head, the weight whereof was a talent of gold with the precious stones, and it was set on David's head. And he brought the spoil of the city in great abundance.

So David and all the people returned unto Jerusalem.

THE KING'S HEART WAS TOWARD ABSALOM

AND IT CAME TO PASS after this, that Absalom, the son of David had a fair sister, whose name was Tamar; and Amnon, the son of David loved her. And Amnon was so vexed, that he fell sick for his sister Tamar, for she was a virgin.

But Amnon had a friend, whose name was Jonadab, the son of Shimeah David's brother: and Jonadab was a very subtle man. And he said unto Amnon, "Why art thou, being the king's son, lean from day to day? wilt thou not tell me?"

And Amnon said unto him, "I love Tamar, my brother Absalom's sister."

And Jonadab said unto him, "Lay thee down on thy bed, and make thyself sick: and when thy father cometh to see thee, say unto him, 'I pray thee, let my sister Tamar come, and give me meat, and dress the meat in my sight, that I may see it, and eat it at her hand.'"

So Amnon lay down, and made himself sick: and when the king was come to see him, Amnon said unto the king, "I pray thee, let Tamar, my sister, come and make me a couple of cakes in my sight, that I may eat at her hand."

Then David sent to Tamar, saying, "Go now to thy brother Amnon's house, and dress him meat."

So Tamar went to her brother Amnon's house; and he was laid down. And she took flour, and kneaded it, and made cakes in his sight, and did bake the cakes. And she took a pan, and poured them out before him: but he refused to eat.

And Amnon said, "Have out all men from me." And they went out every man from him. And Amnon said unto Tamar, "Bring the meat into the chamber, that I may eat of thine hand." And Tamar took the cakes which she had made, and brought them into the chamber to Amnon her brother. And when she had brought them unto him to eat, he took hold of her, and said unto her, "Come lie with me, my sister."

And she answered him, "Nay, my brother, do not force me; for no such thing ought to be done in Israel: do not thou this folly. And I, whither shall I cause my shame to go? and as for thee, thou shalt be as one of the fools in Israel. Now therefore, I pray thee, speak unto the king; for he will not withhold me from thee."

Howbeit, he would not hearken unto her voice: but being stronger than she, forced her, and lay with her. Then Amnon hated her exceedingly; so that the hatred wherewith he hated her was greater than the love wherewith he had loved her. And Amnon said unto her, "Arise, be gone."

And she said unto him, "There is no cause: this evil in sending me away is greater than the other that thou didst unto me."

But he would not hearken unto her. Then he called his servant that ministered unto him, and said, "Put now this woman out from me, and bolt the door after her." Then his servant brought her out, and bolted the door after her.

And Tamar put ashes on her head, and rent her garment of divers colours that was on her, for with such robes were the king's daughters that were virgins apparelled, and laid her hand on her head, and went on crying.

And Absalom, her brother, said unto her, "Hath Amnon thy brother, been with thee? but hold now thy peace, my sister: he is thy brother; regard not this thing." So Tamar remained desolate in her brother Absalom's house.

But when king David heard of all these things, he was very wroth. And Absalom spake unto his brother Amnon neither good nor bad: for Absalom hated Amnon, because he had forced his sister Tamar.

And it came to pass after two full years, that Absalom had sheep-shearers in Baal-hazor, which is beside Ephraim. And Absalom invited all the king's sons.

And Absalom came to the king, and said, "Behold now, thy servant hath sheep-shearers: let the king, I beseech thee, and his servants go with thy servant."

And the king said to Absalom, "Nay, my son, let us not all now go, lest we be chargeable unto thee." And Absalom pressed him: howbeit he would not go, but blessed him.

Then said Absalom, "If not, I pray thee, let my brother Amnon go with us."

And the king said, "Why should he go with thee?" But Absalom pressed him, that he let Amnon and all the king's sons go with him.

Now Absalom had commanded his servants, saying, "Mark ye now when Amnon's heart is merry with wine, and when I say unto you, 'Smite Amnon;' then kill him, fear not; have not I commanded you? be courageous, and be valiant."

And the servants of Absalom did unto Amnon as Absalom had commanded. Then all the king's sons arose, and every man got him up upon his mule, and fled.

And it came to pass, while they were in the way, that tidings came to David, saying, "Absalom hath slain all the king's sons, and there is not one of them left." Then the king arose, and tare his garments, and lay on the earth; and all his servants stood by with their clothes rent.

And Jonadab, the son of Shimeah, David's brother, said, "Let not my lord suppose that they have slain all the king's sons; for Amnon only is dead, for Absalom hath determined this from the day that he forced his sister Tamar. Now therefore, let not my lord the king take the thing to his heart: for Amnon only is dead."

And the young man that kept the watch lifted up his eyes, and behold, there came much people by the way of the hill-side behind him.

And Jonadab said unto the king, "Behold, the king's sons come: as thy servant said, so it is." And as soon as he had made an end of speaking, the king's sons came, and lifted up their voice and wept: and the king also and all his servants wept very sore.

But Absalom fled, and went to Talmai, of Geshur, and was there three years. And David mourned for his son every day. And the soul of king David longed to go forth unto Absalom.

Now Joab perceived that the king's heart was toward Absalom. And Joab sent to Tekoah, and fetched thence a wise woman, and said unto her, " I pray thee, feign thyself, to be a mourner, and put on now mourning apparel, and anoint not thyself with oil, but be as a woman that had a long time mourned for the dead: and come to the king, and speak on this manner unto him." So Joab put the words in her mouth.

And when the woman of Tekoah spake to the king, she fell on her face to the ground, and did obeisance, and said, " Help, O king."

And the king said unto her, " What aileth thee? "

And she answered, " I am indeed a widow woman, and mine husband is dead. And thy handmaid had two sons, and they two strove together in the field, and there was none to part them, but the one smote the other, and slew him. And behold, the whole family is risen against thine handmaid, and they said, ' Deliver him that smote his brother, that we may kill him.' And so they shall quench my coal which is left, and shall not leave to my husband neither name nor remainder upon the earth."

And the king said unto the woman, " Go to thine house, and I will give charge concerning thee." And he said, " As the Lord liveth, there shall not one hair of thy son fall to the earth."

Then the woman said, " Let thine handmaid, I pray thee, speak one word unto my lord the king."

And he said, " Say on."

And the woman said, " Wherefore then hast thou thought such a thing against the people of God? for the king doth speak this thing as one which is faulty, in that the king doth not fetch home again his banished. For we must needs die, and as water spilt on the ground, which cannot be gathered up again; neither doth God respect any person: yet doth he devise means, that his banished be not expelled from him. Therefore I am come to speak of this thing unto my lord the king: for the king will hear, to deliver his handmaid out of the hand of the man that would destroy me and my son together out of the inheritance of God. For as an angel of God, so is my lord the king to discern good and bad: therefore the Lord thy God will be with thee."

Then the king said unto the woman, "Hide not from me, I pray thee, the thing that I shall ask thee."

And the woman said, "Let my lord the king now speak."

And the king said, "Is not the hand of Joab with thee in all this?"

And the woman said, "As thy soul liveth, my lord the king, none can turn to the right hand or to the left from aught that the king hath spoken: for thy servant Joab, he bade me, and he put all these words in the mouth of thine handmaid: and my lord is wise, according to the wisdom of an angel of God, to know all things that are in the earth."

And the king said unto Joab, "Behold now, I have done this thing: go therefore, bring the young man Absalom again."

And Joab fell to the ground on his face, and bowed himself, and thanked the king: and Joab said, "Today thy servant knoweth that I have found grace in thy sight, my lord, O king, in that the king hath fulfilled the request of his servant." So Joab arose and went to Geshur, and brought Absalom to Jerusalem.

And the king said, "Let him turn to his own house, and let him not see my face." So Absalom returned to his own house, and saw not the king's face.

And unto Absalom there were born three sons, and one daughter, whose name was Tamar: she was a woman of fair countenance.

So Absalom dwelt two full years in Jerusalem, and saw not

the king's face. Therefore Absalom sent for Joab, to have sent him to the king; but he would not come to him: and when he sent again the second time, he would not come.

Therefore Absalom said unto his servants, "See, Joab's field is near mine, and he hath barley there; go and set it on fire." And Absalom's servants set the field on fire.

Then Joab arose, and came to Absalom, and said, "Wherefore have thy servants set my field on fire?"

And Absalom answered Joab, "Behold, I sent unto thee, saying, 'Come hither, that I may send thee to the king, to say, "Wherefore am I come from Geshur? it had been good for me to have been there still: now therefore let me see the king's face; and if there be any iniquity in me, let him kill me."'"

So Joab came to the king, and told him. And when David called for Absalom, he came to the king, and bowed himself on his face to the ground before the king: and the king kissed Absalom.

O ABSALOM, MY SON, MY SON!

In all Israel there was none so much praised as Absalom for his beauty: from the sole of his foot even to the crown of his head there was no blemish in him. And when he shaved his head, for at every year's end he shaved it because the hair was heavy on him, he weighed the hair of his head at two hundred shekels after the king's weight.

And it came to pass, that Absalom prepared him chariots and horses, and fifty men to run before him. And Absalom rose up early, and stood beside the way of the gate. And when any man that had a controversy came to the king for judgment, Absalom called unto him, and said, "Of what city art thou?"

And he said, "Thy servant is of one of the tribes of Israel."

And Absalom said unto him, "See, thy matters are good and right; but there is no man deputed of the king to hear thee."

Absalom said moreover, "Oh that I were made judge in the land, that every man which hath any suit or cause might come unto me, and I would do him justice!" And when any man came nigh to do him obeisance, he put forth his hand, and took him, and kissed him. And on this manner did Absalom to all Israel that came to the king for judgment: so Absalom stole the hearts of the men of Israel.

And it came to pass, that Absalom said unto the king, "I pray thee, let me go and pay my vow, which I have vowed unto the Lord, in Hebron. For thy servant vowed a vow while I abode in Syria, saying, 'If the Lord shall bring me indeed to Jerusalem, then I will serve the Lord.'"

And the king said unto him, "Go in peace." So he arose and went to Hebron.

But Absalom sent spies throughout all the tribes of Israel, saying, "As soon as ye hear the sound of the trumpet, then ye shall say, 'Absalom reigneth in Hebron.'"

And with Absalom went two hundred men out of Jerusalem; and they went in their simplicity, and they knew not any thing. And Absalom sent for Ahithophel the Gilonite, David's counsellor, from his city while he offered sacrifices. And the conspiracy was strong; for the people increased with Absalom.

And there came a messenger to David, saying, "The hearts of the men of Israel are after Absalom."

And David said unto all his servants that were with him at Jerusalem, "Arise, and let us flee; for we shall not else escape from Absalom: make speed to depart, lest he overtake us suddenly, and bring evil upon us, and smite the city with the edge of the sword."

And the king's servants said, "Behold, thy servants are ready to do whatsoever my lord the king shall appoint."

And the king went forth, and all his household. And the king left ten women which were concubines to keep the house. And the king went forth, and all the people after him, and tarried in a place that was far off. And all his servants, and six hundred men which came after him from Gath, passed on before the king.

Then said the king to Ittai the Gittite, "Wherefore goest thou also with us? return to thy place; for thou art a stranger, and also an exile. Whereas thou camest but yesterday, should I this day make thee go up and down with us? seeing I go whither I may; return thou, and take back thy brethren: mercy and truth be with thee."

And Ittai answered the king, and said, "As the Lord liveth, and as my lord the king liveth, surely in what place my lord the king shall be, whether in death or life, even there also will thy servant be."

And David said to Ittai, "Go and pass over." And Ittai the Gittite passed over, and all his men, and all the little ones that were with him.

And all the country wept with a loud voice, and all the people passed over: the king also himself passed over the brook Kidron, toward the way of the wilderness.

And lo, Zadok also, and all the Levites were with him, bearing the ark of the covenant of God: and they set down the ark of God until all the people had done passing out of the city.

And the king said unto Zadok, "Carry back the ark of God into the city: if I shall find favour in the eyes of the Lord, he will bring me again, and show me both it, and his habitation: but if he thus say, 'I have no delight in thee;' behold, here am I, let him do to me as seemeth good unto him."

The king said also unto Zadok the priest, "Art not thou a seer? return into the city in peace, and your two sons with you, Ahimaaz thy son, and Jonathan the son of Abiathar. See, I will tarry in the plain of the wilderness, until there come word from you to certify me." Zadok therefore and Abiathar carried the ark of God again to Jerusalem: and they tarried there.

And David went up by the ascent of mount Olivet, and wept as he went up, and had his head covered, and he went barefoot: and all the people that were with him covered every man his head, and they went up, weeping as they went up.

A Psalm of David when he fled from Absalom, his son:

"Lord, how are they increased that trouble me?
Many are they that rise up against me.
Many there be which say of my soul,
'There is no help for him in God.'

"But thou, O Lord, art a shield for me;
My glory and the lifter up of mine head.
I cried unto the Lord with my voice,
And he heard me out of his holy hill.
I laid me down and slept;
I awaked; for the Lord sustained me.

"I will not be afraid of ten thousands of people,
That have set themselves against me round about.
Arise, O Lord; save me, O my God.
Salvation belongeth unto the Lord:
Thy blessing is upon thy people."

And one told David, saying, "Ahithophel is among the conspirators with Absalom."

And David said, "O Lord, I pray thee, turn the counsel of Ahithophel into foolishness."

And it came to pass, that when David was come to the top of the mount, where he worshipped God, behold, Hushai the Archite came to meet him with his coat rent, and earth upon his head: unto whom David said, "If thou passest on with me, then thou shalt be a burden unto me: but if thou return to the city, and say unto Absalom, 'I will be thy servant, O king; as I have been thy father's servant hitherto, so will I now also be thy servant;' then mayest thou for me defeat the counsel of Ahithophel. And hast thou not there with thee Zadok and Abiathar the priests? therefore it shall be, that what thing soever thou shalt hear out of the king's house, thou shalt tell it to Zadok and Abiathar the priests. Behold, they have there with them their two sons, Ahimaaz, Zadok's son, and Jonathan, Abiathar's son; and by them ye shall send unto me everything that ye can hear."

So Hushai, David's friend came into the city, and Absalom came into Jerusalem.

And when David was a little past the top of the hill, behold, Ziba the servant of Mephibosheth met him, with a couple of asses saddled, and upon them two hundred loaves of bread, and an hundred bunches of raisins, and an hundred of summer fruits, and a bottle of wine.

And the king said unto Ziba, "What meanest thou by these?"

And Ziba said, "The asses be for the king's household to ride on; and the bread and summer fruit for the young men to eat; and the wine, that such as be faint in the wilderness may drink."

And the king said, "And where is thy master's son?"

And Ziba said, "Behold, he abideth at Jerusalem: for he said, 'Today shall the house of Israel restore me the kingdom of my father.'"

Then said the king to Ziba, "Behold, thine are all that pertained unto Mephibosheth."

And Ziba said, "I humbly beseech thee that I may find grace in thy sight, my lord, O king."

And when David came to Bahurim behold, thence came out a man of the family of the house of Saul, whose name was Shimei; he came forth, and cursed as he came. And he cast stones at

David, and at all the servants of king David: and all the people and all the mighty men were on his right hand and on his left.

And thus said Shimei when he cursed, " Come out, come out, thou bloody man, and thou man of Belial: the Lord hath returned upon thee all the blood of the house of Saul, in whose stead thou hast reigned; and the Lord hath delivered the kingdom into the hand of Absalom thy son: and behold, thou art taken in thy mischief, because thou art a bloody man."

Then said Abishai the son of Zeruiah unto the king, " Why should this dead dog curse my lord the king? let me go over, I pray thee, and take off his head."

And the king said, " What have I to do with you, ye sons of Zeruiah? so let him curse, because the Lord hath said unto him, 'Curse David.' Who shall then say, 'Wherefore hast thou done so?' "

And David said to Abishai, and to all his servants, " Behold, my son seeketh my life: how much more now may this Benjamite do it? let him alone, and let him curse; for the Lord hath bidden him. It may be that the Lord will look on mine affliction, and that the Lord will requite me good for this cursing this day."

And as David and his men went by the way, Shimei went along on the hill's side, and cursed as he went, and threw stones at him, and cast dust.

And the king, and all the people that were with him, became weary, and refreshed themselves there.

And Absalom, and all the men of Israel, came to Jerusalem, and Ahithophel with him. And it came to pass, when Hushai, David's friend, was come unto Absalom, that Hushai said unto Absalom, " God save the king, God save the king."

And Absalom said to Hushai, " Is this thy kindness to thy friend? why wentest thou not with thy friend? "

And Hushai said unto Absalom, " Nay, but whom the Lord, and this people, and all the men of Israel choose, his will I be, and with him will I abide. And whom should I serve? should I not serve in the presence of David's son? as I have served in thy father's presence, so will I be in thy presence."

Then said Absalom to Ahithophel, "Give counsel among you what we shall do."

And Ahithophel said unto Absalom, "Go in unto thy father's concubines, which he hath left to keep the house; and all Israel shall hear that thou art abhorred of thy father: then shall the hands of all that are with thee be strong."

So they spread a tent upon the top of the house; and Absalom went in unto his father's concubines in the sight of all Israel.

Moreover, Ahithophel said unto Absalom, "Let me now choose out twelve thousand men, and I will arise and pursue after David this night: and I will come upon him while he is weary and weak-handed, and will make him afraid: and all the people that are with him shall flee; and I will smite the king only: and I will bring back all the people unto thee: so all the people shall be in peace."

And the saying pleased Absalom well, and all the elders of Israel. Then said Absalom, "Call now Hushai, and let us hear likewise what he saith."

And when Hushai was come, Absalom spake unto him, saying, "Ahithophel hath spoken after this manner: shall we do after his saying? if not, speak thou."

And Hushai said unto Absalom, "The counsel that Ahithophel hath given is not good at this time. For, thou knowest thy father and his men, that they be mighty men, and they be chafed in their minds, as a bear robbed of her whelps in the field: and thy father is a man of war, and will not lodge with the people. Behold, he is hid now in some pit, or in some other place. And all Israel knoweth that thy father is a mighty man, and they which be with him are valiant men. Therefore I counsel that all Israel be generally gathered unto thee, from Dan even to Beer-sheba, as the sand that is by the sea for multitude; and thou go to battle in thine own person. So shall we come upon him in some place where he shall be found, and we will light upon him as the dew falleth on the ground: and of him and of all the men that are with him there shall not be left so much as one. Moreover, if he be gotten into a city, then shall all Israel bring ropes to that city, and we will draw it into the river, until there be not one small stone found there."

And Absalom and all the men of Israel said, " The counsel of Hushai is better than the counsel of Ahithophel." For the Lord appointed to defeat the good counsel of Ahithophel, that He might bring evil upon Absalom.

Then said Hushai unto Zadok and to Abiathar the priests, " Thus and thus did Ahithophel counsel Absalom and the elders of Israel: and thus and thus have I counselled. Now therefore send quickly, and tell David, saying, ' Lodge not this night in the plains of the wilderness, but speedily pass over; lest the king be swallowed up, and all the people that are with him.' "

Now Jonathan and Ahimaaz stayed by Enrogel, for they might not be seen to come into the city. Nevertheless, a lad saw them, and told Absalom. But they went away quickly, and came to a man's house in Bahurim, which had a well in his court; whither they went down. And the woman spread a covering over the well's mouth, and spread ground corn thereon; and the thing was not known.

And when Absalom's servants came to the woman of the house, they said, " Where are Ahimaaz and Jonathan? "

And the woman said, " They be gone over the brook of water." And when they had sought them and could not find them, they returned to Jerusalem.

And after they were departed, Ahimaaz and Jonathan came up out of the well, and went and told king David, and said, " Arise, and pass quickly over the water: for thus hath Ahithophel counselled against you."

Then David arose, and all the people that were with him, and they passed over Jordan before the morning light.

And when Ahithophel saw that his counsel was not followed, he saddled his ass, and arose, and got him home to his house, to his city, and put his household in order, and hanged himself, and died, and was buried in the sepulchre of his father.

And Absalom made Amasa captain of the host instead of Joab. And Absalom passed over Jordan, he and all the men of Israel with him, and pitched in the land of Gilead.

Then David came to Mahanaim. And it came to pass, when David was come to Mahanaim, that Shobi the son of Nahash of the children of Ammon, and Machir, and Barzillai the Gileadite, brought beds, and basins, and earthen vessels, and wheat, and barley, and flour, and parched corn, and beans, and lentiles, and parched pulse, and honey, and butter, and sheep, and cheese of kine, for David, and for the people that were with him, to eat: for they said, "The people are hungry, and weary, and thirsty, in the wilderness."

And David numbered the people that were with him, and set captains of thousands and captains of hundreds over them. And David sent forth a third part of the people under the hand of Joab, and a third part under the hand of Abishai, Joab's brother, and a third part under the hand of Ittai the Gittite.

And the king said unto the people, "I will surely go forth with you myself also."

But the people answered, "Thou shalt not go forth: for if we flee away, they will not care for us; neither if half of us die, will they care for us: but now thou art worth ten thousand of us: therefore now succour us out of the city."

And the king said unto them, "What seemeth you best I will do." And the king stood by the gate side, and all the people came out by hundreds and by thousands. And the king commanded Joab and Abishai and Ittai, saying, "Deal gently for my sake with the young man, even with Absalom." And all the people heard when the king gave all the captains charge concerning Absalom.

So the people went out into the field against Israel: and the battle was in the wood of Ephraim, where the people of Israel were slain before the servants of David, and there was there a great slaughter that day of twenty thousand men. For the battle was there scattered over the face of all the country. And the wood devoured more people that day than the sword devoured.

And Absalom met the servants of David. And Absalom rode upon a mule, and the mule went under the thick boughs of a great oak, and his head caught hold of the oak, and he was taken up between the heaven and the earth; and the mule that was under him went away.

And a certain man saw it, and told Joab, and said, "Behold, I saw Absalom hanged in an oak."

And Joab said unto the man, "And behold, thou sawest him, and why didst thou not smite him there to the ground? and I would have given thee ten shekels of silver, and a girdle."

And the man said, "Though I should receive a thousand shekels of silver in mine hand, yet would I not put forth mine hand against the king's son: for in our hearing the king charged thee and Abishai and Ittai, saying, 'Beware that none touch the young man Absalom.' Otherwise I should have wrought falsehood against mine own life: for there is no matter hid from the king, and thou thyself wouldest have set thyself against me."

Then said Joab, "I may not tarry thus with thee." And he took three darts in his hand, and thrust them through the heart of Absalom, while he was yet alive in the midst of the oak. And ten young men that bare Joab's armour compassed about and smote Absalom and slew him.

And Joab blew the trumpet, and the people returned from pursuing after Israel: for Joab held back the people. And they took Absalom, and cast him into a great pit in the wood, and laid a very great heap of stones upon him: and all Israel fled.

Then said Joab to Cushi, "Go, tell the king what thou hast seen." And Cushi bowed himself unto Joab, and ran.

And David sat between the two gates: and the watchman went up to the roof over the gate unto the wall, and lifted up his eyes, and looked, and behold a man running alone. And the watchman cried, and told the king. And the king said, "If he be alone there is tidings in his mouth." And he came apace, and drew near.

And behold, Cushi came; and Cushi said, "Tidings, my lord the king: for the Lord hath avenged thee this day of all them that rose up against thee."

And the king said unto Cushi, "Is the young man Absalom safe?"

And Cushi answered, "The enemies of my lord the king, and all that rise against thee to do thee hurt, be as that young man is."

And the king was much moved, and went up to the chamber over the gate, and wept: and as he went, thus he said, "O my son Absalom! my son, my son Absalom! would God I had died for thee, O Absalom, my son, my son!"

And it was told Joab, "Behold, the king weepeth and mourneth for Absalom." And the victory that day was turned into mourning unto all the people: for the people heard say how the king was grieved for his son. And the people got them by stealth that day into the city, as people being ashamed steal away when they flee in battle.

But the king covered his face, and the king cried with a loud voice, "O my son Absalom! O Absalom, my son, my son!"

And Joab came into the house to the king, and said, "Thou hast shamed this day the faces of all thy servants, which have saved thy life, and the lives of thy sons and of thy daughters, and the lives of thy wives, in that thou lovest thine enemies, and hatest thy friends: for thou hast declared this day, that thou regardest neither princes nor servants: for this day I perceive, that if Absalom had lived, and all we had died, then it had pleased thee well. Now therefore arise, go forth, and speak comfortably unto thy servants, for I swear by the Lord, if thou go not forth, there will not tarry one with thee this night; and that will be worse unto thee than all the evil that befell thee from thy youth until now."

Then the king arose, and sat in the gate. And they told the people saying, "Behold, the king doth sit in the gate." And all the people came before the king.

And the king sent to Zadok and to Abiathar the priests, saying, "Speak unto the elders of Judah, saying, 'Why are ye the last to bring the king back to his house? seeing the speech of all Israel is come to the king. Ye are my brethren, ye are my bones and my flesh: wherefore then are ye the last to bring back the king?'"

And he bowed the heart of all the men of Judah, even as the heart of one man; so that they sent this word unto the king, "Return thou, and all thy servants." So the king returned, and came to Jordan. And Judah came to Gilgal, to go to meet the king, to conduct the king over Jordan.

And there went over a ferry-boat to carry over the king's household, and to do what he thought good.

And Shimei the son of Gera, hasted and came down with the men of Judah to meet king David. And there were a thousand men of Benjamin with him, and Ziba the servant of the house of Saul, and his fifteen sons and his twenty servants, with him, and they went over Jordan before the king.

And Shimei fell down before the king, as he was come over Jordan, and said, "Let not my lord impute iniquity unto me, neither do thou remember that which thy servant did perversely the day that my lord the king went out of Jerusalem, that the king should take it to his heart. For thy servant doth know that I have sinned; therefore behold, I am come the first this day of all the house of Joseph to meet my lord the king."

But Abishai said, "Shall not Shimei be put to death for this, because he cursed the Lord's anointed?"

And David said, " Shall there any man be put to death this day in Israel? for do not I know that I am this day king over Israel? " Therefore the king said unto Shimei, " Thou shalt not die."

And Mephibosheth the son of Jonathan came down to meet the king, and had neither dressed his feet, nor trimmed his beard, nor washed his clothes, from the day the king departed until the day he came again in peace.

And the king said unto him, " Wherefore wentest not thou with me, Mephibosheth? "

And he answered, " My lord, O king, my servant deceived me: for thy servant said, 'I will saddle me an ass, that I may ride thereon, and go to the king; because thy servant is lame.' And he hath slandered thy servant unto my lord the king; but my lord the king is as an angel of God: do therefore what is good in thine eyes. Thou didst set thy servant among them that did eat at thine own table. What right therefore have I yet to cry any more unto the king? "

And the king said unto him, " Why speakest thou any more of thy matters? I have said, 'Thou and Ziba divide the land.' "

And Mephibosheth said unto the king, " Yea, let him take all, forasmuch as my lord the king is come again in peace unto his own house."

And David came to his house at Jerusalem; and the king took the ten women his concubines, whom he had left to keep the house, and put them in ward, and fed them. So they were shut up unto the day of their death, living in widowhood.

And David spake unto the Lord the words of this song in the day that the Lord had delivered him out of the hand of all his enemies; and he said:

" The Lord is my rock, and my fortress, and my deliverer;
The God of my rock; in him will I trust:
He is my shield, and the horn of my salvation,
My high tower, and my refuge, my saviour;
Thou savest me from violence.

When the waves of death compassed me,
The floods of ungodly men made me afraid;
The sorrows of hell compassed me about;
The snares of death prevented me;

In my distress I called upon the Lord, and cried to my
God:
And he did hear my voice out of his temple,
And my cry did enter into his ears.
He sent from above, he took me;
He drew me out of many waters:
He delivered me from my strong enemy,
And from them that hated me:
For they were too strong for me.
They prevented me in the day of my calamity:
But the Lord was my stay.
For who is God, save the Lord?
And who is a rock, save our God?
God is my strength and power:
And he maketh my way perfect.
Thou hast also given me the shield of thy salvation:
And thy gentleness hath made me great."

GOD SAVE KING SOLOMON!

NOW KING DAVID was old and stricken in years; and his son Adonijah, the son of Haggith, exalted himself, saying, "I will be king." And he prepared him chariots and horsemen, and fifty men to run before him: he was a very goodly man; and his mother bare him after Absalom. And he conferred with Joab the son of Zeruiah, and with Abiathar the priest: and they, following Adonijah, helped him.

But Zadok the priest, and Benaiah the son of Jehoiada, and Nathan the prophet, and Shimei, and Rei, and the mighty men which belonged to David, were not with Adonijah.

And Adonijah slew sheep, and oxen, and fat cattle, and called all his brethren, the king's sons, and all the men of Judah, the king's servants. But Nathan the prophet, and the mighty men, and Solomon, his brother, he called not.

Wherefore Nathan spake unto Bath-sheba, the mother of Solomon, saying, "Hast thou not heard that Adonijah the son of Haggith doth reign, and David our lord knoweth it not? Now therefore come, let me, I pray thee, give thee counsel, that thou mayest save thine own life, and the life of thy son Solomon. Go, and get thee in unto king David, and say unto him, 'Didst not thou, my lord, O king, swear unto thine handmaid, saying, "Assuredly Solomon thy son shall reign after me, and he shall sit upon my throne"? why then doth Adonijah reign?' Behold, while thou yet talkest there with the king, I also will come in after thee, and confirm thy words."

And Bath-sheba went in unto the king into the chamber. And she bowed and did obeisance unto the king. And the king said, "What wouldest thou?"

And she said unto him, "My lord, thou swarest by the Lord thy God unto thine handmaid, saying, 'Assuredly Solomon thy son shall reign after me, and he shall sit upon my throne.' And now, behold Adonijah reigneth; and my lord, thou knowest it not. And he hath slain oxen, and fat cattle, and sheep in abundance, and hath called all the sons of the king, and Abiathar the priest, and Joab the captain of the host, but Solomon thy servant hath he not called. And thou, my lord, O king, the eyes of all Israel are upon thee, that thou shouldest tell them who shall sit on the throne of my lord the king after him. Otherwise it shall come to pass, when my lord the king shall sleep with his fathers, that I and my son Solomon shall be counted offenders."

And lo, while she yet talked with the king, Nathan the prophet also came in. And he bowed himself before the king with his face to the ground. And Nathan said, "My lord, O king, hast thou said, 'Adonijah shall reign after me, and he shall sit upon my throne?' For he is gone down this day, and hath slain oxen, and fat cattle, and sheep in abundance, and hath called all the king's sons, and the captains of the host, and Abiathar, the priest, and behold, they eat and drink before him, and say, 'God save king Adonijah.' But me, even me thy servant, and Zadok the priest, and Benaiah, and thy servant Solomon, hath he not called. Is this thing done by my lord the king, and thou hast not showed unto thy servant who should sit on the throne of my lord the king after him?"

Then king David answered and said, "Call Bath-sheba." And she came into the king's presence, and stood before the king. And the king sware, and said, "As the Lord liveth, that hath redeemed my soul out of all distress, even as I sware unto thee by the Lord God of Israel, saying, 'Assuredly Solomon thy son shall reign after me, and he shall sit upon my throne in my stead;' even so will I certainly do this day."

Then Bath-sheba bowed with her face to the earth, and did reverence to the king, and said, "Let my lord king David live for ever."

And king David said, "Call me Zadok the priest, and Nathan

the prophet, and Benaiah the son of Jehoiada." And they came before the king. The king said unto them, "Take you the servants of your lord, and cause Solomon my son to ride upon mine own mule, and bring him down to Gihon: And let Zadok the priest and Nathan the prophet anoint him there king over Israel. And blow ye the trumpet, and say, 'God save king Solomon.' Then ye shall come up after him, that he may come and sit upon my throne; for he shall be king in my stead; and I have appointed him to be ruler over Israel and over Judah."

And Benaiah the son of Jehoiada answered and said, "Amen! As the Lord hath been with my lord the king, even so be he with Solomon, and make his throne greater than the throne of my lord king David."

So Zadok, and Nathan, and Benaiah went down, and caused Solomon to ride upon king David's mule, and brought him to Gihon. And Zadok the priest took an horn of oil out of the tabernacle, and anointed Solomon. And they blew the trumpet, and all the people said, "God save king Solomon."

And all the people came up after him and the people piped with pipes, and rejoiced with great joy, so that the earth rent with the sound of them.

And Adonijah and all the guests that were with him heard it as they had made an end of eating. And when Joab heard the sound of the trumpet, he said, "Wherefore is this noise of the city being in an uproar?"

And while he yet spake, behold, Jonathan the son of Abiathar the priest came, and said to Adonijah, "Verily our lord king David hath made Solomon king. And the king hath sent with him Zadok the priest, and Nathan the prophet, and Benaiah the son of Jehoiada, and the Cherethites, and the Pelethites, and they have caused him to ride upon the king's mule; and Zadok, and Nathan have anointed him king in Gihon: and they are come up from thence rejoicing, so that the city rang again. This is the noise that ye have heard. And also Solomon sitteth on the throne of the kingdom. And moreover the king's servants came to bless our lord king David, saying, 'God make the name of Solomon better than thy name, and make his throne greater than thy throne.' And the king bowed himself and said, 'Blessed be the Lord God of Israel, which hath given one to sit on my throne this day, mine eyes even seeing it.'"

And Adonijah feared because of Solomon, and arose, and went, and caught hold on the horns of the altar. And it was told Solomon, saying, "Behold, Adonijah feareth king Solomon: for lo, he hath caught hold on the horns of the altar, saying, 'Let king Solomon swear unto me today that he will not slay his servant with the sword.'"

And Solomon said, "If he will show himself a worthy man, there shall not an hair of him fall to the earth; but if wickedness shall be found in him, he shall die."

So king Solomon sent, and they brought him down from the altar. And he came and bowed himself to king Solomon. And Solomon said unto him, "Go to thine house."

THINE, O LORD, IS THE GREATNESS, AND THE POWER, AND THE GLORY, AND THE VICTORY, AND THE MAJESTY

AND DAVID assembled all the princes of Israel, the princes of the tribes, and the captains of the companies that ministered to the king, and the captains over the thousands, and captains over hundreds, and the stewards over all the substance and possession of the king, and of his sons, and the officers, and with the mighty men, and with all the valiant men unto Jerusalem.

Then David the king stood up upon his feet, and said, "Hear me, my brethren, and my people! As for me, I had it in mine heart to build an house of rest for the ark of the covenant of the Lord, and for the footstool of our God, and had made ready for the building. But God said unto me, 'Thou shalt not build an house for my name, because thou hast been a man of war, and hast shed blood.' Howbeit the Lord God of Israel chose me before all the house of my father to be king over Israel for ever: for he hath chosen Judah to be the ruler; and of the house of Judah, the house of my father; and among the sons of my father he liked me to make me king over all Israel: and of all my sons, (for the Lord hath given me many sons,) he hath chosen Solomon my son to sit upon the throne of the kingdom of the Lord over Israel.

"And he said to me, 'Solomon thy son, he shall build my house and my courts: for I have chosen him to be my son, and I will be his father. Moreover I will establish his kingdom for ever, if he be constant to do my commandments and my judgments, as at this day.'

"And thou, Solomon my son, know thou the God of thy father, and serve him with a perfect heart, and with a willing mind: for the Lord searcheth all hearts, and understandeth all the imaginations of the thoughts: if thou seek him, he will be found of thee; but if thou forsake him, he will cast thee off for ever. Take heed now; for the Lord hath chosen thee to build an house for the sanctuary: be strong, and of good courage and do it: fear not, nor be dismayed, for the Lord God, even my God, will be with thee; he will not fail thee, nor forsake thee, until thou hast finished all the work for the service of the house of the Lord."

Then David gave to Solomon his son the pattern of all that he had by the Spirit, of the courts of the house of the Lord. "All this," said David, "the Lord made me understand in writing, even all the works of this pattern."

Furthermore David said unto all the congregation, " Now I have prepared with all my might for the house of my God, the gold for things to be made of gold, and the silver for things of silver, and the brass for things of brass, the iron for things of iron, and wood for things of wood; onyx-stones, stones to be set, glistering stones of divers colors, and all manner of precious stones, and marble in abundance. Moreover, because I have set my affection to the house of my God, I have given of mine own gold and silver to the house of my God, over and above all that I have prepared for the holy house, even three thousand talents of gold, of the gold of Ophir, and seven thousand talents of refined silver to overlay the walls of the houses withal, for all manner of work to be made by the hands of artificers. And thou mayest add thereto. There are workmen with thee in abundance, hewers and workers of stone and timber, and all manner of cunning men for every manner of work. And who is willing to consecrate his service this day unto the Lord? Arise, therefore, and be doing, and the Lord be with thee."

Then the chief of the fathers and princes of the tribes of Israel, and the captains of thousands and of hundreds, with the rulers over the king's work, offered willingly, and gave for the service of the house of God. Then the people rejoiced, because with perfect heart they offered willingly to the Lord: and David the king also rejoiced with great joy.

Wherefore David blessed the Lord before all the congregation and David said, " Blessed be thou, Lord God of Israel our father, for ever and ever. Thine, O Lord is the greatness, and the power, and the glory, and the victory, and the majesty: for all that is in the heaven and in the earth is thine; thine is the kingdom, O Lord, and thou art exalted as head above all. Both riches and honor come of thee, and thou reignest over all; and in thine hand it is to make great, and to give strength unto all. Now therefore, our God, we thank thee, and praise thy glorious name.

"But who am I, and what is my people, that we should be able to offer so willingly after this sort? for all things come of thee, and of thine own have we given thee. For, O Lord our God, all this store that we have prepared to build thee an house for thine holy name cometh of thine hand, and is all thine own.

"I know also, my God, that thou triest the heart, and hast pleasure in uprightness. As for me, in the uprightness of mine heart I have willingly offered all these things. And now I have seen with joy thy people, which are present here, to offer willingly unto thee. O Lord God of Abraham, Isaac, and of Israel, our fathers, keep this for ever in the imagination of the thoughts of the heart of thy people, and prepare their heart unto thee. And give Solomon my son a perfect heart, to keep thy commandments, thy testimonies, and thy statutes, and to do all these things, and to build the palace, for which I have made provision."

And David said to all the congregation, "Now bless the Lord your God." And all the congregation blessed the Lord God of their fathers, and bowed down their heads, and worshipped the Lord, and king.

And they sacrificed sacrifices, and offered burnt-offerings unto the Lord, and did eat and drink before the Lord on that day with great gladness. And they made Solomon the son of David king the second time, and anointed him unto the Lord to be the chief governor, and Zadok to be priest.

And Solomon sat on the throne of the Lord as king instead of David his father, and prospered; and all Israel obeyed him. And all the princes, and the mighty men, and all the sons of king David, submitted themselves unto Solomon the king. And the Lord magnified Solomon exceedingly in the sight of all Israel, and bestowed upon him such royal majesty as had not been on any king before him in Israel.

David the son of Jesse reigned over all Israel forty years. And now the days of David drew nigh that he should die; and he charged Solomon his son, saying, "I go the way of all the earth: be strong therefore, and show thyself a man. And keep the charge of the Lord thy God, to walk in his ways, to keep his statutes, and his commandments, and his judgments, and his testimonies, as it is written in the law of Moses, that thou mayest prosper in all that thou doest, and whithersoever thou turnest thyself."

Now these be the last words of David, the son of Jesse, the sweet psalmist of Israel.

"The Spirit of the Lord spake by me,
And his word was in my tongue.
The God of Israel said,
'He that ruleth over men must be just,
Ruling in the fear of God.
And he shall be as the light of the morning
When the sun riseth,
Even a morning without clouds;
As the tender grass springing out of the earth
By clear shining after rain.'"

So David slept with his fathers, and was buried in the city of David. He died in a good old age, full of days, riches, and honour. And Solomon his son reigned in his stead.

"O Lord,

Behold, heaven and the heaven of heavens
cannot contain Thee."

THE SECOND BOOK OF CHRONICLES

THE FIRST AND SECOND BOOKS OF KINGS

THE PROPHETS

Amos, Hosea, Micah, Isaiah I, Zephaniah,

Jeremiah, and from Lamentations

BEHOLD, I HAVE GIVEN THEE A WISE AND AN UNDERSTANDING HEART

And Solomon the son of David was strengthened in his kingdom, and the Lord his God was with him, and magnified him exceedingly. And Solomon loved the Lord, walking in the statutes of David his father.

Then Solomon spake unto all Israel, to the captains of thousands and of hundreds, and to the judges, and to every governor in all Israel, and all the congregation went with him, to the high place that was at Gibeon, for the tabernacle of the congregation of God was there, which Moses the servant of the Lord had made in the wilderness. And Solomon went up thither to the brazen altar before the Lord, which was at the tabernacle of the congregation, and offered a thousand burnt-offerings upon it.

In that night the Lord appeared to Solomon in a dream: and God said, "Ask what I shall give thee."

And Solomon said, "Thou hast showed unto thy servant David my father great mercy, according as he walked before thee in truth, and in righteousness, and in uprightness of heart with thee; and thou hast kept for him this great kindness, that thou hast given him a son to sit on his throne, as it is this day.

"And now, O Lord my God, thou hast made thy servant king instead of David my father: and I am but a little child: I know not how to go out or come in. And thy servant is in the midst of thy people which thou hast chosen, a great people, that cannot be numbered nor counted for multitude. Give therefore thy servant an understanding heart to judge thy people, that I may discern between good and bad: for who is able to judge this thy so great a people?"

And the speech pleased the Lord, that Soloman had asked this thing. And God said unto him, " Because thou hast asked this thing, and hast not asked for thyself long life; neither hast asked riches for thyself, nor hast asked the life of thine enemies: but hast asked for thyself understanding to discern judgment; behold, I have done according to thy word, lo, I have given thee a wise and an understanding heart; so that there was none like thee before thee, neither after thee shall any arise like unto thee. And I have also given thee that which thou hast not asked, both riches, and honour; so that there shall not be any among the kings like unto thee all thy days. And if thou wilt walk in my ways, to keep my statutes and my commandments, as thy father David did walk, then I will lengthen thy days."

And Solomon awoke; and behold, it was a dream. Then Solomon returned from his journey to the high place at Gibeon, and came to Jerusalem, and stood before the ark of the covenant of the Lord, and offered up burnt-offerings, and offered peace-offerings, and made a feast to all his servants.

Then came there two women, that were harlots, unto the king, and stood before him. And the one woman said, "O my lord, I and this woman dwell in one house; and I was delivered of a child with her in the house. And it came to pass the third day after I was delivered, that this woman was delivered also: and we were together, there was no stranger with us in the house. And this woman's child died in the night, because she overlaid it. And she arose at midnight, and took my son from beside me, while thine handmaid slept, and laid it in her bosom, and laid her dead child in my bosom. And when I arose in the morning to give my child suck, behold, it was dead: but when I had considered it in the morning, behold, it was not my son, which I did bear."

And the other woman said, "Nay; but the living is my son, the dead is thy son."

And the first said, "No; but the dead is thy son, and the living is my son." Thus they spake before the king.

Then said the king, "The one saith, 'This is my son that liveth, and thy son is dead;' and the other saith, 'Nay; but thy son is the dead, and my son is the living.'"

Then said the king, "Bring me a sword." And they brought him a sword. And the king said, "Divide the living child in two, and give half to the one, and half to the other."

Then spake the woman whose the living child was unto the king, for she yearned for her son, and she said, "O my lord, give her the living child, and in no wise slay it."

But the other said, "Let it be neither mine nor thine, but divide it."

Then the king answered and said, "Give the first the living child, and in no wise slay it: she is the mother thereof."

And all Israel heard of the judgment which the king had judged; and they feared the king: for they saw that the wisdom of God was in him, to do judgment.

THE HOUSE WHICH I BUILD IS GREAT FOR GREAT IS OUR GOD

And Hiram king of Tyre sent his servants with greetings unto Solomon; for he had heard that they had anointed him king in the room of his father; for Hiram was ever a lover of David.

And Solomon sent to Hiram saying, "Now the Lord my God hath given me rest on every side, so that there is neither adversary nor evil occurrent. And behold, I purpose to build an house unto the name of the Lord my God, as the Lord spake unto David my father, saying, 'Thy son, whom I will set upon thy throne in thy room, he shall build an house unto my name.'

And as thou didst deal with David my father, and didst send him cedars to build him an house to dwell therein, even so deal with me.

"Behold, I build an house to the name of the Lord my God, to dedicate it to him, and to burn before him sweet incense. And the house which I build is great: for great is our God above all gods. But who is able to build him an house, seeing the heaven and heaven of heavens cannot contain him? Who am I then that I should build him an house, save only to burn sacrifice before him?

"Send me now therefore a man cunning to work in gold, and in silver, and in brass, and in iron, and in purple, and crimson, and blue, to grave with the cunning men that are with me in Judah, and in Jerusalem, whom David my father did provide.

"Send me also cedar-trees, fir-trees, and algum-trees out of Lebanon: for I know that thy servants have skill to cut timber in Lebanon. And behold, my servants shall be with thy servants, even to prepare me timber in abundance: for the house which I am about to build shall be wonderful and great.

"And behold, I will give to thy servants, the hewers that cut timber, twenty thousand measures of beaten wheat, and twenty thousand measures of barley, and twenty thousand baths of wine, and twenty thousand baths of oil."

And it came to pass when Hiram heard the words of Solomon, that he rejoiced greatly, and said, "Blessed be the Lord this day, which hath given unto David a wise son over this great people."

Then Hiram king of Tyre answered in writing, which he sent to Solomon, "Because the Lord hath loved his people, he hath made thee king over them. Blessed be the Lord God of Israel, that made heaven and earth, who hath given to David the king a wise son, endued with prudence and understanding, that might build an house for the Lord, and an house for his kingdom.

"I have considered the things which thou sentest to me for: and now I have sent a cunning man, endued with understanding, skillful to work in gold, and in silver, in brass, in iron, in stone, and in timber, in purple, in blue, and in fine linen, and in crimson; also to grave any manner of graving, and to find out every device which shall be put to him.

"And I will do all thy desire concerning timber of cedar, and concerning timber of fir. And we will cut wood out of Lebanon, as much as thou shalt need; and we will bring it to thee in floats by sea to Joppa; and thou shalt carry it up to Jerusalem. And thou shalt accomplish my desire in giving food for my household. Now therefore the wheat, and the barley, and the oil, and the wine which my lord hath spoken of, let him send unto his servants."

And Solomon gave Hiram twenty thousand measures of wheat for food to his household, and twenty thousand measures of pure oil; this gave Solomon to Hiram year by year. And there was peace between Hiram and Solomon; and they two made a league together.

And Solomon numbered all the strangers that were in the land of Israel, and he set threescore and ten thousand of them to be bearers of burdens, and fourscore thousand to be hewers in the mountain, and three thousand and six hundred overseers to set the people a-work. And the king commanded, and they brought great stones, costly stones, and hewed stones, to lay the foundation of the house. And Solomon's builders, and Hiram's builders, and the stone-squarers, did hew them: so they prepared timber and stones to build the house. Thus Solomon began to build the house of the Lord at Jerusalem.

In the four hundred and eightieth year after the children of Israel were come out of the land of Egypt, in the fourth year of Solomon's reign over Israel, he began to build the house of the Lord.

And the house which king Solomon built for the Lord measured three score cubits in length, and the breadth thereof twenty cubits, and the heighth thereof thirty cubits.

And the house when it was in building, was built of stone made ready before it was brought thither; so that there was neither hammer nor ax nor any tool of iron heard in the house while it was in building.

And Solomon built the walls of the house within with boards of cedar, both the floor and the walls and the ceiling; and covered the floor with planks of fir.

And he built the walls within for an oracle, for the most holy place. And within the oracle was a space of twenty cubits, wherein the Ark of the Covenant of the Lord was to be placed. And he overlaid the oracle with pure gold. And he drew chains of gold across before the oracle. And he made the veil of blue, and purple, and crimson, and fine linen, and wrought cherubims thereon.

And Solomon made two cherubims and he set the cherubims within the oracle, and they stretched forth their wings so that the wing of one touched the wing of the other in the midst of the oracle. And he overlaid the cherubims with gold.

And he carved all the walls of the house round about with carved figures of cherubims and palm trees and open flowers. And Solomon overlaid the house within with pure gold. And the floor of the house he overlaid with gold within and without. And he reared up pillars before the temple, one on the right hand and one on the left. And he made the court of the priests, and the great court, and doors for the court, and overlaid the doors of them with brass.

And he made the molten sea, and it was round, ten cubits from brim to brim. And it stood upon twelve oxen, three looking in each direction; and the sea was set upon them. And the sea and the oxen were cast of bright brass. And the brim of the sea was wrought like the brim of a cup, with flowers of lilies; it contained two thousand baths. And the sea was for the priests to wash in to purify themselves. And he set the sea on the right side of the temple over against the south.

And Solomon made all the vessels that pertained unto the house of the Lord: the altar of incense that was by the oracle, he overlaid with pure gold. And he made ten candlesticks of gold, and set them in the temple, five on the right hand, and five on the left. And he made ten tables of gold whereupon the shew-bread was; and set them five on the right side and five on the left; and there were bowls, and snuffers, and basons, and spoons, and censers, and pots and shovels of pure gold. And Solomon left the vessels unweighed, because there were exceeding many, neither was their weight known.

Moreover, Solomon made an altar of brass for the sacrifice; and the pots and the shovels and the basons all were of bright brass. And he made also ten lavers, and put five on the right hand, and five on the left to wash in them such things as were offered for the burnt-offering. But the molten sea was for the priests to wash in.

Thus all the work that Solomon made for the house of the Lord was finished: and Solomon brought in all the things that David, his father, had dedicated; and the silver and the gold, and all the instruments, put he among the treasures of the house of God. In the eleventh year was the house finished throughout.

But Solomon was also building his own house. And it was all built of costly hewed stones. And he made a porch for the throne where he might judge, even the porch of judgment.

And Solomon made affinity with Pharaoh, king of Egypt, and took Pharaoh's daughter, and brought her into the city of David. And he also made an house for Pharaoh's daughter, whom he had taken to wife. So was ended all the work that king Solomon made.

THE HEAVENS CANNOT CONTAIN THEE: HOW MUCH LESS THIS HOUSE WHICH I HAVE BUILT!

THEN SOLOMON assembled the elders of Israel, and all the heads of the tribes, and the chief of the fathers of the children of Israel, unto Jerusalem, to bring up the Ark of the Covenant of the Lord, out of the city of David, which is Zion.

And all the elders of Israel came; and the Levites took up the Ark. And they brought the Ark, and the tabernacle of the congregation, and all the holy vessels that were in the tabernacle. Also king Solomon, and all the congregation of Israel that were assembled before the Ark, sacrificed sheep and oxen.

And the priests brought in the Ark of the Covenant of the Lord into the oracle, the most holy place, even under the wings of the cherubims: for the cherubims spread forth their wings over the place of the Ark, and the cherubims covered the Ark, and the staves thereof. There was nothing in the Ark save the two tables of stone, the Ten Commandments, which Moses put therein at Horeb, when the Lord made a covenant with the children of Israel when they came out of Egypt. And they set up the veil and covered the Ark of the testimony.

And it came to pass, when the priests were come out of the holy place, also the Levites which were the singers, being arrayed in white linen, when they lifted up their voice with the trumpets and cymbals and instruments of music, and praised the Lord saying: " For he is good; for his mercy endureth for ever:" that the house was filled with a cloud, even the house of the Lord, so that the priests could not stand to minister by reason of the cloud; for the glory of the Lord filled the house of God.

And the king turned his face, and blessed the whole congregation of Israel; and all the congregation of Israel stood. And

Solomon stood before the altar of the Lord in the presence of all the congregation, and spread forth his hands, and kneeled down upon his knees before the congregation, and spread forth his hands toward heaven, and said,

"O Lord God of Israel, there is no God like thee in the heaven, nor in the earth; which keepest covenant, and showest mercy unto thy servants, that walk before thee with all their hearts. But will God in very deed dwell with men on the earth? Behold, heaven and the heaven of heavens cannot contain thee: how much less this house which I have built! Have respect therefore to the prayer of thy servant, and to his supplication, O Lord my God, to hearken unto the cry and the prayer which thy servant prayeth before thee: that thine eyes may be open upon this house day and night. Hearken therefore unto the supplications of thy servant, and of thy people Israel, which they shall make toward this place. Hear thou from thy dwelling-place, even from heaven, and when thou hearest, forgive.

"When thy people Israel be smitten down before the enemy because they have sinned against thee, and shall turn again to thee, and confess thy name, and pray, and make supplication unto thee in this house, then hear thou in heaven, and forgive the sin of thy people Israel, and bring them again unto the land which thou gavest unto their fathers.

"When heaven is shut up, and there is no rain, because they have sinned against thee; if they pray toward this place, and confess thy name, and turn from their sin, then hear thou in heaven, and forgive the sin of thy servants, and of thy people Israel, and teach them the good way wherein they should walk, and give rain upon the land which thou hast given unto thy people for an inheritance.

"If there be in the land famine, if there be pestilence, blasting, mildew, locust, or if there be caterpillar; if their enemy besiege them in the land of their cities; whatsoever plague, whatsoever sickness there be, what prayer and supplication soever be made by any man, or by all thy people Israel, which shall know every man the plague of his own heart, and spread forth his hands toward this house, then hear thou in heaven thy dwelling-place, and forgive, and do, and give to every man according to his ways, whose heart thou knowest. For thou, even thou only, knowest the hearts of all the children of men; that they may fear thee all the days that they live in the land which thou gavest unto our fathers.

"Now, my God, let, I beseech thee, thine eyes be open, and let thine ears be attent unto the prayer that is made in this place. Now therefore arise, O Lord God, into thy resting-place, thou, and the ark of thy strength: let thy priests, O Lord God, be clothed with salvation, and let thy saints rejoice in goodness."

And when Solomon had made an end of praying all this prayer and supplication unto the Lord, he arose, and stood and blessed all the congregation of Israel with a loud voice, saying, "Blessed be the Lord, that hath given rest unto his people Israel, according to all that he promised: there hath not failed one word of all his good promise, which he promised by the hand of Moses, his servant. The Lord our God be with us, as he was with our fathers: let him not leave us, nor forsake us: that he may incline our hearts unto him to walk in all his ways, and keep his commandments, and his statutes, and his judgments, which he commanded our fathers; that all the people of the earth may know that the Lord is God, and that there is none else. Let your heart therefore be perfect with the Lord our God, to walk in his statutes, and to keep his commandments, as at this day."

And the king, and all Israel with him, offered sacrifice before the Lord. So the king and all the people dedicated the house of God.

Thus Solomon finished the house of the Lord, and the king's house; and all that came into Solomon's heart to make in the house of the Lord, and in his own house, he prosperously effected.

THE QUEEN OF SHEBA HEARD OF THE FAME OF SOLOMON

So Solomon was king over all Israel, and reigned over all kingdoms from the river unto the land of the Philistines, and unto the border of Egypt. They brought presents, and served Solomon all the days of his life, for he had dominion over all the region on this side the river, and he had peace on all sides round about him. And Judah and Israel dwelt safely, every man under his vine and under his fig-tree, from Dan even to Beer-Sheba, all the days of Solomon.

And God gave Solomon wisdom and understanding exceeding much, and largeness of heart, even as the sand that is on the sea-shore. And Solomon's wisdom excelled the wisdom of all the children of the east country, and all the wisdom of Egypt. And there came of all people to hear the wisdom of Solomon, from all kings of the earth, which had heard of his wisdom.

And they brought every man his present, vessels of silver, and vessels of gold, and raiment, harness, and spices, horses, and mules, a rate year by year. And all the kings of Arabia and governors of the country brought gold and silver to Solomon. And Solomon made a great throne of ivory, and overlaid it with pure gold. And there were six steps to the throne, with a footstool of gold. And twelve lions stood there on the one side and on the other upon the six steps. There was not the like made in any kingdom. And all the drinking vessels of king Solomon were of gold, and all the vessels of the house of the forest of Lebanon were of pure gold, for the king's ships went to Tarshish with the servants of Hiram, bringing gold, and silver, ivory, and apes, and peacocks. And king Solomon passed all the kings of the earth in riches and wisdom.

And when the queen of Sheba heard of the fame of Solomon, she came to prove Solomon with hard questions at Jerusalem, with a very great company, and camels that bare spices, and gold in abundance, and precious stones: and when she was come to Solomon, she communed with him of all that was in her heart. And Solomon told her all her questions; there was nothing hid from Solomon which he told her not.

And when the queen of Sheba had seen the wisdom of Solomon, and the house that he had built, and the meat of his table, and the sitting of his servants, and the attendance of his ministers, and their apparel; his cup-bearers also, and their apparel; and his ascent by which he went up into the house of the Lord; there was no more spirit in her.

And she said to the king, "It was a true report which I heard in mine own land of thine acts, and of thy wisdom: howbeit, I believed not their words, until I came, and mine eyes had seen it: and behold, the one half of the greatness of thy wisdom was not told me, for thou exceedest the fame that I heard. Happy are thy men, and happy are these thy servants, which stand continually before thee, and hear thy wisdom. Blessed be the Lord thy God, which delighted in thee to set thee on his throne, to be king for the Lord thy God: because thy God loved Israel, to establish them for ever, therefore made he thee king over them, to do judgment and justice."

And she gave the king an hundred and twenty talents of gold, and of spices very great store, and precious stones; there came no more such abundance of spices as these which the queen of Sheba gave to king Solomon.

And king Solomon gave unto the queen of Sheba all her desire, whatsoever she asked, besides that which Solomon gave her of his royal bounty. So she turned and went to her own country, she and her servants.

THE PROVERBS OF SOLOMON, KING OF ISRAEL

And all of the kings of the earth sought the presence of Solomon, to hear his wisdom that God had put in his heart. And he spake three thousand proverbs: and his songs were a thousand and five. And he spake of trees, from the cedar-tree that is in Lebanon, even unto the hyssop that springeth out of the wall; and he spake also of beasts, and of fowl, and of creeping things, and of fishes. For he was wiser than all men; and his fame was in all nations round about.

(The wisdom of king Solomon may be read in the book of Proverbs.)

"A wise man will hear, and will increase learning."

BUT WHEN SOLOMON WAS OLD, HE LOVED MANY STRANGE WOMEN

Better a poor and a wise child than an old and foolish king, who will no more be admonished.

But king Solomon loved many strange women, together with the daughter of Pharaoh, women of the nations concerning which the Lord said unto the children of Israel, "Ye shall not go in to them, neither shall they come in unto you: for surely they will turn away your heart after their gods." Solomon clave unto these in love.

And it came to pass, when Solomon was old, that his wives turned away his heart, and his heart was not perfect with the Lord his God, as was the heart of David his father. And Solomon did evil in the sight of the Lord, and did build high places for the gods of all his strange wives.

And the Lord was angry with Solomon, because his heart was turned away from the Lord God of Israel, which had appeared unto him twice, and had commanded him concerning this thing. But he kept not that which the Lord commanded.

Wherefore the Lord said unto Solomon, " Forasmuch as this is done of thee, and thou hast not kept my covenant and my statutes which I have commanded thee, I will surely rend the kingdom from thee, and will give it to thy servant. Notwithstanding, in thy days I will not do it for David thy father's sake, but I will rend it out of the hand of thy son. Howbeit, I will not rend away all the kingdom; but will give one tribe to thy son, for David my servant's sake, and for Jerusalem's sake which I have chosen."

Now Jeroboam the son of Nebat, Solomon's servant, was a mighty man of valour. And Solomon seeing the young man, that he was industrious, made him ruler over all the charge of the house of Joseph.

And it came to pass at that time, when Jeroboam went out of Jerusalem, that the prophet Ahijah found him in the way. And Jeroboam had clad himself with a new garment; and they two were alone in the field. And Ahijah caught the new garment that was on him, and rent it in twelve pieces, and said to Jeroboam, " Take thee ten pieces, for thus saith the Lord, the God of Israel, 'Behold, I will rend the kingdom out of the hand of Solomon, and will give ten tribes to thee, because Solomon has forsaken me, and has worshipped other gods, and has not walked in my ways, to do that which is right in mine eyes, and to keep my statutes and my judgments, as did David his father. Howbeit, I will not take the whole kingdom out of his hand, but he shall have one tribe for my servant David's sake, and for Jerusalem's sake, the city which I have chosen out of all the tribes of Israel. I will make Solomon prince all the days of his life for David my servant's sake, whom I chose, because he kept my commandments and my statutes. But I will take the kingdom out of his son's hand, and will give it unto thee, even ten tribes. And unto his son will I give one tribe, that David my servant may have a light alway before me in Jerusalem, the city which I have chosen to put my name there. And I will take thee, and thou shalt reign according to all that thy soul desireth, and shalt be king over Israel. And it shall be, if thou wilt hearken unto all that I command thee, and wilt walk in my ways, and do that is right in my sight, to keep my statutes and my commandments, as David my servant did, that I will be with thee, and build thee a sure house, as I built for David, and will give Israel unto thee.' "

Solomon sought therefore to kill Jeroboam, and Jeroboam arose, and fled into Egypt, and was in Egypt until the death of Solomon.

And the time that Solomon reigned in Jerusalem over all Israel was forty years. And Solomon slept with his fathers, and was buried in the city of David his father. And Rehoboam his son reigned in his stead.

ISRAEL REBELLED AGAINST THE HOUSE OF DAVID

And Rehoboam went to Shechem: for to Shechem came all Israel to make him king.

And it came to pass, when Jeroboam the son of Nebat, who was in Egypt, whither he had fled from the presence of Solomon, heard it, that Jeroboam returned out of Egypt. And they sent and called him.

So Jeroboam and all Israel came and spake to Rehoboam, saying, "Thy father made our yoke grievous: now therefore ease thou somewhat the grievous servitude of thy father, and his heavy yoke that he put upon us, and we will serve thee."

And he said unto them, "Depart yet for three days, then come again to me." And the people departed.

And king Rehoboam consulted with the old men that stood before Solomon his father while he yet lived, and said, "How do ye advise that I may answer this people?"

And they spake unto him, saying, "If thou be kind to this people, and please them, and speak good words to them, they will be thy servants for ever."

But he forsook the counsel which the old men gave him, and took counsel with the young men that were brought up with him, that stood before him. And he said unto them, "What advice give ye, that we may return answer to this people, which have spoken to me, saying, 'Ease somewhat the yoke that thy father did put upon us'?"

And the young men that were brought up with him, spake unto him, saying, "Thus shalt thou answer the people, 'My little finger shall be thicker than my father's loins. For whereas my father put a heavy yoke upon you, I will put more to your yoke: my father chastised you with whips, but I will chastise you with scorpions.'"

So Jeroboam and all the people came to Rehoboam on the third day, as the king bade. And king Rehoboam forsook the counsel of the old men, and answered them roughly after the advice of the young men, saying, "My father made your yoke heavy, but I will add thereto; my father chastised you with whips, but I will chastise you with scorpions." So the king hearkened not unto the people.

And when all Israel saw that the king would not hearken unto them, the people answered the king, saying, "What portion have we in David? neither have we inheritance in the son of Jesse: to your tents, O Israel; now see to thine own house, David." So Israel departed unto their tents.

Then king Rehoboam sent Adoram, who was over the tribute; and all Israel stoned him with stones, that he died.

So Israel rebelled against the house of David unto this day. But as for the children of Israel which dwelt in the cities of Judah, Rehoboam reigned over them.

And it came to pass when all Israel heard that Jeroboam was come again, that they sent and called him unto the congregation, and made him king over all Israel. There was none that followed the house of David, but the tribe of Judah only.

And when Rehoboam was come to Jerusalem, he assembled all the house of Judah, with the tribe of Benjamin, an hundred and four score thousand chosen men, which were warriors, to fight against the house of Israel, to bring the kingdom again to Rehoboam the son of Solomon.

But the word of God came unto Shemaiah the man of God, saying, "Speak unto Rehoboam the son of Solomon, king of Judah, and unto all the house of Judah and Benjamin, and to the remnant of the people, saying, 'Thus saith the Lord, "Ye shall not go up, nor fight against your brethren the children of Israel. Return every man to his house; for this thing is from me." ' "

They hearkened therefore to the word of the Lord, and returned, according to the word of the Lord.

JEROBOAM, KING OF ISRAEL MADE TWO CALVES OF GOLD

Then Jeroboam built Shechem in mount Ephraim, and dwelt therein. And Jeroboam said in his heart, "If this people go up to do sacrifice in the house of the Lord at Jerusalem, then shall the heart of this people turn again unto Rehoboam king of Judah, and they shall kill me, and the kingdom return to the house of David."

Whereupon Jeroboam made two calves of gold, and said unto the people, " It is too much for you to go up to Jerusalem: behold thy gods, O Israel, which brought thee up out of the land of Egypt." And he set the one in Bethel, and the other put he in Dan. And he made priests of the lowest of the people, which were not of the sons of Levi.

And Jeroboam ordained a feast in the eighth month, on the fifteenth day of the month, like unto the feast that is in Judah. And he offered upon the altar, and sacrificed unto the calves that he had made, and ordained a feast unto the children of Israel.

And behold, there came a man of God out of Judah unto Bethel. And he cried against the altar and said, "O altar, altar! thus saith the Lord: ' Behold, a child shall be born unto the house of David, Josiah by name; and upon thee shall he offer the priests of the high places that burn incense upon thee, and men's bones shall be burnt upon thee.' And this is the sign which the Lord hath spoken: ' Behold, the altar shall be rent, and the ashes that are upon it shall be poured out.' "

And Jeroboam stood by the altar to burn incense. And it came to pass when he heard the saying of the man of God, he put forth his hand to lay hold on the man of God, and his hand which he put forth, dried up, so that he could not pull it in again to him. The altar also was rent, and the ashes poured out from the altar, according to the sign which the man of God had given by the word of the Lord.

And Jeroboam said unto the man of God, " Entreat now the face of the Lord thy God, and pray for me, that my hand may be restored to me again."

And the man of God besought the Lord, and Jeroboam's hand was restored, and became as it was before. And Jeroboam said unto the man of God, " Come home with me, and refresh thyself, and I will give thee a reward."

And the man of God said unto him, " If thou wilt give me half thine house, I will not go in with thee, neither will eat bread nor drink water in this place: for so it was charged me by the word of the Lord, saying, ' Eat no bread, nor drink water, nor turn again by the same way that thou camest.' " So he went another way, and returned not by the way that he came to Bethel.

After this thing Jeroboam made again the lowest of the people priests of the high places. Whosoever would, he consecrated him, and he became one of the priests of the high places. And this thing became sin unto the house of Jeroboam, even to cut it off, and to destroy it from off the face of the earth.

THE HOUSE OF JEROBOAM CUT OFF

At that time Abijah the son of Jeroboam fell sick. And Jeroboam said to his wife, "Arise, I pray thee and disguise thyself, that thou be not known to be the wife of Jeroboam; and get thee to Shiloh: behold, there is Ahijah, the prophet, which told me that I should be king over this people. And take with thee ten loaves, and cracknels, and honey, and go to him. He shall tell thee what shall become of the child."

And Jeroboam's wife did so, and arose, and went to Shiloh, and came to the house of Ahijah.

But Ahijah could not see; for his eyes were set by reason of his age. And the Lord said unto Ahijah, "Behold, the wife of Jeroboam cometh to ask a thing of thee for her son, for he is sick. Thus shalt thou say unto her, for it shall be, when she cometh in, that she shall feign herself to be another woman."

And it was so, when Ahijah heard the sound of her feet as she came in at the door, that he said, "Come in, thou wife of Jeroboam; why feignest thou thyself to be another? for I am sent to thee with heavy tidings. Go tell Jeroboam, thus saith the Lord God of Israel, 'I exalted thee from among the people, and made thee prince over my people Israel, and rent the kingdom away from the house of David, and gave it thee, yet thou hast done evil above all that were before thee. For thou hast gone and made thee other gods, and molten images, to provoke me to anger, and hast cast me behind thy back. Therefore behold, I will bring evil upon the house of Jeroboam, and will take away the remnant of the house of Jeroboam, as a man taketh away dung, till it be all gone.' Arise thou therefore, get thee to thine own house: and when thy feet enter into the city, the child shall die. And all Israel shall mourn for him and bury him; for he only of Jeroboam shall come to the grave. Moreover, the Lord shall raise him up a king over Israel, who shall cut off the house of Jeroboam that day. For the Lord shall smite Israel, as a reed is shaken in the water, and he shall root up Israel out of this good land, which he gave to their fathers, and shall scatter them beyond the river. And he shall give Israel up because of the sins of Jeroboam, who did sin, and who made Israel to sin."

And Jeroboam's wife arose, and departed, and came to Tirzah, and when she came to the threshold of the door, the child died. And they buried him; and all Israel mourned for him, according to the word of the Lord, which he spake by the hand of his servant Ahijah the prophet.

"YE HAVE FORSAKEN ME, THEREFORE HAVE I ALSO LEFT YOU"

AND IT CAME TO PASS, when Rehoboam, king of Judah, had established the kingdom, and had strengthened himself, he forsook the law of the Lord, and all Judah with him.

And it came to pass, that in the fifth year of king Rehoboam, Shishak of Egypt came up against Jerusalem with twelve hundred chariots, and threescore thousand horsemen; and the people were without number that came with him out of Egypt. And Shishak took the fenced cities which pertained to Judah, and came to Jerusalem.

Then came Shemaiah, the prophet, to Rehoboam, and to the princes of Judah, that were gathered together to Jerusalem because of Shishak, and said unto them, "Thus saith the Lord, 'Ye have forsaken me, therefore have I also left you in the hand of Shishak.'"

Whereupon the princes of Judah, and the king humbled themselves; and they said, "The Lord is righteous."

And when the Lord saw that they humbled themselves, the word of the Lord came to Shemaiah, saying, "They have humbled themselves; therefore I will not destroy them, but I will grant them some deliverance; and will not destroy them altogether, by the hand of Shishak. Nevertheless they shall be his servants."

So Shishak king of Egypt came up against Jerusalem, and took away the treasures of the house of the Lord, and the treasures of the king's house. He took all. He carried away also the shields of gold which Solomon had made. Instead of which, king Rehoboam made shields of brass, and committed them to the hands of the chief of the guard, that kept the entrance of the king's house.

Rehoboam was one and forty years old when he began to reign, and he reigned seventeen years in Jerusalem, and he prepared not his heart to seek the Lord. And there were wars between Rehoboam and Jeroboam continually.

And Rehoboam slept with his fathers, and was buried in the city of David. And Abijah his son reigned in his stead.

O CHILDREN OF ISRAEL, FIGHT NOT AGAINST THE LORD

Now in the eighteenth year of king Jeroboam's reign over Israel, began Abijah, the son of Rehoboam, to reign over Judah. And there was war between Abijah and Jeroboam.

And Abijah set the battle in array with an army of valiant men of war, even four hundred thousand chosen men: Jeroboam also set the battle in array against him with eight hundred thousand chosen men, being mighty men of valour.

And Abijah stood up upon mount Zemaraim, which is in mount Ephraim, and said, "Hear me, thou Jeroboam, and all Israel! Ought ye not to know that the Lord God of Israel gave the kingdom over Israel to David for ever, even to him and to his sons by a covenant of salt? Yet Jeroboam the son of Nebat, the servant of Solomon the son of David, is risen up, and hath rebelled against his Lord. And there are gathered unto him vain men, the children of Belial, and strengthened themselves against Rehoboam the son of Solomon, when Rehoboam was young and tender-hearted, and could not withstand them.

"And now ye think to withstand the kingdom of the Lord in the hand of the sons of David; and ye be a great multitude, and there are with you golden calves, which Jeroboam made you for gods. Have ye not cast out the priests of the Lord, the sons of Aaron, and the Levites, and have made you priests after the manner of the nations of other lands? so that whosoever cometh to consecrate himself with a young bullock and seven rams, the same may be a priest of them that are no gods?

"But as for us, the Lord is our God, and we have not forsaken him; and the priests, which minister unto the Lord, are the sons of Aaron, and the Levites wait upon their business. And they burn unto the Lord every morning and every evening burnt-sacrifices and sweet incense; the shew-bread also set they in order upon the pure table; and the candlestick of gold with the lamps thereof to burn every evening. For we keep the charge of the Lord our God; but ye have forsaken him.

"And behold, God himself is with us for our captain, and his priests with sounding trumpets to cry alarm against you. O children of Israel, fight ye not against the Lord God of your fathers; for ye shall not prosper."

But Jeroboam caused an ambushment to come about behind them: so Jeroboam was before Judah, and the ambushment was behind them. And when Judah looked back, behold, the battle was before and behind.

And Judah cried unto the Lord, and the priests sounded with the trumpets. Then the men of Judah gave a shout; and as the men of Judah shouted, it came to pass, that God smote Jeroboam and all Israel before Judah and Abijah. And the children of Israel fled before Judah: and God delivered them into their hand. And Abijah and his people slew them with a great slaughter; so there fell down slain of Israel five hundred thousand chosen men.

Thus the children of Israel were brought under at that time, and the children of Judah prevailed, because they relied upon the Lord God of their fathers.

And Abijah pursued after Jeroboam, and took cities from him, Bethel with the towns thereof, and Jeshanah with the towns thereof, and Ephraim with the towns thereof. Neither did Jeroboam recover strength again in the days of Abijah. But Abijah waxed mighty. In his days the land was quiet ten years.

So Abijah slept with his fathers, and they buried him in the city of David. And Asa his son reigned in his stead.

In the second year of Asa, king of Judah, Jeroboam died. And it came to pass that Baasha smote all the house of Jeroboam; and he left not Jeroboam any that breathed, until he had destroyed him, according unto the saying of the Lord, which he spake by his servant Ahijah; because of the sins of Jeroboam which he sinned, and which he made Israel sin.

And there was war between Asa king of Judah and Baasha king of Israel all their days.

BE STRONG,
AND YOUR WORK SHALL BE REWARDED

And Asa did that which was good and right in the eyes of the Lord his God: for he took away the altars of the strange gods, and the high places, and brake down the images, and cut down the groves. And he commanded Judah to seek the Lord God of their fathers, and to do the law and the commandment. And the kingdom was quiet before him.

And he built fenced cities in Judah; for the land had rest. Therefore he said unto Judah, "Let us build these cities, and make about them walls, and towers, gates, and bars, while the land is yet before us, because we have sought the Lord our God, and he hath given us rest on every side." So they built and prospered.

And Asa had an army of men that bare targets and spears, out of Judah three hundred thousand; and out of Benjamin, that bare shields and drew bows, two hundred and fourscore thousand: all these were mighty men of valour.

And there came out against them Zerah, the Ethiopian, with an host of a thousand thousand, and three hundred chariots. Then Asa went out against him, and they set the battle in array.

And Asa cried unto the Lord his God, and said, "Lord it is nothing with thee to help, whether with many, or with them that have no power: help us, O Lord our God, for we rest on thee, and in thy name we go against this multitude. O Lord, thou art our God; let not man prevail against thee."

So the Lord smote the Ethiopians before Asa, and before Judah. And the Ethiopians fled. And Asa and the people that were with him pursued them unto Gerar. And the Ethiopians were overthrown that they could not recover themselves, for they were destroyed before the Lord.

And Asa smote all the cities round about Gerar; and they spoiled the cities. They smote also the tents of cattle, and carried away sheep and camels in abundance, and returned to Jerusalem.

And the spirit of God came upon Azariah, the son of Oded. And he went out to meet Asa, and said unto him, "Hear ye me, Asa, and all Judah and Benjamin: The Lord is with you, while ye be with him. And if ye seek him, he will be found of you; but if ye forsake him, he will forsake you. Now for a long season Israel hath been without the true God, and without a teaching priest, and without law. And in those times there was no peace to him that went out, nor to him that came in, but great vexations were upon all the inhabitants of the countries. And nation was destroyed of nation, and city of city. Be ye strong therefore, and let not your hands be weak; for your work shall be rewarded."

And when Asa heard these words, and the proprecy of Oded the prophet, he took courage, and put away the abominable idols out of all the land of Judah and Benjamin, and out of the cities which he had taken from mount Ephraim, and renewed the altar of the Lord, that was before the porch of the Lord.

And he gathered all Judah and Benjamin, and the strangers with them out of Ephraim and Manasseh, and out of Simeon: for they fell to him out of Israel in abundance, when they saw that the Lord his God was with him.

So they gathered themselves together at Jerusalem in the third month, in the fifteenth year of the reign of Asa. And they entered into a covenant to seek the Lord God of their fathers with all their heart and with all their soul. And they sware unto the Lord with a loud voice, and with shouting, and with trumpets, and with cornets. And all Judah rejoiced at the oath: for they had sworn with all their heart, and sought him with their whole desire, and he was found of them. And the Lord gave them rest round about.

And also Asa the king, removed Maachah, his mother, from being queen, because she had made an idol in a grove. And Asa cut down her idol, and stamped it, and burnt it at the brook Kidron.

And Asa brought into the house of God the things that his father had dedicated, and that he himself had dedicated, silver, and gold, and vessels. And there was no more war unto the five and thirtieth year of the reign of Asa.

ASA SOUGHT NOT TO THE LORD, BUT TO THE PHYSICIANS

IN THE SIX and thirtieth year of the reign of Asa, Baasha king of Israel came up against Judah, and built Ramah, to the intent that he might let none go out or come in to Asa king of Judah.

Then Asa brought out silver and gold out of the treasures of the house of the Lord and of the king's house, and sent to Ben-hadad king of Syria, that dwelt at Damascus, saying, "There is a league between me and thee, as there was between my father and thy father: behold, I have sent thee silver and gold; go break thy league with Baasha, king of Israel, that he may depart from me."

And Ben-hadad hearkened unto king Asa, and sent the captains of his armies against the cities of Israel; and they smote Ijon, and Dan, and Abelmaim, and all the store-cities of Naphtali.

And it came to pass, when Baasha heard it, that he left off building of Ramah, and let his work cease. Then Asa the king carried away the stones of Ramah, and the timber thereof, wherewith Baasha was building, and built therewith Geba and Mizpah.

And at that time Hanani the seer came to Asa king of Judah, and said unto him, "Because thou hast relied on the king of Syria, and not relied on the Lord thy God, therefore is the host of the king of Syria escaped out of thine hand. Were not the Ethiopians and the Lubims a huge host, with very many chariots and horsemen? yet, because thou didst rely on the Lord, he delivered them into thine hand. For the eyes of the Lord run to and fro throughout the whole earth, to show himself strong in the behalf of them whose heart is perfect toward him. Herein thou hast done foolishly: therefore from henceforth thou shalt have wars."

Then Asa was wroth with the seer, and put him in a prison-house; for he was in a rage with him because of this thing. And Asa oppressed some of the people the same time.

And Asa in the thirty and ninth year of his reign was diseased in his feet, until his disease was exceeding great; yet in his disease he sought not to the Lord, but to the physicians.

And Asa slept with his fathers, and died in the one and fortieth year of his reign. And they buried him in his own sepulchres which he had made for himself in the city of David, and laid him in the bed which was filled with sweet odours, and divers kinds of spices prepared by the apothecaries' art: and they made a very great burning for him.

And Jehoshaphat his son reigned in his stead, and strengthened himself against Israel.

JEHOSHAPHAT, KING OF JUDAH, WALKED IN THE COMMANDMENTS OF GOD AND PROSPERED

AND JEHOSHAPHAT, Asa's son, reigned in Judah, and strengthened himself against Israel. And he placed forces in all the fenced cities of Judah, and set garrisons in the land of Judah, and in the cities of Ephraim, which Asa his father had taken.

And the Lord was with Jehoshaphat, because he sought the Lord God of his fathers, and walked in His commandments, and not after the doings of Israel. Therefore the Lord established the kingdom in his hand; and all Judah brought to Jehoshaphat presents; and he had riches and honour in abundance. And his heart was lifted up in the ways of the Lord. Moreover he took away the high places and groves out of Judah.

Also in the third year of his reign he sent his princes, to teach in the cities of Judah. And with them he sent Levites; and they had the book of the law of the Lord with them, and went about throughout all the cities of Judah, and taught the people.

And the fear of the Lord fell upon all the kingdoms of the lands that were round about Judah, so that they made no war against Jehoshaphat. Also some of the Philistines brought him presents, and tribute-silver; and the Arabians brought him flocks.

And Jehoshaphat waxed great exceedingly; and he built in Judah castles, and cities of store. And he had much business in the cities of Judah.

BUT THE KINGS OF ISRAEL WALKED IN THEIR SINS, AND DIED

THEN THE WORD of the Lord came to Jehu the prophet to speak against Baasha, king of Israel, saying, "Forasmuch as I exalted thee out of the dust, and made thee prince over my people Israel, and thou hast walked in the way of Jeroboam, and hast made my people Israel to sin, behold I will take away thy house like the house of Jeroboam the son of Nebat."

So Baasha slept with his fathers, and was buried in Tirzah; and his son Elah reigned in his stead.

And Elah's servant, Zimri, captain of half his chariots, conspired against Elah as he was in Tirzah drinking himself drunk in the house of his steward. And Zimri went in and smote him and killed him, and reigned in his stead.

And it came to pass, when Zimri began to reign, as soon as he sat on his throne, that he slew all the house of Baasha. He left not one, neither of his kinsfolks, nor of his friends. Thus did

Zimri destroy all the house of Baasha, according to the word of the Lord, which he spake against Baasha by Jehu the prophet.

And Zimri reigned in Tirzah. And the people were encamped against the Philistines. And the people that were encamped heard say, "Zimri hath conspired, and hath also slain king Elah." Wherefore all Israel made Omri the captain of the host, king over Israel that day in the camp.

And Omri went up from Gibbethon, and all Israel with him, and they besieged Tirzah. And it came to pass, when Zimri saw that the city was taken, that he went into the palace of the king's house, and burnt the king's house over him with fire and died.

Then were the people of Israel divided into two parts; half of the people followed Tibni to make him king, and half followed Omri. But the people that followed Omri prevailed against the people that followed Tibni, so Tibni died, and Omri reigned.

But Omri wrought evil in the eyes of the Lord, and did worse than all that were before him. So Omri slept with his fathers, and was buried in Samaria. And Ahab the son of Omri reigned over Israel.

And Ahab did more evil than all the kings of Israel that were before him. And it came to pass, as if it had been a light thing for him to walk in the sins of his fathers, that he took to wife Jezebel, the daughter of the king of the Zidonians, and went and served Baal, and worshipped him. And Ahab reared up an altar for Baal in the house of Baal, which he had built in Samaria, and he made a grove.

And Jezebel cut off the prophets of the Lord, but the prophets of Baal were four hundred and fifty, and the prophets of the grove four hundred which ate at Jezebel's table. And Elijah the Tishbite only remained a prophet of the Lord.

THE WORD OF THE LORD IN THY MOUTH IS TRUTH

And Elijah the Tishbite, who was of the inhabitants of Gilead, said unto Ahab, "As the Lord God of Israel liveth, before whom I stand, there shall not be dew nor rain these years, but according to my word."

And the word of the Lord came unto Elijah, saying, "Get thee hence, and turn thee eastward, and hide thyself by the brook Cherith, that is before Jordan. And it shall be, that thou shalt drink of the brook; and I have commanded the ravens to feed thee there."

So he went and did according unto the word of the Lord: for he went and dwelt by the brook Cherith, that is before Jordan. And the ravens brought him bread and flesh in the mornings, and bread and flesh in the evening; and he drank of the brook.

And it came to pass after a while, that the brook dried up, because there had been no rain in the land. And the word of the Lord came unto Elijah, saying, "Arise, get thee to Zarephath, which belongeth to Zidon, and dwell there: behold, I have commanded a widow woman there to sustain thee."

So he arose and went to Zarephath. And when he came to the gate of the city, behold, the widow woman was there gathering of sticks; and he called to her, and said, "Fetch me, I pray thee, a little water in a vessel, that I may drink." And as she was going to fetch it, he called to her, and said, "Bring me, I pray thee, a morsel of bread in thine hand."

And she said, "As the Lord thy God liveth, I have not a cake, but a handful of meal in a barrel, and a little oil in a cruse; and behold, I am gathering two sticks, that I may go in and dress it for me and my son, that we may eat it, and die."

And Elijah said unto her, " Fear not; go and do as thou hast said, but make me thereof a little cake first, and bring it unto me, and after make for thee and for thy son. For thus saith the Lord God of Israel, ' The barrel of meal shall not waste, neither shall the cruse of oil fail, until the day that the Lord sendeth rain upon the earth.' "

And she went and did according to the saying of Elijah; and she, and he, and her house, did eat many days. And the barrel of meal wasted not, neither did the cruse of oil fail, according to the word of the Lord, which he spake by Elijah.

And it came to pass after these things, that the son of the woman, the mistress of the house, fell sick; and his sickness was so sore, that there was no breath left in him.

And she said unto Elijah, " What have I to do with thee, O thou man of God? art thou come unto me to call my sin to remembrance, and to slay my son? "

And he said unto her, " Give me thy son." And he took him out of her bosom, and carried him up into a loft, where he abode, and laid him upon his own bed.

And he cried unto the Lord, and said, " O Lord my God, I pray thee, let this child's soul come into him again." And the Lord heard the voice of Elijah and the soul of the child came into him again, and he revived.

And Elijah took the child, and brought him down out of the chamber into the house, and delivered him unto his mother. And Elijah said, " See, thy son liveth."

And the woman said to Elijah, " Now by this I know that thou art a man of God, and the word of the Lord in thy mouth is Truth."

"HOW LONG HALT YE BETWEEN TWO OPINIONS? "

AND AS ELIJAH had said there was neither dew nor rain three years, and there was a sore famine in Samaria. And Ahab king of Israel called Obadiah, who was the governor of his house. (Now Obadiah feared the Lord greatly: for when Jezebel cut off the prophets of the Lord, Obadiah took an hundred prophets, and hid them by fifty in a cave, and fed them with bread and water.)

And Ahab said unto Obadiah, " Go into the land unto all the fountains of water, and unto all brooks, peradventure we may find grass to save the horses and mules alive, that we lose not all the beasts." So they divided the land between them to pass throughout it. Ahab went one way by himself, and Obadiah went another way by himself.

And it came to pass after many days, that the word of the Lord came to Elijah, saying, " Go, show thyself unto Ahab; and I will send rain upon the earth." And Elijah went to show himself unto Ahab.

And as Obadiah was in the way, behold, Elijah met him. And Obadiah knew him, and fell on his face, and said, " Art thou my lord Elijah? "

And he answered him, " I am: go tell Ahab, ' Behold, Elijah is here.' "

And Obadiah said, " What have I sinned, that thou wouldst deliver thy servant into the hand of Ahab, to slay me? As the Lord thy God liveth, there is no nation or kingdom whither Ahab hath not sent to seek thee. And when they said, ' He is not here;' he took an oath of the kingdom and nation, that they had found thee not. And now thou sayest, ' Go, tell thy lord,

" Behold, Elijah is here." ' And it shall come to pass, as soon as I am gone from thee, that the Spirit of the Lord shall carry thee whither I know not; and so when I come and tell Ahab, and he cannot find thee, he shall slay me. But I thy servant fear the Lord from my youth. Was it not told my lord what I did when Jezebel slew the prophets of the Lord, how I hid an hundred men of the Lord's prophets by fifty in a cave, and fed them with bread and water? And now thou sayest, 'Go, tell thy lord, " Behold, Elijah is here;" ' and he shall slay me."

And Elijah said, " As the Lord of hosts liveth, before whom I stand, I will surely show myself unto Ahab today."

So Obadiah went to meet Ahab, and told him. And Ahab went to meet Elijah. And it came to pass when Ahab saw Elijah, that Ahab said unto him, " Art thou he that troubleth Israel? "

And Elijah answered, " I have not troubled Israel; but thou, and thy father's house, in that ye have forsaken the commandments of the Lord, and thou hast followed Baalim. Now therefore send, and gather to me all Israel unto mount Carmel, and the prophets of Baal four hundred and fifty, and the prophets of the groves four hundred, which eat at Jezebel's table."

So Ahab sent unto all the children of Israel, and gathered the prophets together unto mount Carmel.

And Elijah came unto all the people, and said, " How long halt ye between two opinions? if the Lord be God, follow him: but if Baal, then follow him." And the people answered him not a word.

Then said Elijah unto the people, " I, even I only, remain a prophet of the Lord; but Baal's prophets are four hundred and fifty men. Let them therefore give us two bullocks; and let them choose one bullock for themselves, and cut it in pieces, and lay it on wood, and put no fire under. And I will dress the other bullock, and lay it on wood, and put no fire under. And call ye on the name of your gods, and I will call on the name of the Lord: and the God that answereth by fire, let him be God."

And all the people answered and said, "It is well spoken."

And Elijah said unto the prophets of Baal, "Choose you one bullock for yourselves, and dress it first; for ye are many. And call on the name of your gods, but put no fire under."

And they took the bullock which was given them, and they dressed it, and called on the name of Baal from morning even until noon, saying, "O Baal, hear us." But there was no voice, nor any that answered. And they leaped upon the altar which was made.

And it came to pass at noon, that Elijah mocked them, and said, "Cry aloud: for he is a god; either he is talking, or he is pursuing, or he is in a journey, or peradventure he sleepeth and must be awaked."

And they cried aloud, and cut themselves after their manner with knives and lancets, till the blood gushed out upon them. And it came to pass, when mid-day was past, and they prophesied until the time of the offering of the evening sacrifice, that there was neither voice, nor any to answer, nor any that regarded.

And Elijah said unto all the people, "Come near unto me." And all the people came near unto him. And he repaired the altar of the Lord that was broken down. And he took twelve stones, according to the number of the tribes of the sons of Jacob, and with the stones he built an altar in the name of the Lord. And he made a trench about the altar, as great as would contain two measures of seed. And he put the wood in order, and cut the bullock in pieces, and laid him on the wood, and said, "Fill four barrels with water, and pour it on the burnt-sacrifice, and on the wood."

And he said, "Do it the second time." And they did it the second time. And he said, "Do it the third time." And they did it the third time. And the water ran round about the altar. And he filled the trench also with water.

And it came to pass at the time of the offering of the evening sacrifice, that Elijah the prophet came near and said, " Lord God of Abraham, Isaac, and of Israel, let it be known this day that thou art God in Israel, and that I am thy servant, and that I have done all these things at thy word. Hear me, O Lord, hear me, that this people may know that thou art the Lord God, and that thou hast turned their heart back again."

Then the fire of the Lord fell, and consumed the burnt-sacrifice, and the wood, and the stones, and the dust, and licked up the water that was in the trench.

And when all the people saw it, they fell on their faces, and they said, " The Lord, he is the God! the Lord, he is the God."

And Elijah said unto them, " Take the prophets of Baal; let not one of them escape." And they took them; and Elijah brought them down to the brook Kishon, and slew them there.

And Elijah said unto Ahab, " Get thee up, eat and drink; for there is a sound of abundance of rain." So Ahab went up to eat and to drink.

And Elijah went up to the top of Carmel; and he cast himself down upon the earth, and put his face between his knees, and said to his servant. " Go up now, look toward the sea."

And he went up, and looked, and said, " There is nothing."

And Elijah said, " Go again seven times."

And it came to pass at the seventh time, that he said, " Behold, there ariseth a little cloud out of the sea, like a man's hand."

And Elijah said, " Go up, say unto Ahab, ' Prepare thy chariot, and get thee down, that the rain stop thee not.' "

And it came to pass in the meanwhile, that the heaven was black with clouds and wind, and there was a great rain. And Ahab rode, and went to Jezreel.

And the hand of the Lord was on Elijah; and he girded up his loins, and ran before Ahab to the entrance of Jezreel.

A STILL SMALL VOICE

And Ahab told Jezebel all that Elijah had done, and withal how he had slain all the prophets with the sword.

Then Jezebel sent a messenger unto Elijah, saying, "So let the gods do to me, and more also, if I make not thy life as the life of one of them by tomorrow about this time."

And when Elijah heard that, he arose, and went for his life, and came to Beer-sheba, which belongeth to Judah, and left his servant there. But he himself went a day's journey into the wilderness, and came and sat down under a juniper tree. And he requested for himself that he might die; and said, "It is enough; now, O Lord take away my life; for I am not better than my fathers."

And as he lay and slept under a juniper tree, behold, then an angel touched him, and said unto him, "Arise and eat." And he looked, and behold, there was a cake baken on the coals and a cruse of water at his head: and he did eat and drink, and laid him down again.

And the angel of the Lord came again the second time, and touched him, and said, "Arise and eat, because the journey is too great for thee." And he arose, and did eat and drink, and went in the strength of that meat forty days and forty nights unto Horeb the mount of God.

And he came thither unto a cave, and lodged there; and behold, the word of the Lord came to him, and said unto him, "What doest thou here, Elijah?"

And Elijah said, "I have been very jealous for the Lord God of hosts: for the children of Israel have forsaken thy covenant, thrown down thine altars, and slain thy prophets with the sword; and I, even I only, am left; and they seek my life, to take it away."

And he said, "Go forth, and stand upon the mount before the Lord." And behold, the Lord passed by, and a great and strong wind rent the mountains, and brake in pieces the rocks, before the Lord; but the Lord was not in the wind. And after the wind an earthquake, but the Lord was not in the earthquake. And after the earthquake a fire, but the Lord was not in the fire. And after the fire a still small voice.

And it was so, when Elijah heard it, that he wrapped his face in his mantle, and went out, and stood in the entering in of the cave. And behold, there came a voice unto him, and said, "What doest thou here, Elijah?"

And Elijah said, "I have been very jealous for the Lord God of hosts: because the children of Israel have forsaken thy covenant, thrown down thine altars, and slain thy prophets with the sword; and I, even I only, am left; and they seek my life, to take it away."

And the Lord said unto him, "Go, return on thy way to the wilderness of Damascus: and when thou comest, anoint Hazael to be king over Syria: and Jehu the son of Nimshi shalt thou anoint to be king over Israel: and Elisha the son of Shaphat shalt thou anoint to be prophet in thy room. And it shall come to pass, that him that escapeth the sword of Hazael shall Jehu slay: and him that escapeth from the sword of Jehu shall Elisha slay. Yet I have left me seven thousand in Israel, all the knees which have not bowed unto Baal, and every mouth which hath not kissed him."

So Elijah departed thence, and found Elisha the son of Shaphat, who was ploughing with twelve yoke of oxen before him, and he with the twelfth: and Elijah passed by him, and cast his mantle upon him.

And Elisha left the oxen, and ran after Elijah and said, "Let me, I pray thee, kiss my father and my mother, and then I will follow thee."

And Elijah said, "Go back: for what have I done to thee?"

And Elisha returned back from Elijah, and took a yoke of oxen, and slew them, and boiled their flesh, and gave unto the people, and they did eat. Then he arose, and went after Elijah, and ministered unto him.

THE VINEYARD OF NABOTH

And it came to pass after these things, that Naboth the Jezreelite had a vineyard, which was in Jezreel, hard by the palace of Ahab king of Israel.

And Ahab spake unto Naboth, saying, "Give me thy vineyard, that I may have it for a garden of herbs, because it is near unto my house: and I will give thee for it a better vineyard than it; or if it seem good to thee, I will give thee the worth of it in money."

And Naboth said to Ahab, "The Lord forbid it me, that I should give the inheritance of my fathers unto thee."

And Ahab came into his house heavy and displeased, because Naboth had said, "I will not give thee the inheritance of my fathers." And he laid him down upon his bed, and turned away his face, and would eat no bread.

But Jezebel his wife came to him, and said unto him, "Why is thy spirit so sad, that thou eatest no bread?"

And he said unto her, "Because I spake unto Naboth the Jezreelite, and said unto him, 'Give me thy vineyard for money; or else, if it please thee, I will give thee another vineyard for it': and he answered, 'I will not give thee my vineyard.'"

And Jezebel his wife said unto him, "Dost thou now govern the kingdom of Israel? arise, and eat bread, and let thine heart be merry: I will give thee the vineyard of Naboth the Jezreelite."

So she wrote letters in Ahab's name, and sealed them with his seal, and sent the letters unto the elders and to the nobles that were in his city, dwelling with Naboth. And she wrote in the letters, saying, "Proclaim a fast, and set Naboth on high among the people: and set two men, sons of Belial, before him, to bear witness against him, saying, 'Thou didst blaspheme God and the king.' And then carry him out and stone him, that he may die."

And the men of his city, even the elders and the nobles who were the inhabitants in his city, did as Jezebel had sent unto them, and as it was written in the letters which she had sent unto them. They proclaimed a fast, and set Naboth on high among the people. And there came in two men, children of Belial, and sat before him: and the men of Belial witnessed against him, even against Naboth, in the presence of the people, saying, "Naboth did blaspheme God and the king." Then they carried him forth out of the city, and stoned him with stones, that he died.

Then they sent to Jezebel, saying, "Naboth is stoned, and is dead."

And it came to pass, when Jezebel heard that Naboth was stoned, and was dead, that Jezebel said to Ahab, "Arise, take possession of the vineyard of Naboth the Jezreelite, which he refused to give thee for money: for Naboth is not alive, but dead."

And when Ahab heard that Naboth was dead, Ahab rose up to go down to the vineyard of Naboth the Jezreelite, to take possession of it.

And the word of the Lord came to Elijah the Tishbite, saying, "Arise, go down to meet Ahab king of Israel, which is in Samaria: behold, he is in the vineyard of Naboth, whither he is gone down to possess it. And thou shalt speak unto him saying, 'Thus saith the Lord, "Hast thou killed, and also taken possession?" Thus saith the Lord, "In the place where dogs licked the blood of Naboth shall dogs lick thy blood, even thine." ' "

And Ahab said to Elijah, " Hast thou found me, O mine enemy? "

And Elijah answered, " I have found thee: because thou hast sold thyself to work evil in the sight of the Lord. Behold, I will bring evil upon thee, and will take away thy posterity, for the provocation wherewith thou hast provoked me to anger, and made Israel to sin. And of Jezebel also spake the Lord, saying, ' The dogs shall eat Jezebel by the wall of Jezreel.' "

There was none like unto Ahab, which did sell himself to work wickedness in the sight of the Lord, whom Jezebel his wife stirred up.

And it came to pass, when Ahab heard those words, that he rent his clothes, and put sackcloth upon his flesh, and fasted, and lay in sackcloth, and went softly.

And the word of the Lord came to Elijah the Tishbite, saying, " Seest thou how Ahab humbleth himself before me? because he humbleth himself before me, I will not bring the evil in his days: but in his son's days will I bring the evil upon his house."

SHOULDEST THOU HELP THE UNGODLY?

NOW JEHOSHAPHAT had riches and honour in abundance. And it came to pass, that Jehoshaphat king of Judah, came down and joined affinity with Ahab king of Israel. And Ahab killed sheep and oxen for him in abundance, and for the people that were with him.

And Ahab king of Israel said unto Jehoshaphat king of Judah, " Wilt thou go with me to battle to Ramoth-gilead? "

And Jehoshaphat said, "I am as thou art, my people as thy people, my horses as thy horses and we will be with thee in the war. Inquire, I pray thee, at the word of the Lord today."

Then the king of Israel gathered the prophets together, about four hundred men, and said unto them, "Shall I go against Ramoth-gilead to battle, or shall I forbear?"

And they said, "Go up; for the Lord shall deliver it into the hand of the king."

And Jehoshaphat said, "Is there not here a prophet of the Lord besides, that we might inquire of him?"

And Ahab said, "There is yet one man, Micaiah, the son of Imlah, by whom we may inquire of the Lord: but I hate him: for he doth not prophesy good concerning me, but evil."

And Jehoshaphat said, "Let not the king say so."

Then Ahab called for one of his officers and said, "Fetch quickly Micaiah the son of Imlah."

And Ahab king of Israel and Jehoshaphat king of Judah sat either of them on his throne clothed in their robes, and all the prophets prophesied before them.

And Zedekiah had made him horns of iron, and said, "Thus saith the Lord, 'With these thou shalt push Syria until they be consumed!'"

And all the prophets prophesied so, saying, "Go up to Ramoth-gilead, and prosper: for the Lord shall deliver it into the hand of the king."

And the messenger that went to call Micaiah spake to him, saying, "Behold, the words of the prophets declare good to the king with one assent; let thy word therefore, I pray thee, be like one of theirs, and speak thou good."

And Micaiah said, "As the Lord liveth, even what my God saith, that will I speak."

And when Micaiah was come to the king, the king said, "Micaiah, shall we go to Ramoth-gilead to battle, or shall I forbear?"

And Micaiah said, "Go ye up, and prosper, and they shall be delivered into your hand."

And the king said to him, "How many times shall I adjure thee that thou say nothing but the truth to me in the name of the Lord?"

Then Micaiah said, "I did see all Israel scattered upon the mountains, as sheep that have no shepherd: and the Lord said, 'These have no master; let them return therefore every man to his house in peace.'"

And Ahab said to Jehoshaphat, "Did I not tell thee, that he would not prophesy good unto me, but evil?"

Again Micaiah said, "Therefore hear the word of the Lord: I saw the Lord sitting upon his throne, and all the host of heaven standing on his right hand and on his left. And the Lord said, 'Who shall entice Ahab king of Israel, that he may go up and fall at Ramoth-gilead?'

"And one spake saying after this manner, and another after that manner. Then there came out a spirit, and stood before the Lord, and said, 'I will entice him.'

"And the Lord said unto him, 'Wherewith?'

"And he said, 'I will go out, and be a lying spirit in the mouth of all his prophets.'

"And the Lord said, 'Thou shalt entice him, and thou shalt also prevail: go out and do even so.'

"Now therefore behold, the Lord hath put a lying spirit in the mouth of these thy prophets, and the Lord hath spoken evil against thee."

Then Zedekiah came near, and smote Micaiah upon the cheek, and said, "Which way went the Spirit of the Lord from me to speak unto thee?"

And Micaiah said, "Behold, thou shalt see on that day when thou shalt go into an inner chamber to hide thyself."

Then the king of Israel said, "Take ye Micaiah, and carry him back to Amon the governor of the city, and to Joash the king's son, and say, 'Put this fellow in the prison, and feed him with bread of affliction and with water of affliction, until I return in peace.'"

And Micaiah said, "If thou certainly return in peace, then hath not the Lord spoken by me. Hearken, all ye people."

So Ahab king of Israel and Jehoshaphat the king of Judah went up to Ramoth-gilead. And Ahab said unto Jehoshaphat, "I will disguise myself, and will go to the battle; but put thou on thy robes." So Ahab disguised himself; and they went to the battle.

Now the king of Syria had commanded the captains of the chariots that were with him, saying, "Fight ye not with small or great, save only with the king of Israel."

And it came to pass, when the captains of the chariots saw Jehoshaphat, that they said, "It is the king of Israel." Therefore they compassed about him to fight: but Jehoshaphat cried out, and the Lord helped him; and God moved them to depart from him, for it came to pass, that, when the captains of the chariots perceived that it was not the king of Israel, they turned back again from pursuing him.

And a certain man drew a bow at a venture, and smote the king of Israel between the joints of the harness: wherefore he said unto the driver of his chariot, "Turn thine hand, and carry me out of the host; for I am wounded."

And the battle increased that day. And Ahab the king was stayed up in his chariot against the Syrians, and died at even. And there went a proclamation throughout the host about the going down of the sun, saying, "Every man to his city and every man to his own country."

So Ahab the king of Israel died, and was brought to Samaria; and they buried him in Samaria. And Ahaziah his son reigned in his stead.

And Jehoshaphat the king of Judah returned to his house in peace to Jerusalem.

And Jehu the son of Hanani the seer went out to meet him, and said to king Jehoshaphat, "Shouldest thou help the ungodly, and love them that hate the Lord? therefore is wrath upon thee from before the Lord. Nevertheless, there are good things found in thee, in that thou hast taken away the groves out of the land, and hast prepared thine heart to seek God."

And Jehoshaphat dwelt at Jerusalem: and he went out again through the people from Beer-sheba to mount Ephraim, and brought them back unto the Lord God of their fathers. And he set judges in the land throughout all the fenced cities of Judah, city by city. And said to the judges, "Take heed what ye do; for ye judge not for man, but for the Lord, who is with you in judgment. Wherefore now let the fear of the Lord be upon you: take heed and do it: for there is no iniquity with the Lord our God, nor respect of persons, nor taking of gifts."

Moreover, in Jerusalem did Jehoshaphat set of the Levites, and of the priests, and of the chief of the fathers of Israel, for the judgment of the Lord, and for controversies, when they returned to Jerusalem. And he charged them saying, "Thus shall ye do in the fear of the Lord, faithfully, and with a perfect heart. Deal courageously, and the Lord shall be with the good."

BE NOT AFRAID, THE BATTLE IS NOT YOURS, BUT GOD'S

IT CAME TO PASS after this, that the children of Moab, and the children of Ammon, and with them other beside the Ammonites, came against Jehoshaphat to battle.

Then there came some that told Jehoshaphat, saying, "There cometh a great multitude against thee from beyond the sea on this side Syria; and behold, they be in Hazazon-tamar."

And Jehoshaphat feared, and set himself to seek the Lord, and proclaimed a fast throughout all Judah. And Judah gathered themselves together, to ask help of the Lord; even out of all the cities of Judah they came to seek the Lord.

And Jehoshaphat stood in the congregation of Judah and Jerusalem, in the house of the Lord, before the new court, and said, "O Lord God of our fathers, art not thou God in heaven? and rulest not thou over all the kingdoms of the heathen? and in thine hand is there not power and might, so that none is able to withstand thee? Art not thou our God, who didst drive out the inhabitants of this land before thy people Israel, and gavest it to the seed of Abraham thy friend for ever? And they dwelt therein, and have built thee a sanctuary therein for thy name, saying, 'If when evil cometh upon us, as the sword, judgment, or pestilence, or famine, we stand before this house, and in thy presence, (for thy name is in this house) and cry unto thee in our affliction, then thou wilt hear and help.' And now, behold, the children of Ammon and Moab, and mount Seir, whom thou wouldest not let Israel invade, when they came out of the land of Egypt, but turned from them, and destroyed them not. Behold, I say, how they reward us, to come to cast us out of thy possession, which thou hast given us to inherit. O our God, wilt thou not judge them? for we have no might against this great company that cometh against us; neither know we what to do: but our eyes are upon thee."

And all Judah stood before the Lord, with their little ones, their wives and their children. Then upon Jahaziel, the son of Zechariah, a Levite came the Spirit of the Lord in the midst of the congregation; and he said, "Hearken ye, all Judah, and ye inhabitants of Jerusalem, and thou king Jehoshaphat, thus saith the Lord unto you, 'Be not afraid nor dismayed by reason of this great multitude; for the battle is not yours, but God's. Tomorrow go ye down against them: behold, they come up by the cliff of Ziz; and ye shall find them at the end of the brook, before the wilderness of Jeruel. Ye shall not need to fight in this battle: set yourselves, stand ye still, and see the salvation of the Lord with you, O Judah and Jerusalem; fear not, nor be dismayed; tomorrow go out against them: for the Lord will be with you.'"

And Jehoshaphat bowed his head with his face to the ground; and all Judah and the inhabitants of Jerusalem fell before the Lord, worshipping the Lord. And the Levites stood up to praise the Lord God of Israel with a loud voice on high.

And they rose early in the morning, and went forth into the wilderness of Tekoa: and as they went forth, Jehoshaphat stood and said, "Hear me, O Judah, and ye inhabitants of Jerusalem: Believe in the Lord your God, so shall ye be established; believe his prophets, so shall ye prosper."

And when he had consulted with the people, he appointed singers unto the Lord, and that should praise the beauty of holiness, as they went out before the army, and to say, "Praise the Lord; for his mercy endureth for ever."

And when they began to sing and to praise, the Lord set ambushments against the children of Ammon, Moab, and mount Seir, which were come against Judah; and they were smitten. For the children of Ammon and Moab stood up against the inhabitants of mount Seir, utterly to slay and destroy them; and when they had made an end of the inhabitants of Seir, every one helped to destroy another.

And when Judah came toward the watchtower in the wilderness, they looked unto the multitude, and behold, they were dead bodies fallen to the earth, and none escaped. And when Jehoshaphat and his people came to take away the spoil of them, they found among them in abundance both riches, and precious jewels, which they stripped off for themselves, more than they could carry away. And they assembled themselves in the valley of Berachah, for there they blessed the Lord.

Then they returned, every man of Judah and Jerusalem, and

Jehoshaphat in the fore-front of them, to go again to Jerusalem with joy; for the Lord had made them to rejoice over their enemies. And they came to Jerusalem with psalteries and harps and trumpets unto the house of the Lord.

And the fear of God was on all the kingdoms of those countries, when they had heard that the Lord fought against the enemies of Judah. So the realm of Jehoshaphat was quiet: for his God gave him rest round about.

And Jehoshaphat reigned over Judah: he was thirty and five years old when he began to reign, and he reigned twenty and five years in Jerusalem. And he walked in the way of Asa his father, and departed not from it, doing that which was right in the sight of the Lord.

WHY GO YE TO INQUIRE OF BAAL-ZEBUB?

And Ahaziah, the son of Ahab, began to reign over Israel in Samaria the seventeenth year of Jehoshaphat, king of Judah, and reigned two years over Israel. And he did evil in the sight of the Lord, and walked in the way of his father Ahab, and in the way of his mother Jezebel, for he served Baal, and worshipped him, and provoked to anger the Lord God of Israel, according to all that his father had done. And Moab rebelled against Israel after the death of Ahab.

And Ahaziah fell down through a lattice in his upper chamber that was in Samaria, and was sick: and he sent messengers, and said unto them, "Go, inquire of Baal-zebub, the god of Ekron, whether I shall recover of this disease."

But the angel of the Lord said to Elijah the Tishbite, "Arise, go up to meet the messengers of the king of Israel, and say unto them, 'Is it not because there is not a God in Israel, that ye go to inquire of Baal-zebub the god of Ekron? Now therefore thus saith the Lord, "Thou shalt not come down from that bed on which thou art gone up, but shalt surely die."' " And Elijah departed.

And when the messengers turned back unto Ahaziah, he said unto them, "Why are ye now turned back?"

And they said unto him, "There came a man up to meet us, and said unto us, 'Go, turn again unto the king that sent you, and say unto him, "Thus saith the Lord, 'Is it not because there is not a God in Israel, that thou sendest to inquire of Baal-zebub the god of Ekron? therefore thou shalt not come down from that bed on which thou art gone up, but shalt surely die.'" ' "

And Ahaziah said unto them, "What manner of man was he which came up to meet you, and told you these words?"

And they answered him, "He was an hairy man, and girt with a girdle of leather about his loins."

And Ahaziah said, "It is Elijah the Tishbite."

Then the king sent unto Elijah a captain of fifty with his fifty. And the captain went up to Elijah: and behold, he sat on the top of an hill. And the captain spake unto him, "Thou man of God, the king hath said, 'Come down.' "

And Elijah answered and said to the captain of fifty, "If I be a man of God, then let fire come down from heaven, and consume thee and thy fifty." And there came down fire from heaven, and consumed the captain and his fifty.

Again also Ahaziah sent unto Elijah another captain of fifty with his fifty. And the captain said unto Elijah, "O man of God, thus hath the king said, 'Come down quickly.' "

And Elijah answered and said unto them, "If I be a man of God, let fire come down from heaven, and consume thee and thy fifty." And the fire of God came down from heaven, and consumed him and his fifty.

And Ahaziah sent again a captain of the third fifty with his fifty. And the third captain of fifty went up, and came and fell on his knees before Elijah, and besought him, and said unto him, "O man of God, I pray thee, let my life, and the life of these fifty thy servants, be precious in thy sight. Behold, there came fire down from heaven, and burnt up the two captains of the former fifties with their fifty: therefore let my life now be precious in thy sight."

And the angel of the Lord said unto Elijah, "Go down with him: be not afraid of him." And Elijah arose, and went down with him unto the king.

And Elijah said unto Ahaziah, "Thus saith the Lord, 'Forasmuch as thou hast sent messengers to inquire of Baal-zebub the god of Ekron, is it not because there is no God in Israel to inquire of his word? therefore thou shalt not come down off that bed on which thou art gone up, but shalt surely die.'"

So Ahaziah died according to the word of the Lord which Elijah had spoken. And because he had no son, Joram, the son of Ahab, reigned in his stead.

JEHORAM FORSOOK THE LORD GOD OF HIS FATHERS

Now Jehoshaphat, king of Judah, slept with his fathers, and was buried with his fathers in the city of David. And in the fifth year of Joram the son of Ahab king of Israel, Jehoram the son of Jehoshaphat king of Judah began to reign.

And Jehoram had six brethren, the sons of Jehoshaphat. And their father gave them great gifts of silver, and of gold, and of precious things, with fenced cities of Judah; but the kingdom gave he to Jehoram, because he was the first-born.

Now when Jehoram was risen up to the kingdom of his father, he strengthened himself, and slew all of his brethren with the sword, and divers also of the princes of Judah. And he walked in the way of the kings of Israel, like as did the house of Ahab, for he had the daughter of Ahab to wife.

And Jehoram wrought that which was evil in the eyes of the Lord. And the Edomites revolted from under the dominion of Judah, and made themselves a king. The same time also did Libnah revolt from under his hand; because he had forsaken the Lord God of his fathers. Moreover, he made high places in the mountains of Judah, and caused the inhabitants of Jerusalem to commit fornication, and compelled Judah thereto.

And there came a writing to Jehoram from Elijah the prophet, saying, "Because thou hast not walked in the ways of Jehoshaphat thy father, but hast walked in the way of the kings of Israel, and also hast slain thy brethren which were better than thyself, behold, thou shalt have great sickness by disease of thy bowels."

Moreover, the Philistines, and the Arabians, that were near the Ethopians, came up into Judah, and brake into it, and carried away all the substance that was found in the king's house, and his sons also, and his wives; so that there was never a son left him, save only Ahaziah the youngest of his sons.

And it came to pass, after the end of two years that Jehoram died of sore diseases. And his people made no burning for him, like the burning of his fathers. He reigned in Jerusalem eight years, and departed without being desired.

And the inhabitants of Jerusalem made Ahaziah, Jehoram's youngest son king in his stead: for the band of men that came with the Arabians to the camp had slain all the eldest.

THE CHARIOT OF FIRE, AND HORSES OF FIRE

AND IT CAME TO PASS, when the Lord would take up Elijah into heaven by a whirlwind, that Elijah went with Elisha from Gilgal.

And Elijah said unto Elisha, "Tarry here, I pray thee; for the Lord hath sent me to Bethel."

And Elisha said unto him, "As the Lord liveth, and as thy soul liveth, I will not leave thee."

So they went down to Bethel. And the sons of the prophets that were at Bethel came forth to Elisha, and said unto him, "Knowest thou that the Lord will take away thy master from thy head today?"

And he said, "Yea, I know it: hold ye your peace."

And Elijah said unto him, "Elisha, tarry here, I pray thee; for the Lord hath sent me to Jericho."

And Elisha said, "As the Lord liveth, and as thy soul liveth, I will not leave thee."

So they came to Jericho. And the sons of the prophets that were at Jericho came to Elisha, and said unto him, "Knowest thou that the Lord will take away thy master from thy head today?"

And he answered, "Yea, I know it; hold your peace."

And Elijah said unto him, "Tarry, I pray thee here; for the Lord hath sent me to Jordan."

And Elisha said, "As the Lord liveth, and as thy soul liveth, I will not leave thee." And they two went on.

And fifty men of the sons of the prophets went, and stood to view afar off: and they two stood by Jordan. And Elijah took his mantle, and wrapped it together, and smote the waters, and they were divided hither and thither, so that they two went over on dry ground.

And it came to pass, when they were gone over, that Elijah said unto Elisha, "Ask what I shall do for thee, before I be taken away from thee."

And Elisha said, "I pray thee, let a double portion of thy spirit be upon me."

And Elijah said, "Thou hast asked a hard thing: nevertheless, if thou see me when I am taken from thee, it shall be so unto thee; but if not, it shall not be so."

And it came to pass, as they still went on, and talked, that behold, there appeared a chariot of fire, and horses of fire, and parted them both asunder; and Elijah went up by a whirlwind into heaven.

And Elisha saw it, and he cried, "My father, my father, the chariot of Israel, and the horsemen thereof!" And he saw him no more: and he took hold of his own clothes, and rent them in two pieces.

And he took the mantle of Elijah that fell from him, and smote the waters, and said, "Where is the Lord God of Elijah?" And when he also had smitten the waters, they parted hither and thither; and Elisha went over.

And when the sons of the prophets which were to view at Jericho saw him, they said, "The spirit of Elijah doth rest on Elisha." And they came to him, and bowed themselves to the ground before him. And they said unto him, "Behold, now, there be with thy servants fifty strong men: let them go, we pray thee, and seek thy master, lest peradventure the Spirit of the Lord hath taken him up, and cast him upon some mountain, or into some valley."

And Elisha said, "Ye shall not send."

And when they urged him till he was ashamed, he said, "Send." They sent therefore fifty men; and they sought three days, but found him not. And when they came again to Elisha (for he tarried at Jericho), he said unto them, "Did I not say unto you, 'Go not?'"

And the men of the city said unto Elisha, "Behold, I pray thee, the situation of this city is pleasant, as my Lord seeth: but the water is naught, and the ground is barren."

And Elisha said, "Bring me a new cruse, and put salt therein." And they brought it to him.

And he went forth unto the spring of the waters, and cast the salt in there, and said, "Thus saith the Lord, I have healed these waters; there shall not be from thence any more death or barren land." So the waters were healed according to the saying of Elisha which he spake.

And Elisha went from thence to mount Carmel, and from thence he returned to Samaria.

WHAT HAST THOU IN THE HOUSE?

NOW THERE cried a certain woman of the wives of the sons of the prophets unto Elisha, saying, "Thy servant my husband is dead; and thou knowest that thy servant did fear the Lord: and the creditor is come to take unto him my two sons to be bond-men."

And Elisha said unto her, "What shall I do for thee? Tell me, what hast thou in the house?"

And she said, "Thine handmaid hath not anything in the house save a pot of oil."

Then he said, "Go, borrow thee vessels abroad of all thy neighbours, even empty vessels; borrow not a few. And when thou art come in, thou shalt shut the door upon thee and upon thy sons, and shalt pour out into all those vessels, and thou shalt set aside that which is full."

So she went from him, and shut the door upon her and upon her sons, who brought the vessels to her; and she poured out. And it came to pass, when the vessels were full, that she said unto her son, "Bring me yet a vessel."

And he said unto her, "There is not a vessel more." And the oil stayed.

Then she came and told the man of God. And he said, "Go, sell the oil, and pay thy debt, and live thou and thy children of the rest."

IT IS WELL

AND IT FELL on a day, that Elisha passed to Shunem, where was a great woman, and she constrained him to eat bread. And so it was, that as oft as he passed by, he turned in thither to eat bread.

And she said unto her husband, "Behold now, I perceive that this is an holy man of God, which passeth by us continually. Let us make a little chamber, I pray thee, on the wall; and let us set for him there a bed, and a table, and a stool, and a candlestick: and it shall be, when he cometh to us, that he shall turn in thither."

And it fell on a day, that Elisha came thither, and he turned into the chamber, and lay there. And he said to Gehazi, his servant, "Call this Shunammite." And when he had called her, she stood before him. And Elisha said unto him, "Say unto her now, 'Behold, thou hast been careful for us with all this care; what is to be done for thee? Wouldst thou be spoken for to the king, or to the captain of the host?'"

And she answered, "I dwell among mine own people."

And Elisha said, "What then is to be done for her?"

And Gehazi answered, "Verily she hath no child, and her husband is old."

And Elisha said, "Call her." And when he had called her, she stood in the door. And Elisha said, "About this season according to the time of life, thou shalt embrace a son."

And she said, "Nay, my lord, thou man of God, do not lie unto thine handmaid." And the woman conceived and bare a son at that season that Elisha had said unto her according to the time of life.

And when the child was grown, it fell on a day, that he went out to his father to the reapers. And he said unto his father, "My head, my head!"

And his father said to a lad, "Carry him to his mother."

And when he had taken him, and brought him to his mother, he sat on her knees till noon, and then died. And she went up, and laid him on the bed of the man of God, and shut the door upon him, and went out.

And she called unto her husband, and said, "Send me, I pray thee, one of the young men, and one of the asses, that I may run to the man of God, and come again."

And her husband said, "Wherefore wilt thou go to him today? It is neither new moon, nor sabbath."

And she said, "It shall be well."

Then she saddled an ass, and said to her servant, "Drive and go forward; slack not thy riding for me, except I bid thee." So she went and came unto the man of God to mount Carmel.

And it came to pass, when the man of God saw her afar off, that he said to Gehazi his servant, "Behold, yonder is that Shunammite. Run now, I pray thee, to meet her, and say unto her, 'Is it well with thee? is it well with thy husband? is it well with the child?'"

And she answered, "It is well."

And when she came to the man of God to the hill, she caught him by the feet: but Gehazi came near to thrust her away. And the man of God said, "Let her alone; for her soul is vexed within her; and the Lord hid it from me, and hath not told me."

Then she said, "Did I desire a son of my lord? Did I not say, 'Do not deceive me?'"

Then he said to Gehazi, "Gird up thy loins; take my staff in thine hand, and go thy way: if thou meet any man, salute him not, and if any salute thee, answer him not again: and lay my staff upon the face of the child."

And the mother of the child said, "As the Lord liveth, and as thy soul liveth, I will not leave thee." And he arose, and followed her.

And Gehazi passed on before them, and laid the staff upon the face of the child; but there was neither voice, nor hearing. Wherefore he went again to meet Elisha, and told him, saying, "The child is not awaked."

And when Elisha was come into the house, behold, the child was dead, and laid upon his bed. He went in therefore, and shut the door upon them twain, and prayed unto the Lord. And he went up and stretched himself upon the child, and the flesh of the child waxed warm. Then he returned, and walked in the house to and fro; and went up, and stretched himself upon him: and the child sneezed and opened his eyes.

And Elisha called Gehazi, and said, "Call this Shunammite." So he called her. And when she was come in unto him, Elisha said, "Take up thy son."

Then she went in, and fell at his feet, and bowed herself to the ground, and took up her son, and went out.

O THOU MAN OF GOD, THERE IS DEATH IN THE POT

AND ELISHA came again to Gilgal. And there was a dearth in the land; and the sons of the prophets were sitting before him, and he said unto his servant, "Set on the great pot, and seethe pottage for the sons of the prophets."

And one went out into the field to gather herbs, and found a wild vine, and gathered thereof wild gourds his lap full, and came and shred them into the pot of pottage: for they knew them not.

So they poured out for the men to eat. And it came to pass, as they were eating of the pottage, that they cried out, and said, "O thou man of God, there is death in the pot." And they could not eat thereof.

But Elisha said, "Then bring meal." And he cast it into the pot; and he said, "Pour out for the people, that they may eat." And there was no harm in the pot.

And there came a man from Baal-shalisha, and brought the man of God bread of the first-fruits, twenty loaves of barley, and full ears of corn in the husk thereof. And Elisha said, "Give unto the people, that they may eat."

And his servitor said, "What! should I set this before an hundred men?"

Elisha said again, "Give the people, that they may eat: for thus saith the Lord, 'They shall eat, and shall leave thereof.'"

So he set it before them, and they did eat, and left thereof according to the word of the Lord.

GO AND WASH IN JORDAN SEVEN TIMES

Now Naaman, captain of the host of the king of Syria, was a great man with his master, and honourable, because by him the Lord had given deliverance unto Syria. He was also a mighty man of valour, but he was a leper.

And the Syrians had gone out by companies, and had brought away captive out of the land of Israel a little maid; and she waited on Naaman's wife. And she said unto her mistress, "Would God my lord were with the prophet that is in Samaria! for he would recover him of his leprosy."

And one went in, and told his lord, saying, "Thus and thus said the maid that is of the land of Israel."

And the king of Syria said, "Go to! go! and I will send a letter unto the king of Israel, saying, 'Now when this letter is come unto thee, behold, I have therewith sent Naaman, my servant, to thee, that thou mayest recover him of his leprosy.'"

And Naaman departed, and took with him ten talents of silver and six thousand pieces of gold, and ten changes of raiment. And he brought the letter to the king of Israel.

And it came to pass, when the king of Israel had read the letter, that he rent his clothes, and said, "Am I God, to kill and to make alive, that this man doth send unto me to recover a man of his leprosy? Wherefore consider, I pray you, and see how he seeketh a quarrel against me."

And it was so, when Elisha, the man of God, had heard that the king of Israel had rent his clothes, that he sent to the king, saying, "Wherefore hast thou rent thy clothes? let Naaman come now to me, and he shall know that there is a prophet in Israel."

So Naaman came with his horses and with his chariot, and stood at the door of the house of Elisha. And Elisha sent a messenger unto him, saying, "Go and wash in Jordan seven times, and thy flesh shall come again to thee, and thou shalt be clean."

But Naaman was wroth, and went away, and said, "Behold, I thought, 'He will surely come out to me, and stand, and call on the name of the Lord his God, and strike his hand over the place, and recover the leper.' Are not Abana and Pharpar, rivers of Damascus, better than all the waters of Israel? may I not wash in them, and be clean?" So he turned and went away in a rage.

And his servants came near, and spake unto him, and said, "My father, if the prophet had bid thee do some great thing, wouldest thou not have done it? how much rather then, when he saith to thee, 'Wash, and be clean?'"

Then went Naaman down, and dipped himself seven times in Jordan, according to the saying of the man of God: and his flesh came again like unto the flesh of a little child, and he was clean. And he returned to the man of God, he and all his company, and came and stood before him: and he said, "Behold, now I know that there is no God in all the earth, but in Israel: now therefore, I pray thee, take a blessing of thy servant."

But Elisha said, "As the Lord liveth, before whom I stand, I will receive none." And Naaman urged him to take it; but he refused.

And Elisha said unto him, "Go in peace." So Naaman departed from him a little way.

But Gehazi, the servant of Elisha the man of God, said, "Behold, my master hath spared Naaman this Syrian, in not receiving at his hands that which he brought: but as the Lord liveth, I will run after him, and take somewhat of him." So Gehazi followed after Naaman.

And when Naaman saw him running after him, he lighted down from the chariot to meet him, and said, "Is all well?"

And Gehazi said, "All is well. My master hath sent me, saying, 'Behold, even now there be come to me from mount Ephraim two young men of the sons of the prophets: give them, I pray thee, a talent of silver, and two changes of garments.' "

And Naaman said, "Be content, take two talents." And Naaman urged him, and bound two talents of silver in two bags, with two changes of garments, and laid them upon two of his servants; and they bare them before him.

And when Gehazi came to the tower, he took them from their hand, and bestowed them in the house: and he let the men go, and they departed.

But Gehazi went in, and stood before his master: and Elisha said unto him, " Whence comest thou, Gehazi? "

And Gehazi said, " Thy servant went no whither."

And Elisha said unto him, " Went not mine heart with thee, when the man turned again from his chariot to meet thee? Is it a time to receive money, and to receive garments, and oliveyards and vineyards, and sheep, and oxen, and men-servants, and maid-servants? The leprosy therefore of Naaman shall cleave unto thee and unto thy seed for ever."

And Gehazi went out from his presence a leper as white as snow.

AND THE IRON DID SWIM

AND THE SONS of the prophets said unto Elisha, " Behold now, the place where we dwell with thee is too strait for us. Let us go, we pray thee, unto Jordan, and take thence every man a beam, and let us make us a place there, where we may dwell."

And Elisha answered, " Go ye."

And one said, "Be content, I pray thee, and go with thy servants."

And he answered, "I will go." So Elisha went with them.

And when they came to Jordan, they cut down wood. But as one was felling a beam, the axe-head fell into the water: and he cried, and said, "Alas, master! for it was borrowed."

And the man of God said, "Where fell it?"

And he showed him the place. And Elisha cut down a stick, and cast it in thither; and the iron did swim. Therefore said Elisha, "Take it up to thee." And he put out his hand and took it.

THE MOUNTAIN WAS FULL OF HORSES AND CHARIOTS OF FIRE

THEN THE KING of Syria warred against Israel, and took counsel with his servants, saying, "In such and such a place shall be my camp."

And Elisha, the man of God, sent unto Joram, the king of Israel, saying, "Beware that thou pass not such a place; for thither the Syrians are come down." And the king of Israel sent to the place which the man of God told him and warned him of, and saved himself there, twice.

Therefore the heart of the king of Syria was sore troubled for this thing; and he called his servants, and said unto them, "Will ye not show me which of us is for the king of Israel?"

And one of his servants said, "None, my lord, O king; but Elisha, the prophet that is in Israel, telleth the king of Israel the words that thou speakest in thy bed-chamber."

And the king of Syria said, "Go, and spy where he is, that I may send and fetch him."

And it was told him, saying, " Behold, he is in Dothan."

Therefore sent the king thither horses, and chariots, and a great host: and they came by night, and compassed the city about.

And when the servant of the man of God was risen early, and gone forth, behold, an host compassed the city both with horses and chariots. And he said unto Elisha, " Alas, my master! how shall we do? "

And Elisha answered, " Fear not: for they that be with us are more than they that be with them." And Elisha prayed, and said, " Lord, I pray thee, open his eyes, that he may see."

And the Lord opened the eyes of the young man; and he saw: and behold, the mountain was full of horses and chariots of fire round about Elisha.

And when the Syrians came down to him, Elisha prayed unto the Lord, and said, " Smite this people, I pray thee, with blindness." And he smote them with blindness according to the word of Elisha.

And Elisha said unto them, " This is not the way, neither is this the city: follow me, and I will bring you to the man whom ye seek." But he led them to Samaria.

And it came to pass, when they were come into Samaria, that Elisha said, " Lord, open the eyes of these men, that they may see." And the Lord opened their eyes, and they saw; and behold, they were in the midst of Samaria.

And the king of Israel said unto Elisha, when he saw them, " My Father, shall I smite them? shall I smite them? "

And Elisha answered, " Thou shalt not smite them: wouldest thou smite those whom thou hast taken captive with thy sword and thy bow? Set bread and water before them, that they may eat and drink, and go to their master."

And he prepared great provision for them: and when they had eaten and drunk, he sent them away, and they went to their master.

THE NOISE OF A GREAT HOST

AND IT CAME TO PASS after this, that Benhadad king of Syria gathered all his host, and went up, and besieged Samaria. And there was a great famine in Samaria: and behold, they besieged it, until an ass's head was sold for fourscore pieces of silver, and dove's dung for five pieces of silver.

And as Joram, the king of Israel, was passing by upon the wall, there cried a woman unto him, saying, "Help, my lord, O king!"

And the king said unto her, "If the Lord do not help thee, whence shall I help thee? out of the barn-floor, or out of the wine-press?" And he said, "What aileth thee?"

And she answered, "This woman said unto me, 'Give thy son, that we may eat him today, and we will eat my son tomorrow.'"

And it came to pass, when the king heard the words of the woman, that he rent his clothes; and he passed by upon the wall, and the people looked, and behold, he had sackcloth upon his flesh. Then he said, "God do so and more also to me, if the head of Elisha the son of Shaphat shall stand on him this day."

But Elisha sat in his house, and the elders sat with him; and the king sent a man from before him. But ere the messenger came to him, Elisha said to the elders, "See ye how this son of a murderer hath sent to take away mine head? look, when the messenger cometh, shut the door, and hold him fast at the door; is not the sound of his master's feet behind him?"

And while he yet talked with them, behold, the messenger came down unto him, and said, "Behold, this evil is of the Lord; what should I wait for the Lord any longer?"

Then said Elisha, "Hear ye the word of the Lord; thus saith the Lord, 'Tomorrow about this time shall a measure of fine flour be sold for a shekel, and two measures of barley for a shekel, in the gate of Samaria.'"

Then a lord on whose hand the king leaned answered the man of God, and said, "Behold, if the Lord would make windows in heaven, this thing might be."

And Elisha said, "Behold, thou shalt see it with thine eyes, but shalt not eat thereof."

Now there were four leprous men at the entering in of the gate; and they said one to another, "Why sit we here until we die? If we say, 'We will enter into the city,' then the famine is in the city, and we shall die there: and if we sit still here, we die also. Now therefore come, and let us fall unto the host of the Syrians; if they save us alive, we shall live; and if they kill us, we shall but die." And they rose up in the twilight to go unto the camp of the Syrians: and when they were come to the uttermost part of the camp of Syria, behold, there was no man there.

For the Lord had made the host of the Syrians to hear a noise of chariots, and a noise of horses, even the noise of a great host: and they said one to another, "Lo, the king of Israel hath hired against us the kings of the Hittites, and the kings of the Egyptians, to come upon us." Wherefore they arose and fled in the twilight, and left their tents, and their horses, and their asses, even the camp as it was, and fled for their life.

And when the lepers came to the uttermost part of the camp, they went into one tent, and did eat and drink, and carried thence silver, and gold, and raiment, and went and hid it; and came again, and entered into another tent, and carried thence also, and went and hid it.

Then they said one to another, "We do not well: this day

is a day of good tidings, and we hold our peace: if we tarry till the morning light, some mischief will come upon us: now therefore come, that we may go and tell the king's household." So they came and called unto the porter of the city; and they told them, saying, "We came to the camp of the Syrians, and, behold, there was no man there, neither voice of man, but horses tied, and asses tied, and the tents as they were."

And the porters told it to the king's house within. And the king arose in the night, and said unto his servants, "I will now show you what the Syrians have done to us. They know that we be hungry; therefore are they gone out of the camp, to hide themselves in the field, saying, 'When they come out of the city, we shall catch them alive, and get into the city.'"

And one of his servants answered and said, "Let some take, I pray thee, five of the horses that remain, which are left in the city, for behold, they are even as all the multitude of the Israelites that are consumed, and let us send and see."

They took therefore two chariot horses; and the king sent after the host of the Syrians, saying, "Go and see." And they went after them unto Jordan: and lo, all the way was full of garments and vessels, which the Syrians had cast away in their haste. And the messengers returned, and told the king.

And the people went out, and spoiled the tents of the Syrians. So a measure of fine flour was sold for a shekel, and two measures of barley for a shekel, according to the word of the Lord.

And the king appointed the lord on whose hand he leaned to have the charge of the gate: and the people trode upon him in the gate, and he died, as the man of God had said, who spake when the king came down to him: and he said, "Behold, thou shalt see it with thine eyes, but shalt not eat thereof." And so it fell out unto him: for the people trode upon him in the gate, and he died.

THOU SHALT BE KING OVER SYRIA, AND I KNOW THE EVIL THOU WILT DO UNTO ISRAEL

And Elisha came to Damascus. And Ben-hadad the king of Syria was sick; and it was told him, saying, "The man of God is come hither."

And the king said unto Hazael, "Take a present in thine hand, and go, meet the man of God, and inquire of the Lord by him, saying, 'Shall I recover of this disease?'"

So Hazael went to meet Elisha, and took a present with him, even of every good thing of Damascus, forty camels' burden, and came and stood before him, and said, "Thy son Ben-hadad, king of Syria hath sent me to thee, saying, 'Shall I recover of this disease?'"

And Elisha said unto Hazael, "Go, say unto him, 'Thou mayest certainly recover:' howbeit, the Lord hath showed me, that he shall surely die."

And Hazael settled his countenance steadfastly, until he was ashamed: and the man of God wept.

And Hazael said, "Why weepeth my lord?"

And Elisha answered, "Because I know the evil that thou wilt do unto the children of Israel: their strong holds wilt thou set on fire, and their young men wilt thou slay with the sword, and wilt dash their children, and rip up their women with child."

And Hazael said, "But what! is thy servant a dog, that he should do this great thing?"

And Elisha answered, "The Lord hath showed me that thou shalt be king over Syria."

And Hazael departed from Elisha, and came to Ben-hadad, his master, who said unto him, "What said Elisha to thee?"

And Hazael answered, "He told me that thou shouldest surely recover."

And it came to pass on the morrow, that Hazael took a thick cloth, and dipped it in water, and spread it on Ben-hadad's face, so that he died: and Hazael reigned in his stead.

RESTORE ALL THAT WAS HERS

Now Elisha had spoken unto the woman, whose son he had restored to life, saying, "Arise, and go thou and thine household, and sojourn wheresoever thou canst sojourn: for the Lord hath called for a famine; and it shall also come upon the land seven years."

And the woman had gone with her household, and sojourned in the land of the Philistines seven years. And it came to pass at the seven years' end, that the woman returned out of the land of the Philistines; and she went forth to cry unto king Joram for her house, and for her land.

And the king talked with Gehazi, the servant of the man of God, saying, "Tell me, I pray thee, all the great things that Elisha hath done."

And it came to pass, as Gehazi was telling the king how Elisha had restored a dead body to life, that behold, the woman, whose son he had restored to life, cried to the king for her house and for her land. And Gehazi said, "My lord, O king, this is the woman, and this is her son, whom Elisha restored to life."

And when the king asked the woman, she told him. So the king appointed unto her a certain officer, saying, "Restore all that was hers, and all the fruits of the field since the day that she left the land, even until now."

THE LORD BEGAN TO CUT ISRAEL SHORT

Now Ahaziah, the son of Jehoram, king of Judah, reigned. And he reigned one year in Jerusalem. And he did evil in the sight of the Lord like the house of Ahab, for he was son-in-law of the house of Ahab, and they were his counsellors after the death of his father to his destruction. His mother Athalia, the daughter of Omri, also was his counsellor to do wickedly.

And he walked after their counsel, and went with Joram, king of Israel, to war against Hazael, king of Syria, at Ramoth-gilead. And the Syrians wounded Joram, and king Joram went back to be healed in Jezreel of the wounds which the Syrians had given him. And Ahaziah, king of Judah, went down to see Joram in Jezreel because he was sick.

And Elisha the prophet called one of the children of the prophets, and said unto him, " Gird up thy loins, and take this box of oil in thine hand, and go to Ramoth-gilead: and when thou comest thither, look out there Jehu son of Jehoshaphat, the son of Mimshi, and go in, and make him arise up from among his brethren, and carry him to an inner chamber; then take the box of oil, and pour it on his head, and say, 'Thus saith the Lord, " I have anointed thee king over Israel." ' Then open the door, and flee, and tarry not."

So the young prophet went to Ramoth-gilead, and when he came, behold, the captains of the host were sitting; and he said, " I have an errand to thee, O captain."

And Jehu said, " Unto which of all of us? "

And he said, " To thee, O captain."

And Jehu arose, and went into the house; and the prophet

poured the oil on his head, and said unto him, "Thus saith the Lord God of Israel, 'I have anointed thee king over the people of the Lord, even over Israel. And thou shalt smite the house of Ahab thy master, that I may avenge the blood of my servants the prophets, and the blood of all the servants of the Lord, at the hand of Jezebel. For the whole house of Ahab shall perish, and the dogs shall eat Jezebel, and there shall be none to bury her.'" And the young prophet opened the door and fled.

Then Jehu came forth, and one said unto him, "Is all well? wherefore came this mad fellow to thee?"

And Jehu said, "Thus spake he to me, saying, 'Thus saith the Lord, "I have anointed thee king over Israel."'"

Then they hasted, and took every man his garment, and blew with trumpets, saying, "Jehu is king."

So Jehu the son of Nimshi, conspired against Joram. But king Joram was in Jezreel to be healed of the wounds which the Syrians had given him when he fought with Hazael king of Syria. And Jehu said, "If it be your minds, then let none go forth nor escape out of the city to go to tell it in Jezreel."

So Jehu rode in a chariot, and went to Jezreel; for Joram lay there. And Ahaziah, king of Judah, was come down to see Joram. And there stood a watchman on the tower in Jezreel, and he spied the company of Jehu as he came, and said, "I see a company."

And Joram said, "Take an horseman and send to meet them, and let him say, 'Is it peace?'"

So there went one on horseback to meet Jehu, and said, "Thus saith the king, 'Is it peace?'"

And Jehu said, "What hast thou to do with peace? turn thee behind me."

And the watchman told, saying, "The messenger came to them, but he cometh not again."

Then Joram sent out a second on horseback, which came to Jehu and said, "Thus saith the king, 'Is it peace?'"

And Jehu answered, "What hast thou to do with peace? turn thee behind me."

And the watchman told, saying, "He came even unto them, and cometh not again: and the driving is like the driving of Jehu the son of Nimshi; for he driveth furiously."

And Joram said, "Make ready." And his chariot was made ready. And Joram king of Israel, and Ahaziah king of Judah went out, each in his chariot, and they went out against Jehu, and met him in the portion of the vineyard of Naboth the Jezreelite.

And it came to pass, when Joram saw Jehu, that he said, "Is it peace, Jehu?"

And Jehu answered, "What peace, so long as the whoredoms of thy mother Jezebel and her witchcrafts are so many?"

And Joram turned his hands, and fled, and said to Ahaziah, "There is treachery, O Ahaziah." And Jehu drew a bow with his full strength, and smote Joram between his arms, and he sunk down in his chariot.

Then said Jehu to Bidkar his captain, "Take up, and cast Joram in the portion of the field of Naboth the Jezreelite: for remember how that, when I and thou rode together after Ahab, his father, the Lord laid this burden upon him: 'Surely I have seen yesterday the blood of Naboth, and the blood of his sons, and I will requite thee in this plat, saith the Lord.' Now therefore take and cast him into the plat of ground, according to the word of the Lord."

But when Ahaziah the king of Judah saw this, he fled by the way of the garden-house. And Jehu followed after him, and said, "Smite him also in the chariot." And they did so, and he fled to Megiddo, and died there. And his servants carried him in a chariot to Jerusalem, and buried him in his sepulchre with his fathers in the city of David.

And when Jehu was come to Jezreel, Jezebel heard of it; and she painted her face, and tired her head, and looked out at a window. And as Jehu entered in at the gate, she said, "Had Zimri peace, who slew his master?"

And Jehu lifted up his face to the window, and said, "Who is on my side? who?" And there looked out to him two or three eunuchs. And he said, "Throw Jezebel down." So they threw her down, and he trode her under foot.

And when Jehu was come in, he said, "Go, see now this cursed woman, and bury her, for she is a king's daughter."

And they went to bury her: but they found no more of her than the skull, and the feet, and the palms of her hands. Wherefore they came again, and told Jehu, and he said, "This is the word of the Lord, which he spake by his servant Elijah the Tishbite, saying, 'In the portion of Jezreel shall dogs eat Jezebel.'"

So Jehu slew all that remained of the house of Ahab in Jezreel, and all his great men, and his kinsfolks, and his priests, until he left none remaining. And he arose and departed, and came to Samaria, and he slew all that remained unto Ahab in Samaria.

And Jehu gathered all the people together, and said unto them, "Ahab served Baal a little; but Jehu shall serve him much. Now therefore call unto me all the prophets of Baal, all his servants, and all his priests; let none be wanting: for I have a great sacrifice to do to Baal; whosoever shall be wanting he shall not live." But Jehu did it in subtilty, to the intent that he might destroy the worshippers of Baal.

And Jehu said, "Proclaim a solemn assembly for Baal." And they proclaimed it. And Jehu sent through all Israel: and all the worshippers of Baal came, so that there was not a man left that came not. And they came into the house of Baal: and the house of Baal was full from one end to another.

And Jehu said unto him that was over the vestry, "Bring forth vestments for all the worshippers of Baal." And he brought them forth vestments. And Jehu went into the house of Baal, and said unto the worshippers of Baal, "Search, and look that there be here with you none of the servants of the Lord, but the worshippers of Baal only."

And it came to pass, as soon as he had made an end of offering the burnt-offering, that Jehu said to the guard and to the captains, " Go in, and slay them; let none come forth." And they smote them with the edge of the sword. And they brought forth the images out of the house of Baal, and burned them. And they brake down the image of Baal, and brake down the house of Baal. Thus Jehu destroyed Baal out of Israel.

But Jehu took no heed to walk in the law of the Lord God of Israel with all his heart, for the golden calves that were in Bethel, and that were in Dan remained. And the Lord began to cut Israel short; and Hazael smote them in all the coasts of Israel.

WHY TRANSGRESS YE THE COMMANDMENTS OF THE LORD, THAT YE CANNOT PROSPER?

NOW WHEN ATHALIAH, the mother of Ahaziah king of Judah, saw that her son was dead, she arose, and destroyed all the seed royal of the house of Judah.

But Jehosheba, sister of Ahaziah and wife of Jehoiada, the priest, took Joash, the son of Ahaziah, and stole him from among the king's sons that were slain, and hid him and his nurse in a bed-chamber, from Athaliah so that she slew him not. And Joash was hid with them in the house of God six years. And Athaliah reigned over the land of Judah.

And the seventh year Jehoiada, the priest, sent and fetched the rulers over hundreds, with the captains and the guard, and brought them to him into the house of the Lord, and made a covenant with them, and took an oath of them in the house of the Lord, and showed them Joash the king's son.

And the captains over the hundreds did according to all things that Jehoiada the priest commanded. And they went about in Judah, and gathered the Levites out of all the cities of Judah, and the chief of the fathers of Israel, and they came to Jerusalem. And Jehoiada said unto them, " Behold, the king's son shall reign as the Lord hath said of the sons of David. This is the thing that ye shall do: A third part of you shall be keepers of the watch of the king's house; that it be not broken down. And two parts of all you shall keep the watch of the house of the Lord about the king. And ye shall compass the king round about, every man with his weapons in his hand."

Moreover, Jehoiada the priest delivered to the captains of hundreds spears, and bucklers, and shields, that had been king David's which were in the house of God. And he set all the people, every man having his weapon in his hand, from the right side of the temple to the left side of the temple.

Then they brought out the king's son, and put upon him the crown, and gave him the testimony, and made him king. And Jehoiada and his sons anointed him, and said, " God save the king."

Now when Athaliah heard the noise of the people running and praising the king, she came into the house of the Lord, and she looked, and behold, the king stood at his pillar, and the princes with the trumpets by the king; and all the people of the land rejoiced, and sounded with trumpets; also the singers with instruments of music, and such as were taught to sing praise. Then Athaliah rent her clothes, and said, " Treason, treason! "

But Jehoiada the priest commanded the officers of the host, and said unto them, " Have her forth without the ranges: and him that followeth her, kill with the sword." For the priest had said, "Let her not be slain in the house of the Lord." So they laid hands on her; and when she was come to the entering of the horsegate by the king's house, they slew her there.

And Jehoiada made a covenant between him, and between all the people, and between the king, that they should be the Lord's people. Then all the people went to the house of Baal, and brake it down, and brake his altars and his images in pieces, and slew Mattan the priest of Baal before the altar.

And Jehoiada appointed the Levites to offer the burnt-offerings of the Lord, as it is written in the law of Moses, with rejoicing and with singing, as it was ordained by David.

And all of the people of the land brought the king from the house of the Lord into the king's house, and set him upon the throne of the kingdom. And all the people rejoiced; and the city was quiet after that they had slain Athaliah with the sword.

Joash was seven years old when he began to reign, and he reigned forty years in Jerusalem. And he did that which was right in the sight of the Lord all the days of Jehoiada the priest.

And it came to pass that Joash was minded to repair the house of the Lord, for the sons of Athaliah, that wicked woman, had broken up the house of God; and also all the dedicated things of the house of the Lord did she bestow upon Baalim.

And at the king's commandment they made a chest, and set it without at the gate of the house of the Lord. And they made a proclamation through Judah and Jerusalem, to bring in to the Lord the collection that Moses, the servant of God, laid upon Israel in the wilderness. And all the princes and all the people rejoiced, and brought in, and cast into the chest. Thus did they day by day, and gathered money in abundance.

And king Joash and Jehoiada hired masons and carpenter, and also such as wrought iron and brass to mend the house of the Lord. So the workmen wrought, and the work was perfected by them, and they set the house of God in his state, and strengthened it. And they offered burnt-offerings in the house of the Lord continually all the days of Jehoiada.

But Jehoiada waxed old, and was full of days when he died; an hundred and thirty years old. And they buried him in the city of David among the kings, because he had done good in Israel, both toward God, and toward his house.

Now after the death of Jehoiada came the princes of Judah, and made obeisance to the king. Then the king hearkened unto them. And they left the house of the Lord God of their fathers, and served groves and idols: and wrath came upon Judah and Jerusalem for their trespass.

And the Spirit of God came upon Zechariah the son of Jehoiada the priest, which stood above the people, and said unto them, "Thus saith God, 'Why transgress ye the commandments of the Lord, that ye cannot prosper? because ye have forsaken the Lord, He hath also forsaken you.'"

And they conspired against him, and stoned him with stones at the commandment of king Joash, in the court of the house of the Lord. Thus Joash, the king, remembered not the kindness which Jehoiada had done to him, but slew his son.

And it came to pass at the end of the year, that the host of Syria came up against Judah and Jerusalem, and destroyed all the princes from among the people, and sent all the spoil of them unto the king of Damascus. For the army of the Syrians came with a small company of men, and the Lord delivered a very great host into their hand, because they had forsaken the Lord God of their fathers.

And when they were departed from Joash (for they left him in great diseases), his own servants conspired against him for the blood of the sons of Jehoiada the priest, and slew him on his bed, and he died; and they buried him in the city of David, but they buried him not in the sepulchres of the kings. And Amaziah his son reigned in his stead.

JOASH, KING OF ISRAEL, WEPT OVER ELISHA

AND THE TIME Jehu reigned over Israel in Samaria was twenty and eight years. And Jehu slept with his fathers: and they buried him in Samaria.

And Jehoahaz the son of Jehu began to reign over Israel, and reigned seventeen years. And he did that which was evil in the sight of the Lord. And the anger of the Lord was kindled against Israel, and he delivered them into the hand of Hazael, king of Syria, and the king of Syria oppressed them, and made them like the dust of the threshing field.

Nevertheless they departed not from their sins, but walked therein. And Hazael, king of Syria, oppressed Israel all the days of Jehoahaz. And Jehoahaz slept with his fathers, and they buried him in Samaria. And Joash, his son, reigned in his stead.

And Hazael, king of Syria, died; and Ben-hadad, his son, reigned in his stead.

Now Elisha was fallen sick of his sickness whereof he died. And Joash the king of Israel came down unto him, and wept over his face, and said, " O my father, my father! ' the chariot of Israel, and the horsemen thereof! ' "

And Elisha said unto him, " Take bow and arrows." And he took unto him bow and arrows. And Elisha said, "Put thine hand upon the bow." And he put his hand upon it: And Elisha put his hands upon the king's hands. And Elisha said, " Open the window eastward." And he opened it. Then Elisha said, " Shoot." And he shot. And Elisha said, "The arrow of the Lord's deliverance, and the arrow of deliverance from Syria: for thou shalt smite the Syrians in Aphek, till thou hast consumed them."

And Elisha said, "Take the arrows." And he took them. And Elisha said unto the king of Israel, "Smite upon the ground." And he smote thrice and stayed.

And the man of God was wroth with him, and said, "Thou shouldest have smitten five or six times; then hadst thou smitten Syria till thou hadst consumed it: whereas now thou shalt smite Syria but thrice." And Elisha died and they buried him.

And Joash, the son of Jehoahaz, took again out of the hand of Ben-hadad the son of Hazael, the cities, which he had taken out of the hand of Jehoahaz his father by war. Three times did Joash beat him, and recovered the cities of Israel.

WHY HAST THOU SOUGHT GODS THAT COULD NOT DELIVER THEIR OWN PEOPLE?

IN THE SECOND YEAR of Joash, king of Israel, reigned Amaziah, the son of Joash, king of Judah. Amaziah was twenty and five years old when he began to reign. And he did that which was right in the sight of the Lord, but not with a perfect heart: the high places were not taken away; as yet the people did sacrifice, and burnt incense on the high places.

And it came to pass, as soon as the kingdom was confirmed in his hand, that he slew his servants which had slain the king his father.

Moreover, Amaziah gathered Judah together, and made them captains over thousands, and captains over hundreds, according to the houses of their fathers, throughout all Judah and Benjamin: and he numbered them from twenty years old and above, and found them three hundred thousand choice men, able to go forth to war, that could handle spear and shield. He hired also an hundred thousand mighty men of valour out of Israel for an hundred talents of silver.

But there came a man of God to him, saying, "O king, let not the army of Israel go with thee; for the Lord is not with Israel. God shall make thee fall before the enemy: for God hath power to help, and to cast down."

And Amaziah said to the man of God, "But what shall we do for the hundred talents which I have given to the army of Israel?"

And the man of God answered, "The Lord is able to give thee much more than this."

Then Amaziah separated them, to-wit, the army that was come to him out of Israel, to go home again: wherefore their anger was greatly kindled against Judah, and they returned home in great anger.

And Amaziah strengthened himsedf, and led forth his people, and went to the valley of Salt and smote ten thousand of the children of Seir. But the soldiers of the army which Amaziah sent back, fell upon the cities of Judah, and smote three thousand of them, and took much spoil.

Now it came to pass, after that Amaziah was come from the slaughter of the Edomites, that he brought the gods of the children of Seir, and set them up to be his gods, and bowed himself before them, and burned incense unto them.

Wherefore the Lord sent unto him a prophet which said unto him, " Why hast thou sought after the gods of the people, which could not deliver their own people out of thine hand? "

And the king said unto him, " Art thou the king's counsel? forbear; why shouldest thou be smitten? "

Then the prophet forbare, and said, " I know that God hath determined to destroy thee, because thou hast done this, and hast not hearkened unto my counsel."

Then Amaziah, king of Judah, sent to Joash, king of Israel, saying, " Come, let us see one another in the face."

And Joash answered, saying, " Lo, thou hast smitten the Edomites; and thine heart lifteth thee up to boast: abide now at home; why shouldest thou meddle to thine hurt, that thou shouldest fall, even thou, and Judah with thee? "

But Amaziah would not hear. So Joash the king of Israel went up; and they saw one another in the face at Beth-shemesh, which belongeth to Judah. And Judah was put to the worse before Israel and they fled every man to his tent.

And Joash took Amaziah at Beth-shemesh, and brought him to Jerusalem, and brake down the wall of Jerusalem, four hundred cubits. And he took all the gold and silver, and all the vessels that were found in the house of God, and the treasures of the king's house, the hostages also, and returned to Israel.

Now after the time that Amaziah did turn away from following the Lord, the people made a conspiracy against him in Jerusalem; and he fled to Lachish; but they sent to Lachish after him, and slew him there. And they brought him on horses; and he was buried at Jerusalem with his fathers in the city of David.

WHEN UZZIAH WAS STRONG HIS HEART WAS LIFTED UP TO HIS DESTRUCTION

AND ALL THE PEOPLE of Judah took Uzziah and made him king in the room of his father Amaziah. Sixteen years old was Uzziah when he began to reign, and he reigned fifty and two years in Jerusalem. And he sought God in the days of Zechariah, who had understanding in the visions of God, and as long as he sought the Lord, God made him to prosper.

And he went forth and warred against the Philistines. And God helped him against the Philistines, and against the Arabians. And the Ammonites gave gifts to Uzziah. And his name was spread abroad even to the entering in of Egypt; for he strengthened himself exceedingly.

Moreover, Uzziah built towers in Jerusalem, and fortified them. Also he built towers in the desert, and digged many wells, for he had much cattle, both in the low country, and in the plains; husbandmen also, and vine-dressers in the mountains, and in Carmel: for he loved husbandry.

Moreover, Uzziah had an host of fighting men, that went out to war by bands. And Uzziah prepared for all the host, shields, and spears, and helmets, and harbegeons, and bows, and slings to cast stones. And he made in Jerusalem engines, invented by cunning men, to be upon the towers and upon the bulwarks, to shoot arrows and great stones withal. And his name spread far abroad; for he was marvellously helped, till he was strong.

But when he was strong, his heart was lifted up to his destruction: for he transgressed against the Lord his God, and went into the temple of the Lord to burn incense upon the altar of incense.

And Azariah the priest went in after him, and with him fourscore priests of the Lord, that were valiant men: and they withstood Uzziah the king, and said unto him, "It appertaineth not unto thee, Uzziah, to burn incense unto the Lord, but to the priests, the sons of Aaron, that are consecrated to burn incense. Go out of the sanctuary; for thou hast trespassed; neither shall it be for thine honour from the Lord God."

Then Uzziah was wroth, and had a censer in his hand to burn incense; and while he was wroth with the priests, the leprosy even rose up in his forehead before the priests in the house of the Lord. And all the priests looked upon him, and behold, he was leprous in his forehead, and they thrust him out from thence. Yea, himself hasted to go out, because the Lord had smitten him.

And Uzziah the king was a leper and dwelt in a separate house, and Jothan his son was over the king's house, judging the people of the land.

HEAR THE WORD OF THE LORD

And Joash, king of Israel, slept with his fathers, and was buried in Samaria with the kings of Israel. And Jeroboam, the son of Joash began to reign in Israel and reigned forty and one years.

And the Lord saw the affliction of Israel, that it was bitter; for there was not any shut up, nor any left, nor any helper for Israel. And the Lord said not that he would blot out the name of Israel from under heaven; but he saved them by the hand of Jeroboam the son of Joash. And Jeroboam restored the coast of Israel from the entering of Hamath unto the sea of the plain, according to the word of the Lord God of Israel.

But Jeroboam did that which was evil in the sight of the Lord: he departed not from the sins of his fathers who made Israel to sin.

And the word of the Lord came to Amos, the herdsman of Tekoa, and he spake prophecies which he saw concerning Israel in the days of Jeroboam, and he said:

"Behold, the Lord stood upon a wall made by a plumbline, with a plumbline in his hand. And the Lord said unto me, 'Amos, what seest thou?' And I said, 'A plumbline.' Then said the Lord, 'Behold, I will set a plumbline in the midst of my people Israel; I will not again pass by them any more; and the high places of Isaac shall be desolate, and the sanctuaries of Israel shall be laid waste and I will rise against the house of Jeroboam with the sword.'"

Then Amaziah the priest of Bethel sent to Jeroboam, king of Israel, saying, "Amos hath conspired against thee in the midst of the house of Israel: the land is not able to bear all his words. For thus Amos saith, 'Jeroboam shall die by the sword, and Israel shall surely be led away captive out of their own land.' "

And Amaziah said unto Amos: "O thou seer, go, flee thee away into the land of Judah, and there eat bread, and prophesy there. But prophesy not again any more at Bethel; for it is the king's chapel, and it is the king's court."

Then answered Amos, and said to Amaziah: "I was no prophet, neither was I a prophet's son; but I was a herdsman, and a gatherer of sycamore fruit. And the Lord took me as I followed the flock, and the Lord said unto me, 'Go, prophesy unto my people Israel.' Now therefore hear thou the word of the Lord: thou sayest, 'Prophesy not against Israel, and drop not thy word against the house of Isaac.' Therefore thus saith the Lord: 'Thy wife shall be a harlot in the city; and thy sons and thy daughters shall fall by the sword, and thy land shall be divided by line; and thou shalt die in a polluted land; and Israel shall surely go into captivity forth of this land.' "

And Amos spoke again and said, "Thus hath the Lord God showed unto me: and behold a basket of summer fruit. And He said, 'Amos, what seest thou?' And I said, 'A basket of summer fruit.' Then said the Lord unto me, 'The end is come upon my people Israel: I will not again pass by them any more.

"'And it shall come to pass in that day,' saith the Lord God, 'That I will cause the sun to go down at noon, and I will darken the earth in the clear day: and I will turn your feasts into mourning, and all your songs into lamentation; and I will bring up sackcloth upon all loins, and baldness upon every head; and I will make it as the mourning of an only son, and the end thereof as a bitter day.

"'Behold, the days come,' saith the Lord God, 'That I will send a famine in the land, not a famine of bread, nor a thirst for water, but of hearing the words of the Lord: and they shall wander from sea to sea, and from the north even to the east, they shall run to and fro to seek the word of the Lord, and shall not find it. In that day shall the fair virgins and the young men faint for thirst. They that swear by the sin of Samaria, and say, " Thy god, O Dan, liveth;" and, " The manner of Beer-sheba liveth;" even they shall fall, and never rise up again.' "

And Amos said, " Thus saith the Lord unto the house of Israel,

' Seek ye me, and ye shall live;
Seek him that maketh the seven stars and Orion,
And turneth the shadow of death into the morning.
Seek good, and not evil, that ye may live;
And so the Lord, the God of hosts,
Shall be with you, as ye have spoken.
Hate the evil, and love the good,
And establish judgment in the gate:
It may be that the Lord God of hosts
Will be gracious unto the remnant of Joseph.' "

And Amos said:

" Prepare to meet thy God, O Israel!
For lo, he that formeth the mountains,
And createth the wind,
And declareth unto man what is his thought,
That maketh the morning darkness,
And treadeth upon the high places of the earth,
The Lord, The God of hosts, is his name."

THERE IS NO TRUTH, NOR MERCY, NOR KNOWLEDGE OF GOD IN THE LAND

But Jeroboam departed not from all the sins of his fathers, who made Israel to sin. And Jeroboam slept with his fathers, and Zachariah his son reigned in his stead.

In the thirty and eighth year of Uzziah, king of Judah, did Zachariah the son of Jeroboam reign over Israel six months. And he did that which was evil in the sight of the Lord, and Shallum, the son of Jabesh, conspired against him and smote him before the people, and slew him, and reigned in his stead. And he reigned a full month, for Menahem, the son of Gadi, went up from Tirzah and came to Samaria, and smote Shallum, and slew him, and reigned in his stead.

And Menahem did that which was evil. He smote Tiphsah, and all that were therein, and the coasts thereof from Tirzah, because they opened not to him, therefore he smote it. And all the women that were with child, he ripped up.

And Pul the king of Assyria came against the land. And Menahem gave Pul a thousand talents of silver, that his hand might be with him to confirm the kingdom in his hand. And Menahem exacted the money from Israel, even of all the mighty men of wealth, of each man fifty shekels of silver, to give to the king of Assyria. So the king of Assyria turned back, and stayed not there in the land.

In the fiftieth year of Uzziah king of Judah, Menahem slept with his fathers, and Pekahiah his son reigned in his stead. And he did that which was evil, and Pekah the son of Remaliah, a captain of his, conspired against him, and smote him in the palace of the king's house, and reigned in his room.

And the word of the Lord came unto the prophet Hosea, and he said:

" Hear the word of the Lord, ye children of Israel:
For the Lord hath a controversy with the inhabitants of the land,
Because there is no truth, nor mercy, nor knowledge of God in the land.
By swearing, and lying, and killing, and stealing, and committing adultery,
They break out, and blood toucheth blood.
Therefore shall the land mourn,
And everyone that dwelleth therein shall languish,
With the beasts of the field, and the fowls of heaven;
Yea, the fishes of the sea also shall be taken away.
My people are destroyed for lack of knowledge:
Because thou hast rejected knowledge,
I will also reject thee;
Seeing thou hast forgotten the law of thy God,
I will also forget thy children."

And Hosea said: " Thus saith the Lord:

" ' Israel hath cast off the thing that is good:
The enemy shall pursue him.
They have set up kings, but not by me:
They have made princes, and I knew it not:
Of their silver and their gold have they made them idols,
That they may be cut off.

" ' For they have sown the wind,
And they shall reap the whirlwind.
Israel is swallowed up.
I have written to him the great things of my law,

But they were counted as a strange thing,
For Israel hath forgotten his Maker.

" 'Oh Israel, thou hast destroyed thyself;
But in me is thine help.

" 'Who is wise, and he shall understand these things?
Prudent, and he shall know them?
For the ways of the Lord are right,
And the just shall walk in them:
But the transgressors shall fall therein.' "

THE VISION OF ISAIAH, THE PROPHET, AND HIS CALL

In the second year of Pekah, the son of Remaliah, king of Israel, Uzziah, king of Judah, slept with his fathers, and they buried him with his fathers in the field of the burial which belonged to the kings, for they said, "He is a leper." And Jotham his son reigned in his stead.

And the prophet Isaiah had a vision, and he said:

"In the year that king Uzziah died I saw also the Lord sitting upon a throne, high and lifted up, and his train filled the temple. Above it stood the seraphims: each one had six wings; with twain he covered his face, and with twain he covered his feet, and with twain he did fly. And one cried unto another, and said, 'Holy, holy, holy, is the Lord of Hosts: the whole earth is full of his glory.' And the posts of the door moved at the voice of him that cried, and the house was filled with smoke.

"Then said I, 'Woe is me! for I am undone; because I am a man of unclean lips, and I dwell in the midst of a people of unclean lips: for mine eyes have seen the king, the Lord of hosts.'

"Then flew one of the seraphims unto me, having a live coal in his hand, which he had taken with the tongs from off the altar: and he laid it upon my mouth, and said, 'Lo, this hath touched thy lips; and thine iniquity is taken away, and thy sin purged.'

"Also I heard the voice of the Lord, saying, 'Whom shall I send, and who will go for us?'

"Then said I, 'Here am I; send me.'

"And He said, 'Go, and tell this people, "Hear ye indeed, but understand not; and see ye indeed, but perceive not." Make the heart of this people fat, and make their ears heavy, and shut their eyes; lest they see with their eyes, and hear with their ears, and understand with their heart, and convert, and be healed.'

"Then said I, 'Lord, how long?'

"And He answered, 'Until the cities be wasted without inhabitant, and the houses without man, and the land be utterly desolate; and the Lord have removed men far away, and there be a great forsaking in the midst of the land. But yet in it shall be a tenth, and it shall return, and shall be eaten: as a teil-tree, and as an oak whose substance is in them, when they cast their leaves: so the holy seed shall be the substance thereof.'"

THE DAYS OF JOTHAM, KING OF JUDAH

JOTHAM was twenty and five years old when he began to reign, and he reigned sixteen years in Jerusalem. And he did that which was right in the sight of the Lord, according to all that his father Uzziah did: howbeit, he entered not into the temple of the Lord. And the people did corruptly.

He built the high gate of the house of the Lord, and on the wall of Ophel he built much. Moreover, he built cities in the mountains of Judah, and in the forests he built castles and towers.

He fought against the king of the Ammonites, and prevailed against them. And the children of Ammon gave him the same year, an hundred talents of silver, and ten thousand measures of wheat, and ten thousand of barley. So much did the children of Ammon pay him both the second year, and the third.

So Jotham became mighty, because he prepared his ways before the Lord his God. And Jotham slept with his fathers, and they buried him in the city of David: and Ahaz his son reigned in his stead.

MICAH

THE WORD of the Lord that came to Micah the Morasthite in the days of Jotham, Ahaz, and Hezekiah, kings of Judah, which he saw concerning Samaria and Jerusalem.

HEARKEN, O EARTH, AND ALL THAT THEREIN IS!

Hear, all ye people!
Hearken, O earth, and all that therein is:
And let the Lord God be witness against you,
The Lord from his holy temple.
For, behold, the Lord cometh forth out of his place,
And will come down, and tread upon the high places
of the earth.
And the mountain shall be molten under him,
And the valleys shall be cleft, as wax before the fire,
And as the waters that are poured down a steep place.

For the transgression of Jacob is all this,
And for the sins of the house of Israel.
What is the transgression of Jacob? is it not Samaria?
And what are the high places of Judah? are they not
Jerusalem?
Therefore I will make Samaria as an heap of the field,
And as plantings of a vineyard:
And I will pour down the stones thereof into the valley,
And I will discover the foundations thereof.
And all the graven images thereof shall be beaten to pieces,
And all the hires thereof shall be burned with the fire,
And all the idols thereof will I lay desolate:
For she gathered it of the hire of an harlot,

And they shall return to the hire of an harlot.
Therefore I will wail and howl,
I will go stripped and naked:
I will make wailing like the dragons,
And mourning as the owls.
For her wound is incurable;
For it is come unto Judah;
He is come unto the gate of my people,
Even to Jerusalem.

Woe to them that devise iniquity, and work evil upon
their beds!
When the morning is light, they practise it,
Because it is in the power of their hand.
And they covet fields, and take them by violence;
And houses, and take them away:
So they oppress a man and his house,
Even a man and his heritage.
The women of my people have ye cast out from their
pleasant houses;
From their children have ye taken away my glory for ever.
Arise ye, and depart; for this is not your rest:
Because it is polluted, it shall destroy you,
Even with a sore destruction.
Thus saith the Lord concerning the prophets that make my
people err,
That bite with their teeth, and cry, " Peace ";
And he that putteth not into their mouths;
They even prepare war against him.
Therefore night shall be unto you,
That ye shall not have a vision;
And it shall be dark unto you,
That ye shall not divine;
And the sun shall go down over the prophets,

And the days shall be dark over them.
Then shall the seers be ashamed,
And the diviners confounded:
Yea, they shall all cover their lips;
For there is no answer of God.

But truly I am full of power by the spirit of the Lord,
And of judgment, and of might,
To declare unto Jacob his transgression,
And to Israel his sin.
Hear this, I pray you, ye heads of the house of Jacob,
And princes of the house of Israel,
That abhor judgment, and pervert all equity.
They build up Zion with blood,
And Jerusalem with iniquity.
The heads thereof judge for reward,
And the priests thereof teach for hire,
And the prophets thereof divine for money:
Yet will they lean upon the Lord, and say,
"Is not the Lord among us? none evil can come upon us."
Therefore shall Zion for your sake be plowed as a field,
And Jerusalem shall become heaps,
And the mountain of the house as the high places of
the forest.

THE HOUSE OF THE LORD

But in the last days it shall come to pass,
That the mountain of the house of the Lord
Shall be established in the top of the mountains,
And it shall be exalted above the hills;
And people shall flow unto it.

And many nations shall come, and say,
" Come, and let us go up to the mountain of the Lord,
And to the house of the God of Jacob;
And he will teach us of his ways,
And we will walk in his paths:
For the law shall go forth of Zion,
And the word of the Lord from Jerusalem.

And he shall judge among many people,
And rebuke strong nations afar off;
And they shall beat their swords into plowshares,
And their spears into pruninghooks:
Nation shall not lift up a sword against nation,
Neither shall they learn war any more.

But they shall sit every man under his vine and under his
fig tree;
And none shall make them afraid:
For the mouth of the Lord of hosts hath spoken it.
For all people will walk every one in the name of his god,
And we will walk in the name of the Lord our God for
ever and ever.

" In that day," saith the Lord,
" Will I assemble her that halteth,
And I will gather her that is driven out,
And her that I have afflicted;
And I will make her that halteth a remnant,
And her that was cast far off a strong nation:
And the Lord shall reign over them in mount Zion from
henceforth, even for ever."

HE THAT IS TO BE RULER OVER ISRAEL

"Thou Beth-lehem Ephratah,
Though thou be little among the thousands of Judah,
Yet out of thee shall he come forth unto me that is to be ruler of Israel;
Whose goings forth have been from of old, from everlasting.
And he shall stand and feed in the strength of the Lord,
In the majesty of the name of the Lord his God;
And they shall abide;
For now shall he be great unto the ends of the earth."

WHAT DOTH THE LORD REQUIRE OF THEE?

Hear, all ye people!
Hearken, O earth!
And all that therein is:

Wherewith shall I come before the Lord,
And bow myself before the high God?
Shall I come before him with burnt-offerings,
With calves of a year old?

Will the Lord be pleased with thousands of rams,
Or with ten thousands of rivers of oil?
Shall I give my firstborn for my transgression,
The fruit of my body for the sin of my soul?

He hath showed thee, O man, what is good;
And what doth the Lord require of thee,
But to do justly, and to love mercy,
And to walk humbly with thy God.

JUDAH WAS BROUGHT LOW BECAUSE OF AHAZ

IN THE SEVENTEENTH YEAR of Pekah, king of Israel, Ahaz the son of Jotham, king of Judah, began to reign. Twenty years old was Ahaz when he began to reign in Jerusalem. But he did not that which was right in the sight of the Lord his God, but walked in the ways of the kings of Israel, yea, and made his son to pass through the fire, according to the abominations of the heathen. And he sacrificed also, and burnt incense in the high places, and on the hills, and under every green tree, and made also molten images for Baalim.

And it came to pass that Rezin, king of Syria, and Pekah, king of Israel, went up toward Jerusalem to war against it. And it was told Ahaz saying, " Syria is confederate with Israel." And Ahaz' heart was moved, and the heart of his people, as the trees of the wood are moved with the wind.

Then said the Lord unto the prophet, Isaiah, " Go forth to meet Ahaz, and say unto him, ' Take heed, and be quiet; fear not, neither be faint-hearted for the two tails of these smoking firebrands. Because Syria and Israel have taken evil counsel against thee, saying, " Let us go up against Judah, and vex it, and let us make a breach therein, and set a king in the midst of it, even the son of Tabeal." Thus saith the Lord, " It shall not stand, neither shall it come to pass. For the head of Syria is Damascus, and the head of Damascus is Rezin; and the head of Ephraim is Samaria, and the head of Samaria is Pekah. And within threescore and five years shall Ephraim be broken, that it be not a people. If ye will not believe, surely ye shall not be established." ' "

And Isaiah said, " Ask thee a sign of the Lord thy God; ask it either in the depth, or in the height above."

But Ahaz said, "I will not ask, neither will I tempt the Lord."

And Isaiah said, "Hear ye not, O house of David; is it a small thing for you to weary men, but will ye weary my God also? Therefore the Lord himself shall give you a sign: 'Behold, a virgin shall conceive, and bear a son, and shall call his name Immanuel. Butter and honey shall he eat, that he may know to refuse the evil, and choose the good. For before the child shall know to refuse the evil, and choose the good, the land that thou abhorrest shall be forsaken of both her kings. The Lord shall bring upon thee, and upon thy people, and upon thy father's house days that have not come, from the day that Israel departed from Judah; even the king of Assyria.'"

Then Rezin, king of Syria, and Pekah, king of Israel came up to Jerusalem to war: and they besieged Ahaz. And the king of Syria smote Ahaz and carried away a great multitude, and brought them to Damascus. And the king of Israel smote Ahaz with a great slaughter. For Pekah slew in Judah an hundred and twenty thousand in one day, because they had forsaken the Lord God of their fathers. And Israel carried away captive two hundred thousand, women, sons, and daughters, and took also much spoil, and brought the spoil to Samaria.

But a prophet of the Lord was there, whose name was Oded: and he went out before the host that came to Samaria, and said, "Behold, because the Lord God of your fathers was wroth with Judah, he delivered them into your hand, and ye have slain them in a rage that reacheth up unto heaven. And now ye purpose to keep the children of Judah and Jerusalem for bond-men and bond-women unto you: but are there not with you sins against the Lord your God? Now hear me therefore, and deliver the captives again, which ye have taken captive of your brethren; for the fierce wrath of the Lord is upon you."

Then certain of the heads of the children of Ephraim stood up against them that came from the war, and said unto them, "Ye shall not bring in the captives hither: for whereas we have offended against the Lord already, ye intend to add more to our sins and to our trespass: for our trespass is great, and there is fierce wrath against Israel."

So the armed men left the captives and the spoil before the princes and the congregation. And the heads of the children of Ephraim rose up, and took the captives, and with the spoil clothed all that were naked among them, and arrayed them, and shod them, and gave them to eat and to drink, and anointed them, and carried all the feeble of them upon asses, and brought them to Jericho, the city of palm-trees, to their brethren. Then they returned to Samaria.

At that time Hoshea the son of Elah made a conspiracy against Pekah king of Israel, and smote him, and slew him, and reigned in his stead, in the twelfth year of Ahaz king of Judah.

And king Ahaz sent unto the king of Assyria to help him, for again the Edomites had come and smitten Judah, and carried away captives. The Philistines also had invaded the cities of the low country, and of the south of Judah, and they dwelt there. For the Lord brought Judah low because of Ahaz: for he made Judah naked, and transgressed sore against the Lord. So Ahaz sent messengers to the king of Assyria saying, "I am thy servant and thy son: come up and save me out of the hand of the king of Syria."

And the Lord spake unto Isaiah again, saying, "Forasmuch as this people refuseth the waters of Shiloah that go softly, now therefore behold the Lord bringeth upon them the waters of the river, strong and many, even the king of Assyria, and all his glory: and he shall come up over all his channels, and go over all his banks; and he shall pass through Judah; he shall overflow and reach even to the neck; and the stretching out of his wings shall fill the breadth of thy land, O Immanuel. Associate yourselves, O ye people, and ye shall be broken in pieces; and give ear, all ye far countries. For the Lord spake thus to me with a strong hand, and instructed me that I should not walk in the way of this people saying, ' Say ye not, A confederacy, to all them to whom this people shall say, A confederacy; neither fear ye their fear, nor be afraid. Sanctify the Lord of hosts himself; and let him be your fear, and let him be your dread. And He shall be for a sanctuary. And when they shall say unto you, " Seek unto them that have familiar spirits, and unto wizards that peep, and that mutter;" should not a people seek unto their God? to the law and to the testimony? If they speak not according to this word, it is because there is no light in them. And they shall look unto the earth, and behold trouble and darkness, and dimness of anguish, and they shall be driven to darkness.' "

But Ahaz took the silver and gold that was found in the house of the Lord, and in the treasures of the king's house, and sent it for a present to the king of Assyria. And the king of Assyria hearkened unto him: for he went up against Damascus, and took it, and carried the people of it captive to Kir, and slew Rezin. But he helped Ahaz not.

And in the time of his distress did Ahaz trespass yet more against the Lord. For he sacrificed unto the gods of Damascus, which smote him. And he said, " Because the gods of the kings of Syria help them, therefore will I sacrifice to them, that they may help me." But they were the ruin of him.

And Ahaz gathered together the vessels of the house of God, and cut in pieces the vessels of the house of the Lord, and he made altars in every corner of Jerusalem. And in every city of Judah he made high places to burn incense unto other gods, and provoked to anger the Lord God of his fathers.

And Ahaz slept with his fathers, and they buried him in the city, even in Jerusalem: but they brought him not into the sepulchres of the kings of Judah. And Hezekiah his son reigned in his stead.

ISAIAH

THE VISION of Isaiah the son of Amoz, which he saw concerning Israel and Judah in the days of Uzziah, Jotham, Ahaz and Hezekiah:

CEASE TO DO EVIL! LEARN TO DO WELL!

Hear, O heavens, and give ear, O earth:
For the Lord hath spoken:

I have nourished and brought up children,
And they have rebelled against me.
The ox knoweth his owner,
And the ass his master's crib;
But Israel doth not know,
My people doth not consider.

Ah sinful nation, a people laden with iniquity,
A seed of evildoers, children that are corrupters!
They have forsaken the Lord,
They have provoked the Holy One of Israel unto anger,
They are gone away backward.

Why should ye be stricken any more?
Ye will revolt more and more;
The whole head is sick, and the whole heart faint,
From the sole of the foot even unto the head there is
no soundness in it,

But wounds, and bruises, and putrefying sores;
They have not been closed, neither bound up,
Neither mollified with ointment.
Your country is desolate,
Your cities are burned with fire;
Your land, strangers devour it in your presence,
And it is desolate as overthrown by strangers.
And the daughter of Zion is left as a cottage in a vineyard,
As a lodge in a garden of cucumbers,
As a besieged city.
Except the Lord of hosts had left unto us a very small
remnant,
We should have been as Sodom,
We should have been like unto Gomorrah.

Hear the word of the Lord, ye rulers of Sodom!
Give ear unto the law of our God, ye people of Gomorrah!
To what purpose is the multitude of your sacrifices unto
me? saith the Lord.
I am full of the burnt offerings of rams, and of fed beasts;
And I delight not in the blood of bullocks, or of lambs,
or of he-goats.

When ye come to appear before me,
Bring no more vain oblations;
Incense is an abomination unto me;
The new moons and sabbaths, the calling of assemblies,
I cannot away with;
It is iniquity, even the solemn meeting.
Your new moons and your appointed feasts my soul
hateth;
They are a trouble unto me;
I am weary to bear them.

And when ye spread forth your hands,
I will hide mine eyes from you;
Yea, when ye make many prayers, I will not hear;
Your hands are full of blood.

Wash you, make you clean;
Put away the evil of your doings from before mine eyes;
Cease to do evil!
Learn to do well!
Seek judgment, relieve the oppressed,
Judge the fatherless, plead for the widow.

Come now, and let us reason together, saith the Lord:
Though your sins be as scarlet,
They shall be as white as snow;
Though they be red like crimson,
They shall be as wool.
If ye be willing and obedient,
Ye shall eat the good of the land:
But if ye refuse and rebel,
Ye shall be devoured with the sword:
For the mouth of the Lord hath spoken it.

BECAUSE THE DAUGHTERS OF ZION ARE HAUGHTY

Because the daughters of Zion are haughty,
And walk with stretched forth necks and wanton eyes,
Walking and mincing as they go,
And making a tinkling with their feet:
Therefore the Lord will smite with a scab
The crown of the head of the daughters of Zion.

In that day the Lord will take away
The bravery of their tinkling ornaments about their feet,
And their cauls, and their round tires like the moon,
And the chains, and the bracelets, and the mufflers,
The bonnets, and the ornaments of the legs,
And the headbands, and the tablets, and the earrings,
The rings, and the nose jewels,
The changeable suits of apparel,
And the mantles, and the wimples, and the crisping pins,
The glasses, and the fine linen, and the hoods, and the veils.

And it shall come to pass,
That instead of sweet smell there shall be stink;
And instead of a girdle a rent;
And instead of well-set hair baldness;
And instead of a stomacher a girding of sackcloth;
And burning instead of beauty.

Thy men shall fall by the sword,
And thy mighty in war,
And her gates shall lament and mourn;
And she being desolate shall sit upon the ground.

And in that day
Seven woman shall take hold of one man,
Saying, " We will eat our own bread,
And wear our own apparel:
Only let us be called by thy name,
To take away our reproach."

THE FRUIT OF THEIR DOINGS

Say ye to the righteous,
That it shall be well with him;
For they shall eat the fruit of their doings.

Woe unto the wicked!
It shall be ill with him;
For the reward of his hands shall be given him.

WOE TO THE DRUNKARDS OF EPHRAIM

Woe to the crown of pride,
To the drunkards of Ephraim,
Whose glorious beauty is a fading flower
Which are on the head of the fat valleys
Of them that are overcome with wine!
The crown of pride,
The drunkards of Ephraim,
Shall be trodden under feet.

But they also have erred through wine,
And through strong drink are out of the way;
The priest and the prophet have erred through strong drink,
They are swallowed up of wine,
They are out of the way through strong drink;
They err in vision,
They stumble in judgment.

For all tables are full of vomit and filthiness,
So that there is no place clean.

TREMBLE, YE WOMEN THAT ARE AT EASE!

Rise up, ye women that are at ease,
Hear my voice, ye careless daughters;
Give ear unto my speech.

Many days and years shall ye be troubled,
Ye careless daughters:
For the vintage shall fail,
The gathering shall not come.

Tremble, ye women that are at ease;
Be troubled, ye careless ones:
Strip you, and make you bare,
And gird sackcloth upon your loins.

Upon the land of my people
Shall come up thorns and briers;
Yea, upon all the houses of joy in the joyous city.
Because the palaces shall be forsaken;
The multitude of the city shall be left.

Until the spirit be poured upon us from on high;
And the work of righteousness shall be peace;
And the effect of righteousness
Quietness and assurance for ever.

CEASE YE FROM MAN
WHOSE BREATH IS IN HIS NOSTRILS

The lofty looks of man shall be humbled,
And the haughtiness of men shall be bowed down,
And the Lord alone shall be exalted in that day.
For the day of the Lord of hosts
Shall be upon every one that is proud and lofty,
And upon every one that is lifted up;
And he shall be brought low.
And the loftiness of man shall be bowed down,
And the haughtiness of men shall be made low;
And the Lord shall be exalted in that day.

And the idols he shall utterly abolish.
In that day a man shall cast his idols of silver, and
his idols of gold,
Which they made each one for himself to worship,
To the moles and to the bats;
To go into the clefts of the rocks,
And into the tops of the ragged rocks,
For fear of the Lord, and for the glory of his majesty,
When He ariseth to shake terribly the earth.

Cease ye from man, whose breath is in his nostrils;
For wherein is he to be accounted of?

WOE UNTO THEM THAT CALL EVIL GOOD

Woe unto them that call evil good, and good evil;
That put darkness for light, and light for darkness;
That put bitter for sweet, and sweet for bitter!
Woe unto them that are wise in their own eyes,
And prudent in their own sight!
Woe unto them that are mighty to drink wine,
And men of strength to mingle strong drink;
Which justify the wicked for reward,
And take away the righteousness of the righteous from him!

Therefore as the fire devoureth the stubble,
And the flame consumeth the chaff,
So their root shall be as rottenness,
And their blossom shall go up as dust;
Because they have cast away the law of the Lord of hosts,
And despised the word of the Holy One of Israel.

IN QUIETNESS AND IN CONFIDENCE SHALL BE YOUR STRENGTH

Woe to the rebellious children, saith the Lord,
That take counsel, but not of me;
And that cover with a covering,
But not of my Spirit,
That they may add sin to sin:
That walk to go down into Egypt,
And have not asked at my mouth;

To strengthen themselves in the strength of Pharaoh,
And to trust in the shadow of Egypt!

Therefore shall the strength of Pharaoh be your shame,
And the trust in the shadow of Egypt your confusion.
For the Egyptians shall help in vain,
And to no purpose:
Therefore have I cried concerning this,
Their strength is to sit still.

Now go, write it before them in a table,
And note it in a book,
That it may be for the time to come for ever and ever:
That this is a rebellious people, lying children,
Children that will not hear the law of the Lord:
Which say to the seers, " See not;"
And to the Prophets, " Prophesy not unto us right things,
Speak unto us smooth things, prophesy deceits:
Get you out of the way,
Turn aside out of the path,
Cause the Holy One of Israel to cease from before us."

Wherefore thus saith the Holy One of Israel,
" Because ye despise the Word,
And trust in oppression and perverseness,
And stay thereon:
Therefore this iniquity shall be to you as a breach ready to fall,
Swelling out in a high wall,
Whose breaking cometh suddenly at an instant."
And he shall break it as the breaking of the potter's vessel,
That is broken in pieces;
He shall not spare.

For thus saith the Lord God, the Holy One of Israel:
" In returning and rest shall ye be saved;
In quietness and in confidence shall be your strength:"
And ye would not.
But ye said, " No; for we will flee upon horses;"
Therefore shall ye flee:
And, " We will ride upon the swift;"
Therefore shall they that pursue you be swift.
One thousand shall flee at the rebuke of one;
At the rebuke of five shall ye flee:
Till ye be left as a beacon upon the top of a mountain,
And as an ensign on a hill.

FOR PRECEPT MUST BE UPON PRECEPT

Whom shall he teach knowledge?
And whom shall he make to understand doctrine?
For precept must be upon precept,
Precept upon precept;
Line upon line, line upon line;
Here a little and there a little:

For with stammering lips and another tongue will he speak
to this people,
To whom he said, " This is the rest wherewith ye may
cause the weary to rest;
And this is the refreshing:"
Yet they would not hear.

But the word of the Lord was unto them
Precept upon precept, precept upon precept;
Line upon line, line upon line;
Here a little, and there a little.

Wherefore hear the word of the Lord,
Ye scornful men that rule this people which are in
Jerusalem:
Because ye have said,
" We have made a covenant with death,
And with hell are we at agreement,
When the overflowing scourge shall pass through,
It shall not come unto us;
For we have made lies our refuge,
And under falsehood have we hid ourselves."

Therefore thus saith the Lord God,
" Behold, I lay in Zion for a foundation a stone,
A tried stone, a precious corner stone, a sure foundation;
He that believeth shall not make haste.
Judgment also will I lay to the line,
And righteousness to the plummet:
And the hail shall sweep away the refuge of lies,
And the waters shall overflow the hiding place.
And your covenant with death shall be disannulled,
And your agreement with hell shall not stand;
When the overflowing scourge shall pass through,
Then ye shall be trodden down by it."

BECAUSE THOU HAST FORGOTTEN GOD

Because thou hast forgotten the God of thy salvation,
And hast not been mindful of the rock of thy strength,
Therefore shalt thou plant pleasant plants,
And shall set it with strange slips:
In the day shalt thou make thy plant to grow,
And in the morning shalt thou make thy seed to flourish:
But the harvest shall be a heap in the day of grief
And of desperate sorrow.

"OH ISRAEL, THOU HAST DESTROYED THYSELF"

HOSHEA, the son of Elah, reigned in Samaria over Israel nine years. And he did that which was evil in the sight of the Lord. And it came to pass that Shalmaneser king of Assyria came up against Samaria, and besieged it, and at the end of three years took it. And Hoshea became servant to the king of Assyria, and gave him presents. That was in the fourth year of the reign of Hezekiah, king of Judah.

And the king of Assyria found conspiracy in Hoshea, king of Israel, for he had sent messengers to So, king of Egypt, and brought no present to the king of Assyria, as he had done year by year; therefore the king of Assyria shut him up, and bound him in prison.

Then the king of Assyria came up throughout all the kingdom of Israel, and took Samaria and carried the people of Israel away into Assyria, and placed them in Halah, and Habor by the river of Gozan, and in the cities of the Medes.

For the children of Israel had sinned against the Lord their God, because they had not obeyed the voice of the Lord, but had transgressed His covenant and all that Moses the servant of the Lord commanded, and would not hear them nor do them. And they walked in the statutes of the heathen whom the Lord cast out from before the children of Israel. For they served idols, whereof the Lord had said unto them, "Ye shall not do this thing."

Yet the Lord testified against Israel, and against Judah by all the prophets, and by all the seers, saying, "Turn ye from your evil ways, and keep my commandments, and my statutes, according to all the law which I commanded your fathers, and which I sent to you by my servants the prophets."

Notwithstanding, they would not hear, but hardened their necks, like to the neck of their fathers that did not believe in the Lord their God. And they rejected his statutes, and his covenant that he made with their fathers, and they followed vanity, and became vain, and went after the heathen that were round about them, and made them molten images, even two calves, and made a grove, and worshipped all the host of heaven, and served Baal. And they caused their sons and their daughters to pass through the fire, and used divination and enchantments, and sold themselves to do evil in the sight of the Lord, and they left all of the commandments of the Lord their God.

Therefore the Lord removed them out of his sight: there was none left but the tribe of Judah only. And the Lord rejected all the seed of Israel, and afflicted them, and delivered them into the hand of spoilers, until he had cast them out of his sight. So Israel was carried away captive out of their own land.

And the king of Assyria brought men from Babylon, and from Cuthah, and from Ava, and from Hamath, and from Spharvaim, and placed them in the cities of Samaria instead of the children of Israel; and they possessed Samaria, and dwelt in the cities thereof.

HEZEKIAH WROUGHT THAT WHICH WAS GOOD, AND RIGHT, AND TRUTH BEFORE THE LORD, AND PROSPERED

HEZEKIAH the son of Ahaz began to reign when he was five and twenty years old, and he reigned nine and twenty years in Jerusalem. And he did that which was right in the sight of the Lord, according to all that David had done.

He, in the first year of his reign, opened the doors of the house of the Lord, and repaired them. And he brought in the priests and the Levites, and said unto them, "Hear me, ye Levites! Sanctify now yourselves, and sanctify the house of the Lord God of your fathers, and carry forth the filthiness out of the holy place. For our fathers have trespassed, and done that which was evil in the eyes of the Lord our God, and have forsaken him, and have turned away their faces from the habitation of the Lord, and turned their backs. Also they have shut up the doors of the porch, and put out the lamps, and have not burned incense nor offered burnt-offerings in the holy place unto the God of Israel. Wherefore the wrath of the Lord was upon Judah and Jerusalem, and he hath delivered them to trouble. For lo, our fathers have fallen by the sword, and our sons and our daughters and our wives are in captivity for this. Now it is in mine heart to make a covenant with the Lord God of Israel, that his fierce wrath may turn away from us. My sons, be not now negligent: for the Lord hath chosen you to stand before him, to serve him, and that ye should minister unto him, and burn incense."

Then the Levites arose, and they gathered their brethren, and sanctified themselves, and came, according to the commandment of the king, to cleanse the house of the Lord. And the priests went into the inner part of the house, and brought out all the uncleanness that they found in the temple into the court. And the Levites took it, to carry it out into the brook Kidron.

Then they went in to Hezekiah the king, and said, "We have cleansed all the house of the Lord, and the altar of burnt-offering, with all the vessels thereof, and the shew-bread table, with all the vessels thereof. Moreover all the vessels, which king Ahaz in his reign did cast away in his transgression, have we prepared and sanctified, and behold, they are before the altar of the Lord."

Then Hezekiah the king rose early, and gathered the rulers of the city, and went up to the house of the Lord. And they brought a sin-offering for the kingdom, and for the sanctuary, and for Judah. And the sons of Aaron offered them on the altar of the Lord to make an atonement for all Israel: for the king commanded that the burnt-offering and the sin-offering should be made for all Israel.

And when the burnt-offering began, the song of the Lord began also, and they sang praises with gladness, and they bowed their heads and worshipped. And all this continued until the burnt-offering was finished.

Then Hezekiah said, "Now ye have consecrated yourselves unto the Lord, come near and bring sacrifices and thank-offerings into the house of the Lord." And the congregation brought in sacrifices and thank-offerings; and, as many as were of a free heart, burnt-offerings.

So the service of the house of the Lord was set in order. And Hezekiah rejoiced, and all the people, that God had prepared the people; for the thing was done suddenly.

And Hezekiah sent to all Israel and Judah, and wrote letters also to Ephraim and Manasseh, that they should come to the house of the Lord at Jerusalem, to keep the passover unto the Lord God of Israel.

So the posts went with the letters from the king and his princes throughout all Israel and Judah, according to the commandment of the king, saying, " Ye children of Israel, turn again unto the Lord God of Abraham, Isaac, and Israel, and he will return to the remnant of you that are escaped out of the hand of the kings of Assyria. Now be not stiffnecked, as your fathers were, but yield yourselves unto the Lord, and enter into his sanctuary, which he hath sanctified for ever; and serve the Lord your God, that the fierceness of his wrath may turn away from you. For if ye turn again unto the Lord, your brethren and your children shall find compassion before them that lead them captive, so that they shall come again into this land: For the Lord your God is gracious and merciful, and will not turn away his face from you, if ye return unto him."

So the posts passed from city to city through the country of Ephraim and Manasseh even unto Zebulun: but they laughed them to scorn, and mocked them.

Nevertheless, some of them humbled themselves, and came to Jerusalem. Also in Judah the hand of God gave them one heart to do the commandment of the king. And there assembled at Jerusalem much people to keep the feast of unleavened bread, a very great congregation.

And they kept the feast of unleavened bread seven days with great gladness; and they praised the Lord day by day. And the whole assembly took counsel to keep other seven days: and they kept other seven days with gladness. So there was great joy in Jerusalem. For since the time of Solomon the son of David there was not the like in Jerusalem. And the priests and the Levites arose and blessed the people.

Now when all this was finished, all Israel that were present went out to the cities of Judah, and brake the images in pieces, and cut down the high places and the altars out of all Judah and Benjamin, in Ephraim also and Manasseh, until they had utterly destroyed them all. Then all the children of Israel returned every man to his possession, into their own cities.

And Hezekiah commanded the people that dwelt in Jerusalem

to give the portion to the priests and the Levites, that they might be encouraged in the law of the Lord. And as soon as the commandment went abroad they brought in abundance the first-fruits of corn, wine, and oil, and honey, and all of the increase of the field; and the tithe of all things brought they in abundantly, and also the tithe of oxen and sheep, and of holy things, and laid them by heaps.

And when Hezekiah and the princes came and saw the heaps, they blessed the Lord, and his people. Then Hezekiah commanded to prepare chambers in the house of the Lord; and they prepared them, and brought in the offerings and the tithes, and the dedicated things faithfully.

Thus Hezekiah wrought that which was good and right and truth before the Lord his God. And in every work that he began in the service of the house of God, and in the law, and in the commandments, to seek his God, he did it with all his heart, and prospered.

THE LORD SAVED HEZEKIAH AND THE INHABITANTS OF JERUSALEM FROM SENNACHERIB

After these things, and the establishment thereof, Sennacherib king of Assyria came, and entered into Judah, and encamped against the fenced cities, and thought to win them for himself.

And when Hezekiah saw that Sennacherib was come, and that he was purposed to fight against Jerusalem, he took counsel with his princes and his mighty men to stop the waters of the fountains which were without the city. So there were gathered much people together, who stopped all the fountains, and the brook that ran through the midst of the land, saying, " Why should the kings of Assyria come, and find much water? "

Also Hezekiah strengthened himself, and built up all the wall that was broken, and raised it up to the towers, and another wall without, and repaired Millo in the city of David, and made darts and shields in abundance.

And Hezekiah set captains of war over the people, and gathered them together to him in the street of the gate of the city, and spake comfortably to them, saying, " Be strong and courageous; be not afraid nor dismayed for the king of Assyria, nor for all the multitude that is with him: for there be more with us than with him. With him is an arm of flesh; but with us is the Lord our God to help us, and to fight our battles."

After this did Sennacherib, king of Assyria, send his servants, Tartan and Rabsaris and Rab-shakeh from Lachish to king Hezekiah, with a great host against Jerusalem, but he himself laid siege against Lachish.

And Tartan, Rabsaris and Rab-shakeh came and stood by the conduit of the upper pool which is in the highway of the fuller's field. And when they had called to Hezekiah, he sent out to them Eliakim, which was over the household, and Shebna, the scribe, and Joah the recorder.

And Rab-shakeh said unto them, "Speak ye now to Hezekiah: Thus saith the great king of Assyria. 'Now on whom dost thou trust, that thou rebellest against me? Now behold, thou trustest even upon Egypt, on which if a man lean, it will go into his hand, and pierce it; so is Pharaoh king of Egypt unto all that trust on him. Now therefore, I pray thee, give pledges to my lord king of Assyria, and I will deliver thee two thousand horses, if thou be able on thy part to set riders upon them. Am I now come up without the Lord against this place to destroy it? The Lord said to me, " Go up against this land, and destroy it." Doth not Hezekiah persuade you to give over yourselves to die by famine, and by thirst, saying, "The Lord our God shall deliver us out of the hand of the king of Assyria? " Know ye not what I and my fathers have done unto all the people of other lands? Now therefore let not Hezekiah deceive you, nor persuade you on this manner, neither yet believe him: for no god of any nation or kingdom was able to deliver his people out of mine hand, and out of the hand of my fathers: how much less shall your God deliver you out of mine hand? ' "

Then they cried with a loud voice, in the Jew's speech, unto the people of Jerusalem that were on the wall, to affright them, and to trouble them; that they might take the city. And they spake against the God of Jerusalem, as against the gods of the people of the earth, which were the work of the hands of man. But the people held their peace, and answered them not a word: for the king's commandment was, saying, "Answer them not."

Then came Eliakim, Shebna, and Joah to Hezekiah with their clothes rent, and told him the words of Rab-shakeh. And it came to pass, when king Hezekiah heard it, that he rent his clothes, and covered himself with sackcloth, and went into the house of the Lord. And he sent the elders of the priests, covered with sackcloth to Isaiah the prophet.

So the servants of king Hezekiah came to Isaiah, and said unto him, " Thus saith Hezekiah, ' This day is a day of trouble, and of rebuke, and blasphemy. Wherefore lift up thy prayer for the remnant that are left.' "

And Isaiah said unto them, " Thus shall ye say to your master, 'Thus saith the Lord,

" Woe to them that go down to Egypt for help;
And stay on horses, and trust in chariots,
Because they are many;
And in horsemen, because they are very strong;
But they look not unto the Holy One of Israel,
Neither seek the Lord!
Now the Egyptians are men, and not God;
And their horses are flesh, and not spirit.

When the Lord shall stretch out his hand,
Both he that helpeth shall fall,
And he that is holpen shall fall down,
And they shall fail together.

" As birds flying,
So will the Lord of hosts defend Jerusalem;
Defending also he will deliver it;
And passing over he will preserve it." ' "

And Isaiah said, " Say to your master, 'Thus saith the Lord, " Be not afraid of the words which thou hast heard, with which the servants of the king of Assyria have blasphemed me. Behold, I will send a blast upon him, and he shall hear a rumour, and shall return to his own land; and I will cause him to fall by the sword in his own land." ' "

But Rab-shakeh also wrote letters to rail on the Lord God of Israel, and to speak against him saying, " Let not thy God in whom thou trustest deceive thee, saying, ' Jerusalem shall not be delivered into the hand of the king of Assyria.' Behold, thou hast heard what the kings of Assyria have done to all lands, by destroying them utterly: and shalt thou be delivered? "

And Hezekiah received the letter of the hand of the messengers, and read it: and Hezekiah went up into the house of the Lord, and spread the letter before the Lord. And he prayed, and said, " O Lord God of Israel, which dwellest between the cherubims, thou art the God, even thou alone, of all the kingdoms of the earth; thou hast made heaven and earth. Lord, bow down thine ear, and hear; open thine eyes and see; and hear the words of Sennacherib, which he hath sent to reproach the living God. Of a truth, Lord, the kings of Assyria have destroyed the nations and their lands, and have cast their gods into the fire: for they were no gods, but the work of men's hands, wood and stone: therefore they have destroyed them. Now, therefore, O Lord our God, I beseech thee, save thou us out of his hand, that all the kingdoms of the earth may know that thou art the Lord God, even thou only."

Then Isaiah sent to Hezekiah, saying, "Thus saith the Lord God of Israel, 'That which thou hast prayed to me, against Sennacherib, king of Assyria, I have heard.' This is the word which the Lord hath spoken concerning Sennacherib: 'Whom hast thou reproached and blasphemed? and against whom hast thou exalted thy voice, and lifted up thine eyes on high? even against the Holy One of Israel. But I know thy abode, and thy going out, and thy coming in, and thy rage against me. Because thy rage against me, and thy tumult is come up into mine ears. Therefore,' thus saith the Lord, concerning the king of Assyria, 'He shall not come into this city, nor shoot an arrow there, nor come before it with shield, nor cast a bank against it. By the way that he came, by the same shall he return, and shall not come into this city,' saith the Lord. 'For I will defend this city, to save it, for mine own sake, and for my servant David's sake.'"

And it came to pass that night, that the angel of the Lord went out, and smote in the camp of the Assyrians an hundred fourscore and five thousand: and when they arose early in the morning, behold, they were all dead corpses.

So Sennacherib, king of Assyria, departed, and went and returned, and dwelt at Nineveh. And it came to pass, as he was worshipping in the house of Nisroch his god, that his sons smote him with the sword: and they escaped into the land of Armenia: and Esar-haddon his son reigned in his stead.

Thus the Lord saved Hezekiah and the inhabitants of Jerusalem from the hand of Sennacherib the king of Assyria, and from the hand of all other, and guided them on every side.

And many brought gifts unto the Lord to Jerusalem, and presents to Hezekiah king of Judah: so that he was magnified in the sight of all nations from thenceforth.

A SONG OF PRAISE

Great is the Lord, and greatly to be praised
In the city of our God,
In the mountain of his holiness.
Beautiful for situation,
The joy of the whole earth is mount Zion,
On the sides of the north,
The city of the great King.
God is known in her palaces for a refuge.
For lo, the kings were assembled,
They passed by together.
They saw it, and so they marvelled;
They were troubled, and hasted away.
Fear took hold of them there,
And pain, as of a woman in travail.
As we have heard,
So have we seen in the city of the Lord of hosts,
In the city of our God:
God will establish it for ever.
Let mount Zion rejoice,
Let the daughters of Judah be glad,
Because of thy judgments.
Walk about Zion, and go round about her:
Tell the towers thereof.
Mark well her bulwarks,
Consider her palaces;
That ye may tell it to the generation following.
For this God is our God for ever and ever.

"THE LORD WAS READY TO SAVE ME"

IN THOSE DAYS was Hezekiah sick unto death. And Isaiah the prophet the son of Amoz came unto him, and said unto him, "Thus saith the Lord, 'Set thine house in order: for thou shalt die, and not live.' "

Then Hezekiah turned his face toward the wall, and prayed unto the Lord, and said, "Remember now, O Lord, I beseech thee, how I have walked before thee in truth and with a perfect heart, and have done that which is good in thy sight." And Hezekiah wept sore.

And it came to pass, afore Isaiah was gone out into the middle court, that the word of the Lord came to him, saying, "Turn again, and tell Hezekiah the captain of my people, 'Thus saith the Lord, the God of David thy father, "I have heard thy prayer, I have seen thy tears: behold, I will heal thee: on the third day thou shalt go up unto the house of the Lord. And I will add unto thy days fifteen years; and I will deliver thee and this city out of the hand of the king of Assyria; and I will defend this city for mine own sake, and for my servant David's sake." ' "

And Hezekiah said unto Isaiah, "What shall be the sign that the Lord will heal me, and that I shall go up into the house of the Lord the third day?"

And Isaiah said, "This sign shalt thou have of the Lord: Shall the shadow go forward ten degrees, or go back ten degrees?"

And Hezekiah answered, "It is a light thing for the shadow to go down ten degrees: nay, but let the shadow return backward ten degrees."

And Isaiah the prophet cried unto the Lord: and he brought the shadow ten degrees backward, by which it had gone down in the dial of Ahaz.

And Isaiah said, "Take a lump of figs." And they took and laid it on the boil, and Hezekiah recovered.

THE SONG OF HEZEKIAH

The writing of Hezekiah king of Judah, when he had been sick, and was recovered of his sickness:

" I said in the cutting off of my days, ' I shall go to the gates of the grave:
I am deprived of the residue of my years.'
I said, ' I shall not see the Lord, even the Lord, in the land of the living:
I shall behold man no more with the inhabitants of the world.'
Mine age is departed,
And is removed from me as a shepherd's tent:
I have cut off like a weaver my life:
He will cut me off with pining sickness:
From day even to night wilt thou make an end of me.
I reckoned till morning, that, as a lion, so will he break all my bones:
From day even to night wilt thou make an end of me.
Like a crane or a swallow, so did I chatter:
I did mourn as a dove:
Mine eyes fail with looking upward:
O Lord, I am oppressed: undertake for me.
What shall I say?
He hath both spoken unto me,
And himself hath done it:
I shall go softly all my years in the bitterness of my soul.
O Lord, by these things men live,
And in all these things is the life of my spirit:
So wilt thou recover me, and make me to live.
Behold, for peace I had great bitterness:
But thou hast in love to my soul delivered it from the pit of corruption:

For thou hast cast all my sins behind thy back.
For the grave cannot praise thee,
Death cannot celebrate thee:
They that go down into the pit cannot hope for thy truth.
The living, the living he shall praise thee,
As I do this day:
The father to the children shall make known thy truth.
The Lord was ready to save me:
Therefore we will sing my songs to the stringed
  instruments
All the days of our life in the house of the Lord.

And Hezekiah had exceeding much riches and honour: and he made himself treasuries for silver, and for gold, and for precious stones, and for spices, and for shields, and for all manner of pleasant jewels: storehouses also for the increase of corn, and wine, and oil; and stalls for all manner of beasts, and cotes for flocks. Moreover, he provided him cities, and possessions of flocks and herds in abundance: For God had given him substance very much.

This same Hezekiah also stopped the upper water-course of Gihon, and brought it straight down to the west side of the city of David. And Hezekiah prospered in all his works.

At that time Merodach-baladan, the son of Baladan, king of Babylon, sent letters and a present to Hezekiah: for he had heard that Hezekiah had been sick and was recovered.

And Hezekiah was glad of them, and showed them the house of his precious things, the silver, and the gold, and the spices, and the precious ointment, and all the house of his armour, and all that was found in his treasures: there was nothing in his house nor in all his dominion, that Hezekiah showed them not.

Then came Isaiah the prophet unto king Hezekiah, and said unto him, " What said these men? and from whence came they unto thee? "

And Hezekiah said, " They are come from a far country, even from Babylon."

And Isaiah said, " What have they seen in thine house? "

And Hezekiah answered, " All the things that are in mine house have they seen: there is nothing among my treasures that I have not showed them."

And Isaiah said unto Hezekiah, " Hear the word of the Lord. 'Behold, the days come, that all that is in thine house, and that which thy fathers have laid up in store unto this day, shall be carried into Babylon: nothing shall be left,' saith the Lord. And thy sons shall they take away; and they shall be eunuchs in the palace of the king of Babylon."

Then said Hezekiah unto Isaiah, " Good is the word of the Lord which thou hast spoken." And he said, " Is it not good, if peace and truth be in my days? "

And Hezekiah slept with his fathers, and they buried him in the chiefest of the sepulchres of the sons of David: and all Judah and the inhabitants of Jerusalem did him honour at his death: and Manasseh his son reigned in his stead.

A GREAT LIGHT

ISAIAH, the prophet, foretold the coming of the Christ, and the effect of his coming, and he said: "And the work of righteousness shall be peace; and the effect of righteousness quietness and assurance for ever." And Isaiah said:

THE PRINCE OF PEACE

The people that walked in darkness
Have seen a great light;
They that dwell in the land of the shadow of death,
Upon them hath the light shined.

For unto us a child is born,
Unto us a son is given;
And the government shall be upon his shoulders.
And his name shall be called
Wonderful, Counsellor, The mighty God,
The everlasting Father, The Prince of Peace.

Of the increase of his government and peace
There shall be no end,
Upon the throne of David, and upon his kingdom,
To order it and to establish it
With judgment and with justice
From henceforth even for ever.

The zeal of the Lord of hosts will perform this.

THE SPIRIT OF THE LORD SHALL REST UPON HIM

And there shall come forth a rod out of the stem of Jesse,
And a Branch shall grow out of his roots,
And the Spirit of the Lord shall rest upon him;
The spirit of wisdom and understanding,
The spirit of counsel and might,
The spirit of knowledge and of the fear of the Lord;
And shall make him of quick understanding in the fear of the Lord;
And he shall not judge after the sight of his eyes,
Neither reprove after the hearing of his ears;
But with righteousness shall he judge the poor
And reprove with equity for the meek of the earth.
And he shall smite the earth with the rod of his mouth,
And with the breath of his lips shall he slay the wicked.
And righteousness shall be the girdle of his loins,
And faithfulness the girdle of his reins.
The wolf also shall dwell with the lamb,
And the leopard shall lie down with the kid;
And the calf and the young lion and the fatling together;
And a little child shall lead them.
And the cow and the bear shall feed;
Their young ones shall lie down together;
And the lion shall eat straw like the ox;
And the sucking child shall play on the hole of the asp,
And the weaned child shall put his hand on the cockatrice's den.
They shall not hurt nor destroy in all my holy mountain;
For the earth shall be full of the knowledge of the Lord,
As the waters cover the sea.

THE WAY OF HOLINESS

The wilderness and the solitary place shall be glad for
them;
And the desert shall rejoice, and blossom as the rose.
It shall blossom abundantly,
And rejoice even with joy and singing;
The glory of Lebanon shall be given unto it,
The excellency of Carmel and Sharon,
They shall see the glory of the Lord,
And the excellency of our God.

Strengthen ye the weak hands and confirm the feeble
knees.
Say to them that are of a fearful heart,
" Be strong, fear not;
Behold, your God will come with vengeance,
Even God with a recompence;
He will come and save you."

Then the eyes of the blind shall be opened,
And the ears of the deaf shall be unstopped;
Then shall the lame man leap as an hart,
And the tongue of the dumb sing;
For in the wilderness shall waters break out,
And streams in the desert.
And the parched ground shall become a pool,
And the thirsty land springs of water.
And an highway shall be there, and a way,
And it shall be called The Way of Holiness;
The unclean shall not pass over it;
But it shall be for those:

The wayfaring men, though fools, shall not err therein.
No lion shall be there,
Nor any ravenous beast shall go up thereon,
It shall not be found there;
But the redeemed shall walk there.

And the ransomed of the Lord shall return,
And come to Zion with songs and everlasting joy upon
their heads;
They shall obtain joy and gladness,
And sorrow and sighing shall flee away.

THE INHABITANT SHALL NOT SAY, "I AM SICK"

Look upon Zion, the city of our solemnities:
Thine eyes shall see Jerusalem a quiet habitation,
A tabernacle that shall not be taken down;
Not one of the stakes thereof shall ever be removed,
Neither shall any of the cords thereof be broken.

But there the glorious Lord
Will be unto us a place of broad rivers and streams;
Wherein shall go no galley with oars,
Neither shall gallant ship pass thereby.

For the Lord is our judge,
The Lord is our lawgiver,
The Lord is our king;
He will save us.

And the inhabitant shall not say, "I am sick:"
The people shall be forgiven their iniquity.

THE MOUNTAIN OF THE LORD'S HOUSE

And it shall come to pass in the last days,
That the mountain of the Lord's house
Shall be established in the top of the mountains,
And shall be exalted above the hills;
And all nations shall flow into it.
And many people shall go and say,
" Come ye, and let us go up to the mountain of the Lord,
To the house of the God of Jacob;
And he will teach us of his ways,
And we will walk in his paths;
For out of Zion shall go forth the law,
And the word of the Lord from Jerusalem."
And he shall judge among the nations,
And shall rebuke many people:
And they shall beat their swords into plowshares,
And their spears into pruninghooks;
Nation shall not lift up sword against nation,
Neither shall they learn war any more.
" O house of Jacob, come ye,
And let us walk in the light of the Lord."

GOD WILL WIPE AWAY TEARS FROM OFF ALL FACES

And in this mountain shall the Lord of hosts
Make unto all people a feast of fat things,
A feast of wines on the lees,
Of fat things full of marrow,
Of wines on the lees well refined.

And he will destroy in this mountain
The face of the covering cast over all people,
And the veil that is spread over all nations.

He will swallow up death in victory;
And the Lord God will wipe away tears from off all faces;
And the rebuke of his people shall he take away from off
all the earth:
For the Lord hath spoken it.

And it shall be said in that day,
" Lo, this is our God;
We have waited for him, and he will save us:
This is the Lord, we have waited for him;
We will be glad, and rejoice in his salvation."

For in this mountain shall the hand of the Lord rest.

THEY WOULD NOT HEARKEN

MANASSEH, the son of Hezekiah, was twelve years old when he began to reign, and he reigned fifty and five years in Jerusalem.

And he did that which was evil, like unto the abominations of the heathen. Moreover Manasseh shed innocent blood very much; for he filled Jerusalem with innocent blood from one end to the other.

And the Lord spake unto Manasseh and to his people, but they would not hearken. Wherefore the Lord brought upon them the host of the king of Assyria, which took Manasseh among the thorns, and bound him with fetters, and carried him to Babylon. And when he was in affliction, he besought the Lord his God, and humbled himself greatly, and prayed to him, and God heard his supplication, and brought him again to Jerusalem. Then Manasseh knew that the Lord he was God.

After this Manasseh built a wall without the city of David, and raised it up to a very great height, and put captains of war in all the fenced cities of Judah. And he repaired the altar of the house of the Lord, and sacrificed thereon peace offerings and thank offerings, and commanded Judah to serve the Lord God of Israel.

So Manasseh slept with his fathers, and they buried him in his own house; and Amon his son reigned in his stead.

Amon reigned two years in Jerusalem. But he did that which was evil, and walked not in the way of the Lord. And his servants conspired against him, and slew him in his own house. And the people made Josiah his son, king in his stead.

O JERUSALEM, WASH THINE HEART FROM WICKEDNESS!

JOSIAH was eight years old when he began to reign, and he reigned in Jerusalem one and thirty years. And he did that which was right in the sight of the Lord, for while he was yet young, he began to seek after the God of David. And he began to purge Judah and Jerusalem from the high places, and the groves, and the carved images, and the molten images.

And in the days of Josiah, the word of the Lord came to Jeremiah, the son of Hilkiah of the priests, and the Lord said, "Before I formed thee, and before thou camest forth out of the womb, I sanctified thee, and I ordained thee a prophet unto the nations."

And Jeremiah said, "Ah, Lord God! Behold, I cannot speak: for I am a child."

But the Lord said, "Say not, I am a child: for thou shalt go to all that I shall send thee, and whatsoever I command thee thou shalt speak. Be not afraid of their faces: for I am with thee to deliver thee."

Then the Lord put forth His hand and touched Jeremiah's mouth and said, "Behold, I have put my words in thy mouth. See I have this day set thee over the nations and over the kingdoms to root out, and to pull down, and to destroy, and to throw down, to build, and to plant."

Moreover the Lord said, "Jeremiah, what seest thou?"

And Jeremiah said, "I see a rod of an almond tree."

Then said the Lord, "Thou hast well seen: for I will hasten my word to perform it."

And the word of the Lord came the second time, saying, " What seest thou? "

And Jeremiah said, " I see a seething pot; and the face thereof is toward the north."

Then the Lord said, "Out of the north an evil shall break forth upon all the inhabitants of the land. For lo, the kingdoms of the north shall come against all the cities of Judah. And I will utter my judgments against them touching all their wickedness. Thou therefore, gird up thy loins, and arise, and speak unto them all that I command thee: be not dismayed at their faces, for behold, I have made thee this day a defenced city, and an iron pillar, against the people of the land, and they shall fight against thee, but they shall not prevail against thee; for I am with thee to deliver thee."

And in the eighteenth year of the reign of Josiah, when he had purged the land, Josiah sent Shaphan, the scribe, and others to repair the house of the Lord his God. And they delivered the money which the Levites had gathered from all Judah and Benjamin, into the hand of the workmen that had the oversight of the work of the house of the Lord. And as they wrought to repair the house of the Lord, Hilkiah, the priest, found a book of the law of the Lord given by Moses.

And Shaphan carried the book to king Josiah saying, " Hilkiah, the priest, hath given me a book." And Shaphan read it before the king.

And it came to pass, that when king Josiah heard the words of the law, that he rent his clothes, and he commanded Hilkiah and Shaphan, saying, " Go and inquire of the Lord for me, and for them that are left in Israel and Judah concerning the words of the book that is found, for great is the wrath of the Lord that is poured out upon us, because our fathers have not kept the word of the Lord, to do after all that is written in this book."

And they went to Huldah the prophetess. Now she dwelt in

Jerusalem in the college, and they spake to her to that effect. And she answered them, "Thus saith the Lord: Behold, I will bring evil upon this place, and upon the inhabitants thereof, even all the curses that are written in the book which they have read before the king of Judah. Because they have forsaken me, therefore my wrath will be poured out upon this place, and shall not be quenched. And as for the king of Judah, who sent you to inquire of the Lord, so shall ye say unto him 'Thus saith the Lord God of Israel: Because thine heart was tender, and thou didst humble thyself before God when thou heardest his words, and didst rend thy clothes and weep before me, I have heard thee: Behold, I will gather thee to thy fathers, and thou shalt be gathered to thy grave in peace, neither shall thine eyes see all the evil that I will bring upon this place, and upon the inhabitants of the same.'"

Then king Josiah sent and gathered together all the elders of Judah and Jerusalem. And the king went up into the house of the Lord, and all the men of Judah, and the inhabitants of Jerusalem, and the priests and the Levites, and all the people great and small, and the king read in their ears all the words of the book that was found in the house of the Lord.

And Zephaniah, the prophet, and uncle of the king stood before them and said: "This is the word of the Lord which came to me, Zephaniah:

> " This is the word of the Lord:
> I will utterly consume all things from off the land,"
>   saith the Lord;
> "I will stretch out mine hand upon Judah,
> And upon the inhabitants of Jerusalem;
> And I will cut off the remnant of Baal from this place,
> And them that worship the host of heaven,
> And them that are turned back from the Lord,
> And those that have not sought the Lord,
> Nor inquired for him.

"Hold thy peace at the presence of the Lord God;
For the day of the Lord is at hand;
That day is a day of wrath,
A day of trouble and distress;
A day of waste and desolation,
A day of darkness and gloominess,
A day of clouds and thick darkness,
And I will bring distress upon men,
That they walk like blind men
Because they have sinned against the Lord,
And their blood shall be poured out as dust.
Neither their silver nor their gold shall be able to deliver
them in the day of the Lord's wrath;
But the whole land shall be devoured by the fire of
His jealousy.
For he shall make a speedy riddance of all them that
dwell in the land.

"Gather yourselves together,
Yea, gather together, O nation not desired;
Before the decree bring forth.
Before the day pass as the chaff,
Before the fierce anger of the Lord come upon you,
Before the day of the Lord's anger come upon you.
Seek ye the Lord, all ye meek of the earth,
Which have wrought His judgment;
Seek righteousness, seek meekness;
It may be ye shall be hid in the day of the Lord's anger."

And Jeremiah, the prophet, spake before all the people and to king Josiah, and said, "The word of the Lord came to me saying, 'Go and cry in the ears of Jerusalem, saying:

"'"Thus saith the Lord: What iniquity have your fathers found in me, that they are gone far from me, and have walked after vanity, and are become vain? Hath a nation changed their gods, which are yet no gods? But my people have changed their glory for that which doth not profit. Be astonished, O ye heavens, at this, and be horribly afraid; be ye very desolate, saith the Lord. For my people have committed two evils; they have forsaken Me, the fountain of living waters, and hewed them out cisterns, broken cisterns, that can hold no water. Thine own wickedness shall correct thee, and thy backslidings shall reprove thee. Know therefore and see that it is an evil thing and bitter, that thou hast forsaken the Lord thy God, and that my fear is not in thee.

" ' "If thou wilt return, O Israel, saith the Lord, Return unto Me; and if thou wilt put away thine abominations out of my sight, then shalt thou not remove. O Jerusalem, wash thine heart from wickedness, that thou mayest be saved. How long shall thy vain thoughts lodge within thee?" ' "

And king Josiah stood in his place, and made a covenant before the Lord, to walk after the Lord, and to keep his commandments with all his heart, and with all his soul, and to perform the words of the covenant which are written in this book. And all the people stood by the covenant.

And Josiah took away all the abominations out of all the countries that pertained to the children of Israel, and made all that were present in Israel to serve the Lord their God. Moreover, the workers with familiar spirits, and the wizzards and the images, and the idols, and all the abominations that were spied in the land of Judah and Jerusalem, did Josiah put away that he might perform the words of the law which were written in the book that Hilkiah the priest found in the house of the Lord.

And the king commanded the people saying, " Keep the passover unto the Lord your God as it is written in the book." So the service was prepared, and the priests stood in their place, and the Levites in their course, according to the king's commandment. And the children of Israel kept the passover and the feast of unleavened bread seven days. And there was no passover like to that kept in Israel from the days of Samuel the prophet. In the eighteenth year of the reign of Josiah was this passover kept.

After this did Pharaoh-Necho, king of Egypt, go up against the king of Assyria to the river Euphrates. And Josiah went out against him. But Necho sent ambassadors to Josiah, saying, "What have I to do with thee, thou king of Judah? I come not against thee this day, but against the house wherewith I have war."

Nevertheless Josiah would not turn his face, but disguised himself that he might fight with him, and hearkened not unto the words of Necho, and came to fight in the valley of Megiddo. And the archers shot at king Josiah; and the king said to his servants, "Have me away for I am sore wounded." His servants therefore took him and brought him to Jerusalem, and he died, and was buried in one of the sephulchres of his fathers.

And Jeremiah, the prophet, lamented for Josiah. And all Judah and Jerusalem mourned for him. And all the singing men and the singing women spake of Josiah in their lamentations.

And the people of the land took Jehoahaz, the son of Josiah, and anointed him, and made him king in his father's stead.

LET NOT THE WISE MAN GLORY IN HIS WISDOM

JEHOAHAZ was twenty and three years old when he began to reign, and he reigned three months in Jerusalem. And Pharaoh-Necho, the king of Egypt, put him in bands at Riblah, that he might not reign in Jerusalem, and put the land to a tribute of an hundred talents of silver, and a talent of gold.

And Pharaoh-Necho made Eliakin, the son of Josiah, king over Judah and Jerusalem, and turned his name to Jehoiakim, and took Jehoahaz away to Egypt, and he died there.

And Jehoiakim gave the silver and the gold to Pharaoh; but he taxed the land to give the money according to the commandment of Pharaoh. He exacted the silver and the gold of the people of the land.

And Jehoiakim did that which was evil in the sight of the Lord. And in the beginning of his reign, came this word from the Lord to Jeremiah concerning all of the people of Judah, saying, " Stand in the court of the Lord's house, and speak unto all the cities of Judah, which come to worship in the Lord's house, all the words that I command thee to speak unto them; diminish not a word.

" Proclaim there, ' Hear the word of the Lord, all ye of Judah, that enter in at these gates to worship the Lord. Amend your ways and your doings, and I will cause you to dwell in this place. Trust ye not in lying words; for if ye throughly amend your ways and your doings, then I will cause you to dwell in this place, in the land that I gave to your fathers, for ever and ever.

" 'Will ye steal, murder, and commit adultery, and swear falsely, and burn incense unto Baal, and walk after other gods whom ye know not and come and stand before me in this house? Is this house, which is called by my name, become a den of robbers in your eyes?

" 'And now because ye have done all of these works,' saith the Lord, 'Therefore will I do unto this house, which is called by my name, as I have done to Shiloh. And I will cast you out of my sight. This is a nation that obeyed not the voice of the Lord their God nor received correction. Truth is perished and cut off from their mouth. I will cause to cease from the cities of Judah, and from the streets of Jerusalem, the voice of mirth, and the voice of gladness, the voice of the bridegroom, and the voice of the bride, for the land shall be desolate.' "

Now it came to pass, when Jeremiah had made an end of speaking all that the Lord had commanded him to speak, the priests, and the prophets and all the people took him saying, "Thou shalt surely die. Why hast thou prophesied in the name of the Lord, saying, 'This house shall be like Shiloh, and this city shall be desolate without an inhabitant?' " And all the people were gathered against Jeremiah in the house of the Lord.

Then spake the priests and the prophets to all the people, saying, "This man is worthy to die; for he hath prophesied against this city, as ye have heard with your ears."

Then spake Jeremiah unto all the people, saying, "Hear now this, O foolish people, and without understanding; which have eyes and see not; which have ears, and hear not: Your iniquities have turned away these things, and your sins have withholden good things from you. The Lord sent me to prophesy against this house and against this city all the words that ye have heard. Therefore now amend your ways and your doings and obey the voice of the Lord your God: and the Lord will repent him of the evil that he hath pronounced against you. As for me, behold, I am in your hand: do with me as seemeth good and meet unto you. But know ye for certain, that if ye put me to death, ye shall surely bring innocent blood upon yourselves, and upon this city, and upon the inhabitants thereof. For of a truth the Lord hath sent me unto you to speak all these words in your ears."

Then said the princes and all the people, "This man is not worthy to die: for he hath spoken to us in the name of the Lord our God."

Then rose up certain of the elders of the land, and spake, saying, "Micah, the prophet in the days of Hezekiah, king of Judah, spake, saying, 'Zion shall be plowed like a field, and Jerusalem shall become heaps.' Did Hezekiah put him to death? Did he not fear the Lord, and besought the Lord, and the Lord repented him of the evil which he had pronounced against them? Thus might we procure great evil against our souls."

And Jeremiah said, "Thus saith the Lord, 'Let not the wise man glory in his wisdom, neither let the mighty man glory in his might, let not the rich man glory in his riches: but let him that glorieth, glory in this, that he understandeth and knoweth me, that I am the Lord which exercise lovingkindness, judgment, and righteousness, in the earth, for in these things I delight,' saith the Lord."

O EARTH, EARTH, EARTH, HEAR THE WORD OF THE LORD

THE WORD came to Jeremiah from the Lord saying, "Arise, and go down to the potter's house, and there I will cause thee to hear my words."

Then Jeremiah went down to the potter's house, and behold, the potter wrought a work on the wheels. And the vessel that he made of clay was marred in the hand of the potter: so he made it again another vessel, as seemed good to the potter to make it.

Then the word of the Lord came to Jeremiah saying, "O house of Israel, cannot I do with you as this potter? Behold, as the clay is in the potter's hand, so are ye in mine hand, O house of Israel. At what instant I shall speak concerning a nation, and concerning a kingdom to pluck up, and to pull down, and to destroy it: if that nation turn from their evil, I will repent of the evil that I thought to do unto them."

Then said the Lord, "Go down to the house of Jehoiakim the king of Judah, and speak there this word. 'The House of Israel and the house of Judah have dealt very treacherously against me. They have belied the Lord, and said, "It is not he; neither shall evil come upon us; neither shall we see sword nor famine; and the prophets shall become wind, and the word is not in them." Hear the word of the Lord, O king of Judah that sittest upon the throne of David, thou and thy servants, and thy people that enter in by these gates.' Thus saith the Lord, 'Execute ye judgment and righteousness, and deliver the spoiled out of the hand of the oppressor, and do no wrong, do no violence to the stranger, to the fatherless nor the widow, neither shed innocent blood.

"'But if ye will not hear these words, I swear by myself,' saith the Lord, 'that this house shall become a desolation and I will cast you out of this land into a land that ye know not, neither ye nor your fathers; and there shall ye serve other gods day and night.

"'Lo, I will bring a nation upon you from far, O house of Israel; it is a mighty nation, it is an ancient nation; a nation whose language thou knowest not, neither understandest what they say. And they shall eat up thine harvest, and thy bread, which thy sons and thy daughters should eat; they shall eat up thy flocks and thine herds; they shall eat up thy vines and thy fig trees; they shall impoverish thy fenced cities, wherein thou trustest. And I will give thee into the hand of them that seek thy life, and into the hand of them whose face thou fearest, even into the hand of Nebuchadnezzar, king of Babylon, and into the hand of the Chaldeans.

" 'Behold, I will bring upon this people, even the fruit of their thoughts, because they have not hearkened unto my words nor to my law, but rejected it; and I will send a sword after them, till I have consumed them.

" 'Then shall the cities of Judah and the inhabitants of Jerusalem go and cry unto the gods unto whom they offer incense; but they shall not save them at all in the time of their trouble. For according to the number of thy cities are thy gods, O Judah. Shall a man make gods unto himself, and they are no gods?

" 'But the Lord is the true God; he is the living God, and an everlasting king. He hath made the earth by his power; he hath established the world by his wisdom, and stretched out the heavens by his discretion. Blessed is the man that trusteth in the Lord, and whose hope the Lord is. For he shall be as a tree planted by the waters, and that spreadeth out her roots by the river, and shall not see when heat cometh, but her leaf shall be green; and shall not be careful in the year of drought, neither shall cease from yielding fruit. O Lord, the hope of Israel, all that forsake thee shall be ashamed because they have forsaken the Lord, the fountain of living water.' "

But the people said, "There is no hope, but we will walk after our own devices, and we will every one do the imagination of his evil heart."

Then said they, "Come, and let us devise devices against Jeremiah; for the law shall not perish from the priest, nor counsel from the wise, nor the word from the prophet. Come, and let us smite him with the tongue, and let us not give heed to any of his words."

And Jeremiah said, "Give heed to me, O Lord, and hearken to the voice of them that contend with me. Shall evil be recompensed for good? for they have digged a pit for my soul. Remember that I stood before thee to speak good for them, and to turn away thy wrath from them. Yea, Lord, thou knowest all their counsel against me to slay me."

Now Pashur, who was chief governor in the house of the Lord, heard that Jeremiah prophesied these things. Then Pashur smote Jeremiah, the prophet, and put him in the stocks that were in the gate of Benjamin, which was by the house of the Lord. And it came to pass on the morrow, that Pashur brought forth Jeremiah out of the stocks.

Then said Jeremiah unto him, "Thus saith the Lord, 'Behold, I will make thee a terror to thyself and to all thy friends: and they shall fall by the sword of their enemies, and thine eyes shall behold it. And I will give Judah into the hand of the king of Babylon, and he shall carry them captive into Babylon and shall slay them with the sword. Moreover, I will deliver all the strength of this city, and all the labours thereof, and all the precious things thereof, and all the treasures of the kings of Judah will I give into the hand of their enemies, which shall spoil them and take them and carry them to Babylon. And thou, Pashur, and all that dwell in thine house shall go into captivity; and thou shalt come to Babylon, and there thou shalt die, and shalt be buried there, thou, and all thy friends, to whom thou hast prophesied lies.'

"Therefore, thus saith the Lord concerning Jehoiakim, the son of Josiah, king of Judah, 'Thine eyes and thine heart are not but for thy covetousness, and for to shed innocent blood, and for oppression, and for violence, to do it. They shall not lament for him. He shall be buried with the burial of an ass, drawn and cast forth beyond the gates of Jerusalem. I spake unto thee in thy prosperity, but thou saidst, "I will not hear." This hath been thy manner from thy youth, that thou obeyedst not my voice. The wind shall eat up all thy pastors, and thy lovers shall go into captivity: surely shalt thou be ashamed and confounded for all thy wickedness. And I will give thee into the hand of them that seek thy life, and into the hand of them whose face thou fearest, even into the hand of Nebuchadnezzar, king of Babylon, and into the hand of the Chaldeans. I will cast thee out into another country, and there shall ye die.'

"Hear ye, and give ear; be not proud: for the Lord hath spoken. Give glory to the Lord your God, before he cause darkness, and before your feet stumble upon the dark mountains, and while ye look for light, he turn it into the shadow of death, and make it gross darkness. But if ye will not hear, my soul shall weep in secret places for your pride; and mine eye shall weep sore, and run down with tears, because the Lord's flock is carried away captive. Say unto the king and to the queen, 'Humble yourselves, sit down. Lift up your eyes, and behold them that come from the north: where is the flock that was given thee, thy beautiful flock?'

"O earth, earth, earth, hear the word of the Lord."

THE ROLL OF A BOOK

And Jeremiah was shut up in prison. And it came to pass, in the fourth year of Jehoiakim that this word came unto Jeremiah from the Lord, saying, "Take thee a roll of a book, and write therein all the words that I have spoken unto thee against Israel."

Then Jeremiah called Baruch, the scribe, and Baruch wrote upon a roll of a book all the words the Lord had spoken to Jeremiah. And Jeremiah said, "I am shut up; I cannot go into the house of the Lord. Therefore, go thou, and read in the roll which thou hast written the words of the Lord in the ears of all the people upon the fasting day. And also thou shalt read them in the ears of all Judah that come out of their cities. It may be they will return every one from his evil way: for great is the fury that the Lord hath pronounced against this people."

And Baruch did according to all that Jeremiah commanded him, reading in the book the words of the Lord in the Lord's house.

When Mechaiah, the scribe, heard the words of the Lord, he went down to the king's house, and lo, all the princes sat there. And Mechaiah declared unto them all the words that Baruch had read in the ears of the people. Therefore all the princes sent unto Baruch saying, "Take in thine hand the roll wherein thou hast read and come." So Baruch came unto them.

They said unto him, "Sit down now and read it in our ears." So Baruch read it in their ears.

Now it came to pass, when they had heard the words, they were afraid, and said, "We will surely tell the king." And they asked Baruch, "How didst thou write all these words?"

And Baruch answered, "Jeremiah pronounced them unto me, and I wrote them with ink in the book."

Then said the princes, "Go hide thee! and Jeremiah also, and let no man know where ye be."

And the princes went to king Jehoiakim, and told him of the book. So the king sent to fetch the roll, and it was read in the ears of the king, and all the princes.

Now Jehoiakim sat in the winter house, and there was a fire burning on the hearth before him. And when Jehudi (the priest) had read three or four leaves, he cut it with a pen knife and cast it into the fire, until all the roll was consumed in the fire. Yet they were not afraid, nor rent their garments, neither the king nor any of his servants that heard all these words.

But Jehoiakim, the king, commanded them to take Baruch and Jeremiah, and say, "Why hast thou written therein saying, 'The king of Babylon shall certainly come and destroy this land and shall cause to cease from thence man and beast?'" But the Lord had hidden them so they could not be found.

Then the word of the Lord came to Jeremiah, saying, "Take another roll and write all the words that were in the first roll which Jehoiakim, the king hath burned." Then took Jeremiah another roll and Baruch wrote therein from the mouth of Jeremiah all the words of the book which Jehoiakim had burned in the fire.

TWO BASKETS OF FIGS

JEHOIAKIM reigned eleven years in Jerusalem, and the abominations which he did are written in the book of the kings of Israel. And against him came up Nebuchadnezzar, king of Babylon, and bound him in fetters to carry him to Babylon, and he died, and Jehoiachin, his son, reigned in his stead.

And Jehoiachin did that which was evil in the sight of the Lord, according to all that his father had done. And when the year was expired, Nebuchadnezzar, king of Babylon, came against the city, and his servants did besiege it. And Jehoiachin went out to Nebuchadnezzar, he, and his mother, and his servants, and his princes, and his officers, and Nebuchadnezzar carried away Jehoiachin and all that were with him, the mighty of the land, those carried he into captivity from Jerusalem to Babylon. And he carried out thence all the treasures of the house of the Lord, and the treasures of the king's house, and cut in pieces all the vessels of gold which Solomon, king of Israel, had made in the temple of the Lord.

And Nebuchadnezzar made Zedekiah, Jehoiakim's brother, king in Judah and Jerusalem. But neither Zedekiah nor his servants nor the people of the land did hearken unto the words of the Lord, which He spake by His prophet Jeremiah.

Now after Nebuchadnezzar had carried away captive Jehoiachin the son of Jehoiakim, and the princes of Judah with the carpenters and smiths, and had brought them to Babylon, the Lord showed Jeremiah, and behold, two baskets of figs were set before the temple of the Lord: One basket had very good figs, even like the figs that are first ripe; and the other basket had very naughty figs, which could not be eaten they were so bad.

Then said the Lord unto Jeremiah, " What seest thou, Jeremiah? "

And he said, " Figs: the good figs very good, and the evil figs very evil, that cannot be eaten, they are so bad."

Again the word of the Lord came unto Jeremiah, saying, "Thus saith the Lord, the God of Israel, ' Like these good figs, so will I acknowledge them that are carried away captive out of Judah, whom I have sent out of this place into the land of the Chaldeans, for their good. For I will set mine eyes upon them for good, and I will bring them again to this land: and I will build them, and not pull them down, and I will plant them, and not pluck them up. And I will give them an heart to know me, that I am the Lord, and they shall be my people, and I will be their God: for they shall return unto me with their whole heart.

"' And as the evil figs, which cannot be eaten they are so evil, so will I give Zedekiah, the king of Judah and his princes, and the residue of Jerusalem that remain in this land, them I will deliver to be removed into all kingdoms of the earth, for their hurt to be a reproach and a proverb.' "

YE SHALL SEEK ME, AND FIND ME WHEN YE SEARCH FOR ME WITH ALL YOUR HEART

Now these are the words of the letter that Jeremiah, the prophet, sent from Jerusalem unto the elders which were carried away captives, and to the priests, and to the prophets, and to all the people whom Nebuchadnezzar had carried away captive from Jerusalem to Babylon:

"Thus saith the Lord of hosts, the God of Israel, unto all that are carried away captives, whom I have caused to be carried away from Jerusalem unto Babylon: 'Build ye houses, and dwell in them; and plant gardens and eat the fruit of them; take ye wives, and beget sons and daughters; and take wives for your sons, and give your daughters to husbands, that they may bear sons and daughters; that ye may be increased there, and not diminished. And seek the peace of the city whither I have caused you to be carried away captives, and pray unto the Lord for it: for in the peace thereof shall ye have peace.'

"For thus saith the Lord of hosts, the God of Israel, 'Let not your prophets and your diviners, that be in the midst of you, deceive you, for they prophesy falsely unto you in my name: I have not sent them.'

"For thus saith the Lord, 'After seventy years be accomplished at Babylon, I will visit you, and perform my good word toward you in causing you to return to this place. For I know the thoughts that I think toward you,' saith the Lord, 'thoughts of peace, and not of evil to give you an expected end. Then shall ye call upon me, and ye shall go and pray unto me, and I will hearken unto you. And ye shall seek me, and find me, when ye shall search for me with all your heart.

"'And I will be found of you,' saith the Lord: 'and I will turn away your captivity, and I will gather you from all the nations, and from all the places whither I have driven you; and I will bring you again into the place whence I caused you to be carried away captive.'"

Then Shemaiah the Nehelamite sent letters from Babylon unto all the people at Jerusalem, and to Zephaniah the priest, and to all the priests, saying, "Why hast thou not reproved Jeremiah which maketh himself a prophet unto you? For he sent letters unto us in Babylon, saying, 'This captivity is long: build ye houses, and dwell in them; and plant gardens, and eat the fruit of them.'"

And Zephaniah the priest read this letter in the ears of Jeremiah the prophet.

Then came the word of the Lord unto Jeremiah, saying, "Send to all them of the captivity, saying, 'Because Shemaiah hath prophesied unto you, and I sent him not, and he caused you to trust in a lie, therefore I will punish Shemaiah and his seed; he shall not have a man to dwell among this people; neither shall he behold the good that I will do for my people, because he hath taught rebellion against the Lord.'"

OBEY, I BESEECH THEE, THE VOICE OF THE LORD

Now the Chaldeans besieged Jerusalem again, and Zedekiah the king sent unto Jeremiah, saying, "Pray now unto the Lord our God for us."

Then Pharaoh's army came forth out of Egypt, and when the Chaldeans heard tidings of them, they departed from Jerusalem.

Then came the word of the Lord unto Jeremiah, saying, "Thus shall ye say unto Zedekiah, the king of Judah, that sent you unto me to enquire of me: 'Behold, Pharaoh's army which is come forth to help you, shall return to Egypt into their own land. And the Chaldeans shall come again, and fight against this city, and take it, and burn it with fire. For though ye had smitten the whole army of the Chaldeans that fight against you, and there remained but the wounded men among them, yet should they rise up every man in his tent and burn this city with fire.' "

And it came to pass, that when the army of Chaldeans was broken up from Jerusalem for fear of Pharaoh's army, then Jeremiah went forth out of Jerusalem to go into the land of Benjamin to separate himself thence in the midst of the people. And when he was in the gate of Benjamin, a captain of the ward was there, who took Jeremiah, saying, "Thou fallest away to the Chaldeans."

Then said Jeremiah, "It is false; I fall not away to the Chaldeans." But the captain hearkened not unto him, but took him and brought him to the princes.

Therefore the princes said unto king Zedekiah, "We beseech thee let this man be put to death, for he has said, 'Thus saith the Lord, "He that remaineth in this city shall die by the sword, by the famine, and by the pestilence; but he that goeth forth to the Chaldeans shall live. This city shall surely be given into the hand of the king of Babylon's army, which shall take it." ' Thus he weakeneth the hands of the men of war that remain in this city, and the hands of all the people, in speaking such words unto them. For this man seeketh not the welfare of this people."

Then Zedekiah the king said, "Behold, he is in your hand: for the king is not he that can do anything against you."

Then the princes took Jeremiah, and cast him into the dungeon that was in the court of the prison; and they let down Jeremiah with cords. And in the dungeon there was no water, but mire; so Jeremiah sunk in the mire.

Now when Ebedmelech the Ethiopian, one of the eunuchs, which was in the king's house, heard that they had put Jeremiah in the dungeon, he went forth and spake to the king, saying, "My lord the king, these men have done evil in all that they have done to Jeremiah the prophet, whom they have cast into the dungeon; and he is like to die for hunger in the place where he is."

Then king Zedekiah commanded Ebedmelech, saying, "Take thirty men with thee and take up Jeremiah the prophet out of the dungeon, before he die."

So Ebedmelech took the men with him, and took old rags and let them down by cords into the dungeon to Jeremiah, and said, "Put these rags under thine armholes under the cords." And Jeremiah did so. So they drew up Jeremiah with cords, and took him up out of the dungeon: and Jeremiah remained in the court of the prison.

Then Zedekiah the king sent, and took Jeremiah, and said unto him, "I will ask thee a thing; hide nothing from me."

Then Jeremiah said, "If I declare it unto thee, wilt thou not surely put me to death? and if I give thee counsel, wilt thou not hearken unto me?"

So Zedekiah sware secretly unto Jeremiah, saying, "As the Lord liveth that made us, I will not put thee to death, neither will I give thee into the hand of these men that seek thy life."

Then said Jeremiah, "Thus saith the Lord, the God of Israel: 'If thou wilt assuredly go forth unto the king of Babylon's princes, then thy soul shall live, and this city shall not be burned with fire; and thou shalt live and thine house. But if thou wilt not go forth to the king of Babylon's princes, then shall this city be given into the hand of the Chaldeans, and they shall burn it with fire, and thou shalt not escape out of their hand.'"

And Zedekiah said, "I am afraid of the Jews that are fallen to the Chaldeans, lest they deliver me into their hand, and they mock me."

But Jeremiah said, "They shall not deliver thee. Obey, I

beseech thee, the voice of the Lord, which I speak unto thee: so it shall be well with thee, and thy soul shall live. But if thou refuse to go forth, this is the word that the Lord hath showed me: They shall bring out thy wives and thy children to the Chaldeans; and thou shalt not escape out of their hand, but shall be taken, and thou shalt cause this city to be burned with fire."

Then said Zedekiah unto Jeremiah, "Let no man know of these words and thou shalt not die."

Then came all the princes unto Jeremiah and asked him, and he said, "I presented my supplication before the king, that he would not cause me to return to the dungeon to die there."

So they left off speaking with him. So Jeremiah abode in the court of the prison until the day that Jerusalem was taken.

And Jeremiah said:

Mine enemies chased me sore,
Like a bird, without cause.
They had cut off my life in the dungeon,
And cast a stone upon me.
Waters flowed over mine head;
Then I said, "I am cut off."

Then I called upon thy name, O Lord,
Out of the low dungeon.
Thou hast heard my voice;
Thou drewest near in the day that I called upon thee;
Thou saidst, "Fear not!"
O Lord, thou hast pleaded the causes of my soul;
Thou hast redeemed my life.

THE PUNISHMENT OF THINE INIQUITY IS ACCOMPLISHED, O JERUSALEM

AND NOW NEBUCHADNEZZAR, king of Babylon, came against the army of Pharaoh-Necho which was by the river Euphrates in Carchemish, and smote him. And Pharaoh, the king of Egypt, came not again any more out of his land: for Nebuchadnezzar had taken from the river of Egypt unto the river Euphrates all that pertained unto the king of Egypt.

And it came to pass in the ninth year of his reign, that Zedekiah rebelled against Nebuchadnezzar, king of Babylon. And Nebuchadnezzar came, he and all his army, against Jerusalem, and pitched against it, and built forts against it round about.

And the famine was sore in the land. And Jeremiah said, "Ah Lord God! Behold, thou hast made the heaven and the earth by thy great power and stretched out arm, and there is nothing too hard for thee. Thine eyes are open upon all the ways of men, to give every one according to his ways, and according to the fruit of his doings. Thus saith the Lord, 'He that remaineth in this city shall die by the sword, by the famine, and by the pestilence; but he that goeth forth to the Chaldeans shall live.' "

And the famine was sore in the city, so that there was no bread for the people of the land.

And Jeremiah lamented:

" How is the gold become dim?
How is the most fine gold changed?
The stones of the sanctuary are poured out in the top
    of every street;

The precious sons of Zion comparable to fine gold
How are they esteemed as earthen pitchers,
The work of the hands of the potter!
They that did feed delicately are desolate in the streets;
They that were brought up in scarlet embrace dunghills.
Their visage is blacker than a coal;
They are not known in the streets;
Their skin cleaveth to their bones;
It is withered, it is become like a stick.
They that be slain with the sword
Are better than they that be slain with hunger:
For these pine away, stricken through for want of the
fruits of the field.

The punishment of thine iniquity is accomplished,
O daughter of Zion."

"Therefore let mine eyes run down with tears night and day, and let them not cease: for the virgin daughter of my people is broken with a great breach, and with a grievous blow. If I go forth into the field, then behold the slain with the sword! and if I enter into the city then behold, them that are sick with famine."

So the city was besieged two years, and the famine prevailed. And in the eleventh year of the reign of king Zedekiah, the city was broken up, and all the men of war fled, and went forth out of the city by night, by way of the gate which was by the king's garden; and they went by the way of the plain. But the army of the Chaldeans pursued after king Zedekiah, and overtook him in the plains of Jericho; and all his army was scattered from him.

Then they took Zedekiah, and carried him up unto Nebuchadnezzar. And the king of Babylon slew the sons of Zedekiah before his eyes. He slew also all the princes of Judah. Then he put out the eyes of Zedekiah and bound him in chains, and carried him to Babylon, and put him in prison till the day of his death.

Now Nebuzaradan, captain of the guard, which served the king of Babylon, came into Jerusalem, and burned the house of the Lord, and the king's house, and all the houses of Jerusalem, and all the houses of the great men, burned he with fire. And the pillars of brass, and the brazen sea that were in the house of the Lord, did the Chaldeans break in pieces and carried the brass of them to Babylon. And all the vessels of brass, and such things as were of gold and of silver, Nebuzaradan took these, and brought them to Nebuchadnezzar. And all the army of the Chaldeans that were with the captain of the guard, brake down all the walls of Jerusalem round about.

And Nebuzaradan took the people of Judah and brought them to Nebuchadnezzar to Riblah. And the king of Babylon smote them, and put them to death in Riblah in the land of Hamath. Thus the tribe of Judah was carried away captive out of his own land.

Now Nebuchadnezzar had given charge concerning Jeremiah to Nebuzaradan, saying, "Take him and look well to him, and do him no harm; but do unto him even as he shall say unto thee."

So Nebuzaradan took Jeremiah out of the court of the prison, and said unto him, "I loose thee this day from the chains that were upon thine hand. If it seem good unto thee to come with me unto Babylon, come; and I will look well unto thee; but if it seem ill unto thee to come with me into Babylon, forbear. Or you may go back to Gedaliah, whom the king of Babylon hath made governor over Judah, and dwell with him among the people: or go wheresoever it seemeth convenient unto thee to go. Behold, all the land is before thee." So the captain of the guard gave Jeremiah food and a reward, and let him go.

Now Nebuzaradan had carried away captive most of the

people of Judah, but he left certain of the poor of the land for vinedressers and for husbandmen. And Nebuchadnezzar had made Gedaliah ruler over the people that remained in the land. Then went Jeremiah unto Gedaliah, and dwelt with him among the people that were left.

And Jeremiah lamented:

JERUSALEM HATH GRIEVOUSLY SINNED

How doth the city sit solitary, that was full of people!
How is she become as a widow! she that was great among the nations,
And princess among the provinces, how is she become tributary!

She weepeth sore in the night, and her tears are on her cheeks;
Among all her lovers she hath none to comfort her;
All her friends have dealt treacherously with her, they are become her enemies.

Judah is gone into captivity because of affliction, and because of great servitude;
She dwelleth among the heathen, she findeth no rest:
All her persecutors overtook her between the straits.

And from the daughter of Zion all her beauty is departed;
Her princes are become like harts that find no pasture,
And they are gone without strength before the pursuer.

Jerusalem remembered in the days of her affliction and of her miseries all her pleasant things that she had in the days of old;

When her people fell into the hand of the enemy, and none did help her,
The adversaries saw her, and did mock at her sabbaths.

Jerusalem hath grievously sinned; therefore she is removed.
All that honoured her despise her, because they have seen her nakedness;
Yea, she sigheth, and turneth backward.

For these things I weep; mine eye, mine eye runneth down with water,
Because the comforter that should relieve my soul is far from me;
My children are desolate, because the enemy prevailed.

The Lord is righteous; for I have rebelled against his commandment;
Hear, I pray you, all people, and behold my sorrow;
My virgins and my young men are gone into captivity.

OH, REMNANT OF JUDAH, GO YE NOT INTO EGYPT

Now it came to pass, that Ishmael of the seed royal, and ten men with him came to Gedaliah, and they did eat bread together. Then arose Ishmael and the ten men with him, and smote Gedaliah with the sword, and slew him, whom the king of Babylon had made governor over the land. Ishmael slew also all the Jews that were found there, and the men of war.

But when Johanan, the captain of the forces, heard of all the evil that Ishmael had done, they went to fight with him, and found him by the great waters that are in Gibeon. And all the people that were with Ishmael were glad, and went unto Johanan. But Ishmael escaped and went to the Ammonites.

Then Johanan and all the people came near and said unto Jeremiah, "We beseech thee, pray for us unto the Lord thy God, that the Lord may show us the way wherein we should walk, and we will obey the voice of the Lord our God to whom we sent thee."

And it came to pass, after ten days that the word of the Lord came to Jeremiah, saying, "Thus saith the Lord, 'If ye will abide in this land, then I will build you and not pull you down, and I will plant you and not pluck you up, for I am with you to save you, and I will show my mercy unto you. But if ye wholly set your faces to enter into Egypt, and go and sojourn there, then shall the sword which ye feared, overtake you, and the famine whereof ye are afraid shall follow close after you there in Egypt; and there ye shall die. Oh, ye remnant of Judah, Go ye not into Egypt.' "

And when Jeremiah had made an end of speaking unto all the people, then spake Johanan and all the proud men, saying unto Jeremiah, "Thou speakest falsely: the Lord our God hath not sent thee to say, 'Go not into Egypt to sojourn there.' "

So Johanan and the captains of the forces took all the remnant of Judah, even men, women and children, and every person that Nebuzaradan had left with Gedaliah, and also Jeremiah the prophet, and came into the land of Egypt: for they obeyed not the voice of the Lord.

Then came the word of the Lord unto Jeremiah, saying, "Take great stones in thine hand, and hide them in the clay in the brick kiln, which is at the entry of Pharaoh's house, in the sight of the men of Judah, and say unto them, 'Thus saith the God of Israel, "Behold, Nebuchadnezzar, the king of Babylon, shall set his throne upon these stones, and spread his pavilion over them. And when he cometh he shall smite the land of Egypt; and he shall deliver such as are for death to death; and such as are for captivity to captivity; and such as are for the sword to the sword. And he shall array himself with the land of Egypt, as a shepherd putteth on his garment; and he shall go forth from thence in peace.

" ' " And behold, all the men of Judah that are in the land of Egypt, shall be consumed by the sword and by the famine, until there be an end of them. Yet a small number that escape the sword shall return out of the land of Egypt into the land of Judah. Therefore, hear ye the word of the Lord, all Judah that dwell in Egypt." ' "

I HAVE LOVED THEE WITH AN EVERLASTING LOVE

THIS WORD came to Jeremiah from the Lord, saying, " Write thee all the words that I have spoken unto thee in a book. For lo, the days come, that I will bring again the captivity of my people Israel and Judah, and I will cause them to return to the land that I gave to their fathers, and they shall possess it.

" For lo, I will raise and cause to come up against Babylon an assembly of great nations from the north country, and they shall set themselves in array against her, and she shall be taken.

"In those days, the children of Israel shall come, they and the children of Judah together, going and weeping: they shall go and seek the Lord their God. And I will reveal unto them the abundance of peace and Truth.

" Am I a God at hand, and not a God afar off? Can any hide himself in secret places that I shall not see him? Do not I fill heaven and earth?

“Therefore fear thou not, O my servant Jacob, neither be dismayed, O Israel! for lo I will save thee from afar, and thy seed
from the land of th captivity. They shall come with weeping,
and with supp ons will I lead them. I will cause them to walk
and with waters in a straight way, wherein they shall not
by the riv am a father to Israel. Yea, I have loved thee with
stumbl ing Love; therefore with loving kindness have I
an ee.

Therefore, they shall come and sing in the height of Zion, and
all flow together to the goodness of the Lord, for wheat, and
for wine, and for oil, and for the young of the flock and of the
herd: and their soul shall be as a watered garden; and they shall
not sorrow any more at all.

“Behold, the days come that I will make a new covenant with the house of Israel, and with the house of Judah: I will put my law in their inward parts, and write it in their hearts; and will be their God, and they shall be my people. And they shall teach no more every man his neighbour, and every man his brother, saying, ‘Know the Lord:’ for they shall all know me, from the least of them unto the greatest of them:

“Behold the days come, that I will raise unto David a righteous branch, and a King shall reign and prosper, and shall execute judgment and justice in the earth. In his days Judah shall be saved, and Israel shall dwell safely: and this is his name whereby he shall be called, THE LORD OUR RIGHTEOUSNESS.”

Thus far are the words of Jeremiah.

" Behold, I even I,
Will both search my sheep, and seek them out."

THE BOOK OF EZEKIEL

The Prophet

I SAW BRIGHTNESS AS OF THE GLORY OF THE LORD

NOW IT CAME TO PASS, in the fifth year of King Jehoiachin's captivity, that the word of the Lord came expressly unto Ezekiel, the priest, in the land of the Chaldeans by the river Chebar, and Ezekiel said:

"As I was among the captives by the river Chebar, the heavens were opened, and I saw visions of God. And I looked, and, behold, a whirlwind came out of the north, a great cloud, and a fire infolding itself, and a brightness was about it, and out of the midst thereof as the colour of amber.

"Also out of the midst thereof came the likeness of four living creatures. And this was their appearance: they had the likeness of a man, and every one had four faces, and every one had four wings. Their wings were joined one to another; they turned not when they went; they went every one straight forward.

"As for the likeness of their faces, they four had the face of a man, and the face of a lion, on the right side; and they four had the face of an ox on the left side; they four also had the face of an eagle. Thus were their faces: and their wings were stretched upward. And they went every one straight forward: whither the spirit was to go, they went.

"Their appearance was like burning coals of fire, and the fire was bright, and out of the fire went forth lightning. And the living creatures ran and returned as the appearance of a flash of lightning.

"Now as I beheld the living creatures, behold one wheel upon the earth. And they four had one likeness: and their appearance and their work was as it were a wheel in the middle of a wheel. And when the living creatures went, the wheels went by them; and when the living creatures were lifted up from the earth, the wheels were lifted up: for the spirit of the living creatures was in the wheels.

"And when they went, I heard the noise of their wings, like the noise of great waters, and as the voice of the Almighty. And I saw as it were the appearance of fire, and it had brightness round about. This was the appearance of the likeness of the glory of the Lord. And when I saw it, I fell upon my face, and I heard a voice of one that spoke.

"And he said unto me, 'Son of man stand upon thy feet, and I will speak unto thee.' And the Spirit entered into me and set me upon my feet.

"And he said, 'Son of man, I send thee to the children of Israel, to a rebellious nation that hath rebelled against me and transgressed against me even unto this very day.

"'I do send thee unto them; and thou shalt say unto them, "Thus saith the Lord God." And they, whether they will hear, or whether they will forbear, (for they are a rebellious house,) yet shall they know that there hath been a prophet among them.

"'And thou, son of man, be not afraid of them, neither be afraid of their words, though briers and thorns be with thee, and thou dost dwell among scorpions; be not afraid of their words, nor be dismayed at their looks.

"'But thou, son of man, be not thou rebellious like that rebellious house: open thy mouth, and eat that I give thee.'

"And when I looked, behold, an hand was sent unto me; and, lo, a roll of a book was therein. And he spread it before me; and it was written within and without: and there was written therein lamentations, and mourning, and woe. And he said, 'Son of man, eat that thou findest; eat this roll, and go speak unto the house of Israel.'

"So I opened my mouth, and he caused me to eat that roll. And he said unto me, 'Son of man, thou art not sent unto a people of strange speech and hard language whose words thou canst not understand. Surely had I sent thee to them, they would have hearkened unto thee. But the house of Israel will not hearken unto thee; for they will not hearken to me.

" 'Son of man, all my words that I shall speak unto thee receive in thine heart, and hear with thine ears. And go, get thee to them of the captivity, unto the children of thy people, and speak unto them, "Thus saith the Lord God," whether they will hear, or whether they will forbear.'

"Then the spirit took me up, and I heard behind me a voice of a great rushing, saying, 'Blessed be the glory of the Lord from his place.' I heard also the noise of the wings of the living creatures that touched one another, and the noise of the wheels over against them, and a noise of a great rushing.

"So the spirit lifted me up, and took me away, and I went in bitterness, in the heat of my spirit; but the hand of the Lord was strong upon me. Then I came to them of the captivity that dwelt by the river Chebar, and I sat where they sat, and remained there perplexed among them seven days.

"And it came to pass at the end of seven days, that the word of the Lord came unto me, saying, 'Son of man, I have made thee a watchman unto the house of Israel: therefore hear the word at my mouth, and give them warning from me.

" 'When I say unto the wicked, "Thou shalt surely die;" and thou givest him not warning, nor speakest to warn the wicked from his wicked way to save his life; the same wicked man shall die in his iniquity; but his blood will I require at thine hand. Yet if thou warn the wicked, and he turn not from his wickedness, nor from his wicked way he shall die in his iniquity; but thou hast delivered thy soul.

" 'Again, when a righteous man doth turn from his righteousness, and commit iniquity, he shall die; because thou hast not given him warning, he shall die in his sin, and his righteousness which he hath done shall not be remembered; but his blood will I require at thine hand. Nevertheless, if thou warn the righteous man, that the righteous sin not, and he doth not sin, he shall surely live, because he is warned; also thou hast delivered thy soul.'

"And the hand of the Lord was there upon me; and he said unto me, 'Arise, go forth into the plain, and I will there talk with thee.'

"Then I arose, and went forth into the plain: and, behold the glory of the Lord stood there, as the glory which I saw by the river of Chebar: and I fell on my face. Then the spirit entered into me, and set me upon my feet, and spake with me, and said unto me, 'Go, shut thyself within thine house. But thou, O son of man, behold, they shall put bands upon thee, and shall bind thee with them, and thou shalt not go out among them: and I will make thy tongue cleave to the roof of thy mouth, that thou shalt be dumb, and shalt not be to them a reprover: for they are a rebellious house. But when I speak with thee, I will open thy mouth, and thou shalt say unto them, "Thus saith the Lord God; He that heareth, let him hear; and he that forbeareth, let him forbear: for they are a rebellious house." '"

WALK IN MY STATUTES, AND KEEP MY ORDINANCES, AND DO THEM

AGAIN the word of the Lord came unto me, saying, "Son of man, thy brethren, the men of thy kindred, and all the house of Israel wholly, are they unto whom the inhabitants of Jerusalem have said, 'Get you far from the Lord; unto us is this land given in possession.'

"Therefore say, 'Thus saith the Lord God. "Although I have cast them far off among the heathen, and although I have scattered them among the countries, yet will I be to them as a little sanctuary in the countries where they shall come."

"Therefore say, 'Thus saith the Lord, I will even gather you from the people, and assemble you out of the countries where ye have been scattered, and I will give you the land of Israel. And they shall come thither, and they shall take away all the detestable things thereof and all the abominations thereof from thence. And I will give them one heart, and I will put a new spirit within you; and I will take the stony heart out of their flesh, and will give them an heart of flesh: that they may walk in my statutes, and keep mine ordinances, and do them: and they shall be my people, and I will be their God.

"'But as for them whose heart walketh after the heart of their detestable things and their abominations, I will recompense their way upon their own heads,'" saith the Lord God.

Then I spake unto them of the captivity all the things that the Lord had showed me.

TURN YOURSELVES FROM YOUR IDOLS

THEN CAME certain of the elders of Israel unto me, Ezekiel, and sat before me. And the word of the Lord came unto me, saying,

"Son of man, these men have set up their idols in their heart, and put the stumbling block of their iniquity before their face: should I be enquired of at all by them?

"Therefore speak unto them, and say unto them, 'Thus saith the Lord God: "Every man that setteth up his idols in his heart, and putteth the stumbling block of his iniquity before his face, and cometh to the prophet, I the Lord will answer him that cometh according to the multitude of his idols."'

"Therefore say unto them, 'Repent, and turn yourselves from your idols, and turn away your faces from all your abominations.'"

TURN YOURSELVES, AND LIVE YE

The word of the Lord came unto me again, saying, "What mean ye, that ye use this proverb concerning the land of Israel, saying, 'The fathers have eaten sour grapes, and the children's teeth are set on edge?' As I live," saith the Lord, "Ye shall not have occasion any more to use this proverb in Israel.

"Yet say ye, 'Why doth not the son bear the iniquity of the father?'

"When the son hath done that which is lawful and right, and hath kept all my statutes, and hath done them, he shall surely live. The soul that sinneth, it shall die. The son shall not bear the iniquity of the father, neither shall the father bear the iniquity of the son: the righteousness of the righteous shall be upon him, and the wickedness of the wicked shall be upon him.

"But if the wicked will turn from all his sins that he hath committed, and keep all my statutes, and do that which is lawful and right, he shall surely live, he shall not die. All his transgressions that he hath committed, they shall not be mentioned unto him: in his righteousness that he hath done he shall live. Have I any pleasure at all that the wicked should die? and not that he should return from his ways and live? Because he considereth, and turneth away from all his transgressions that he hath committed, he shall surely live, he shall not die.

"When a righteous man turneth away from his righteousness, and committeth iniquity, and dieth in them; for his iniquity that he hath done shall he die.

" Yet ye say, ' The way of the Lord is not equal.'

" Hear now, O house of Israel: Is not my way equal? Are not your ways unequal? Therefore I will judge you, O house of Israel, every one according to his ways.

" Repent, and turn yourselves from all your transgressions; so iniquity shall not be your ruin. Cast away from you all your transgressions, whereby ye have transgressed; and make you a new heart, and a new spirit: for why will ye die, O house of Israel? For I have no pleasure in the death of him that dieth," saith the Lord God: " Wherefore turn yourselves, and live ye."

A LAMENTATION FOR TYRUS

THE WORD of the Lord came again unto me, Ezekiel, saying, " Now thou son of man, take up a lamentation for Tyrus, and say unto Tyrus:

' O thou that art situate at the entry of the sea,
Which art a merchant of the people for many isles,
Thus saith the Lord God:
" O Tyrus, thou hast said, ' I am of perfect beauty.'

' " Thy borders are in the midst of the seas,
Thy builders have perfected thy beauty.
They have made all thy ship boards of fir trees of Senir;
They have taken cedars from Lebanon to make masts for thee.
Of the oaks of Bashan have they made thine oars;
The company of the Ashurites have made thy benches of ivory,
Brought out of the isles of Chittim.

'"Judah, and the land of Israel, they were thy merchants:
They traded in thy market wheat of Minnith,
And pannag, and honey, and oil, and balm.
Damascus was thy merchant in the multitude of the wares
of thy making,
For the multitude of all riches;
In the wine of Helbon, and white wool.
Arabia, and all the princes of Kedar,
They traded with thee in lambs, and rams, and goats:
In these were they thy merchants.
The merchants of Sheba and Raamah, they were thy
merchants:
They traded in thy fairs with chief of all spices,
And with all precious stones, and gold.
The ships of Tarshish did sing of thee in thy market;
And thou wast replenished, and made very glorious in the
midst of the seas.

'"Thy rowers have brought thee into great waters;
The east wind hath broken thee in the midst of the seas.
Thy riches, and thy fairs, and thy merchandise,
Thy mariners, and thy pilots, and thy calkers,
And the occupiers of thy merchandise,
And all thy men of war, that are in thee,
And in all thy company which is in the midst of thee,
Shall fall into the midst of the seas in the day of thy ruin.

'"The suburbs shall shake at the sound of the cry of thy
pilots.
And all that handle the oar,
The mariners, and all the pilots of the sea,
Shall come down from their ships,
They shall stand upon the land,
And shall cause their voice to be heard against thee,

And shall cry bitterly,
And shall cast up dust upon their heads,
They shall wallow themselves in the ashes.
And in their wailing they shall take up a lamentation
for thee,
And lament over thee, saying,
'What city is like Tyrus,
Like the destroyed in the midst of the sea? ' " ' "

A LAMENTATION FOR PHARAOH KING OF EGYPT

AND IT CAME TO PASS in the twelfth year, that the word of the Lord came unto me, saying, "Son of man, take up a lamentation for Pharaoh king of Egypt, and say unto him:

" 'Thou art like a young lion of the nations,
And thou art as a whale in the seas:
And thou camest forth with thy rivers,
And troubledst the waters with thy feet,
And fouledst their rivers.'

"Thus saith the Lord God:
'I will therefore spread out my net over thee with a
company of many people,
And they shall bring thee up in my net.
Then I will leave thee upon the land;
I will cast thee forth upon the open field,
And will cause all the fowls of heaven to remain upon thee,
And I will fill the beasts of the whole earth with thee.
And I will lay thy flesh upon the mountains,
And fill the valleys with thy height.

I will also water with thy blood the land wherein thou
 swimmest, even to the mountains;
And the rivers shall be full of thee.

" 'And when I shall put thee out,
I will cover the heaven,
And make the stars thereof dark;
I will cover the sun with a cloud,
And the moon shall not give her light.
All the bright lights of heaven will I make dark over thee,
And set darkness upon thy land,'
Saith the Lord God.

" 'Yea, I will make many people amazed at thee,
And their kings shall be horribly afraid for thee,
When I shall brandish my sword before them;
And they shall tremble at every moment,
Every man for his own life,
In the day of thy fall.'

" For thus saith the Lord God;
' The sword of the king of Babylon shall come upon thee.
By the swords of the mighty will I cause thy multitude to
 fall,
The terrible of the nations, all of them;
And they shall spoil the pomp of Egypt,
And all the multitude thereof shall be destroyed.

" ' When I shall make the land of Egypt desolate,
And the country shall be destitute of that whereof it was
 full,
When I shall smite all them that dwell therein,
Then shall they know that I am the Lord.
This is the lamentation wherewith they shall lament her:

The daughters of the nations shall lament her;
They shall lament for her, even for Egypt,
And for all her multitude,'
Saith the Lord God."

I WILL BOTH SEARCH MY SHEEP, AND SEEK THEM OUT

AND IT CAME TO PASS in the twelfth year of our captivity, that one that had escaped out of Jerusalem came unto me, saying, "The city is smitten."

Now the hand of the Lord was upon me Ezekiel in the evening, before he that was escaped came, and I had not opened my mouth until he came to me in the morning, and my mouth was opened, and I was no more dumb. Then the word of the Lord came unto me, saying, "Son of man, prophesy against the shepherds of Israel; prophesy, and say unto them:

"'Woe be to the shepherds of Israel that do feed themselves!
Should not the shepherds feed the flocks?
Ye eat the fat, and ye clothe you with the wool;
Ye kill them that are fed, but ye feed not the flock.
The diseased have ye not strengthened,
Neither have ye healed that which was sick,
Neither have ye bound up that which was broken,
Neither have ye brought again that which was driven
away,
Neither have ye sought that which was lost;
But with force and with cruelty have ye ruled them.

" 'And they were scattered because there is no shepherd:
And they became meat to all the beasts of the field,
When they were scattered.
My sheep wandered through all the mountains,
And upon every high hill:
Yea, my flock was scattered upon all the face of the earth,
And none did search or seek after them.
Therefore, ye shepherds, hear the word of the Lord:
" As I live," saith the Lord God,
" Surely because my flock became a prey,
And my flock became meat to every beast of the field,
Because there was no shepherd,
Neither did my shepherds search for my flock,
But the shepherds fed themselves, and fed not my flock,
Therefore, O ye shepherds, I am against the shepherds,
And I will deliver my flock from their mouth.

" ' " Behold, I, even I, will both search my sheep, and seek them out.
As a shepherd seeketh out his flock
In the day that he is among his sheep that are scattered;
So will I seek out my sheep,
And will deliver them out of all places
Where they have been scattered in the cloudy and dark day.

" ' "And I will bring them out from the people,
And gather them from the countries,
And will bring them to their own land,
And feed them upon the mountains of Israel by the rivers,
And in all the inhabited places of the country.
I will feed them in a good pasture,
And upon the high mountains of Israel shall their fold be:
There shall they lie in a good fold,

And in fat pastures shall they feed upon the mountains
of Israel.

"'" I will feed my flock, and I will cause them to lie down,"
Saith the Lord God.
"'I will seek that which was lost,
And bring again that which was driven away,
And will bind up that which was broken,
And will strengthen that which was sick.
But the fat and the strong, I will feed with judgment.

"'"As for you, O my flock,
Behold, I judge between cattle and cattle.
Seemeth it a small thing unto you to have eaten up the
good pasture,
But ye must tread down with your feet the residue of your
pasture?
And to have drunk of the deep waters,
But ye must foul the residue with your feet?
And as for my flock,
They eat that which ye have trodden with your feet;
And they drink that which ye have fouled with your feet.

"'" Behold, I, even I, will judge between the fat cattle and
between the lean cattle.
Because ye have thrust with side and with shoulder,
And pushed all the diseased with your horns,
Till ye have scattered them abroad,
Therefore will I save my flock,
And they shall no more be a prey.
And I will judge between cattle and cattle.
And I will set up one shepherd over them,
And he shall feed them, even my servant David;
He shall feed them, and he shall be their shepherd.

And I the Lord will be their God,
And my servant David a prince among them.
I the Lord have spoken it.

" ' "And I will make with them a covenant of peace,
And will cause the evil beasts to cease out of the land:
And they shall dwell safely in the wilderness,
And sleep in the woods.
And I will make them and the places round about my hill
a blessing.
And I will cause the shower to come down in his season;
There shall be showers of blessing.
And the tree of the field shall yield her fruit,
And the earth shall yield her increase,
And they shall be safe in their land,
And shall know that I am the Lord,
When I have broken the bands of their yoke,
And delivered them out of the hand
Of those that served themselves of them.

" ' "And they shall no more be a prey to the heathen,
Neither shall the beast of the land devour them;
But they shall dwell safely,
And none shall make them afraid.
And I will raise up for them a plant of renown,
And they shall be no more consumed with hunger in the
land,
Neither bear the shame of the heathen any more.
Thus shall they know that I the Lord their God am with
them,
And that they, even the house of Israel, are my people.
And ye my flock,
The flock of my pasture, are men,
And I am your God," ' saith the Lord God."

THE NAME OF THE CITY SHALL BE, THE LORD IS THERE

IN THE TWENTY-FIFTH YEAR of our captivity, the hand of the Lord was upon me, Ezekiel, and in visions, God brought me into the land of Israel, and set me upon a very high mountain, by which was, as it were, the frame of a city on the south.

And he brought me thither, and behold, there was a man, whose appearance was like the appearance of brass, with a line of flax in his hand, and a measuring reed; and he stood in the gate. And he said unto me, "Son of man, behold with thine eyes, and hear with thine ears, and set thine heart upon all that I shall show thee. And declare all that thou seest to the house of Israel."

And behold a wall on the outside of the house round about, and in the man's hand a measuring reed: so he measured the breadth and height of the building. And he measured all the gates, height and breadth, the porches and all the posts and pillars, and all the chambers and the arches and windows thereof.

Afterward he brought me to the Temple, and he measured its gates, its posts and porches, and the doors and windows and chambers. Afterward, he brought me to the gate, even the gate of the Temple that looketh toward the east.

And behold, the glory of the God of Israel came from the way of the east: and his voice was like the noise of many waters, and the earth shined with his glory. And the visions were like the vision that I saw by the river Chebar; and I fell upon my face.

And the glory of the Lord came into the temple by way of the gate whose prospect is toward the east. So the spirit took me up, and brought me into the inner court, and behold, the glory of the Lord filled the house.

And I heard him speaking unto me out of the house, and the man stood by me. And he said unto me, " Son of man, the place of my throne, where I will dwell in the midst of the children of Israel for ever, and my holy name, shall the house of Israel no more defile, neither they nor their kings by their whoredom, nor by the carcases of their kings in the high places. Now let them put away their iniquities, and I will dwell in the midst of them for ever. Thou, son of man, show the house of Israel that they may be ashamed of their iniquities. And if they be ashamed of all that they have done, show them the form of the house, and the fashion thereof, and all the laws thereof. And write it in their sight, that they may keep all the ordinances thereof, and do them. This is the law of the house: Upon the top of the mountain, the whole limit thereof round about shall be most Holy. Behold, this is the law of the house."

Afterward he brought me again unto the door of the house; and, behold, waters issued out from under the threshold of the house eastward; for the front of the house stood toward the east, and the waters came down from under the right side of the house, at the south side of the altar.

Then brought he me out of the gate northward, and led me about by the way that looketh eastward; and, behold, there ran out waters on the right side. And the man went forth, and measured a thousand cubits and brought me through the waters; the waters were to the ankles. Again he measured a thousand, and brought me through the waters; the waters were to the knees. Again he measured a thousand, and brought me through; the waters were to the loins. Afterward he measured a thousand; and it was a river that I could not pass over: for the waters were risen, waters to swim in, a river that could not be passed over.

And he said unto me, " Son of man, hast thou seen this? " Then he brought me, and caused me to return to the brink of the river. Now when I had returned, behold, at the bank of the river were very many trees on the one side and on the other.

Then said he unto me, " These waters issue out toward the east country, and go down into the desert, and go into the sea: which being brought forth into the sea, the waters shall be healed. And it shall come to pass, that everything that liveth, which moveth, whithersoever the rivers shall come, shall live; and there shall be a very great multitude of fish, because these waters shall come thither; for they shall be healed; and every thing shall live whither the river cometh.

" And it shall come to pass that the fishers shall stand upon it; they shall spread forth their nets, and their fish shall be according to their kinds as the fish of the great sea, exceeding many. And by the river upon the bank thereof, on this side and on that side shall grow all trees for meat, whose leaf shall not fade, neither shall the fruit thereof be consumed: it shall bring forth new fruit according to his months, because their waters issued out of the sanctuary: and the fruit thereof shall be for meat, and the leaf thereof for healing.

" Thus saith the Lord God, 'This shall be the border, whereby ye shall inherit the land according to the twelve tribes of Israel. And ye shall inherit it, one as well as another: concerning which I lifted up mine hand to give it unto your fathers; and this land shall fall unto you for inheritance. And it shall come to pass, that ye shall divide it by lot for an inheritance unto you, and to the strangers that sojourn among you, which shall beget children among you: and they shall be unto you as born in the country among the children of Israel; they shall have inheritance with you among the tribes of Israel. And it shall come to pass, that in what tribe the stranger sojourneth, there shall ye give him his inheritance,' saith the Lord God. And they shall not sell of it, neither exchange, nor alienate the first-fruits of the land: for it is holy unto the Lord.

" And the city shall be in the midst thereof. And they that

serve the city shall serve it out of all the tribes of Israel. And the gates of the city shall be after the names of the tribes of Israel: northward there shall be three gates; eastward three gates; on the south side three gates; and at the west side three gates: a gate for each of the twelve tribes of Israel. And the name of the city from that day shall be, 'THE LORD IS THERE.'"

“ Comfort ye my people.”

ISAIAH II

or

The Unknown Prophet

ISAIAH II

The Unknown Prophet, or sometimes called the Second Isaiah, wrote comfortingly to the children of Israel in captivity, saying:

COMFORT YE MY PEOPLE

" Comfort ye, comfort ye my people,"
Saith your God;
" Speak ye comfortably to Jerusalem,
And cry unto her,
That her warfare is accomplished,
That her iniquity is pardoned:
For she hath received of the Lord's hand
Double for all her sins."

The voice of him that crieth in the wilderness,
" Prepare ye the way of the Lord,
Make straight in the desert a highway for our God.
Every valley shall be exalted,
And every mountain and hill shall be made low:
And the crooked shall be made straight,
And the rough places plain:
And the glory of the Lord shall be revealed,
And all flesh shall see it together:
For the mouth of the Lord hath spoken it."

The voice said, " Cry."
And he said, " What shall I cry? "
" All flesh is grass,
And all the goodliness thereof is as the flower of the field:

The grass withereth, the flower fadeth:
But the word of our God shall stand for ever."

O Zion, that bringest good tidings,
Get thee up into the high mountain;
O Jerusalem, that bringest good tidings,
Lift up thy voice with strength;
Lift it up,
Be not afraid;
Say unto the cities of Judah,
" Behold, your God! "

Behold, the Lord God will come with strong hand,
And his arm shall rule for him:
Behold, his reward is with him,
And his work before him.
He shall feed his flock like a shepherd:
He shall gather the lambs with his arm,
And carry them in his bosom,
And shall gently lead those that are with young.

THE SPIRIT OF THE LORD

Who hath measured the waters in the hollow of his hand,
And meted out heaven with the span,
And comprehended the dust of the earth in a measure,
And weighed the mountains in scales,
And the hills in a balance?

Who hath directed the Spirit of the Lord,
Or being his counsellor hath taught him?
With whom took he counsel,
And who instructed him,

And taught him in the path of judgment,
And taught him knowledge,
And showed to him the way of understanding?

Behold, the nations are as a drop of a bucket,
And are counted as the small dust of the balance:
Behold, he taketh up the iles as a very little thing.
All nations before him are as nothing;
And they are counted to him less than nothing, and vanity.

To whom then will ye liken God?
Or what likeness will ye compare unto him?
Have ye not known? have ye not heard?
Hath it not been told you from the beginning?
Have ye not understood from the foundations of the earth?
It is he that sitteth upon the circle of the earth,
That stretcheth out the heavens as a curtain,
And spreadeth them out as a tent to dwell in;
That bringeth the princes to nothing;
He maketh the judges of the earth as vanity.

" To whom then will ye liken me,
Or shall I be equal? " saith the Holy One.
Lift up your eyes on high,
And behold who hath created these things,
That bringeth out their host by number:
He calleth them all by names
By the greatness of his might,
For that he is strong in power,
Not one faileth.

Hast thou not known?
Hast thou not heard,
That the everlasting God,

The Lord, the Creator of the ends of the earth,
Fainteth not, neither is weary?
There is no searching of his understanding.

He giveth power to the faint;
And to them that have no might he increaseth strength,
Even the youths shall faint and be weary,
And the young men shall utterly fall:
But they that wait upon the Lord shall renew their
strength;
They shall mount up with wings as eagles;
They shall run, and not be weary;
And they shall walk, and not faint.

THE LORD HATH OPENED MINE EAR

The Lord God hath given me the tongue of the learned,
That I should know how to speak a word in season to him
that is weary;
He wakeneth morning by morning,
He wakeneth mine ear to hear as the learned;
The Lord God hath opened mine ear.

FEAR THOU NOT

Fear thou not; for I am with thee:
Be not dismayed; for I am thy God:
I will strengthen thee; yea, I will help thee;
Yea, I will uphold thee with the right hand of my
righteousness.

Behold, all they that were incensed against thee
Shall be ashamed and confounded:

They shall be as nothing;
And they that strive with thee shall be as nothing,
And as a thing of nought.

For I the Lord thy God will hold thy right hand,
Saying unto thee, " Fear not; I will help thee."
Behold, I will make thee a new sharp threshing instrument
having teeth:
Thou shalt thresh the mountains, and beat them small,
And shalt make the hills as chaff.
Thou shalt fan them, and the wind shall carry them away,
And the whirlwind shall scatter them:
And thou shalt rejoice in the Lord,
And shalt glory in the Holy One of Israel.

When the poor and needy seek water,
And there is none, and their tongue faileth for thirst,
I the Lord will hear them,
I the God of Israel will not forsake them.
I will open rivers in high places,
And fountains in the midst of the valleys:
I will make the wilderness a pool of water,
And the dry land springs of water.

I will plant in the wilderness the cedar,
The shittah tree, and the myrtle, and the oil tree;
I will set in the desert the fir tree,
And the pine, and the box tree together.
That they may see, and know, and consider and understand
together,
That the hand of the Lord hath done this,
And the Holy One of Israel hath created it.

BEHOLD MY SERVANT

Behold my servant, whom I uphold;
Mine elect, in whom my soul delighteth;
I have put my spirit upon him:
He shall bring forth judgment to the Gentiles.
He shall not cry, nor lift up,
Nor cause his voice to be heard in the street.
A bruised reed shall he not break,
And the smoking flax shall he not quench;
He shall bring forth judgment unto truth.
He shall not fail nor be discouraged,
Till he have set judgment in the earth:
And the isles shall wait for his law.

A LIGHT OF THE GENTILES

Thus saith God the Lord,
He that created the heavens, and stretched them out;
He that spread forth the earth,
And that which cometh out of it;
He that giveth breath unto the people upon it,
And spirit to them that walk therein:
" I the Lord have called thee in righteousness,
And will hold thine hand,
And will keep thee,
And give thee for a covenant of the people,
For a light of the Gentiles;
To open the blind eyes,
To bring out the prisoners from the prison,
And them that sit in darkness out of the prison house.
I am the Lord; that is my name:

And my glory will I not give to another,
Neither my praise to graven images.
Behold, the former things are come to pass,
And new things do I declare:
Before they spring forth I tell you of them."
Sing unto the Lord a new song,
And his praise from the end of the earth.
Let the wilderness and the cities thereof lift up their voice,
Let the inhabitants of the rock sing,
Let them shout from the top of the mountains.
Let them give glory unto the Lord.
And I will bring the blind by a way that they knew not;
I will lead them in paths that they have not known:
I will make darkness light before them, and crooked things straight.
These things will I do unto them, and not forsake them.
Hear, ye deaf; and look, ye blind, that ye may see.
The Lord is well pleased for his righteousness' sake;
He will magnify the law, and make it honourable.

FEAR NOT: FOR I AM WITH THEE

Thus saith the Lord that created thee, O Jacob,
And he that formed thee, O Israel,
" Fear not: for I have redeemed thee,
I have called thee by thy name,
Thou art mine.

" When thou passest through the waters,
I will be with thee;
And through the rivers,
They shall not overflow thee;
When thou walkest through the fire,

Thou shalt not be burned;
Neither shall the flame kindle upon thee.

" Since thou wast precious in my sight,
Thou hast been honourable,
And I have loved thee.
Fear not: for I am with thee;
I will bring thy seed from the east,
And gather thee from the west;
I will say to the north, ' Give up;'
And to the south, ' Keep not back; '
Bring my sons from far,
And my daughters from the ends of the earth;
Even every one that is called by my name;
For I have created him for my glory,
I have formed him,
Yea, I have made him."

Bring forth the blind people that have eyes,
And the deaf that have ears.
Let all the nations be gathered together,
And let the people be assembled;
Who among them can declare this,
And show us former things?
Let them bring forth their witnesses,
That they may be justified;
Or let them hear and say, " It is Truth."

" Ye are my witnesses," saith the Lord,
"And my servant whom I have chosen;
That ye may know and believe me,
And understand that I am he;
Before me there was no God formed,
Neither shall there be after me.

" I, even I, am the Lord;
And beside me there is no saviour.
I have declared, and have saved,
And I have showed,
When there was no strange god among you;
Therefore ye are my witnesses," saith the Lord,
" That I am God.

" Yea, before the day was I am he;
And there is none that can deliver out of my hand;
I will work, and who shall let it?
I am the Lord, your Holy One,
The creator of Israel, your King.
This people have I formed for myself,
They shall show forth my praise."

THE ARMY AND THE POWER ARE EXTINCT

Thus saith the Lord, which maketh a way in the sea,
And a path in the mighty waters;
Which bringeth forth the chariot and horse,
The army and the power;
"They shall lie down together,
They shall not rise;
They are extinct,
They are quenched as tow.

" Remember ye not the former things,
Neither consider the things of old.
Behold, I will do a new thing;
Now it shall spring forth;
Shall ye not know it?
I will even make a way in the wilderness,
And rivers in the desert.

" The beast of the field shall honour me,
The dragons and the owls:
Because I give waters in the wilderness,
And rivers in the desert,
To give drink to my people, my chosen.
This people have I formed for myself;
They shall show forth my praise."

I HAVE BLOTTED OUT THY TRANSGRESSIONS

Thus saith the Lord the King of Israel,
" I am the first, and I am the last;
And beside me there is no God.

" I will pour water upon him that is thirsty,
And floods upon the dry ground:
I will pour my spirit upon thy seed,
And my blessing upon thine offspring.

" Fear ye not, neither be afraid:
Have not I told thee from that time, and have declared it?
Ye are even my witnesses.
Is there a God beside me?
Yea, there is no God; I know not any.

" I have blotted out as a thick cloud, thy transgressions,
And as a cloud, thy sins:
Return unto me;
For I have redeemed thee."

Sing, O ye heavens; for the Lord hath done it:
Shout, ye lower parts of the earth:
Break forth into singing, ye mountains,

O forest, and every tree therein:
For the Lord hath redeemed Jacob,
And glorified himself in Israel.

I MADE THE EARTH, AND CREATED MAN UPON IT

Thus saith the Lord to his anointed,
Whose right hand I have holden,
To subdue nations before him;
To open before him the two leaved gates;
And the gates shall not be shut:

"I will go before thee,
And make the crooked places straight;
I will break in pieces the gates of brass,
And cut in sunder the bars of iron;
And I will give thee the treasures of darkness,
And hidden riches of secret places,
That thou mayest know that I, the Lord,
Which call thee by thy name,
Am the God of Israel.

"I am the Lord, and there is none else,
There is no God beside me;
I girded thee, though thou hast not known me;
That they may know from the rising of the sun, and from the west,
That there is none beside me.
I am the Lord, and there is none else.

"I form the light, and create darkness;
I make peace, and create evil;

I the Lord do all these things.
Drop down, ye heavens, from above;
And let the skies pour down righteousness;
Let the earth open,
And let them bring forth salvation,
And let righteousness spring up together;
I the Lord have created it.

" Woe unto him that striveth with his Maker!
Let the potsherd strive with the potsherds of the earth.
Shall the clay say to him that fashioneth it,
' What makest thou? '
Or thy work, ' He hath no hands? '
Woe unto him that saith unto his father,
' What begettest thou? '
Or to the woman, ' What hast thou brought forth? ' "

Thus saith the Lord, the Holy One of Israel, and his
Maker,
"Ask me of things to come concerning my sons,
And concerning the work of my hands
Command ye me."

" I have made the earth, and created man upon it;
I, even my hands, have stretched out the heavens,
And all their host have I commanded.
I have raised him up in righteousness,
And I will direct all his ways.
He shall build my city,
And he shall let go my captives,
Not for price nor reward,"
Saith the Lord of hosts.

UNTO ME EVERY KNEE SHALL BOW

Thus saith the Lord that created the heavens,
God himself that formed the earth and made it;
He hath established it,
He created it not in vain,
He formed it to be inhabited:

" I am the Lord; and there is none else.
I have not spoken in secret,
In a dark place of the earth:
I said not unto the seed of Jacob,
' Seek ye me in vain; '
I the Lord speak righteousness,
I declare things that are right.

" Assemble yourselves and come;
Draw near together, ye that are escaped of the nations;
They have no knowledge that set up the wood of their graven image,
And pray unto a god that cannot save.

" Tell ye, and bring them near;
Yea, let them take counsel together:
Who hath declared this from ancient time?
Who hath told it from that time?
Have not I, the Lord?
And there is no God else beside me;
A just God and a Saviour;
There is none beside me.

" Look unto me, and be ye saved,
All the ends of the earth:
For I am God, and there is none else.

I have sworn by myself,
The word is gone out of my mouth in righteousness,
And shall not return,
That unto me every knee shall bow,
Every tongue shall swear."

I AM GOD, AND THERE IS NONE ELSE

Hearken unto me, O house of Jacob:
To whom will ye liken me,
And make me equal,
And compare me,
That we may be like?

They lavish gold out of the bag,
And weigh silver in the balance,
And hire a goldsmith;
And he maketh it a god:
They fall down, yea, they worship.
They bear him upon the shoulder,
They carry him, and set him in his place,
And he standeth:
From his place shall he not remove,
One shall cry unto him,
Yet can he not answer,
Nor save him out of his trouble.
Remember this, and show yourselves men:
Bring it again to mind, O ye transgressors.

Remember the former things of old:
For I am God, and there is none else;
I am God, and there is none like me,
Declaring the end from the beginning,

And from ancient times the things that are not yet done,
Saying, " My counsel shall stand,
And I will do all my pleasure:
Yea, I have spoken it,
I will also bring it to pass;
I have purposed it,
I will also do it."

Hearken unto me, ye stouthearted,
That are far from righteousness:
I bring near my righteousness;
It shall not be far off,
And my salvation shall not tarry;
And I will place salvation in Zion
For Israel my glory.

THE LORD GOD WILL HELP ME

The Lord God will help me;
Therefore shall I not be confounded:
Therefore have I set my face like a flint,
And I know that I shall not be ashamed.

Behold, the Lord God will help me;
Who is he that shall condemn me?
Lo, they all shall wax old as a garment;
The moth shall eat them up.

Who is among you that feareth the Lord,
That obeyeth the voice of his servant,
That walketh in darkness, and hath no light?
Let him trust in the name of the Lord, and stay upon his
God.

MY HOUSE SHALL BE CALLED A HOUSE OF PRAYER

Thus saith the Lord,
" Keep ye judgment, and do justice:
For my salvation is near to come,
And my righteousness to be revealed.
Blessed is the man that doeth this,
And the son of man that layeth hold on it;
That keepeth the sabbath from polluting it,
And keepeth his hand from doing any evil.
Them will I bring to my holy mountain,
And make them joyful in my house of prayer:
Their burnt offerings and their sacrifices shall be accepted upon mine altar;
For mine house shall be called an house of prayer for all people."

THOU ART OUR FATHER

I will mention the lovingkindness of the Lord,
And the praises of the Lord,
According to all that the Lord hath bestowed on us,
And the great goodness toward the house of Israel,
Which he hath bestowed on them according to his mercies,
And according to the multitude of his loving kindnesses.
For he said, Surely they are my people,
Children that will not lie:
So he was their Saviour.
In all their affliction he was afflicted,
And the angel of his presence saved them:
In his love and in his pity he redeemed them;
And he bare them, and carried them all the days of old.

Doubtless thou art our Father,
Though Abraham be ignorant of us,
And Israel acknowledge us not:
Thou, O Lord, art our Father, our Redeemer;
Thy name is from everlasting.

WHAT HE HATH PREPARED

Since the beginning of the world
Men have not heard,
Nor perceived by the ear,
Neither hath the eye seen,
O God, beside thee,
What he hath prepared
For him that waiteth for him.

I WILL NOT FORGET THEE

Sing, O heavens;
And be joyful, O earth!
And break forth into singing, O mountains:
For the Lord hath comforted his people,
And will have mercy upon his afflicted.

But Zion said, " The Lord hath forsaken me,
And my Lord hath forgotten me."
" Can a woman forget her sucking child,
That she should not have compassion on the son of her
womb?
Yea, they may forget,
Yet will I not forget thee.

"Behold, I have graven thee upon the palms of my hands;
Thy walls are continually before me.
And all flesh shall know that I the Lord am thy Saviour
And thy Redeemer, the mighty One of Jacob."

SORROW AND MOURNING SHALL FLEE AWAY

The redeemed of the Lord shall return,
And come with singing unto Zion;
And everlasting joy shall be upon their head:
They shall obtain gladness and joy;
And sorrow and mourning shall flee away.

AWAKE, AWAKE, PUT ON STRENGTH

Awake, awake; put on thy strength, O Zion;
Put on thy beautiful garments, O Jerusalem, the holy city:
For henceforth there shall no more come into thee the
uncircumcised and the unclean.
Shake thyself from the dust;
Arise, and sit down, O Jerusalem:
Loose thyself from the bands of thy neck,
O captive daughter of Zion.

How beautiful upon the mountains
Are the feet of him that bringeth good tidings,
That publisheth peace;
That bringeth good tidings of good,
That publisheth salvation;
That saith unto Zion, "Thy God reigneth!"

Thy watchmen shall lift up the voice;
With the voice together shall they sing:

For they shall see eye to eye,
When the Lord shall bring again Zion.

Break forth into joy,
Sing together, ye waste places of Jerusalem:
For the Lord hath comforted his people,
He hath redeemed Jerusalem.

TO WHOM IS THE ARM OF THE LORD REVEALED

Who hath believed our report?
And to whom is the arm of the Lord revealed?
For he shall grow up before him as a tender plant,
And as a root out of a dry ground.

He is despised and rejected of men;
A man of sorrows, and acquainted with grief;
And we hid as it were our faces from him;
He was despised, and we esteemed him not.

Surely he hath borne our griefs,
And carried our sorrows:
Yet we did esteem him stricken,
Smitten of God, and afflicted.

But he was wounded for our transgressions,
He was bruised for our iniquities:
The chastisement of our peace was upon him;
And with his stripes we are healed.

All we like sheep have gone astray;
We have turned every one to his own way;
And the Lord hath laid on him
The iniquity of us all.

He was oppressed, and he was afflicted,
Yet he opened not his mouth:
He is brought as a lamb to the slaughter,
And as a sheep before her shearers is dumb,
So he openeth not his mouth.

He was taken from prison and from judgment:
And who shall declare his generation?
For he was cut off out of the land of the living:
For the transgression of my people was he stricken.

And he made his grave with the wicked,
And with the rich in his death;
Because he had done no violence,
Neither was any deceit in his mouth.
By his knowledge shall my righteous servant justify many;
For he shall bear their iniquities.

Therefore will I divide him a portion with the great,
And he shall divide the spoil with the strong:
Because he hath poured out his soul unto death;
And he was numbered with the transgressors;
And he bare the sin of many,
And made intercession for the transgressors.

NO WEAPON THAT IS FORMED AGAINST THEE SHALL PROSPER

Sing, O barren, thou that didst not bear;
Break forth into singing, and cry aloud,
Thou that didst not travail with child:
For more are the children of the desolate
Than the children of the married wife, saith the Lord.

Enlarge the place of thy tent,
And let them stretch forth the curtains of thine habitation:
Spare not, lengthen thy cords, and strengthen thy stakes.
For thou shalt break forth on the right hand and on the
left;
And thy seed shall inherit the Gentiles,
And make the desolate cities to be inhabited.

Fear not; for thou shalt not be ashamed:
Neither be thou confounded;
For thou shalt not be put to shame:
For thou shalt forget the shame of thy youth,
And shalt not remember the reproach of thy widowhood
any more.
For thy Maker is thine husband;
The Lord of hosts is his name;
And thy Redeemer the Holy One of Israel;
The God of the whole earth shall he be called.

For the Lord hath called thee
As a woman forsaken and grieved in spirit,
And as a wife of youth, when thou wast refused,
Saith thy God.
For a small moment have I forsaken thee:
But with great mercies will I gather thee.

In a little wrath I hid my face from thee for a moment;
But with everlasting kindness will I have mercy on thee,
Saith the Lord thy Redeemer.
For this is as the waters of Noah unto me:
For as I have sworn that the waters of Noah
Should no more go over the earth;
So have I sworn that I would not be wroth with thee,
Nor rebuke thee.

For the mountains shall depart,
And the hills be removed;
But my kindness shall not depart from thee,
Neither shall the covenant of my peace be removed,
Saith the Lord that hath mercy on thee.

O thou afflicted,
Tossed with tempest, and not comforted,
Behold, I will lay thy stones with fair colours,
And lay thy foundations with sapphires.
And I will make thy windows of agates,
And thy gates of carbuncles,
And all thy borders of pleasant stones.
And all thy children shall be taught of the Lord;
And great shall be the peace of thy children.

In righteousness shalt thou be established:
Thou shalt be far from oppression;
For thou shalt not fear:
And from terror; for it shall not come near thee.
Behold, they shall surely gather together,
But not by me:
Whosoever shall gather together against thee
Shall fall for thy sake.

No weapon that is formed against thee shall prosper;
And every tongue that shall rise against thee in judgment
Thou shalt condemn.
This is the heritage of the servants of the Lord,
And their righteousness is of me,
Saith the Lord.

HO, EVERY ONE THAT THIRSTETH, COME YE TO THE WATERS

Ho, every one that thirsteth, come ye to the waters,
And he that hath no money; come ye, buy, and eat;
Yea, come, buy wine and milk without money and
without price.
Wherefore do you spend money for that which is not
bread?
And your labour for that which satisfieth not?
Hearken diligently unto me, and eat ye that which is good,
And let your soul delight itself in fatness.

Incline your ear, and come unto me;
Hear, and your soul shall live;
And I will make an everlasting covenant with you,
Even the sure mercies of David.
Behold, I have given him for a witness to the people,
A leader and commander to the people.
Behold, thou shalt call a nation that thou knowest not,
And nations that knew not thee shall run unto thee
because of the Lord thy God,
And for the Holy One of Israel; for he hath glorified thee.

Seek ye the Lord while he may be found,
Call ye upon him while he is near:
Let the wicked forsake his way,
And the unrighteous man his thoughts;
And let him return unto the Lord,
And he will have mercy upon him;
And to our God,
For he will abundantly pardon.

For my thoughts are not your thoughts,
Neither are your ways my ways, saith the Lord.

For as the heavens are higher than the earth,
So are my ways higher than your ways,
And my thoughts than your thoughts.

For as the rain cometh down, and the snow from heaven,
And returneth not thither, but watereth the earth,
And maketh it bring forth and bud,
That it may give seed to the sower, and bread to the eater;
So shall my word be that goeth forth out of my mouth:
It shall not return unto me void,
But it shall accomplish that which I please,
And it shall prosper in the thing whereto I sent it.

For ye shall go out with joy, and be led forth with peace;
The mountains and the hills shall break forth before you
into singing,
And all the trees of the field shall clap their hands.
Instead of the thorn shall come up the fir tree,
And instead of the brier shall come up the myrtle tree:
And it shall be to the Lord for a name,
For an everlasting sign that shall not be cut off.

PEACE, PEACE TO HIM THAT IS NEAR

Thus saith the high and lofty One that inhabiteth eternity,
Whose name is Holy;
" I dwell in the high and holy place,
With him also that is of a contrite and humble spirit,
To revive the spirit of the humble,
And to revive the heart of the contrite ones.
I have seen his ways, and will heal him:
I will lead him also, and restore comforts unto him.

Peace, peace to him that is far off,
And to him that is near," saith the Lord;
" And I will heal him."

" But the wicked are like the troubled sea,
When it cannot rest,
Whose waters cast up mire and dirt.
There is no peace," saith my God, " to the wicked."

THE LORD'S HAND IS NOT SHORTENED THAT IT CANNOT SAVE

Behold, the Lord's hand is not shortened, that it cannot save,
Neither his ear heavy, that it cannot hear;
But your iniquities have separated between you and your God,
And your sins have hid his face from you, that he will not hear.

For your hands are defiled with blood, and your fingers with iniquity;
Your lips have spoken lies, your tongue hath muttered perverseness.
None calleth for justice, nor any pleadeth for Truth;
They trust in vanity, and speak lies;
They conceive mischief, and bring forth iniquity.
Their feet run to evil, and they make haste to shed innocent blood;
Their thoughts are thoughts of iniquity;
Wasting and destruction are in their paths.
The way of peace they know not,

And there is no judgment in their goings.
They have made them crooked paths;
Whosoever goeth therein shall not know peace.
Therefore is judgment far from us,
Neither doth justice overtake us.

We wait for light, but behold obscurity;
For brightness, but we walk in darkness.
We grope for the wall like the blind,
And we grope as if we had no eyes;
We stumble at noon day as in the night;
We are in desolate places as dead men,
For our transgressions are multiplied before thee,
And our sins testify against us;
For our transgressions are with us,
And as for our iniquities, we know them.

In transgressing and lying against the Lord,
And departing away from our God,
Speaking oppression and revolt,
Conceiving and uttering from the heart words of falsehood,
Judgment is turned away backward,
And justice standeth afar off,
For truth is fallen in the street,
And equity cannot enter.

Yea, truth faileth; and he that departeth from evil maketh himself a prey;
The Lord saw it, and it displeased him that there was no judgment;
Therefore his arm brought salvation unto him,
And his righteousness, it sustained him,
For he put on righteousness as a breastplate,

And an helmet of salvation upon his head.
When the enemy shall come in like a flood,
The Spirit of the Lord shall lift up a standard against him.
And the Redeemer shall come to Zion,
And unto them that turn from transgression in Jacob,
Saith the Lord.

THY LIGHT IS COME

Arise, shine; for thy light is come,
And the glory of the Lord is risen upon thee.
For, behold, the darkness shall cover the earth,
And gross darkness the people:
But the Lord shall arise upon thee,
And his glory shall be seen upon thee.
And the Gentiles shall come to thy light,
And kings to the brightness of thy rising.
And they shall call thee, The City of the Lord,
The Zion of the Holy One of Israel.

Violence shall no more be heard in thy land,
Wasting nor destruction within thy borders;
But thou shalt call thy walls Salvation,
And thy gates Praise.

The sun shall be no more thy light by day;
Neither for brightness shall the moon give light unto thee:
But the Lord shall be unto thee an everlasting light,
And thy God thy glory.
The sun shall no more go down;
Neither shall thy moon withdraw itself:
For the Lord shall be thine everlasting light,
And the days of thy mourning shall be ended.

THE SPIRIT OF THE LORD IS UPON ME

The Spirit of the Lord God is upon me;
Because the Lord hath anointed me to preach good tidings
unto the meek;
He hath sent me to bind up the brokenhearted,
To proclaim liberty to the captives,
And the opening of the prison to them that are bound:
To proclaim the acceptable year of the Lord,
To comfort all that mourn;

To appoint unto them that mourn in Zion,
To give unto them beauty for ashes,
The oil of joy for mourning,
The garment of praise for the spirit of heaviness;
That they might be called trees of righteousness,
The planting of the Lord,
That he might be glorified.

And they shall build the old wastes,
They shall raise up the former desolations,
And they shall repair the waste cities,
The desolations of many generations.
For I the Lord love judgment;
I will direct their work in Truth,
And I will make an everlasting covenant with them.
I will greatly rejoice in the Lord,
My soul shall be joyful in my God;
For he hath clothed me with the garments of salvation,
He hath covered me with the robe of righteousness.
As a bridegroom decketh himself with ornaments,
And as a bride adorneth herself with her jewels.

For as the earth bringeth forth her bud,
And as the garden causeth the things that are sown in it
to spring forth;

So the Lord God will cause righteousness and praise
To spring forth before all the nations.

MY SERVANT SHALL DEAL PRUDENTLY

Behold, my servant shall deal prudently,
He shall be exalted and extolled,
And be very high.

I CREATE NEW HEAVENS AND A NEW FAITH

Behold, I create new heavens and a new earth:
And the former shall not be remembered,
Nor come into mind.
But be ye glad and rejoice forever in that which I create:
For, behold, I create Jerusalem a rejoicing,
And her people a joy.

And I will rejoice in Jerusalem,
And joy in her people;
And the voice of weeping shall be no more heard in her,
Nor the voice of crying.
There shall be no more thence an infant of days,
Nor an old man that hath not filled his days.

And they shall build houses, and inhabit them;
And they shall plant vineyards, and eat the fruit of them.
They shall not build, and another inhabit;
They shall not plant, and another eat:
For as the days of a tree are the days of my people,
And mine elect shall long enjoy the work of their hands.

And it shall come to pass,
That before they call, I will answer;
And while they are yet speaking, I will hear.

The wolf and the lamb shall feed together,
And the lion shall eat straw like the bullock:
And dust shall be the serpent's meat.
They shall not hurt nor destroy in all my holy mountain,
Saith the Lord.

ALL SHALL WORSHIP BEFORE ME

Thus saith the Lord,
The heaven is my throne, and the earth is my footstool:
Where is the house that ye build unto me?
And where is the place of my rest?
For all those things hath mine hand made,
And all those things have been, saith the Lord:
But to this man will I look,
Even to him that is poor and of a contrite spirit,
And trembleth at my word.
Hear the word of the Lord,
Ye that tremble at his word.

As one whom his mother comforteth,
So will I comfort you;
And ye shall be comforted in Jerusalem.
For I know their works and their thoughts:
It shall come, that I will gather all nations and tongues;
And they shall come and see my glory.
For as the new heavens and the new earth, which I shall make,
Shall remain before me, saith the Lord,
So shall your seed and your name remain.
And it shall come to pass,
That from one new moon to another,
And from one sabbath to another,
Shall all flesh come to worship before me, saith the Lord.

The Wise Shall Understand

"And they that be wise
Shall shine as the brightness of the firmament;
And they that turn many to righteousness
As the stars for ever and ever."

THE BOOK OF DANIEL
The Prophet

NEBUCHADNEZZAR DREAMED DREAMS

Now in the reign of Jehoiakim when Nebuchadnezzar besieged Jerusalem, he carried away to Babylon captives and vessels of the house of the Lord, and placed the vessels in the house of his god.

And Nebuchadnezzar spake unto Ashpenaz, the master of the eunuchs, that he should bring certain of the captives of Israel, of the king's seed, and of the princes, children in whom was no blemish, but well favored, and skillful in all wisdom, and understanding science, and to whom they might teach the learning and the tongue of the Chaldeans. And the king appointed them a daily provision of the king's meat, and of the wine which he drank; so nourishing them three years, that at the end they might stand before the king.

Now among these were Daniel, whom the prince of the eunuchs named Belteshazzar, also Shradrach, Meshach, and Abednego. But Daniel purposed in his heart that he would not defile himself with the portion of the king's meat, nor with the wine which he drank: therefore he requested of the prince of the eunuchs that he might not defile himself.

Now God had brought Daniel into favour and tender love with the prince of the eunuchs, who said unto Daniel, "I fear my lord the king, who hath appointed your meat and your drink: for why should he see your faces worse liking than the children which are of your sort? then shall ye make me endanger my head to the king."

Then said Daniel, "Prove thy servants, I beseech thee, ten days; and let them give us pulse to eat, and water to drink. Then let our countenances be looked upon before thee, and the countenance of the children that eat of the portion of the king's meat: and as thou seest, deal with thy servants." So he consented to them in this matter, and proved them ten days. And at the end of ten days their countenances appeared fairer and fatter in flesh than all the children which did eat the portion of the king's meat. So he took away their portion, and gave them pulse.

And God gave them knowledge and skill in all learning and wisdom; and Daniel had understanding in all visions and dreams. And at the end of three years, the prince of the eunuchs brought them in before Nebuchadnezzar. And the king communed with them; and among them all was found none like Daniel.

And Nebuchadnezzar dreamed dreams, wherewith his spirit was troubled, and his sleep brake from him. Then he commanded to call the magicians, and the astrologers, and the sorcerers, and the Chaldeans, for to show him his dream. And they came and stood before him.

And the king said unto them, "I have dreamed a dream, and my spirit was troubled to know the dream."

Then spake the Chaldeans, "O king, live for ever: tell thy servants the dream, and we will show the interpretation."

The king answered, "The thing is gone from me: if ye will not make known unto me the dream, with the interpretation thereof, ye shall be cut in pieces, and your houses shall be made a dunghill. But if ye show the dream, and the interpretation thereof, ye shall receive of me gifts and rewards and great honour: therefore show me the dream, and the interpretation thereof."

The Chaldeans answered the king, "There is not a man upon the earth that can show the king's dream: therefore there is no king, lord nor ruler, that asked such things of any magician, or astrologer, or Chaldean. And it is a rare thing that the king requireth, and there is none that can show it, except the gods, whose dwelling is not with flesh."

For this cause king Nebuchadnezzar was angry and very

furious, and commanded to destroy all the wise men of Babylon. And the decree went forth that the wise men should be slain: and they sought Daniel and his fellows to be slain.

Then Daniel answered the captain of the king's guard, " Why is the decree so hasty from the king? " And the captain made the thing known to Daniel. Then Daniel went in, and desired of the king that he would give him time, and that he would show the king the interpretation.

Then Daniel went to his house, and desired mercies of the God of heaven concerning this secret. And the secret was revealed unto Daniel in a night vision. Then Daniel blessed the God of heaven, and he said, " Blessed be the name of God for ever and ever: He giveth wisdom unto the wise, and knowledge to them that know understanding. He revealeth the deep and secret things, and the light dwelleth with him. I thank thee and praise thee, O God."

Then Daniel went in unto the captain of the guard, and said unto him, " Destroy not the wise men of Babylon, but bring me in before king Nebuchadnezzar and I will show unto the king the interpretation."

Then the captain brought Daniel in before the king in haste, and said, " I have found a man of the captives of Judah, that will make known unto the king the interpretation."

The king said to Daniel, " Art thou able to make known unto me the dream which I have seen, and the interpretation thereof? "

Daniel answered, "The secret which the king hath demanded cannot the wise men, the astrologers, the magicians, the soothsayers, show unto the king. But there is a God in heaven that revealeth secrets, and maketh known to king Nebuchadnezzar what shall be in the latter days. Thy dream, and visions of thy head upon thy bed, are these: As for thee, O king, thy thoughts came into thy mind upon thy bed, what should come to pass hereafter; and he that revealeth secrets maketh known to thee what shall come to pass.

worship the golden image that Nebuchadnezzar the king hath set up. And whoso falleth not down and worshippeth shall the same hour be cast into the midst of a burning fiery furnace."

Therefore when all the people heard the sound of the cornet and all kinds of music, all the people fell down and worshipped the golden image that Nebuchadnezzar had set up.

Wherefore, certain of the Chaldeans came near, and accused the Jews, and said to the king, "O king, live for ever. Thou, O king, hast made a decree, that every man that shall hear the sound of the music, shall fall down and worship the golden image; and whoso falleth not down and worshippeth, should be cast into the midst of a burning fiery furnace. There are certain Jews whom thou hast set over the affairs of the province of Babylon, Shadrach, Meshach, and Abednego; these men, O king, have not regarded thee; they serve not thy gods, nor worship the golden image which thou hast set up."

Then Nebuchadnezzar in his rage and fury commanded to bring Shadrach, Meshach, and Abednego, and they brought them before the king. And the king said unto them, "Is it true, O Shadrach, Meshach, and Abednego, that ye do not serve my gods, nor worship the golden image which I have set up? If ye worship not, ye shall be cast into the midst of a burning fiery furnace; and who is that God that shall deliver you out of my hands?"

Shadrach, Meshach, and Abednego, answered the king, "O Nebuchadnezzar, we are not careful to answer thee in this matter. If it be so, our God whom we serve is able to deliver us from the burning fiery furnace, and he will deliver us out of thine hand, O king. But if not, be it known unto thee, O king, that we will not serve thy gods, nor worship the golden image which thou hast set up."

Then was Nebuchadnezzar full of fury, and the form of his visage was changed, and he commanded that they should heat the furnace seven times more than it was wont to be heated. And he commanded the most mighty men that were in his army to bind Shadrach, Meshach, and Abednego, and cast them into the fiery furnace. Then these men were bound in their coats, their hosen, and their hats, and their other garments, and were cast into the midst of the furnace. And because the furnace was exceeding hot, the flame slew those men that took them up.

And Shadrach, Meshach, and Abednego, fell down bound into the midst of the burning fiery furnace. Then the king was astonished, and rose up in haste, and said unto his counsellors, "Did not we cast three men bound into the midst of the fire?"

They answered, "True, O king."

And the king said, "Lo, I see four men loose, walking in the midst of the fire, and they have no hurt; and the form of the fourth is like the Son of God." Then Nebuchadnezzar came near to the mouth of the furnace and said, "Shadrach, Meshach, and Abednego, ye servants of the most high God, come forth." Then these men came forth from the midst of the fire.

And the princes, governors, and captains, and the king's counsellors, being gathered together, saw these men, upon whose bodies the fire had no power, nor was an hair of their head singed, neither were their coats changed, nor the smell of fire had passed on them.

Then Nebuchadnezzar spake, and said, "Blessed be the God of Shadrach, Meshach, and Abednego, who hath sent his angel, and delivered his servants that trusted in him, and have changed the king's word, and yielded their bodies, that they might not serve nor worship any god, except their own God. Therefore, I make a decree, that no people, nation, and language, speak any thing amiss against the God of Shadrach, Meshach, and Abednego; because there is no other God that can deliver after this sort."

Then the king promoted Shadrach, Meshach, and Abednego, in the province of Babylon.

I NEBUCHADNEZZAR PRAISE AND EXTOL AND HONOUR THE KING OF HEAVEN

PEACE be multiplied unto all people, nations and languages that dwell in all the earth:

I, Nebuchadnezzar, thought it good to show the signs and wonders that the high God hath wrought toward me. How great are his signs! and how mighty are his wonders! His kingdom is an everlasting kingdom, and his dominion is from generation to generation.

I, Nebuchadnezzar, was at rest in mine house, and flourishing in my palace. I saw a dream which made me afraid, and the thoughts upon my bed and the visions of my head troubled me. Therefore made I a decree to bring in all the wise men of Babylon before me that they might make known unto me the interpretation of the dream. Then came in the wise men, and I told the dream before them; but they did not make known unto me the interpretation.

But at last Daniel came in before me, and I told him the dream, saying, " O Daniel, master of the magicians, because I know that no secret troubleth thee, tell me the visions of my dream that I have seen, and the interpretation thereof. This was my vision: I saw, and behold, a tree in the midst of the earth, and the height thereof was great. The tree grew, and was strong, and the height thereof reached unto heaven, and the sight thereof to the end of all the earth. The leaves of the tree were fair, and the fruit much, and in it was meat for all. The beasts of the field had shadow under it, and the fowls of heaven dwelt in the boughs thereof, and all flesh was fed of it.

"I saw in the vision, and behold, a watcher came down from heaven: He cried aloud, and said thus, 'Hew down the tree, and cut off his branches, shake off the leaves, and scatter his fruit: let the beasts get away from under it, and the fowls from his branches. Nevertheless leave the stump of his roots in the earth, even with a band of iron and brass, in the tender grass of the field; and let it be wet with dew of heaven, and let his portion be with the beasts in the grass of the earth. Let his heart be changed from man's, and let a beast's heart be given unto him; and let seven times pass over him.'

"This dream I king Nebuchadnezzar have seen. Now thou, O Daniel, declare the interpretation, for the spirit of the holy gods is in thee."

Then Daniel was perplexed for one hour, and his thoughts troubled him. And the king said, "Let not the dream, or the interpretation thereof trouble thee."

And Daniel answered, "My lord, the dream be to them that hate thee, and to thine enemies. The tree that thou sawest, which grew, and was strong, whose height reached unto the heaven, and the sight thereof to all the earth, it is thou, O king, that art grown and become strong: for thy greatness is grown, and reacheth unto heaven, and thy dominion to the end of the earth. And whereas the king saw an holy one coming down from heaven, and saying, 'Hew the tree down, and destroy it; yet leave the stump of the roots in the earth, even with a band of iron and brass, in the tender grass of the field; and let it be wet with the dew of heaven, till seven times pass over him.'

"This is the interpretation, O king, and this is the decree of the most High. They shall drive thee from men, and thy dwelling shall be with the beasts of the field, and they shall make thee to eat grass as oxen, and they shall wet thee with the dew of heaven, and seven times shall pass over thee, till thou know that the most High ruleth in the kingdom of men, and giveth it to whomsoever he will. And whereas they commanded to leave the stump of the tree roots; thy kingdom shall be sure unto thee, after thou shalt know that the heavens do rule.

"Whereas, O king, let my counsel be acceptable unto thee, and break off thy sins by righteousness, and thine iniquities by showing mercy to the poor; it may be a lengthening of thy tranquillity."

All this came upon the king Nebuchadnezzar. At the end of twelve months he walked in the palace of the kingdom of Babylon, and said, "Is not this great Babylon, that I have built for the house of the kingdom by the might of my power, and for the honour of my majesty?"

While the word was in the king's mouth, there fell a voice from heaven, saying, "O king Nebuchadnezzar, to thee it is spoken: The kingdom is departed from thee. And they shall drive thee from men, and thy dwelling shall be with the beasts of the field, until thou know that the most High ruleth in the kingdom of men, and giveth it to whomsoever he will."

The same hour was the thing fulfilled, and Nebuchadnezzar was driven from men, and did eat grass as oxen, and his body was wet with the dew of heaven, till his hairs were grown like eagles' feathers, and his nails like birds' claws.

And at the end of the days, I Nebuchadnezzar, lifted up mine eyes unto heaven, and mine understanding returned to me, and I blessed the most High, and praised and honoured him that liveth for ever, whose dominion is an everlasting dominion, and his kingdom is from generation to generation. And all the inhabitants of the earth do according to his will, and none can stay his hand, or say unto him "What doest thou?"

At the same time my reason returned unto me; and for the glory of my kingdom, my honour and brightness returned unto me; and my counsellors and my lords sought unto me; and I was established in my kingdom, and excellent majesty was added unto me.

Now, I Nebuchadnezzar, praise and extol and honour the King of heaven, all whose works are truth, and his ways judgment; and those that walk in pride he is able to abase.

THOU ART WEIGHED IN THE BALANCE

BELSHAZZAR the king made a great feast to a thousand of his lords, and drank wine before the thousand. And Belshazzar commanded to bring the gold and silver vessels which his father, Nebuchadnezzar, had taken out of the temple in Jerusalem.

Then they brought the golden vessels that were taken out of the temple of the house of God which was at Jerusalem, and the king, and his princes, his wives, and his concubines, drank in them. They drank wine, and praised the gods of gold, and of silver, of brass, of iron, of wood, and of stone.

In the same hour came forth fingers of a man's hand, and wrote over against the candlestick upon the plaster of the wall of the king's palace: and the king saw the part of the hand that wrote. Then the king's countenance was changed, and his thoughts troubled him, so that the joints of his loins were loosed, and his knees smote one against another.

The king cried aloud to bring in the astrologers, the Chaldeans, and the soothsayers. And the king said to the wise men of Babylon, "Whosoever shall read this writing, and show me the interpretation thereof, shall be clothed with scarlet, and have a chain of gold about his neck, and shall be the third ruler in the kingdom." But the wise men could not read the writing, nor make known to the king the interpretation.

Then was king Belshazzar greatly troubled, and his countenance was changed in him, and his lords were dismayed.

Now the queen, by reason of the words of the king, came into the banquet house, and said, "O king, live for ever: let not thy thoughts trouble thee, nor let thy countenance be changed. There is a man in thy kingdom, in whom is the spirit of the holy gods. And in the days of thy father light and understanding and wisdom were found in him, whom the king Nebuchadnezzar made master of the wise men. Now let Daniel be called, and he will show the interpretation."

Then was Daniel brought in before king Belshazzar. And the king said, "Art thou that Daniel which is of the children of the captivity of Judah, whom king Nebuchadnezzar, my father, brought out of Jewry? I have heard of thee, that the spirit of the gods is in thee, and that light and understanding and excellent wisdom is found in thee. And now the wise men have been brought in before me, that they should read this writing, but they could not show the interpretation of the thing. Now if thou canst read the writing, and make known the interpretation, thou shalt be clothed with scarlet, and have a chain of gold about thy neck, and shalt be the third ruler in the kingdom."

Then Daniel answered, "Let thy gifts be to thyself, and give thy rewards to another; yet I will read the writing unto the king, and make known to him the interpretation.

"O thou king Belshazzar, the most high God gave Nebuchadnezzar thy father a kingdom, and majesty, and glory, and honour; and for the majesty that he gave him, all people, nations, and languages, trembled and feared before him. But when his heart was lifted up, and his mind hardened in pride, he was deposed from his kingly throne, and they took his glory from him. And he was driven from the sons of men; and his heart was made like the beasts, and his dwelling was with the wild asses; and they fed him with grass like oxen, and his body was wet with the dew of heaven, till he knew that the most high God ruled in the kingdom of men, and that he appointed over it whomsoever he will.

"And thou his son, O Belshazzar hast not humbled thine heart, though thou knowest all this, but hast lifted up thyself against the Lord of heaven. And they have brought the vessels of his house before thee, and thou, and thy lords, and thy wives, and thy concubines, have drunk wine in them; and thou hast praised the gods of silver, and gold, of brass, iron, wood, and stone, which see not, nor hear, nor know; and the God in whose hand thy breath is, and whose are all thy ways, hast thou not glorified.

"Then was the part of the hand sent from him; and this writing was written. And this is the writing that was written, MENE, MENE, TEKEL, UPHARSIN. This is the interpretation of the thing: MENE; God hath numbered thy kingdom, and finished it. TEKEL: Thou art weighed in the balances, and art found wanting. PERES: Thy kingdom is divided, and given to the Medes and Persians."

Then commanded Belshazzar, and they clothed Daniel with scarlet, and put a chain of gold about his neck, and made a proclamation concerning him, that he should be the third ruler in the kingdom.

In that night was Belshazzar the king of the Chaldeans slain. And Darius the Median took the kingdom, being about three score and two years old.

GOD SENT HIS ANGEL, AND SHUT THE LIONS' MOUTHS

IT PLEASED DARIUS to set over the kingdom an hundred and twenty princes which should be over the whole kingdom. And over these, three presidents, of whom Daniel was first. Daniel was preferred above the presidents and princes, because an excellent spirit was in him; and the king thought to set him over the whole realm.

Then the presidents and princes sought to find occasion against Daniel concerning the kingdom, but they could find none because he was faithful. Then said these men, "We shall not find any occasion against Daniel, except we find it against him concerning the law of his God."

Then these presidents and princes assembled together to the king, and said unto him, " King Darius, live for ever. All the presidents of the kingdom, and the princes have consulted together to establish a royal statute, and to make a firm decree, that whosoever shall ask a petition of any God or man for thirty days, save of thee, O king, he shall be cast into the den of lions. Now, O king, establish the decree, and sign the writing, that it be not changed, according to the law of the Medes and Persians, which altereth not." Wherefore king Darius signed the writing.

Now when Daniel knew that the writing was signed, he went into his house; and his windows being open in his chamber toward Jerusalem, he kneeled upon his knees three times a day, and prayed, and gave thanks before his God, as he had done before.

Then these men assembled and found Daniel praying and making supplication before his God. And they came and said to the king, " Hast thou not signed a decree, that every man that shall ask a petition of any God or man within thirty days, save of thee, O king, shall be cast into the den of lions? "

The king answered, " The thing is true according to the law of the Medes and Persians, which altereth not."

Then they said, " That Daniel, which is of the children of the captivity of Judah, regardeth not thee, O king, nor the decree that thou hast signed, but maketh his petition three times a day."

Then king Darius, when he heard these words, was sore displeased with himself, and set his heart on Daniel to deliver him: and he laboured till the going down of the sun to deliver him.

Then these men assembled unto the king and said, " Know, O king, that the law of the Medes and Persians is: That no decree nor statute which the king establisheth may be changed."

So the king commanded, and they brought Daniel, and cast him into the den of lions. And the king said unto Daniel, " Thy God, whom thou servest continually, he will deliver thee."

And a stone was brought, and laid upon the mouth of the den; and the king sealed it with his own signet, and with the signet of his lords; that the purpose might not be changed concerning Daniel. Then the king went to his palace, and passed the night fasting; neither were instruments of music brought before him; and his sleep went from him.

Then the king arose very early in the morning, and went in haste unto the den of lions. And when he came to the den, he cried with a lamentable voice unto Daniel, and said, " O Daniel, servant of the living God, whom thou servest continually, is thy God able to deliver thee from the lions? "

Then Daniel said unto the king, " O king, live for ever. My God hath sent his angel, and hath shut the lions' mouths, that they have not hurt me: forasmuch as before him innocency was found in me; and also before thee have I done no hurt."

Then was the king exceeding glad, and commanded that they should take Daniel up out of the den. So Daniel was taken up out of the den, and no manner of hurt was found upon him, because he believed in God.

And the king commanded, and they brought those men which had accused Daniel, and they cast them into the den of lions. And the lions had the mastery of them, and brake all their bones in pieces before they came to the bottom of the den.

Then king Darius wrote unto all people, nations, and languages, that dwell in all the earth; " Peace be multiplied unto you. I make a decree, that in every dominion of my kingdom men tremble and fear before the God of Daniel; for he is the living God, and steadfast for ever, and his kingdom is that which shall not be destroyed, and his dominion shall be even unto the end. He delivereth and rescueth, and he worketh signs and wonders in heaven and in earth, and He hath delivered Daniel from the power of the lions."

So Daniel prospered in the reign of Darius, and also in the reign of Cyrus the Persian.

THE SON OF MAN WAS GIVEN DOMINION, AND GLORY, AND A KINGDOM

In the first year of Belshazzar, king of Babylon, Daniel had a dream and visions of his head upon his bed: then he wrote the dream, and told the sum of the matter:

Daniel spake and said: "I saw in my vision by night, and behold, the Ancient of days did sit, whose garment was white as the snow, and the hair of his head like the pure wool: His throne was like the fiery flame, and his wheels as burning fire. A fiery stream issued and came forth from before him: thousand thousands ministered unto him, and ten thousand times ten thousand stood before him: the judgment was set, and the books were opened.

"And I saw in the night visions, and, behold, one like the Son of man came with the clouds of heaven, and came to the Ancient of days, and they brought him near before him. And there was given him dominion, and glory, and a kingdom, that all people, nations, and languages, should serve him: his dominion is an everlasting dominion, which shall not pass away, and his kingdom that which shall not be destroyed.

"And the kingdom and dominion, and the greatness of the kingdom under the whole heaven, shall be given to the people of the saints of the most High, whose kingdom is an everlasting kingdom, and all dominions shall serve and obey him.

"As for me Daniel, my cogitations much troubled me, and my countenance changed in me; but I kept the matter in my heart."

FOR THE LORD OUR GOD IS RIGHTEOUS IN ALL HIS WORKS

In the first year of Darius the son of Ahasuerus, of the seed of the Medes, which was made king over the realm of the Chaldeans, in the first year of his reign, I Daniel understood by books the number of the years, whereof the word of the Lord came to Jeremiah the prophet, that he would accomplish seventy years in the desolations of Jerusalem. And I set my face unto the Lord God, to seek by prayer and supplications, with fasting, and sackcloth, and ashes, and I prayed unto the Lord my God, and made my confession, and said:

" O Lord, the great and dreadful God, keeping the covenant and mercy to them that love him, and to them that keep his commandments; O Lord, righteousness belongeth unto thee, but unto us confusion of faces, as at this day – to the men of Judah, and to the inhabitants of Jerusalem, and unto all Israel, that are near, and that are far off, through all the countries whither thou hast driven them, because of their trespass that they have trespassed against thee.

" O Lord, to us belongeth confusion of face, to our kings, to our princes, and to our fathers, because we have sinned against thee. To the Lord our God belong mercies and forgiveness, though we have rebelled against thee. Neither have we obeyed the voice of the Lord our God, to walk in his laws which he set before us by his servants the prophets.

" Yea, all Israel have transgressed thy law, even by departing, that they might not obey thy voice. Therefore the curse is poured upon us, and the oath that is written in the law of Moses, the servant of God, because we have sinned against him.

And he hath confirmed his words, which he spake against us, and against our judges that judged us, by bringing upon us a great evil: for under the whole heaven hath not been done, as hath been done upon Jerusalem. As it is written in the law of Moses, all this evil is come upon us: yet made we not our prayer before the Lord our God, that we might turn from our iniquities, and understand thy Truth, for the Lord our God is righteous in all his works which he doeth. And now, O Lord, according to all thy righteousness, I beseech thee, let thine anger and thy fury be turned away from thy city Jerusalem, thy holy mountain.

"Now therefore, O our God, hear the prayer of thy servant, and his supplications, and cause thy face to shine upon thy sanctuary that is desolate. O my God, incline thine ear, and hear; open thine eyes, and behold our desolations, and the city which is called by thy name: for we do not present our supplications before thee for our righteousness, but for thy great mercies. O Lord, hear; O Lord, forgive; O Lord, hearken and do; defer not, for thine own sake, O my God: for thy city and thy people are called by thy name."

And while I was speaking, and praying, and confessing my sin and the sin of my people Israel, and presenting my supplication before the Lord my God for the holy mountain of my God; yea, while I was speaking in prayer, even the man Gabriel, being caused to fly swiftly, touched me about the time of the evening oblation.

And he informed me, and talked with me, and said, "O Daniel, I am now come forth to give thee skill and understanding. At the beginning of thy supplications the commandment came forth, and I am come to show thee; for thou art greatly beloved: therefore understand the matter, and consider the vision. Seventy weeks are determined upon thy people and upon thy holy city, to finish the transgression, and to make an end of sins, and to make reconciliation for iniquity, and to bring in everlasting righteousness, and to seal up the vision and the prophecy, and to anoint the most Holy. Know therefore, and understand, that from the going forth of the commandment to restore and to build Jerusalem unto the Messiah the Prince shall be seven weeks, and threescore and two weeks: the street shall be built again, and the wall, even in troublous times."

THE WISE SHALL UNDERSTAND

IN THE THIRD YEAR of Cyrus, king of Persia, a thing was revealed unto Daniel, and the thing was true, but the time appointed was long: and he understood the thing, and had understanding of the vision.

In those days I, Daniel, was mourning three full weeks. I ate no pleasant bread, neither came flesh nor wine in my mouth, neither did I anoint myself at all, till three whole weeks were fulfilled. And in the four and twentieth day of the first month, as I was by the side of the great river, which is Hiddekel, I lifted up mine eyes, and looked, and behold a certain man clothed in linen, whose loins were girded with fine gold of Uphaz: His body also was like the beryl, and his face as the appearance of lightning, and his eyes as lamps of fire, and his arms and his feet like in colour to polished brass, and the voice of his words like the voice of a multitude.

And I, Daniel, alone saw the vision: for the men that were with me saw not the vision; but a great quaking fell upon them, so that they fled to hide themselves. Therefore I was left alone, and saw this great vision, and there remained no strength in me. Yet heard I the voice of his words: and when I heard the voice of his words, then was I in a deep sleep on my face, and my face toward the ground.

And, behold, an hand touched me, which set me upon my knees and upon the palms of my hands. And he said unto me, "O Daniel, a man greatly beloved, understand the words that I speak unto thee, and stand upright, for unto thee am I sent." And when he had spoken this word unto me, I stood trembling.

Then said he unto me, "Fear not, Daniel: for from the first day that thou didst set thine heart to understand, and to chasten thyself before thy God, thy words were heard, and I am come for thy words. Now I am come to make thee understand what shall befall thy people in the latter days: for yet the vision is for many days."

And when he had spoken such words unto me, I set my face toward the ground, and I became dumb. And, behold, one like the similitude of the sons of men touched my lips; then I opened my mouth, and spake, and said unto him that stood before me, "O my lord, by the vision my sorrows are turned upon me, and I have retained no strength, neither is there breath left in me."

Then there came again and touched me one like the appearance of a man, and he strengthened me, and said, "O man greatly beloved, fear not: peace be unto thee, be strong, yea, be strong."

And when he had spoken unto me, I was strengthened, and said, "Let my lord speak; for thou hast strengthened me."

Then said he, "Knowest thou wherefore I come unto thee? I will show thee that which is noted in the scripture of truth. Behold, there shall stand up yet three kings in Persia; and the fourth shall be far richer than they all; and by his strength through his riches he shall stir up all against the realm of Grecia. And a mighty king shall stand up, that shall rule with great dominion, and do according to his will. And when he shall stand up, his kingdom shall be broken, and shall be divided toward the four winds of heaven; and not to his posterity, nor according to

“ Thou art of purer eyes than to behold evil.”

THE BOOK OF HABAKKUK

The Prophet

THOU ART OF PURER EYES THAN TO BEHOLD EVIL

The burden which the prophet Habakkuk did see:

Lo, the Chaldeans, that bitter and hasty nation,
March through the breadth of the land,
To possess the dwelling places that are not theirs.
They are terrible and dreadful:
Their horses also are swifter than the leopards,
And are more fierce than the evening wolves.
Their horsemen come from far;
They fly as the eagle that hasteth to eat.
They come for violence;
They gather the captives as the sand.
They scoff at the kings,
And princes are a scorn unto them.
They deride every stronghold, and take it,
And offend, imputing this his power unto his god.

Art Thou not from everlasting,
O Lord my God, mine Holy One?
O Lord, Thou hast ordained them for judgment;
And, O mighty God,
Thou hast established them for correction.
Thou art of purer eyes than to behold evil,
And canst not look on iniquity.

THE EARTH SHALL BE FILLED WITH THE KNOWLEDGE OF THE GLORY OF THE LORD

I will stand upon my watch,
And set me upon the tower,
And will watch to see what he will say unto me,
And what I shall answer when I am reproved.

And the Lord answered me, and said,
" Write the vision,
And make it plain upon tables,
That he may run that readeth it.
For the vision is yet for an appointed time,
But at the end it shall speak, and not lie:
Though it tarry, wait for it;
Because it will surely come, it will not tarry.
For the just shall live by faith."

Woe to him that increaseth that which is not his!
Because thou hast spoiled many nations,
All the remnant of the people shall spoil thee;
Because of men's blood,
And for the violence of the land,
Of the city, and of all that dwell therein.

Woe to him that coveteth an evil covetousness to his house,
That he may set his nest on high;
For the stone shall cry out of the wall,
And the beam out of the timber shall answer it.
Woe to him that buildeth a town with blood,
And establisheth a city by iniquity!

Behold, is it not of the Lord of hosts
That the people shall labour in the very fire,
And the people weary themselves for very vanity?

For the earth shall be filled
With the knowledge of the glory of the Lord,
As the waters cover the sea.

THE LORD IS IN HIS HOLY TEMPLE

What profiteth the graven image
That the maker thereof hath graven it,
The molten image, and a teacher of lies,
That the maker of his work trusteth therein,
To make dumb idols?
Woe to him that saith to the wood, " Awake ";
And to the dumb stone, " Arise, it shall teach! "
Behold, it is laid over with gold and silver,
And there is no breath at all in the midst of it.

But the Lord is in his holy temple:
Let all the earth keep silence before him.

I WILL REJOICE IN THE LORD

Although the fig tree shall not blossom,
Neither shall fruit be in the vines;
Though the labour of the olive shall fail,
And the fields shall yield no meat;
Though the flock shall be cut off from the fold,
And there shall be no herd in the stalls:
Yet I will rejoice in the Lord,
I will joy in the God of my salvation.

BY THE RIVERS OF BABYLON

By the rivers of Babylon,
There we sat down, yea, we wept,
When we remembered Zion.
We hanged our harps
Upon the willows in the midst thereof.
For there they that carried us away captive required
of us a song,
And they that wasted us required of us mirth, saying,
" Sing us one of the songs of Zion."
How shall we sing the Lord's song
In a strange land?
If I forget thee, O Jerusalem,
Let my right hand forget her cunning.
If I do not remember thee,
Let my tongue cleave to the roof of my mouth;
If I prefer not Jerusalem above my chief joy.

Psalm 137

his dominion which he ruled: for his kingdom shall be plucked up. . . .

" And at that time shall Michael stand up, the great prince which standeth for the children of thy people: and there shall be a time of trouble, such as never was since there was a nation even to that same time: and at that time thy people shall be delivered every one that shall be found written in the book. And many of them that sleep in the dust of the earth shall awake, some to everlasting life, and some to shame and everlasting contempt.

" And they that be wise shall shine as the brightness of the firmament; and they that turn many to righteousness as the stars for ever and ever. But thou, O Daniel, shut up the words, and seal the book, even to the time of the end: many shall run to and fro, and knowledge shall be increased."

" Then I, Daniel, looked, and behold, there stood other two, the one on this side of the bank of the river, and the other on that side of the bank of the river. And one said to the man clothed in linen, which was upon the waters of the river, ' How long shall it be to the end of these wonders? '

" And I heard the man clothed in linen, which was upon the waters of the river, when he held up his right hand and his left hand unto heaven, and sware by him that liveth for ever, that it shall be for a time, times, and an half; and when he shall have accomplished to scatter the power of the holy people, all these things shall be finished.

" And I heard, but I understood not: then said I, ' O my Lord, what shall be the end of these things? '

" And he said, ' Go thy way, Daniel: for the words are closed up and sealed till the time of the end. Many shall be purified, and made white, and tried; but the wicked shall do wickedly: and none of the wicked shall understand; but the wise shall understand. And from the time that the daily sacrifice shall be taken away, and the abomination that maketh desolate set up, there shall be a thousand two hundred and ninety days. Blessed is he that waiteth, and cometh to the thousand three hundred and five and thirty days. But go thou thy way till the end be: for thou shalt rest, and stand in thy lot at the end of the days.' "

" Not by might, nor by power, but by my Spirit,"
saith the Lord.

THE BOOK OF EZRA

With selections from the Prophets,

Haggai and Zechariah

GOD HATH CHARGED ME TO BUILD HIM A TEMPLE IN JERUSALEM

Now in the first year of Cyrus, king of Persia, as Jeremiah, the prophet, had prophesied, the Lord stirred up Cyrus, and he made a proclamation throughout all of his kingdom, and also put it in writing, saying:

" Thus saith Cyrus, the king of Persia: The Lord God of heaven hath given me all the kingdoms of the earth, and he hath charged me to build him an house at Jerusalem, which is in Judah. Who is there among you, of all his people, God being with you, who will go up to Jerusalem, and build the house of the Lord God of Israel? "

Then rose up the chief of the fathers of Judah, and the priests and Levites, with all them whose spirit God had stirred up, to go up to build the house of the Lord in Jerusalem. And all their brethren strengthened their hands with vessels of silver, with gold, with goods, and with beasts, and with precious things, besides a free will offering.

Also Cyrus the king brought forth the vessels of the house of the Lord, which Nebuchadnezzar had brought out of Jerusalem, and had put in the house of his gods. The vessels of gold and of silver were five thousand four hundred. These did Cyrus the king bring forth to return to Jerusalem from Babylon.

And the whole congregation was forty two thousand three hundred, besides their servants and their maids, who came again unto Judea from Babylon, and they dwelt in their own cities, and all Israel in their cities.

Then in the second year of their return from Babylon, the word of the Lord came to Zerubbabel the governor of Judah by Haggai, the prophet, who said: " Thus speaketh the Lord of hosts, saying, ' This people say " The time is not come, the time is not come, the time that the Lord's house should be built." ' " Is it time for you to dwell in your own houses, and his house to lie waste? "

And Haggai said:

" Now therefore," thus saith the Lord of hosts:
" Consider your ways.
Ye have sown much, and bring in little;
Ye eat, but ye have not enough;
Ye drink, but ye are not filled with drink;
Ye clothe you, but there is none warm;
And he that earneth wages
Earneth wages to put it into a bag with holes."

Thus saith the Lord of hosts:
" Consider your ways.
Go up to the mountain, and bring wood, and build the house;
And I will take pleasure in it,
And I will be glorified," saith the Lord.

" Ye looked for much, and lo, it came to little;
Why? Because of mine house that is waste,
And ye run every man to his own house.
Therefore the heaven over you is stayed from dew,
And the earth is stayed from her fruit,
And I called for a drought upon the land,
And upon the mountains,
And upon men, and upon cattle,
And upon all the labour of the hands."

Then Zerubbabel, the governor of Judah, with all the remnant of the people obeyed the voice of the Lord and the words of Haggai the prophet. And they gathered themselves together as one man to Jerusalem. Then stood up Zerubbabel and others and builded an altar for the burnt-offerings unto the Lord as it is written in the law of Moses. And they set the altar upon his bases; for fear was upon them because of the people of those countries. And they offered burnt-offerings unto the Lord morning and evening; and they kept the feast of tabernacles, and offered burnt-offerings as the duty of every day required. They also gave money unto the masons and carpenters to bring cedar trees from Lebanon according to the grant they had from Cyrus king of Persia.

And in the second year of their coming out of the captivity to Jerusalem, began Zerubbabel and the others to set forward the work of the house of the Lord.

And when the builders had laid the foundation of the temple, they set the priests in their apparel with trumpets, and the Levites with cymbals to praise the Lord. And they sang together, praising and giving thanks unto the Lord, "Because he is good, For his mercy endureth forever."

And all the people shouted with a great shout when they praised the Lord because the foundation of the house of the Lord was laid. But many of the priests and Levites and of the chief of the fathers, who were ancient men that had seen the first temple, wept with a loud voice when they saw the foundation, and many shouted aloud for joy; so the people could not discern the noise of the shout of joy from the noise of weeping.

And the word of the Lord came to Haggai, saying, "Speak now to Zerubbabel and to all the people and say, 'Who is left among you that saw this house in her first glory? And how do you see it now? Is it not in your eyes as nothing, in comparison? Yet be strong, O Zerubbabel, and be strong, all ye people of the land, and work: for I am with you,' saith the Lord of hosts. 'The silver is mine and the gold is mine, and the glory of this latter house shall be greater than the former; and in this place will I give peace.' "

Now when the adversaries of Judah and Benjamin heard that the children of the captivity builded the temple unto the Lord God of Israel, they came to Zerubbabel and to the chief of the fathers, and said unto them, "Let us build with you: for we seek your God, as ye do; and we do sacrifice unto him."

But Zerubbabel and the rest of the fathers of Israel, said, "Ye have nothing to do with us to build an house unto our God; but we ourselves will build unto the Lord God of Israel, as Cyrus the king of Persia hath commanded us."

Then the people of the land troubled them in building. And hired counsellors against them, to frustrate their purpose, all the days of Cyrus king of Persia, even unto the reign of Darius king of Persia. And this is a copy of the letter they sent unto the king Darius:

"Be it known unto the king, that the Jews which came up from thee to us in Jerusalem are building walls and foundations. Be it known unto the king, that if this city be builded, and the walls set up again, then they will not pay toll, tribute, and custom, and so thou shalt damage the revenue of the kings. We have sent and certified the king, that search may be made in the book of the records of thy fathers: so shalt thou know that this city is a rebellious city, and hurtful unto kings and provinces, and that they have moved sedition within the same of old time; for which cause was this city destroyed. We certify the king that if this city be builded again, and the walls set up, thou shalt have no portion on this side of the river."

Then king Darius sent an answer:

"To the chancellor, and to the scribe, and to the rest of their companions that dwell in Samaria, and unto the rest beyond the river: Peace, and at such a time:

"The letter which ye sent unto us hath been plainly read before me. And I commanded, and search hath been made, and it is found that this city of old time hath made insurrection against kings, and that rebellion and sedition have been made therein. There have been mighty kings also over Jerusalem, which have ruled over all countries beyond the river; and toll, tribute, and custom, was paid unto them. Give ye now commandment to cause these men to cease, and that this city be not builded, until another commandment shall be given from me. Take heed now that ye fail not to do this: why should damage grow to the hurt of the kings?"

Now when the copy of the king's letter was read before the scribe and his companions, they sent up in haste to Jerusalem unto the Jews, and made them to cease by force and power. Then ceased the work of the house of God at Jerusalem.

Then the prophets, Haggai, and Zechariah, prophesied unto the Jews that were in Judah and Jerusalem in the name of the God of Israel.

And Zechariah said, "This is the word of the Lord unto Zerubbabel, saying, 'Not by might, nor by power, but by my Spirit,' saith the Lord of hosts. 'The hands of Zerubbabel have laid the foundation of this house; his hands shall finish it; and thou shalt know that the Lord of hosts hath sent me unto you.'" Then rose up Zerubbabel and the others, and began to build the house of God, and the prophets of God helped them.

At the same time came to them Tatnai the governor on this side the river and his companions, and said unto them, "Who hath commanded you to build this house, and to make up this wall? What are the names of the men who make this building?"

And they sent a letter to Darius the king wherein was written:

"Unto Darius the king, all peace: Be it known unto the king, that we went into the province of Judea to the house of the great God, which is builded with great stones, and timber is laid in the walls, and this work goeth fast on, and prospereth in their hands. Then we asked those elders, 'Who commanded you to build this house, and to make up these walls?' And they returned us this answer: 'In the first year of Cyrus the king of Babylon, he made a decree to build this house of God.' Now therefore let there be search made in the king's treasure house there in Babylon, whether it be so, and let the king send his pleasure to us concerning this matter."

Then Darius the king made a decree, and search was made in the house of the rolls, where the treasures were laid up in Babylon. And there was found a roll, and therein was a record thus written: " In the first year of Cyrus the king, he made a decree concerning the house of God at Jerusalem: Let the house be builded, and let the foundation thereof be strongly laid; the height thereof threescore cubits, and the breadth thereof threescore cubits; with three rows of great stones, and a row of new timber: and let the expenses be given out of the king's treasure."

And Darius said, " Now therefore, Tatnai, governor beyond the river, and your companions, Let the work of this house of God alone! Let the governor of the Jews and the elders of the Jews build this house of God in his place. Moreover I make a decree that from the tribute beyond the river expenses be given unto these men forthwith, that they may not be hindered. And that which they have need of for the burnt-offerings, be given them from day to day without fail. That they may offer sacrifices of sweet savours unto the God of heaven, and pray for the life of the king, and of his sons. Also I make a decree, to destroy any people that shall put their hand to destroy this house of God. I Darius have made a decree; let it be done with speed."

Then Tatnai, governor on this side the river, and his companions did speedily what Darius the king had decreed.

And the elders of the Jews builded, and they prospered through the help of Haggai and Zechariah the prophets. And they builded, and finished the house of God according to the commandment of the God of Israel.

And the children of Israel, the priests and the Levites, and the rest of the children of the captivity kept the dedication of this house of God with joy.

And Zechariah the prophet said unto all of the people, " Thus saith the Lord, 'Behold, I will save my people from the east country, and from the west country. And I will bring them, and they shall dwell in the midst of Jerusalem. And they shall be my people, and I will be their God, in Truth and in righteousness. And Jerusalem shall be called a city of Truth, and the mountain of the Lord of hosts the holy mountain. And the streets of the city shall be full of boys and girls playing in the streets thereof.

" 'Let your hands be strong, ye that hear these words by the mouth of the prophets which were in the days that the foundation of the house of the Lord was laid, that the temple might be built. For before these days there was no hire for man nor any hire for beast, neither was there any peace to him that went out or came in because of affliction.

" 'But now the seed shall be prosperous, the vine shall give the fruit, and the ground shall give her increase, and the heavens shall give their dew, and I will cause the remnant of the people to possess all these things. And it shall come to pass as ye were a curse among the heathen, O house of Judah and house of Israel, so will I save you and ye shall be a blessing. Fear not, but let your hands be strong.

" 'These are the things that ye shall do: Speak ye every man the truth to his neighbor. Execute the judgment of Truth and peace in your gates. And let none of you imagine evil in your hearts against his neighbor. And love no false oath.

" 'And it shall come to pass, that there shall come people, and the inhabitants of many cities, saying, " Let us go speedily to pray before the Lord and to seek the Lord of hosts." Yea, many people and strong nations shall come to seek the Lord in Jerusalem, and to pray before the Lord, saying, " We will go with you; for we have heard that God is with you." ' "

And the children of Israel, which had come out of the captivity, kept the feast of unleavened bread seven days with joy, for the Lord made them joyful, and strengthened them.

REJOICE GREATLY, O DAUGHTER OF ZION

THE WORD of the Lord that came unto Zechariah, the prophet:

Rejoice greatly, O daughter of Zion;
Shout, O daughter of Jerusalem.
Behold, thy King cometh unto thee:
He is just, and having salvation;
Lowly, and riding upon an ass,
And upon a colt, the foal of an ass.

And I will cut off the chariot from Ephraim,
And the horse from Jerusalem,
And the battle bow shall be cut off;
And he shall speak peace unto the heathen;
And his dominion shall be from sea even to sea,
And from the river even to the ends of the earth.

And the Lord shall be seen over them,
And his arrow shall go forth as the lightning.
And the Lord their God shall save them in that day
As the flock of his people;
For they shall be as the stones of a crown,
Lifted up as an ensign upon his land.
For how great is his goodness,
And how great is his beauty.

THE TWO ANOINTED ONES

THIS IS THE WORD of the Lord that came unto Zechariah the prophet:

The angel of the Lord came and waked me, as a man that is wakened out of his sleep. And said unto me, "What seest thou?"

And I said, "I have looked, and behold a candlestick all of gold, with a bowl upon the top of it, and his seven lamps thereon, and seven pipes to the seven lamps, which are upon the top thereof: And two olive trees by it, one on the right side of the bowl, and the other upon the left side thereof."

So I answered and spake to the angel that talked with me, saying, "What are these, my lord?"

Then the angel that talked with me answered and said unto me, "Knowest thou not what these be?"

And I said, "No, my lord."

Then he answered, saying, "This is the word of the Lord, saying, 'Not by might, nor by power, but by my Spirit,' saith the Lord of hosts."

Then I said unto him, "What be these two olive trees upon the right side of the candlestick and upon the left side thereof? And what be these two olive branches, which through the two golden pipes empty the golden oil out of themselves?"

And he answered me and said, "Knowest thou not what these be?"

And I said, "No, my lord."

Then said he, "These are the two anointed ones, that stand by the Lord of the whole earth."

EZRA THE SCRIBE CAME TO JERUSALEM

Now after these things, in the reign of Artaxerxes the king of Persia, Ezra the scribe came to Jerusalem from Babylon. For Ezra had prepared his heart to seek the law of the Lord, and to do it, and teach in Israel statutes and judgments.

Now this is a copy of the letter that king Artaxerxes gave to Ezra the scribe:

"Artaxerxes, king of kings, unto Ezra the scribe of the law of the God of heaven, perfect peace, and at such a time:

"I make a decree, that all they of the people of Israel, of the priests and Levites, in my realm, which are minded of their own free will to go up to Jerusalem, go with thee. Forasmuch as thou art sent by the king and his seven counsellors, to enquire concerning Judah and Jerusalem, and to carry the silver and gold, which the king and his counsellors have freely offered unto the God of Israel, with the freewill offering of the people and of the priests for the house of thy God in Jerusalem. That thou mayest buy speedily with this money bullocks and rams for the offerings upon the altar. And whatsoever shall seem good to thee and to thy brethren, to do with the rest of the silver and the gold, do for the service of the house of thy God. And thou, Ezra, set magistrates and judges, which may judge all the people that are beyond the river, all such as know the laws of God; and teach ye them that know them not."

And Ezra said, "Blessed be the Lord God of our fathers, which hath put such a thing as this in the king's heart, to beautify the house of the Lord in Jerusalem; and hath extended mercy unto me before the king and his counsellors."

Then Ezra gathered together those that went up to Jerusalem with him from Babylon. And they abode in their tents three days by the river. And Ezra proclaimed a fast and prayer before God to seek a right way for them and all their substance. For he was ashamed to require of the king a band of soldiers and horsemen to help them against the enemy in the way, because he had said unto the king: "The hand of our God is upon all them for good that seek him; but his power and his wrath is against all them that forsake him." So they fasted and besought God, and he was intreated of them.

Then Ezra separated twelve of the chief of the priests, and ten of their brethren with them. And he weighed into their hand all of the gold and silver, and gold and silver vessels, and said unto them, "Ye are holy unto the Lord, and the vessels are holy also. Watch ye, and keep them, until ye weigh them before the chief of the priests and the Levites at Jerusalem in the chambers of the house of the Lord." So the priests and the Levites took the silver and the gold to bring them to Jerusalem.

Then Ezra and all that were with him departed from the river to go to Jerusalem. And the hand of God was upon them, and He delivered them from the hand of the enemy. And they came to Jerusalem and abode there three days. And on the fourth day the silver and gold and the vessels were weighed in at the house of God. And all the children of those which were come out of the captivity, offered burnt-offerings unto the God of Israel.

Now when these things were done, the princes came to Ezra, saying, "The people of Israel and the priests and the Levites, have not separated themselves from the people of the lands, the Canaanites, the Hittites, the Perizzites, the Jebusites, the Ammonites, the Moabites, the Egyptians, and the Amorites. For they have taken their daughters for themselves and their sons, so that the holy seed is mingled with the people of these lands; yea, the princes and rulers have been chief in this trespass."

And when Ezra heard this, he rent his garments and his mantle, and plucked off the hair of his head, and of his beard, and sat down dismayed. Then were assembled unto him every one that trembled at the words of the God of Israel. And at the evening sacrifice Ezra fell upon his knees, and spread out his hands unto the Lord, and said: " O my God, I am ashamed and blush to lift up my face to thee, for our iniquities are increased over our head. O Lord God of Israel, thou art righteous, and we cannot stand before thee because of this."

Now when Ezra had prayed, and when he had confessed, weeping and casting himself down before the house of God, there assembled unto him a very great congregation of men and women and children; for the people wept very sore.

And Sechaniah said unto Ezra, " We have trespassed against our God, and have taken strange wives of the people of the land: yet now there is hope in Israel concerning this thing. Now therefore let us make a covenant with our God to put away all the wives, and such as are born of them according to thy council, and let it be done according to the law. Arise: for this matter belongeth unto thee; we also will be with thee; be of good courage and do it."

Then Ezra arose from before the house of God, but he did eat no bread, nor drink water for he mourned because of the transgression. And they made a proclamation throughout Judah and Jerusalem unto all the children of the captivity that they should gather themselves together unto Jerusalem. Then all the men of Judah and Benjamin gathered together unto Jerusalem. And all the people sat in the street of the house of God, trembling, because of this matter and because of the rain.

And Ezra stood up, and said, " Ye have transgressed, and have taken strange wives. Now therefore make confession unto the Lord God of your fathers, and do his pleasure: separate yourselves from the people of the land and from the strange wives."

And all the people answered with a loud voice, and said, " As thou hast said, so must we do. But the people are many and it is a time of much rain. Let them which have taken strange wives come at appointed times, and with them the elders of every city, and the judges thereof, until the fierce wrath of our God for this matter be turned from us."

And the children of the captivity did so. And Ezra, with certain chief of the fathers, sat down in the first day of the tenth month to examine the matter. And they made an end with all the men that had taken strange wives by the first day of the first month. And some of them had wives by whom they had children.

" Arise, and build the wall."

THE BOOK OF NEHEMIAH

ARISE AND BUILD THE WALL

Now it came to pass, that Nehemiah was in Shushan the palace in Babylon in the days of Artaxerxes the king of Persia, when there came certain men of Judah; and Nehemiah asked them concerning the Jews that had escaped, which were left of the captivity, and concerning Jerusalem.

And they said, "The remnant that are there are in great affliction and reproach: the wall of Jerusalem is broken down, and the gates thereof are burned with fire." When Nehemiah heard these words, he sat down and wept, and mourned certain days and fasted, and prayed before the God of heaven.

And it came to pass in the month Nisan, that wine was brought before king Artaxerxes, and Nehemiah took up the wine and gave it to the king. And the king said, "Why is thy countenance sad, seeing thou art not sick? this is nothing else but sorrow of heart."

And Nehemiah said, "Let the king live forever: why should not my countenance be sad, when the city, the place of my fathers' sepulchers, lieth waste, and the gates thereof are consumed with fire? "

Then the king said, " For what dost thou make request? "

And Nehemiah said, " If it please the king, that thou wouldst sent me unto Judah, unto the city of my fathers' sepulchers, that I may build the wall."

And the king said, " For how long shall thy journey be? and when wilt thou return? " So it pleased the king to send him, and he set a time.

And Nehemiah said, " If it please the king, let letters be given me to the governors beyond the river, that they may convey me over till I come into Judah. And also a letter unto the keeper of the king's forest, that he may give me timber to make beams for the gates of the palace which appertained to the house of God, and for the wall of the city." And the king granted it, and sent captains of the army and horsemen with Nehemiah.

Then Nehemiah came to the governors beyond the river, and gave them the king's letters. When Sanballat the Horonite, and Tobiah the Ammonite heard of it, it grieved them exceedingly that there was come a man to seek the welfare of the children of Israel.

So Nehemiah came to Jerusalem, and was there three days. And he arose in the night, and a few men with him, and he went by night, and viewed the walls of Jerusalem which were broken down, and the gates thereof were consumed with fire. And he turned back, and entered by the gate of the valley, and so returned. And the rulers knew not whither he went, or what he did, neither had he told the Jews, nor the priests, nor anyone.

Then he said unto them, "Ye see the distress that we are in, how Jerusalem lieth waste, and the gates thereof are burned with fire. Come, and let us build up the wall of Jerusalem, that we be no more a reproach." And he told them that the hand of God was upon him, and of the king's words.

And they said, "Let us rise up and build." So they strengthened their hands for this work.

But when Sanballat and the others heard it, they laughed them to scorn, and despised them, and said, "What is this that ye do? will ye rebel against the king?"

Then Nehemiah answered them, "The God of heaven, he will prosper us; therefore, we his servants will arise and build: but ye have no portion, nor right, nor memorial, in Jerusalem."

But when Sanballat heard that they builded the wall, he was wroth, and took great indignation, and mocked the Jews. And he spake before his brethren, the army of Samaria, and said, "What do these feeble Jews? will they fortify themselves? will they sacrifice? will they make an end in a day? will they revive the stones out of the heaps of the rubbish which are burned?"

Now Tobiah the Ammonite was by him, and he said, "Even that which they build, if a fox go up, he shall even break down their stone wall."

So the Jews built the wall; and all the wall was joined together unto the half thereof: for the people had a mind to work.

But it came to pass, that when Sanballat and Tobiah heard that the walls of Jerusalem were made up, and that the breaches began to be stopped, then they were very wroth, and conspired all of them together to come and fight against Jerusalem, and hinder it.

Nevertheless the Jews made their prayer unto God, and set a watch against them day and night. And the adversaries said, "They shall not know, neither see, till we come in the midst among them, and slay them, and cause the work to cease."

Therefore Nehemiah set people both on the lower places behind the wall and on the higher places with swords and spears, and bows. And he said unto the people, "Be not afraid of them: remember the Lord is great, and fight for your brethren, your sons, and your daughters, your wives, and your houses."

And it came to pass, from that time forth that half of the people wrought in the work, and the other half held the spears, the shields, and the bows, and the harbergeons. And they which builded on the wall and they that bare burdens, every one, with one of his hands wrought in the work, and with the other hand held a weapon. For the builders, every one had his sword girded by his side, and so builded. And he that sounded the trumpet was beside Nehemiah.

And Nehemiah said unto the nobles, and to the rulers, and to the rest of the people, "The work is great and large, and we are separated upon the wall, one far from another. In what place therefore ye hear the sound of the trumpet, resort thither: our God shall fight for us. And let everyone with his servant lodge within Jerusalem, that in the night they may be a guard to us."

So they laboured in the work: and half of them held the spears from the rising of the morning till the stars appeared. And neither Nehemiah nor any of the men, put off their clothes, saving that every one put them off for washing.

Now it came to pass when Sanballat and Tobiah and the rest of their enemies heard that the wall was being built and that no breach was left therein, except that the doors were not set upon the gates, Sanballat sent unto Nehemiah saying, "Come and let us meet together in one of the villages of the plain," but he thought to do him mischief.

And Nehemiah sent messengers unto him, saying, "I am doing a great work, so that I cannot come down; why should the work cease whilst I leave it, and come down to you?"

Yet four times they sent messages of this sort, and Nehemiah answered them after the same manner. Then sent Sanballat his servant the fifth time with an open letter in his hand, wherein was written, "It is reported among the heathen, that thou and the Jews think to rebel; for which cause thou buildest the wall, that thou mayest be their king. And thou hast also appointed prophets to preach of thee at Jerusalem, saying, 'There is a king in Judah;' and now it shall be reported to the king according to these words. Come now therefore, and let us take counsel together."

Then Nehemiah sent unto him, saying, "There are no such things done as thou sayest, but thou feignest them out of thine own heart."

Afterward came Shemariah, and he said, "Let us meet together in the house of God, within the temple, and let us shut the doors of the temple; for they will come to slay thee; yea, in the night will they come to slay thee."

And Nehemiah said, "Should such a man as I flee? and who is there that would go into the temple to save his life? I will not go in." And, lo, Nehemiah perceived that God had not sent him, but Sanballat had hired him.

So the wall was finished in fifty and two days. And it came to pass, that when all the enemies heard thereof, and all the heathen that were about the city, they were much cast down in their own eyes; for they perceived that this work was wrought of God.

Now the city was large and great; but the people were few within, and the houses were not builded. So when the wall was built, Nehemiah said, " Let not the gates of Jerusalem be opened until the sun be hot, and while they stand by, let them shut the doors and bar them; and appoint watches of the inhabitants of Jerusalem, every one in his watch, and every one near his house." And Nehemiah gave his brother Hanani charge over Jerusalem, for he was a faithful man, and feared God above many.

So the priests and the Levites and some of the people of Israel dwelt in their own cities. And when the seventh month came all the people gathered themselves together as one man into the street that was before the water gate. And they spake unto Ezra the scribe to bring the book of the law of Moses.

And Ezra the scribe stood upon a pulpit of wood, and he opened the book, and when he opened it, all the people stood up, and Ezra blessed the Lord the great God, and said, " Blessed be thy glorious name: Thou even thou art Lord alone: thou hast made heaven, the heaven of heavens, with all their host, the earth, and all things that are therein, the seas and all that is therein, and thou preservest them all; and the host of heaven worshippeth thee."

And all the people answered, " Amen, Amen! " with lifting up of their hands, and they worshipped the Lord with their faces to the ground.

So Ezra read in the book of the law of God distinctly from the morning until midday, before men and women and those that could understand, and the ears of the people were attentive unto the book of the law: and Ezra gave the sense and caused the people to understand the reading.

And Nehemiah and Ezra and the Levites taught the people, and said unto them, " This day is holy unto the Lord your God: mourn not nor weep." For all the people wept when they heard the words of the law. And they said," Send portions unto them for whom nothing is prepared; for this day is holy unto our Lord; neither be ye sorry; for the joy of the Lord is your strength."

Also that day at the dedication of the wall of Jerusalem, they offered great sacrifices and rejoiced; for God had made them rejoice with great joy. So that the joy of Jerusalem was heard even afar off.

And the rulers of the people dwelt at Jerusalem. But the rest of the people cast lots, to bring one of ten to dwell in Jerusalem, the holy city, and nine parts to dwell in other cities. And the people blessed all the men that willingly offered themselves to dwell at Jerusalem.

And in the thirty second year of Artaxerxes, Nehemiah came again unto the king in Babylon, and after certain days, he obtained permission of the king, and returned to Jerusalem.

In those days Nehemiah saw Jews that had married wives of Ashdod, of Ammon, and of Moab: and their children spoke half in the speech of Ashdod and could not speak in the Jew's language, but according to the language of each people. And Nehemiah contended with them and smote certain of them, and plucked off their hair, and made them swear by God, saying, " Ye shall not give your daughters unto their sons, nor take their daughters unto your sons, or for yourselves, or transgress against our God in marrying strange wives." And when they heard the law, they separated from Israel all the mixed multitude.

And Nehemiah saw in Judah some treading wine presses on the sabbath, and bringing in sheaves, and lading asses, also wine, grapes and figs, and all manner of burdens, which they brought into Jerusalem on the sabbath day. And Nehemiah commanded that when it began to be dark before the sabbath, that the gates should be shut, and that they should not be opened till after the sabbath, that no burden be brought into Jerusalem on the sabbath day.

And Neremiah saw merchants and sellers of all kind of ware, lodged outside the wall, and he commanded them, " Why lodge ye about the wall? if ye do so again, I will lay hands on you." From that time forth they came no more on the sabbath.

And Nehemiah said, "Remember me, O my God, concerning this, and wipe not out my good deeds that I have done for the house of my God. Remember me, O my God, for good."

" I will sacrifice unto Thee with the voice of thanksgiving;
I will pay that that I have vowed."

THE BOOK OF JONAH

JONAH

NOW THE WORD of the Lord came unto Jonah the son of Amittai, saying, " Arise, go to Nineveh, that great city, and cry against it; for their wickedness is come up before me."

But Jonah rose up to flee unto Tarshish from the presence of the Lord, and went down to Joppa; and he found a ship going to Tarshish; so he paid the fare thereof, and went down into it, to go with them unto Tarshish from the presence of the Lord.

But the Lord sent out a great wind into the sea, and there was a mighty tempest in the sea, so that the ship was like to be broken. Then the mariners were afraid, and cried every man unto his god, and cast forth the wares that were in the ship into the sea, to lighten it of them. But Jonah was gone down into the sides of the ship; and he lay, and was fast asleep.

So the shipmaster came to him, and said unto him, " What meanest thou, O sleeper? arise, call upon thy God, if so be that God will think upon us, that we perish not."

And they said every one to his fellow, " Come, and let us cast lots, that we may know for whose cause this evil is upon us." So they cast lots, and the lot fell upon Jonah.

Then said they unto him, " Tell us, we pray thee, for whose cause this evil is upon us, what is thine occupation? and whence comest thou? what is thy country? and of what people art thou? "

And he said unto them, " I am a Hebrew; and I fear the Lord, the God of heaven, which hath made the sea and the dry land."

Then were the men exceedingly afraid, and said unto him, " Why hast thou done this? " For the men knew that he fled from the presence of the Lord, because he had told them. Then said they unto him, " What shall we do unto thee, that the sea may be calm unto us?" for the sea wrought, and was tempestuous.

And he said unto them, "Take me up, and cast me forth into the sea; so shall the sea be calm unto you: for I know that for my sake this great tempest is upon you."

Nevertheless the men rowed hard to bring it to the land; but they could not: for the sea wrought, and was tempestuous against them. Wherefore they cried unto the Lord, and said, "We beseech thee, O Lord, we beseech thee, let us not perish for this man's life, and lay not upon us innocent blood: for thou, O Lord, hast done as it pleased thee."

So they took up Jonah, and cast him forth into the sea: and the sea ceased from her raging. Then the men feared the Lord exceedingly, and offered a sacrifice unto the Lord, and made vows.

Now the Lord had prepared a great fish to swallow up Jonah. And Jonah was in the belly of the fish three days and three nights. Then Jonah prayed unto the Lord his God out of the fish's belly and said,

"I cried by reason of mine affliction unto the Lord,
And he heard me;
Out of the belly of hell cried I,
And thou heardest my voice.
For thou hadst cast me into the deep,
In the midst of the seas;
And the floods compassed me about:
All thy billows and thy waves passed over me.
Then I said, 'I am cast out of thy sight;
Yet I will look again toward thy holy temple.'
The waters compassed me about, even to the soul:
The depth closed me round about,
The weeds were wrapped about my head.
I went down to the bottoms of the mountains;

The earth with her bars was about me for ever:
Yet hast thou brought up my life from corruption,
O Lord my God.
When my soul fainted within me, I remembered the Lord:
And my prayer came in unto thee,
Into thine holy temple.
They that observe lying vanities forsake their own mercy.
But I will sacrifice unto thee with the voice of
thanksgiving;
I will pay that that I have vowed.
Salvation is of the Lord."

And the Lord spoke unto the fish, and it vomited out Jonah upon the dry land.

And the word of the Lord came unto Jonah the second time, saying, "Arise, go unto Nineveh, that great city, and preach unto it the preaching that I bid thee."

So Jonah arose, and went unto Nineveh, according to the word of the Lord. Now Nineveh was an exceedingly great city of three days' journey. And Jonah began to enter into the city a day's journey, and he cried, and said, "Yet forty days, and Nineveh shall be overthrown."

So the people of Nineveh believed God, and proclaimed a fast, and put on sackcloth, from the greatest of them even to the least of them. For the word came unto the king of Nineveh, and he arose from his throne, and he laid his robe from him, and covered him with sackcloth, and sat in ashes. And he caused it to be proclaimed and published through Nineveh by the decree of the king and his nobles, saying,

"Let neither man nor beast, herd nor flock, taste anything: let them not feed, nor drink water: but let man and beast be covered with sackcloth, and cry mightily unto God: yea, let them turn every one from his evil way, and from the violence that is in their hands. Who can tell if God will turn and repent, and turn away from his fierce anger, that we perish not? "

And God saw their works, that they turned from their evil way; and God repented of the evil that he had said that he would do unto them; and he did it not.

But it displeased Jonah exceedingly, and he was very angry. And he prayed unto the Lord, and said, "I pray thee, O Lord, was not this my saying, when I was yet in my country? Therefore I fled before unto Tarshish: for I knew that thou art a gracious God, and merciful, slow to anger, and of great kindness, and repentest thee of the evil. Therefore now, O Lord, take, I beseech thee, my life from me; for it is better for me to die than to live."

Then said the Lord, " Doest thou well to be angry? "

So Jonah went out of the city, and sat on the east side of the city, and there made him a booth, and sat under it in the shadow, till he might see what would become of the city.

And the Lord God prepared a gourd, and made it to come up over Jonah, that it might be a shadow over his head, to deliver him from his grief. So Jonah was exceedingly glad of the gourd.

But when the morning rose the next day, a worm smote the gourd that it withered.

And it came to pass, when the sun did arise, the sun beat upon the head of Jonah, that he fainted, and wished in himself to die, and said, " It is better for me to die than to live."

And God said to Jonah, "Doest thou well to be angry? "

And Jonah said, " I do well to be angry, even unto death."

Then said the Lord, " Thou hast had pity on the gourd, for the which thou hast not laboured, neither madest it grow; which came up in a night, and perished in a night. And should not I spare Nineveh, that great city, wherein are more than sixscore thousand persons, that cannot discern between their right hand and their left hand; and also much cattle? "

"I will pour out my Spirit."

THE BOOK OF JOEL

"I WILL POUR MY SPIRIT"

THE WORD of the Lord that came to Joel, the son of Pethuel.

Hear this, ye old men,
And give ear, all ye inhabitants of the land:

That which the palmerworm hath left hath the locust eaten;
And that which the locust hath left hath the cankerworm eaten;
And that which the cankerworm hath left hath the caterpillar eaten.
Awake, ye drunkards, and weep;
And howl, ye drinkers of wine.
For a nation is come upon my land,
Strong, and without number,
Whose teeth are the teeth of a lion.
He hath laid my vine waste, and barked my fig tree;
He hath made it clean bare, and cast it away;
The branches thereof are made white.
The field is wasted, the land mourneth.
Be ye ashamed, O ye husbandmen;
Howl, O ye vinedressers,
Because joy is withered away from the sons of men.

Call a solemn assembly,
Gather the elders and all the inhabitants of the land
Into the house of the Lord your God,
And cry unto the Lord.

Alas for the day! for the day of the Lord is at hand,
And as destruction from the Almighty shall it come.
Is not the meat cut off before our eyes,
Yea, joy and gladness from the house of our God?
O Lord, to thee will I cry:
For the fire hath devoured the pastures of the wilderness,
And the flame hath burned all the trees of the field.
The beasts of the field cry also unto thee:
For the rivers of waters are dried up,
And the fire hath devoured the pastures of the wilderness.

Blow ye the trumpet in Zion,
And sound an alarm in my high mountain:
Let all the inhabitants of the land tremble;
For the day of the Lord cometh, for it is nigh at hand:
A day of darkness and of gloominess,
A day of clouds and of thick darkness,
As the morning spread upon the mountains.
The people shall be much pained;
All faces shall gather blackness.
They shall run to and fro in the city;
They shall run upon the wall,
They shall climb up upon the houses;
They shall enter in at the windows like a thief.
The earth shall quake before them;
The heavens shall tremble;
The sun and the moon shall be dark,
And the stars shall withdraw their shining.

The Lord shall utter his voice:
For the day of the Lord is great and very terrible,
Who can abide it?
Therefore saith the Lord,
"Turn ye even to me with all your heart,

And with fasting, and with weeping, and with mourning.
And rend your heart, and not your garments,
And turn unto the Lord your God:
For he is gracious and merciful,
Slow to anger, and of great kindness."

Blow the trumpet in Zion,
Sanctify a fast, call a solemn assembly:
Gather the people, sanctify the congregation,
Assemble the elders, gather the children.
Let the priests, and the ministers of the Lord, weep,
And let them say, " Spare thy people, O Lord,
And give not thine people to reproach,
That the heathen should rule over them."
The Lord will answer and say unto his people,
" Behold, I will send you corn, and wine, and oil,
And ye shall be satisfied therewith,
And I will no more make you a reproach among the heathen."

Fear not, O land! be glad and rejoice:
For the Lord will do great things.
Be glad, ye children of Zion,
And rejoice in the Lord your God,
For he hath given you the former rain moderately,
And he will cause to come down for you the rain,
The former rain, and the latter rain in the first month.
" And I will restore unto you the years that the locust hath eaten;
And ye shall eat in plenty, and be satisfied,
And praise the name of the Lord your God,
That hath dealt wondrously with you.
And ye shall know that I am the Lord your God, and none else:

And it shall come to pass,
That I will pour out my Spirit upon all flesh:
And your sons and your daughters shall prophesy,
And your old men shall dream dreams,
And your young men shall see visions.
And it shall come to pass,
That whosoever shall call on the name of the Lord,
Shall be delivered.

" For behold, in those days, and in that time,
When I shall bring again the captivity of Judah and
Jerusalem,
I will also gather all nations.
Proclaim ye this among the Gentiles:
Assemble yourselves, and come!
Put ye in the sickle, for the harvest is ripe;
Come, get you down, for the press is full."
Multitudes, multitudes in the valley of decision:
For the day of the Lord is near in the valley of decision.
The sun and the moon shall be darkened,
And the stars shall withdraw their shining;
And the heavens and the earth shall shake.
But the Lord will be the hope of his people,
And the strength of the children of Israel.
And it shall come to pass in that day,
That the mountains shall drop down new wine,
And the hills shall flow with milk,
And all the rivers of Judah shall flow with waters,
And a fountain shall come forth of the house of the Lord:
For the Lord dwelleth in Zion.

" I am the Lord, I change not."

THE BOOK OF MALACHI

The Prophet

I WILL OPEN THE WINDOWS OF HEAVEN, AND POUR YOU OUT A BLESSING

THE BURDEN of the word of the Lord to Israel, by Malachi, the prophet:

Have we not all one Father? Hath not One God created us? Why do we deal treacherously, every man against his brother?

"Behold, I will send my messenger, and he shall prepare the way before me: and the Lord, whom ye seek, shall suddenly come to his Temple, even the messenger of the covenant, whom ye delight in, behold, he shall come," saith the Lord of hosts.

But who may abide the day of his coming? and who shall stand when he appeareth? For he is like a refiner's fire, and like fuller's soap: and he shall sit as a refiner and purifier of silver. And he shall purify the sons of Levi, and purge them as gold and silver, that they may offer unto the Lord an offering in righteousness. Then shall the offering of Judah and Jerusalem be pleasant unto the Lord, as in the days of old, as in former years.

"And I will come near to you in judgment; and I will be a swift witness against the sorcerers, and against the adulterers, and against false swearers, and against those that oppress the hireling in his wages, the widow, and the fatherless, and that turn aside the stranger from his right, and fear not me," saith the Lord of hosts. "For I am the Lord, I change not. Return unto me, and I will return unto you," saith the Lord.

"Bring ye all the tithes into the storehouse, that there may be meat in mine house, and prove me now herewith," saith the Lord of hosts, "if I will not open you the windows of heaven, and pour you out a blessing, that there shall not be room enough to receive it."

Then they that feared the Lord spoke often one to another: and the Lord hearkened, and heard it, and a book of remembrance was written before him for them that feared the Lord, and that thought upon his name.

"And they shall be mine," saith the Lord of hosts, "in that day when I make up my jewels; and I will spare them, as a man spareth his own son that serveth him. Then shall ye return, and discern between the righteous and the wicked, between him that serveth God and him that serveth him not. For, behold, the day cometh that shall burn as an oven; and all the proud, yea, and all that do wickedly, shall be stubble. But unto you that fear my name shall the Sun of righteousness arise with healing in his wings.

"Remember ye the law of Moses my servant, which I commanded unto him in Horeb for all Israel, with statutes and judgments. Behold, I will send you Elijah the prophet, before the coming of the great and dreadful day of the Lord; and he shall turn the heart of the fathers to the children, and the heart of the children to their fathers."

“ Who knoweth whether thou art come to
the kingdom for such a time as this.”

THE BOOK OF ESTHER

ESTHER

" Who knoweth whether thou art come to
the kingdom for such a time as this."

NOW IT CAME TO PASS in the days when king Ahasuerus sat on the throne of his kingdom (this is Ahasuerus which reigned from India unto Ethiopia, over an hundred and seven and twenty provinces), he made a feast unto all his princes and his servants. He showed the riches of his glorious kingdom, and the honour of his excellent majesty many days, even an hundred and four score days.

And when these days were expired, the king made a feast unto all the people that were present in Shushan the palace, both great and small. Also Vashti the queen made a feast for the women in the royal house.

In the court of the garden of the king's palace, were white, green, and blue hangings fastened with cords of fine linen to silver rings and pillars of marble. The beds were of gold and silver upon a pavement of red, and blue, and white and black marble. And they gave them drink in vessels of gold.

On the seventh day, when the heart of the king was merry with wine, he commanded the seven chamberlains to bring Vashti, the queen, before the king, to show the people and the princes her beauty, for she was fair to look upon. But Queen Vashti refused to come at the king's commandment. Therefore was the king very wroth, and his anger burned in him.

Then the king said to the wise men, which knew the times, " What shall we do unto Queen Vashti according to law, because she hath not performed the commandment of the king? "

And Memucan answered, "Vashti the queen hath not done

wrong to the king only, but also to all the princes, and to all the people that are in all the provinces of king Ahasuerus. For all women shall despise their husbands when it shall be reported, 'King Ahasuerus commanded the queen to be brought in before him, but she came not.' If it please the king let there go a royal commandment from him, that Vashti come no more before king Ahasuerus; and let the king give her royal estate unto another that is better than she. And when the king's decree shall be published throughout all his empire, all wives shall give to their husbands honour, both great and small."

And the saying pleased the king and the princes; and the king sent letters into all the provinces that every man should bear rule in his own house.

After these things, when the wrath of king Ahasuerus was appeased, then said the king's servants, "Let there be fair young virgins sought for the king. And let the maiden which pleaseth the king be queen instead of Vashti." And the thing pleased the king; and he did so.

Now there were in Shushan the palace, Mordecai, a certain Jew, who had been carried away captive from Jerusalem, and Esther, his uncle's daughter, whom Mordecai took for his own daughter after the death of her mother and father. And the maid was fair and beautiful.

So it came to pass, when the king's commandment was heard, and when many maidens were gathered together unto Shushan the palace, that Esther was brought also unto the king's house, to the custody of Hegai, keeper of the women. And the maiden pleased Hegai, and she obtained kindness of him, and he gave her seven maidens out of the king's house, and he gave her and her maids the best place in the house of the women.

Esther had not showed her people nor her kindred; for Mordecai had charged her that she should not show it. And Mordecai walked every day before the court of the women's house to know how Esther did, and what should become of her.

Then came every maiden before the king. And the king loved Esther, and she obtained grace and favour in his sight more than all the virgins, so that he set the royal crown upon her head, and made her queen instead of Vashti. Then the king made a great feast, even Esther's feast; and he gave gifts according to the state of the king.

In those days while Mordecai sat in the king's gate, two of the king's chamberlains were wroth and sought to lay hand on king Ahasuerus. And the thing was known to Mordecai, who told it unto Esther the queen; and Esther told the king in Mordecai's name. When it was found out therefore, the chamberlains were both hanged on a tree; and it was written in the book of the chronicles.

After these things did king Ahasuerus promote Haman, and set his seat above all the princes that were with him. And all the king's servants, that were in the king's gate, bowed, and reverenced Haman, for the king had so commanded. But Mordecai bowed not, nor did him reverence. And when Haman saw that Mordecai bowed not, nor did him reverence, than was Haman full of wrath. And he thought scorn to lay hands on Mordecai alone, wherefore Haman sought to destroy all the Jews that were throughout the whole kingdom of Ahasuerus, for Mordecai had told that he was a Jew.

And Haman said unto king Ahasuerus, "There is a certain people scattered abroad and dispersed among the people in all the provinces of thy kingdom: and their laws are diverse from all people; neither keep they the king's laws. If it please the king, let it be written that they may be destroyed; and I will pay ten thousand talents of silver to the hands of those that have charge of the business."

And the king took his ring from his hand, and gave it unto Haman, the Jew's enemy, and the king said unto Haman, "The silver is given to thee, the people also, to do with them as it seemeth good to thee."

Then were the king's scribes called and there was written all that Haman commanded, to the governors and to the rulers of every province; in the name of king Ahasuerus was it written, and sealed with the king's ring. And the letters were sent by posts into all the king's provinces, to destroy, to kill, and to cause to perish, all Jews, both young and old, little children and women, in one day, even upon the thirteenth day of the twelfth month, and to take the spoil of them for a prey. The posts went out, being hastened by the king's commandment, and the decree was given in Shushan the palace. And the king and Haman sat down to drink; but the city Shushan was perplexed.

When Mordecai perceived all that was done, Mordecai rent his clothes, and put on sackcloth with ashes, and went out into the midst of the city, and cried with a loud and bitter cry. And in every province, whithersoever the king's commandment and his decree came, there was great mourning among the Jews, and fasting, and weeping, and wailing; and many lay in sackcloth and ashes.

So Esther's maids and her chamberlains came and told it her. Then was the queen exceedingly grieved; and she sent one of the king's chamberlains, whom he had appointed to attend upon her, to Mordecai, to know what it was, and why it was.

And Mordecai told him all that had happened, and of the sum of money that Haman had promised to pay to destroy the Jews. Also he gave him the copy of the decree to show it unto Esther, and to charge her that she should go in unto the king, to make supplication unto him for her people.

And the chamberlain came and told Esther the words of Mordecai. Again Esther sent word to Mordecai, "All the king's servants, and the people of the king's provinces, do know, that whosoever, whether man or woman, shall come unto the king into the inner court, who is not called, there is a law to put him to death, except the king shall hold out the golden sceptre, that he may live; but I have not been called to come in unto the king these thirty days." And they told Mordecai Esther's words.

Then Mordecai commanded to answer Esther, "Think not of thyself. If thou holdest thy peace at this time, then shall deliverence arise to the Jews from another place; but who knoweth whether thou art come to the kingdom for such a time as this?"

Then Esther bade them return Mordecai this answer, "Go, gather together all the Jews that are present in Shushan, and fast ye for me, and neither eat nor drink three days, night or day; I also and my maidens will fast likewise: and so will I go in unto the king, which is not according to the law; and if I perish, I perish." So Mordecai went his way, and did according to all that Esther commanded him.

Now it came to pass on the third day, that Esther put on her royal apparel, and stood in the inner court of the king's house, and the king sat upon his royal throne. And when the king saw Esther the queen standing in the court, she obtained favour in his sight; and the king held out to Esther the golden sceptre that was in his hand. So Esther drew near, and touched the top of the sceptre.

Then said the king, "What wilt thou, Queen Esther? and what is thy request? it shall be given thee to the half of the kingdom."

And Esther answered, "If it seem good unto the king, let the king and Haman come this day unto the banquet that I have prepared for him."

Then the king said, "Cause Haman to make haste, that he may do as Esther hath said." So the king and Haman came to the banquet that Esther had prepared. And the king said unto Esther at the banquet, "What is thy petition? and it shall be granted thee; and what is thy request? even to the half of the kingdom it shall be performed."

Then answered Esther, "My petition and my request is: if I have found favour in the sight of the king, and if it pleases the king to grant my petition, and to perform my request, let the king and Haman come to the banquet that I shall prepare for them, and I will do tomorrow as the king hath said."

Then went Haman forth that day joyful and with a glad heart; but when Haman saw Mordecai in the king's gate, that he stood not up, nor moved for him, he was full of indignation against Mordecai. Nevertheless Haman refrained himself; and when he came home, he sent and called for his friends, and Zeresh his wife. And Haman told them of the glory of his riches, and all the things wherein the king had promoted him. Haman said moreover, "Yea, Esther the queen did let no man come in with the king unto the banquet that she had prepared but myself; and tomorrow am I invited also with the king. Yet all this availeth me nothing, so long as I see Mordecai, the Jew, sitting at the king's gate."

Then said Zeresh his wife and all his friends unto him, "Let a gallows be made of fifty cubits high, and tomorrow speak thou unto the king that Mordecai may be hanged thereon; then go thou in merrily with the king unto the banquet." And the thing pleased Haman; and he caused the gallows to be made.

On that night could not the king sleep, and he commanded to bring the book of the chronicles; and they were read before the king. And it was found written, that Mordecai had told of two of the king's chamberlains, the keepers of the door, who sought to lay hand on king Ahasuerus. And the king said, "What honour and dignity hath been done to Mordecai for this?"

The king's servants said, "Nothing has been done for him."

And the king said, "Who is in the court?"

Now Haman was come into the outward court to speak unto the king to hang Mordecai on the gallows that he had prepared for him. And the king's servants said, "Behold, Haman standeth in the court."

And the king said, "Let him come in." So Haman came in. And the king said unto him, "What shall be done unto the man whom the king delighteth to honour?"

Now Haman thought in his heart, "To whom would the king delight to do honour more than to myself?" And Haman answered, "For the man whom the king delighteth to honour, let the royal apparel be brought which the king useth to wear, and the horse that the king rideth upon, and the crown royal which is set upon his head; and let this apparel and horse be delivered to the hand of one of the king's most noble princes, that they may array the man whom the king delighteth to honour, and bring him on horseback through the street of the city, and proclaim before him, 'Thus shall it be done to the man whom the king delighteth to honour.'"

Then said the king to Haman, "Make haste, and take the apparel and the horse, as thou hast said, and do even so to Mordecai the Jew, that sitteth at the king's gate; let nothing fail of all that thou hast spoken."

Then took Haman the apparel and the horse, and arrayed Mordecai, and brought him on horseback through the streets of the city, and proclaimed before him, "Thus shall it be done unto the man whom the king delighteth to honour." And Mordecai came again to the king's gate.

But Haman hasted to his house mourning, and having his head covered. And Haman told Zeresh his wife, and all his friends everything that had befallen him. And while they were yet talking came the king's chamberlains, and hasted to bring Haman unto the banquet that Esther had prepared.

So the king and Haman came to banquet with Esther the queen. And the king said unto Esther on the second day, "What is thy petition, Queen Esther? and it shall be granted thee; and what is thy request? and it shall be performed even to the half of the kingdom."

Then the queen answered and said, "If I have found favour in thy sight, O king, and if it please the king, let my life be given me at my petition, and my people at my request. For we are sold, I and my people, to be destroyed, to be slain, and to perish."

Then the king said, "Who is he, and where is he, that durst presume in his heart to do so?"

And Esther said, "The adversary and enemy is this wicked Haman."

Then Haman was afraid before the king and the queen. And the king arising from the banquet in his wrath went into the palace garden. And Haman stood up to make request for his life to Esther the queen; for he saw there was evil determined against him by the king.

Then the king returned out of the palace garden, and one of the chamberlains said, "Behold the gallows fifty cubits high, which Haman had made for Mordecai, standeth in the house of Haman."

Then the king said, "Hang him thereon." So they hanged Haman on the gallows that he had prepared for Mordecai.

On that day did king Ahasuerus give the house of Haman unto Esther the queen. And Mordecai came before the king, for Esther had told what he was unto her. And the king took off his ring, which he had taken from Haman, and gave it unto Mordecai. And Esther set Mordecai over the house of Haman.

And Esther spake yet again before the king, and fell down at his feet, and besought him with tears to put away the mischief of Haman, and she said, "If it please the king, and if I have found favour in his sight, and the thing seem right before the king, let it be written to reverse the letters devised by Haman which he wrote to destroy the Jews which are in all the king's provinces. For how can I endure to see the evil that shall come unto my people? or how can I endure to see the destruction of my kindred?"

Then the king said unto Esther the queen and to Mordecai, "Behold, I have given Esther the house of Haman, and him have they hanged upon the gallows, because he laid his hand upon the Jews. Write ye also for the Jews, as it liketh you, in the king's name, and seal it with the king's ring; for the writing which is written in the king's name, and sealed with the king's ring, may no man reverse."

Then were the king's scribes called and it was written according to all that Mordecai commanded unto the Jews, and to the rulers of the provinces which are from India unto Ethiopia. And he wrote in the king's name, and sealed it with the king's ring, and sent letters by posts on horseback, and riders on mules, camels, and young dromedaries; wherein the king granted the Jews which were in every city to gather themselves together, and to stand for their life, to destroy, to slay, and to cause to perish, all the power of the people and province that would assault them, both little ones and women, and to take the spoil of them for a prey. So the posts went out, being hasted and pressed on by the king's commandment. And the decree was given in Shushan the palace.

And the Jews gathered themselves together in their cities throughout all the provinces of the king Ahasuerus. And no man could withstand them; for the fear of them fell upon all people. And the Jews had joy and gladness, a feast and a good day.

And Mordecai wrote letters unto all the Jews that were in all the provinces of the king Ahasuerus, both nigh and far, that they should keep the fourteenth day of the month Adar, and also the fifteenth day, every year as the days wherein the Jews rested from their enemies, and the month which was turned unto them from sorrow to joy, and from mourning into a good day.

Then Esther the queen wrote with all authority to confirm this second letter, and her decree confirmed these matters, and it was written in the book.

" I have heard of Thee by the hearing of the ear;
But now mine eye seeth Thee."

THE BOOK OF JOB

JOB

THERE WAS A MAN in the land of Uz, whose name was Job; and that man was perfect and upright, and one that feared God, and eschewed evil. And there were born unto him seven sons and three daughters. His substance also was seven thousand sheep, and three thousand camels, and five hundred yoke of oxen, and five hundred she asses, and a very great household; so that this man was the greatest of all the children of the east.

Now there was a day when the sons of God came to present themselves before the Lord, and Satan came also among them.

And the Lord said unto Satan, " Whence comest thou? "

Then Satan answered the Lord, and said,

" From going to and fro in the earth,
And from walking up and down in it."

And the Lord said unto Satan,

" Hast thou considered my servant Job?
For there is none like him in the earth,
A perfect and an upright man,
One that feareth God, and escheweth evil."

Then Satan answered the Lord, and said,

" Doth Job fear God for nought?
Hast not thou made a hedge about him,
And about his house,
And about all that he hath, on every side?

Thou hast blessed the work of his hands,
And his substance is increased in the land.
But put forth thine hand now,
And touch all that he hath,
And he will curse thee to thy face."

And the Lord said unto Satan,

"Behold, all that he hath is in thy power;
Only upon himself put not forth thine hand."

So Satan went forth from the presence of the Lord.

And it fell on a day when Job's sons and his daughters were eating and drinking wine in their eldest brother's house, that there came a messenger unto Job, and said,

"The oxen were plowing,
And the asses feeding beside them;
And the Sabeans fell upon them, and took them away;
Yea, they have slain the servants with the edge of the sword;
And I only am escaped alone to tell thee."

While he was yet speaking, there came also another and said,

"The fire of God is fallen from heaven,
And hath burned up the sheep, and the servants, and consumed them;
And I only am escaped alone to tell thee."

While he was yet speaking, there came also another and said,

"The Chaldeans made three bands,
And fell upon the camels, and have taken them away,

Yea, and slain the servants with the edge of the sword;
And I only am escaped alone to tell thee."

While he was yet speaking, there came also another, and said,

" Thy sons and thy daughters were eating
And drinking wine in their eldest brother's house;
And, behold, there came a great wind from the wilderness
And smote the four corners of the house,
And it fell upon the young men, and they are dead;
And I only am escaped alone to tell thee."

Then Job arose, and rent his mantle, and shaved his head, and fell down upon the ground, and worshipped; and he said,

" Naked came I out of my mother's womb,
And naked shall I return thither;
The Lord gave, and the Lord hath taken away;
Blessed be the name of the Lord."

In all this Job sinned not, nor charged God foolishly.

Again there was a day when the sons of God came to present themselves before the Lord, and Satan came also among them to present himself before the Lord. And the Lord said unto Satan,

" From whence comest thou? "

And Satan answered the Lord, and said,

" From going to and fro in the earth,
And from walking up and down in it."

And the Lord said unto Satan,

"Hast thou considered my servant Job?
That there is none like him in the earth,
A perfect and upright man,
One that feareth God, and escheweth evil;
And he still holdeth fast his integrity,
Although thou movedst against him,
To destroy him without cause."

And Satan answered the Lord, and said,

"Skin for skin!
Yea, all that a man hath will he give for his life.
But put forth thine hand now,
And touch his bone and his flesh,
And he will curse thee to thy face."

And the Lord said unto Satan, "Behold, he is in thine hand: only spare his life."

So Satan went forth from the presence of the Lord, and smote Job with sore boils from the sole of his foot unto his crown. And Job sat down among the ashes.

Then said his wife unto him,
"Dost thou still hold fast thine integrity?
Curse God, and die."

But Job said unto her,
"Thou speakest as one of the foolish women speaketh,
What? shall we receive good at the hand of God,
And shall we not receive evil?"

In all this did not Job sin with his lips.

Now when Job's three friends heard of all this evil that was come upon him, they came every one from his own place; Eliphaz the Temanite, and Bildad the Shuhite, and Zophar the

Naamathite; for they had made an appointment together to come
to mourn with h… nd to comfort him.
And whe… lifted up their eyes afar off, and knew him
not, the… up their voice, and wept; and they rent every
one …tle, and sprinkled dust upon their heads toward
…o they sat down with him upon the ground seven days
…n …hts, and none spake a word unto him; for they saw
…is grief was very great.

After this opened Job his mouth, and Job spake and said:

“ Let the day perish wherein I was born;
Let that day be darkness;
Let not God regard it from above,
Neither let the light shine upon it.
Wherefore is light given to him that is in misery,
And life unto the bitter in soul.
For the thing which I greatly feared is come upon me,
And that which I was afraid of is come unto me.
I was not in safety,
Neither had I rest,
Neither was I quiet;
Yet trouble came.”

Then Eliphaz the Temanite answered and said:
“ If we assay to commune with thee,
Wilt thou be grieved?
But who can withhold himself from speaking?
Remember, I pray thee, who ever perished, being
innocent?
Or where were the righteous cut off?
Even as I have seen, they that plow iniquity, and sow
wickedness, reap the same.
Now a thing was secretly brought to me,
And mine ear received a little thereof.

In thoughts from the visions of the nig
When deep sleep falleth on men,
Then a spirit passed before my face;
It stood still but I could not discern the form th
And an image was before mine eyes,
There was silence, and I heard a voice, saying,
'Shall mortal man be more just than God?
Shall a man be more pure than his maker?'

"Call now, if there be any that will answer thee;
And to which of the saints wilt thou turn?
For wrath killeth the foolish man,
And envy slayeth the silly one.
Although *affliction* cometh not forth of the dust,
Neither doth trouble spring out of the ground,
Yet man is born unto trouble,
As the sparks fly upward.

"I would seek unto God,
And unto God would I commit my cause,
Which doeth great things and unsearchable,
Marvellous things without number.
Behold, happy is the man whom God correcteth;
Therefore despise not thou the chastening of the
Almighty;
le shall deliver thee in six troubles;
n, in seven there shall no evil touch thee."

nswered and said:
t my grief were thoroughly weighed,
calamity laid in the balances together!
would be heavier than the sand of the sea;
ny words are swallowed up.
d I will hold my tongue;

And cause me to understand wherein I have erred.
My days are swifter than a weaver's shuttle,
And are spent without hope.
O remember that my life is wind;
Mine eyes shall no more see good.
Therefore I will not refrain my mouth;
I will speak in the anguish of my spirit;
I will complain in the bitterness of my soul.
What is man, that thou shouldest magnify him?
And that thou shouldest set thine heart upon him?
And why dost thou not pardon my transgression,
And take away mine iniquity?
For now shall I sleep in the dust;
And thou shalt seek me in the morning,
But I shall not be."

Then answered Bildad the Shuhite, and said:
"How long wilt thou speak these things?
And how long shall the words of thy mouth be like a
strong wind?
If thou wouldest seek unto God betimes,
And make thy supplication to the Almighty;
If thou wert pure and upright,
Surely now he would awake for thee,
And make the habitation of thy righteousness prosperous.
Behold, God will not cast away a perfect man,
Neither will he help the evildoers."

Then Job answered and said,
"I know it is so of a truth;
But how should man be just with God?
Behold, he taketh away, who can hinder him?
Who will say unto him, 'What doest thou?'
If I justify myself, mine own mouth shall condemn me;

If I say, 'I am perfect,' it shall also prove me perverse.
This is one thing, therefore I said it,
He destroyeth the perfect and the wicked.
I will say unto God, 'Do not condemn me;
Thou knowest that I am not wicked;
And there is none that can deliver out of thine hand.'
If I be wicked, woe unto me;
And if I be righteous, yet will I not lift up my head.
I am full of confusion;
Therefore see thou mine affliction;
Are not my days few?
Cease then and let me alone,
That I may take comfort a little,
Before I go whence I shall not return,
Even to the land of darkness and the shadow of death."

Then answered Zophar the Naamathite, and said:
"Should not the multitude of words be answered?
And should a man full of talk be justified?
For thou hast said, 'My doctrine is pure,
And I am clean in thine eyes.'
But Oh that God would speak,
And open his lips against thee;
And he would show thee the secrets of wisdom.
Know therefore that God exacteth of thee less than thine iniquity deserveth.
Canst thou by searching find out God?
Canst thou find out the Almighty unto perfection?
It is as high as heaven; what canst thou do?
Deeper than hell; what canst thou know?
If iniquity be in thine hand, put it far away,
For then shalt thou lift up thy face without spot;
Yea, thou shalt be stedfast, and shalt not fear;
Because thou shalt forget thy misery,

And remember it as waters that pass away.
And thine age shall be clearer than the noonday;
Thou shalt shine forth;
Thou shalt be as the morning.
Also thou shalt lie down, and none shall make thee afraid;
But the eyes of the wicked shall fail,
And they shall not escape."

And Job answered and said:
"No doubt but ye are the people,
And wisdom will die with you.
But I have understanding as well as you;
Lo, mine eye hath seen all this,
Mine ear hath heard and understood it.
What ye know, the same do I know also;
I am not inferior unto you.
Surely I would speak to the Almighty,
And I desire to reason with God.
Man that is born of woman is of few days, and full of trouble.
He cometh forth like a flower, and is cut down;
He fleeth also as a shadow, and continueth not.
And dost thou open thine eyes upon such an one,
And bringest me into judgment with thee?
Who can bring a clean thing out of an unclean?
Not one."

Then answered Eliphaz the Temanite, and said:
"Should a wise man utter vain knowledge,
And fill his belly with the east wind?
What knowest thou, that we know not?
What understandest thou, which is not in us?
Why doth thine heart carry thee away?
And what do thy eyes wink at,

That thou turnest thy spirit against God,
And lettest such words go out of thy mouth?
The wicked man travaileth with pain all his days,
And the number of years is hidden to the oppressor.
Trouble and anguish shall make him afraid;
They shall prevail against him, as a king ready to the battle.
For he stretcheth out his hand against God,
And strengtheneth himself against the Almighty."

Then Job answered and said:
"I have heard many such things;
Miserable comforters are ye all.
I also could speak as ye do,
If your soul were in my soul's stead;
I could heap up words against you,
And shake mine head at you.
Though I speak, my grief is not assuaged;
And though I forbear, what am I eased?
My friends scorn me;
But mine eye poureth out tears unto God.
O that one might plead for a man with God,
As a man pleadeth for his neighbor!
But as for you all, do ye return,
For I cannot find one wise man among you."

Then answered Bildad the Shuhite, and said:
"How long will it be ere ye make an end of words?
Wherefore are we counted as beasts
And reputed vile in your sight?
Yea, the light of the wicked shall be put out,
And the spark of his fire shall not shine.
The light shall be dark in his tabernacle,
And his candle shall be put out with him.
Surely such are the dwellings of the wicked,

And this is the place of him that knoweth not God."

Then Job answered and said:
"How long will ye vex my soul,
And break me in pieces with words?
These ten times have ye reproached me;
Ye are not ashamed that ye make yourselves strange to me.
And be it indeed that I have erred,
Mine error remaineth with myself.
Know now that God hath overthrown me,
And hath compassed me with his net.
Behold, I cry out of wrong, but I am not heard;
I cry aloud, but there is no judgment.
He hath fenced up my way that I cannot pass,
And he hath set darkness in my paths.
He hath stripped me of my glory,
And taken the crown from my head.
He hath destroyed me on every side, and I am gone;
And mine hope hath he removed like a tree.
My kinsfolk have failed,
And my friends have forgotten me.
My bone cleaveth to my skin and to my flesh,
And I am escaped with the skin of my teeth.
Have pity upon me, have pity upon me, O ye my friends;
For the hand of God hath touched me.
O that my words were now written!
Oh that they were printed in a book!
For I know that my redeemer liveth,
Whom I shall see for myself,
And mine eyes shall behold."

Then answered Zophar the Naamathite, and said:
"Knowest thou not this of old,
Since man was placed upon earth,

That the triumphing of the wicked is short,
And the joy of the hypocrite but for a moment?
Though his excellency mount up to the heavens,
And his head reach unto the clouds,
Yet he shall perish for ever;
He shall fly away as a dream,
And shall not be found;
Yea, he shall be chased away as a vision of the night.
The heaven shall reveal his iniquity,
And the earth shall rise up against him.
The increase of his house shall depart,
And his goods shall flow away in the day of his wrath.
This is the portion of a wicked man from God,
And the heritage appointed unto him by God."

But Job answered and said:
" Suffer me that I may speak;
And after that I have spoken, mock on.
As for me, is my complaint to man?
And if it were so, why should not my spirit be troubled?
Wherefore do the wicked live, become old,
Yea, are mighty in power?
Their houses are safe from fear,
Neither is the rod of God upon them.
Therefore they say unto God, 'Depart from us;
For we desire not the knowledge of thy ways.
What is the Almighty, that we should serve him?
And what profit should we have, if we pray unto him? '
Lo, their good is not in their hand:
The counsel of the wicked is far from me.
Shall any teach God knowledge,
Seeing he judgeth those that are high?
One dieth in his full strength,
Being wholly at ease and quiet.

And another dieth in the bitterness of his soul,
And never eateth with pleasure.
They shall lie down alike in the dust.
Behold, I know your thoughts,
And the devices which ye wrongfully imagine against me.
How then comfort ye me in vain,
Seeing in your answers there remaineth falsehood? "

Then Eliphaz the Temanite answered and said:
" Is it any pleasure to the Almighty,
That thou art righteous?
Or is it gain to him, that thou makest thy way perfect?
Will he reprove thee for fear of thee?
Is not thy wickedness great?
And thine iniquities infinite?
Thou hast not given water to the weary to drink,
And thou hast withholden bread from the hungry.
Thou hast sent widows away empty,
And the arms of the fatherless have been broken.
Therefore snares are round about thee;
And sudden fear troubleth thee,
Or darkness that thou canst not see.
Is not God in the height of heaven?
And behold the height of the stars,
How high they are!
Acquaint now thyself with him, and be at peace,
Thereby good shall come unto thee.
Receive, I pray thee, the law from his mouth,
And lay up his words in thine heart.
If thou return to the Almighty,
Thou shalt be built up,
Thou shalt put away iniquity far from thy tabernacles."

Then Job answered and said:
" Oh that I knew where I might find him!
That I might come even to his seat!
I would order my cause before him,
And fill my mouth with arguments.
I would know the words which he would answer me,
And understand what he would say unto me.
Will he plead against me with his great power?
No; but he would put strength in me.
Behold, I go forward, but he is not there;
And backward, but I cannot perceive him.
But he knoweth the way that I take;
When he hath tried me, I shall come forth as gold.
My foot hath held his steps,
His way have I kept, and not declined.
Neither have I gone back from the commandments of his lips;
I have esteemed the words of his mouth more than my necessary food.
But he is in One Mind, and who can turn him?
And what his Soul desireth, even that he doeth.
All the while my breath is in me,
And the spirit of God is in my nostrils,
My lips shall not speak wickedness,
Nor my tongue utter deceit.
Surely there is a vein for the silver,
And a place for gold where they fine it.
Iron is taken out of the earth,
And brass is molten out of the stone.
But where shall wisdom be found?
And where is the place of understanding?
Man knoweth not the price thereof;
Neither is it found in the land of the living.
The depth saith, ' It is not with me ';

And the sea saith, ‘ It is not with me.’
It cannot be gotten for gold,
Neither shall silver be weighed for the price thereof.
Whence then cometh wisdom?
And where is the place of understanding?
God understandeth the way thereof,
And he knoweth the place thereof.
And unto man he said,
‘ Behold, the fear of the Lord, that is wisdom;
And to depart from evil is understanding.’
Oh that I were as in months past,
As in the days when God preserved me;
When his candle shined upon my head,
And when by his light I walked through darkness;
As I was in the days of my youth,
When the secret of God was upon my tabernacle;
When the Almighty was yet with me,
And when my children were about me.
I put on righteousness, and it clothed me:
My judgment was as a robe and a diadem.
I was eyes to the blind, and feet was I to the lame.
I was a father to the poor:
And the cause which I knew not I searched out.
Then said I, I shall die in my nest,
And I shall multiply my days as the sand.
But now, terrors are turned upon me;
They pursue my soul as the wind;
And my welfare passeth away as a cloud.
And now my soul is poured out upon me;
The days of affliction have taken hold upon me.
I cry unto thee, and thou dost not hear me;
I stand up, and thou regardest me not.
When I looked for good, then evil came unto me;
And when I waited for light, there came darkness.

Doth not he see my ways, and count all my steps?
If I walked with vanity, or if my foot hasted to deceit;
Let me be weighed in an even balance,
That God may know mine integrity.
The words of Job are ended."

So these three men ceased to answer Job, because he was righteous in his own eyes. Then was kindled the wrath of Elihu the Buzite; against Job was his wrath kindled, because he justified himself rather than God. Also against his three friends was his wrath kindled, because they had found no answer, and yet had condemned Job.

Now Elihu had waited till Job had spoken, because they were older than he. When Elihu saw that there was no answer in the mouth of these three men, then his wrath was kindled.

And Elihu the Buzite said:
"I am young, and ye are very old;
Wherefore I was afraid, and durst not show you mine
opinion.
I said, 'Days should speak,
And multitude of years should teach wisdom.'
But there is a spirit in man,
And the inspiration of the Almighty giveth them
understanding.
Great men are not always wise;
Neither do the aged understand judgment.
Yea, I attended unto you,
And behold, there was none of you that convinced Job,
Or that answered his words.
Wherefore, Job, I pray thee,
Hear my speeches, and hearken to all my words.
The Spirit of God hath made me,
And the breath of the Almighty hath given me life.

For God speaketh once, yea twice,
Yet man perceiveth it not.
If there be a messenger with him, an interpreter, one among a thousand,
To show unto man his uprightness,
He shall pray unto God, and he shall be favorable unto him;
And he shall see his face with joy;
For he will render unto man his righteousness.
Let us choose to us judgment;
Let us know among ourselves what is good.
For Job hath said, 'I am righteous;
And God hath taken away my judgment.'
Therefore hearken unto me, ye men of understanding,
Far be it from God, that he should do wickedness;
And from the Almighty, that he should commit iniquity.
For the work of man shall he render unto him,
And cause every man to find according to his ways.
Yea, surely God will not do wickedly,
Neither will the Almighty pervert judgment.
Job hath spoken without knowledge,
And his words are without wisdom.
Look unto the heavens, and see;
And behold the clouds which are higher than thou.
He that is perfect in knowledge is with thee.
Behold, God is mighty, and despiseth not any;
He is mighty in strength and wisdom.
Behold, God exalteth by his power;
Who teacheth like him?
Remember that thou magnify his work, which men behold.
Stand still, and consider the wondrous works of God;
The wondrous works of him which is perfect in knowledge.

Touching the Almighty, we cannot find him out;
He is excellent in power, and in judgment, and in plenty of justice;
He will not afflict."

Then the Lord answered Job out of the whirlwind and said:

" Who is this that darkeneth counsel by words without knowledge?
Gird up now thy loins like a man;
For I will demand of thee, and answer thou me.
Where wast thou when I laid the foundations of the earth?
Declare, if thou hast understanding.
Whereupon are the foundations thereof fastened?
Or who laid the corner stone thereof;
When the morning stars sang together,
And all the sons of God shouted for joy?
Or who shut up the sea with doors, when it brake forth,
And said, ' Hitherto shalt thou come, but no further;
And there shall thy proud waves be stayed '?
Hast thou commanded the morning since thy days,
And caused the dayspring to know his place?,
Hast thou entered into the springs of the sea?
Or hast thou walked in the search of the depth?
Hast thou perceived the breadth of the earth?
Declare, if thou knowest it all.
Where is the way where light dwelleth?
And as for darkness, where is the place thereof?
Hast thou entered into the treasures of the snow?
Or hast thou seen the treasures of the hail?
By what way is the light parted,
Which scattereth the east wind upon the earth?
Who hath divided a watercourse for the overflowing waters;

Or a way for the lightning of thunder;
To cause it to rain on the earth, where no man is;
To satisfy the desolate and waste ground,
And to cause the bud of the tender herb to spring forth.
Has the rain a father?
Or who hath begotten the drops of dew?
Canst thou bind the sweet influences of Pleiades,
Or loose the bands of Orion?
Canst thou bring forth Mazzaroth in his season?
Or canst thou guide Arcturus with his sons?
Knowest thou the ordinances of heaven?
Canst thou set the dominion thereof in the earth?
Canst thou lift up thy voice to the clouds,
That abundance of waters may cover thee?
Canst thou send lightnings, that they may go,
And say unto thee, 'Here we are'?
Who hath put wisdom in the inward parts?
Or who hath given understanding to the heart?
Shall he that contendeth with the Almighty instruct him?
He that reproveth God, let him answer it."

Then Job answered the Lord, and said:
"I know that thou canst do every thing,
And that no thought can be withholden from thee.
Who is he that hideth counsel without knowledge?
Therefore have I uttered that I understood not;
Things too wonderful for me, which I knew not.
I have heard of thee by the hearing of the ear;
But now mine eye seeth thee."

And the Lord turned the captivity of Job, when he prayed for his friends; also the Lord gave Job twice as much as he had before. So the Lord blessed the latter end of Job more than his beginning; for he had fourteen thousand sheep, and six thousand camels, and a thousand yoke of oxen, and a thousand she asses. He also had seven sons and three daughters.

After this lived Job an hundred and forty years, and saw his sons, and his sons' sons, even four generations.

" O worship the Lord
In the beauty of holiness."

THE BOOK OF PSALMS

PSALMS OF GUIDANCE

" Lead me, O Lord, in thy righteousness:
Make thy way straight before my face."

BLESSED IS THE MAN

Blessed is the man that walketh not in the counsel of the ungodly,
Nor standeth in the way of sinners,
Nor sitteth in the seat of the scornful.
But his delight is in the law of the Lord,
And in his law doth he meditate day and night.
And he shall be like a tree planted by the rivers of water,
That bringeth forth fruit in his season;
His leaf also shall not wither;
And whatsoever he doeth shall prosper.
The ungodly are not so;
But are like the chaff which the wind driveth away.
Therefore the ungodly shall not stand in the judgment,
Nor sinners in the congregation of the righteous.
For the Lord knoweth the way of the righteous;
But the way of the ungodly shall perish.

DWELL TOGETHER IN UNITY

Behold, how good and how pleasant it is
For brethren to dwell together in unity!
It is like the precious ointment upon the head,
And as the dew that descended upon the mountains.

WHO SHALL ABIDE IN THY TABERNACLE?

Lord, who shall abide in thy tabernacle?
Who shall dwell in thy holy hill?
He that walketh uprightly,
And worketh righteousness,
And speaketh truth in his heart.
He that backbiteth not with his tongue,
Nor doeth evil to his neighbor,
Nor taketh up a reproach against his neighbor.
But he honoureth them that fear the Lord.
He that doeth these things shall never be moved.

THE LOVE OF THE LORD

Come, ye children, hearken unto me;
I will teach you the fear of the Lord.
What man is he that desireth life,
And loveth many days, that he may see good?
Keep thy tongue from evil,
And thy lips from speaking guile.
Depart from evil and do good;
Seek peace, and pursue it.
The eyes of the Lord are upon the righteous,
And his ears are open unto their cry.

FRET NOT THYSELF

Fret not thyself because of evildoers,
Neither be thou envious against the workers of iniquity.
For they shall soon be cut down like the grass,
And wither as the green herb.

Trust in the Lord, and do good;
So shalt thou dwell in the land,
And verily thou shalt be fed.
Delight thyself also in the Lord,
And he shall give thee the desires of thine heart.
Commit thy way unto the Lord:
Trust also in him, and he shall bring it to pass.
And he shall bring forth thy righteousness as the light,
And thy judgment as the noonday.

Rest in the Lord, and wait patiently for him.
Fret not thyself because of him who prospereth in his way,
Because of the man who bringeth wicked devices to pass.
Cease from anger, and forsake wrath;
Fret not thyself in any wise to do evil,
For evildoers shall be cut off:
But those that wait upon the Lord,
They shall inherit the earth.

For yet a little while, and the wicked shall not be:
Yea, thou shalt diligently consider his place, and it shall
 not be.
But the meek shall inherit the earth;
And shall delight themselves in the abundance of peace.
The wicked have drawn out the sword, and have bent
 their bow,

To cast down the poor and needy,
And to slay such as be of upright conversation.
Their sword shall enter into their own heart,
And their bows shall be broken.

The steps of a good man are ordered by the Lord;
And he delighteth in his way.
Though he fall, he shall not be utterly cast down,
For the Lord upholdeth him with his hand.
I have been young, and now am old,
Yet have I not seen the righteous forsaken,
Nor his seed begging bread.
Depart from evil, and do good,
And dwell forever more.

I have seen the wicked in great power,
And spreading himself like a green bay tree.
Yet he passed away, and lo, he was not;
Yea, I sought him, but he could not be found.
Mark the perfect man, and behold the upright:
For the end of that man is peace.

I WILL KEEP MY MOUTH WITH A BRIDLE

I said, I will take heed to my ways,
That I sin not with my tongue;
I will keep my mouth with a bridle.

Lord, make me to know mine end,
And the measure of my days, what it is,
That I may know how frail I am.

Behold, thou hast made my days as an handbreadth;
And mine age is as nothing before thee;
Verily every man at his best state is altogether vanity.

Surely every man walketh in a vain show;
Surely they are disquieted in vain;
He heapeth up riches, and knoweth not who shall gather
them.

And now, Lord, what wait I for?
My hope is in thee.
Deliver me from all my transgressions.

O SEND OUT THY LIGHT

O send out thy light and thy truth;
Let them lead me;
Let them bring me unto thy holy hill,
And to thy tabernacles.

Then will I go unto the altar of God,
Unto God my exceeding joy;
Yea, upon the harp will I praise thee,
O God, my God.

Why art thou cast down, O my soul?
And why art thou disquieted within me?
Hope in God, for I shall yet praise him,
Who is the health of my countenance, and my God.

WHY BOASTEST THOU IN MISCHIEF?

Why boastest thou thyself in mischief, O mighty man?
The goodness of God endureth continually.

Thy tongue deviseth mischiefs, like a sharp razor,
  working deceitfully.
Thou lovest evil more than good,
And lying rather than to speak righteousness.
Thou lovest all devouring words,
O thou deceitful tongue.

God shall likewise destroy thee for ever,
He shall take thee away,
And pluck thee out of thy dwelling place,
And root thee out of the land of the living.

The righteous also shall see, and fear,
And shall laugh at him.
Lo, this is the man that made not God his strength,
But trusted in the abundance of his riches,
And strengthened himself in his wickedness.

THE FOOL

The fool hath said in his heart, "There is no God."

THE UPRIGHT

Blessed is the man that feareth the Lord,
That delighteth greatly in his commandments.
Wealth and riches shall be in his house;
And his righteousness endureth for ever.

Unto the upright there ariseth light in the darkness;
He is gracious, and full of compassion, and righteous.
A good man showeth favour, and lendeth;
He will guide his affairs with discretion.

He shall not be afraid of evil tidings;
His heart is fixed, trusting in the Lord;
His heart is established, he shall not be afraid.
But the desire of the wicked shall perish.

WHO SHALL ASCEND INTO THE HILL OF THE LORD?

Who shall ascend into the hill of the Lord?
Or who shall stand in his holy place?
He that hath clean hands, and a pure heart;
Who hath not lifted up his soul unto vanity,
Nor sworn deceitfully.
He shall receive the blessing from the Lord,
And righteousness from the God of his salvation.

WALK IN THE LAW OF THE LORD

Blessed are the undefiled in the way,
Who walk in the law of the Lord.
Blessed are they that keep his testimonies,
And that seek him with the whole heart.

Make me to go in the path of thy commandments;
For therein do I delight.
Turn away mine eyes from beholding vanity;
And quicken thou me in thy way.

O how love I thy law!
It is my meditation all the day.
Order my steps in thy word;
And let not iniquity have dominion over me.

Thy word is very pure,
Therefore thy servant loveth it.
Thy word is true from the beginning;
And every one of thy righteous judgments endureth
for ever.

I WILL NOT KNOW A WICKED PERSON

I will sing of mercy and judgment:
Unto thee, O Lord, will I sing.

I will behave myself wisely in a perfect way.
I will walk within my house with a perfect heart.

I will set no wicked thing before mine eyes:
I hate the work of them that turn aside; it shall not cleave to me.

A froward heart shall depart from me;
I will not know a wicked person.

Whoso privily slandereth his neighbour, him will I cut off:
Him that hath an high look and a proud heart will not I suffer.

Mine eyes shall be upon the faithful of the land,
That they may dwell with me.

PSALMS OF REJOICING

"This is the day which the Lord hath made:
We will rejoice and be glad in it."

IN THE MORNING, I WILL LOOK UP

My voice shalt thou hear in the morning, O Lord;
In the morning will I direct my prayer unto thee,
 and will look up.
Let all those that put their trust in thee rejoice;
Let them ever shout for joy!
Let them also that love thy name be joyful in thee.
For thou, Lord, wilt bless the righteous;
With favour wilt thou compass him as with a shield.

MAKE A JOYFUL NOISE

Make a joyful noise unto God, all ye lands;
Sing forth the honour of his name;
Make his praise glorious.
All the earth shall worship thee,
And shall sing unto thee;
They shall sing to thy name.

Come and see the works of God:
He ruleth by his power for ever;
His eyes behold the nations.
O bless our God, ye people,
And make the voice of his praise to be heard;
Which holdeth our soul in Life,
And suffereth not our feet to be moved.

BLESSED IS THE NATION

The word of the Lord is right,
And all his works are done in Truth.
He loveth righteousness and judgment;
The earth is full of the goodness of the Lord.

By the word of the Lord were the heavens made,
And all the host of them by the breath of his mouth.
He gathered the waters of the sea together as an heap;
He layeth up the depth in storehouses.

Let all the earth fear the Lord;
Let all the inhabitants of the world stand in awe of him.
For he spake, and it was done;
He commanded, and it stood fast.

The counsel of the Lord standeth for ever,
The thoughts of his heart to all generations.
Blessed is the nation whose God is the Lord,
And the people whom he hath chosen for his own
inheritance.

MY HEART GREATLY REJOICETH

The Lord is my strength and my shield;
My heart trusteth in him, and I am helped;
Therefore my heart greatly rejoiceth,
And my song will praise him.
Save thy people, and bless thine inheritance;
Feed them also, and lift them up for ever.

BLESSED BE THE LORD

God setteth the solitary in families;
He bringeth out those which are bound with chains;
Blessed be the Lord,
Who daily loadeth us with benefits.
He that is our God is the God of salvation,
And unto God the Lord belong the issues from death.
Sing unto God, ye kingdoms of the earth;
O sing praises unto the Lord.

IN THY NAME SHALL THEY REJOICE

O Lord God of hosts, who is a strong Lord like unto thee?
Or to thy faithfulness round about thee?
Thou rulest the raging of the sea;
When the waves thereof arise, thou stillest them.

The heavens are thine, the earth also is thine;
As for the world and the fulness thereof, thou hast founded them.
Justice and judgment are the habitation of thy throne;
Mercy and Truth shall go before thy face.

Blessed is the people that know the joyful sound;
They shall walk, O Lord, in the light of thy countenance.
In thy name shall they rejoice all the day,
And in thy righteousness shall they be exalted.
Blessed is the Lord for evermore.

THE LORD REIGNETH

The Lord reigneth; let the earth rejoice!
Let the multitude of isles be glad thereof.
Ye that love the Lord, hate evil;
He preserveth the souls of his saints;
He delivereth them out of the hand of the wicked.
Light is sown for the righteous,
And gladness for the upright in heart.
Rejoice in the Lord, ye righteous;
And give thanks at the remembrance of his holiness.

OPEN TO ME THE GATES OF RIGHTEOUSNESS

I called upon the Lord in distress;
The Lord answered me, and set me in a large place.
It is better to trust in the Lord than to put confidence in man.
Open to me the gates of righteousness;
I will go into them, and I will praise the Lord,
For thou hast heard me, and art become my salvation.

The stone which the builders refused is become the head stone of the corner.
This is the Lord's doing;
It is marvellous in our eyes.
This is the day which the Lord hath made;
We will rejoice and be glad in it.

IN THE SHADOW OF THY WINGS WILL I REJOICE

O God, thou art my God!
Early will I seek thee;
My soul thirsteth for thee,
My flesh longeth for thee in a dry and thirsty land,
  where no water is;
To see thy power and thy glory, as I have seen thee in
  the sanctuary.

Because thy lovingkindness is better than life,
My lips shall praise thee.
Thus will I bless thee while I live;
I will lift up my hands in thy name.
My soul shall be satisfied as with marrow and fatness;
And my mouth shall praise thee with joyful lips,
When I remember thee upon my bed,
And meditate on thee in the night watches.
Because thou hast been my help,
Therefore in the shadow of thy wings will I rejoice.

PSALMS OF SUSTENANCE

" The Lord is my shepherd:
I shall not want."

I SHALL NOT WANT

The Lord is my shepherd;
I shall not want.
He maketh me to lie down in green pastures;
He leadeth me beside the still waters.
He restoreth my soul;
He leadeth me in the paths of righteousness for his name's sake.
Yea, though I walk through the valley of the shadow of death,
I will fear no evil,
For thou art with me;
Thy rod and thy staff they comfort me.
Thou preparest a table before me in the presence of mine enemies;
Thou anointest my head with oil;
My cup runneth over.
Surely goodness and mercy shall follow me all the days of my life,
And I will dwell in the house of the Lord for ever.

THOU MAINTAINEST MY LOT

Preserve me, O God, for in thee do I put my trust.
The Lord is the portion of mine inheritance and of my cup;
Thou maintainest my lot.
The lines are fallen unto me in pleasant places;
Yea, I have a goodly heritage.

I have set the Lord always before me;
Because he is at my right hand, I shall not be moved.
Therefore my heart is glad, and my glory rejoiceth.
Thou wilt show me the path of life;
In thy presence is fulness of joy;
At thy right hand there are pleasures for evermore.

THEY SHALL BE ABUNDANTLY SATISFIED

O Lord, thou preservest man and beast.
How excellent is thy loving kindness , O God!
Therefore the children of men put their trust under the shadow of thy wings.
They shall be abundantly satisfied with the fatness of thy house;
And thou shalt make them drink of the river of thy pleasures.
For with thee is the fountain of Life;
In thy light shall we see light.
O continue thy loving kindness unto them that know thee.
And thy righteousness to the upright in heart.

MAGNIFY THE LORD

I will bless the Lord at all times;
His praise shall continually be in my mouth.
O magnify the Lord with me,
And let us exalt his name together.

I sought the Lord, and he heard me,
And delivered me from all my fears.
This poor man cried, and the Lord heard him,
And saved him out of all his troubles.

The angel of the Lord encampeth round about them that fear him,
And delivereth them.
O taste and see that the Lord is good;
Blessed is the man that trusteth in him.

O fear the Lord, ye his saints;
For there is no want to them that fear him.
The young lions do lack, and suffer hunger;
But they that seek the Lord shall not want any good thing.

THE LORD SHALL SUSTAIN THEE

Give ear to my prayer, O God,
And hide not thyself from my supplication.
Attend unto me, and hear me!
My heart is sore pained within me,
And the terrors of death are fallen upon me.

I said, Oh that I had wings like a dove!
For then would I fly away and be at rest.
Lo, then would I wander far off,
And remain in the wilderness.
I would hasten my escape from the windy storm and
    tempest.

As for me, I will call upon God,
And the Lord shall save me.
Evening, and morning, and at noon, will I pray and cry
    aloud;
And he shall hear my voice.

Cast thy burden upon the Lord,
And he shall sustain thee;
He shall never suffer the righteous to be moved.

THE LORD RENDERS TO EVERY MAN ACCORDING TO HIS WORK

My soul, wait thou only upon God,
For my expectation is from him.
He only is my rock and my salvation;
He is my defence;
I shall not be moved.

In God is my salvation and my glory;
The rock of my strength, and my refuge is in God.
Trust in him at all times.
Ye people, pour out your heart before him;
God is a refuge for us.

God hath spoken once;
Twice have I heard this,
That power belongeth unto God.
Also unto thee, O Lord, belongeth mercy,
For thou renderest to every man according to his work.

WE SHALL BE SATISFIED WITH THE GOODNESS OF THY HOUSE

O thou that hearest prayer,
Unto thee shall all flesh come.

Blessed is the man whom thou choosest,
And causest to approach unto thee,
That he may dwell in thy courts:
We shall be satisfied with the goodness of thy house,
Even of thy holy temple.

Thou visitest the earth, and waterest it;
Thou greatly enrichest it with the river of God, which is full of water;
Thou preparest them corn, when thou hast so provided for it.
Thou waterest the ridges thereof abundantly;
Thou settlest the furrows thereof;
Thou makest it soft with showers;
Thou blessest the springing thereof.
Thou crownest the year with thy goodness.
And the little hills rejoice on every side.
The pastures are clothed with flocks;
The valleys also are covered over with corn;
They shout for joy, they also sing.

I WILL GO IN THE STRENGTH OF THE LORD

In thee, O Lord, do I put my trust;
Let me never be put to confusion.
Deliver me in thy righteousness,
Incline thine ear unto me, and save me.

Be thou my strong habitation,
Whereunto I may continually resort;
Thou hast given commandment to save me,
For thou art my rock and my fortress.

Thou art my hope, O Lord God;
Thou art my trust from my youth.
Cast me not off in the time of old age;
Forsake me not when my strength faileth.

I will go in the strength of the Lord God;
I will make mention of thy righteousness, even thine only.
O God, thou hast taught me from my youth,
And hitherto have I declared thy wondrous works.

Now also when I am old and grayheaded, O God, forsake me not,
Until I have showed thy strength unto this generation,
And thy power to every one that is to come.
My lips shall greatly rejoice when I sing unto thee;
My tongue also shall talk of thy righteousness all the day long.

THE LORD SHALL GIVE THAT WHICH IS GOOD

I will hear what God the Lord will speak;
For he will speak peace unto his people, and to his saints,
But let them not turn again to folly.
Surely his salvation is nigh them that fear him,
That glory may dwell in our land.

Mercy and Truth are met together;
Righteousness and peace have kissed each other.
Truth shall spring out of the earth;
And righteousness shall look down from heaven.

Yea, the Lord shall give that which is good,
And our land shall yield her increase.
Righteousness shall go before him,
And shall set us in the way of his steps.

THE LORD WILL NOT CAST OFF HIS PEOPLE

O Lord God, to whom vengeance belongeth,
How long shall the wicked triumph?
How long shall they utter and speak hard things?
And all the workers of iniquity boast themselves?

They break in pieces thy people, O Lord,
And afflict thine heritage.
They slay the widow and the stranger, and murder the fatherless.
Yet they say, The Lord shall not see,
Neither shall the God of Jacob regard it.

He that planted the ear, shall he not hear?
He that formed the eye, shall he not see?
He that teacheth man knowledge, shall he not know?
The Lord knoweth the thoughts of man,
That they are vanity.

Blessed is the man whom thou chastenest, O Lord,
And teachest him out of thy law.
For the Lord will not cast off his people,
Neither will he forsake his inheritance.
But judgment shall return unto righteousness;
And all the upright in heart shall follow it.

PSALMS OF GRATITUDE

" Bless the Lord, O my soul,
And forget not all His benefits."

JOY COMETH IN THE MORNING

I will extol thee, O Lord,
For Thou hast lifted me up.
O Lord my God, I cried unto thee,
And thou hast healed me.
O Lord, thou hast brought up my soul from the grave;
Thou hast kept me alive, that I should not go down to the pit.
Sing unto the Lord, O ye saints of his,
And give thanks at the remembrance of his holiness.

Weeping may endure for a night,
But joy cometh in the morning.
Lord, by thy favour thou hast made my mountain to stand strong;
Thou hast turned for me my mourning into dancing;
Thou hast put off my sackcloth, and girded me with gladness,
To the end that my glory may sing praise to thee, and not be silent.
O Lord my God, I will give thanks to thee for ever.

OH HOW GREAT IS THY GOODNESS

Oh how great is thy goodness, which thou hast laid up for them that fear thee;
Which Thou hast wrought for them that trust in thee before the sons of men!
Blessed be the Lord, for he hath shown me his marvellous kindness in a strong city.

THE LORD HATH PUT A NEW SONG IN MY MOUTH

I waited patiently for the Lord,
And he inclined unto me, and heard my cry,
He brought me up also out of an horrible pit, out of the miry clay,
And set my feet upon a rock, and established my goings.
And he hath put a new song in my mouth, even praise unto our God;
Many shall see it, and fear, and shall trust in the Lord.
Many, O Lord my God, are thy wonderful works which thou hast done,
And thy thoughts which are to us-ward;
They cannot be reckoned up in order unto thee;
If I would declare and speak of them,
They are more than can be numbered.
Sacrifice and offering thou didst not desire;
Mine ears hast thou opened;
Burnt offering and sin offering hast thou not required.
Then said I, Lo, I come;
In the volume of the book it is written of me,
I delight to do thy will, O my God;
Yea, thy law is within my heart.

FORGET NOT ALL HIS BENEFITS

Bless the Lord, O my soul!
And all that is within me, bless his holy name.
Bless the Lord, O my soul,
And forget not all his benefits:
Who forgiveth all thine iniquities;
Who healeth all thy diseases;
Who redeemeth thy life from destruction;
Who crowneth thee with loving kindness and tender mercies;
Who satisfieth thy mouth with good things;
So that thy youth is renewed like the eagle's.

The Lord executeth righteousness and judgment for all that are oppressed.
The Lord is merciful and gracious, slow to anger, and plenteous in mercy.
He hath not dealt with us after our sins,
Nor rewarded us according to our iniquities.
For as the heaven is high above the earth,
So great is his mercy toward them that fear him.
So far as the east is from the west,
So far hath he removed our transgressions from us.
Like as a father pitieth his children,
So the Lord pitieth them that fear him.

As for man, his days are as grass;
As a flower of the field, so he flourisheth.
For the wind passeth over it, and it is gone;
And the place thereof shall know it no more.

But the mercy of the Lord is from everlasting to
everlasting upon them that fear him,
And his righteousness unto children's children;
To such as keep his covenant,
And to those that remember his commandments to do
them.

The Lord hath prepared his throne in the heavens;
And his kingdom ruleth over all.
Bless the Lord, all his works in all places of his dominion;
Bless the Lord, O my soul.

WHAT SHALL I RENDER UNTO THE LORD?

Gracious is the Lord, and righteous;
Yea, our God is merciful!
For thou hast delivered my soul from death, mine eyes from tears, and my feet from falling.
I will walk before the Lord in the land of the living.
What shall I render unto the Lord for all his benefits toward me?
I will pay my vows unto the Lord now in the presence of all his people.
I will offer unto thee the sacrifice of thanksgiving,
And will call upon the name of the Lord.

PSALMS OF HUMILITY

" I shall be satisfied,
When I awake with Thy likeness."

WHAT IS MAN, THAT THOU ART MINDFUL OF HIM?

O Lord our Lord, how excellent is thy name in all the earth!
Who hast set thy glory above the heavens.
When I consider thy heavens, the work of thy fingers,
The moon and the stars, which Thou hast ordained,
What is man, that thou art mindful of him?
And the son of man, that Thou visitest him?
For thou hast made him a little lower than the angels,
And hast crowned him with glory and honor.
Thou madest him to have dominion over the works of thy hands;
Thou hast put all things under his feet.
O Lord, our Lord, how excellent is thy name in all the earth!

WHEN I AWAKE WITH THY LIKENESS

I have called upon thee, for thou wilt hear me, O God;
Incline thine ear unto me, and hear my speech;
Show thy marvellous loving kindness,
O thou that savest by thy right hand;
Hide me under the shadow of thy wings.
As for me, I will behold thy face in righteousness;
I shall be satisfied, when I awake with thy likeness.

CLEANSE THOU ME FROM SECRET FAULTS

The heavens declare the glory of God;
And the firmament showeth his handywork.
Day unto day uttereth speech,
And night unto night showeth knowledge.

There is no speech nor language,
Where their voice is not heard.
Their line is gone out through all the earth,
And their works to the end of the world.

The law of the Lord is perfect, converting the soul;
The testimony of the Lord is sure, making wise the simple.
The statutes of the Lord are right, rejoicing the heart;
The commandment of the Lord is pure, enlightening the eyes.

The fear of the Lord is clean, enduring for ever;
The judgments of the Lord are true and righteous altogether.
More to be desired are they than gold, yea, than much fine gold;
And in keeping of them there is great reward.

Who can understand his errors?
Cleanse thou me from secret faults.
Let the words of my mouth, and the meditation of my heart,
Be acceptable in thy sight, O Lord, my strength, and my redeemer.

IT IS GOOD FOR ME TO DRAW NEAR TO GOD

Truly God is good to Israel,
Even to such as are of a clean heart.
But as for me, my feet were almost gone;
My steps had well nigh slipped.
For I was envious at the foolish,
When I saw the prosperity of the wicked;
For they have more than heart could wish.
Thus my heart was grieved,
So foolish was I, and ignorant.

Nevertheless, I am continually with thee;
Thou hast holden me by my right hand.
Thou shalt guide me with thy counsel.
Whom have I in heaven but thee?
And there is none upon earth that I desire beside thee.
My flesh and my heart faileth,
But God is the strength of my heart, and my portion
forever.
It is good for me to draw near to God;
I have put my trust in the Lord God,
That I may declare all thy works.

THE LORD WILL GIVE GRACE AND GLORY

How amiable are thy tabernacles, O Lord of hosts!
My soul longeth, yea, even fainteth for the courts of the Lord;
My heart and my flesh crieth out for the living God.

Yea, the sparrow hath found an house,
And the swallow a nest for herself, where she may lay her young,
Even thine altars, O Lord of hosts, my king, and my God.

Blessed are they that dwell in thy house;
They will be still praising thee.
Blessed is the man whose strength is in thee.

For a day in thy courts is better than a thousand.
I had rather be a doorkeeper in the house of my God,
Than to dwell in the tents of wickedness.

For the Lord God is a sun and shield:
The Lord will give grace and glory;
No good thing will he withhold from them that walk uprightly.

O Lord of hosts, blessed is the man that trusteth in thee.

TEACH ME THY WAY

Give ear, O Lord, unto my prayer;
And attend to the voice of my supplication.
In the day of my trouble, I will call upon thee,
For thou wilt answer me.

All nations whom thou hast made shall come and worship
before thee, O Lord;
And shall glorify thy name,
For thou are great, and doest wondrous things;
Thou art God alone.

Teach me thy way, O Lord;
I will walk in thy Truth;
Unite my heart to fear thy name;
I will praise thee, O Lord my God, with all my heart,
And I will glorify thy name for evermore.

Great is thy mercy toward me:
For thou hast delivered me from the lowest hell.
Thou, O Lord, art a God full of compassion, and gracious,
Longsuffering, and plenteous in mercy and Truth.

LET THE BEAUTY OF THE LORD OUR GOD BE UPON US

Lord, thou hast been our dwelling place in all generations.
Before the mountains were brought forth,
Or ever thou hadst formed the earth and the world,
Even from everlasting to everlasting, thou art God.
For a thousand years in thy sight are but as yesterday
when it is past,
And as a watch in the night.
Let thy work appear unto thy servants,
And thy glory unto their children.
And let the beauty of the Lord our God be upon us;
And establish thou the work of our hands upon us;
Yea, the work of our hands establish thou it.

GREAT PEACE HAVE THEY WHICH LOVE THY LAW

Open thou mine eyes that I may behold wondrous things
out of thy law.
Give me understanding, and I shall keep thy law;
Yea, I shall observe it with my whole heart.
Thy word is a lamp unto my feet,
And a light unto my path.
Thy righteousness is an everlasting righteousness,
And thy law is the Truth.
Great peace have they which love thy law,
And nothing shall offend them.

STILL WITH THEE

O Lord, thou hast searched me, and known me.
Thou knowest my downsitting and mine uprising;
Thou understandest my thought afar off.
Thou compassest my path and my lying down,
And art acquainted with all my ways.
For there is not a word in my tongue,
But, lo, O Lord, thou knowest it altogether.

Whither shall I go from thy spirit?
Or whither shall I flee from thy presence?
If I ascend up into heaven, thou art there;
If I make my bed in hell, behold, thou art there.
If I take the wings of the morning,
And dwell in the uttermost parts of the sea,
Even there shall thy hand lead me,
And thy right hand shall hold me.
If I say, Surely the darkness shall cover me;
Even the night shall be light about me.
Yea, the darkness hideth not from thee;
But the night shineth as the day;
The darkness and the light are both alike to thee.

I will praise thee; for I am fearfully and wonderfully made;
Marvellous are thy works, and that my soul knoweth right well.
How precious also are thy thoughts unto me, O God!
How great is the sum of them!

If I should count them, they are more in number than the
sand;
When I awake, I am still with thee.
Search me, O God, and know my heart;
Try me, and know my thoughts;
And see if there be any wicked way in me,
And lead me in the way everlasting.

TEACH ME TO DO THY WILL

Hear my prayer, O Lord, give ear to my supplications;
In thy faithfulness answer me, and in thy righteousness.
I stretch forth my hands unto thee;
My soul thirsteth after thee, as a thirsty land.
Cause me to hear thy lovingkindness in the morning;
For in thee do I trust;
Cause me to know the way wherein I should walk;
For I lift up my soul unto thee.
Teach me to do thy will,
For thou art my God; thy spirit is good;
Lead me into the land of uprightness.

PSALMS OF THANKSGIVING

" Serve the Lord with gladness:
Come before His presence with singing,
Be thankful unto Him, and bless His name."

BE THANKFUL UNTO HIM

Make a joyful noise unto the Lord, all ye lands.
Serve the Lord with gladness;
Come before his presence with singing.
Know ye that the Lord, he is God;
It is he that hath made us, and not we ourselves;
We are his people, and the sheep of his pasture.

Enter into his gates with thanksgiving,
And into his courts with praise;
Be thankful unto him, and bless his name.
For the Lord is good;
His mercy is everlasting;
And his Truth endureth to all generations.

IT IS GOOD TO GIVE THANKS

It is a good thing to give thanks unto the Lord,
And to sing praises unto thy name, O most High;
To show forth thy lovingkindness in the morning,
And thy faithfulness every night.

For thou, Lord, hast made me glad through thy works;
I will triumph in the works of thy hands.
O Lord, how great are thy works!
And thy thoughts are very deep.

LET US WORSHIP AND BOW DOWN

O come, let us sing unto the Lord;
Let us make a joyful noise to the rock of our salvation.
Let us come before his presence with thanksgiving,
And make a joyful noise unto him with psalms.

For the Lord is a great God,
And a great King above all gods.
In his hand are the deep places of the earth;
The strength of the hills is his also.

The sea is his, and he made it;
And his hands formed the dry land.
O come, let us worship and bow down;
Let us kneel before the Lord our maker.

LET THE HEART OF THEM REJOICE THAT SEEK THE LORD

O give thanks unto the Lord;
Call upon his name;
Make known his deeds among the people.
Sing unto him, sing psalms unto him;
Talk ye of all his wondrous works.
Glory ye in his holy name;
Let the heart of them rejoice that seek the Lord.
Seek the Lord, and his strength;
Seek his face evermore.

O GIVE THANKS UNTO THE LORD

O give thanks unto the Lord; for he is good;
For his mercy endureth forever.
To him who alone doeth great wonders;
For his mercy endureth forever.
To him that by wisdom made the heavens;
For his mercy endureth forever.
To him that stretched out the earth above the waters;
For his mercy endureth forever.
To him that made great lights;
For his mercy endureth forever.
The sun to rule by day;
For his mercy endureth forever.
The moon and stars to rule by night;
For his mercy endureth forever.
O give thanks unto the God of heaven;
For his mercy endureth forever.

GOD IS THE JUDGE

Unto thee, O God, do we give thanks, unto thee do we give thanks;
For that thy name is near thy wondrous works declare.
For promotion cometh neither from the east, nor from the west, nor from the south;
But God is the judge;
He putteth down one, and setteth up another.

PSALMS OF PROTECTION

"Be still, and know that I am God."

A VERY PRESENT HELP

God is our refuge and strength,
A very present help in trouble.
Therefore will not we fear, though the earth be removed,
And though the mountains be carried into the midst of the sea;
Though the waters thereof roar and be troubled,
Though the mountains shake with the swelling thereof.

There is a river, the streams whereof shall make glad the city of God,
The holy place of the tabernacles of the most High.
God is in the midst of her; she shall not be moved:
God shall help her, and that right early.

The heathen raged, the kingdoms were moved;
He uttered his voice, the earth melted.
The Lord of hosts is with us;
The God of Jacob is our refuge.

Come, behold the works of the Lord,
What desolations he hath made in the earth.
He maketh wars to cease unto the end of the earth;
He breaketh the bow, and cutteth the spear in sunder;
He burneth the chariot in the fire.

"Be still, and know that I am God:
I will be exalted among the heathen,
I will be exalted in the earth."
The Lord of hosts is with us;
The God of Jacob is our refuge.

I WILL NOT BE AFRAID

Lord, how are they increased that trouble me!
Many are they that rise up against me.
Many there be which say of my soul,
There is no help for him in God.
But thou, O Lord, art a shield for me;
My glory, and the lifter up of mine head.

I cried unto the Lord with my voice,
And he heard me out of his holy hill.
I laid me down and slept;
I awaked; for the Lord sustained me.

I will not be afraid of ten thousand of people,
That have set themselves against me round about.
Salvation belongeth unto the Lord;
Thy blessing is upon thy people.

THE RIGHTEOUS LORD LOVETH RIGHTEOUSNESS

In the Lord put I my trust:
How say ye to my soul,
Flee as a bird to your mountain?
For lo, the wicked bend their bow,
They make ready their arrow upon the string,
That they may privily shoot at the upright in heart.
The Lord is in his holy temple,
The Lord's throne is in heaven;
His eyes behold the children of men.
The Lord trieth the righteous:
For the righteous Lord loveth righteousness;
His countenance doth behold the upright.

THE LORD DELIVERETH OUT OF ALL TROUBLES

The righteous cry, and the Lord heareth, and delivereth them out of all their troubles.
The Lord is nigh unto them that are of a broken heart;
And saveth such as be of a contrite spirit.
Many are the afflictions of the righteous;
But the Lord delivereth him out of them all.
He keepeth all his bones;
Not one of them is broken.
Evil shall slay the wicked;
And they that hate the righteous shall be desolate.
The Lord redeemeth the soul of his servants;
And none of them that trust in him shall be desolate.

GOD GIRDETH ME WITH STRENGTH

I will love thee, O Lord, my strength!
The Lord is my rock, and my fortress, and my deliverer,
My God, my strength in whom I will trust,
My buckler, and the horn of my salvation, and my high tower.
I will call upon the Lord, who is worthy to be praised;
So shall I be saved from mine enemies.

The sorrows of death compassed me,
And the floods of ungodly men made me afraid.
In my distress I called upon the Lord, and cried unto my God:
He heard my voice out of his temple,
And my cry came before him, even into his ears.

He sent from above, he took me,
He drew me out of many waters.
He delivered me from my strong enemy,
And from them which hated me:
For they were too strong for me.
He brought me forth also into a large place;
He delivered me, because he delighted in me.

The Lord rewarded me according to my righteousness;
According to the cleanness of my hands hath he recompensed me.
For I have kept the ways of the Lord,
And have not wickedly departed from my God.
For all his judgments were before me,
And I did not put away his statutes from me.

With the merciful thou wilt show thyself merciful;
With the upright man thou wilt show thyself upright;
With the pure thou wilt show thyself pure;
For thou wilt save the afflicted people;
But wilt bring down high looks.
For thou wilt light my candle:
The Lord my God will enlighten my darkness.

As for God, his way is perfect;
The word of the Lord is tried;
He is a buckler to all those that trust in him.
For who is God save the Lord?
Or who is a rock save our God?
It is God that girdeth me with strength,
And maketh my way perfect.
The Lord liveth; and blessed be my rock;
And let the God of my salvation be exalted.

MY HEART SHALL NOT FEAR

The Lord is my light and my salvation;
Whom shall I fear?
The Lord is the strength of my life;
Of whom shall I be afraid?
Though an host should encamp against me,
My heart shall not fear;
Though war should rise against me,
In this will I be confident.

One thing have I desired of the Lord,
That will I seek after;
That I may dwell in the house of the Lord all the days of my life,
To behold the beauty of the Lord,
And to enquire in his temple.

For in the time of trouble he shall hide me in his pavilion;
In the secret of his tabernacle shall he hide me;
He shall set me up upon a rock;
Therefore will I offer in his tabernacle sacrifices of joy.

When thou saidst, Seek ye my face;
My heart said unto thee, thy face, Lord, will I seek.
I had fainted unless I had believed to see the goodness of the Lord in the land of the living.
Wait on the Lord! be of good courage, and he shall strengthen thine heart.
Wait, I say, on the Lord!

I WILL NOT FEAR WHAT FLESH CAN DO UNTO ME

Be merciful unto me, O God,
For man would swallow me up;
He, fighting daily, oppresseth me.

Mine enemies would daily swallow me up,
For they be many that fight against me, O thou most
High.
What time I am afraid, I will trust in thee.

In God I will praise his word;
In God I have put my trust;
I will not fear what flesh can do unto me.

THERE SHALL NO EVIL BEFALL THEE

He that dwelleth in the secret place of the most High
Shall abide under the shadow of the Almighty.
I will say of the Lord, he is my refuge and my fortress,
My God, in him will I trust.
Surely he shall deliver thee from the snare of the fowler,
And from the noisome pestilence.
He shall cover thee with his feathers, and under his wings
shalt thou trust;
His Truth shall be thy shield and buckler.

Thou shalt not be afraid for the terror by night,
Nor for the arrow that flieth by day,
Nor for the pestilence that walketh in darkness,

Nor for the destruction that wasteth at noonday.
A thousand shall fall at thy side, and ten thousand at thy
right hand,
But it shall not come nigh thee.
Only with thine eyes shalt thou behold and see the reward
of the wicked.

Because thou hast made the Lord, which is my refuge,
Even the most High, thy habitation,
There shall no evil befall thee,
Neither shall any plague come nigh thy dwelling.
For he shall give his angels charge over thee,
To keep thee in all thy ways;
They shall bear thee up in their hands,
Lest thou dash thy foot against a stone.
Thou shalt tread upon the lion and adder;
The young lion and the dragon shalt thou trample under
feet.

"Because he hath set his love upon me,
Therefore will I deliver him;
I will set him on high,
Because he hath known my name.
He shall call upon me, and I will answer him;
I will be with him in trouble,
I will deliver him, and honor him.
With long life will I satisfy him,
And show him my salvation."

GOD HATH SPOKEN IN HIS HOLINESS

God hath spoken in his holiness;
I will rejoice.
Wilt not thou, O God, give us help from trouble?
For vain is the help of man.
Through God we shall do valiantly.

THE LORD ON HIGH IS MIGHTIER THAN THE MIGHTY WAVES OF THE SEA

The Lord reigneth, he is clothed with majesty;
The Lord is clothed with strength, wherewith he hath girded himself;
The world also is stablished, that it cannot be moved.
Thy throne is established of old;
Thou art from everlasting.
The floods have lifted up. O Lord,
The floods have lifted up their voice;
The floods lift up their waves.
The Lord on high is mightier than the noise of many waters,
Yea, than the mighty waves of the sea.
Thy testimonies are very sure;
Holiness becometh thine house, O Lord, forever.

THOU HAST BEEN A SHELTER FOR ME

Hear my cry, O God; attend unto my prayer.
From the end of the earth will I cry unto thee,
When my heart is overwhelmed;
Lead me to the rock that is higher than I,
For thou hast been a shelter for me,
And a strong tower from the enemy.
I will abide in thy tabernacle for ever;
I will trust in the covert of thy wings.
I will sing praise unto thy name for ever.

HIDE ME FROM THE SECRET COUNSEL OF THE WICKED

Hear my voice, O God, in my prayer:
Preserve my life from fear of the enemy.
Hide me from the secret counsel of the wicked;
From the insurrection of the workers of iniquity,
Who whet their tongue like a sword,
And bend their bows to shoot their arrows, even bitter words,
That they may shoot in secret at the perfect;
Suddenly do they shoot, and fear not.
They encourage themselves in an evil matter;
They commune of laying snares privily;
They say, Who shall see them?
They search out iniquities;
They accomplish a diligent search;

Both the inward thought of every one of them, and the
heart, is deep.
So they shall make their own tongue to fall upon
themselves;
All that see them shall flee away.
And all men shall fear, and shall declare the work of God;
For they shall wisely consider of his doing.
The righteous shall be glad in the Lord, and shall trust in
him;
And all the upright in heart shall glory.

HE THAT KEEPETH THEE WILL NOT SLUMBER

I will lift up mine eyes unto the hills,
From whence cometh my help.
My help cometh from the Lord,
Which made heaven and earth.
He will not suffer thy foot to be moved;
He that keepeth thee will not slumber.
Behold, he that keepeth Israel shall neither slumber nor
sleep.
The Lord is thy keeper;
The Lord is thy shade upon thy right hand.
The sun shall not smite thee by day,
Nor the moon by night.
The Lord shall preserve thee from all evil;
He shall preserve thy soul.
The Lord shall preserve thy going out and thy coming in
From this time forth, and even for evermore.

THEY THAT TRUST IN THE LORD

They that trust in the Lord shall be as mount Zion,
Which cannot be removed, but abideth for ever.
As the mountains are round about Jerusalem,
So the Lord is round about his people from henceforth
even forever.
Do good, O Lord, unto those that be good,
And to them that are upright in their hearts.
As for such as turn aside unto their crooked ways,
The Lord shall lead them forth with the workers of
iniquity;
But peace shall be upon Israel.

EXCEPT THE LORD BUILD THE HOUSE

Except the Lord build the house,
They labour in vain that build it;
Except the Lord keep the city,
The watchman waketh but in vain.

THE LORD WILL PERFECT THAT WHICH CONCERNETH ME

I will praise thee with my whole heart;
I will worship toward thy holy temple,
And praise thy name for thy lovingkindness and for
thy Truth;
For thou hast magnified thy word above all thy name.
In the day when I cried, thou answeredst me,
And strengthened me with strength in my soul.
Though I walk in the midst of trouble,
Thou wilt revive me.
Thou shalt stretch forth thine hand,
And thy right hand shall save me.
The Lord will perfect that which concerneth me;
Thy mercy, O Lord, endureth for ever:
Forsake not the works of thine own hands.

THE EARTH IS THE LORD'S

The earth is the Lord's and the fullness thereof;
The world, and all they that dwell therein.
For he hath founded it upon the seas,
And established it upon the floods.

Lift up your heads, O ye gates!
Even lift them up ye everlasting doors!
And the King of glory shall come in.
Who is this King of glory?
The Lord of hosts,
He is the King of glory.

PSALMS OF FORGIVENESS

" Create in me a clean heart, O God;
And renew a right spirit within me."

ACCORDING TO THY MERCY REMEMBER THOU ME

Unto thee, O Lord, do I lift up my soul.
O my God, I trust in thee!
Show me thy ways, O Lord;
Teach me thy paths.
Lead me in thy Truth, and teach me,
For thou art the God of my salvation,
On thee do I wait all the day.

Remember, O Lord, thy tender mercies and thy
loving kindnesses;
For they have been ever of old.
Remember not the sins of my youth, nor my
transgressions;
According to thy mercy remember thou me for thy
goodness sake, O Lord.
Good and upright is the Lord,
Therefore he will teach sinners in the way;
The meek will he guide in judgment,
And the meek will he teach his way.
All the paths of the Lord are mercy and Truth
Unto such as keep his covenant and his testimonies.

For thy name's sake, O Lord,
Pardon mine iniquity, for it is great.
Mine eyes are ever toward the Lord,
For he shall pluck my feet out of the net.
Let integrity and uprightness preserve me,
For I wait on thee.

THOU FORGAVEST MY SIN

Blessed is he whose transgression is forgiven,
Whose sin is covered.
Blessed is the man unto whom the Lord imputeth not
iniquity,
And in whose spirit there is no guile.

I acknowledged my sin unto thee,
And mine iniquity have I not hid.
I said, I will confess my transgression unto the Lord,
And thou forgavest the iniquity of my sin.

Thou art my hiding place; thou shalt preserve me from
trouble;
Thou shalt compass me about with songs of deliverance.
Be ye not as the horse, or as the mule, which have no
understanding,
Whose mouth must be held in with bit and bridle.

Many sorrows shall be to the wicked;
But he that trusteth in the Lord, mercy shall compass him
about.
Be glad in the Lord, and rejoice, ye righteous;
And shout for joy, all ye that are upright in heart.

THE SACRIFICES OF GOD ARE A BROKEN AND A CONTRITE HEART

Have mercy upon me, O God, according to thy
lovingkindness;
According unto the multitude of thy tender mercies
blot out my transgressions.
Wash me throughly from mine iniquity,
And cleanse me from my sin.

For I acknowledge my transgressions;
And my sin is ever before me.
Behold, thou desirest Truth in the inward parts;
And in the inward part thou shalt make me to know
wisdom.

Purge me with hyssop, and I shall be clean;
Wash me, and I shall be whiter than snow.
Hide thy face from my sins,
And blot out all mine iniquities.

Create in me a clean heart, O God;
And renew a right spirit within me.
Cast me not away from thy presence,
And take not thy holy spirit from me.

Restore unto me the joy of thy salvation;
And uphold me with thy free spirit.
O Lord, open thou my lips,
And my mouth shall show forth thy praise.

For thou desirest not sacrifice, else would I give it;
Thou delightest not in burnt offering.
The sacrifices of God are a broken spirit;
A broken and a contrite heart, O God, thou wilt not
despise.

HOPE THOU IN GOD

As the hart panteth after the water brooks,
So panteth my soul after thee, O God.
My soul thirsteth for God, for the living God;
When shall I come and appear before God?

My tears have been my meat day and night,
While they continually say unto me, Where is thy God?
Deep calleth unto deep at the noise of thy waterspouts;
All thy waves and thy billows are gone over me.

Yet the Lord will command his lovingkindness in the
daytime,
And in the night, his song shall be with me,
And my prayer unto the God of my life.

Why art thou cast down, O my soul?
And why art thou disquieted within me?
Hope thou in God!
For I shall yet praise him, who is the health of my
countenance, and my God.

THOU ART HOLY

My God, my God, why hast thou forsaken me?
Why art thou so far from helping me,
And from the words of my roaring?
O my God, I cry in the daytime, but thou hearest not;
And in the night season, and am not silent.

But thou art holy;
Our fathers trusted in thee;
They trusted, and Thou didst deliver them.
They cried unto thee, and were delivered;
They trusted in thee, and were not confounded.

All the ends of the world shall remember and turn unto the Lord;
And all the kindreds of the nations shall worship before thee.
For the kingdom is the Lord's,
And he is the governor among the nations.
They shall come, and shall declare his righteousness
Unto a people that shall be born.

IN THE SHADOW OF THY WINGS WILL I MAKE MY REFUGE

Be merciful unto me, O God, be merciful unto me!
For my soul trusteth in thee;
Yea, in the shadow of thy wings will I make my refuge,
Until these calamities be overpast.
I will cry unto God most high;
Unto God that performeth all things for me.
God shall send forth his mercy and his Truth.

Be thou exalted, O God, above the heavens;
Let thy glory be above all the earth.
For thy mercy is great unto the heavens,
And thy Truth unto the clouds.
Be thou exalted, O God, above the heavens;
Let thy glory be above all the earth.

GOD HATH SHOWED US LIGHT

I called upon the Lord in distress;
The Lord answered me, and set me in a large place.
The Lord is on my side; I will not fear;
What can man do unto me?
It is better to trust in the Lord
Than to put confidence in man.
The Lord is my strength and song,
And is become my salvation.
I shall not die, but live,
And declare the works of the Lord.

The Lord hath chastened me sore,
But he hath not given me over unto death.
Open to me the gates of righteousness:
I will go into them, and I will praise the Lord.
God is the Lord, which hath showed us light.
O give thanks unto the Lord, for he is good:
For his mercy endureth forever.

IN THE MULTITUDE OF THY MERCY HEAR ME

Save me, O God!
For the waters are come in unto my soul.
I sink in the deep mire, where there is no standing;
I am come into deep waters, where the floods overflow me.
I am weary of my crying; my throat is dried;
Mine eyes fail while I wait for my God.
O God, thou knowest my foolishness;
And my sins are not hid from thee.

But as for me, my prayer is unto thee, O Lord, in an acceptable time;
O God, in the multitude of thy mercy hear me,
In the truth of thy salvation.
Deliver me out of the mire, and let me not sink;
Let me be delivered from them that hate me, and out of the deep waters.
Let not the waterflood overflow me,
Neither let the deep swallow me up,
And let not the pit shut her mouth upon me.

Hear me, O Lord, for thy lovingkindness is good;
Turn unto me according to the multitude of thy tender mercies,

And hide not thy face from thy servant, for I am in
trouble.
Let thy salvation, O God, set me on high.
I will praise the name of God with a song,
And will magnify him with thanksgiving.

WHEREWITHAL SHALL A YOUNG MAN CLEANSE HIS WAY?

Wherewithal shall a young man cleanse his way?
By taking heed thereto according to thy word.
With my whole heart have I sought Thee;
O let me not wander from thy commandments.
Thy word have I hid in mine heart,
That I might not sin against thee.
Open thou mine eyes,
That I may behold wondrous things out of thy law.

Teach me good judgment and knowledge,
For I have believed thy commandments.
Before I was afflicted, I went astray;
But now have I kept thy word.
Thou art good, and doest good; teach me thy statutes.
The law of thy mouth is better unto me than thousands
of gold and silver.
Unless thy law had been my delight,
I should have perished in mine affliction.

O how love I thy law!
It is my meditation all the day.

THEY SHALL REAP IN JOY

They that sow in tears shall reap in joy.
He that goeth forth and weepeth,
Bearing precious seed,
Shall doubtless come again with rejoicing,
Bringing his sheaves with him.

THERE IS FORGIVENESS WITH THEE

Out of the depths have I cried unto thee, O Lord.
Lord, hear my voice;
Let thine ears be attentive to the voice of my
  supplications.
If thou, Lord, shouldest mark iniquities,
O Lord, who shall stand?
But there is forgiveness with thee,
That thou mayest be feared.

I wait for the Lord, my soul doth wait,
And in his word do I hope.
My soul waiteth for the Lord more than they that watch
  for the morning;
I say, more than they that watch for the morning.
For with the Lord there is mercy,
And with him is plenteous redemption.

PSALMS OF PRAISE

" Oh that men would praise the Lord for His goodness,
And for His wonderful works to the children of men."

WORSHIP IN THE BEAUTY OF HOLINESS

Give unto the Lord, O ye mighty,
Give unto the Lord glory and strength.
Give unto the Lord the glory due unto his name;
Worship the Lord in the beauty of holiness.
The Lord will give strength unto his people;
The Lord will bless his people with peace.

GOD A REFUGE

Great is the Lord, and greatly to be praised in the city
of our God,
In the mountain of his holiness.
Beautiful for situation, the joy of the whole earth, is
mount Zion,
On the sides of the north, the city of the great King.
God is known in her palaces for a refuge.

We have thought of thy lovingkindness, O God,
In the midst of thy temple.
According to thy name, O God,
So is thy praise unto the ends of the earth;
Thy right hand is full of righteousness.
For this God is our God for ever and ever.

THE LORD SHALL ENDURE FOREVER

I will praise thee, O Lord, with my whole heart;
I will show forth all thy marvellous works.
I will be glad and rejoice in thee;
I will praise thy name, O thou most High.

The Lord shall endure forever;
He hath prepared his throne for judgment.
And he shall judge the world in righteousness;
He shall minister judgment to the people in uprightness.

The Lord also will be a refuge for the oppressed,
A refuge in times of trouble.
And they that know thy name will put their trust in thee,
For thou, Lord, hast not forsaken them that seek thee.

Sing praises to the Lord, which dwelleth in Zion;
Declare among the people his doings.
The Lord is known by the judgments which he executeth;
The wicked is snared in the work of his own hands.

WHOSO OFFERETH PRAISE GLORIFIETH ME

The mighty God, even the Lord, hath spoken,
And called the earth from the rising of the sun unto the going down thereof.
Out of Zion, the perfection of beauty,
God hath shined.

Our God shall come, and shall not keep silence:
A fire shall devour before him.
And the heavens shall declare his righteousness,
For God is judge himself.

Offer unto God thanksgiving,
And pay thy vows unto the most High.
And call upon me in the day of trouble;
I will deliver thee, and thou shalt glorify me.

Whoso offereth praise glorifieth me;
And to him that ordereth his conversation aright
Will I show the salvation of God.

CAUSE THY FACE TO SHINE UPON US

God be merciful unto us, and bless us;
And cause thy face to shine upon us,
That thy way may be known upon earth,
Thy saving health among all nations.

Let the people praise thee, O God;
Let all the people praise thee.
O let the nations be glad and sing for joy,
For thou shalt judge the people righteously, and govern
the nations upon earth.

Let the people praise thee, O God;
Let all the people praise thee.
Then shall the earth yield her increase;
And God, even our God, shall bless us.

BE THOU EXALTED

O God, my heart is fixed;
I will sing and give praise, even with my glory.
Awake, psaltery and harp;
I myself will awake early.

I will praise thee, O Lord, among the people;
And I will sing praises unto thee among the nations.
For thy mercy is great above the heavens,
And thy Truth reacheth unto the clouds.

Be thou exalted, O God, above the heavens;
And thy glory above all the earth.
Give us help from trouble, for vain is the help of man.
Through God we shall do valiantly,
For it is he that shall tread down our enemies.

THOU ART CLOTHED WITH HONOUR AND MAJESTY

Bless the Lord, O my soul!
O Lord my God, thou art very great;
Thou art clothed with honour and majesty.
Who coverest thyself with light as with a garment;
Who stretchest out the heavens like a curtain;
Who layeth the beams of his chambers in the waters;
Who maketh the clouds his chariot;
Who walketh upon the wings of the wind;
Who laid the foundations of the earth,
That it should not be removed for ever.
He watereth the hills from his chambers;
The earth is satisfied with the fruit of thy works.
He causeth the grass to grow for the cattle,
And herb for the service of man;
That he may bring forth food out of the earth.

O Lord, how manifold are thy works!
In wisdom hast thou made them all;
The earth is full of thy riches.
Thou sendest forth thy Spirit, they are created;
And thou renewest the face of the earth.
The glory of the Lord shall endure for ever;
The Lord shall rejoice in his works.
I will sing unto the Lord as long as I live;
I will sing praise to my God while I have my being.
My meditation of him shall be sweet;
I will be glad in the Lord.
Bless thou the Lord, O my soul.
Praise ye the Lord.

HOLY AND REVEREND IS HIS NAME

I will praise the Lord with my whole heart,
In the assembly of the upright, and in the congregation.
The works of the Lord are great,
Sought out of all them that have pleasure therein.

His work is honourable and glorious:
And his righteousness endureth for ever.
He hath made his wonderful works to be remembered:
The Lord is gracious and full of compassion.

The works of his hands are verity and judgment;
All his commandments are sure.
They stand fast for ever and ever,
And are done in Truth and uprightness.

Holy and reverend is his name:
The fear of the Lord is the beginning of wisdom:
A good understanding have all they that do his
commandments;
His praise endureth for ever.

THE LOVINGKINDNESS OF THE LORD

O give thanks unto the Lord, for he is good!
For his mercy endureth for ever.
Let the redeemed of the Lord say so,
Whom he hath redeemed from the hand of the enemy;
And gathered them out of the lands,
From the east, and from the west, from the north,
  and from the south.
They wandered in the wilderness in a solitary way;
They found no city to dwell in.
Hungry and thirsty, their soul fainted in them.
Then they cried unto the Lord in their trouble,
And he delivered them out of their distresses.
He led them forth by the right way,
That they might go to a city of habitation.
Oh that men would praise the Lord for his goodness,
And for his wonderful works to the children of men!

For he satisfieth the longing soul,
And filleth the hungry soul with goodness.
Such as sit in darkness and in the shadow of death,
Being bound in affliction and iron,
Because they rebelled against the words of God,
And contemned the counsel of the most High,
They fell down, and there was none to help.
Then they cried unto the Lord in their trouble,
And he saved them out of their distresses.
He brought them out of darkness and the shadow of death,
And brake their bands in sunder.
Oh that men would praise the Lord for his goodness,
And for his wonderful works to the children of men!

For he hath broken the gates of brass,
And cut the bars of iron in sunder.
Fools because of their transgression,
And because of their iniquities, are afflicted,
And they draw near unto the gates of death.
Then they cry unto the Lord in their trouble,
And he saveth them out of their distresses.
He sent his word, and healed them,
And delivered them from their destructions.
Oh that men would praise the Lord for his goodness,
And for his wonderful works to the children of men!

They that go down to the sea in ships,
That do business in great waters,
They see the works of the Lord,
And his wonders in the deep.
For he commandeth, and raiseth the stormy wind,
Which lifteth up the waves thereof.
They mount up to the heaven,
They go down again to the depths,
Their soul is melted because of trouble.
Then they cry unto the Lord in their trouble,
And he bringeth them out of their distresses.
He maketh the storm a calm,
So that the waves thereof are still.
Then are they glad because they be quiet;
So he bringeth them unto their desired haven.
Oh that men would praise the Lord for his goodness,
And for his wonderful works to the children of men!

He turneth the wilderness into a standing water,
And dry ground into watersprings.
And there he maketh the hungry to dwell,
That they may prepare a city of habitation,

And sow the fields, and plant vineyards,
Which may yield fruits of increase.
He blesseth them also, so that they are multiplied greatly,
And suffereth not their cattle to decrease.
The righteous shall see it and rejoice;
And all iniquity shall stop her mouth.
Who is wise, and will observe these things,
Even they shall understand the lovingkindness of the Lord.

LET THE WHOLE EARTH BE FILLED WITH HIS GLORY

Blessed be the Lord God, the God of Israel,
Who only doeth wondrous things.
All nations shall call him blessed.
And blessed be his glorious name for ever;
And let the whole earth be filled with his glory.

THE LORD IS ABOVE ALL

Praise the Lord, for the Lord is good!
Sing praises unto his name, for it is pleasant.
For I know that the Lord is great,
And that our Lord is above all gods.
Whatsoever the Lord pleased,
That did he in Heaven, and in earth,
In the seas, and all deep places.
He caused the vapours to ascend from the ends of the earth;
He maketh lightnings for the rain;
He bringeth the wind out of his treasuries.
Thy name, O Lord, endureth for ever;
And thy memorial, O Lord, throughout all generations.

The idols of the heathen are silver and gold,
The work of men's hands.
They have mouths, but they speak not;
Eyes have they, but they see not;
They have ears, but they hear not;
Neither is there any breath in their mouths.
They that make them are like unto them;
So is every one that trusteth in them.
Praise ye the Lord.

HIS UNDERSTANDING IS INFINITE

Praise ye the Lord!
For it is good to sing praises unto our God,
For it is pleasant, and praise is comely.

He healeth the broken in heart, and bindeth up their
wounds.
He telleth the number of the stars;
He calleth them all by their names.
Great is our Lord, and of great power;
His understanding is infinite.

The Lord lifteth up the meek,
He casteth the wicked down to the ground.
Sing unto the Lord with thanksgiving;
Sing praise upon the harp unto our God
Who covereth the heaven with clouds,
Who prepareth rain for the earth,
Who maketh grass to grow upon the mountains.

The Lord taketh pleasure in them that fear him,
In those that hope in his mercy.
Praise the Lord, O Jerusalem!
Praise thy God, O Zion.

THY KINGDOM IS EVERLASTING

I will extol thee, my God, O King;
And I will bless thy name for ever and ever.
Every day will I bless thee;
And I will praise thy name for ever and ever.
Great is the Lord, and greatly to be praised:
And his greatness is unsearchable.
One generation shall praise thy works to another,
And shall declare thy mighty acts.
I will speak of the glorious honour of thy majesty,
And of thy wondrous works.

The Lord is gracious, and full of compassion;
Slow to anger, and of great mercy.
The Lord is good to all,
And his tender mercies are over all his works.
All thy works shall praise thee, O Lord,
And thy saints shall bless thee.
They shall speak of the glory of thy kingdom,
And talk of thy power:
To make known to the sons of men his mighty acts,
And the glorious majesty of his kingdom,
Thy kingdom is an everlasting kingdom,
And thy dominion endureth throughout all generations.

The Lord upholdeth all that fall,
And raiseth up all those that be bowed down.
The eyes of all wait upon thee;
And thou givest them their meat in due season.
Thou openest thine hand,
And satisfiest the desire of every living thing.

The Lord is righteous in all his ways,
And holy in all his works.
The Lord is nigh unto all them that call upon him,
To all that call upon him in Truth.
He will fulfil the desire of them that fear him;
He also will hear their cry, and will save them.
The Lord preserveth all them that love him.

SING UNTO THE LORD A NEW SONG

Praise ye the Lord;
Sing unto the Lord a new song,
And his praise in the congregation of saints.
Let Israel rejoice in him that made him;
Let the children of Zion be joyful in their King.
For the Lord taketh pleasure in his people;
He will beautify the meek with salvation.
Let the high praises of God be in their mouth,
And a twoedged sword in their hand.

THE LORD SHALL REIGN FOREVER

Praise ye the Lord!
Praise the Lord, O my soul!
While I live will I praise the Lord;
I will sing praise unto my God while I have my being.

Put not your trust in princes, nor in the son of man,
In whom there is no help.
Happy is he that hath the God of Jacob for his help,
Whose hope is in the Lord his God:
Which made heaven, and earth, the sea, and all that therein is;
Which keepeth Truth for ever;
Which executeth judgment for the oppressed;
Which giveth food to the hungry.
The Lord looseth the prisoners;
The Lord openeth the eyes of the blind;
The Lord raiseth them that are bowed down;
The Lord loveth the righteous.
The Lord preserveth the strangers;
He relieveth the fatherless and widow;
But the way of the wicked he turneth upside down.

The Lord shall reign for ever,
Even thy God, O Zion unto all generations.
Praise ye the Lord.

HIS NAME ALONE IS EXCELLENT

Praise ye the Lord!

Praise ye the Lord from the heavens;
Praise him in the heights.
Praise ye him, all his angels;
Praise ye him, all his hosts.
Praise ye him, sun and moon;
Praise him, all ye stars of light.
Praise him, ye heavens of heavens,
And ye waters that be above the heavens.
Let them praise the name of the Lord.

For he commanded, and they were created.
He hath also established them for ever and ever;
He hath made a decree which shall not pass.
Praise the Lord from the earth:
Kings of the earth, and all people,
Princes, and all judges of the earth;
Both young men, and maidens,
Old men and children;
Let them praise the name of the Lord,
For his name alone is excellent;
His glory is above the earth and heaven.

Praise ye the Lord.

" A wise man
will hear, and will increase learning:
and a man of understanding shall attain
unto wise counsels."

THE PROVERBS OF SOLOMON,
The son of David, King of Israel.

HAPPY IS THE MAN THAT FINDETH WISDOM

Happy is the man that findeth wisdom,
And the man that getteth understanding.
For the merchandise of it is better than the merchandise
of silver,
And the gain thereof than fine gold.
She is more precious than rubies,
And all the things thou canst desire are not to be
compared unto her.
Length of days is in her right hand,
And in her left hand riches and honor.
Her ways are ways of pleasantness,
And all her paths are peace.
She is a tree of life to them that lay hold upon her,
And happy is every one that retaineth her.
The Lord by wisdom hath founded the earth;
By understanding hath he established the heavens;
By his knowledge the depths are broken up,
And the clouds drop down dew.

WISDOM IS BETTER THAN RUBIES

Doth not wisdom cry?
And understanding put forth her voice?
She standeth in the top of high places,
By the way in the places of the paths.
She crieth at the gates, at the entry of the city,
At the coming in at the doors.

" Unto you, O men, I call;
And my voice is to the sons of man.
O ye simple, understand wisdom:
And, ye fools, be ye of an understanding heart.
Hear; for I will speak of excellent things;
And the opening of my lips shall be right things.
For my mouth shall speak Truth;
And wickedness is an abomination to my lips.
All the words of my mouth are in righteousness;
There is nothing froward or perverse in them.
They are all plain to him that understandeth,
And right to them that find knowledge.
Receive my instruction, and not silver;
And knowledge rather than choice gold.
For wisdom is better than rubies,
And all the things that may be desired are not to be
compared to it."

WHOSO FINDETH ME FINDETH LIFE

I Wisdom dwell with prudence;
Counsel is mine, and sound wisdom;
I am understanding;
I have strength.
I love them that love me,
And those that seek me early shall find me.
Riches and honour are with me;
Yea, durable riches and righteousness.
My fruit is better than gold,
Yea, than fine gold,
And my revenue than choice silver.
I lead in the way of righteousness,
In the midst of the paths of judgment,
That I may cause those that love me to inherit substance,
And I will fill their treasures.

The Lord possessed me in the beginning of his way,
Before his works of old.
I was set up from everlasting, from the beginning, or
ever the earth was.
When there were no depths, I was brought forth,
Before the mountains were settled,
Before the hills was I brought forth.
While as yet he had not made the earth, nor the fields,
Nor the highest part of the dust of the world.
When he prepared the heavens, I was there.
When he set a compass upon the face of the depth;
When he established the clouds above;
When he strengthened the fountains of the deep;
When he gave to the sea his decree,

That the waters should not pass his commandment;
When he appointed the foundations of the earth;
Then I was by him, as one brought up with him,
And I was daily his delight,
Rejoicing always before him,
Rejoicing in the habitable part of his earth,
And my delights were with the sons of men.

Now therefore hearken unto me, O ye children:
For blessed are they that keep my ways.
Hear instruction, and be wise, and refuse it not.
Blessed is the man that heareth me,
Watching daily at my gates,
Waiting at the posts of my doors.
For whoso findeth me findeth life,
And shall obtain favour of the Lord.

TURN YOU AT MY REPROOF

Wisdom crieth without;
She uttereth her voice in the streets;
She crieth in the chief place of concourse,
In the openings of the gates,
In the city she uttereth her words, saying,
" How long, ye simple ones,
Will ye love simplicity?
And the scorners delight in their scorning,
And fools hate knowledge?
Turn you at my reproof!
Behold, I will pour out my spirit unto you,
I will make known my words unto you.
Because I have called, and ye refused,
I have stretched out my hand, and no man regarded.
But ye have set at nought all my counsel,
And would none of my reproof;
When your fear cometh as desolation,
And your destruction cometh as a whirlwind,
When distress and anguish cometh upon you,
Then shall they call upon me,
But I will not answer.
They shall seek me early,
But they shall not find me.
For that they hated knowledge,
And did not choose the fear of the Lord;
They would none of my counsel;
They despised all my reproof;
Therefore shall they eat of the fruit of their own way,
And be filled with their own devices.
For the turning away of the simple shall slay them,
And the prosperity of fools shall destroy them.
But whoso hearkeneth unto me shall dwell safely,
And shall be quiet from the fear of evil."

UNDERSTANDING SHALL KEEP THEE

When wisdom entereth into thine heart,
And knowledge is pleasant unto thy soul,
Discretion shall preserve thee,
Understanding shall keep thee;
To deliver thee from the way of the evil man,
From the man that speaketh froward things,
That thou mayest walk in the way of good men,
And keep the paths of the righteous.
For the upright shall dwell in the land,
And the perfect shall remain in it.
But the wicked shall be cut off from the earth,
And the transgressors shall be rooted out of it.

ON WISDOM

The fear of the Lord is the beginning of wisdom:
And the knowledge of the holy is understanding.

When wisdom entereth into thine heart,
And knowledge is pleasant unto thy soul,
Discretion shall preserve thee,
Understanding shall keep thee.
Wisdom resteth in the heart of him that hath understanding.

Wisdom is the principal thing; therefore get wisdom:
And with all thy getting get understanding.

Wisdom is better than rubies;
And all things that may be desired are not to be compared
to it.

How much better is it to get wisdom than gold:
And to get understanding rather to be chosen than silver.

He that getteth wisdom loveth his own soul;
He that keepeth understanding shall find good.

There is no wisdom nor understanding nor counsel
against the Lord.

ON KNOWLEDGE

The heart of the prudent getteth knowledge;
And the ear of the wise seeketh knowledge.

The hearing ear,
And the seeing eye,
The Lord hath made even both of them.

Apply thine heart unto instruction,
And thine ears to the words of knowledge.

Bow down thine ear,
And hear the words of the wise,
And apply thine heart unto my knowledge.

There is gold, and a multitude of rubies;
But the lips of knowledge are a precious jewel.

A scorner seeketh wisdom, and findeth it not;
But knowledge is easy unto him that understandeth.

The eyes of the Lord preserve knowledge,
And he overthroweth the words of the transgressor.

ON LAW

Where there is no vision, the people perish;
But he that keepeth the law, happy is he.

For the commandment is a lamp,
And the law is light;
And reproofs of instruction are the way of life.

He that keepeth the commandment
Keepeth his own soul.

He that turneth away his ear from hearing the law,
Even his prayer shall be an abomination.

There are many devices in a man's heart;
Nevertheless the counsel of the Lord,
That shall stand.

FORGET NOT MY LAW

My son, forget not my law,
But let thine heart keep my commandments;
For length of days, and long life, and peace,
Shall they add to thee.
Let not mercy and truth forsake thee;
Bind them about thy neck;
Write them upon the table of thine heart;
So shalt thou find favour and good understanding
In the sight of God and man.

ON TRUSTING GOD

Every word of God is pure:
He is a shield unto them that put their trust in him.

The name of the Lord is a strong tower:
The righteous runneth into it, and is safe.

Trust in the Lord with all thine heart,
And lean not unto thine own understanding.
In all thy ways acknowledge him,
And he shall direct thy paths.
Be not wise in thine own eyes;
Fear the Lord, and depart from evil.

ON STRENGTH

If thou faint in the day of adversity
Thy strength is small.

A wise man is strong:
Yea, a man of knowledge increaseth strength.

THE LOVE OF THE LORD

Honor the Lord with thy substance,
And with the first fruits of all thine increase;
So shall thy barns be filled with plenty,
And thy presses shall burst out with new wine.

The fear of the Lord tendeth to life;
And he that hath it shall abide satisfied;
He shall not be visited with evil.

The fear of the Lord is the beginning of knowledge:
But fools despise wisdom and instruction.

The fear of the Lord is to hate evil.

In the fear of the Lord is strong confidence;
And his children shall have a place of refuge.

The fear of the Lord is a fountain of life,
To depart from the snares of death.

ON JUSTICE

To do justice and judgment
Is more acceptable to the Lord than sacrifice.

The path of the just is as the shining light,
That shineth more and more unto the perfect day.

It is joy to the just to do judgment.

ON MERCY

By mercy and Truth iniquity is purged:
And by the fear of the Lord men depart from evil.

The merciful man doeth good to his own soul:
But he that is cruel troubleth his own flesh.

Mercy and Truth preserve the king;
And his throne is upholden by mercy.

He that followeth after righteousness and mercy
Findeth life, righteousness, and honor.

ON VENGEANCE

Say not thou, "I will recompense evil;"
But wait on the Lord, and he shall save thee.

Rejoice not when thine enemy falleth,
And let not thine heart be glad when he stumbleth.

If thine enemy be hungry, give him bread to eat;
And if he be thirsty, give him water to drink;
For thou shalt heap coals of fire upon his head,
And the Lord shall reward thee.

ON HUMILITY

By humility and the fear of the Lord
Are riches, and honor, and life.

The fear of the Lord is the instruction of Wisdom,
And before honor is humility.

All the ways of a man are clean in his own eyes:
But the Lord weigheth the spirits.

Let another man praise thee,
And not thine own mouth,
A stranger, and not thine own lips.

Before destruction the heart of man is haughty,
And before honor is humility.

ON PRIDE

When pride cometh, then cometh shame;
But with the lowly is wisdom.

Pride goeth before destruction,
And a haughty spirit before a fall.

He that is of a proud heart stirreth up strife.

A man's pride shall bring him low;
But honor shall uphold the humble in spirit.

ON TRUTH

The lips of Truth shall be established for ever.

He that speaketh truth showeth forth righteousness:
But a false witness deceit.

A faithful witness will not lie:
But a false witness will utter lies.

A true witness delivereth souls:
But a deceitful witness speaketh lies.

Let not mercy and Truth forsake thee:
So shalt thou find favour and good understanding in the sight of God and man.

THE LIAR

A lying tongue is but for a moment.

A false witness shall not be unpunished,
And he that speaketh lies shall not escape.

Deceit is in the heart of them that imagine evil.

A wicked doer giveth heed to false lips,
And a liar giveth ear to a naughty tongue.

THE WAY

THOU SHALT WALK IN THE WAY SAFELY

Let not understanding depart from before thine eyes:
Keep sound wisdom and discretion,
So shall they be life unto thy soul,
And grace to thy neck.
Then shalt thou walk in the way safely,
And thy foot shall not stumble.
When thou liest down, thou shalt not be afraid;
Yea, thou shalt lie down, and thy sleep shall be sweet.
Be not afraid of sudden fear,
Neither of the desolation of the wicked, when it cometh;
For the Lord shall be thy confidence,
And shall keep thy foot from being taken.

The Lord loveth him that followeth after righteousness.

Good understanding giveth favour;
But the way of transgressors is hard.

The way of the wicked is as darkness:
They know not at what they stumble.

He that walketh uprightly, walketh surely.
Forsake the foolish, and live;
And go in the way of understanding.

The highway of the upright is to depart from evil;
He that keepeth his way preserveth his soul.

The just man walketh in his integrity;
And his children are blessed after him.

When a man's ways please the Lord,
He maketh even his enemies to be at peace with him.

Folly is joy to him that is destitute of wisdom:
But a man of understanding walketh uprightly.

Even a child is known by his doings,
Whether his work is pure,
And whether it be right.

The way of life is above to the wise;
That he may depart from hell beneath.

Whoso walketh uprightly shall be saved:
But he that is perverse in his ways shall fall at once.

Every way of a man is right in his own eyes:
But the Lord pondereth the hearts.

A man's heart deviseth his way:
But the Lord directeth his steps.

The man that wandereth out of the way of understanding
Shall remain in the congregation of the dead.

THE WISE MAN

Give instruction to a wise man, and he will be yet wiser:
Teach a just man, and he will increase in learning.

The wise in heart shall be called prudent;
And the sweetness of the lips increaseth learning.

Hear counsel, and receive instruction,
That thou mayest be wise in thy latter end.

There is treasure to be desired
And oil in the dwelling of the wise:
But a foolish man spendeth it up.

The wise man feareth and departeth from evil:
But a fool rageth, and is confident.

The simple believeth every word:
But the prudent man looketh well to his going.

He that walketh with wise men shall be wise;
But a companion of fools shall be destroyed.

The way of a fool is right in his own eyes:
But he that hearkeneth unto counsel is wise.

The heart of the wise teacheth his mouth,
And addeth learning to his lips.

THE FOOLISH MAN

Speak not in the ears of a fool,
For he will despise the wisdom of thy words.

The heart of him that hath understanding seeketh
knowledge:
But the mouth of fools feedeth on foolishness.

Answer not a fool according to his folly,
Lest thou also be like unto him.

Answer a fool according to his folly,
Lest he be wise in his own eyes.

It is an honor for a man to cease from strife:
But every fool will be meddling.

Every prudent man dealeth with knowledge:
But a fool layeth open his folly.

A fool uttereth all his mind:
But a wise man keepeth it till afterwards.

Seest thou a man wise in his own conceit?
There is more hope of a fool than of him.

As snow in summer, and as rain in harvest,
So honor is not seemly for a fool.

The heart of fools proclaimeth foolishness.

The fear of the Lord is the beginning of knowledge:
But fools despise wisdom and instruction.

THE RIGHT THINKER

As a man thinketh in his heart so is he.

Commit thy works unto the Lord,
And thy thoughts shall be established.

In the way of righteousness is life,
And in the pathway thereof there is no death.

As righteousness tendeth to life,
So he that pursueth evil pursueth it to his own death.

The treasures of wickedness profit nothing,
But righteousness delivereth from death.

The integrity of the upright shall guide them,
But the perverseness of transgressors shall destroy them.

When the righteous are in authority, the people rejoice,
But when the wicked beareth rule, the people mourn.

The fear of the wicked, it shall come upon him;
But the desire of the righteous shall be granted.

The righteous shall never be removed,
But the wicked shall not inhabit the earth.

The light of the righteous rejoiceth;
But the lamp of the wicked shall be put out.

The hope of the righteous shall be gladness.

The thoughts of the righteous are right.

Righteousness exalteth a nation;
But sin is a reproach to any people.

The righteousness of the perfect shall direct his way:
But the wicked shall fall by his own wickedness.

In the house of the righteous is much treasure;
But in the revenues of the wicked is trouble.

Riches profit not in the day of wrath:
But righteousness delivereth from death.

The wicked are overthrown, and are not:
But the house of the righteous shall stand.

The righteousness of the upright shall deliver them:
But transgressors shall be taken in their own naughtiness.

Though hand join in hand,
The wicked shall not be unpunished,
But the seed of the righteous shall be delivered.

The hoary head is a crown of glory,
If it be found in the way of righteousness.

Righteousness keepeth him that is upright in the way.

A righteous man regardeth the life of his beast.

The righteous consider the cause of the poor.

The desire of the righteous is only good.

THE EVIL DOER

Be not thou envious against evil men,
Neither desire to be with them,
For their heart studieth destruction,
And their lips talk of mischief.

He that seeketh mischief,
It shall come upon him.

An evil man seeketh only rebellion.

Do not they err that devise evil?
But mercy and truth shall be to them that devise good.

Fret not thyself because of evil men,
Neither be thou envious at the wicked,
For there shall be no reward to the evil man;
The candle of the wicked shall be put out.

Whoso rewardeth evil for good,
Evil shall not depart from his house.

He that justifieth the wicked,
And he that condemneth the just,
Even they both are abomination to the Lord.

The wicked flee when no man pursueth.

A sound heart is the life of the flesh:
But envy the rottenness of the bones.

He that covereth his sins shall not prosper:
But whoso confesseth and forsaketh them shall have mercy.

ON RIGHT SPEAKING

The preparations of the heart in man,
And the answer of the tongue, is from the Lord.

A word fitly spoken is like apples of gold in pictures of
silver.

A soft answer turneth away wrath:
But grievous words stir up anger.

There is that speaketh like the piercings of a sword,
But the tongue of the wise is health.

The heart of the righteous studieth to answer.

He that keepeth his mouth keepeth his life.

The words of a man's mouth are as deep waters,
And the wellspring of wisdom as a flowing brook.

Whoso keepeth his mouth and his tongue
Keepeth his soul from troubles.

A man hath joy by the answer of his mouth:
And a word spoken in due season, how good is it.

Righteous lips are the delight of kings;
And they love him that speaketh right.

A wholesome tongue is a tree of life.

The words of the pure are pleasant words.

He that hath knowledge spareth his words:
And a man of understanding is of an excellent spirit.

ON CARELESS SPEAKING

A fool's mouth is his destruction,
And his lips are the snare of his soul.

He that answereth a matter before he heareth it,
It is folly and shame unto him.

Seest thou a man that is hasty in his words?
There is more hope of a fool than of him.

Even a fool, when he holdeth his peace, is counted wise,
And he that shutteth his lips is esteemed a man of
understanding.

The tongue of the wise useth knowledge aright:
But the mouth of fools poureth out foolishness.

There is that speaketh like the piercings of a sword:
But the tongue of the wise is health.

He that keepeth his mouth keepeth his life:
But he that openeth wide his lips shall have destruction.

Boast not thyself of tomorrow,
For thou knowest not what a day may bring forth.

THE TALEBEARER

Where no wood is, there the fire goeth out:
So where there is no talebearer the strife ceaseth.

The words of the talebearer are as wounds,
And they go down into the innermost parts of the belly.

He that goeth about as a talebearer revealeth secrets:
Therefore meddle not with him that flattereth with his lips.

The north wind driveth away rain:
So doth an angry countenance a backbiting tongue.

ON FLATTERY

He that rebuketh a man, afterwards shall find more favor
than he that flattereth with his tongue.

A man that flattereth his neighbour
Spreadeth a net for his feet.

A lying tongue hateth those that are afflicted by it:
And a flattering mouth worketh ruin.

ON CONTROLLING SELF

He that is slow to anger is better than the mighty,
And he that ruleth his spirit than he that taketh a city.

He that hath no rule over his own spirit,
Is like a city that is broken down and without walls.

He that is slow to wrath is of great understanding:
But he that is hasty of spirit exalteth folly.

ON ANGER

He that is soon angry dealeth foolishly.

An angry man stirreth up strife,
And a furious man aboundeth in transgression.

A man of great wrath shall suffer punishment.

A wrathful man stirreth up strife:
But he that is slow to anger appeaseth strife.

Make no friendship with an angry man,
And with a furious man thou shalt not go.

Hatred stirreth up strifes,
But love covereth all sins.

ON JOY

He that is of a merry heart hath a continual feast.

A merry heart maketh a cheerful countenance:
But by sorrow of the heart the spirit is broken.

Heaviness in the heart of man maketh it stoop:
But a good word maketh it glad.

To the counsellors of peace is joy.

A merry heart doeth good like a medicine.

ON GIFTS

A gift is a precious stone in the eyes of him that hath it;
Whithersoever it turneth, it prospereth.

A man's gift maketh room for him,
And bringeth him before great men.

Every man is a friend to him that giveth gifts.

Whoso boasteth himself of a false gift
Is like clouds and wind without rain.

DURABLE RICHES

The blessing of the Lord, it maketh rich,
And he addeth no sorrow with it.

There is that maketh himself rich, yet hath nothing:
There is that maketh himself poor, yet hath great riches.

A good name is rather to be chosen than great riches,
And loving favor rather than silver and gold.

The crown of the wise is their riches.

Better a little with the fear of the Lord
Than great treasure and trouble therewith.

How much better is it to get wisdom than gold!
And to get understanding rather to be chosen than silver.

THE POOR

The poor and the deceitful man meet together:
The Lord enlighteneth both their eyes.

He that oppresseth the poor reproacheth his Maker:
But he that honoreth him, hath mercy on the poor.

Better is the poor that walketh in his uprightness,
Than he that is perverse in his ways though he be rich.

The rich and the poor meet together;
The Lord is maker of them all.

MATERIAL RICHES

Labor not to be rich;
Cease from thine own wisdom.
Wilt thou set thine eyes on that which is not?
For riches certainly make themselves wings;
They fly away as an eagle toward heaven.

He that trusteth in his riches shall fall,
But the righteous shall flourish as a branch.

Better a little with righteousness
Than great revenues without right.

The rich ruleth over the poor,
And the borrower is servant to the lender.

Wealth maketh many friends,
But the poor is separated from his neighbor.

He that is greedy of gain troubleth his own house.

He becometh poor that dealeth with a slack hand.

Better is the poor that walketh in his integrity,
Than he that is perverse in his lips, and is a fool.

ON DILIGENCE

The hand of the diligent maketh rich.

The substance of a diligent man is precious.

The thoughts of the diligent tend only to plenteousness.

He that tilleth his land shall be satisfied with bread:
But he that followeth vain persons is void of
understanding.

Be diligent to know the state of thy flocks,
And look well to thy herds,
For riches are not forever.

He that gathereth in summer is a wise son:
But he that sleepeth in harvest is a son that causeth shame.

The hand of the diligent shall bear rule,
But the slothful shall be under tribute.

He that tilleth his land shall have plenty of bread:
But he that followeth after vain persons shall have poverty
enough.

In all labor there is profit:
But the talk of the lips tendeth only to penury.

A man shall be satisfied with good by the fruit of his
mouth:
And the recompence of a man's hands shall be rendered
unto him.

ON SLOTH

CONSIDER THE ANT

Go to the ant, thou sluggard!
Consider her ways, and be wise,
Which having no guide, overseer, or ruler,
Provideth her meat in the summer,
And gathereth her food in the harvest.
How long wilt thou sleep, O sluggard?
When wilt thou arise out of thy sleep?
Yet a little sleep, a little slumber,
A little folding of the hands to sleep;
So shall thy poverty come as one that travelleth,
And thy want as an armed man.

Love not sleep, lest thou come to poverty;
Open thine eyes, and thou shalt be satisfied with bread.

Slothfulness casteth into a deep sleep;
And an idle soul shall suffer hunger.

The soul of the sluggard desireth and hath nothing;
But the soul of the diligent shall be made fat.

He also that is slothful in his work
Is brother to him that is a great waster.

THE FIELD OF THE SLOTHFUL

I went by the field of the slothful,
And by the vineyard of the man void of understanding;
And, lo, it was all grown over with thorns,
And nettles had covered the face thereof,
And the stone wall thereof was broken down.
Then I saw, and considered it well,
I looked upon it, and received instruction.
Yet a little sleep, a little slumber,
A little folding of the hands to sleep,
So shall thy poverty come as one that travelleth;
And thy want as an armed man.

The desire of the slothful killeth him;
For his hands refuse to labor.

A slothful man hideth his hand in his bosom:
And will not so much as bring it to his mouth again.

The sluggard will not plow by reason of the cold:
Therefore shall he beg in harvest, and have nothing.

The way of the slothful man is as an hedge of thorns.

THE WINEBIBBER

Wine is a mocker, and strong drink is raging;
And whosoever is deceived thereby is not wise.

He that loveth pleasure, shall be a poor man;
He that loveth wine and oil shall not be rich.

Be not among winebibbers; among riotous eaters of flesh:
For the drunkard and the glutton shall come to poverty,
And drowsiness shall clothe a man with rags.

WHO HATH WOE?

Who hath woe? Who hath sorrow?
Who hath contentions? Who hath babbling?
Who hath wounds without cause?
Who hath redness of eyes?
They that tarry long at the wine;
They that go to seek mixed wine.
Look not thou upon the wine when it is red,
When it giveth his color in the cup,
When it moveth itself aright.
At last it biteth like a serpent,
And stingeth like an adder,
And thine heart shall utter perverse things.
Yea, thou shalt be as he that lieth down in the midst of the sea,
Or as he that lieth down on the top of a mast.
"They have stricken me," shalt thou say, "and I was not sick;
They have beaten me, and I felt it not;
When shall I awake?"

ON CORRECTION

The fining pot is for silver, and the furnace for gold,
But the Lord trieth the hearts.

The ear that heareth the reproof of life abideth among the wise.

He that refuseth instruction despiseth his own soul:
But he that heareth reproof getteth understanding.

A reproof entereth more into a wise man
Than an hundred stripes into a fool.

Correction is grievous unto him that forsaketh the way;
And he that hateth reproof shall die.

A scorner loveth not one that reproveth him:
Neither will he go unto the wise.

Reprove not a scorner lest he hate thee:
Rebuke a wise man and he will love thee.

He is in the way of life that keepeth instruction:
But he that refuseth reproof erreth.

Poverty and shame shall be to him that refuseth instruction;
But he that regardeth reproof shall be honored.

As an earring of gold,
And an ornament of fine gold,
So is a wise reprover upon an obedient ear.

ON GIVING

Withhold not good from them to whom it is due,
When it is in the power of thine hand to do it.

The righteous giveth and spareth not.

There is that scattereth, and yet increaseth;
And there is that withholdeth more than is meet, but it
tendeth to poverty.

The liberal soul shall be made fat;
And he that watereth shall be watered also himself.

He that hath a bountiful eye shall be blessed;
For he giveth of his bread to the poor.

He that giveth unto the poor shall not lack;
But he that hideth his eyes shall have many a curse.

Whoso stoppeth his ears at the cry of the poor,
He also shall cry himself,
But shall not be heard.

He that hath pity upon the poor lendeth unto the Lord;
And that which he hath given will he pay him again.

THY NEIGHBOR

Say not unto thy neighbor,
" Go, and come again, and tomorrow I will give;"
When thou hast it by thee.

Better is a neighbor that is near
Than a brother that is far off.

Debate thy cause with thy neighbor himself,
And discover not a secret to another.

Be not a witness against thy neighbor without cause;
And deceive not with thy lips:
Say not, " I will do so to him as he hath done to me:
I will render to the man according to his work."

He that despiseth his neighbor sinneth:
But he that hath mercy on the poor happy is he.

Devise not evil against thy neighbor,
Seeing he dwelleth securely by thee.

Withdraw thy foot from thy neighbor's house,
Lest he be weary of thee, and so hate thee.

A FRIEND

A friend loveth at all times.

As in water, face answereth to face
So the heart of man to man.

Ointment and perfume rejoice the heart;
So doth the sweetness of a man's friend by hearty counsel.

Faithful are the wounds of a friend:
But the kisses of an enemy are deceitful.

Thine own friend, and thy father's friend, forsake not.

A man that hath friends must show himself friendly;
And there is a friend that sticketh closer than a brother.

A faithful man shall abound with blessings.

ADVICE TO A PARENT

By mercy and truth iniquity is purged;
And by the fear of the Lord men depart from evil.

Train up a child in the way he should go,
And when he is old, he will not depart from it.

Withhold not correction from the child.

Correct thy son, and he shall give thee rest;
Yea, he shall give delight unto thy soul.

Chasten thy son while there is hope,
And let not thy soul spare for his crying.

The rod and reproof give wisdom;
But a child left to himself bringeth his mother to shame.

Foolishness is bound in the heart of a child;
But the rod of correction shall drive it far from him.

He that handleth a matter wisely shall find good:
And whoso trusteth in the Lord happy is he.

The wise in heart shall be called prudent.

Understanding is a wellspring of life
Unto him that hath it.

He that is slow to anger is better than the mighty;
And he that ruleth his spirit than he that taketh a city.

ADVICE TO A SON

My son, if thine heart be wise,
My heart shall rejoice, even mine.

A wise son maketh a glad father:
But a foolish son is the heaviness of his mother.

Whoso keepeth the law is a wise son.

A wise son heareth his father's instruction,
But a scorner heareth not the rebuke.

Hear thou my son, and be wise,
And guide thine heart in the way.

House and riches are the inheritance of fathers:
And a prudent wife is from the Lord.

Whoso findeth a wife findeth a good thing,
And obtaineth favour of the Lord.

My son, if thou be surety for thy friend,
Thou art snared with the words of thy mouth;
Deliver thyself as a roe from the hand of the hunter,
And as a bird from the hand of the fowler.

Confidence in an unfaithful man in time of trouble,
Is like a broken tooth, and a foot out of joint.

FIND THE KNOWLEDGE OF GOD

My son, if thou wilt receive my words,
And hide my commandments with thee,
So that thou incline thine ear unto wisdom,
And apply thine heart to understanding;
Yea, if thou criest after knowledge,
And liftest up thy voice for understanding,
If thou seekest her as silver,
And searchest for her as for hid treasures,
Then shalt thou understand the fear of the Lord,
And find the knowledge of God.

For the Lord giveth wisdom:
Out of his mouth cometh knowledge and understanding.
He layeth up sound wisdom for the righteous;
He is a buckler to them that walk uprightly.
He keepeth the paths of judgment,
And preserveth the way of his saints.
Then shalt thou understand righteousness, and judgment,
 and equity,
Yea, every good path.

REFRAIN THY FOOT FROM EVIL

My son, if sinners entice thee,
Consent thou not.
If they say, " Come with us, let us lay wait for blood,
Let us lurk privily for the innocent without cause.
We shall find all precious substance,
We shall fill our houses with spoil.
Cast in thy lot among us;
Let us all have one purse."

My son, walk not thou in the way with them;
Refrain thy foot from their path,
For their feet run to evil, and make haste to shed blood.
Surely in vain the net is spread in the sight of any bird.
They lay wait for their own blood;
They lurk privily for their own lives.
So are the ways of every one that is greedy of gain;
Which taketh away the life of the owners thereof.

WHOM THE LORD LOVETH HE CORRECTETH

My son, despise not the chastening of the Lord,
Neither be weary of his correction;
For whom the Lord loveth he correcteth,
Even as a father the son in whom he delighteth.

LET NOT MERCY AND TRUTH FORSAKE THEE

My son, forget not my law,
But let thine heart keep my commandments:
For length of days, and long life, and peace
Shall they add to thee.
Let not mercy and truth forsake thee;
Bind them about thy neck;
Write them upon the table of thine heart:
So shalt thou find favour and good understanding in the sight of God and man.

THOU SHALT WALK IN THE WAY SAFELY

My son, let not understanding depart from before thine eyes:
Keep sound wisdom and discretion,
So shall they be life unto thy soul,
And grace to thy neck.
Then shalt thou walk in thy way safely,
And thy foot shall not stumble.
When thou liest down, thou shalt not be afraid;
Yea, thou shalt lie down, and thy sleep shall be sweet.
Be not afraid of sudden fear,
Neither of the desolation of the wicked, when it cometh.
For the Lord shall be thy confidence,
And shall keep thy foot from being taken.

WHOSO COMMITTETH ADULTERY

My son, keep thy father's commandment,
And forsake not the law of thy mother;
When thou goest, it shall lead thee,
When thou sleepest, it shall keep thee,
And when thou wakest, it shall talk with thee;
To keep thee from the evil woman,
From the flattery of the tongue of a strange woman.
For by means of a whorish woman a man is brought to a piece of bread;
The adulteress will hunt for the precious life.
Can a man take fire in his bosom,
And his clothes not be burned?
Can one go upon hot coals,
And his feet not be burned?
Whoso committeth adultery with a woman lacketh understanding;
He that doeth it destroyeth his own soul.
A wound and dishonour shall he get,
And his reproach shall not be wiped away.

REGARD REPROOF

A fool despiseth his father's instruction,
But he that regardeth reproof is prudent.

KEEP THEE FROM THE STRANGE WOMAN

My son, keep my words, and lay up my commandments with thee.
Keep my commandments, and live,
And my law as the apple of thine eye.
Say unto wisdom, " Thou art my sister;"
And call understanding thy kinswoman,
That they may keep thee from the strange woman,
From the stranger which flattereth with her words.

For at the window of my house I looked through my casement,
And beheld among the simple ones,
I discerned among the youths,
A young man void of understanding,
Passing through the street near her corner,
And he went the way to her house,
In the twilight, in the evening, in the black and dark night.

And, behold, there met him a woman with the attire of an harlot, and subtil of heart.
She is loud and stubborn; her feet abide not in her house;
Now is she without, now in the streets,
And lieth in wait at every corner.

So she caught him, and kissed him,
And with an impudent face said unto him,
" I have peace offerings with me;
This day have I payed my vows.
Therefore came I forth to meet thee,
Diligently to seek thy face, and I have found thee.

I have decked my bed with coverings of tapestry,
With carved works, with fine linen of Egypt.
I have perfumed my bed with myrrh, aloes, and cinnamon.
Come, let us take our fill of love until the morning;
Let us solace ourselves with loves.
For the goodman is not at home,
He is gone on a long journey;
He hath taken a bag of money with him, and will come
home on the day appointed."

With her much fair speech she caused him to yield,
With the flattering of her lips she forced him.
He goeth after her straightway,
As an ox goeth to the slaughter,
Or as a fool to the correction of the stocks;
Till a dart strike through his liver;
As a bird hasteth to the snare,
And knoweth not that it is for his life.

Hearken unto me now therefore, O ye children,
And attend to the words of my mouth.
Let not thine heart decline to her ways,
Go not astray in her paths,
For she hath cast down many wounded;
Yea, many strong men have been slain by her.
Her house is the way to hell,
Going down to the chambers of death.

WISDOM IS THE PRINCIPAL THING

Hear, ye children, the instruction of a father,
And attend to know understanding.
For I give you good doctrine,
Forsake not my law.

Get wisdom, get understanding: forget it not;
Neither decline from the words of my mouth.
Forsake her not, and she shall preserve thee:
Love her, and she shall keep thee.
Wisdom is the principal thing;
Therefore get wisdom,
And with all thy getting, get understanding.

I have taught thee in the way of wisdom;
I have led thee in right paths.
When thou goest, thy steps shall not be straitened;
And when thou runnest, thou shalt not stumble.
Take fast hold of instruction, let her not go;
Keep her, for she is thy life.

Enter not into the path of the wicked,
And go not in the way of evil men.
For they eat the bread of wickedness,
And drink the wine of violence.
But the path of the just is as the shining light,
That shineth more and more unto the perfect day.
The way of the wicked is as darkness,
They know not at what they stumble.

KEEP THY HEART WITH ALL DILIGENCE

My son, attend to my words:
Incline thine ear unto my sayings.
Let them not depart from thine eyes;
Keep them in the midst of thine heart,
For they are life unto those that find them,
And health to all their flesh.

Keep thy heart with all diligence;
For out of it are the issues of life.
Put away from thee a froward mouth,
And perverse lips put far from thee.

Let thine eyes look right on,
And let thine eyelids look straight before thee.
Ponder the path of thy feet,
And let all thy ways be established.
Turn not to the right hand nor to the left;
Remove thy foot from evil.

ADVICE TO A DAUGHTER

A gracious woman retaineth honor.

Every wise woman buildeth her house;
But the foolish plucketh it down with her hands.

As a jewel of gold in a swine's snout,
So is a fair woman which is without discretion.

A continual dropping in a very rainy day
And a contentious woman are alike.

Better is a dry morsel, and quietness therewith,
Than an house full of sacrifices with strife.

Better a dinner of herbs where love is
Than a stalled ox and hatred therewith.

It is better to dwell in the wilderness,
Than with a contentious and angry woman.

It is better to dwell in the corner of the housetop
Than with a brawling woman in a wide house.

A foolish woman is clamorous;
She is simple, and knoweth nothing.

A virtuous woman is a crown to her husband:
But she that maketh ashamed is as rottenness in his bones.

A VIRTUOUS WOMAN

Who can find a virtuous woman?
For her price is far above rubies.
The heart of her husband doth safely trust in her,
So that he shall have no need of spoil.
She will do him good and not evil all the days of her life.

She seeketh wool, and flax,
And worketh willingly with her hands.
She is like the merchants' ships;
She bringeth her food from afar.

She riseth also while it is yet night,
And giveth meat to her household, and a portion to her maidens.
She considereth a field, and buyeth it;
With the fruit of her hands she planteth a vineyard.

She girdeth her loins with strength,
She strengtheneth her arms.
She perceiveth that her merchandise is good;
Her candle goeth not out by night.

She layeth her hands to the spindle,
And her hands hold the distaff.
She stretcheth out her hand to the poor;
Yea, she reacheth forth her hands to the needy.

She is not afraid of the snow for her household,
For all her household are clothed with scarlet.
She maketh herself coverings of tapestry;
Her clothing is silk and purple.

Her husband is known in the gates,
When he sitteth among the elders of the land.
She maketh fine linen, and selleth it;
And delivereth girdles unto the merchant.

Strength and honor are her clothing;
And she shall rejoice in time to come.
She openeth her mouth with wisdom;
And in her tongue is the law of kindness.

She looketh well to the ways of her household,
And eateth not the bread of idleness.
Her children arise up, and call her blessed;
Her husband also, and he praiseth her.

Many daughters have done virtuously,
But thou excellest them all.
Favor is deceitful, and beauty is vain;
But a woman that feareth the Lord, she shall be praised.
Give her of the fruit of her hand,
And let her own works praise her in the gates.

ON BUILDING

Through wisdom is an house builded,
And by understanding it is established;
And by knowledge shall the chambers be filled
With all precious and pleasant riches.

WHAT IS HIS NAME?

Who hath ascended up into heaven, or descended?
Who hath gathered the wind in his fists?
Who hath established all the ends of the earth?
What is his name,
And what is his son's name,
If thou canst tell?

SEVEN THINGS HATEFUL TO GOD

These six things doth the Lord hate:
Yea, seven are an abomination unto him:
A proud look,
A lying tongue,
And hands that shed innocent blood,
A heart that deviseth wicked imaginations,
Feet that be swift in running to mischief,
A false witness that speaketh lies,
And he that soweth discord among brethren.

FOUR THINGS TOO WONDERFUL FOR ME

There be three things which are too wonderful for me,
Yea, four which I know not:
The way of an eagle in the air;
The way of a serpent upon a rock;
The way of a ship in the midst of the sea;
And the way of a man with a maid.

FOUR THINGS EXCEEDING WISE

There be four things which are little upon the earth,
But they are exceeding wise:
The ants are a people not strong,
Yet they prepare their meat in the summer;
The conies are but a feeble folk,
Yet make they their houses in the rocks;
The locusts have no king,
Yet go they forth all of them by bands;
The spider taketh hold with her hands,
And is in king's palaces.

" Fear God, and keep His commandments:
For this is the whole duty of man."

ECCLESIASTES

The words of the Preacher, the son of David,
King of Jerusalem

VANITY: EMPTINESS

"Vanity of vanities," saith the Preacher, "vanity of vanities; all is vanity."

What profit hath a man of all his labour which he taketh under the sun? One generation passeth away, and another generation cometh: but the earth abideth for ever.

The sun also ariseth, and the sun goeth down, and hasteth to his place where he arose. The wind goeth toward the south, and turneth about unto the north; it whirleth about continually, and the wind returneth again according to his circuits. All the rivers run into the sea; yet the sea is not full; unto the place from whence the rivers come, thither they return again.

All things are full of labour; man cannot utter it: the eye is not satisfied with seeing, nor the ear filled with hearing.

The thing that hath been, it is that which shall be; and that which is done is that which shall be done: and there is no new thing under the sun. Is there any thing whereof it may be said, "See, this is new?" It hath been already of old time, which was before us.

There is no remembrance of former things; neither shall there be any remembrance of things that are to come with those that shall come after.

WISDOM EXCELLETH FOLLY AS FAR AS LIGHT EXCELLETH DARKNESS

I the Preacher was king over Israel in Jerusalem. And I gave my heart to seek and search out by wisdom concerning all things that are done under heaven. I have seen all the works that are done under the sun; and, behold, all is vanity and vexation of spirit.

I communed with mine own heart, saying, "Lo, I am come to great estate, and have gotten more wisdom than all they that have been before me in Jerusalem": yea, my heart had great experience of wisdom and knowledge. And I gave my heart to know wisdom, and to know madness and folly: I perceived that this also is vexation of spirit.

I said in mine heart, "Go to now, I will prove thee with mirth, therefore enjoy pleasure." I sought in mine heart to give myself unto wine, yet acquainting mine heart with wisdom; and to lay hold on folly, till I might see what was that good for the sons of men, which they should do under the heaven all the days of their life.

I made me great works; I builded me houses; I planted me vineyards: I made me gardens and orchards, and I planted trees in them of all kind of fruits: I made me pools of water, to water therewith the wood that bringeth forth trees: I got me servants and maidens, and had servants born in my house; also I had great possessions of great and small cattle above all that were in Jerusalem before me: I gathered me also silver and gold, and the peculiar treasure of kings and of the provinces: I gat me men singers and women singers, and the delights of the sons of men, as musical instruments, and that of all sorts. So I was great, and increased more than all that were before me in Jerusalem: also my wisdom remained with me. And whatsoever mine eyes desired I kept not from them, I withheld not my heart from any joy; for my heart rejoiced in all my labour: and this was my portion of all my labour.

Then I looked on all the works that my hands had wrought, and on the labour that I had laboured to do: and, behold, all was vanity and vexation of spirit, and there was no profit under the sun.

And I turned myself to behold wisdom, and madness, and folly; then I saw that wisdom excelleth folly, as far as light excelleth darkness.

And moreover, because the Preacher was wise, he still taught the people knowledge; yea, he gave good heed, and sought out, and set in order many proverbs. The preacher sought to find out acceptable words: and that which was written was upright, even words of Truth.

WISDOM IS BETTER THAN WEAPONS OF WAR

There was a little city, and few men within it; and there came a great king against it, and besieged it, and built great bulwarks against it. Now there was found in it a poor wise man, and he by his wisdom delivered the city; yet no man remembered that same poor man.

Then said I, Wisdom is better than strength: nevertheless the poor man's wisdom is despised, and his words are not heard. The words of wise men are heard in quiet more than the cry of him that ruleth among fools.

Wisdom is better than weapons of war.

WORDS OF THE WISE

The words of the wise spoken in quiet
Are heard more than the cry of him that ruleth
among fools.

The wise man's eyes are in his head;
But the fool walketh in darkness.

Keep thy foot when thou goest to the house of God,
And be more ready to hear, than to give the sacrifice
of fools:
For they consider not that they do evil.

The words of a wise man's mouth are gracious:
But the lips of a fool will swallow up himself.

It is better to hear the rebuke of the wise,
Than for a man to hear the song of fools;
For as the crackling of thorns under a pot,
So is the laughter of the fool.

In the multitude of dreams and many words
There are also divers vanities:
But fear thou God.

Wisdom is good with an inheritance:
And by it there is profit to them that see the sun.

Consider the work of God!
In the day of prosperity be joyful,
But in the day of adversity consider.

There is an evil which I have seen under the sun,
As an error which proceedeth from the ruler:
Folly is set in great dignity,
And the rich sit in low place.

I have seen servants upon horses,
And princes walking as servants upon the earth.

Be not hasty in thy spirit to be angry,
For anger resteth in the bosom of fools.

A wise man's heart is at his right hand;
But a fool's heart at his left.
Yea also, when he that is a fool walketh by the way,
His wisdom faileth him,
And he saith to every one that he is a fool.

Though a sinner do evil an hundred times,
And his days be prolonged,
Yet surely I know that it shall be well with them that
fear God, which fear before him:
But it shall not be well with the wicked,
Neither shall he prolong his days, which are as a shadow;
Because he feareth not before God.

If the clouds be full of rain,
They empty themselves upon the earth:
And if the tree fall toward the south, or toward the north,
In the place where the tree falleth, there it shall be.

He that observeth the wind shall not sow;
And he that regardeth the clouds shall not reap.

By much slothfulness the building decayeth;
And through idleness of the hands the house droppeth
through.

Better is a handful with quietness,
Than both hands full with travail and vexation of spirit.

Better is a poor and wise child,
Than an old and foolish king,
Who will no more be admonished.

The profit of the earth is for all;
The king himself is served by the field.

A good name is better than precious ointment.

Wisdom strengtheneth the wise
More than ten mighty men which are in the city.

A man's wisdom maketh his face to shine;
And the boldness of his face shall be changed.

Say not thou, "What is the cause that the former days
  were better than these?"
For thou dost not enquire wisely concerning this.

There is a sore evil which I have seen under the sun,
Namely riches kept for the owners thereof to their hurt.

He that loveth silver shall not be satisfied with silver;
Nor he that loveth abundance with increase.

When thou vowest a vow unto God, defer not to pay it;
For he hath no pleasure in fools:
Pay that which thou hast vowed.
Better is it that thou shouldst not vow,
Than that thou shouldest vow and not pay.

For wisdom is a defence,
And money is a defence:

But the excellency of knowledge is,
That wisdom giveth life to them that have it.

That which is far off, and exceeding deep,
Who can find it out?
I applied mine heart to know,
And to search, and to seek out wisdom, and the reason of things,
Lo, this only have I found,
That God hath made man upright:
But they have sought out many inventions.

Whoso keepeth the commandment shall feel no evil thing:
And a wise man's heart discerneth both time and judgment.

I know that whatsoever God doeth, it shall be forever:
Nothing can be put to it, nor any thing taken from it:
And God doeth it, that men should fear before him.
That which hath been is now;
And that which is to be hath already been;
And God requireth that which is past.

For all this I considered in my heart,
Even to declare all this,
That the righteous, and the wise, and their works,
Are in the hand of God.

For God giveth to a man that is good in his sight
Wisdom, and knowledge, and joy.

Let us hear the conclusion of the whole matter:
Fear God, and keep his commandments:
For this is the whole duty of man.
For God shall bring every work into judgment,
With every secret thing,
Whether it be good, or whether it be evil.

REMEMBER NOW THY CREATOR

Remember now thy Creator in the days of thy youth,
While the evil days come not,
Nor the years draw nigh, when thou shalt say,
" I have no pleasure in them ";
While the sun, or the light, or the moon, or the stars,
Be not darkened,
Nor the clouds return after the rain:
In the day when the keepers of the house shall tremble,
And the strong men shall bow themselves,
And the grinders cease because they are few,
And those that look out of the windows be darkened,
And the doors shall be shut in the streets,
When the sound of the grinding is low,
And he shall rise up at the voice of the bird,
And all the daughters of musick shall be brought low;
Also when they shall be afraid of that which is high,
And fears shall be in the way,
And the almond tree shall flourish,
And the grasshopper shall be a burden,
And desire shall fail:
Because man goeth to his long home,
And the mourners go about the streets:
Or ever the silver cord be loosed,
Or the golden bowl be broken,
Or the pitcher be broken at the fountain,
Or the wheel broken at the cistern.
Then shall the dust return to the earth as it was:
And the spirit shall return unto God who gave it.

THE TIME OF THE SINGING OF BIRDS

My beloved spake, and said unto me,
" Rise up, my love, my fair one, and come away.
For lo, the winter is past, the rain is over and gone;
The flowers appear on the earth,
The time of the singing of birds is come,
And the voice of the turtle is heard in our land.
The fig tree putteth forth her green figs,
And the vines with the tender grape give a good smell.
Arise, my love, my fair one, and come away."

From the Song of Songs which is Solomon's.

The New Testament

" Thou shalt love the Lord thy God with all thy heart, and with all thy soul, and with all thy mind. This is the first and great commandment. And the second is like unto it, Thou shalt love thy neighbor as thyself. On these two commandments hang all the law and the prophets."

Christ Jesus

The Light Shineth

THE FOUR GOSPELS

MATTHEW, MARK, LUKE AND JOHN

Combined into One Story in the Words of

The King James Version of the Bible

Arranged by

ERMA WOOD CARLSON

FOREWORD

The purpose of The Light Shineth is to give a chronological story of the life of Jesus the Christ in the words of the King James Version of the Bible. By weaving the four Gospels, Matthew, Mark, Luke, and John, together into a unified whole, the full beauty and power of Jesus' life is realized. All of Jesus' words and works have been included, and only undue repetition and genealogies omitted.

The four Gospels do not always agree in the details of a story. This is illustrated in the story of blind Bartimaeus. As related in Mark's Gospel, when Jesus "went out of Jericho . . . blind Bartimaeus, the son of Timaeus, sat by the highway side begging;" according to Luke's Gospel, "as he was come nigh unto Jericho, a certain blind man sat by the way side begging;" according to Matthew, " as they departed from Jericho . . . two blind men sitting by the wayside . . ."; the incident is not related in John's Gospel. In cases of this kind, either the story that is the best known, or the one that seemed the most logical is used, with parts of the others added to make it complete.

The List of References shows all references selected, and the order in which they are combined.

THY WORD IS TRUTH

" And the Word was made flesh,
and dwelt among us."

John

A MAN SENT FROM GOD WHOSE NAME WAS JOHN

> There was a man sent from God, whose name was John. The same came for a witness, to bear witness of the Light, that all men through him might believe. He was not that Light, but was sent to bear witness of that Light.

There were in the days of Herod, the king of Judea, a certain priest named Zacharias, and his wife, and her name was Elizabeth. And they were both righteous before God, walking in all the commandments and ordinances of the Lord, blameless. And they had no child, and they both were now well stricken in years.

According to the custom of the priest's office, Zacharias' lot was to burn incense when he went into the temple of the Lord. And the whole multitude of the people prayed without at the time of incense. And it came to pass, that while he executed the priest's office before God, there appeared unto him an angel of the Lord standing on the right side of the altar of incense. And when Zacharias saw him, he was troubled, and fear fell upon him.

But the angel said unto him, "Fear not, Zacharias; for thy prayer is heard; and thy wife Elizabeth shall bear thee a son, and thou shalt call his name John. And thou shalt have joy and gladness; and many shall rejoice at his birth. For he shall be great in the sight of the Lord, and many of the children of Israel shall he turn to the Lord their God. And he shall go before him in the spirit and power of Elijah, to turn the hearts of the fathers to the children, and the disobedient to the wisdom of the just; to make ready a people prepared for the Lord."

And Zacharias said unto the angel, "Whereby shall I know this? for I am an old man, and my wife well stricken in years."

And the angel answering, said unto him, "I am Gabriel, that stand in the presence of God; and am sent to speak unto thee, and to show thee these glad tidings. And behold thou shalt be dumb, and not able to speak, until the day that these things shall be performed, because thou believest not my words, which shall be fulfilled in their season."

And the people waited for Zacharias, and marvelled that he tarried so long in the temple. And when he came out, he could not speak unto them; and they perceived that he had seen a vision in the temple; for he beckoned unto them, and remained speechless. And he departed to his own house.

And after those days, his wife Elizabeth brought forth a son. And her neighbours and her cousins heard how the Lord had showed great mercy upon her, and they rejoiced with her. And it came to pass, that on the eighth day they came to name the child; and they called him Zacharias, after the name of his father.

And his mother answered and said, "Not so; but he shall be called John."

And they said unto her, "There is none of thy kindred that is called by this name." And they made signs to his father how he would have him called.

And he asked for a writing table, and wrote saying, "His name is John." And they marvelled all. And his mouth was opened immediately, and his tongue loosed, and he spake, and praised God.

And Zacharias was filled with the Holy Ghost, and prophesied, saying, "Blessed be the Lord God of Israel; for he hath visited and redeemed his people, and hath raised up an horn of salvation for us in the house of his servant David; as he spake by the mouth of his holy prophets, which have been since the world began: that we should be saved from our enemies, and from the hand of all that hate us; that he would grant unto us, that we, being delivered out of the hand of our enemies might serve him without fear, in holiness and righteousness before him, all the days of our life. And thou, child, shalt be called the prophet of the Highest: for thou shalt go before the face of the Lord to prepare his ways; to give knowledge of salvation unto his people by the remission of their sins, through the tender mercy of our God; whereby the dayspring from on high hath visited us, to give light to them that sit in darkness and in the shadow of death, to guide our feet into the way of peace."

And fear came on all that dwelt round about them; and all these sayings were noised abroad throughout all the hill country of Judea. And all they that heard them, laid them up in their hearts, saying, "What manner of child shall this be!"

And the hand of the Lord was with him. And the child grew, and waxed strong in spirit, and was in the deserts till the day of his showing unto Israel.

UNTO US A CHILD IS BORN

All things were made by God; and without him was not anything made that was made. In him was Life; and the Life was the Light of men. And the Light shineth in darkness; and the darkness comprehended it not. That was the true Light, which lighteth every man that cometh into the world.

NOW THE BIRTH of Jesus Christ was on this wise: The angel Gabriel was sent from God unto a city of Galilee, named Nazareth, to a virgin espoused to a man whose name was Joseph, of the house of David; and the virgin's name was Mary. And the angel came in unto her, and said, "Hail, thou that art highly favored, the Lord is with thee; blessed art thou among women." And when she saw him, she was troubled at his saying, and cast in her mind what manner of salutation this should be.

And the angel said unto her, "Fear not, Mary; for thou hast found favour with God. And behold, thou shalt bring forth a son, and shalt call his name Jesus. And of his kingdom there shall be no end. He shall be great, and shall be called the Son of the Highest; and the Lord God shall give unto him the throne of his father David. And he shall reign over the house of Jacob for ever; and of his kingdom there shall be no end."

Then said Mary unto the angel, "How shall this be, seeing I am not a wife?"

And the angel answered and said unto her, "The power of the Highest shall overshadow thee; therefore thy son shall be called the Son of God. And behold, thy cousin Elizabeth, who was called barren, hath conceived a son in her old age; for with God nothing shall be impossible."

And Mary said, " My soul doth magnify the Lord, and my spirit hath rejoiced in God my Saviour. Be it unto me according to thy word." And the angel departed from her.

When Mary was espoused to Joseph, before they came together, she was found with child. Then Joseph her husband, being a just man, and not willing to make her a public example, was minded to put her away privily. But while he thought on these things, behold, the angel of the Lord appeared unto him in a dream, saying, " Joseph, thou son of David, fear not to take unto thee Mary thy wife: for that which is conceived in her is of the Holy Ghost. And she shall bring forth a son, and thou shalt call his name Jesus: for he shall save his people from their sins." Then Joseph being raised from sleep did as the angel of the Lord had bidden him, and took unto him Mary, his wife.

Now all this was done, that it might be fulfilled which was spoken of the Lord by the prophet, saying, " Behold, a virgin shall be with child, and shall bring forth a son, and they shall call his name Emmanuel, which being interpreted is, God with us."

And it came to pass in those days, that there went out a decree from Caesar Augustus, that all the world should be taxed. And all went to be taxed, every one into his own city. And Joseph also, with Mary his espoused wife, being great with child, went up from Galilee, out of the city of Nazareth, into Judea, unto the city of David which is called Bethlehem, because he was of the house and lineage of David. And so it was, that while they were there, the days were accomplished that Mary should be delivered; and she brought forth her first-born son, and wrapped him in swaddling-clothes, and laid him a manger; because there was no room for them in the inn.

And there were in the same country shepherds abiding in the field, keeping watch over their flock by night. And lo, the angel of the Lord came upon them, and the glory of the Lord shone round about them; and they were sore afraid.

And the angel said unto them, "Fear not; for behold, I bring you good tidings of great joy, which shall be to all people. For unto you is born this day, in the city of David, a Saviour, which is Christ the Lord. And this shall be a sign unto you; Ye shall find the babe wrapped in swaddling-clothes, lying in a manger."

And suddenly there was with the angel a multitude of the heavenly host praising God, and saying, "Glory to God in the highest, and on earth peace, good will toward men."

And it came to pass, as the angels were gone away from them into heaven, the shepherds said one to another, "Let us now go even unto Bethlehem, and see this thing which is come to pass, which the Lord hath made known unto us."

And they came with haste, and found Mary and Joseph, and the babe lying in a manger. And when they had seen it, they made known abroad the saying which was told them concerning this child. And all they that heard it, wondered at those things which were told them by the shepherds. But Mary kept all these things, and pondered them in her heart. And the shepherds returned, glorifying and praising God for all the things that they had heard and seen, as it was told unto them.

Now when Jesus was born in Bethlehem of Judea in the days of Herod the king, behold, there came wise men from the east to Jerusalem, saying, "Where is he that is born King of the Jews? for we have seen his star in the east, and are come to worship him."

When Herod the king had heard these things, he was troubled, and all Jerusalem with him. And when he had gathered all the chief priests and scribes of the people together, he demanded of them where Christ should be born.

And they said unto him, "In Bethlehem of Judea; for thus it is written by the prophet, 'And thou Bethlehem, in the land of Juda, art not the least among the princes of Juda; for out of thee shall come a Governor, that shall rule my people Israel.'"

Then Herod, when he had privily called the wise men inquired of them diligently what time the star appeared. And he sent them to Bethlehem, and said, "Go and search diligently for the young child; and when ye have found him, bring me word again, that I may come and worship him also."

When they had heard the king, they departed; and lo, the star, which they saw in the east, went before them, till it came and stood over where the young child was. When they saw the star, they rejoiced with exceeding great joy. And when they were come into the house, they saw the young child with Mary his mother, and fell down, and worshipped him; and when they had opened their treasures, they presented unto him gifts: gold, and frankincense, and myrrh. And being warned of God in a dream that they should not return to Herod, they departed into their own country another way.

And when they were departed, behold, the angel of the Lord appeared to Joseph in a dream, saying, "Arise, and take the young child and his mother, and flee into Egypt, and be thou there until I bring thee word; for Herod will seek the young child to destroy him." When Joseph arose, he took the young child and his mother by night, and departed into Egypt.

Then Herod, when he saw that he was mocked of the wise men, was exceeding wroth, and sent forth, and slew all the children that were in Bethlehem, and in all the coasts thereof, from two years old and under, according to the time which he had diligently inquired of the wise men.

But when Herod was dead, behold, an angel of the Lord appeared in a dream to Joseph in Egypt, saying, "Arise, and take the young child and his mother, and go into the land of Israel; for they are dead which sought the young child's life."

And he arose, and took the young child and his mother, and came into the land of Israel. And he came and dwelt in a city called Nazareth.

A LIGHT TO LIGHTEN THE GENTILES

And the child's name was called Jesus, which was so named of the angel before he was conceived. And Joseph and Mary brought him to Jerusalem to present him to the Lord (as it is written in the law, "Every male shall be called holy to the Lord"), and to offer a sacrifice according to that which is said in the law of the Lord, "A pair of turtledoves, or two young pigeons."

And behold, there was a man in Jerusalem, whose name was Simeon; and the same man was just and devout, waiting for the consolation of Israel. And it was revealed unto him by the Holy Ghost, that he should not see death, before he had seen the Lord's Christ.

And he came by the Spirit into the temple; and when the parents brought in the child Jesus, to do for him after the custom of the law, then took he him up in his arms, and blessed God, and said, "Lord, now lettest thou thy servant depart in peace, according to thy word; for mine eyes have seen thy salvation, which thou hast prepared before the face of all people; a light to lighten the Gentiles, and the glory of thy people Israel."

And Joseph and Mary marvelled at those things which were spoken of him.

And Simeon blessed them, and said unto Mary, "Behold, this child is set for the fall and rising again of many in Israel; and for a sign which shall be spoken against. Yea, a sword shall pierce through thy own soul also, that the thoughts of many hearts may be revealed."

And there was one Anna, a prophetess; and she was of a great age, and departed not from the temple, but served God with fastings and prayers night and day. And she, coming in that instant, gave thanks likewise unto the Lord, and spake of Jesus to all them that looked for redemption in Jerusalem.

And when Joseph and Mary had performed all things according to the law of the Lord, they returned into Galilee, to their own city Nazareth.

MY FATHER'S BUSINESS

AND THE CHILD, Jesus, grew, and waxed strong in spirit, filled with wisdom; and the grace of God was upon him.

Now his parents went to Jerusalem every year at the feast of the passover. And when he was twelve years old, they went up to Jerusalem after the custom of the feast. And when they had fulfilled the days, as they returned, the child Jesus tarried behind in Jerusalem; and Joseph and Mary knew not of it. But they, supposing him to have been in the company, went a day's journey; and they sought him among their kinsfolk and acquaintance. And when they found him not, they turned back again to Jerusalem, seeking him.

And it came to pass, that after three days they found him in the temple sitting in the midst of the doctors, both hearing them, and asking them questions. And all that heard him were astonished at his understanding and answers.

And when they saw him, they were amazed; and his mother said unto him, " Son, why hast thou thus dealt with us? behold, thy father and I have sought thee sorrowing."

And he said unto them, " How is it that ye sought me? wist ye not that I must be about my Father's business? "

And they understood not the saying which he spake unto them. And he went down with them, and came to Nazareth, and was subject unto them; but his mother kept all these sayings in her heart. And Jesus increased in wisdom and stature, and in favour with God and man.

MY BELOVED SON

IT IS WRITTEN in the prophets, "Behold, I send my messenger before thy face which shall prepare thy way before thee."

Now in the fifteenth year of the reign of Tiberius Caesar, the word of the Lord came unto John, the son of Zacharias, in the wilderness. And he came into all the country about Jordan preaching the baptism of repentance for the remission of sins, and saying, "Repent ye; for the kingdom of heaven is at hand." And John was clothed with camel's hair, and with a girdle of skin about his loins; and he did eat locust and wild honey.

Then went out to him Jerusalem, and all Judea, and all the region round about Jordan, and were baptized of him in Jordan, confessing their sins. And the Jews sent priests and Levites from Jerusalem to ask him, "Who art thou?"

And he confessed, "I am not the Christ."

And they asked him, "What then? Art thou Elijah?"

And he saith, "I am not."

"Art thou that prophet?"

And he answered, "No."

Then said they unto him, "Who art thou? that we may give an answer to them that sent us. What sayest thou of thyself?"

He said, "I am the voice of one crying in the wilderness, 'Prepare ye the way of the Lord, make his paths straight.' Every valley shall be filled, and every mountain and hill shall be brought low; and the crooked shall be made straight, and the rough ways shall be made smooth; and all flesh shall see the salvation of God."

But when he saw many of the Pharisees and Sadducees come to his baptism, he said, "O generation of vipers, who hath warned you to flee from the wrath to come? Bring forth therefore fruits worthy of repentance, and begin not to say within yourselves, 'We have Abraham to our father;' for I say unto you, that God is able of these stones to raise up children unto Abraham. And now also the axe is laid unto the root of the trees; every tree, therefore, which bringeth not forth good fruit, is hewn down and cast into the fire."

And the people asked him saying, "What shall we do then?"

He answered and said unto them, "He that hath two coats, let him impart to him that hath none; and he that hath meat, let him do likewise."

Then came also publicans to be baptized, and said unto him, "Master, what shall we do?"

And he said unto them, "Exact no more than that which is appointed you."

And the soldiers likewise demanded of him, saying, "And what shall we do?"

And he said unto them, "Do violence to no man, neither accuse any falsely; and be content with your wages."

And as the people were in expectation, and all men mused in their hearts of John, whether he were the Christ, or not, they asked him, "Why baptizest thou then, if thou be not that Christ, nor Elijah, nor that prophet?"

And John answered, saying unto them all, "I indeed baptize you with water; but one mightier than I cometh, the latchet of whose shoes I am not worthy to unloose; he shall baptize you with the Holy Ghost, and with fire; whose fan is in his hand, and he will throughly purge his floor, and will gather the wheat into his garner; but the chaff he will burn with fire unquenchable." And many other things in his exhortation preached he unto the people.

The next day John saw Jesus coming unto him, and said, "Behold, the Lamb of God, which taketh away the sins of the world! This is he of whom I said, 'After me cometh a man which is preferred before me;' for he was before me, and I knew him not; but that he should be made manifest to Israel, therefore am I come baptizing with water. He that sent me to baptize with water, the same said unto me, 'Upon whom thou shalt see the Spirit descending and remaining on him, the same is he which baptizeth with the Holy Ghost'. And I saw the Spirit descending from heaven like a dove, and it abode upon him. And I bare record that this is the Son of God."

Then came Jesus to be baptized of him; but John forbade him, saying, "I have need to be baptized of thee, and comest thou to me?"

And Jesus answering said unto him, "Suffer it to be so now; for thus it becometh us to fulfill all righteousness." Then John baptized him.

And Jesus, when he was baptized, went up straightway out of the water and prayed; and lo, the heavens were opened unto him, and the Spirit of God descended like a dove and lighted upon him, and a voice came from heaven which said, "Thou art my beloved Son: in thee I am well pleased."

AND GOD ONLY SHALT THOU SERVE

AND JESUS being full of the Holy Ghost, returned from Jordan, and was led by the Spirit into the wilderness. And he was there in the wilderness forty days, tempted of Satan; and was with the wild beasts. And in those days he did eat nothing. And when he had fasted forty days and forty nights, he was afterward an hungered.

And the devil said unto him, "If thou be the Son of God, command that these stones be made bread."

But Jesus answered and said, "It is written, 'Man shall not live by bread alone, but by every word that proceedeth out of the mouth of God.'"

And the devil brought him to Jerusalem, and set him on a pinnacle of the temple, and said unto him, "If thou be the Son of God, cast thyself down from hence. For it is written, 'He shall give his angels charge over thee, to keep thee; and in their hands they shall bear thee up, lest at any time thou dash thy foot against a stone.'"

Jesus said unto him, "It is written again, 'Thou shalt not tempt the Lord thy God.'"

And the devil, taking him up into an high mountain, showed him, in a moment of time, all the kingdoms of the world and the glory of them. And the devil said unto him, "All this power will I give thee, and the glory of them, for that is delivered unto me and to whomsoever I will give it. If thou therefore wilt fall down and worship me, all shall be thine."

And Jesus answered and said unto him, "Get thee behind me, Satan; for it is written, 'Thou shalt worship the Lord thy God, and him only shalt thou serve.'"

And when the devil had ended all the temptation, he departed from him for a season; and behold, angels came and ministered unto him.

And Jesus returned in the power of the Spirit into Galilee; and from that time he began to preach, saying, " The time is fulfilled, and the kingdom of God is at hand; repent ye, and believe the gospel." And there went out a fame of him through all the region round about. And he taught in their synagogues, being glorified of all.

THE WORKS THAT I DO

"The works that I do in my Father's name,
They bear witness of me.
If I do not the works of my Father,
Believe me not;
But if I do, though ye believe not me,
Believe me for the very works' sake.
He that believeth on me,
The works that I do shall he do also;
And greater works than these shall he do,
Because I go unto my Father."

Christ Jesus

THIS DAY IS THIS SCRIPTURE FULFILLED

And Jesus began to be about thirty years of age, being, as was supposed, the son of Joseph. And he came to Nazareth where he had been brought up; and as his custom was he went into the synagogue on the Sabbath day, and stood up to read. And there was delivered unto him the book of the prophet Isaiah. And when he had opened the book, he found the place where it was written:

" The Spirit of the Lord is upon me, because he hath anointed me to preach the gospel to the poor; he hath sent me to heal the broken-hearted, to preach deliverance to the captives, and recovering of sight to the blind, to set at liberty them that are bruised. To preach the acceptable year of the Lord."

And Jesus closed the book, and he gave it again to the minister, and sat down. And the eyes of all them that were in the synagogue were fastened on him. And he said unto them, " This day is this scripture fulfilled in your ears."

And they were astonished, and all wondered at the gracious words which proceeded out of his mouth. And they said, " Whence hath this man this wisdom and these mighty works? Is not this Joseph, the carpenter's son? Is not his mother called Mary? and his brethren, James, and Joses, and Simon, and Judas? And his sisters, are thy not all with us? Whence then hath this man all these things? " And they were offended in him.

And Jesus said, " Verily I say unto you, no prophet is accepted in his own country. But I tell you of a truth, many widows were in Israel in the days of Elijah, when the heaven was shut up three years and six months, when great famine was throughout all the land; but unto none of them was Elijah sent, save unto

Sarepta, a city of Sidon, unto a woman that was a widow. And many lepers were in Israel in the time of Elisha the prophet; and none of them was cleansed, saving Naaman the Syrian."

And all they in the synagogue, when they heard these things, were filled with wrath, and rose up, and thrust him out of the city, and led him unto the brow of the hill whereon their city was built, that they might cast him down headlong. But he passing through the midst of them went his way.

THEY FORSOOK ALL AND FOLLOWED HIM

AND LEAVING NAZARETH, Jesus came and dwelt in Capernaum which is upon the sea coast. And Jesus walking by the sea of Galilee, saw two ships standing by the sea; and he saw two brethren, Simon, called Peter, and Andrew his brother, casting a net into the sea; for they were fishers. And he entered into one of the ships, which was Simon's, and he said unto Simon, "Launch out into the deep, and let down your nets."

And Simon answering said unto him, "Master, we have toiled all the night, and have taken nothing; nevertheless at thy word, I will let down the net."

And when they had done this, they enclosed a great multitude of fishes; and their net broke. And they beckoned unto their partners, which were in the other ship, that they should come and help them. And they came, and filled both ships, so that they began to sink.

When Simon Peter saw it, he fell down at Jesus' knees, saying, "Depart from me; for I am a sinful man, O Lord." For he was astonished, and all that were with him, at the draught of the fishes they had taken.

And Jesus said unto Simon, "Fear not; follow me, and I will make you fishers of men." And when they had brought their ships to land, they forsook all, and followed him.

And going on from thence, Jesus saw two other brethren, James the son of Zebedee and John, his brother, in a ship with Zebedee their father, mending their nets; and he called them. And they left their father, Zebedee, in the ship with hired servants and followed him.

They said unto him, "Master, where dwellest thou?"

Jesus saith unto them, "Come and see." They came and saw where he dwelt, and abode with him that day, for it was about the tenth hour.

The day following, Jesus went forth into Galilee, and found Philip, and said unto him, "Follow me." Now Philip was of Bethsaida, the city of Andrew and Peter.

Philip found Nathanael and said unto him, "We have found him of whom Moses in the law and the prophets did write, Jesus of Nazareth, the son of Joseph."

And Nathanael said unto him, "Can any good thing come out of Nazareth?"

Philip said unto him, "Come and see."

Jesus saw Nathanael coming to him and said of him, "Behold, an Israelite indeed, in whom is no guile."

Nathanael said unto him, "Whence knowest thou me?"

Jesus answered, "Before Philip called thee, when thou wast under the fig tree, I saw thee."

Nathanael said unto him, "Master, thou art the Son of God; thou art the King of Israel."

Jesus answered him, "Because I said unto thee, 'I saw thee under the fig tree,' believest thou? Thou shalt see greater things than these. Verily, verily, I say unto you, hereafter ye shall see heaven open, and the angels of God ascending and descending upon the Son of man."

BEGINNING OF MIRACLES

AND THE THIRD DAY there was a marriage in Cana of Galilee; and the mother of Jesus was there, and both Jesus was called, and his disciples, to the marriage.

And when they wanted wine, the mother of Jesus said unto him, " They have no wine."

Jesus said unto her, " Woman, what have I to do with thee? Mine hour is not yet come."

His mother said unto the servants, " Whatsoever he saith unto you, do it."

And there were set there six waterpots of stone. And Jesus saith unto them, " Fill the waterpots with water." And they filled them up to the brim. And he saith unto them, " Draw out now, and bear unto the governor of the feast." And they bare it.

When the ruler of the feast had tasted the water that was made wine, and knew not whence it was (but the servants which drew the water knew), the governor of the feast called the bridegroom, and said unto him, " Every man at the beginning doth set forth good wine, and when men have well drunk that which is worse; but thou hast kept the good wine until now."

This beginning of miracles did Jesus in Cana of Galilee, and manifested forth his glory; and his disciples believed on him.

ONE HAVING AUTHORITY

After this Jesus went down to Capernaum, he, and his mother, and his brethren, and his disciples. And straightway on the Sabbath day he entered into the synagogue and taught. And they were astonished at his doctrine; for he taught them as one that had authority, and not as the scribes.

And there was in their synagogue a man with an unclean spirit; and he cried out, saying, "Let us alone; what have we to do with thee, thou Jesus of Nazareth? art thou come to destroy us? I know thee who thou art, the Holy One of God."

And Jesus rebuked him, saying, "Hold thy peace, and come out of him." And when the unclean spirit had thrown him in the midst, he came out of him and hurt him not.

And they were all amazed, insomuch that they questioned among themselves saying, "What thing is this? What new doctrine is this? for with authority commandeth he even the unclean spirits, and they do obey him."

And when they were come out of the synagogue, Jesus entered into the house of Simon and Andrew, with James and John. But Simon's wife's mother lay sick of a fever, and they told him of her. And he came and took her by the hand, and lifted her up; and immediately the fever left her, and she arose and ministered unto them.

And the fame of Jesus went out into every place of the country round about. And at evening, when the sun did set, they brought unto him all that were diseased, and them that were possessed with devils; and all the city was gathered together at the door. All they that had any sick with divers diseases brought them unto him; and he laid his hands on every one of them, and healed them.

And in the morning, rising up a great while before day, he went out, and departed into a solitary place, and there prayed. And Simon and they that were with him followed after him. And when they had found him, they said unto him, "All men seek for thee."

And he said, "Let us go into the next towns, that I may preach there also; for therefore came I forth."

And when it was day, the people sought him, and came unto him, and stayed him, that he should not depart from them. And he said unto them, "I must preach the kingdom of God to other cities also; for therefore am I sent."

And there came a leper to him, beseeching him, and kneeling down to him, and saying unto him, "Lord, if thou wilt, thou canst make me clean."

And Jesus moved with compassion, put forth his hand, and touched him, and said unto him, "I will; be thou clean." And as soon as he had spoken, immediately the leprosy departed from him, and he was clean. And Jesus said unto him, "See thou tell no man; but go thy way, show thyself to the priest, and offer the gift that Moses commanded, for a testimony unto them."

But so much the more went there a fame abroad of him; and great multitudes came together to hear, and to be healed by him of their infirmities. And Jesus went about all the cities and villages, teaching in their synagogues, and preaching the gospel of the kingdom, and healing every sickness and every disease among the people. But when he saw the multitudes, he was moved with compassion on them, because they fainted, and were scattered abroad, as sheep having no shepherd. Then saith he unto his disciples, "The harvest truly is plenteous, but the labourers are few; pray ye therefore the Lord of the harvest, that he will send forth labourers into his harvest."

RISE UP AND WALK

AND AGAIN Jesus entered into Capernaum after some days; and it was noised that he was in the house. And straightway many were gathered together, insomuch that there was no room to receive them, no, not so much as around the door; and he preached the word unto them.

And behold, men brought in a bed a man which was taken with a palsy; and they sought means to bring him in, and to lay him before Jesus. And when they could not find by what way they might bring him in because of the multitude, they went upon the housetop, and let him down through the tiling with his couch into the midst before Jesus. When Jesus saw their faith, he said unto the sick of the palsy, "Son, thy sins be forgiven thee."

But there were certain of the scribes sitting there and reasoning in their hearts, "Why doth this man thus speak blasphemies? who can forgive sins but God only?"

And Jesus knowing their thoughts said, "Wherefore think ye evil in your hearts? Whether is easier to say, 'Thy sins be forgiven thee;' or to say, 'Rise up and walk?' But that ye may know that the Son of man hath power upon earth to forgive sins," he said unto the sick of the palsy, "I say unto thee, 'Arise, and take up thy couch, and go unto thine house.'" And immediately he rose up before them, and took up that whereon he lay, and departed to his own house, glorifying God.

And they were all amazed, and they glorified God which had given such power unto men; and they were filled with fear, saying, "We have seen strange things this day."

I WILL HAVE MERCY AND NOT SACRIFICE

After these things Jesus went forth, and saw a publican, named Matthew, sitting at the receipt of custom; and Jesus said unto him, "Follow me." And he left all, and rose up, and followed him.

And Matthew made a great feast in his own house; and there was a great company of publicans and others that sat down with them. And when the Pharisees saw it, they said unto Jesus' disciples, "Why eateth your master with publicans and sinners?"

But when Jesus heard that, he said unto them, "They that be whole need not a physician, but they that are sick. But go ye, and learn what that meaneth: I will have mercy and not sacrifice; for I am not come to call the righteous, but sinners to repentance."

And they said unto him, "Why do the disciples of John fast often, and make prayers, and likewise the disciples of the Pharisees; but thine eat and drink?"

And Jesus said unto them, "Can ye make the children of the bridechamber fast, while the bridegroom is with them? But the days will come when the bridegroom shall be taken away from them, and then they shall fast in those days. No man putteth a piece of new cloth unto an old garment, for that which is put in to fill it up taketh from the garment, and the rent is made worse. Neither do men put new wine into old bottles; else the bottles break, and the wine runneth out, and the bottles perish; but they put new wine into new bottles, and both are preserved."

And when Jesus departed thence, two blind men followed him, crying, and saying, "Thou son of David; have mercy on us."

And when Jesus was come into the house, the blind men came to him; and Jesus saith unto them, "Believe ye that I am able to do this?"

They said unto him, "Yea, Lord."

Then touched he their eyes, saying, "According to your faith be it unto you." And their eyes were opened; and Jesus straitly charged them, saying, "See that no man know it."

As they went out, behold, they brought to Jesus a dumb man possessed with a devil. And when the devil was cast out, the dumb spake; and the multitude marvelled, saying, "It was never so seen in Israel." And they spread abroad his fame in all that country.

DO GOOD ON THE SABBATH DAYS

And it came to pass on the second sabbath after the first, that Jesus went through the corn fields; and his disciples were an hungered, and began to pluck the ears of corn, and did eat, rubbing them in their hands.

And certain of the Pharisees said unto them, "Why do ye that which is not lawful to do on the sabbath days?"

And Jesus answering them said, "Have ye not read what David did, when he was an hungered, and they that were with him; how he entered into the house of God, and did eat the shewbread, which was not lawful for him to eat, neither for them which were with him, but only for the priests? But if ye had known what this meaneth, 'I will have mercy, and not sacrifice,' ye would not have condemned the guiltless. The sabbath was made for man, and not man for the sabbath. Therefore, the Son of man is Lord also of the sabbath." And he departed and went into their synagogue.

And behold, there was a man there which had a withered hand. And the scribes and Pharisees watched Jesus, whether he would heal on the sabbath day. And they asked him saying, "Is it lawful to heal on the sabbath days?" that they might accuse him.

But Jesus knew their thoughts and said to the man which had the withered hand, "Rise up, and stand forth in the midst;" and he arose and stood forth.

Then said Jesus unto them, "I will ask you one thing: is it lawful on the sabbath days to do good, or to do evil? to save life, or to destroy it? What man shall there be among you, that shall have one sheep, and if it fall into a pit on the sabbath day, will he not lay hold on it and lift it out? How much then is a man better than a sheep? Wherefore it is lawful to do well on the sabbath days." And when he had looked round about on them with anger, being grieved for the hardness of their hearts, he said unto the man, "Stretch forth thine hand." And he stretched it forth, and it was restored whole, like as the other.

And the scribes and Pharisees were filled with madness, and communed one with another what they might do to Jesus. But when Jesus knew it, he withdrew himself from thence; and great multitudes followed him, and he healed them all.

Then was brought unto him one possessed with a devil, blind, and dumb; and he healed him, insomuch that the blind and dumb both spake and saw. And the people were amazed and said, "Is not this the son of David?"

But when the Pharisees heard it they said, "This fellow doth cast out devils but by Beelzebub the prince of the devils."

And Jesus knew their thoughts, and said unto them, "Every kingdom divided against itself is brought to desolation; and every city or house divided against itself shall not stand. And if Satan cast out Satan, he is divided against himself; how shall then his kingdom stand? And if I by Beelzebub cast out devils, by whom do your children cast them out? therefore they shall be your judges. But if I with the finger of God cast out devils, no doubt the kingdom of God is come upon you.

"When a strong man armed keepeth his palace, his goods are in peace; but when a stronger than he shall come upon him, and overcome him, he taketh from him all his armour wherein he trusted, and divideth his spoils. He that is not with me is against me; and he that gathereth not with me scattereth abroad.

"When the unclean spirit is gone out of a man, he walketh through dry places seeking rest, and finding none, he saith, 'I will return unto my house whence I came out.' And when he cometh, he findeth it swept and garnished. Then goeth he, and taketh with himself seven other spirits more wicked than himself, and they enter in and dwell there; and the last state of that man is worse than the first.

"Wherefore I say unto you, all manner of sin and blasphemy shall be forgiven unto men; but the blasphemy against the Holy Ghost shall not be forgiven unto men. And whosoever speaketh a word against the Son of man, it shall be forgiven him; but whosoever speaketh against the Holy Ghost, it shall not be forgiven him, neither in this world, neither in the world to come.

"Either make the tree good, and his fruit good, or else make the tree corrupt, and his fruit corrupt; for the tree is known by his fruit. For a good tree bringeth not forth corrupt fruit; neither doth a corrupt tree bring forth good fruit. For every tree is known by his own fruit. For of thorns men do not gather figs, nor of a bramble bush gather they grapes. O generation of vipers, how can ye, being evil, speak good things? for out of the abundance of the heart the mouth speaketh. A good man out of the good treasure of his heart bringeth forth good things; and an evil man out of the evil treasure bringeth forth evil things. But I say unto you, that every idle word that men shall speak, they shall give account thereof in the day of judgment. For by thy words thou shalt be justified, and by thy words thou shalt be condemned."

And the scribes which came down from Jerusalem said, " He hath an unclean spirit."

And when his friends heard of it they went out to lay hold on him, for they said, " He is beside himself."

Then came to him his mother and his brethren, and could not come near him for the press, and sent unto him calling him. And it was told him, " Thy mother and thy brethren stand without, desiring to see thee."

And he answered and said unto them, " My mother and my brethren are these which hear the word of God, and do it. For whosoever shall do the will of my Father which is in heaven, the same is my brother, and sister and mother."

But Jesus withdrew himself with his disciples, and he went out into a mountain to pray, and continued all night in prayer to God. And when it was day, he called unto him his disciples; and of them he chose twelve, whom also he ordained, that they should be with him, and that he might send them forth to preach: Simon, whom he also named Peter, and Andrew his brother, James and John, Philip and Bartholomew (sometimes called Nathanael), Matthew and Thomas, James the son of Alphaeus, and Simon called Zelotes, and Judas the brother of James, and Judas Iscariot, which also was the traitor.

BLESSED ARE YE

AND JESUS came down with his disciples and stood in the plain; and a great multitude of people out of all Judaea and Jerusalem, and from the sea coast of Tyre and Sidon, came to hear him, and to be healed of their diseases. And the whole multitude sought to touch him; for there went virtue out of him, and healed them all. And seeing the multitudes, Jesus went up into a mountain; and when he was set, his disciples came unto him. And he opened his mouth, and taught them saying:

"Blessed are the poor in spirit; for theirs is the kingdom of heaven.

"Blessed are they that mourn; for they shall be comforted.

"Blessed are the meek; for they shall inherit the earth.

"Blessed are they which do hunger and thirst after righteousness; for they shall be filled.

"Blessed are the merciful; for they shall obtain mercy.

"Blessed are the pure in heart; for they shall see God.

"Blessed are the peace-makers; for they shall be called the children of God.

"Blessed are they which are persecuted for righteousness sake; for theirs is the kingdom of heaven.

"Blessed are ye when men shall revile you and persecute you, and shall say all manner of evil against you falsely, for my sake. Rejoice, and be exceeding glad; for great is your reward in heaven; for so persecuted they the prophets which were before you.

"Ye are the salt of the earth; but if the salt have lost his savour, wherewith shall it be salted? it is thenceforth good for nothing, but to be cast out, and to be trodden under foot of men.

For every one shall be salted with fire, and every sacrifice shall be salted with salt. Salt is good; but if the salt have lost his saltness, wherewith will ye season it? Have salt in yourselves, and have peace one with another.

"Ye are the light of the world. A city that is set on an hill cannot be hid. Neither do men light a candle, and put it under a bushel, but on a candlestick; and it giveth light unto all that are in the house. Let your light so shine before men, that they may see your good works, and glorify your Father which is in heaven.

"Think not that I am come to destroy the law, or the prophets: I am not come to destroy, but to fulfill. For verily I say unto you, till heaven and earth pass, one jot or one tittle shall in no wise pass from the law, till all be fulfilled. Whosoever therefore shall break one of these least commandments, and shall teach men so, he shall be called the least in the kingdom of heaven; but whosoever shall do and teach them, the same shall be called great in the kingdom of heaven. For I say unto you, that except your righteousness shall exceed the righteousness of the scribes and Pharisees, ye shall in no case enter into the kingdom of heaven.

"Ye have heard that it was said by them of old time, 'Thou shalt not kill'; and, 'Whosoever shall kill shall be in danger of the judgment.' But I say unto you, that whosoever is angry with his brother without a cause shall be in danger of the judgment; and whosoever shall say to his brother, 'Raca,' shall be in danger of the council; but whosoever shall say, 'Thou fool,' shall be in danger of hell fire. Therefore if thou bring thy gift to the altar, and there rememberest that thy brother hath ought against thee; leave there thy gift before the altar, and go thy way; first be reconciled to thy brother, and then come and offer thy gift.

"Agree with thine adversary quickly, whiles thou art in the

way with him; lest at any time the adversary deliver thee to the judge, and the judge deliver thee to the officer, and thou be cast into prison. Verily I say unto thee, thou shalt by no means come out thence, till thou hast paid the uttermost farthing.

"Ye have heard that it was said by them of old time, 'Thou shalt not commit adultery.' But I say unto you, that whosoever looketh on a woman to lust after her hath committed adultery with her already in his heart. And if thy right eye offend thee, pluck it out, and cast it from thee: it is better for thee to enter into the kingdom of God with one eye, than having two eyes to be cast into hell fire. And if thy right hand offend thee, cut it off, and cast it from thee: for it is profitable for thee that one of thy members should perish, and not that thy whole body should be cast into hell. And if thy foot offend thee, cut it off; it is better for thee to enter halt into life, than having two feet to be cast into hell, into the fire that never shall be quenched. It hath been said, 'Whosoever shall put away his wife, let him give her a writing of divorcement.' But I say unto you, whosoever shall put away his wife, and marry another, committeth adultery against her. And if a woman shall put away her husband, and be married to another, she committeth adultery.

"Again, ye have heard that it hath been said by them of old time, 'Thou shalt not forswear thyself, but shall perform unto the Lord thine oaths.' But I say unto you, swear not at all; neither by heaven, for it is God's throne; nor by the earth, for it is his footstool; neither by Jerusalem, for it is the city of the great King; neither shalt thou swear by thy head, because thou canst not make one hair white or black. But let your communication be, 'Yea, yea;' and, 'Nay, nay;' for whatsoever is more than these cometh of evil.

"Ye have heard that it hath been said, 'An eye for an eye, and a tooth for a tooth.' But I say unto you, that ye resist not evil; but whosoever shall smite thee on thy right cheek, turn to him the other also. And if any man will sue thee at the law, and take away thy coat, let him have thy cloke also. And whosoever shall compel thee to go a mile, go with him twain. Give to every man that asketh of thee; and of him that taketh away thy goods, ask them not again; and from him that would borrow of thee turn not thou away. And as ye would that men should do to you, do ye also to them likewise.

"Ye have heard that it hath been said, 'Thou shalt love thy neighbour, and hate thine enemy.' But I say unto you, love your enemies, bless them that curse you, do good to them that hate you, and pray for them which despitefully use you, and persecute you. Be ye therefore merciful, as your Father also is merciful. For if ye love them which love you, what thank have ye? for sinners also love those that love them. And if ye do good to them which do good to you, what thank have ye? for sinners also do even the same. And if ye lend to them of whom ye hope to receive, what thank have ye? for sinners also lend to sinners, to receive as much again. But love ye your enemies, and do good, and lend, hoping for nothing again; and your reward shall be great, and ye shall be the children of your Father which is in heaven: for he is kind unto the unthankful and to the evil, and maketh his sun to rise on the evil and on the good, and sendeth rain on the just and on the unjust. Be ye therefore perfect, even as your Father which is in heaven is perfect.

"Take heed that ye do not your alms before men, to be seen of them; otherwise ye have no reward of your Father which is in heaven. Therefore when thou doest thine alms, do not sound a trumpet before thee, as the hypocrites do in the synagogues and in the streets, that they may have glory of men. Verily I say unto you, they have their reward. But when thou doest alms, let not thy left hand know what thy right hand doeth; that thine alms may be in secret; and thy Father which seeth in secret himself shall reward thee openly. Give, and it shall be given unto you; good measure, pressed down, and shaken together, and running over, shall men give into your bosom. For with the same measure that ye mete withal, it shall be measured to you again.

"And when thou prayest, thou shalt not be as the hypocrites are: for they love to pray standing in the synagogues and in the corners of the streets, that they may be seen of men. Verily I say unto you, They have their reward. But thou, when thou prayest, enter into thy closet, and when thou hast shut thy door, pray to thy Father which is in secret; and thy Father which seeth in secret shall reward thee openly. And when ye pray, use not vain repetitions, as the heathen do; for they think that they shall be heard for their much speaking. Be not ye therefore like unto them: for your Father knoweth what things ye have need of before ye ask him. After this manner therefore pray ye:

"Our Father which art in heaven,
Hallowed be thy Name.
Thy kingdom come,
Thy will be done in earth, as it is in heaven.
Give us this day our daily bread.
And forgive us our debts, as we forgive our debtors.
And lead us not into temptation,
But deliver us from evil:
For thine is the kingdom, and the power, and the glory,
for ever.
Amen.

"Moreover, when ye fast, be not as the hypocrites, of a sad countenance; for they disfigure their faces, that they may appear unto men to fast. Verily I say unto you, they have their reward. But thou, when thou fastest, anoint thine head, and wash thy face; that thou appear not unto men to fast, but unto thy Father which is in secret; and thy Father which is in secret, shall reward thee openly.

"Judge not, that ye be not judged. For with what judgment ye judge, ye shall be judged; and with what measure ye mete, it shall be measured to you again. Judge not, and ye shall not be judged; condemn not, and ye shall not be condemned; forgive, and ye shall be forgiven.

"Can the blind lead the blind? shall they not both fall into the ditch? And why beholdest thou the mote that is in thy brother's eye, but perceivest not the beam that is in thine own eye? Either how canst thou say to thy brother, 'Brother, let me pull out the mote that is in thine eye,' when thou thyself beholdest not the beam that is in thine own eye? Thou hypocrite, cast out first the beam out of thine own eye, and then shalt thou see clearly to pull out the mote that is in thy brother's eye.

"The light of the body is the eye; therefore when thine eye is single, thy whole body also is full of light; but when thine eye is evil, thy body also is full of darkness. If therefore the light that is in thee be darkness, how great is that darkness! Take heed therefore that the light which is in thee be not darkness. If the whole body therefore be full of light, having no part dark, the whole shall be full of light, as when the bright shining of a candle doth give thee light.

"Give not that which is holy unto the dogs, neither cast ye your pearls before swine, lest they trample them under their feet, and turn again and rend you.

"Beware of false prophets, which come to you in sheep's clothing, but inwardly they are ravening wolves. Ye shall know them by their fruits. Do men gather grapes of thorns, or figs of thistles? Even so every good tree bringeth forth good fruit; but a corrupt tree bringeth forth evil fruit. A good tree cannot bring forth evil fruit, neither can a corrupt tree bring forth good fruit. Every tree that bringeth not forth good fruit is hewn down, and cast into the fire. Wherefore by their fruits ye shall know them.

"And why call ye me, 'Lord, Lord,' and do not the things which I say? Not every one that saith unto me, 'Lord, Lord,' shall enter into the kingdom of heaven; but he that doeth the will of my Father which is in heaven. Enter ye in at the strait gate; for wide is the gate, and broad is the way, that leadeth to destruction, and many there be which go in thereat; because strait is the gate, and narrow is the way, which leadeth unto life, and few there be that find it. Many will say to me in that day, 'Lord, Lord, have we not prophesied in thy name? and in thy name have cast out devils? and in thy name done many wonderful works?' And then I will profess unto them, 'I never knew you; depart from me, ye that work iniquity.'

"Therefore whosoever cometh to me, and heareth my sayings, and doeth them, I will show you to whom he is like. He is like a man which built an house, and digged deep, and laid the foundation on a rock. And the rain descended, and the floods came, and the winds blew, and beat upon that house; and it fell not; for it was founded upon a rock.

"And every one that heareth these sayings of mine, and doeth them not, shall be likened unto a foolish man, that without a foundation, built his house upon the sand; and the rain descended, and the floods came, and the winds blew, and beat upon that house; and it fell, and great was the fall of it."

And it came to pass, when Jesus had ended these sayings, the people were astonished at his doctrine, for he taught them as one having authority and not as the scribes.

SPEAK THE WORD ONLY

AND WHEN JESUS was come down from the mountain, great multitudes followed him, and he entered into Capernaum. And a certain centurion's servant, who was dear unto him, was sick, and ready to die. And the centurion came unto Jesus, beseeching him, and saying, "Lord, my servant lieth at home sick of the palsy, grievously tormented."

And Jesus saith unto him, "I will come and heal him."

The centurion answered and said, "Lord, I am not worthy that thou shouldst come under my roof; but speak the word only, and my servant shall be healed. For I also am a man set under authority, having under me soldiers; and I say unto one, 'Go,' and he goeth; and to another, 'Come,' and he cometh; and to my servant, 'Do this,' and he doeth it."

When Jesus heard these things, he marvelled at him, and turned him about, and said unto the people that followed, "I say unto you, I have not found so great faith, no, not in Israel." And Jesus said unto the centurion, "Go thy way; and as thou hast believed, so be it done unto thee." And his servant was healed in that selfsame hour.

And it came to pass the day after, that Jesus went into a city called Nain; and many of his disciples went with him, and much people. Now when he came nigh to the gate of the city, behold, there was a dead man carried out, the only son of his mother, and she was a widow; and much people of the city was with her.

And when the Lord saw her, he had compassion on her, and said unto her, "Weep not." And he came and touched the bier; and they that bare him stood still. And Jesus said, "Young man, I say unto thee, Arise." And he that was dead sat up, and began to speak. And Jesus delivered him to his mother.

And there came a fear on all; and they glorified God, saying that, "A great prophet is risen up among us;" and that, "God hath visited his people." And this rumor of him went forth throughout all Judaea, and throughout all the region round about.

THAT WHICH IS BORN OF THE SPIRIT IS SPIRIT

And the Jews' passover was at hand, and Jesus went up to Jerusalem, and found in the temple those that sold oxen and sheep and doves, and the changers of money sitting. And when he had made a scourge of small cords, he drove them all out of the temple, and the sheep, and the oxen; and poured out the changers' money, and overthrew the tables; and said unto them that sold doves, "Take these things hence; make not my Father's house an house of merchandise."

And the disciples remembered that it was written, "The zeal of thine house hath eaten me up."

Then answered the Jews and said unto him, "What sign showest thou unto us, seeing that thou doest these things?"

Jesus answered and said unto them, "Destroy this temple, and in three days I will raise it up."

Then said the Jews, "Forty and six years was this temple in building, and wilt thou rear it up in three days?"

But he spake of the temple of his body. When therefore he was risen from the dead, his disciples remembered that he had said this unto them; and they believed the scripture, and the word which Jesus had said.

Now when he was in Jerusalem at the passover, in the feast day, many believed in his name, when they saw the miracles which he did. But Jesus did not commit himself unto them, because he knew all men, and needed not that any should testify of man; for he knew what was in man.

There was a man of the Pharisees, named Nicodemus, a ruler of the Jews. The same came to Jesus by night, and said unto him, "Rabbi, we know that thou art a teacher come from God; for no man can do these miracles that thou doest except God be with him."

Jesus answered and said unto him, "Verily, verily, I say unto thee, except a man be born again, he cannot see the kingdom of God."

Nicodemus saith unto him, "How can a man be born when he is old? can he enter the second time into his mother's womb, and be born?"

Jesus answered, "Verily, verily, I say unto thee, except a man be born of water and of the Spirit, he cannot enter into the kingdom of God. That which is born of the flesh is flesh; and that which is born of the Spirit is spirit. Marvel not that I said unto thee, 'Ye must be born again.' The wind bloweth where it listeth, and thou hearest the sound thereof, but canst not tell whence it cometh, and whither it goeth; so is every one that is born of the Spirit."

Nicodemus answered and said unto him, "How can these things be?"

Jesus answered and said unto him, "Art thou a master of Israel, and knowest not these things? Verily, verily, I say unto thee, we speak that we do know, and testify that we have seen; and ye receive not our witness. If I have told you earthly things, and ye believe not, how shall ye believe, if I tell you of heavenly things?

"No man hath ascended up to heaven, but he that came down from heaven. As Moses lifted up the serpent in the wilderness, even so must the Son of man be lifted up; that whosoever believeth in him should not perish, but have eternal life. For God so loved the world, that he gave his only begotten Son, that whosoever believeth in him should not perish, but have everlasting life. For God sent not his Son into the world to condemn the world; but that the world through him might be saved. He that believeth on him is not condemned; but he that believeth not is condemned already, because he hath not believed in the name of the only begotten Son of God. And this is the condemnation, that light is come into the world, and men loved darkness rather than light, because their deeds were evil. For every one that doeth evil hateth the light, neither cometh to the light lest his deeds should be reproved. But he that doeth truth cometh to the light, that his deeds may be made manifest, that they are wrought in God."

GOD GIVETH NOT THE SPIRIT BY MEASURE

AFTER THESE THINGS came Jesus and his disciples into the land of Judaea; and there he tarried with them, and baptized; though Jesus himself baptized not, but his disciples.

And John also was baptizing in Aenon near to Salim because there was much water there. Then there arose a question between some of John's disciples and the Jews about purifying. And they came unto John, and said, "Rabbi, he that was with thee beyond Jordan, to whom thou barest witness, behold, the same baptizeth, and all men come to him."

John answered and said, "A man can receive nothing, except it be given him from heaven. Ye yourselves bear me witness that I said, 'I am not the Christ, but I am sent before him.' He that hath the bride is the bridegroom; but the friend of the bridegroom, which standeth and heareth him, rejoiceth greatly because of the bridegroom's voice; this my joy therefore is fulfilled. He must increase, but I must decrease. He that cometh from above is above all; he that is of the earth is earthly, and speaketh of the earth; he that cometh from heaven is above all. And what he hath seen and heard, that he testifieth; and no man receiveth his testimony. He that hath received his testimony hath set to his seal that God is true. For he whom God hath sent speaketh the words of God; for God giveth not the Spirit by measure unto him. The Father loveth the Son, and hath given all things into his hand. He that believeth on the Son hath everlasting life; and he that believeth not the Son shall not see life."

When therefore Jesus knew how the Pharisees had heard that he baptized more disciples than John, he left Judaea. But Herod, the king, being reproved by John for all the evils which Herod had done, added yet this above all, that he shut up John in prison.

Now when Jesus had heard that John was cast into prison, he departed into Galilee. And Jesus went about all Galilee, teaching in their synagogues, and preaching the gospel of the kingdom, and healing all manner of sickness and all manner of diseases among the people. And his fame went throughout all Syria; and they brought unto him all sick people that were taken with divers diseases and torments, and those which were possessed with devils, and those which were lunatick, and those that had the palsy; and he healed them.

And the disciples of John showed him all of these things. And John calling unto him two of his disciples sent them to Jesus, saying, "Art thou he that should come? or look we for another?"

And in that same hour Jesus cured many of their infirmities and plagues, and of evil spirits; and unto many that were blind he gave sight. Then Jesus answering said unto them, "Go your way, and tell John what things ye have seen and heard;

how that the blind see, the lame walk, the lepers are cleansed, the deaf hear, the dead are raised, to the poor the gospel is preached. And blessed is he, whosoever shall not be offended in me."

And when the messengers of John were departed, Jesus began to speak unto the people concerning John, "What went ye out in the wilderness for to see? A reed shaken with the wind? But what went ye out for to see? A man clothed in soft raiment? Behold, they that are gorgeously apparelled, and live delicately are in king's courts. But what went ye out for to see? A prophet? Yea, I say unto you, and much more than a prophet. For this is he, of whom it is written, 'Behold, I send my messenger before thy face, which shall prepare thy way before thee.' Verily I say unto you, among them that are born of women there hath not risen a greater than John the Baptist. For all the prophets and the law, prophesied until John. And if ye will receive it, this is Elijah which was to come. Whereunto then shall I liken the men of this generation? and to what are they like? They are like children sitting in the market place, and calling one to another and saying, 'We have piped unto you, and ye have not danced; we have mourned to you, and ye have not wept.' For John the Baptist came neither eating bread nor drinking wine, and ye say, 'He hath a devil.' The Son of man is come eating and drinking; and ye say, 'Behold, a gluttonous man, and a winebibber; a friend of publicans and sinners!' But Wisdom is justified of all her children. He that hath ears to hear let him hear."

Now Herod, the king, feared John, knowing that he was a just man and an holy. For Herod had sent forth and laid hold upon John, and bound him in prison, for Herodias' sake, his brother Philip's wife; for he had married her. For John had said unto Herod, "It is not lawful for thee to have thy brother's wife." Therefore Herodias had a quarrel against John, and would have killed him; but she could not.

And a day came that Herod on his birthday made a supper

to his lords. And the daughter of Herodias came in, and danced, and pleased Herod, and them that sat with him. The king said unto the damsel, " Ask of me whatsoever thou wilt, and I will give it thee." And he sware unto her, " Whatsoever thou shalt ask of me, I will give it thee, unto the half of my kingdom."

And she went forth and said unto her mother, " What shall I ask? "

And Herodias said, " The head of John the Baptist."

And she came in straightway with haste, and said, " Give me here John Baptist's head in a charger."

And the king was exceeding sorry, nevertheless, for his oath's sake, and them which sat with him at meat, he would not reject her. And immediately the king sent an executioner and beheaded John in the prison, and brought his head in a charger, and gave it to the damsel; and the damsel gave it to her mother.

And when John's disciples heard of it, they came and took up John, and laid him in a tomb; and went and told Jesus. When Jesus heard of it he departed into a desert place apart.

WORSHIP THE FATHER IN SPIRIT AND IN TRUTH

JESUS LEFT JUDAEA, and he must needs go through Samaria. Then cometh he to a city of Samaria, which is called Sychar, near to the parcel of ground that Jacob gave to his son Joseph. Now Jacob's well was there. Jesus therefore, being wearied with his journey, sat thus on the well; and it was about the sixth hour. There cometh a woman of Samaria to draw water; Jesus saith unto her, " Give me to drink," for his disciples were gone away into the city to buy meat.

Then saith the woman of Samaria unto him, " How is it that thou, being a Jew, askest drink of me, which am a woman of Samaria? for the Jews have no dealings with the Samaritans."

Jesus answered and said unto her, " If thou knewest the gift of God, and who it is that saith to thee, ' Give me to drink,' thou wouldest have asked of him, and he would have given thee living water."

The woman saith unto him, "Sir, thou hast nothing to draw with, and the well is deep; from whence then hast thou that living water? Art thou greater than our father Jacob, which gave us the well, and drank thereof himself, and his children, and his cattle? "

Jesus answered and said unto her, " Whosoever drinketh of this water shall thirst again; but whosoever drinketh of the water that I shall give him shall never thirst; but the water that I shall give him shall be in him a well of water springing up into everlasting life."

The woman saith unto him, " Sir, give me this water, that I thirst not, neither come hither to draw."

Jesus saith unto her, " Go, call thy husband, and come hither."

The woman answered and said, " I have no husband."

Jesus said unto her, " Thou hast well said, ' I have no husband;' for thou hast had five husbands; and he whom thou now hast is not thy husband; in that saidst thou truly."

The woman saith unto him, " Sir, I perceive that thou art a prophet. Our fathers worshipped in this mountain; and ye say, that in Jerusalem is the place where men ought to worship."

Jesus saith unto her, " Woman, believe me, the hour cometh, when ye shall neither in this mountain, nor yet at Jerusalem, worship the Father. Ye worship, ye know not what; we know what we worship; for salvation is of the Jews. But the hour cometh, when the true worshippers shall worship the Father in spirit, and in truth; for the Father seeketh such to worship him.

God is a Spirit; and they that worship him must worship him in Spirit and in truth."

The woman saith unto him, "I know that Messias cometh, which is called Christ; when he is come, he will tell us all things."

Jesus saith unto her, "I that speak unto thee am he."

And upon this came his disciples, and marvelled that he talked with the woman; yet no man said, "What seekest thou?" or, "Why talkest thou with her?"

The woman then left her waterpot, and went her way into the city, and saith to the men, "Come, see a man which told me all things that ever I did; is not this the Christ?" Then they went out of the city, and came unto him.

In the meanwhile his disciples prayed him, saying, "Master, eat."

But he said unto them, "I have meat to eat that ye know not of."

Therefore said the disciples one to another, "Hath any man brought him ought to eat?"

Jesus saith unto them, "My meat is to do the will of him that sent me, and to finish his work. Say not ye, 'There are yet four months, and then cometh harvest?' Behold, I say unto you, 'Lift up your eyes, and look on the fields; for they are white already to harvest.' And he that reapeth receiveth wages, and gathereth fruit unto life eternal; that both he that soweth and he that reapeth may rejoice together. And herein is that saying true, 'One soweth, and another reapeth.' I sent you to reap that whereon ye bestowed no labour; other men laboured, and ye are entered into their labours."

And many of the Samaritans of that city believed on him for the saying of the woman, which testified, "He told me all that ever I did."

So when the Samaritans were come unto him, they besought him that he would tarry with them; and he abode there two days. And many more believed because of his own word; and said unto the woman, "Now we believe, not because of thy saying; for we have heard him ourselves, and know that this is indeed the Christ, the Saviour of the world."

Now after two days he departed thence, and went into Galilee.

GO THY WAY, THY SON LIVETH

Then when Jesus was come into Galilee, the Galilaeans received him, having seen all the things that he did at Jerusalem at the feast; for they also went unto the feast.

So Jesus came again into Cana of Galilee, where he made the water wine. And there was a certain nobleman, whose son was sick at Capernaum. When he heard that Jesus was come out of Judaea into Galilee, he went unto him, and besought him that he would come down, and heal his son; for he was at the point of death.

Then said Jesus unto him, "Except ye see signs and wonders, ye will not believe."

The nobleman saith unto him, "Sir, come down ere my child die."

Jesus saith unto him, "Go thy way, thy son liveth." And the man believed the word that Jesus had spoken unto him, and he went his way.

And as he was now going down, his servants met him, and told him, saying, "Thy son liveth." Then enquired he of them the hour when he began to amend. And they said unto him, "Yesterday at the seventh hour the fever left him."

So the father knew that it was at the same hour, in the which Jesus said unto him, "Thy son liveth;" and himself believed, and his whole house.

This is again the second miracle that Jesus did, when he was come out of Judaea into Galilee.

THE SEED IS THE WORD OF GOD

And Jesus began again to teach by the sea side, and great multitudes were gathered together unto him, so that he went into a ship and sat; and the whole multitude stood on the shore.

And he taught them many things by parables, and said unto them, "Hearken; behold, a sower went forth to sow his seed. And it came to pass, as he sowed, some seed fell by the way side, and the fowls of the air came and devoured it up. And some fell on stony ground, where it had not much earth; and immediately it sprang up, because it had no depth of earth; but when the sun was up, it was scorched; and because it had no root, it withered away. And some fell among thorns, and the thorns grew up, and choked it, and it yielded no fruit. But other fell into good ground, and brought forth fruit, some an hundredfold, some sixtyfold, and some thirtyfold. Who hath ears to hear, let him hear."

And they that were about him with the twelve, said unto him, "Why speakest thou unto them in parables?"

He answered and said, "Because it is given unto you to know the mysteries of the kingdom of heaven, but to them it is not given. For whosoever hath, to him shall be given, and he shall have more abundance; but whosoever hath not, from him shall be taken away even that he hath. Therefore speak I to them in parables; because they seeing see not; and hearing they hear not, neither do they understand. And in them is fulfilled the prophecy of Isaiah, which saith, 'By hearing ye shall hear, and shall not understand; and seeing ye shall see, and shall not perceive. For this people's heart is waxed gross, and their ears are dull of hearing, and their eyes they have closed; lest at any time they should see with their eyes, and hear with their ears, and should understand with their heart, and should be converted, and I should heal them.' But blessed are your eyes, for they see; and your ears, for they hear."

And his disciples asked him saying, "What might this parable be?"

And he said unto them, "Know ye not this parable? how then will ye know all parables? Hear ye therefore, the parable of the sower:

"The seed is the word of God. When any one heareth the word of the kingdom, and understandeth it not, then cometh the wicked one, and catcheth away that which was sown in his heart, lest he should believe and be saved. This is he which received seed by the wayside.

"But he that receiveth the seed into stony places is he that heareth the word, and with joy receiveth it. Yet hath he not root in himself, but endureth for a while; afterwards when tribulation or persecution ariseth because of the word, immediately he is offended.

"He also that received seed among the thorns is he that heareth the word, and the cares of this world, and the deceitfulness of riches, and pleasures of this life, and the lusts of other things entering in, choke the word and he becometh unfruitful.

"But he that received seed into good ground is he that heareth the word, and understandeth it, and in an honest and good heart keepeth it, and bringeth forth fruit with patience, some an hundredfold, some sixtyfold, and some thirtyfold."

And he said unto them, "No man when he hath lighted a candle, putteth it under a bushel, or under a bed, but setteth it on a candlestick, that they which enter in may see the light. For there is nothing hid, which shall not be manifested; neither was any thing kept secret, but that it should come abroad. Take heed therefore how ye hear; with what measure ye mete it shall be measured to you; and unto you that hear shall more be given. For whosoever hath to him shall be given; and whosoever hath not, from him shall be taken even that which he seemeth to have."

Another parable put he forth unto them, saying, "So is the kingdom of God, as if a man should cast seed into the ground; and should sleep, and rise night and day, and the seed should spring and grow up, he knoweth not how. For the earth bringeth forth fruit of herself; first the blade, then the ear, after that the full corn in the ear. But when the fruit is brought forth, immediately he putteth in the sickle, because the harvest is come."

Another parable put he forth unto them saying, "The Kingdom of heaven is likened unto a man which sowed good seed in his field; but while men slept, his enemy came and sowed tares among the wheat, and went his way. But when the blade was sprung up, and brought forth fruit, then appeared the tares also.

"So the servants of the householder came and said unto him, 'Sir, didst not thou sow good seed in thy field? from whence then hath it tares?'

"He said unto them, 'An enemy hath done this.'

"The servants said, 'Wilt thou then that we go and gather them up?'

"But he said, 'Nay; lest while ye gather up the tares, ye root up also the wheat with them. Let both grow together until the harvest; and in the time of harvest I will say to the reapers, 'Gather ye together first the tares, and bind them in bundles to burn them; but gather the wheat into my barn.'"

And with many such parables spake he the word unto them, as they were able to hear it. But without a parable spake he not unto them, that it might be fulfilled which was spoken by the prophet saying, "I will open my mouth in parables; I will utter things which have been kept secret from the foundation of the world."

Then Jesus sent the multitude away, and his disciples came unto him, saying, "Declare unto us the parable of the tares of the field."

He answered them, "He that soweth the good seed is the Son of man; the field is the world; the good seed are the children of the kingdom; but the tares are the children of the wicked one; the enemy that sowed them is the devil; the harvest is the end of the world; and the reapers are the angels. As therefore the tares are gathered and burned in the fire, so shall it be in the end of this world. The Son of man shall send forth his angels, and they shall gather out of his kingdom all things that offend, and them which do iniquity, and shall cast them into a furnace of fire; there shall be wailing and gnashing of teeth. Then shall the righteous shine forth as the sun in the kingdom of their Father. Who hath ears to hear, let him hear."

PEACE, BE STILL

AND THE SAME DAY, when the even was come, Jesus saith unto the disciples, " Let us pass over unto the other side of the sea." And they launched forth.

But as they sailed, Jesus fell asleep. And there arose a great storm of wind, and the waves beat into the ship, and they were filled with water, and were in jeopardy. And Jesus was in the hinder part of the ship asleep on a pillow; and they came to him and awoke him, saying, " Master, carest thou not that we perish? "

And Jesus arose, and rebuked the wind, and the raging of the water, and said, " Peace, be still," and they ceased, and there was a great calm.

And Jesus said unto his disciples, " Why are ye so fearful? How is it that ye have no faith? "

But the men marvelled, saying, " What manner of man is this, that even the winds and the sea obey him! "

THEY FOUND THE MAN CLOTHED AND IN HIS RIGHT MIND

AND JESUS and the disciples came over unto the other side of the sea; and they arrived at the country of the Gadarenes. And when Jesus was come out of the ship, immediately there met him a man with an unclean spirit, which wore no clothes, neither abode in any house, but who had his dwelling among the tombs. And no man could bind him, no not with chains; because he had been often bound with fetters and chains, and the chains had been plucked asunder by him, and the fetters broken in pieces. Neither could any man tame him. And always, night and day, he was in the mountains, and in the tombs, crying and cutting himself with stones.

When he saw Jesus, he cried out, and fell down before him, and with a loud voice said, "What have I to do with thee, Jesus, thou Son of God most high? I beseech thee, torment me not."

For Jesus said unto him, "Come out of the man, thou unclean spirit." And Jesus asked him, saying, "What is thy name?"

And he answered saying, "My name is Legion; for we are many," because many devils were entered into him.

And there was there an herd of many swine feeding on the mountain. And all the devils besought Jesus, saying, "Send us unto the swine, that we may enter into them." And forthwith, Jesus gave them leave, and the unclean spirits went out, and entered into the swine, and the herd ran violently down a steep place into the sea, (they were about two thousand) and were choked in the sea. And they that fed the swine fled, and told it in the city and in the country.

And behold, the whole city came out to meet Jesus, to see what was done. And they came, and found the man out of whom the devils were departed, sitting at the feet of Jesus, clothed, and in his right mind. Then the whole multitude of the country of the Gadarenes round about besought Jesus to depart from them, for they were taken with great fear.

And when Jesus was come into the ship, he that had been possessed with the devil prayed him that he might be with him. But Jesus sent him away saying, "Go home to thy friends, and tell them how great things the Lord hath done for thee, and hath had compassion on thee." And he departed, and began to publish in Decapolis how great things Jesus had done for him; and all men did marvel.

THE DAMSEL IS NOT DEAD

AND WHEN JESUS was passed over again by ship unto the other side, the people gladly received him, for they were all waiting for him.

And behold, there cometh one of the rulers of the synagogue, Jairus by name. And when he saw Jesus, he fell at his feet and besought him greatly, saying, " My little daughter lieth at the point of death; I pray thee, come and lay thy hands on her, that she may be healed; and she shall live." For he had one only daughter about twelve years of age, and she lay a dying.

And Jesus went with him; and much people followed him, and thronged him. And a certain woman which had an issue of blood twelve years, and had suffered many things of many physicians, and had spent all that she had, and was nothing bettered, but rather grew worse, when she had heard of Jesus, came in the press behind and touched the hem of his garment. For she said within herself, " If I may but touch his garment, I shall be whole." And immediately her issue of blood staunched; and she felt in her body that she was healed of that plague.

And Jesus immediately turned him about in the press, and said, " Who touched my clothes? "

When all denied, Peter and they that were with him said, " Master, the multitude throng thee, and press thee, and sayest thou, ' Who touched me? ' "

And Jesus said, " Somebody hath touched me;" and he looked round about to see her that had done this thing. But the woman fearing and trembling, knowing what was done in her, came and fell down before him, and told him all the truth.

And he said unto her, " Daughter, be of good comfort; thy faith hath made thee whole; go in peace."

While he yet spake, there cometh one from the ruler of the synagogue's house, saying to him, " Thy daughter is dead; trouble not the Master."

As soon as Jesus heard the word that was spoken, he saith unto the ruler of the synagogue, " Be not afraid, only believe, and she shall be made whole."

And when Jesus came into the ruler's house, and saw the tumult and them that wept and wailed greatly, he saith unto them, " Why make ye this ado, and weep? The damsel is not dead, but sleepeth." And they laughed him to scorn, knowing that she was dead.

And when he had put them all out, he taketh the father and mother of the damsel, and Peter and James and John, and entered in where the damsel was lying. And he took her by the hand, and called, saying, " Maid, arise." And her spirit came again, and she arose straightway, and he commanded that something should be given her to eat.

And her parents were astonished; but he charged them that they should tell no man what was done.

WILT THOU BE MADE WHOLE?

After this there was a feast of the Jews; and Jesus went up to Jerusalem. Now there is at Jerusalem by the sheep market a pool, which is called in the Hebrew tongue Bethesda having five porches. In these lay a great multitude of impotent folk, of blind, halt, withered, waiting for the moving of the water. For an angel went down at a certain season into the pool, and troubled the water; whosoever then first after the troubling of the water stepped in was made whole of whatsoever disease he had.

And a certain man was there, which had an infirmity thirty and eight years. When Jesus saw him lie, and knew that he had been now a long time in that case, he saith unto him, "Wilt thou be made whole?"

The impotent man answered him, "Sir, I have no man, when the water is troubled, to put me into the pool; but while I am coming another steppeth down before me."

Jesus saith unto him, "Rise, take up thy bed, and walk." And immediately the man was made whole, and took up his bed, and walked; and on the same day was the sabbath.

The Jews therefore said unto him that was cured, "It is the sabbath day; it is not lawful for thee to carry thy bed."

He answered them, "He that made me whole, the same said unto me, 'Take up thy bed, and walk.'"

Then asked they him, "What man is that which said unto thee, 'Take up thy bed, and walk?'"

And he that was healed wist not who it was; for Jesus had conveyed himself away, a multitude being in that place.

Afterward Jesus findeth him in the temple, and said unto him, "Behold, thou art made whole; sin no more, lest a worse thing come unto thee."

The man departed, and told the Jews that it was Jesus, which had made him whole. And therefore did the Jews persecute Jesus, and sought to slay him, because he had done these things on the sabbath day.

But Jesus answered them, "My Father worketh hitherto, and I work."

Therefore the Jews sought the more to kill him, because he not only had broken the sabbath, but said also that God was his Father, making himself equal with God.

Then answered Jesus and said unto them, "Verily, verily, I say unto you, the Son can do nothing of himself, but what he seeth the Father do; for what things soever he doeth, these also doeth the Son likewise. For the Father loveth the Son, and showeth him all things that himself doeth; and he will show him greater works than these that ye may marvel. For as the Father raiseth up the dead, and quickeneth them, even so the Son quickeneth whom he will. For the Father judgeth no man, but hath committed all judgment unto the Son; that all men should honour the Son, even as they honour the Father. He that honoureth not the Son honoureth not the Father which hath sent him.

"Verily, verily, I say unto you, He that heareth my word, and believeth on him that sent me, hath everlasting life, and shall not come into condemnation; but is passed from death unto life. Verily, verily, I say unto you, the hour is coming, and now is, when the dead shall hear the voice of the Son of God; and they that hear shall live. For as the Father hath life in himself, so hath he given to the Son to have life in himself; and hath given him authority to execute judgment also, because he is the Son of man. Marvel not at this; for the hour is coming, in the which all that are in the graves shall hear his voice, and shall come forth; they that have done good unto the resurrection of life; and they that have done evil, unto the resurrection of Judgment.

"I can of mine own self do nothing; as I hear, I judge, and my judgment is just; because I seek not mine own will, but the will of the Father which hath sent me. If I bear witness of myself, my witness is not true. There is another that beareth witness of me; and I know that the witness which he witnesseth of me is true. Ye sent unto John, and he bare witness unto the truth. But I receive not testimony from man; but these things I say, that ye might be saved. John was a burning and a shining light; and ye were willing for a season to rejoice in his light. But I have greater witness than that of John, for the works which the Father hath given me to finish, the same works that I do, bear witness of me, that the Father hath sent me. And the Father himself, which hath sent me, hath borne witness of me. Ye have neither heard his voice at any time, nor seen his shape. And ye have not his word abiding in you; for whom he hath sent, him ye believe not.

"Search the scriptures, for in them ye think ye have eternal life; and they are they which testify of me. And ye will not come to me, that ye might have life. I receive not honour from men. But I know you, that ye have not the love of God in you. I am come in my Father's name, and ye receive me not; if another shall come in his own name, him ye will receive. How can ye believe, which receive honour one of another, and seek not the honour that cometh from God only? Do not think that I will accuse you to the Father; there is one that accuseth you, even Moses, in whom ye trust. For had ye believed Moses, ye would have believed me; for he wrote of me. But if ye believe not his writings how shall ye believe my words?"

After these things Jesus went over the sea of Galilee, which is the sea of Tiberias.

HEAL THE SICK, CLEANSE THE LEPERS, RAISE THE DEAD, CAST OUT DEVILS

AND WHEN JESUS had called unto him his twelve disciples, he gave them power against unclean spirits, to cast them out, and to heal all manner of sickness and all manner of disease. And he sent them to preach the kingdom of God, and to heal the sick. Now the names of the twelve disciples are these: Simon Peter, and Andrew his brother; James and John his brother; Philip and Bartholomew; Thomas, and Matthew;

James the son of Alphaeus, and Lebbaeus, whose surname was Thaddaeus; Simon the Canaanite, and Judas Iscariot.

These twelve Jesus sent forth, and commanded them, saying: "Go not into the way of the Gentiles, and into any city of the Samaritans enter ye not; but go rather to the lost sheep of the house of Israel. And as ye go, preach, saying, 'The kingdom of heaven is at hand.' Heal the sick, cleanse the lepers, raise the dead, cast out devils; freely ye have received, freely give.

"Take nothing for your journey. Provide neither gold, nor silver, nor brass in your purses, nor script for your journey, neither two coats, neither shoes, nor yet staves; for the workman is worthy of his meat. And into whatsoever city or town ye shall enter, enquire who in it is worthy; and there abide till ye go hence. And when ye come into an house salute it. And if the house is worthy, let your peace come upon it; but if it be not worthy, let your peace return to you. And whosoever shall not receive you, nor hear your words, when ye depart out of that house or city, shake off the dust of your feet. Verily I say unto you, it shall be more tolerable for the land of Sodom and Gomorrah in the day of judgment, than for that city.

"Behold, I send you forth as sheep in the midst of wolves; be ye therefore wise as serpents, and harmless as doves. But beware of men; for they will deliver you up to the councils, and they will scourge you in their synagogues; and ye shall be brought before governors and kings for my sake, for a testimony against them and the Gentiles. But when they deliver you up, take no thought how or what ye shall speak; for it shall be given you in that same hour what ye shall speak. For it is not ye that speak, but the spirit of your Father which speaketh in you. And ye shall be hated of all men for my name's sake; but he that endureth to the end shall be saved. The disciple is not above his master, nor the servant above his lord. It is enough for the disciple that he be as his master, and the servant as his lord. If they have called the master of the house

Beelzebub, how much more shall they call them of his household? Fear them not therefore; for there is nothing covered that shall not be revealed; and hid, that shall not be known.

"Whosoever therefore shall confess me before men, him will I confess also before my Father which is in heaven. But whosoever shall deny me before men, him will I also deny before my Father which is in heaven. He that receiveth you receiveth me, and he that receiveth me receiveth him that sent me. He that receiveth a prophet in the name of a prophet shall receive a prophet's reward; and he that receiveth a righteous man in the name of a righteous man shall receive a righteous man's reward. And whosoever shall give to drink unto one of these little ones a cup of cold water only in the name of a disciple, verily I say unto you, he shall in no wise lose his reward.

"What I tell you in darkness, that speak ye in light; and what ye hear in the ear, that preach ye upon the house tops. And fear not them which kill the body, but are not able to kill the soul. Are not five sparrows sold for two farthings, and not one of them is forgotten before God? But even the very hairs of your head are all numbered. Fear not therefore; ye are of more value than many sparrows."

And the disciples departed, and went through the towns preaching the gospel, and healing everywhere.

BUT ONE THING IS NEEDFUL

And when Jesus had made an end of commanding his twelve disciples, he departed thence to teach and to preach in their cities.

Now it came to pass as he went, that he entered into a certain village. And a certain woman named Martha received him into her house. And she had a sister called Mary which also sat at Jesus' feet and heard his word.

But Martha was cumbered about much serving, and came to him and said, " Lord, dost thou not care that my sister hath left me to serve alone? bid her therefore that she help me."

And Jesus answered and said unto her, " Martha, Martha, thou art careful and troubled about many things; but one thing is needful; and Mary hath chosen that good part, which shall not be taken away from her."

HOW MANY LOAVES HAVE YE?

AND THE DISCIPLES, when they were returned, gathered themselves together unto Jesus, and told him all things, both what they had done, and what they had taught.

And Jesus said unto them, " Come ye yourselves apart unto a desert place, and rest awhile," for there were many coming and going, and they had no leisure so much as to eat. And they departed into a desert place privately.

And the people saw them departing, and many knew Jesus, and they ran and followed him on foot out of the cities. When Jesus lifted up his eyes and saw a great multitude come unto him, he was moved with compassion toward them, because they were as sheep not having a shepherd. And he began to teach them many things; and he spake unto them of the kingdom of God, and healed them that had need of healing.

And when it was evening, his disciples came unto him, and said, " This is a desert place, and now the time is far spent. Send them away that they may go into the country round about and into the villages and buy themselves bread; for they have nothing to eat."

But Jesus said unto them, " They need not depart; give ye them to eat."

And they said unto him, " Shall we go and buy two hundred pennyworth of bread, and give them to eat? "

Philip answered, " Two hundred pennyworth of bread is not sufficient for them, that every one of them may take a little."

Jesus saith unto them, " How many loaves have ye? go and see."

Andrew saith unto him, " There is a lad here, which hath five barley loaves, and two small fishes; but what are they among so many? "

Jesus said, " Bring them hither to me." And he commanded the multitude to sit down on the grass. And they sat down in ranks by hundreds and fifties. And Jesus took the five loaves and the two fishes, and looking up to heaven, he blessed and brake, and gave to his disciples, and the disciples to the multitude. And they did all eat, and were filled.

When they were filled, Jesus said unto his disciples, " Gather up the fragments that remain that nothing be lost." And they took up of the fragments that remained twelve baskets full. And they that had eaten were about five thousand men, besides women and children.

And those men, when they had seen the miracle that Jesus did, said, " This is of a truth that prophet that should come into the world."

When Jesus therefore perceived that they would come and take him by force, to make him a king, he straightway constrained his disciples to get into a ship, and to go over the sea toward Capernaum, while he sent the multitude away. And when he had sent the multitude away, he went up into a mountain apart to pray. And when the evening was come, he was there alone.

JESUS CAME UNTO THEM WALKING ON THE SEA

AND THE DISCIPLES went down unto the sea, and entered into a ship, and went over the sea toward Capernaum. And it was now dark, and Jesus had not come to them. And the sea arose by reason of a great wind that blew. And the ship was now in the midst of the sea, tossed with waves; for the wind was contrary.

And in the fourth watch of the night, when the disciples had rowed about twenty or thirty furlongs, they saw Jesus walking on the sea, and drawing nigh unto the ship. And when they saw him walking on the sea, they were troubled, saying, "It is a spirit," and they cried out for fear.

But straightway Jesus spake unto them saying, "Be of good cheer; it is I; be not afraid."

And Peter answered him and said, "Lord, if it be thou, bid me come unto thee on the water."

And Jesus said, "Come."

And when Peter was come down out of the ship, he walked on the water, to go to Jesus. But when he saw the wind boisterous, he was afraid; and beginning to sink, he cried, saying, "Lord, save me."

And immediately Jesus stretched forth his hand, and caught him, and said unto him, "O thou of little faith, wherefore didst thou doubt?"

And when they were come into the ship, the wind ceased; and immediately the ship was at the land whither they went. Then they that were in the ship were sore amazed beyond measure, and wondered, and came and worshipped him, saying, "Of a truth thou art the Son of God."

And when they were come out of the ship, straightway the people knew Jesus, and ran through the whole region round about, and began to carry about in beds those that were sick, where they heard he was. And whithersoever he entered into villages, or cities, or country, they laid the sick in the streets, and besought him that they might touch if it were but the border of his garment; and as many as touched were made perfectly whole.

I AM THE LIVING BREAD

THE DAY following, when the people which stood on the other side of the sea saw that Jesus was not there, neither his disciples, they also took shipping, and came to Capernaum seeking Jesus. And when they had found him, they said unto him, "Rabbi, when camest thou thither?"

Jesus answered them, "Verily, I say unto you, ye seek me, not because ye saw the miracles, but because ye did eat of the loaves, and were filled. Labour not for the meat which perisheth, but for the meat which endureth unto everlasting life, which the Son of man shall give unto you; for him hath God the Father sealed."

Then said they, "What shall we do, that we might work the works of God?"

Jesus answered, "This is the work of God, that ye believe on him whom he hath sent."

They said therefore unto him, "What sign showest thou then, that we may see and believe thee? what dost thou work? Our fathers did eat manna in the desert; as it is written, 'He gave them bread from heaven to eat.'"

Then Jesus said unto them, "Verily, verily, I say unto you,

Moses gave you not the bread from heaven; but my Father giveth you the true bread from heaven. For the bread of God is he which cometh down from heaven, and giveth life unto the world."

Then said they, "Lord, evermore give us this bread."

And Jesus said unto them, "I am the bread of life; he that cometh to me shall never hunger; and he that believeth on me shall never thirst. But I said unto you, that ye also have seen me, and believe not. All that the Father giveth me shall come to me; and him that cometh to me I will in no wise cast out. For I came down from heaven, not to do mine own will, but the will of him that sent me. And this is the Father's will which hath sent me, that of all which he hath given me I should lose nothing, but should raise it up again at the last day. And this is the will of him that sent me, that every one which seeth the Son, and believeth on him, may have everlasting life; and I will raise him up at the last day."

The Jews then murmured at him, because he said, "I am the bread which came down from heaven." And they said, "Is not this Jesus, the son of Joseph, whose father and mother we know? how is it then that he saith, 'I came down from heaven?'"

Jesus therefore answered and said unto them, "Murmur not among yourselves. No man can come to me, except the Father which hath sent me draw him; and I will raise him up at the last day. It is written in the prophets, 'And they shall all be taught of God.' Every man therefore that hath heard, and hath learned of the Father, cometh unto me. Not that any man hath seen the Father, save he which is of God, he hath seen the Father. Verily, verily, he that believeth on me hath everlasting life. I am that bread of life. Your fathers did eat manna in the wilderness, and are dead. This is the bread which cometh down from heaven, that a man may eat thereof, and not die. I am the living bread which came down from heaven; if any man eat of this bread, he shall live for ever; and the bread that I will give is my flesh, which I will give for the life of the world."

The Jews therefore strove among themselves, saying, "How can this man give us his flesh to eat?"

Then Jesus said unto them, "Verily, verily, I say unto you, except ye eat the flesh of the Son of man, and drink his blood, ye have no life in you. Whoso eateth my flesh, and drinketh my blood, hath eternal life; and I will raise him up at the last day. For my flesh is meat indeed, and my blood is drink indeed. He that eateth my flesh, and drinketh my blood, dwelleth in me, and I in him. As the living Father hath sent me, and I live by the Father; so he that eateth me, even he shall live by me. This is that bread which came down from heaven; not as your fathers did eat manna, and are dead; he that eateth of this bread shall live for ever."

Many therefore of his disciples, when they heard this, said, "This is an hard saying; who can hear it?"

When Jesus knew in himself that his disciples murmured at it, he said unto them, "Doth this offend you? What and if ye shall see the Son of man ascend up where he was before? It is the spirit that quickeneth; the flesh profiteth nothing; the words that I speak unto you, they are spirit, and they are life. But there are some of you that believe not. Therefore said I unto you, that no man can come unto me, except it were given unto him of my Father." For Jesus knew from the beginning who they were that believed not, and who should betray him. From that time many of his disciples went back, and walked no more with him.

Then said Jesus unto the twelve, "Will ye also go away?"

Then Simon Peter answered him, "Lord, to whom shall we go? thou hast the words of eternal life. And we believe and are sure that thou art that Christ, the Son of the living God."

THE THINGS WHICH DEFILE

THEN CAME to Jesus scribes and Pharisees, which were of Jerusalem. And when they saw some of his disciples eat bread with defiled, that is to say unwashen, hands, they found fault. For the Pharisees, and all the Jews, except they wash their hands oft, eat not, holding the tradition of the elders. And when they come from the market, except they wash, they eat not. And many other things they hold, as the washing of cups and pots, brazen vessels, and of tables.

Then the Pharisees and scribes asked Jesus, "Why do thy disciples transgress the tradition of the elders? for they wash not their hands when they eat bread."

But Jesus answered and said unto them, "Why do ye also transgress the commandment of God by your tradition? For God commanded, saying, 'Honour thy father and mother;' and, 'He that curseth father or mother, let him die the death.' But ye say, 'Whosoever shall say to his father or his mother, "It is a gift, by whatsoever thou mightest be profited by me;" and honour not his father or his mother, he shall be free.' And ye suffer him no more to do ought for his father or his mother. Thus have ye made the commandment of God of none effect by your tradition. And many such like things do ye. Full well ye reject the commandment of God, that ye may keep your own tradition. Ye Pharisees make clean the outside of the cup and the platter; but your inward part is full of ravening and wickedness. Ye fools, did not he that made that which is without make that which is within also? Well did Isaiah prophesy of you, saying, 'This people draweth nigh unto me with their mouth, and honoureth me with their lips; but their heart is far from me. In vain do they worship me, teaching for doctrines the commandments of men.' "

And he called all the people unto him, and said unto them, "Hearken unto me every one of you, and understand: There is nothing from without a man, that entering into him can defile him; but the things which come out of him, those are they which defile the man."

Then came his disciples, and said unto him, "Knowest thou that the Pharisees were offended, after they heard this saying?"

But Jesus answered and said, "Every plant, which my heavenly Father hath not planted, shall be rooted up. Let them alone; they be blind leaders of the blind. And if the blind lead the blind, both shall fall into the ditch."

Then one of the lawyers said unto him, "Master, thus saying, thou reproachest us also."

And Jesus said, "Woe unto you also, ye lawyers! for ye lade men with burdens grievous to be borne, and ye yourselves touch not the burdens with one of your fingers. Woe unto you, lawyers! for ye have taken away the key of knowledge; ye entered not in yourselves, and them that were entering in ye hindered."

And as he said these things unto them, the scribes and the Pharisees began to urge him vehemently, and to provoke him to speak of many things; laying wait for him, and seeking to catch something out of his mouth, that they might accuse him.

And when Jesus entered into the house from the people, his disciples asked him concerning this parable.

And Jesus said, "Are ye also yet without understanding? Do ye not perceive that whatsoever thing from without entereth into the man, it cannot defile him; because it entereth not into his heart, but goeth into the belly and is cast out. But those things which proceed out of the mouth come forth from the heart, and they defile the man. For from within, out of the heart of men, proceed evil thoughts, adulteries, fornications, murders, thefts, covetousness, wickedness, deceit, lasciviousness, an evil eye, blasphemy, pride, foolishness; all these evil things come from within. These are the things which defile a man; but to eat with unwashen hands defileth not a man."

BE IT UNTO THEE EVEN AS THOU WILT

AND JESUS went thence, and departed into the coasts of Tyre and Sidon, and would have no man know it, but he could not be hid. For behold, a woman of Canaan whose young daughter had an unclean spirit, heard of him; and she came and fell at his feet, and cried unto him, saying, "Have mercy on me, O Lord, thou son of David; my daughter is grievously vexed with a devil."

But Jesus answered her not a word. And his disciples came and besought him, saying, "Send her away; for she crieth after us."

But he said, "I am not sent but unto the lost sheep of the house of Israel."

Then came she and worshipped him saying, "Lord help me."

But Jesus answered and said, "It is not meet to take the children's bread, and cast it to dogs."

And she said, "Truth, Lord, yet the dogs eat of the crumbs which fall from their master's table."

Then Jesus answered and said unto her, "O woman, great is thy faith; be it unto thee even as thou wilt." And her daughter was made whole from that very hour.

And again departing from the coasts of Tyre and Sidon, Jesus came unto the sea of Galilee. And they brought unto him one that was deaf, and had an impediment in his speech; and they besought Jesus to put his hand upon him. And Jesus took him aside from the multitude, and put his fingers into his ears, and he spit, and touched his tongue; and looking up to heaven, he sighed and said, " Ephphatha," that is " Be opened." And straightway his ears were opened, and the string of his tongue was loosed, and he spake plain.

And he charged them that they should tell no man; but the more he charged them, so much the more a great deal they published it; and they were beyond measure astonished, saying, " He hath done all things well; he maketh both the deaf to hear and the dumb to speak."

And Jesus went up into a mountain, and sat down there. And great multitudes came unto him, having with them those that were lame, blind, dumb, maimed, and many others, and cast them down at Jesus' feet; and he healed them; insomuch that the multitude wondered when they saw the dumb to speak, the maimed to be whole, the lame to walk, and the blind to see; and they glorified the God of Israel.

And the multitude being very great, and having nothing to eat, Jesus called his disciples unto him, and said, "I have compassion on the multitude, because they have now been with me three days, and have nothing to eat; and I will not send them away fasting, lest they faint in the way."

And his disciples said unto him, "Whence should we have so much bread in the wilderness as to fill so great a multitude? "

And Jesus asked them, " How many loaves have ye? "

And they said, " Seven, and a few little fishes."

And he commanded the multitude to sit down on the ground. And he took the seven loaves and the fishes, and gave thanks, and brake them, and gave to his disciples, and the disciples to the multitude. And they did all eat and were filled; and they took up of the broken meat that was left seven baskets full. And they that did eat were four thousand men, besides women and children.

And Jesus sent away the multitude and took ship, and came into the coasts of Magdala.

BEWARE OF HYPOCRISY

THEN THE PHARISEES also with the Sadducees came, and tempting, desired Jesus that he would show them a sign from heaven.

He answered and said unto them, "When it is evening, ye say, 'It will be fair weather, for the sky is red;' and in the morning, 'It will be foul weather today; for the sky is red and lowring.' When ye see a cloud rise out of the west, straightway ye say, 'There cometh a shower,' and so it is. And when ye see the south wind blow, ye say, 'There will be heat,' and it cometh to pass. O ye hypocrites, ye can discern the face of the sky, but can ye not discern the signs of the times? A wicked and adulterous generation seeketh after a sign, and there shall no sign be given unto it, but the sign of the prophet Jonah. For as Jonah was three days and three nights in the whale's belly, so shall the Son of man be three days and three nights in the heart of the earth. The men of Nineveh shall rise in judgment with this generation, and shall condemn it; because they repented at the preaching of Jonah, and behold, a greater than Jonah is here. The queen of the south shall rise up in the judgment with this generation, and shall condemn it; for she came from the uttermost parts of the earth to hear the wisdom of Solomon, and, behold, a greater than Solomon is here."

And he left them, and entering into the ship again, departed to the other side. Then Jesus said unto the disciples, "Take heed and beware of the leaven of the Pharisees and of the Sadducees."

Now the disciples had forgotten to take bread, neither had they in the ship with them more than one loaf. And they reasoned among themselves saying, "It is because we have taken no bread."

Which when Jesus perceived, he said, "O ye of little faith, why reason ye among yourselves because ye have brought no bread? Perceive ye not yet, neither understand? Have ye your hearts yet hardened? Having eyes, see ye not? and having ears, hear ye not? and do ye not remember? When I brake the five loaves among five thousand, how many baskets full of fragments took ye up?"

They said unto him, "Twelve."

"And when the seven among four thousand, how many baskets full of fragments took ye up?"

And they said, "Seven."

"How is it that ye do not understand that I spake it not to you concerning bread, but that ye should beware of the leaven of the Pharisees, which is hypocrisy. For there is nothing covered that shall not be revealed, neither hid, that shall not be known. And I say unto you my friends, be not afraid of them that kill the body, and after that have no more that they can do. But I will forewarn you whom ye shall fear: Fear him, which after he hath killed hath power to cast into hell. Yea, I say unto you, fear him."

Then understood they how that he bade them not beware of the leaven of bread, but of the doctrines of the Pharisees and of the Sadducees.

And he came to Bethsaida; and they brought a blind man unto him, and besought him to touch him. And Jesus took the blind man by the hand, and led him out of the town; and when he had spit on his eyes, and put his hands upon him, he asked him if he saw ought.

And the man looked up, and said, "I see men as trees walking."

After that Jesus put his hands again upon his eyes, and made him look up; and he was restored, and saw every man clearly.

And Jesus sent him away to his house, saying, "Neither go into the town, nor tell it to any in the town."

BEHOLD, I GIVE UNTO YOU POWER

AFTER THESE THINGS Jesus appointed other seventy also, and sent them two and two before his face into every city and place whither he himself would come.

Therefore said he unto them, "The harvest truly is great, but the labourers are few; pray ye therefore, the Lord of the harvest, that he would send forth labourers into his harvest.

"Go your ways: behold, I send you forth as lambs among wolves. Carry neither purse, nor script, nor shoes; and salute no man by the way. And into whatsoever house ye enter, first say, 'Peace be to this house.' And if the son of peace be there, your peace shall rest upon it; if not, it shall return to you again. And in the same house remain, eating and drinking such things as they give; for the labourer is worthy of his hire. Go not from house to house. And into whatsoever city ye enter, and they receive you, eat such things as are set before you. And heal the sick that are therein, and say unto them, 'The kingdom of God is come nigh unto you.' But into whatsoever city ye enter, and they receive you not, go your ways out into the streets of the same, and say, 'Even the very dust of your city, which cleaveth on us, we do wipe off against you. Notwithstanding be ye sure of this: that the kingdom of God is come nigh unto you.' Verily, I say unto you, it shall be more tolerable for the land of Sodom and Gomorrah in the day of judgment, than for that city. Woe unto thee, Chorazin! woe unto thee, Bethsaida! for if the mighty works had been done in Tyre and Sidon which have been done in you, they had a great while ago repented, sitting in sackcloth and ashes. But it shall be more tolerable for Tyre and Sidon at the judgment than for you. And thou Capernaum, which art exalted unto heaven, shalt be brought down to hell; for if the mighty works, which have been done in thee, had been done in Sodom, it would have remained until this day. But

I say unto you, that it shall be more tolerable for the land of Sodom in the day of judgment than for thee. He that heareth you heareth me; and he that despiseth you despiseth me; and he that despiseth me despiseth him that sent me."

And the seventy returned again with joy, saying, "Lord, even the devils are subject unto us through thy name."

And Jesus said unto them, "I beheld Satan as lightning fall from heaven. Behold, I give unto you power to tread on serpents and scorpions, and over all the power of the enemy; and nothing shall by any means hurt you. Notwithstanding in this rejoice not, that the spirits are subject unto you; but rather rejoice because your names are written in heaven."

In that hour Jesus rejoiced in spirit, and said, "I thank thee, O Father, Lord of heaven and earth, that thou hast hid these things from the wise and prudent and hast revealed them unto babes; even so, Father, for so it seemed good in thy sight. All things are delivered unto me of my Father; and no man knoweth who the Son is, but the Father; and who the Father is but the Son, and he to whom the Son will reveal him. Come unto me, all ye that labour and are heavy laden, and I will give you rest. Take my yoke upon you, and learn of me; for I am meek and lowly in heart, and ye shall find rest unto your souls. For my yoke is easy, and my burden is light."

And he turned to his disciples and said privately, "Blessed are the eyes which see the things that ye see; for I tell you, that many prophets and kings have desired to see those things which ye see, and have not seen them; and to hear those things which ye hear, and have not heard them. And the days will come, when ye shall desire to see one of the days of the Son of man, and ye shall not see it. And they shall say to you, 'See here;' or, 'See there;' go not after them, nor follow them. For as the lightning, that lighteneth out of the one part under heaven, shineth unto the other part under heaven, so shall also the Son of man be in his day. But first must he suffer many things, and be rejected of this generation."

LORD, TEACH US TO PRAY

AND IT CAME TO PASS, that as Jesus was praying in a certain place, when he ceased, one of his disciples said unto him, "Lord, teach us to pray, as John also taught his disciples."

And Jesus said unto them, "When ye pray say: Our Father, which art in heaven, Hallowed be thy name. Thy kingdom come. Thy will be done in earth, as it is in heaven. Give us this day our daily bread. And forgive us our debts, as we forgive our debtors. And lead us not into temptation, but deliver us from evil. For thine is the kingdom, and the power, and the glory, for ever. Amen.

"And when ye stand praying, forgive, if ye have ought against any; that your Father also which is in heaven may forgive your trespasses. For if ye forgive men their trespasses, your heavenly Father will also forgive you; but if ye do not forgive, neither will your Father which is in heaven forgive your trespasses.

"And when thou prayest, thou shalt not be as the hypocrites are; for they love to pray standing in the synagogues and in the corners of the streets, that they may seen of men. Verily, I say unto you, they have their reward. But thou, when thou prayest, enter into thy closet, and when thou hast shut thy door, pray to thy Father which is in secret; and thy Father which seeth in secret shall reward thee openly.

"And when ye pray, use not vain repetitions as the heathen do; for they think that they shall be heard for their much speaking. Be not ye therefore like unto them; for your Father knoweth what things ye have need of, before ye ask him.

"Again I say unto you, that if two of you shall agree on earth as touching any thing that they shall ask, it shall be done for them of my Father which is in heaven. For where two or three are gathered together in my name, there am I in the midst of them.

"Which of you shall have a friend, and shall go unto him at midnight, and say unto him, 'Friend, lend me three loaves; for a friend of mine in his journey is come to me, and I have nothing to set before him?' And he from within shall answer and say, 'Trouble me not; the door is now shut, and my children are with me in bed; I cannot rise and give thee.' I say unto you, though he will not rise and give him because he is his friend, yet because of his importunity he will rise and give him as many as he needeth.

"And I say unto you: Ask, and it shall be given you; seek, and ye shall find; knock, and it shall be opened unto you. For every one that asketh, receiveth; and he that seeketh findeth; and to him that knocketh it shall be opened. If a son ask bread of any of you that is a father, will he give him a stone? Or if he ask a fish, will he for a fish, give him a serpent? If ye then, being evil, know how to give good gifts unto your children, how much more shall your Father which is in heaven give good things to them that ask him? Therefore, all things whatsoever ye would that men should do to you, do ye even so to them; for this is the law and the prophets."

And the disciples said, "Lord, increase our faith."

And Jesus said, "If ye had faith as a grain of mustard seed, ye might say unto this sycamine tree, 'Be thou plucked up by the root, and be thou planted in the sea;' and it would obey you. Therefore I say unto you, what things soever ye desire, when ye pray, believe that ye receive them, and ye shall have them.

"No man can serve two masters for either he will hate the one, and love the other, or else he will hold to the one, and despise the other. Ye cannot serve God and mammon. Therefore I say unto you, take no thought for your life, what ye shall eat, or what ye shall drink, nor yet for your body what ye shall put on. The life is more than meat and the body is more than raiment. Behold the fowls of the air; for they sow not, neither do they reap, nor gather into barns; yet your heavenly Father feedeth them. Are ye not much better than they? Which of you by taking thought can add one cubit unto his stature? If ye then be not able to do that thing which is least, why take ye thought for the rest? And why take ye thought for raiment? Consider the lilies of the field, how they grow; they toil not, neither do they spin; and yet I say unto you, that even Solomon in all his glory was not arrayed like one of these. Wherefore if God so clothe the grass of the field, which today is, and tomorrow is cast into the oven, shall he not much more clothe you, O ye of little faith? Therefore, take no thought saying, 'What shall we eat?' or, 'What shall we drink?' or, 'Wherewithal shall we be clothed?' For all these things do the nations of the world seek after; and your heavenly Father knoweth that ye have need of all these things. But seek ye first the kingdom of God, and his righteousness, and all these things shall be added unto you. Fear not, little flock; for it is your Father's good pleasure to give you the kingdom.

"Lay not up for yourselves treasures upon earth, where moth and rust doth corrupt, and where thieves break through and steal. But lay up for yourselves treasures in heaven, where neither moth nor rust doth corrupt, and where thieves do not break through and steal; for where your treasure is, there will your heart be also. Sell that ye have, and give alms; provide yourselves bags which wax not old, a treasure in the heavens that faileth not."

HOW OFT SHALL I FORGIVE MY BROTHER?

He that hateth his brother is in darkness, and walketh in darkness, and knoweth not wither he goeth, because that darkness hath blinded his eyes.

THEN SAID JESUS unto his disciples, "Take heed to yourselves: If thy brother trespass against thee, rebuke him; and if he repent, forgive him. And if he trespass against thee seven times in a day, and seven times in a day turn again to thee, saying, 'I repent;' thou shalt forgive him.

"Moreover if thy brother shall trespass against thee, go and tell him his fault between thee and him alone; if he shall hear thee, thou hast gained thy brother. But if he will not hear thee, then take with thee one or two more, that in the mouth of two or three witnesses every word may be established. And if he shall neglect to hear them, tell it unto the church; but if he neglect to hear the church, let him be unto thee as an heathen man and a publican. Verily I say unto you, whatsoever ye shall bind on earth shall be bound in heaven; and whatsoever ye shall loose on earth shall be loosed in heaven."

Then came Peter to Jesus, and said, "Lord, how oft shall my brother sin against me, and I forgive him? till seven times?"

Jesus saith unto him, "I say not unto thee, 'Until seven times;' but until seventy times seven. Therefore is the kingdom of heaven likened unto a certain king which would take account of his servants. And when he had begun to reckon one was brought unto him, which owed him ten thousand talents. But forasmuch as he had not to pay, his lord commanded him to be sold, and his wife, and children, and all that he had, and payment to be made.

"The servant therefore fell down, and worshipped him, saying, 'Lord, have patience with me, and I will pay thee all.' Then the lord of that servant was moved with compassion, and loosed him, and forgave him the debt.

"But the same servant went out, and found one of his fellowservants, which owed him an hundred pence; and he laid hands on him, and took him by the throat, saying, 'Pay me that thou owest.'

"And his fellowservant fell down at his feet, and besought him, saying, 'Have patience with me, and I will pay thee all.' And he would not; but went and cast him into prison, till he should pay the debt. So when his fellowservants saw what was done, they were very sorry, and came and told unto their lord all that was done.

"Then his lord, after that he had called him, said unto him, 'O thou wicked servant, I forgave thee all that debt, because thou desiredst me; shouldest not thou also have had compassion on thy fellowservant, even as I had pity on thee?' And his lord was wroth, and delivered him to the tormenters, till he should pay all that was due unto him.

"So likewise shall my heavenly Father do also unto you, if ye from your hearts forgive not every one his brother their trespasses."

JUDGE RIGHTEOUS JUDGMENT

After these things Jesus would not walk in Jewry, because the Jews sought to kill him. And he went out from thence, and came into Nazareth, his own country, and his disciples followed him.

And when the sabbath day was come, he began to teach in the synagogue; and many hearing him were astonished, saying,

" From whence hath this man these things? and what wisdom is this which is given unto him, that even such mighty works are wrought by his hands? Is not this the carpenter, the son of Mary? "

And Jesus said unto them, " Ye will surely say unto me this proverb, ' Physician heal thyself; whatsoever we have heard done in Capernaum do also here in thy country.' But a prophet is not without honour, but in his own country, and among his own kin, and in his own house."

And he did not many mighty works there because of their unbelief, save that he laid his hands upon a few sick folk and healed them. And he marvelled because of their unbelief. And he went round about the villages teaching.

Now the Jews' feast of tabernacles was at hand. Jesus' brethren therefore said unto him, " Depart hence and go into Judea, that thy disciples also may see the works that thou doest. For there is no man that doeth any thing in secret, and himself seeketh to be known openly. If thou doest these things, show thyself to the world." For neither did his brethren believe in him.

Jesus said unto them, " My time is not yet come; but your time is always ready. The world cannot hate you; but me it hateth, because I testify of it, that the works thereof are evil. Go ye up unto this feast; I go not up yet unto this feast, for my time is not yet full come." When he said these words unto them, he abode still in Galilee. But when his brethren were gone up, then went Jesus also up unto the feast, not openly, but as it were in secret.

Then the Jews sought him at the feast, and said, " Where is he? "

And there was much murmuring among the people concerning him, for some said, " He is a good man."

Others said, " Nay, but he deceiveth the people." Howbeit no man spake openly of him for fear of the Jews.

Now about the midst of the feast Jesus went up into the temple, and taught. And the Jews marvelled, saying, "How knoweth this man letters, having never learned?"

Jesus answered them, and said, "My doctrine is not mine, but his that sent me. If any man will do his will, he shall know of the doctrine, whether it be of God, or whether I speak of myself. He that speaketh of himself seeketh his own glory; but he that seeketh his glory that sent him, the same is true, and no unrighteousness is in him. Did not Moses give you the law, and yet none of you keepeth the law? Why go ye about to kill me?"

The people answered and said, "Thou hast a devil; who goeth about to kill thee?"

Jesus answered them, "I have done one work, and ye all marvel. Are ye angry at me because I have made a man every whit whole on the sabbath day? Judge not according to the appearance, but judge righteous judgment."

Then said some of them of Jerusalem, "Is not this he, whom they seek to kill? But lo, he speaketh boldly, and they say nothing unto him. Do the rulers know indeed that this is the very Christ? Howbeit, we know this man whence he is; but when Christ cometh no man knoweth whence he is."

Then cried Jesus in the temple as he taught, saying, "Ye both know me, and ye know whence I am; and I am not come of myself, but he that sent me is true, whom ye know not. But I know him, for I am from him, and he hath sent me." Then sought they to take him, but no man laid hands on him, because his hour was not yet come.

And many of the people believed on him, and said, "When Christ cometh, will he do more miracles than these which this man hath done?" The Pharisees heard that the people murmured such things concerning him, and the Pharisees and the chief priests sent officers to take him.

Then said Jesus unto them, "Yet a little while am I with you, and then I go unto him that sent me. Ye shall seek me, and shall not find me; and where I am, thither ye cannot come."

Then said the Jews among themselves, "Whither will he go, that we shall not find him? will he go unto the dispersed among the Gentiles, and teach the Gentiles? What manner of saying is this that he said, 'Ye shall seek me, and shall not find me;' and, 'Where I am, thither ye cannot come?' "

In the last day, that great day of the feast, Jesus stood and cried, saying, "If any man thirst, let him come unto me, and drink. He that believeth on me, as the scripture hath said, out of his belly shall flow rivers of living water." (But this spake he of the Spirit, which they that believe on him should receive.)

Many of the people therefore when they heard this saying, said, "Of a truth this is the Prophet."

Others said, "This is the Christ."

But some said, "Shall Christ come out of Galilee? Hath not the scripture said, that Christ cometh of the seed of David, and out of the town of Bethlehem, where David was?" So there was a division among the people because of him. And some of them would have taken him, but no man laid hands on him.

Then came the officers to the chief priests and Pharisees; and the Pharisees said unto them, "Why have ye not brought him?"

The officers answered, "Never man spake like this man."

Then answered the Pharisees, "Are ye also deceived? Have any of the rulers or of the Pharisees believed on him? But this people who knoweth not the law are cursed."

Nicodemus saith unto them (He that came to Jesus by night being one of them), "Doth our law judge any man, before it hear him, and know what he doeth?"

They answered and said unto him, "Art thou also of Galilee? Search and look; for out of Galilee ariseth no prophet."

And every man went unto his own house. And Jesus went unto the mount of Olives.

YE SHALL KNOW THE TRUTH

AND EARLY in the morning Jesus came again into the temple, and all the people came unto him; and he sat down, and taught them.

And the scribes and Pharisees brought unto him a woman taken in adultery; and when they had set her in the midst, they said unto him, "Master, this woman was taken in adultery, in the very act. Now Moses in the law commanded us, that such should be stoned; but what sayest thou?" This they said, tempting him, that they might have to accuse him.

But Jesus stooped down and with his finger wrote on the ground, as though he heard them not. So when they continued asking him, he lifted up himself, and said unto them, "He that is without sin among you, let him first cast a stone at her." And again he stooped down, and wrote on the ground.

And they which heard it, being convicted by their own conscience, went out one by one, beginning at the eldest, even unto the last; and Jesus was left alone, and the woman standing in the midst.

When Jesus had lifted up himself, and saw none but the woman, he said unto her, "Woman, where are those thine accusers? hath no man condemned thee?"

She said, "No man, Lord."

And Jesus said unto her, "Neither do I condemn thee; go, and sin no more."

Then spake Jesus again unto the people, saying, "I am the light of the world; he that followeth me shall not walk in darkness, but shall have the light of life."

The Pharisees therefore said unto him, "Thou bearest record of thyself; thy record is not true."

Jesus answered them, "Though I bear record of myself,

yet my record is true; for I know whence I came, and whither I go; but ye cannot tell whence I come, and whither I go. Ye judge after the flesh; I judge no man. And yet if I judge, my judgment is true; for I am not alone, but I and the Father that sent me. It is also written in your law, that the testimony of two men is true. I am one that bear witness of myself, and the Father that sent me beareth witness of me."

Then said they unto him, "Where is thy Father?"

Jesus answered, "Ye neither know me, nor my Father; if ye had known me, ye should have known my Father also. Ye are from beneath; I am from above; ye are of this world; I am not of this world. I said therefore unto you, that ye shall die in your sins; for if ye believe not that I am he, ye shall die in your sins."

Then said they unto him, "Who art thou?"

And Jesus saith unto them, "Even the same that I said unto you from the beginning. I have many things to say and to judge of you; but he that sent me is true; and I speak to the world those things which I have heard of him. When ye have lifted up the Son of man, then shall ye know that I am he, and that I do nothing of myself; but as my Father hath taught me, I speak these things. And he that sent me is with me; the Father hath not left me alone; for I do always those things that please him."

And as he spake these words, many believed on him.

Then said Jesus to those Jews which believed on him, "If ye continue in my word, then are ye my disciples indeed; and ye shall know the truth, and the truth shall make you free."

They answered him, "We be Abraham's seed, and were never in bondage to any man; how sayest thou, 'Ye shall be made free?'"

Jesus answered them, "Verily, verily, I say unto you, whosoever committeth sin is the servant of sin. And the servant abideth not in the house for ever; but the Son abideth ever.

If the Son therefore shall make you free, ye shall be free indeed. I know that ye are Abraham's seed; but ye seek to kill me, because my word hath no place in you. I speak that which I have seen with my Father; and ye do that which ye have seen with your father."

They answered and said unto him, "Abraham is our father."

Jesus saith unto them, "If ye were Abraham's children, ye would do the works of Abraham. But now ye seek to kill me, a man that hath told you the truth, which I have heard of God; this did not Abraham. Ye do the deeds of your father."

Then said they to him, "We have one Father, even God."

Jesus said unto them, "If God were your Father, ye would love me; for I proceeded forth and came from God; neither came I of myself, but he sent me. Why do ye not understand my speech? even because ye cannot hear my word. Ye are of your father the devil, and the lusts of your father ye will do. He was a murderer from the beginning, and abode not in the truth, because there is no truth in him. When he speaketh a lie, he speaketh of his own; for he is a liar, and the father of it. And because I tell you the truth, ye believe me not. Which of you convinceth me of sin? And if I say the truth, why do ye not believe me? He that is of God heareth God's words; ye therefore hear them not, because ye are not of God."

Then answered the Jews, and said unto him, "Say we not well that thou art a Samaritan, and hast a devil?"

Jesus answered, "I have not a devil; but I honour my Father, and ye do dishonour me. And I seek not mine own glory; there is one that seeketh and judgeth. Verily, verily, I say unto you, if a man keep my saying, he shall never see death."

Then said the Jews unto him, "Now we know that thou hast a devil. Abraham is dead, and the prophets; and thou sayest, 'If a man keep my saying, he shall never taste of death.' Art thou greater than our father Abraham, which is dead? and the prophets are dead; whom makest thou thyself?"

Jesus answered, " If I honour myself, my honour is nothing. It is my Father that honoureth me, of whom ye say that he is your God; yet ye have not known him. But I know him, and if I should say, ' I know him not,' I shall be a liar like unto you; but I know him, and keep his saying. Your father Abraham rejoiced to see my day; and he saw it, and was glad."

Then said the Jews unto him, " Thou art not yet fifty years old, and hast thou seen Abraham? "

Jesus said unto them, " Verily, verily, I say unto you, before Abraham was, I am."

Then took they up stones to cast at him; but Jesus hid himself, and went out of the temple, going through the midst of them, and so passed by.

I AM COME THAT THEY WHICH SEE NOT MIGHT SEE

AND AS JESUS passed by, he saw a man which was blind from his birth. And his disciples asked him, saying, " Master, who did sin, this man, or his parents, that he was born blind? "

Jesus answered, " Neither hath this man sinned, nor his parents; but that the works of God should be made manifest in him. I must work the works of him that sent me, while it is day; the night cometh when no man can work. As long as I am in the world, I am the light of the world."

When he had thus spoken, he spat on the ground, and made clay of the spittle, and he anointed the eyes of the blind man with the clay, and said unto him, " Go, wash in the pool of Siloam " (which is by interpretation, " Sent "). He went his way therefore, and washed, and came seeing.

The neighbours therefore, and they which before had seen him that he was blind, said, " Is not this he that sat and begged? "

Some said, " This is he."

Others said, " He is like him."

But he said, " I am he."

Therefore said they unto him, " How were thine eyes opened? "

He answered and said, " A man that is called Jesus made clay, and anointed mine eyes, and said unto me, ' Go to the pool of Siloam, and wash;' and I went and washed, and I received sight."

Then said they unto him, " Where is he? "

He said, " I know not."

And they brought to the Pharisees him that aforetime was blind. Then again the Pharisees also asked him how he had received his sight.

He said unto them, " He put clay upon mine eyes, and I washed, and do see."

And it was the sabbath day when Jesus made the clay, and opened his eyes. Therefore said some of the Pharisees, " This man is not of God, because he keepeth not the sabbath day."

Others said, " How can a man that is a sinner do such miracles? " And there was a division among them.

They say unto the blind man again, " What sayest thou of him? "

He said, " He is a prophet."

But the Jews did not believe concerning him, that he had been blind, and received his sight, until they called the parents of him that had received his sight. And they asked them saying, " Is this your son, who ye say was born blind? How then doth he now see? "

His parents answered them and said, " We know that this is our son, and that he was born blind. But by what means he now seeth, we know not; or who hath opened his eyes, we know not.

He is of age, ask him; he shall speak for himself." These words spake his parents, because they feared the Jews; for the Jews had agreed already, that if any man did confess Christ, he should be put out of the synagogue. Therefore said his parents, " He is of age, ask him."

Then again called they the man that was blind, and said unto him, " Give God the praise; we know that this man is a sinner."

He answered and said, " Whether he be a sinner or no, I know not; one thing I know, that, whereas I was blind, now I see."

Then said they to him again, " What did he to thee? How opened he thine eyes? "

He answered them, " I have told you already, and ye did not hear; wherefore would ye hear it again? Will ye also be his disciples? "

Then they reviled him, and said, " Thou art his disciple; but we are Moses' disciples. We know that God spake unto Moses; as for this fellow, we know not from whence he is."

The man answered and said unto them, " Why herein is a marvellous thing, that ye know not from whence he is, and yet he hath opened mine eyes. Now we know that God heareth not sinners; but if any man be a worshipper of God, and doeth his will, him he heareth. Since the world began was it not heard that any man opened the eyes of one that was born blind. If this man were not of God, he could do nothing."

They answered and said unto him, " Thou wast altogether born in sins; and dost thou teach us? " And they cast him out.

Jesus heard that they had cast him out; and when he had found him, he said unto him, " Dost thou believe on the Son of God? "

He answered and said, " Who is he, Lord, that I might believe on him? "

And Jesus said unto him, " Thou hast both seen him, and it is he that talketh with thee."

And he said, " Lord, I believe." And he worshipped him.

And Jesus said, " I am come into this world, that they which see not might see."

And some of the Pharisees heard these words, and said unto Jesus, " Are we blind also? "

Jesus said unto them, " If ye were blind, ye should have no sin; but now ye say, 'We see;' therefore your sin remaineth. Verily, verily I say unto you, he that entereth not by the door into the sheepfold, but climbeth up some other way, the same is a thief and a robber. But he that entereth in by the door is the shepherd of the sheep. To him the porter openeth; and the sheep hear his voice, and he calleth his own sheep by name, and leadeth them out. And when he putteth forth his own sheep, he goeth before them, and the sheep follow him, for they know his voice. And a stranger will they not follow, but will flee from him, for they know not the voice of strangers." This parable spake Jesus unto them, but they understood not what things they were which he spake unto them.

Then said Jesus unto them again, " Verily, verily, I say unto you, I am the door of the sheep. All that ever came before me are thieves and robbers, but the sheep did not hear them. I am the door; by me if any man enter in, he shall be saved, and shall go in and out, and find pasture. The thief cometh not, but for to steal, and to kill, and to destroy; I am come that they might have life, and that they might have it more abundantly. I am the good shepherd; the good shepherd giveth his life for the sheep. But he that is an hireling, and not the shepherd, whose own the sheep are not, seeth the wolf coming, and leaveth the sheep, and fleeth; and the wolf catcheth them, and scattereth the sheep. The hireling fleeth, because he is an hireling, and careth not for the sheep. I am the good shepherd, and know my sheep, and am known of mine. As the Father knoweth me, even so know I the Father; and I lay down my life for the sheep. And other sheep I have, which are not of this fold; them also I must bring, and they shall hear my voice, and there shall be one fold, and one shepherd. Therefore doth my Father love me, because I lay down my life, that I might take it again. No man taketh it from me, but I lay it down of myself. I have power to lay it down, and I have power to take it again. This commandment have I received of my Father."

There was a division therefore again among the Jews for these sayings, and many of them said, " He hath a devil, and is mad; why hear ye him? "

Others said, " These are not the words of him that hath a devil. Can a devil open the eyes of the blind? "

Then came the Jews round about him, and said unto him, " How long dost thou make us to doubt? If thou be the Christ, tell plainly."

Jesus answered them, " I told you, and ye believed not; the works that I do in my Father's name, they bear witness of me. But ye believe not, because ye are not of my sheep, as I said unto you. My sheep hear my voice, and I know them, and they follow me; and I give unto them eternal life; and they shall never perish, neither shall any man pluck them out of my hand. My father, which gave them me, is greater than all; and no man is able to pluck them out of my Father's hand. I and my Father are one."

Then the Jews took up stones again to stone him.

Jesus answered them, " Many good works have I showed you from my Father; for which of those works do ye stone me? "

The Jews answered him, saying, " For a good work we stone thee not; but for a blasphemy; and because that thou, being a man, makest thyself God."

Jesus answered them, " Is it not written in your law, ' I said, Ye are gods? ' If he called them gods, unto whom the word of God came, and the scripture cannot be broken, say ye of him, whom the Father hath sanctified, and sent into the world, ' Thou blasphemest;' because I said, ' I am the Son of God? ' If I do not the works of my Father, believe me not. But if I do, though ye believe not me, believe the works, that ye may know and believe, that the Father is in me, and I in him."

Therefore they sought again to take him; but he escaped out of their hand, and went away again beyond Jordan into the place where John at first baptized, and there he abode.

And many resorted unto him, and said, "John did no miracle; but all things that John spake of this man were true." And many believed on him there.

I AM THE RESURRECTION, AND THE LIFE

Now a certain man was sick, named Lazarus, of Bethany, the town of Mary and her sister Martha. Therefore his sisters sent unto Jesus, saying, "Lord, behold, he whom thou lovest is sick."

When Jesus heard that, he said, "This sickness is not unto death, but for the glory of God, that the Son of God might be glorified thereby."

Now Jesus loved Martha, and her sister, and Lazarus. When he had heard therefore that Lazarus was sick, he abode two days still in the same place where he was. Then after that saith he to his disciples, "Let us go into Judaea again."

His disciples said unto him, "Master, the Jews of late sought to stone thee; and goest thou thither again?"

Then said Thomas unto his fellow disciples, "Let us also go, that we may die with him."

Jesus answered, "Are there not twelve hours in the day? If any man walk in the day, he stumbleth not, because he seeth the light of this world. But if a man walk in the night he stumbleth, because there is no light in him." These things said he; and after that he saith unto them, "Our friend Lazarus sleepeth; but I go, that I may wake him out of sleep."

Then said his disciples, "Lord, if he sleep, he shall do well." Howbeit Jesus spake of his death, but they thought that he had spoken of taking of rest in sleep.

Then said Jesus unto them plainly, "Lazarus is dead. And I am glad for your sakes that I was not there, to the intent ye may believe; nevertheless let us go unto him." Then when Jesus came, he found that Lazarus had lain in the grave four days already.

Now Bethany was nigh unto Jerusalem, about fifteen furlongs off, and many of the Jews came to Martha and Mary, to comfort them concerning their brother. Then Martha, as soon as she heard that Jesus was coming went and met him; but Mary sat still in the house.

Then said Martha unto Jesus, "Lord, if thou hadst been here, my brother had not died. But I know, that even now, whatsoever thou wilt ask of God, God will give it thee."

Jesus saith unto her, "Thy brother shall rise again."

Martha saith unto him, "I know that he shall rise again in the resurrection at the last day."

Jesus said unto her, "I am the resurrection, and the life; he that believeth in me, though he were dead, yet shall he live. And whosoever liveth and believeth in me shall never die. Believest thou this?"

She saith unto him, "Yea, Lord; I believe that thou art the Christ, the Son of God, which should come into the world."

And when she had so said, she went her way, and called Mary, her sister, secretly, saying, "The Master is come, and calleth for thee." As soon as she heard that, Mary arose quickly, and came unto him.

The Jews then which were with her in the house, and comforted her, when they saw Mary, that she rose up hastily and went out, followed her, saying, "She goeth unto the grave to weep there."

Then when Mary was come where Jesus was, and saw him, she fell down at his feet, saying unto him, "Lord, if thou hadst been here, my brother had not died."

When Jesus therefore saw her weeping, and the Jews also weeping which came with her, he groaned in the spirit, and was troubled, and said, "Where have ye laid him?"

They said unto him, "Lord, come and see."

Jesus wept. Then said the Jews, "Behold how he loved him!"

And some of them said, "Could not this man, which opened

the eyes of the blind have caused that even this man should not have died? "

Jesus therefore again groaning in himself cometh to the grave. It was a cave, and a stone lay upon it. Jesus said, " Take ye away the stone."

Martha, the sister of him that was dead, saith unto him, " Lord, by this time he stinketh, for he hath been dead four days."

Jesus saith unto her, " Said I not unto thee, that if thou wouldest believe, thou shouldest see the glory of God? " Then they took away the stone from the place where the dead was laid.

And Jesus lifted up his eyes, and said, " Father, I thank thee that thou hast heard me. And I knew that thou hearest me always, but because of the people which stand by I said it, that they may believe that thou hast sent me." And when he thus had spoken, he cried with a loud voice, " Lazarus, come forth." And he that was dead came forth, bound hand and foot with grave-clothes, and his face was bound about with a napkin.

Jesus saith unto them, " Loose him, and let him go."

Then many of the Jews which came to Mary, and had seen the things which Jesus did, believed on him. But some of them went their ways to the Pharisees, and told them what things Jesus had done.

Then gathered the chief priests and the Pharisees a council, and said, " What do we? for this man doeth many miracles. If we let him thus alone, all men will believe on him, and the Romans shall come and take away both our place and nation."

And one of them, named Caiaphas, being the high priest that same year, said unto them, " Ye know nothing at all, nor consider that it is expedient for us, that one man should die for the people, and that the whole nation perish not." And this spake he, not of himself, but he prophesied that Jesus should die for that nation, and not for that nation only, but that also he should gather together in one the children of God that were scattered abroad. Then from that day forth they took counsel together for to put him to death.

Jesus therefore walked no more openly among the Jews, but went thence unto a country near to the wilderness, and there continued with his disciples.

WHOM SAY YE THAT I AM?

AND JESUS went out, and his disciples, into Caesarea Philippi; and when he came into the coasts of Caesarea Philippi, he asked his disciples, saying, "Whom do men say that I the Son of man am?"

And they said, "Some say that thou art John the Baptist, some, Elijah, and others, Jeremias, or one of the prophets."

Jesus saith unto them, "But whom say ye that I am?"

And Simon Peter answered and said, "Thou art the Christ, the son of the living God."

And Jesus said unto him, "Blessed art thou, Simon Bar-jona, for flesh and blood hath not revealed it unto thee, but my Father which is in heaven. And I say unto thee, that thou art Peter, and upon this rock will I build my church, and the gates of hell shall not prevail against it. And I will give unto thee the keys of the kingdom of heaven; and whatsoever thou shalt bind on earth shall be bound in heaven; and whatsoever thou shalt loose on earth shall be loosed in heaven."

Then charged he his disciples that they should tell no man that he was Jesus the Christ. And he began to teach them, that the Son of man must suffer many things, and be rejected of the elders, and of the chief priests and scribes, and be killed, and after three days rise again.

Then Peter began to rebuke him, saying, "Be it far from thee, Lord; this shall not be unto thee."

But Jesus turned, and said unto Peter, "Get thee behind me, Satan, thou art an offence unto me, for thou savourest not the things that be of God, but the things that be of men."

Then said Jesus unto his disciples, "Whosoever will come after me, let him deny himself, and take up his cross daily, and follow me. For whosoever will save his life shall lose it, and whosoever will lose his life for my sake shall find it. For what is a man profited, if he shall gain the whole world, and lose his own soul? or what shall a man give in exchange for his soul? For whosoever shall be ashamed of me and of my words, of him shall the Son of man be ashamed, when he shall come in his own glory, and in his Father's, and of the holy angels. For the Son of man shall come in the glory of his Father with his angels, and then he shall reward every man according to his works. But I tell you of a truth, there be some standing here, which shall not taste of death, till they see the kingdom of God come with power."

THE CHRIST, THE SON OF THE LIVING GOD

AND AFTER six days Jesus taketh with him Peter and James, and John, and leadeth them up into an high mountain apart by themselves to pray. And as he prayed, he was transfigured before them: the fashion of his countenance was altered, and his face did shine as the sun, and his raiment was white and glistering, exceeding white as snow as no fuller on earth could white them. And behold, there talked with him two men, which were Moses and Elijah; who appeared in glory, and spake of his decease which he should accomplish at Jerusalem.

But Peter and they that were with him were heavy with sleep; and when they were awake, they saw his glory, and the two men that stood with him. And it came to pass, as they departed from him, Peter said unto Jesus, " Master, it is good for us to be here; and if thou wilt, let us make three tabernacles, one for thee, and one for Moses, and one for Elijah," for he wist not what to say, for they were sore afraid.

While he yet spake, behold, a bright cloud overshadowed them, and behold, a voice out of the cloud said, " This is my beloved Son in whom I am well pleased; hear ye him." And when the disciples heard it, they fell on their faces, and were sore afraid.

And Jesus came and touched them, and said, " Arise, and be not afraid." And when they had lifted up their eyes, they saw no man any more, save Jesus only with themselves.

And as they came down from the mountain, Jesus charged them saying, "Tell the vision to no man, until the Son of man be risen again from the dead."

And they kept that saying with themselves, questioning one with another what the rising from the dead should mean.

And his disciples asked him, saying, " Why then say the scribes that Elijah must first come? "

And Jesus answered and said unto them, " Elijah truly shall first come, and restore all things. But I say unto you, that Elijah is come already, and they knew him not, but have done unto him whatsoever they listed. Likewise shall also the Son of man suffer of them."

Then the disciples understood that he spake unto them of John the Baptist. And they kept it close, and told no man in those days any of those things which they had seen.

ALL THINGS ARE POSSIBLE TO HIM THAT BELIEVETH

AND IT CAME TO PASS, that on the next day, when they were come down from the hill, Jesus saw a great multitude about his disciples, and the scribes questioning with them. And straightway all the people, when they beheld Jesus, were greatly amazed, and running to him saluted him. And he asked the scribes, "What question ye with them?"

And one of the multitude answered, kneeling down to him and saying, "Master, I beseech thee, look upon my son, for he is mine only child. He is lunatick, and sore vexed, and ofttimes he falleth into the fire, and oft into the water. And I brought him to thy disciples, and they could not cure him."

Then Jesus answered and said, "O faithless and perverse generation, how long shall I be with you? how long shall I suffer you? Bring him hither to me." And they brought him unto Jesus, and straightway he fell on the ground and wallowed foaming.

And Jesus asked his father, "How long is it ago since this came unto him?"

And he said, "Of a child. And wheresoever the spirit taketh him, it teareth him; and he foameth, and gnasheth with his teeth, and pineth away. But if thou canst do any thing, have compassion on us, and help us."

Jesus said unto him, "If thou canst believe; all things are possible to him that believeth."

And straightway the father of the child cried out, and said with tears, "Lord, I believe; help thou mine unbelief."

And Jesus rebuked the foul spirit saying, "Thou dumb and deaf spirit, I charge thee, come out of him, and enter no more into him."

And the spirit cried, and rent him sore, and came out of him; and he was as one dead, insomuch that many said, "He is dead."

But Jesus took him by the hand and lifted him up; and the child was cured from that very hour; and Jesus delivered him again to his father. And they were all amazed at the mighty power of God.

But while they wondered every one at all things which Jesus did, he said unto his disciples, "Let these sayings sink down into your ears; for the Son of man shall be delivered into the hands of men." But they understood not this saying, and it was hid from them, that they perceived it not. And they feared to ask him of that saying.

Then came the disciples to Jesus apart, and said, "Why could not we cast him out?"

And Jesus said unto them, "Because of your unbelief; for verily I say unto you, if ye have faith as a grain of mustard seed, ye shall say unto this mountain, 'Remove hence to yonder place;' and it shall remove, and nothing shall be impossible unto you. Howbeit this kind goeth not out but by prayer and fasting."

And John answered him saying, "Master, we saw one casting out devils in thy name, and he followeth not us; and we forbad him, because he followeth not us."

But Jesus said, "Forbid him not; for there is no man which shall do a miracle in my name, that can lightly speak evil of me. For he that is not against us is for us. For whosoever shall give you a cup of water to drink in my name, because ye belong to Christ, verily I say unto you, he shall not lose his reward."

And they departed thence, and passed through Galilee; and Jesus would not that any man should know it.

OF SUCH IS THE KINGDOM OF HEAVEN

AND WHEN JESUS and the disciples were come to Capernaum, they that received tribute money came to Peter, and said, "Doth not your master pay tribute?"

Peter saith, "Yes."

And when Peter was come into the house, Jesus prevented him saying, "What thinkest thou, Peter? of whom do the kings of the earth take custom or tribute? of their own children or of strangers?"

Peter saith unto him, "Of strangers."

Jesus saith, "Then are the children free. Notwithstanding, lest we should offend them, go thou to the sea, and cast an hook, and take up the fish that first cometh up; and when thou hast opened his mouth, thou shalt find a piece of money; take that and give unto them for me and thee."

And being in the house, Jesus asked his disciples, "What was it that ye disputed among yourselves by the way?"

But they held their peace; for by the way they had disputed among themselves who should be the greatest.

And Jesus perceiving the thought of their heart sat down and called the twelve and saith unto them, "If any man desire to be first, the same shall be last of all, and the servant of all. The kings of the Gentiles exercise lordship over them, and they that exercise authority upon them are called benefactors. But ye shall not be so; but he that is greatest among you, let him be as the younger; and he that is chief, as he that doth serve. For whether is greater, he that sitteth at meat, or he that serveth? is not he that sitteth at meat? But I am among you as he that serveth. Which of you, having a servant plowing or feeding cattle, will say unto him by and by, when he is come from the field, ' Go and sit down to meat? ' And will not rather say unto him, ' Make ready wherewith I may sup, and gird thyself, and serve me till I have eaten and drunken; and afterward thou shalt eat and drink? ' Doth he thank that servant because he did the things that were commanded him? I trow not. So likewise ye, when ye shall have done all those things which are commanded you, say, ' We are unprofitable servants; we have done that which was our duty to do.' "

Then were brought unto Jesus little children, that he should put his hands on them and pray; and the disciples rebuked them.

But when Jesus saw it he was much displeased, and said unto them, " Suffer the little children to come unto me, and forbid them not, for of such is the kingdom of God. Verily I say unto you, whosoever shall not receive the kingdom of God as a little child, he shall not enter therein." And he took them up in his arms, and put his hands on them and blessed them.

And he took a child and set him in the midst of his disciples, and when he had taken him in his arms, he said unto them, " Verily I say unto you, except ye be converted, and become as little children, ye shall not enter into the kingdom of heaven. Whosoever therefore shall humble himself as this little child, the same is greatest in the kingdom of heaven. Whosoever shall receive one of such children in my name, receiveth me; and whosoever shall receive me, receiveth not me, but him that sent me.

" It is impossible but that offenses should come, but woe unto him through whom they come! Whoso shall offend one of these little ones which believe in me, it were better for him that a millstone were hanged about his neck, and that he were drowned in the depth of the sea. Take heed that ye despise not one of these little ones; for I say unto you, that in heaven their angels do always behold the face of my Father which is in heaven."

FORSAKE ALL, AND FOLLOW ME

AND WHEN JESUS was gone forth in the way, there came one running, and kneeled to him, and asked him, " Good Master, what shall I do that I may inherit eternal life? "

And Jesus said unto him, " Why callest thou me good? There is none good but one, that is God; but if thou wilt enter into life, keep the commandments."

He saith unto him, " Which? "

Jesus said, " Thou knowest the commandments, ' Thou shalt do no murder, Thou shalt not commit adultery, Thou shalt not steal, Thou shalt not bear false witness, Honour thy father and thy mother,' and ' Thou shalt love thy neighbour as thyself.' "

The young man saith unto him, " Master, all these have I kept from my youth up; what lack I yet? "

Then Jesus beholding him loved him, and said unto him, " One thing thou lackest. If thou wilt be perfect, go and sell that thou hast, and give to the poor, and thou shalt have treasure in heaven, and come, take up thy cross and follow me."

But when the young man heard that saying, he was very sorrowful, for he had great possessions, and he went away grieved.

And Jesus looked round about, and said unto his disciples, " How hardly shall they that have riches enter into the kingdom of God." And the disciples were astonished at his words.

But Jesus saith unto them, " Children, how hard it is for them that trust in riches to enter into the kingdom of God! It is easier for a camel to go through the eye of a needle, than for a rich man to enter into the kingdom of God."

And they were astonished out of measure, saying among themselves, " Who then can be saved? "

And he said, " The things which are impossible with men are possible with God, for with God all things are possible."

Then Peter said, " Lo we have left all and followed thee."

And Jesus said unto them, " He that loveth father or mother more than me is not worthy of me; and he that loveth son or daughter more than me is not worthy of me. He that taketh not his cross and followeth after me, is not worthy of me. He that findeth his life shall lose it; and he that loseth his life for my sake shall find it. Verily I say unto you, there is no man that hath left house, or parents, or brethren, or wife, or children, for the kingdom of God's sake, who shall not receive an hundred fold in this present time, and in the world to come life everlasting. And ye which have followed me in the regeneration when the Son of man shall sit in the throne of his glory, ye also shall sit upon twelve thrones, judging the twelve tribes of Israel. And every one that hath forsaken houses, or brethren, or sisters, or father, or mother, or wife, or children, or lands, for my name's sake, shall receive an hundred fold, and shall inherit everlasting life. And whosoever doth not bear his cross, and come after me, cannot be my disciple.

" For which of you, intending to build a tower, sitteth not down first, and counteth the cost, whether he have sufficient to finish? Lest haply, after he hath laid the foundation, and is not able to finish it, all that behold it, begin to mock him, saying, 'This man began to build, and was not able to finish.'

" Or what king, going to make war against another king, sitteth not down first, and consulteth whether he be able with ten thousand to meet him that cometh against him with twenty thousand? Or else, while the other is yet a great way off, he sendeth an ambassage, and desireth conditions of peace. So likewise, whosoever he be of you that forsaketh not all that he hath, he cannot be my disciple."

And it came to pass, that as they went in the way, a certain scribe came and said, "Master, I will follow thee withersoever thou goest."

And Jesus said unto him, "The foxes have holes, and the birds of the air have nests, but the Son of man hath not where to lay his head."

And Jesus said unto another, "Follow me."

But he said, "Lord, suffer me first to go bury my father."

Jesus said unto him, "Let the dead bury their dead; but go thou and preach the kingdom of God."

And another also said, "Lord, I will follow thee, but let me first go bid them farewell which are at home at my house."

And Jesus said unto him, "No man, having put his hand to the plow, and looking back, is fit for the kingdom of God."

BEWARE OF COVETOUSNESS

AND JESUS arose from thence, and cometh into the coasts of Judaea by the farther side of Jordan. And the people resort unto him again, and as he was wont, he taught them again. And there were gathered together an innumerable multitude of people, insomuch that they trode one upon another.

And one of the company said unto Jesus, "Master, speak to my brother, that he divide the inheritance with me."

And Jesus said unto him, "Man, who made me a judge or a divider over you? Take heed, and beware of covetousness; for a man's life consisteth not in the abundance of the things which he possesseth."

And he spake a parable unto them saying, "The ground of a certain rich man brought forth plentifully. And he thought within himself saying, 'What shall I do, because I have no room where to bestow my fruits? ' And he said, 'This will I do: I will pull down my barns, and build greater; and there will I bestow all my fruits and my goods. And I will say to my soul, "Soul, thou hast much goods laid up for many years; take thine ease, eat, drink, and be merry." And God said unto him, 'Thou fool, this night thy soul shall be required of thee; then whose shall those things be, which thou hast provided? ' So is he that layeth up treasure for himself, and is not rich toward God."

And the Pharisees also, who were covetous, heard all these things, and they derided him.

And Jesus said unto them, "Ye are they which justify yourselves before men, but God knoweth your hearts; for that which is highly esteemed among men is abomination in the sight of God. The law and the prophets were until John; since that time the kingdom of God is preached, and every man presseth into it. And it is easier for heaven and earth to pass, then one tittle of the law to fail.

"There was a certain rich man which was clothed in purple and fine linen, and fared sumptuously every day. And there was a certain beggar named Lazarus, which was laid at his gate, full of sores, desiring to be fed with the crumbs which fell from the rich man's table. And it came to pass, that the beggar died, and was carried by the angels into Abraham's bosom. The rich man also died, and was buried. And in hell he lifted up his eyes, being in torments, and saw Abraham afar off and Lazarus in his bosom.

"And he cried and said, 'Father Abraham, have mercy on me, and send Lazarus, that he may dip the tip of his finger in water and cool my tongue, for I am tormented in this flame.'

"But Abraham said, 'Son, remember that thou in thy lifetime receivedst thy good things, and likewise Lazarus evil things; but now he is comforted, and thou art tormented. And beside all this, between us and you there is a great gulf fixed, so that they which would pass from hence to you cannot; neither can they pass to us that would come from thence.'

"Then he said, 'I pray thee therefore, father, that thou wouldest send him to my father's house, for I have five brethren, that he may testify unto them lest they also come into this place of torment.'

"Abraham said, 'They have Moses and the prophets, let them hear them.'

"And he said, 'Nay, father Abraham, but if one went unto them from the dead, they will repent.'

"And Abraham said unto him, 'If they hear not Moses and the prophets, neither will they be persuaded, though one rose from the dead.'"

And Jesus said also unto his disciples, "There was a certain rich man, which had a steward, and the same was accused unto him that he had wasted his goods. And he called him and said unto him, 'How is it that I hear this of thee? give an account of thy stewardship, for thou mayest be no longer steward.'

"Then the steward said within himself, 'What shall I do? for my lord taketh away from me the stewardship. I cannot dig; to beg I am ashamed. I am resolved what to do, that when I am put out of the stewardship, they may receive me into their houses.'

"So he called every one of his lord's debtors unto him, and said unto the first, 'How much owest thou unto my lord?'

"And he said, 'An hundred measures of oil.'

"And he said unto him, 'Take thy bill, and sit down quickly, and write fifty.' Then said he to another, 'And how much owest thou?'

"And he said, 'An hundred measures of wheat.'

"And he said unto him, 'Take thy bill, and write fourscore.'

"And the lord commended the unjust steward, because he had done wisely, for the children of this world are in their generation wiser than the children of light. And I say unto you, make to yourselves friends of the mammon of unrighteousness; that, when ye fail, they may receive you into everlasting habitations.

"He that is faithful in that which is least is faithful also in much; and he that is unjust in the least is unjust also in much. If therefore ye have not been faithful in the unrighteous mammon, who will commit to your trust the true riches? And if ye have not been faithful in that which is another man's, who shall give you that which is your own? No servant can serve two masters; for either he will hate the one, and love the other, or else he will hold to the one, and despise the other. Ye cannot serve God and mammon."

Then said Peter unto him, "Lord, speakest thou this parable unto us, or even to all?"

And Jesus said, "Who then is that faithful and wise steward, whom his lord shall make ruler over his household, to give them their portion of meat in due season? Blessed is that servant, whom his lord when he cometh shall find so doing. Of a truth I say unto you, that he will make him ruler over all that he hath. But if that servant say in his heart, 'My lord delayeth his coming,' and shall begin to beat the menservants and maidens, and to eat and drink and be drunken, the lord of that servant will come in a day when he looketh not for him, and at an hour when he is not aware, and will cut him in sunder, and will appoint him his portion with the unbelievers. And that servant which knew his lord's will, and prepared not himself, neither did according to his will, shall be beaten with many stripes. But he that knew not, and did commit things worthy of stripes, shall be beaten with few stripes. For unto whomsoever much is given, of him shall be much required; and to whom men have committed much, of him they will ask the more."

THY SINS ARE FORGIVEN

AND ONE OF THE Pharisees desired Jesus that He should eat with him. And Jesus went unto the Pharisee's house, and sat down to meat. And behold, a woman in the city, which was a sinner, when she knew that Jesus sat at meat in the Pharisee's house, brought an alabaster box of ointment, and stood at his feet behind him weeping, and began to wash his feet with tears, and to wipe them with the hairs of her head, and kissed his feet, and anointed them with the ointment.

Now when the Pharisee which had bidden Jesus saw it, he spake within himself, saying, "This man, if he were a prophet, would have known who and what manner of woman this is that toucheth him; for she is a sinner."

And Jesus answering said unto him, "Simon, I have somewhat to say unto thee."

And he said, "Master, say on."

"There was a certain creditor which had two debtors; the one owed five hundred pence, and the other fifty. And when they had nothing to pay, he frankly forgave them both. Tell me therefore, which of them will love him most?"

And Simon answered and said, "I suppose that he, to whom he forgave most."

And Jesus said unto him, "Thou hast rightly judged." And he turned to the woman, and said unto Simon, "Seest thou this woman? I entered into thine house, thou gavest me no water for my feet; but she has washed my feet with tears, and wiped them with the hairs of her head. Thou gavest me no kiss; but this woman since the time I came in hath not ceased to kiss my feet. My head with oil thou didst not anoint; but this woman hath anointed my feet with ointment. Wherefore I say unto thee, her sins, which are many, are forgiven; for she loved much; but to whom little is forgiven, the same loveth little."

And he said unto her, "Thy sins are forgiven."

And they that sat at meat with him began to say within themselves, "Who is this that forgiveth sins also?"

And Jesus said to the woman, "Thy faith hath saved thee; go in peace."

And it came to pass afterward, that Jesus went throughout every city and village, preaching and showing the glad tidings of the kingdom of God; and the twelve were with him. And certain women, which had been healed of evil spirits and infirmities, Mary called Magdalene, out of whom went seven devils, and Joanna the wife of Chuza, Herod's steward, and Susanna, and many others, ministered unto him of their substance.

THOU ART LOOSED FROM THINE INFIRMITY

AND JESUS was teaching in one of the synagogues on the sabbath. And behold, there was a woman which had a spirit of infirmity eighteen years, and was bowed together, and could in no wise lift up herself.

And when Jesus saw her, he called her to him, and said unto her, "Woman, thou art loosed from thine infirmity." And he laid his hands on her, and immediately she was made straight, and glorified God.

And the ruler of the synagogue answered with indignation, because that Jesus had healed on the sabbath day, and said unto the people, "There are six days in which men ought to work; in them therefore come and be healed, and not on the sabbath day."

Jesus then answered him, and said, "Thou hypocrite, doth not each one of you on the sabbath loose his ox or his ass from the stall, and lead him away to watering? And ought not this woman, being a daughter of Abraham, whom Satan hath bound, lo, these eighteen years, be loosed from this bond on the sabbath day?"

And when he had said these things, all his adversaries were ashamed, and all the people rejoiced for all the glorious things that were done by him.

THE GREAT SUPPER

AND AS JESUS went into the house of one of the chief Pharisees to eat bread on the sabbath day, they watched him. And behold, there was a certain man before him which had the dropsy. And Jesus spake unto the lawyers and Pharisees, saying, "Is it lawful to heal on the sabbath day?" And they held their peace.

And Jesus took him, and healed him, and let him go, and answered them, saying, "Which of you shall have an ass or an ox fallen into a pit, and will not straightway pull him out on the sabbath day?" And they could not answer him again to these things.

And Jesus put forth a parable to those which were bidden, when he marked how they chose out the chief rooms, saying unto them, "When thou art bidden of any man to a wedding, sit not down in the highest room lest a more honourable man than thou be bidden, and he that bade thee and him come and say to thee, 'Give this man place,' and thou begin with shame to take the lowest room. But when thou art bidden, go and sit down in the lowest room, that when he that bade thee cometh, he may say unto thee, 'Friend, go up higher;' then shalt thou have worship in the presence of them that sit at meat with thee. For whosoever exalteth himself shall be abased, and he that humbleth himself shall be exalted."

Then said Jesus also to him that bade him, "When thou makest a dinner or a supper, call not thy friends, nor thy brethren, neither thy kinsmen, nor thy rich neighbours, lest they also bid thee again, and a recompense be made thee. But when thou makest a feast, call the poor, the maimed, the lame, the blind, and thou shalt be blessed, for thou shalt be recompensed at the resurrection of the just."

And when one of them that sat at meat with him heard these things, he said unto him, "Blessed is he that shall eat bread in the kingdom of God."

Then said Jesus unto him, "The kingdom of heaven is like unto a certain man that made a great supper, and bade many; and sent his servant at supper time to say to them that were bidden, 'Come, for all things are now ready.'

"And they all with one consent began to make excuse. The first said unto him, 'I have bought a piece of ground, and I must needs go and see it; I pray thee have me excused.'

"And another said, 'I have bought five yoke of oxen, and I go to prove them; I pray thee have me excused.'

"And another said, 'I have married a wife, and therefore I cannot come.'

"So that servant came, and showed his lord these things. Then the master of the house being angry said to his servant, 'Go out quickly into the streets and lanes of the city, and bring in hither the poor, and the maimed, and the halt, and the blind.'

"And the servant said, 'Lord, it is done as thou hast commanded and yet there is room.'

"And the lord said unto the servant, 'Go out into the highways and hedges, and compel them to come in, that my house may be filled. For I say unto you, that none of those men which were bidden shall taste of my supper, for they which were bidden were not worthy.'"

THE SON OF MAN CAME TO SAVE THAT WHICH WAS LOST

THEN DREW NEAR unto Jesus all the publicans and sinners for to hear him. And the Pharisees and scribes murmured, saying, " This man receiveth sinners, and eateth with them."

And Jesus said, " The Son of man is come to save that which was lost."

And he spake this parable unto them saying, " How think ye? If a man have an hundred sheep, and one of them be gone astray, doth he not leave the ninety and nine, and goeth into the mountains, and seeketh that which is gone astray, until he find it? And when he hath found it, he layeth it on his shoulders, and rejoiceth more of that sheep than of the ninety and nine which went not astray. And when he cometh home, he calleth his friends and neighbours, saying unto them, ' Rejoice with me, for I have found my sheep which was lost.' I say unto you, that likewise joy shall be in heaven over one sinner that repenteth, more than over ninety and nine just persons which need no repentance. It is not the will of your Father which is in heaven that one of these should perish.

" Either what woman having ten pieces of silver, if she lose one piece, doth not light a candle, and sweep the house, and seek diligently till she find it? And when she hath found it, she calleth her friends and her neighbours together, saying, ' Rejoice with me, for I have found the piece which I had lost.' Likewise, I say unto you, there is joy in the presence of the angels of God over one sinner that repenteth."

And he said, " A certain man had two sons. And the younger

of them said to his father, 'Father, give me the portion of goods that falleth to me.'

"And not many days after the younger son gathered all together, and took his journey into a far country, and there wasted his substance with riotous living. And when he had spent all, there arose a mighty famine in that land, and he began to be in want. And he went and joined himself to a citizen of that country, and he sent him into his fields to feed swine. And he would fain have filled his belly with the husks that the swine did eat; and no man gave unto him.

"And when he came to himself, he said, 'How many hired servants of my father's have bread enough and to spare, and I perish with hunger! I will arise and go to my father, and will say unto him, 'Father, I have sinned against heaven, and before thee, and am no more worthy to be called thy son; make me as one of thy hired servants.' And he arose and came to his father.

"But when he was yet a great way off, his father saw him, and had compassion, and ran, and fell on his neck, and kissed him. And the son said unto him, 'Father, I have sinned against heaven, and in thy sight, and am no more worthy to be called thy son.'

"But the father said to his servants, 'Bring forth the best robe, and put it on him; and put a ring on his hand, and shoes on his feet. And bring hither the fatted calf, and kill it; and let us eat and be merry; for this my son was dead, and is alive again; he was lost, and is found.' And they began to be merry.

"Now his elder son was in the field and as he came and drew nigh to the house, he heard music and dancing. And he called one of the servants and asked what these things meant. And the servant said unto him, 'Thy brother is come; and thy father hath killed the fatted calf, because he hath received him safe and sound.'

"And he was angry, and would not go in; therefore came his father out, and intreated him. And he answering said to his father, 'Lo, these many years do I serve thee, neither transgressed I at any time thy commandments; and yet thou never gavest me a kid, that I might make merry with my friends. But as soon as this thy son was come, which hath devoured thy living with harlots, thou hast killed for him the fatted calf.'

" And his father said unto him, 'Son, thou art ever with me, and all that I have is thine. It was meet that we should make merry, and be glad, for this thy brother was dead, and is alive again; and was lost, and is found.' "

THE KINGDOM OF GOD IS WITHIN YOU

And when Jesus was demanded of the Pharisees, when the kingdom of God should come, he answered them and said, " The kingdom of God cometh not with observation; neither shall they say, 'Lo here!' or, 'Lo there!' for, behold, the kingdom of God is within you."

Then said Jesus, " Unto what is the kingdom of God like? and whereunto shall I resemble it? It is like a grain of mustard seed, which indeed is the least of all seeds, which a man took and cast into his garden; and it grew, and waxed a great tree, and the fowls of the air lodged in the branches of it."

And again he said, " Whereunto shall I liken the kingdom of God? It is like leaven, which a woman took and hid in three measures of meal, till the whole was leavened.

" Again the kingdom of heaven is like unto treasure hid in a field; the which when a man hath found, he hideth, and for joy thereof goeth and selleth all that he hath, and buyeth that field.

" Again the kingdom of heaven is like unto a merchant man, seeking goodly pearls; who, when he had found one pearl of great price, went and sold all that he had, and bought it.

"And the kingdom of heaven is like unto a man that is an householder, which went out early in the morning to hire labourers into his vineyard. And when he had agreed with the labourers for a penny a day, he sent them into his vineyard. And he went out about the third hour, and saw others standing idle in the marketplace, and said unto them, 'Go ye also into the vineyard, and whatsoever is right I will give you.' And they went their way.

"Again he went out about the sixth and ninth hour, and did likewise. And about the eleventh hour he went out, and found others standing idle, and saith unto them, 'Why stand ye here all the day idle?'

"They say unto him, 'Because no man hath hired us.'

"He said unto them, 'Go ye also into the vineyard; and whatsoever is right, that shall ye receive.'

"So when even was come, the lord of the vineyard saith unto his steward, 'Call the labourers, and give them their hire, beginning from the last unto the first.' And when they came that were hired about the eleventh hour, they received every man a penny.

"But when the first came, they supposed that they should have received more; and they likewise received every man a penny. And when they had received it, they murmured against the goodman of the house, saying, 'These last have wrought but one hour, and thou hast made them equal unto us, which have borne the burden and heat of the day.'

"But he answered one of them, and said, 'Friend, I do thee no wrong; didst thou not agree with me for a penny? Take that thine is, and go thy way; I will give unto this last even as unto thee. Is it not lawful for me to do what I will with mine own? Is thine eye evil because I am good?' So the last shall be first, and the first last; for many be called, but few chosen.

"Then shall the kingdom of heaven be likened unto ten virgins, which took their lamps, and went forth to meet the bridegroom. And five of them were wise, and five were foolish. They that were foolish took their lamps, and took no oil with them. But the wise took oil in their vessels with their lamps. While the bridegroom tarried, they all slumbered and slept. And at midnight there was a cry made, 'Behold, the bridegroom cometh; go ye out to meet him.'

"Then all those virgins arose, and trimmed their lamps. And the foolish said unto the wise, 'Give us of your oil, for our lamps are gone out.'

"But the wise answered, saying, 'Not so; lest there be not enough for us and you; but go ye rather to them that sell, and buy for yourselves.'

"And while they went to buy, the bridegroom came; and they that were ready went in with him to the marriage, and the door was shut. Afterward came also the other virgins, saying, 'Lord, lord, open to us.'

"But he answered and said, 'Verily I say unto you, I know you not.' Watch therefore, for ye know neither the day nor the hour wherein the Son of man cometh.

"Again the kingdom of heaven is like unto a net, that was cast into the sea, and gathered of every kind; which, when it was full, they drew to shore, and sat down, and gathered the good into vessels, but cast the bad away. So shall it be at the end of the world; the angels shall come forth, and sever the wicked from among the just, and shall cast them into the furnace of fire."

Then said one unto him, "Lord, are there few that be saved?"

And he said unto them, "Strive to enter in at the strait gate; for many, I say unto you, will seek to enter in and shall not be able. When once the master of the house is risen up, and hath shut to the door and ye begin to stand without, and to knock at the door, saying, 'Lord, Lord, open unto us,' and he shall answer and say unto you, 'I know you not whence ye are,' then shall ye begin to say, 'We have eaten and drunk in thy presence, and thou hast taught in our streets.' But he shall say, 'I tell you, I know you not whence ye are; depart from me, all ye workers of iniquity.' There shall be weeping and gnashing of teeth, when ye shall see Abraham, and Isaac, and Jacob, and all the prophets in the kingdom of God, and you yourselves thrust out. And they shall come from the east and from the west, and from the north, and from the south, and shall sit down in the kingdom of God. And, behold, there are last which shall be first, and there are first which shall be last."

Jesus saith unto them, "Have ye understood all these things?"

They say unto him, "Yea, Lord."

Then saith he unto them, "Therefore every scribe which is instructed into the kingdom of heaven is like unto a man that is an householder, which bringeth forth out of his treasure things new and old."

HOW OFTEN WOULD I HAVE GATHERED THY CHILDREN TOGETHER!

THE SAME DAY there came certain of the Pharisees, saying unto Jesus, "Get thee out, and depart hence, for Herod will kill thee."

Now Herod the king, had heard of all that was done by Jesus, for his name was spread abroad. And Herod was perplexed, because that it was said of some that Elijah had appeared, and of others, that one of the old prophets was risen again. But when Herod heard thereof, he said, "It is John whom I beheaded; he is risen from the dead, and therefore mighty works show forth themselves in him."

And Jesus said unto them, "Go ye, and tell that fox, 'Behold, I cast out devils, and I do cures today and tomorrow, and the third day I shall be perfected. Nevertheless I must walk today, and tomorrow, and the day following; for it cannot be that a prophet perish out of Jerusalem!'

"O Jerusalem, Jerusalem which killest the prophets, and stonest them that are sent unto thee; how often would I have gathered thy children together, as a hen doth gather her brood under her wings, and ye would not! Behold, your house is left unto you desolate; and verily I say unto you, ye shall not see me, until the time come when ye shall say, 'Blessed is he that cometh in the name of the Lord.'"

LOVE IS THE FULFILLING OF THE LAW

" To this end was I born,
And for this cause came I into the world,
That I should bear witness unto the Truth.
Every one that is of the Truth heareth my voice."

Christ Jesus

ON THE WAY GOING UP TO JERUSALEM

AND THE JEW'S passover was nigh at hand; and many went out of the country up to Jerusalem before the passover, to purify themselves. And the chief priests and the scribes spake among themselves as they stood in the temple, " What think ye, that Jesus will come to the feast? " And they sought how they might take him by craft and put him to death. But they said, " Not on the feast day, lest there be an uproar of the people."

Now before the feast of the passover, when Jesus knew that his hour was come that he should depart out of this world unto the Father, having loved his own which were in the world, he loved them unto the end. And it came to pass that he steadfastly set his face to go to Jerusalem. And he went through the cities and villages, teaching, and journeying toward Jerusalem.

And the disciples were amazed, and as they followed, they were afraid. And Jesus took them apart in the way, and began to tell them what things should happen unto him, saying, " Behold, we go up to Jerusalem, and all things that are written by the prophets concerning the Son of man shall be accomplished. And he shall be betrayed unto the chief priests and unto the scribes, and they shall condemn him to death, and shall deliver him to the Gentiles; and he shall be mocked, and spitefully entreated, and spitted on; and they shall scourge him, and put him to death; and the third day he shall rise again." But the disciples understood not that saying, and were afraid to ask him.

And James and John the sons of Zebedee, came unto Jesus

saying, " Master, we would that thou shouldst grant unto us that we may sit, one on thy right hand, and the other on thy left hand in thy glory."

But Jesus said unto them, " Ye know not what ye ask; can ye drink of the cup that I drink of? and be baptized with the baptism that I am baptized with? "

And they said unto him, " We can."

And Jesus said unto them, " Ye shall drink indeed of my cup, and be baptized with the baptism that I am baptized with; but to sit on my right hand and on my left, is not mine to give, but it shall be given to them for whom it is prepared of my Father."

And when the ten heard it, they were moved with indignation against the two brethren.

But Jesus called them unto him, and said, " Whosoever will be great among you, let him be your minister; and whosoever will be chief among you, let him be your servant, even as the Son of man came not to be ministered unto, but to minister, and to give his life a ransom for many. Ye are they which have continued with me in my temptations. And I appoint unto you a kingdom, as my Father hath appointed unto me, that ye may eat and drink at my table in my kingdom, and sit on thrones judging the twelve tribes of Israel."

And they were on the way going up to Jerusalem, and Jesus went before them. And it came to pass that they passed through the midst of Samaria and Galilee. And Jesus sent messengers before his face; and they entered into a village of the Samaritans, to make ready for him. And the people did not receive him, because his face was as though he would go to Jerusalem. And when his disciples, James and John, saw this, they said, " Lord, wilt thou that we command fire to come down from heaven, and consume them, even as Elijah did? "

But Jesus turned and rebuked them, and said, " Ye know not what manner of spirit ye are of. For the Son of man is not come to destroy men's lives, but to save them." And they went to another village.

And as Jesus entered into a certain village, there met him ten men that were lepers, which stood afar off, and lifted up their voices and said, " Master, have mercy on us."

And when he saw them, he said unto them, " Go show yourselves unto the priests."

And it came to pass that as they went they were cleansed. And one of them, when he saw that he was healed, turned back, and with a loud voice glorified God, and fell down on his face at Jesus' feet, giving him thanks. And he was a Samaritan.

And Jesus said, "Were there not ten cleansed? but where are the nine? There are not found that returned to give glory to God, save this stranger." And he said unto him, " Arise, go thy way; thy faith hath made thee whole."

And it came to pass, that as Jesus was come nigh unto Jericho with his disciples and a great multitude of people, blind Bartimaeus, the son of Timaeus, sat by the highway side begging. And hearing the multitude pass by, he asked what it meant. And they told him that Jesus of Nazareth passeth by.

And he cried, saying, " Jesus, thou son of David, have mercy on me." And they which went before rebuked him, that he should hold his peace. But he cried so much the more, "Thou son of David, have mercy on me."

And Jesus stood still, and commanded him to be called. And they called the blind man saying unto him, " Be of good comfort, rise, he calleth thee." And he arose and came to Jesus.

And Jesus said unto him, " What wilt thou that I should do unto thee? "

The blind man said, " Lord, that I might receive my sight."

And Jesus said, " Go thy way; thy faith hath made thee whole." And immediately he received his sight, and followed Jesus in the way, glorifying God; and all the people, when they saw it gave praise unto God.

And Jesus entered Jericho. And behold, there was a man named Zacchaeus, which was the chief among the publicans, and he was rich. And he sought to see Jesus who he was, and could not for the press, because he was little of stature. And he ran before and climbed up into a sycomore tree to see him, for he was to pass that way.

And when Jesus came to the place, he looked up, and saw Zacchaeus, and said unto him, "Zacchaeus, make haste and come down, for today I must abide at thy house." And he made haste, and came down, and received him joyfully.

And when the people saw it, they murmured, saying, "Jesus is gone to be guest with a man that is a sinner."

And Zacchaeus stood and said unto Jesus, "Behold, Lord, the half of my goods I give to the poor; and if I have taken anything from any man by false accusation, I restore him fourfold."

And Jesus said unto him, "This day is salvation come to this house, forasmuch as he also is a son of Abraham. For the Son of man is come to seek and to save that which was lost." And as the people heard these things, Jesus added and spake a parable, because he was nigh to Jerusalem, and because they thought that the kingdom of God should immediately appear.

He said therefore, "A certain nobleman went into a far country to receive for himself a kingdom and to return. And he called his servants, and said unto them, 'Occupy till I come.' And unto one he gave five talents, and to another two, and to another one; to every one according to his several ability, and straightway took his journey.

"Then he that had received the five talents went and traded with the same, and made them other five talents. And likewise he that had received two, he also gained other two. But he that had received one went and digged in the earth, and hid his lord's money.

"After a long time the lord of those servants cometh, and reckoneth with them. And so he that had received five talents came and brought other five talents, saying, ' Lord, thou deliveredst unto me five talents: behold, I have gained beside them five talents more.'

" His lord said unto him, ' Well done, thou good and faithful servant, thou hast been faithful over a few things, I will make thee ruler over many things; enter thou into the joy of thy lord.'

" He also that had received two talents came and said, ' Lord, thou deliveredst unto me two talents: behold, I have gained two other talents beside them.'

" His lord said unto him, ' Well done, good and faithful servant, thou hast been faithful over a few things, I will make thee ruler over many things; enter thou into the joy of thy lord.'

" Then he which had received the one talent came and said, ' Lord, I knew thee that thou art an hard man, reaping where thou hast not sown, and gathering where thou hast not strawed; and I was afraid, and went and hid thy talent in the earth; lo, there thou hast that is thine."

" His lord answered and said unto him, ' Thou wicked and slothful servant, out of thine own mouth will I judge thee. Thou knewest that I reap where I sowed not, and gather where I have not strawed. Wherefore then gavest not thou my money into the bank, that at my coming I might have required mine own with usury? Take therefore the talent from him, and give it unto him which hath ten talents, and cast the unprofitable servant into outer darkness. For unto every one that hath shall be given, and he shall have abundance; but from him that hath not shall be taken away even that which he hath.' "

And when Jesus had thus spoken, he went before, ascending up to Jerusalem.

MARY ANOINTED THE FEET OF JESUS

NOW BETHANY was nigh unto Jerusalem about fifteen furlongs off. Then Jesus six days before the passover came to Bethany, where Lazarus was which had been dead, whom he raised from the dead. There they made him a supper, and Martha served, but Lazarus was one of them that sat at the table with Jesus.

Then took Mary an alabaster box of ointment of spikenard, very precious, and she broke the box, and anointed the feet of Jesus, and wiped his feet with her hair; and the house was filled with the odour of the ointment.

And there were some that had indignation within themselves, and said, "Why was this waste of the ointment made?"

Then said one of his disciples, Judas Iscariot, "Why was not this ointment sold for three hundred pence, and given to the poor?" This he said, not that he cared for the poor, but because he was a thief and had the bag, and bare what was put therein.

And Jesus said, "Let her alone; why trouble ye her? She hath wrought a good work on me. For ye have the poor with you always, and whensoever ye will, ye may do them good, but me ye have not always. She hath done what she could; she is come aforehand to anoint my body to the burying. Verily I say unto you, wheresoever this gospel shall be preached throughout the whole world, this also that she hath done shall be spoken of for a memorial of her."

Much people of the Jews therefore knew that Jesus was there, and they came not for Jesus' sake only, but that they might see Lazarus also, whom he had raised from the dead.

But the chief priests consulted that they might put Lazarus also to death, because that by reason of him many of the Jews went away, and believed on Jesus.

HOSANNA IN THE HIGHEST

On the next day, Jesus sent two of his disciples, saying, "Go ye into the village, in which at your entering ye shall find a colt tied, whereon yet never man sat; loose him, and bring him hither. And if any man ask you, 'Why do ye loose him?' thus shalt ye say unto him, 'Because the Lord hath need of him,' and straightway he will send him."

And they that were sent went their way, and found even as Jesus had said unto them. And as they were loosing the colt, the owners thereof said unto them, "Why loose ye the colt?"

And they said, "The Lord hath need of him." And they let them go.

And they brought him to Jesus, and they cast their garments upon the colt, and they set Jesus thereon; that it might be fulfilled which was spoken by the prophet, saying, "Tell the daughter of Sion, 'Behold, thy King cometh unto thee, meek, and sitting upon an ass.'"

And as he went, they spread their clothes in the way. And when he was come nigh the descent of the mount of Olives, the whole multitude of the disciples began to rejoice and praise God with a loud voice for all the mighty works that they had seen, saying, "Blessed be the King that cometh in the name of the Lord; peace in heaven, and glory in the highest."

And some of the Pharisees from among the multitude said unto Jesus, "Master, rebuke thy disciples."

And he answered and said unto them, "I tell you that if these should hold their peace, the stones would immediately cry out."

And when Jesus was come near Jerusalem, he beheld the city,

and wept over it, saying, " If thou hadst known, even thou, at least in this thy day, the things which belong unto thy peace! but now they are hid from thine eyes. For the days shall come upon thee, that thine enemies shall cast a trench about thee, and compass thee round, and keep thee in on every side, and shall lay thee even with the ground, and thy children within thee; and they shall not leave in thee one stone upon another; because thou knewest not the time of thy visitation."

And much people that were come to the feast, when they heard that Jesus was coming to Jerusalem, took branches of palm trees, and went forth to meet him, and cried, " Hosanna! Blessed is the King of Israel that cometh in the name of the Lord."

And many spread their garments in the way; and others cut down branches off the trees, and strawed them in the way, and they that went before, and they that followed, cried saying, " Hosanna! Blessed is he that cometh in the name of the Lord. Blessed be the kingdom of our father David, that cometh in the name of the Lord; Hosanna in the highest! "

And when Jesus was come into Jerusalem, all the city was moved, saying, " Who is this? "

And the multitude said, " This is Jesus the prophet of Nazareth of Galilee."

The Pharisees therefore said among themselves, " Perceive ye how ye prevail nothing. Behold, the world is gone after him."

And there were certain Greeks among them, that came to worship at the feast, saying, " We would see Jesus." And Andrew and Philip told Jesus.

And Jesus answered them saying, "The hour is come, that the Son of man should be glorified. Verily, verily, I say unto you, except a corn of wheat fall into the ground and die, it abideth alone; but if it die, it bringeth forth much fruit. He that loveth his life shall lose it; and he that hateth his life in this world shall keep it unto life eternal. If any man serve me, let him follow me, and where I am, there shall also my servant be; if any man serve me, him will my Father honour. Now is my soul troubled, and what shall I say? Father, save me from this hour? but for this cause came I unto this hour. Father, glorify thy name."

Then came there a voice from heaven, saying, "I have both glorified it, and will glorify it again."

The people therefore, that stood by and heard it, said, "It thundered; " others said, "An angel spake to him."

Jesus answered and said, "This voice came not because of me, but for your sakes. Now is the judgment of this world; now shall the prince of this world be cast out. And I, if I be lifted up from the earth, will draw all men unto me."

The people answered him, "We have heard out of the law that Christ abideth for ever; and how sayest thou, 'The Son of man must be lifted up? ' who is this Son of man? "

Then Jesus said unto them, "Yet a little while is the light with you. Walk while ye have the light, lest darkness come upon you; for he that walketh in darkness knoweth not whither he goeth. While ye have light, believe in the light, that ye may be the children of light."

These things spake Jesus, and departed, and went into the temple of God. And when he had looked round about upon all things, he began to cast out them that sold and bought in the temple, and overthrew the tables of the money changers, and the seats of them that sold doves, and said unto them, "Is it not written, 'My house shall be called of all nations the house of prayer? ' but ye have made it a den of thieves."

And the blind and the lame came to him in the temple, and he healed them. And when the chief priests and the scribes saw the wonderful things that he did, and the children crying in the temple, and saying, "Hosanna to the son of David," they were sore displeased and said unto him, "Hearest thou what these say? "

And Jesus saith unto them, "Yea; have ye never read, 'Out of the mouth of babes and sucklings thou hast perfected praise?'"

And the chief priests and elders said, "By what authority dost thou these things? and who gave thee this authority?"

And Jesus answered and said unto them, "I also will ask you one thing, which if ye tell me, I in like wise will tell you by what authority I do these things. The baptism of John, whence was it? from heaven, or of men?"

And they reasoned with themselves, saying, "If we shall say, 'From Heaven,' he will say unto us, 'Why did ye not then believe him?' But if we shall say, 'Of men,' we fear the people, for all hold John as a prophet."

And they answered Jesus and said, "We cannot tell."

And he said unto them, "Neither tell I you by what authority I do these things. But what think ye? A certain man had two sons; and he came to the first and said, 'Son, go work today in my vineyard.' He answered and said, 'I will not,' but afterward he repented, and went. And he came to the second, and said likewise. And he answered and said, 'I go, sir;' and went not. Whether of them twain did the will of his father?"

They say unto him, "The first."

Jesus saith unto them, "Verily I say unto you, that the publicans and the harlots go into the kingdom of God before you. For John came unto you in the way of righteousness, and ye believed him not; but the publicans and the harlots believed him. And ye, when ye had seen it, repented not afterward, that ye might believe him.

"Hear another parable: There was a certain householder, which planted a vineyard, and hedged it round about, and digged a winepress in it, and built a tower, and let it out to husbandmen, and went into a far country. And when the time of the fruit drew near, he sent to the husbandmen a servant, that he might receive from the husbandmen of the fruit of the vineyard. And they caught the servant, and beat him, and sent him away empty.

And again he sent unto them another servant; and at him they cast stones, and wounded him in the head, and sent him away shamefully handled. And again he sent another, and him they killed; and many others, beating some, and killing some. Then said the lord of the vineyard, 'What shall I do? I will send my beloved son; it may be they will reverence him when they see him.' But when the husbandmen saw the son, they said among themselves, 'This is the heir; come, let us kill him, and let us seize on his inheritance.' And they caught him, and cast him out of the vineyard, and slew him. What therefore shall the lord of the vineyard do unto them? He shall come and destroy these husbandmen, and shall give the vineyard to others."

And when they heard it, they said, "God forbid."

Jesus saith unto them, "Did ye never read in the scriptures, 'The stone which the builders rejected, the same is become the head of the corner; this is the Lord's doing, and it is marvelous in our eyes?' Therefore say I unto you, the Kingdom of God shall be taken from you and given to a nation bringing forth the fruits thereof. And whosoever shall fall on this stone shall be broken; but on whomsoever it shall fall, it will grind him to powder."

And the chief priests and Pharisees sought to lay hold on him, but feared the people, for they knew that he had spoken the parable against them; and they left him, and went their way.

And now the eventide was come, Jesus went out unto Bethany with the twelve; and he lodged there.

WHICH IS THE GREAT COMMANDMENT?

AND ON THE MORROW when they were come from Bethany, Jesus was hungry. And when he saw a fig tree in the way, he came to it, and found nothing thereon, but leaves only, and said unto it, " Let no fruit grow on thee henceforward for ever." And his disciples heard it.

And they came to Jerusalem, and Jesus went into the temple. And the chief priests and the scribes watched him, and sent forth spies which should feign themselves just men, that they might entangle him in his talk.

And they asked him saying, " Master, we know that thou sayest and teachest rightly, neither acceptest thou the person of any, but teachest the way of God truly. Tell us therefore, what thinkest thou? Is it lawful to give tribute unto Caesar, or not? "

But Jesus perceived their wickedness and said, " Why tempt ye me, ye hypocrites? Show me the tribute money." And they brought unto him a penny. And he saith unto them, " Whose is this image and superscription? "

They say unto him, " Caesar's."

Then saith he unto them, " Render therefore unto Caesar the things which are Caesar's; and unto God the things that are God's." When they had heard these words, they marvelled, and left him, and went their way.

Then came unto him the Sadducees, which say there is no resurrection; and they asked him saying, " Master, Moses said, ' If a man die, having no children, his brother shall marry his wife, and raise up children unto his brother.' Now there were seven brethren; and the first took a wife, and dying left no children. And the second took her, and died, neither left he any children; and the third likewise. And the seven had her and left no children; last of all the woman died also. In the resurrection therefore, when they shall rise, whose wife shall she be of them? for the seven had her to wife."

Jesus said unto them, "Ye do err, not knowing the scriptures, nor the power of God. The children of this world marry, and are given in marriage. But they which shall be accounted worthy to obtain that world, and the resurrection from the dead, neither marry, nor are given in marriage. Neither can they die any more, for they are equal unto the angels, and are the children of God, being the children of the resurrection. Have ye not read that which was spoken unto you by God, saying, 'I am the God of Abraham, and the God of Isaac, and the God of Jacob?' God is not the God of the dead, but of the living, for all live unto him." And when the multitude heard this they were astonished at his doctrine.

But when the Pharisees had heard that Jesus had put the Sadducees to silence, they were gathered together, and asked him, "Is it lawful for a man to put away his wife?" tempting him.

And he answered them, "What did Moses command you?"

And they said, "Moses suffered to write a bill of divorcement, and to put her away."

And Jesus said unto them, "Moses for the hardness of your hearts suffered you to put away your wives. But from the beginning of creation God made them male and female. For this cause shall a man leave his father and mother, and cleave to his wife; and they twain shall be one flesh; so then they are no more twain, but one flesh. What therefore God hath joined together, let no man put asunder. Whosoever shall put away his wife, and marrieth another, committeth adultery against her; and if a woman shall put away her husband and be married to another, she committeth adultery; and whosoever marrieth her that is put away from her husband committeth adultery."

His disciples said unto him, "If the case of the man be so with his wife, it is not good to marry."

But Jesus said unto them, "All men cannot receive this saying, save they to whom it is given. He that is able to receive it, let him receive it."

Then one of them which was a lawyer, having heard them reasoning together, and perceiving that Jesus had answered them well, asked him a question, tempting him, and said, "Master, which is the great commandment in the law?"

Jesus said unto him, "The first of all the commandments is, 'Hear, O Israel: the Lord our God is one Lord. And thou shalt love the Lord thy God with all thy heart, and with all thy soul, and with all thy mind, and with all thy strength.' This is the first and great commandment. And the second is like unto it, namely this, 'Thou shalt love thy neighbour as thyself.' On these two commandments hang all the law and the prophets. There is none other commandment greater than these."

But the lawyer willing to justify himself, said unto Jesus, "And who is my neighbour?"

And Jesus answering said, "A certain man went down from Jerusalem to Jericho, and fell among thieves, which stripped him of his raiment, and wounded him, and departed, leaving him half dead. And by chance there came down a certain priest that way, and when he saw him, he passed by on the other side. And likewise a Levite, when he was at the place, came and looked on him, and passed on the other side. But a certain Samaritan, as he journeyed, came where he was; and when he saw him, he had compassion on him, and went to him, and bound up his wounds, pouring in oil and wine, and set him on his own beast, and brought him to an inn, and took care of him. And on the morrow when he departed, he took out two pence, and gave them to the host, and said unto him, 'Take care of him; and whatsoever thou spendest more, when I come again, I will repay thee.' Which now of these three, thinkest thou, was neighbour unto him that fell among thieves?"

And he said, "He that showed mercy on him."

Then said Jesus unto him, " Go and do thou likewise."

And the lawyer said unto him, " Well, Master, thou hast said the truth; for there is one God, and there is none other but he. And to love him with all the heart, and with all the understanding, and with all the soul, and with all the strength, and to love his neighbour as himself, is more than all whole burnt offerings and sacrifices."

And when Jesus saw that he had answered discreetly, he said unto him, " Thou art not far from the kingdom of God."

But though Jesus had done so many miracles before them, yet they believed not on him, that the saying of Isaiah the prophet might be fulfilled, which he spake, " Lord, who hath believed our report? and to whom hath the arm of the Lord been revealed? "

Nevertheless among the chief rulers also, many believed on him; but because of the Pharisees they did not confess him, lest they should be put out of the synagogue; for they loved the praise of men more than the praise of God.

And when even was come Jesus went out of the city unto Bethany.

HIS COMMANDMENT IS LIFE EVERLASTING

And in the morning, Jesus returned into the city; and as they passed by, they saw the fig tree dried up from the roots. And Peter, calling to remembrance, saith unto him, "Master, behold, the fig tree which is withered away."

And Jesus said unto them, "Have faith in God. Verily, I say unto you, if ye have faith and doubt not, ye shall not only do this which is done to the fig tree, but whosoever shall say unto this mountain, 'Be thou removed and be thou cast into the sea, and shall not doubt in his heart, but shall believe that those things which he saith shall come to pass, he shall have whatsoever he saith. Therefore I say unto you, what things soever ye desire, when ye pray, believe that ye receive them, and ye shall have them."

And they came again to Jerusalem; and Jesus taught in the temple, and all the people were very attentive to hear him. And there were present some that told him of the Galilaeans whose blood Pilate had mingled with their sacrifices.

And Jesus said unto them, "Suppose ye that these Galilaeans were sinners above all the Galilaeans because they suffered such things? I tell you, nay; but except ye repent, ye shall all likewise perish. Or those eighteen upon whom the tower in Siloam fell, and slew them; think ye that they were sinners above all men that dwell in Jerusalem? I tell you, nay; but except ye repent, ye shall all likewise perish."

And he spake a parable unto them to this end, that men ought always to pray, and not to faint, saying: "There was in a city a judge, which feared not God, neither regarded man. And there was a widow in that city, and she came unto him, saying, 'Avenge me of mine adversary.' And he would not for a while, but afterward he said within himself, 'Though I fear not God, nor regard man, yet because this widow troubleth me, I will avenge her, lest by her continual coming she weary me.' Hear what the unjust judge saith! And shall not God avenge his own elect, which cry day and night unto him, though he bear long with them? I tell you that he will avenge them speedily. Nevertheless when the Son of man cometh, shall he find faith on the earth?"

He spake also this parable: "A certain man had a fig tree planted in his vineyard, and he came and sought fruit thereon, and found none. Then said he unto the dresser of his vineyard, 'Behold, these three years I am come seeking fruit on this fig tree, and find none; cut it down, why cumbereth it the ground?' And he answering said unto him, 'Lord, let it alone this year also, till I shall dig about it, and dung it. And if it bear fruit well; and if not, then after that thou shalt cut it down.'"

And he spake this parable unto certain which trusted in themselves that they were righteous, and despised others: "Two men went up into the temple to pray, the one a Pharisee, and the other a publican. The Pharisee stood and prayed thus with himself, 'God, I thank thee, that I am not as other men are, extortioners, unjust, adulterers, or even as this publican. I fast twice in the week; I give tithes of all that I possess.'

"And the publican, standing afar off, would not lift up so much as his eyes unto heaven, but smote upon his breast saying, 'God be merciful to me a sinner.' I tell you, this man went down to his house justified rather than the other; for every one that exalteth himself shall be abased, and he that humbleth himself shall be exalted."

And Jesus looked up and saw the rich men casting their gifts into the treasury. And he saw also a certain poor widow casting in thither two mites. And he said, "Of a truth I say unto you, that this poor widow hath cast in more than they all;

for all these have of their abundance cast in unto the offerings of God, but she of her penury hath cast in all the living that she had."

And it came to pass that as Jesus taught the people and preached the gospel, the chief priests and the scribes with the elders came upon him. And Jesus asked them, saying, "What think ye of Christ? whose son is he?"

They said, "The son of David."

And he said unto them, "How say they that Christ is David's son? And David himself saith in the book of Psalms, 'The Lord said unto my Lord, "Sit thou on my right hand, till I make thine enemies thy footstool."' If David then call him Lord, how is he his son?"

And no man was able to answer him a word, neither durst any man from that day forth ask him any more questions.

And Jesus cried and said, "He that believeth on me, believeth not on me, but on him that sent me. And he that seeth me seeth him that sent me. I am come a light into the world, that whosoever believeth on me should not abide in darkness. And if any man hear my words, and believe not, I judge him not; for I came not to judge the world, but to save the world. He that rejecteth me, and receiveth not my words hath one that judgeth him; the word that I have spoken, the same shall judge him in the last day. For I have not spoken of myself, but the Father which sent me, he gave me a commandment, what I should say, and what I should speak. And I know that his commandment is life everlasting; whatsoever I speak therefore, even as the Father said unto me, so I speak.

"I am come to send fire on the earth; and what will I, if it be already kindled? But I have a baptism to be baptised with; and how am I straitened till it be accomplished? Suppose ye that I am come to give peace on earth? I tell you, nay; I came not to send peace but a sword. For I am come to set a man at variance against his father, and the daughter against her mother, and the daughter in law against her mother in law. For from henceforth there shall be five in one house divided, three against two, and two against three. And a man's foes shall be they of his own household."

These things spake Jesus and departed, and went out of the temple.

WATCH AND PRAY

And as Jesus went out of the temple, his disciples came to show him the buildings of the temple; and one of his disciples spoke of how it was adorned with goodly stones and gifts, and said unto him, " Master, see what manner of stones and what buildings are here! "

And Jesus said unto him, " Seest thou these great buildings? Behold, the days will come, in the which there shall not be left one stone upon another that shall not be thrown down."

And at night Jesus went out and abode in the mount that is called the mount of Olives. And as he sat upon the mount of Olives, the disciples came unto him privately saying, " Master, but when shall these things be? and what sign will there be when these things shall come to pass? "

And Jesus answered and said unto them, " Take heed that no man deceive you. For many shall come in my name, saying, 'I am Christ,' and shall deceive many. And when ye shall hear of wars and rumours of wars, be ye not troubled; for such things must needs be. For nation shall rise against nation, and kingdom against kingdom; and there shall be famines, and pestilences, and earthquakes in divers places. These are the beginning of sorrows.

" But take heed to yourselves: then shall they deliver you up to be afflicted, and shall kill you, and ye shall be hated of all nations for my name's sake. And ye shall be brought before rulers and kings for my sake, for a testimony against them. Settle it therefore in your hearts, not to meditate before what ye shall answer. But when they shall lead you and deliver you up, take no thought before hand what ye shall speak, for I will give you a mouth and wisdom, which all your adversaries shall not be able to gainsay nor resist.

"And then shall many be offended, and shall betray one another and shall hate one another. The brother shall betray the brother to death, and the father the son; and children shall rise up against their parents, and shall cause them to be put to death; and ye shall be betrayed both by parents and brethren, and kinsfolk, and friends. And ye shall be hated of all men for my name's sake. And because iniquity shall abound, the love of many shall wax cold. But he that shall endure unto the end, the same shall be saved. In your patience possess ye your souls. And this gospel of the kingdom shall be preached in all the world for a witness unto all nations; and then shall the end come.

"When ye therefore, shall see the abomination of desolation, spoken of by Daniel the prophet, standing where it ought not (let him that readeth understand), then let them that be in Judaea flee to the mountains. Let him which is on the house top not come down to take any thing out of his house. Neither let him which is in the field return back to take his clothes. And woe unto them that are with child, for there shall be great distress in the land. And they shall fall by the edge of the sword, and shall be led away captive into all nations. And pray that your flight be not in the winter; for in those days shall be afflictions, such as was not from the beginning of the creation which God created, unto this time, neither shall be. For these be the days of vengeance that all things which are written may be fulfilled. And except that the Lord had shortened those days, no flesh should be saved; but for the elect's sake, whom he hath chosen, he hath shortened the days. And then if any man shall say to you, 'Lo, here is Christ,' or, 'Lo, he is there,' believe him not. For false Christs and false prophets shall rise, and shall show signs and wonders, to seduce, if it were possible, even the elect. But take heed; behold, I have foretold you all things.

"Immediately after the tribulation of those days shall the sun be darkened, and the moon shall not give her light, and the stars of heaven shall fall, and the powers that are in heaven shall be shaken; and upon the earth distress of nations with perplexity; the sea and waves roaring; men's hearts failing them for fear, and for looking after those things which are coming on the earth; for the powers of heaven shall be shaken.

"And then shall they see the Son of man coming in the clouds with great power and glory. And then shall he send his angels, and shall gather together the elect from the four winds, from the uttermost part of the earth to the uttermost part of heaven. And when these things begin to come to pass, then look up, and lift up your heads, for your redemption draweth nigh.

"Now learn a parable of the fig tree; when her branch is yet tender, and putteth forth leaves, ye know that summer is near. So likewise ye, when ye see these things come to pass, know ye that the kingdom of God is nigh at hand, even at the doors. Heaven and earth shall pass away, but my words shall not pass away. But of that day and that hour knoweth no man, no, not the angels which are in heaven, neither the Son, but the Father.

"Take ye heed, watch and pray! for ye know not when the time is. But as it was in the days of Noah, so shall it be in the days of the Son of man. For as in the days that were before the flood, they did eat, they drank, they married wives, they were given in marriage, until the day that Noah entered into the ark, and the flood came, and destroyed them all. Likewise also as it was in the days of Lot, they did eat, they drank, they bought, they sold, they planted, they builded; but the same day that Lot went out of Sodom it rained fire and brimstone from heaven, and destroyed them all. Even thus shall it be in the day when the Son of man shall be revealed. I tell you in that night there shall be two men in one bed; the one shall be taken, and the other shall be left. Two women shall be grinding together, the one shall be taken, and the other left. Two men shall be in the field; the one shall be taken, the other left. Watch therefore; for ye know not what hour your Lord doth come.

"But know this, that if the goodman of the house had known in what watch the thief would come, he would have watched, and would not have suffered his house to be broken up. Therefore be ye also ready: let your loins be girded about, and your lights burning. Blessed are those servants, whom the lord when he cometh shall find watching. Verily I say unto you, that he shall gird himself, and make them sit down to meat, and will come forth and serve them. And if he shall come in the second watch, or come in the third watch, and find them so, blessed are those servants. And take heed to yourselves, lest at any time your hearts be overcharged with surfeiting, and drunkenness, and cares of this life, and so that day come upon you unawares. For as a snare shall it come on all them that dwell on the face of the whole earth. Watch ye therefore, and pray always, that ye may be accounted worthy to escape all these things that shall come to pass, and to stand before the Son of man.

"Take heed, watch and pray! for ye know not when the time is. Watch ye therefore; lest coming suddenly he find you sleeping. And what I say unto you, I say unto all, Watch!"

FOR ONE IS YOUR FATHER WHICH IS IN HEAVEN

AND ALL THE PEOPLE came early in the morning to Jesus in the temple, for to hear him.

Then spake Jesus to the multitude, and to his disciples, saying, "The scribes and the Pharisees sit in Moses' seat: all therefore whatsoever they bid you observe, that observe and do; but do ye not after their works, for they say, and do not. For they bind heavy burdens and grievous to be borne, and lay them on men's shoulders, but they themselves will not move them with one of their fingers. But all their works they do for to be seen of men; they make broad their phylacteries, and enlarge the borders of their garments, and love the uppermost rooms at feasts, and the chief seats in the synagogues, and greetings in the markets, and to be called of men, 'Rabbi, Rabbi.' But be not ye called, 'Rabbi;' for one is your Master, even Christ, and all ye are brethren. And call no man your father upon the earth, for one is your Father, which is in heaven. But he that is greatest among you shall be your servant. And whosoever shall exalt himself shall be abased; and he that shall humble himself shall be exalted.

"But woe unto you, scribes and Pharisees, hypocrites! for ye shut up the kingdom of heaven against men; for ye neither go in yourselves, neither suffer ye them that are entering to go in. Ye blind guides! for ye devour widow's houses, and for a pretence make long prayers; woe unto you! Ye pay tithe of mint and anise and cummin, and have omitted the weightier matters of the law, judgment, mercy, and faith, and the love of God; these ought ye to have done, and not to leave the other undone. Ye strain at a gnat, and swallow a camel; for ye make clean the outside of the cup and of the platter, but within are full of extortion and excess. Thou blind Pharisee, cleanse first that which is within the cup and platter, that the outside of them may be clean also; for ye are like unto whited sepulchres, which indeed appear beautiful outwardly, but are within full of dead men's bones, and all uncleanness. Even so ye also outwardly appear righteous unto men, but within ye are full of hypocrisy and iniquity.

"Woe unto you, scribes and Pharisees, hypocrites! because ye build the tombs of the prophets, and garnish the sepulchres of the righteous, and say, 'If we had been in the days of our fathers, we would not have been partakers with them in the blood of the prophets.' Wherefore ye be witnesses unto yourselves, that ye are the children of them which killed the prophets. Fill ye up then the measure of your fathers. Ye serpents, ye generation of vipers, how can ye escape the damnation of hell? Wherefore, behold, I send unto you prophets, and wise men, and scribes; and some of them ye shall kill and crucify, and some of them shall ye scourge in your synagogues, and persecute them from city to city; that upon you may come all the righteous blood shed upon the earth, from the blood of righteous Abel unto the blood of Zacharias son of Barachias, whom ye slew between the temple and the altar. Verily I say unto you, all these things shall come upon this generation.

"When the Son of man shall come in his glory, and all the holy angels with him, then shall he sit upon the throne of his glory, and before him shall be gathered all nations. And he shall separate them one from another, as a shepherd divideth his sheep from the goats. And he shall set the sheep on his right hand, but the goats on the left.

"Then shall the King say unto them on his right hand, 'Come, ye blessed of my Father, inherit the kingdom prepared for you from the foundation of the world: for I was an hungred, and ye gave me meat; I was thirsty, and ye gave me drink; I was a stranger, and ye took me in; naked, and ye clothed me; I was sick, and ye visited me; I was in prison, and ye came unto me.'

"Then shall the righteous answer him saying, 'Lord, when saw we thee an hungred, and fed thee? or thirsty, and gave thee drink? When saw we thee a stranger, and took thee in? or naked, and clothed thee? Or when saw we thee sick, or in prison, and came unto thee?'

"And the King shall answer and say unto them, 'Verily I say unto you, inasmuch as ye have done it unto one of the least of these my brethren, ye have done it unto me.'

"Then shall he say also unto them on the left hand, 'Depart from me, ye cursed, into everlasting fire, prepared for the devil and his angels; for I was an hungred, and ye gave me no meat; I was thirsty, and ye gave me no drink; I was a stranger, and ye took me not in; naked, and ye clothed me not; sick, and in prison, and ye visited me not.'

"Then shall they also answer him saying, 'Lord, when saw we thee an hungred, or athirst, or a stranger, or naked, or sick, or in prison, and did not minister unto thee?'

"Then shall he answer them, saying, 'Verily I say unto you, inasmuch as ye did it not to one of the least of these, ye did it not to me.' And these shall go away into everlasting punishment; but the righteous into life eternal."

And Jesus departed from them, and went as he was wont to the mount of Olives; and his disciples followed him.

Then assembled together the chief priests, and the scribes, and the elders of the people, unto the palace of the high priest, who was called Caiaphas, and consulted that they might take Jesus by subtilty, and kill him, for they feared the multitude, because they took Jesus for a prophet.

Now both the chief priests and the Pharisees had given a commandment, that, if any man knew where Jesus was, he should show it, that they might take him. Then entered Satan into Judas, surnamed Iscariot, being of the number of the twelve, and he went his way and communed with the chief priests and captains, how he might betray Jesus unto them. And he said, " What will ye give me, and I will deliver him unto you? "

And they were glad and covenanted with him for thirty pieces of silver. And he promised, and sought opportunity to betray Jesus unto them in the absence of the multitude.

I AM THE WAY, THE TRUTH, AND THE LIFE

And an highway shall be there, and a Way, and it shall be called The Way of holiness. Isaiah.

THEN CAME THE DAY of the feast of unleavened bread, which is called the passover, and the disciples came to Jesus, saying unto him, " Where wilt thou that we prepare for thee to eat the passover? "

And Jesus sent Peter and John saying, " Go ye and prepare us the passover that we may eat. Behold, when ye are entered into the city, there shall a man meet you bearing a pitcher of water; follow him into the house where he entereth in. And ye shall say unto the goodman of the house, ' The Master saith unto thee, " Where is the guest chamber, where I shall eat the passover with my disciples? " ' And he will show you a large upper room furnished and prepared; there make ready for us."

And his disciples went forth, and came into the city, and found as Jesus had said unto them; and they made ready the passover. And in the evening Jesus came with the twelve.

And when the hour was come, he sat down, and the twelve apostles with him. And he said unto them, " With desire I have desired to eat this passover with you before I suffer; for I say unto you, I will not any more eat thereof, until it be fulfilled in the kingdom of God."

And as they did eat, Jesus took bread, and blessed, and brake it, and gave to them and said, " Take, eat; this is my body which is given for you; this do in remembrance of me." And he took the cup, and when he had given thanks, he gave it to them, saying, " Drink ye all of it; for this is my blood of the new testament, which is shed for many for the remission of sins. Verily I say unto you, I will drink no more of the fruit of the vine until that day that I drink it new in the kingdom of God." And they all drank of it.

And supper being ended, Jesus knowing that the Father had given all things into his hands, and that he was come from God and went to God, he riseth, and laid aside his garments, and took a towel and girded himself. After that he poureth water into a bason, and began to wash the disciples' feet, and to wipe them with the towel wherewith he was girded. Then cometh he to Simon Peter, and Peter saith unto him, "Lord, dost thou wash my feet?"

Jesus answered and said unto him, "What I do thou knowest not now, but thou shalt know hereafter."

Peter saith unto him, "Thou shalt never wash my feet."

Jesus answered him, "If I wash thee not, thou hast no part with me."

Simon Peter saith unto him, "Lord, not my feet only, but also my hands and my head."

Jesus saith to him, "He that is washed is clean every whit; and ye are clean."

So after he had washed their feet, and had taken his garments, and was set down again, he said unto them, "Know ye what I have done to you? Ye call me Master and Lord, and ye say well, for so I am. If I then, your Lord and Master, have washed your feet, ye also ought to wash one another's feet. For I have given you an example, that ye should do as I have done to you. Verily, verily, I say unto you, the servant is not greater than his Lord; neither he that is sent greater than he that sent him. If ye know these things, happy are ye if ye do them. I speak not of you all; I know whom I have chosen; but that the scripture may be fulfilled, 'He that eateth bread with me hath lifted up his heel against me.' Now I tell you before it come, that when it is come to pass, ye may believe that I am he."

When Jesus had thus said, he was troubled in spirit, and said, "Verily, verily, I say unto you, that one of you shall betray me."

Then the disciples looked one on another, and they were exceeding sorrowful, and began every one of them to say unto him, "Lord, is it I?"

Jesus answered, "He it is, to whom I shall give a sop, when I have dipped it." And when he had dipped the sop, he gave it to Judas Iscariot. Then said Jesus unto him, "That thou doest, do quickly."

Now no man at the table knew for what intent he spake this unto him. For some of them thought because Judas had the bag, that Jesus had said unto him, "Buy those things that we have need of against the feast;" or, that he should give something to the poor. Judas then having received the sop went immediately out; and it was night.

Therefore when he was gone out, Jesus said, "Little children, yet a little while I am with you. Ye shall seek me, and as I said unto the Jews, 'Whither I go, ye cannot come,' so now I say to you. A new commandment I give unto you, that ye love one another; as I have loved you, that ye also love one another. By this shall all men know that ye are my disciples, if ye have love one to another."

Simon Peter said unto him, "Lord, whither goest thou?"

Jesus answered him, "Whither I go, thou canst not follow me now, but thou shalt follow me afterwards. Let not your heart be troubled, ye believe in God, believe also in me. In my Father's house are many mansions; if it were not so, I would have told you. I go to prepare a place for you. And if I go and prepare a place for you, I will come again and receive you unto myself, that where I am there ye may be also. And whither I go ye know, and the way ye know."

Thomas saith unto him, "Lord, we know not whither thou goest, and how can we know the way?"

Jesus saith unto him, "I am the way, the truth, and the life; no man cometh unto the Father, but by me. If ye had known me, ye should have known my Father also; and from henceforth ye know him, and have seen him."

Philip saith unto him, "Lord, show us the Father, and it sufficeth us."

Jesus saith unto him, "Have I been so long time with you, and yet hast thou not known me, Philip? He that hath seen me, hath seen the Father; and how sayest thou then, 'Show us the Father?' Believest thou not that I am in the Father, and the Father in me? The words that I speak unto you I speak not of myself, but the Father that dwelleth in me, he doeth the works. Believe me that I am in the Father, and the Father in me, or else believe me for the very works' sake. Verily, verily, I say unto you, he that believeth on me, the works that I do shall he do also; and greater works than these shall he do, because I go unto my Father. And whatsoever ye shall ask in my name, that will I do, that the Father may be glorified in the Son. If ye shall ask any thing in my name, I will do it.

"If ye love me, keep my commandments. And I will pray the Father, and he shall give you another Comforter, that he may abide with you for ever; even the Spirit of Truth, whom the world cannot receive, because it seeth him not, neither knoweth him; but ye know him, for he dwelleth with you, and shall be in you. I will not leave you comfortless; I will come to you. Yet a little while, and the world seeth me no more; but ye see me, because I live, ye shall live also. At that day ye shall know that I am in my Father, and ye in me, and I in you. He that hath my commandments, and keepeth them, he it is that loveth me. And he that loveth me shall be loved of my Father, and I will love him, and will manifest myself to him."

Judas saith unto him, not Iscariot, "Lord, how is it that thou wilt manifest thyself unto us, and not unto the world?"

Jesus answered and said unto him, "If a man love me, he

will keep my words. And my Father will love him, and we will come unto him, and make our abode with him. He that loveth me not keepeth not my sayings; and the word which ye hear is not mine, but the Father's which sent me. These things have I spoken unto you, being yet present with you. But the Comforter, which is the Holy Ghost, whom the Father will send in my name, he shall teach you all things, and bring all things to your remembrance, whatsoever I have said unto you.

"I am the true vine, and my Father is the husbandman. Every branch in me that beareth not fruit he taketh away; and every branch that beareth fruit, he purgeth it, that it may bring forth more fruit. Now ye are clean through the word which I have spoken unto you. Abide in me, and I in you. As the branch cannot bear fruit of itself, except it abide in the vine, no more can ye except ye abide in me. I am the vine, and ye are the branches; he that abideth in me, and I in him, the same bringeth forth much fruit, for without me ye can do nothing. If a man abide not in me, he is cast forth as a branch, and is withered; and men gather them, and cast them into the fire, and they are burned. If ye abide in me, and my words abide in you, ye shall ask what ye will, and it shall be done unto you. Herein is my Father glorified, that ye bear much fruit, so shall ye be my disciples. As the Father hath loved me, so have I loved you; continue ye in my love. If ye keep my commandments, ye shall abide in my love, even as I have kept my Father's commandments, and abide in his love.

"These things have I spoken unto you, that my joy might remain in you, and that your joy might be full. This is my commandment, that ye love one another as I have loved you. Greater love hath no man than this, that a man lay down his life for his friends. Ye are my friends, if ye do whatsoever I command you. Henceforth I call you not servants, for the servant knoweth not what his lord doeth. But I have called you friends, for all things that I have heard of my Father, I have made known unto you. Ye have not chosen me, but I have chosen you, and ordained you, that ye should go and bring forth fruit, and that your fruit should remain, that whatsoever ye shall ask of the Father in my name, he may give it you. These things I command you, that ye love one another.

"If the world hate you, ye know that it hated me before it hated you. If ye were of the world, the world would love his own; but because ye are not of the world, but I have chosen you out of the world, therefore the world hateth you. Remember the word that I said unto you, 'The servant is not greater than his lord.' If they have persecuted me, they will also persecute you; if they have kept my saying, they will keep yours also. But all these things will they do unto you for my name's sake, because they know not him that sent me.

"If I had not come and spoken unto them, they had not had sin; but now they have no cloke for their sin. He that hateth me, hateth my Father also. If I had not done among them the works which none other man did, they had not had sin, but now have they both seen and hated both me and my Father. But this cometh to pass, that the word might be fulfilled that is written in their law, 'They hated me without a cause.'

"But when the Comforter is come, whom I will send unto you from the Father, even the Spirit of truth, which proceedeth from the Father, he shall testify of me. And ye also shall bear witness, because ye have been with me from the beginning.

"These things have I spoken unto you, that ye should not be offended. They shall put you out of the synagogues; yea, the time cometh, that whosoever killeth you will think that he doeth God service. And these things will they do unto you, because they have not known the Father, nor me. But these things have I told you, that when the time shall come, ye may remember that I told you of them. And these things I said not unto you at the beginning, because I was with you.

"But now I go my way to him that sent me. Ye have heard

how I said unto you, I go away, and come again unto you. If ye loved me, ye would rejoice, because I said I go unto the Father, for my Father is greater than I. And now I have told you before it come to pass, that when it come to pass, ye might believe. Hereafter I will not talk much with you, for the prince of this world cometh, and hath nothing in me. But that the world may know that I love the Father, and as the Father gave me commandment, even so I do. Peace I leave with you, my peace I give unto you; not as the world giveth, give I unto you. Let not your heart be troubled, neither let it be afraid.

"But because I have said these things unto you, sorrow hath filled your heart. Nevertheless I tell you the truth: it is expedient for you that I go away; for if I go not away, the Comforter will not come unto you. But if I depart, I will send him unto you. And when he is come, he will reprove the world of sin, and of righteousness, and of judgment: of sin, because they believe not on me; of righteousness, because I go to my Father, and ye see me no more; of judgment, because the prince of this world is judged.

"I have yet many things to say unto you, but ye cannot bear them now. Howbeit when he, the Spirit of truth, is come, he will guide you into all truth; for he shall not speak of himself, but whatsoever he shall hear, that shall he speak, and he will show you things to come. He shall glorify me, for he shall receive of mine, and shall show it unto you. All things that the Father hath are mine; therefore said I, that he shall take of mine, and shall show it unto you. A little while and ye shall not see me; and again a little while, and ye shall see me, because I go unto the Father."

Then said some of his disciples among themselves, "What is this that he saith unto us, 'A little while, and ye shall not see me; and again a little while, and ye shall see me,' and 'Because I go to the Father?'" They said therefore, "What is this that he saith, 'A little while?' we cannot tell what he saith."

Now Jesus knew that they were desirous to ask him, and said unto them, "Do ye enquire among yourselves of that I said, 'A little while, and ye shall not see me; and again a little while, and ye shall see me?' Verily, verily, I say unto you, that ye shall weep and lament, but the world shall rejoice; and ye shall be sorrowful, but your sorrow shall be turned into joy. A woman when she is in travail hath sorrow, because her hour is come; but as soon as she is delivered of the child, she remembereth no more the anguish, for joy that a man is born into the world. And ye now therefore have sorrow, but I will see you again, and your heart shall rejoice, and your joy no man taketh from you.

"And in that day, verily, verily, I say unto you, whatsoever ye shall ask the Father in my name, he will give it you. Hitherto have ye asked nothing in my name. Ask, and ye shall receive, that your joy may be full. These things have I spoken unto you in proverbs; but the time cometh when I shall no more speak unto you in proverbs, but I shall show you plainly of the Father. At that day ye shall ask in my name; and I say not unto you, that I will pray the Father for you, for the Father himself loveth you, because ye have loved me, and have believed that I came out from God. I came forth from the Father, and am come into the world; again, I leave the world, and go to the Father."

His disciples said unto him, "Lo, now speakest thou plainly, and speakest no proverb. Now are we sure that thou knowest all things, and needest not that any man should ask thee. By this we believe that thou camest forth from God."

Jesus answered them, "Do ye now believe? Behold, the hour cometh, yea, is now come, that ye shall be scattered, every man to his own, and shall leave me alone; and yet I am not alone, because the Father is with me. These things I have spoken unto you, that in me ye might have peace. In the world ye shall have tribulation; but be of good cheer, I have overcome the world."

These words spake Jesus, and lifted up his eyes to heaven, and said:

"Father, the hour is come; glorify thy Son, that thy Son also may glorify thee: as thou hast given him power over all flesh, that he should give eternal life to as many as thou hast given him. And this is life eternal: that they might know thee the only true God, and Jesus Christ whom thou hast sent. I have glorified thee on the earth; I have finished the work which thou gavest me to do. And now, O Father, glorify thou me with thine own self with the glory which I had with thee before the world was.

"I have manifested thy name unto the men which thou gavest me out of the world; thine they were, and thou gavest them me, and they have kept thy word. Now they have known that all things whatsoever thou hast given me are of thee. For I have given unto them the words which thou gavest me; and they have received them, and have known surely that I came out from thee, and they have believed that thou didst send me. I pray for them. I pray not for the world, but for them which thou hast given me, for they are thine. And all mine are thine, and thine are mine; and I am glorified in them.

"And now I am no more in the world, but these are in the world, and I come to thee. Holy Father, keep through thine own name those whom thou hast given me, that they may be one, as we are. While I was with them in the world, I kept them in thy name. Those that thou gavest me I have kept, and none of them is lost, but the son of perdition, that the scripture might be fulfilled. And now come I to thee. And these things I speak in the world, that they might have my joy fulfilled in themselves. I have given them thy word; and the world hath hated them because they are not of the world, even as I am not of the world. I pray not that thou shouldest take them out of the world, but that thou shouldest keep them from the evil. They are not of the world, even as I am not of the world. Sanctify them through thy truth: thy word is truth. As thou hast sent me into the world, even so have I also sent them into the world. And for their sakes I sanctify myself, that they also might be sanctified through the truth.

" Neither pray I for these alone, but for them also which shall believe on me through their word; that they all may be one, as thou, Father, art in me, and I in thee, that they also may be one in us; that the world may believe that thou hast sent me. And the glory which thou gavest me, I have given them, that they may be one, even as we are one: I in them, and thou in me, that they may be made perfect in one. And that the world may know that thou hast sent me, and hast loved them, as thou hast loved me. Father, I will that they also, whom thou hast given me, be with me where I am, that they may behold my glory, which thou hast given me. For thou lovedst me before the foundation of the world.

" O righteous Father, the world hath not known thee. But I have known thee, and these have known that thou hast sent me. And I have declared unto them thy name, and will declare it, that the love wherewith thou hast loved me may be in them, and I in them. Amen."

And when they had sung an hymn, Jesus said unto them, " All ye shall be offended because of me this night; for it is written, ' I will smite the shepherd, and the sheep shall be scattered.' But after that I am risen, I will go before you into Galilee."

But Peter said unto him, " Though all men shall be offended because of thee, yet will I never be offended. I am ready to go with thee both into prison and unto death. I will lay down my life for thy sake."

Jesus answered him, " Wilt thou lay down thy life for my sake? I tell thee, Peter, the cock shall not crow this day, even in this night, before thou shalt thrice deny that thou knowest me."

But Peter spake the more vehemently, " If I should die with thee, I will not deny thee in any wise."

Likewise also said all the disciples.

And Jesus said, " Peter, behold Satan hath desired to have you that he may sift you as wheat; but I have prayed for thee, that thy faith fail not. And when thou art converted, strengthen thy brethren."

And he said unto them, "When I sent you without purse, and scrip, and shoes, lacked ye anything? "

And they said, " Nothing."

Then said he unto them, " But now, he that hath a purse, let him take it, and likewise his scrip; and he that hath no sword, let him sell his garment, and buy one. For I say unto you, that this that is written must yet be accomplished in me, ' And he was reckoned among the transgressors;' for the things concerning me have an end."

And they said, " Lord, behold, here are two swords."

And he said, " It is enough. Arise, let us go hence."

NOT MY WILL, BUT THINE BE DONE

JESUS WENT FORTH with his disciples over the brook Cedron, where was a garden called Gethsemane, into which he entered, and his disciples followed him. (And Judas also which betrayed him knew the place, for Jesus oftimes resorted thither with his disciples.) And when he was at the place, he said unto them, " Pray that ye enter not into temptation. Sit ye here, while I go and pray yonder."

And he took with him Peter and James and John, and began to be sorrowful and very heavy. Then saith he unto them, " My soul is exceeding sorrowful, even unto death; tarry ye here, and watch with me."

And he went a little farther, and fell on his face, and prayed saying, " O my Father, all things are possible unto thee. If it is possible, remove this cup from me; nevertheless not my will, but thine, be done."

And when he rose up from prayer, and came unto his disciples, he found them sleeping for sorrow, and he said unto them, "Why sleep ye? rise and pray." And he said unto Peter, " Simon, sleepest thou? Could ye not watch with me one hour? Watch and pray that ye enter not into temptation; the spirit indeed is willing, but the flesh is weak."

He went away again the second time, and prayed, saying, " O my Father, if this cup may not pass away from me except I drink it, thy will be done."

And he came and found them asleep again, for their eyes were heavy. And he left them and went away again and prayed the third time. And being in an agony he prayed more earnestly; and his sweat was as it were great drops of blood falling down to the ground. And there appeared an angel unto him from heaven, strengthening him.

Then cometh he to his disciples the third time, and saith unto them, " Sleep on now, and take your rest; it is enough, the hour is come; behold, the Son of man is betrayed into the hands of sinners. Rise up, let us go. Lo, he that betrayeth me is at hand."

And immediately while he yet spake, Judas, having received a band of men and officers from the chief priests and Pharisees, came thither with lanterns and torches and weapons.

Jesus therefore, knowing all things that should come upon him, went forth, and said unto them, " Whom seek ye? "

They answered him, " Jesus of Nazareth."

Jesus saith unto them, " I am he." As soon then as he had said unto them, " I am he," they went backward, and fell to the ground. Then asked he them again, " Whom seek ye? "

And they said, " Jesus of Nazareth."

Now Judas gave them a sign saying, " Whomsoever I shall kiss, that same is he, take him and lead him away safely." And he goeth straightway to Jesus and saith, " Hail, Master," and kissed him.

But Jesus said unto him, " Judas, betrayest thou the Son of man with a kiss? " Then came they and laid their hands on Jesus.

When the disciples saw what would follow, they said, " Lord, shall we smite with the sword? " Then Simon Peter having a sword drew it, and smote the high priest's servant, and cut off his right ear.

But Jesus said unto Peter, " Put up thy sword into the sheath; for all they that take the sword shall perish by the sword. Thinkest thou that I cannot now pray to my Father, and he shall presently give me more than twelve legions of angels? But how then shall the scripture be fulfilled? The cup which my Father hath given me, shall I not drink it? Thus it must be." And he touched the servant's ear and healed him.

Then Jesus said unto the chief priests, and captains of the temple, and the elders, which were come to him, "Be ye come out as against a thief, with swords and staves? When I was daily with you in the temple, ye stretched forth no hands against me; but this is your hour, and the power of darkness. If therefore ye seek me, let these go their way." Then the officers of the Jews took Jesus and bound him, and they led him away to Caiaphas the high priest, where the scribes and elders were assembled.

Then the disciples forsook Jesus and fled. But Simon Peter followed Jesus, and so did John. John was known unto the high priest, and went in with Jesus unto the palace of the high priest. But Peter stood at the door without. Then John went out and spake to her that kept the door, and brought in Peter. And Peter sat with the servants and warmed himself at the fire. Then saith the damsel that kept the door unto Peter, "Art not thou also one of this man's disciples?"

Peter saith, "I am not."

And after a little while one of the servants of the high priest, being his kinsman whose ear Peter had cut off, saith, "Did not I see thee in the garden with him? Art not thou also one of his disciples?"

Peter denied it, and said, "I am not."

And about the space of one hour after another confidently affirmed, "Surely thou art one of them, for thou art a Galilaean, and thy speech betrayeth thee."

Then began Peter to curse and to swear, saying, "I know not the man." And immediately the cock crew, and Jesus turned and looked upon Peter.

And Peter remembered the word of Jesus, how he had said unto him, "Before the cock crow, thou shalt deny me thrice." And Peter went out, and wept bitterly.

I BEAR WITNESS UNTO THE TRUTH

As soon as it was day, the elders of the people and the chief priests and the scribes came together and led Jesus into their council. And all the council sought false witness against Jesus to put him to death, but found none; yea, though many false witnesses came, their witness agreed not together. The high priest then asked Jesus of his disciples, and of his doctrine.

Jesus answered him, " I spake openly to the world; I ever taught in the synagogue, and in the temple whither the Jews always resort; and in secret have I said nothing. Why askest thou me? ask them which heard me, what I have said unto them; behold they know what I said."

And when he had thus spoken, one of the officers which stood by struck Jesus with the palm of his hand, saying, " Answerest thou the high priest so? "

Jesus answered him, " If I have spoken evil, bear witness of the evil; but if well, why smitest thou me? "

And the high priest stood up in the midst, and asked Jesus saying, " Art thou the Christ? tell us! " But Jesus held his peace. And the high priest said unto him, " I adjure thee by the living God, that thou tell us whether thou be the Christ, the son of God."

Jesus saith unto him, " If I tell you, ye will not believe; And if I also ask you, ye will not answer me, nor let me go. Hereafter shall the Son of man sit on the right hand of the power of God."

Then said they all, " Art thou then the Son of God? "

And he said unto them, "Ye say that I am. Nevertheless I say unto you, hereafter shall ye see the Son of man sitting on the right hand of power, and coming in the clouds of heaven."

Then the high priest rent his clothes, saying, "He hath spoken blasphemy; what further need have we of witnesses? Behold, now ye have heard his blasphemy. What think ye?"

They answered and said, "He is guilty of death." Then they did spit in his face and buffeted him; and others smote him with the palms of their hands, saying, "Prophesy unto us, thou Christ, who is he that smote thee?" And when they had bound him, they led him away, and delivered him to Pontius Pilate the governor.

Then Judas, which had betrayed him, when he saw that Jesus was condemned, repented himself, and brought again the thirty pieces of silver to the chief priests and elders, saying, "I have sinned in that I have betrayed the innocent blood."

And they said, "What is that to us? see thou to that."

And Judas cast down the pieces of silver in the temple, and departed, and went and hanged himself.

And the chief priests took the silver pieces, and said, "It is not lawful for to put them in the treasury because it is the price of blood," and they took counsel. And they took the thirty pieces of silver, the price of him that was valued, whom they of the children of Israel did value, and bought with them the potter's field, to bury strangers in. Wherefore that field was called, "The field of blood," unto this day.

And Jesus stood before Pilate the governor. And the chief priests and elders of the people themselves went not into the judgment hall, lest they should be defiled. Pilate then went out unto them and said, "What accusation bring ye against this man?"

They answered, "If he were not a malefactor, we should not have delivered him unto thee. We found this fellow perverting the nation, and forbidding to give tribute to Caesar, saying that he himself is Christ a King." And they accused him of many things.

Then said Pilate unto them, "Take ye him, and judge him according to your law."

The Jews therefore said unto him, "It is not lawful for us to put any man to death."

Then Pilate entered into the judgment hall again, and called Jesus, and said unto him, "Hearest thou how many things they witness against thee?" And Jesus answered him never a word, insomuch that the governor marvelled greatly.

Then Pilate said unto him, "Art thou the King of the Jews?"

Jesus answered him, "Sayest thou this thing of thyself, or did others tell it thee of me?"

Pilate answered, "Am I a Jew? Thine own nation and the chief priests have delivered thee unto me; what hast thou done?"

Jesus answered, "My kingdom is not of this world; if my kingdom were of this world, then would my servants fight, that I should not be delivered to the Jews; but now is my kingdom not from hence."

Pilate therefore said unto him, "Art thou a king then?"

Jesus answered, "Thou sayest that I am a king. To this end was I born, and for this cause came I into the world, that I should bear witness unto the Truth. Every one that is of the truth heareth my voice."

Pilate saith unto him, "What is truth?"

And when he had said this, he went out again unto the Jews, and saith unto them, "I find in him no fault at all." For he knew that for envy they had delivered him.

And they were the more fierce saying, "He stirreth up the people, teaching throughout all Jewry, beginning from Galilee to this place."

When Pilate heard of Galilee, he asked whether the man was a Galilaean. And as soon as he knew that he belonged unto Herod's jurisdiction, he sent him to Herod, who himself was at Jerusalem at that time.

And when Herod saw Jesus, he was exceeding glad; for he was desirious to see him of a long season, because he had heard many things of him, and he hoped to have seen some miracle done by him. Then he questioned with him in many words, but Jesus answered him nothing. And the chief priests and scribes stood and vehemently accused him. And Herod with his men of war set him at nought, and mocked him, and sent him again to Pilate.

Then Pilate therefore took Jesus, and scourged him. And the soldiers platted a crown of thorns, and put it on his head, and they put on him a purple robe, and said, " Hail, King of the Jews! " And they spit upon him, and took a reed, and smote him on the head.

Pilate therefore went forth again, and saith unto the people, " Behold, I bring him forth to you, that ye may know that I find no fault in him." Then came Jesus forth wearing the crown of thorns, and the purple robe. And Pilate said unto them, " Behold the man! "

When the chief priests therefore and officers saw him, they cried out, saying, " Crucify him, crucify him."

Pilate saith unto them, " Take ye him, and crucify him, for I find no fault in him."

The Jews answered him, " We have a law, and by our law he ought to die, because he made himself the Son of God."

When Pilate heard that saying, he was the more afraid; and went again unto the judgment hall, and saith unto Jesus, " Whence art thou? "

But Jesus gave him no answer. Then said Pilate unto him, " Speakest thou not unto me? knowest thou not that I have power to crucify thee, and have power to release thee? "

Jesus answered, " Thou couldest have no power at all against me, except it were given thee from above; therefore he that delivered me unto thee hath the greater sin."

And when Pilate was set down on the judgment seat, his wife sent unto him, saying, " Have thou nothing to do with that just man: for I have suffered many things this day in a dream because of him."

And from thence forth Pilate sought to release him. And when he had called together the chief priests and the rulers and the people, said unto them, "Ye have brought this man unto me, as one that perverteth the people; and, behold, I, having examined him before you, have found no fault in this man touching those things whereof ye accuse him. No, nor yet Herod, for I sent him to him, and lo, nothing worthy of death is found in him. I will chastise him, and release him." For of necessity he must release one unto them at the feast.

But the Jews cried out saying, "If thou let this man go, thou art not Caesar's friend: whosoever maketh himself a king speaketh against Caesar."

When Pilate therefore heard that saying, he brought Jesus forth, and sat down in the judgment seat in a place that is called the Pavement, and he saith unto the Jews, "Behold your King!"

But they cried out, "Away with him, away with him, crucify him."

Pilate saith unto them, "Shall I crucify your King?"

The chief priests answered, "We have no king but Caesar."

And they cried out all at once saying, "Away with this man, and release unto us Barabbas." Barabbas for a certain sedition made in the city and for murder was cast into prison.

When Pilate saw that he could prevail nothing, but that rather a tumult was made, he took water, and washed his hands before the multitude, saying, "I am innocent of the blood of this just person; see ye to it."

Then answered all the people, and said, "His blood be on us, and on our children."

And Pilate answered and said again unto them, "What will ye then that I shall do unto him whom ye call the King of the Jews?"

But they cried saying, "Crucify him, crucify him."

And he said unto them the third time, "Why! what evil hath he done? I have found no cause of death in him; I will therefore chastise him, and let him go."

And they were instant with loud voices, requiring that he might be crucified. And the voices of them and of the chief priests prevailed. And Pilate gave sentence that it should be as they required. And he released unto them Barabbas, that for sedition and murder was cast into prison, whom they had desired; but he delivered Jesus to their will.

TRULY, THIS IS THE SON OF GOD

AND THEY TOOK JESUS, and led him away. And he bearing his cross, went forth into a place called Golgotha, the place of a skull. And as they led Jesus away, they laid hold upon one Simon a Cyrenian, coming out of the country, and on him they laid the cross, that he might bear it after Jesus.

And there followed him a great company of people, and of women which also bewailed and lamented him. But Jesus turning unto them said, "Daughters of Jerusalem, weep not for me, but weep for yourselves, and for your children. For behold, the days are coming, in the which they shall say, 'Blessed are the barren, and the wombs that never bare, and the paps which never gave suck.' Then shall they begin to say to the mountains, 'Fall on us;' and to the hills, 'Cover us.' For if they do these things in a green tree, what shall be done in the dry?"

And there were also two thieves led with him to be put to death. And when they were come to the place which is called Calvary, there they crucified him, and the thieves, one on the right hand and the other on the left. And the scripture was fulfilled, which saith, "And he was numbered with the transgressors."

Then said Jesus, "Father, forgive them for they know not what they do."

And Pilate wrote a title, and put it on the cross. And the writing was, "JESUS OF NAZARETH THE KING OF THE JEWS." And it was written in Hebrew, and Greek, and Latin.

Then said the chief priests of the Jews to Pilate, "Write not, 'The King of the Jews;' but that he said, 'I am King of the Jews.'

Pilate answered, "What I have written I have written."

And they that passed by reviled Jesus wagging their heads, and saying, "Thou that destroyest the temple, and buildest it in three days, save thyself. If thou be the Son of God, come down from the cross."

Likewise also the chief priests mocking him, with the scribes and elders said, "He saved others; himself he cannot save. If he be the King of Israel, let him now come down from the cross, and we will believe him. He trusted in God; let him deliver him now, if he will have him, for he said, 'I am the Son of God.' Let Christ the King of Israel descend now from the cross, that we may see and believe."

And one of the thieves which were hanged, railed on him, saying, "If thou be the Christ, save thyself and us."

But the other rebuked him saying, "Dost thou not fear God, seeing thou art in the same condemnation? And we indeed justly, for we receive the due reward of our deeds; but this man hath done nothing amiss." And he said unto Jesus, "Lord, remember me when thou comest into thy kingdom."

And Jesus said unto him, "Verily I say unto thee, today thou shalt be with me in paradise."

And the soldiers, when they had crucified Jesus, took his garments and made four parts, to every soldier a part; and also his coat; now the coat was without seam, woven from the top throughout. They said therefore among themselves, "Let us not rend it, but cast lots for it, whose it shall be;" that the scripture might be fulfilled which saith, "They parted my raiment among them, and for my vesture they did cast lots."

Now there stood by the cross of Jesus his mother, and his mother's sister, Mary the wife of Cleophas, and Mary Magdalene. When Jesus therefore saw his mother, and John, the disciple standing by, whom he loved, he saith unto his mother, "Woman, behold thy son." Then saith he to John, "Behold thy mother." And John took her unto his own home.

After this Jesus knew that all things were now accomplished that the scripture might be fulfilled.

Now from the sixth hour there was darkness over all the land unto the ninth hour. And about the ninth hour Jesus cried with a loud voice, saying, "E-lo-i, E-lo-i, lama sabachthani?" which is being interpreted, "My God, my God, why hast thou forsaken me?"

Some of them that stood there, when they heard that said, "This man calleth for Elijah."

And straightway one of them ran, and took a sponge, and filled it with vinegar, and put it on a reed, and gave him to drink.

The rest said, "Let be, let us see whether Elijah will come to save him."

When Jesus therefore had received the vinegar, he said, "It is finished." And he cried with a loud voice, "Father, into thy hands I commend my spirit." And he bowed his head, and gave up the ghost.

And behold, the veil of the temple was rent in twain from the top to the bottom; and the earth did quake, and the rocks rent, and there was darkness over all the land.

When the centurion, and they that were with him watching Jesus, saw the earth quake, and those things that were done, they feared greatly, saying, "Truly this was the Son of God."

Then came the soldiers, and brake the legs of the first thief, and of the other which was crucified with him, but when they came to Jesus, and saw that he was dead already, they brake not his legs: but one of the soldiers with a spear pierced his side, and forthwith came thereout blood and water. For these things were done, that the scripture should be fulfilled, "A bone of him shall not be broken." And again another scripture saith, "They shall look on him whom they pierced."

And all the people that came together to that sight, beholding the things which were done, smote their breasts and returned.

And all his acquaintance, and the women that followed him from Galilee, stood afar off, beholding these things.

And after this Joseph of Arimathaea, a rich man who also himself was Jesus' disciple, but secretly for fear of the Jews this man went unto Pilate and begged that he might take away the body of Jesus; and Pilate gave him leave. He came therefore and took the body of Jesus, and wrapped it in linen, and laid it in his own new tomb which he had hewn out of a rock in a garden, wherein never man before was laid. And there came Nicodemus also, which at the first came to Jesus by night, and brought a mixture of myrrh and aloes, about an hundred pound weight. Then took they the body of Jesus, and wound it in linen clothes, with spices, and laid it in the new sepulchre. And they rolled a great stone at the door of the sepulchre, and departed. And that day was the preparation, and the sabbath drew on.

And the women also which came with Jesus from Galilee, among which was Mary Magdalene, and Mary the mother of James and Joses, and the mother of James and John, followed after, and beheld the sepulchre, and how the body was laid. And they returned and prepared spices and ointments; and rested the sabbath day according to the commandment.

Now the chief priests and Pharisees came together unto Pilate saying, " Sir, we remember that that deceiver said while he was yet alive, ' After three days I will rise again.' Command therefore that the sepulchre be made sure until the third day, lest his disciples come by night, and steal him away, and say unto the people, ' He is risen from the dead,' so the last error shall be worse than the first."

Pilate said unto them, " Ye have a watch; go your way, make it as sure as ye can."

So they went and made the sepulchre sure, sealing the stone, and setting a watch.

I ASCEND UNTO MY FATHER AND YOUR FATHER, MY GOD AND YOUR GOD

In the end of the sabbath, as it began to dawn toward the first day of the week, behold, there was a great earthquake, for the angel of the Lord descended from Heaven, and came and rolled back the stone from the door of the sepulchre and sat upon it. His countenance was like lightning, and his raiment white as snow; and for fear of him the keepers did shake, and became as dead men.

And very early in the morning, Mary Magdalene, and Mary the mother of James, and Salome, brought sweet spices which they had prepared that they might come and anoint Jesus, and they came unto the sepulchre at the rising of the sun. And they said among themselves, "Who shall roll us away the stone from the door of the sepulchre?" for it was very great. And when they looked, they saw that the stone was rolled away. And they entered into the sepulchre, and found not the body of the Lord Jesus.

And it came to pass as they were much perplexed thereabout, behold, two men stood by them in shining garments. And as the women were afraid, and bowed down their faces to the earth, they said unto them, "Be not affrighted; ye seek Jesus of Nazareth which was crucified. Why seek ye the living among the dead? He is risen; he is not here. Remember how he spake unto you when he was yet in Galilee, saying, 'The Son of Man must be delivered into the hands of sinful men, and be crucified, and the third day rise again.' Behold the place where they laid him. And go your way, tell his disciples and Peter that he goeth before you into Galilee: there shall ye see him as he said unto you."

And they went out quickly, and fled from the sepulchre; for they trembled and were amazed.

Then Mary Magdalene runneth, and cometh to Simon Peter, and to the other disciple, whom Jesus loved, and saith unto them, "They have taken away the Lord out of the sepulchre, and we know not where they have laid him."

Peter therefore went forth, and John, and they ran both together; and John did outrun Peter, and came first to the sepulchre. And he stooping down, and looking in, saw the linen clothes lying; yet went he not in. Then cometh Simon Peter following him, and went into the sepulchre, and seeth the linen clothes lie, and the napkin, that was about his head, not lying with the linen clothes, but wrapped together in a place by itself. And they departed wondering at that which was come to pass.

But Mary stood without at the sepulchre weeping: and as she wept, she stooped down, and looked into the sepulchre, and seeth two angels in white sitting, the one at the head, and the other at the feet, where the body of Jesus had lain.

And they say unto her, "Woman, why weepest thou?"

She saith unto them, "Because they have taken away my Lord, and I know not where they have laid him." And when she had thus said, she turned herself back, and saw Jesus standing, and knew not that it was Jesus.

Jesus saith unto her, "Woman, why weepest thou? whom seekest thou?"

She, supposing him to be the gardener, saith unto him, "Sir, if thou have borne him hence, tell me where thou hast laid him, and I will take him away."

Jesus saith unto her, "Mary."

She turned herself, and saith unto him, "Rabboni;" which is to say, "Master."

Jesus saith unto her, "Touch me not; for I am not yet ascended to my Father: but go to my brethren, and say unto them, I ascend unto my Father, and your Father; and to my God, and your God."

And she departed quickly with fear and great joy; and did run to bring his disciples word, as they mourned and wept. And she told the disciples that she had seen the Lord, and that he had spoken these things unto her, and her words seemed to them as idle tales, and they believed them not.

Now some of the watch came into the city, and showed unto the chief priests all the things that were done. And when the chief priests had assembled with the elders, and had taken counsel, they gave large money unto the soldiers, saying, "Say ye, 'Jesus' disciples came by night and stole him away, while we slept,' and if this come to the governor's ears, we will persuade him and secure you." So they took the money, and did as they were taught.

And behold, two of the disciples went that same day to a village called Emmaus, which was from Jerusalem about three score furlongs. And they talked together of all these things which had happened. And it came to pass, that while they communed together and reasoned, Jesus himself drew near, and went with them. But their eyes were holden that they should not know him.

And Jesus said unto them, "What manner of communications are these that ye have one to another, as ye walk and are sad? "

And one of them answering said, " Art thou only a stranger in Jerusalem, and hast not known the things which are come to pass there in these days? "

And Jesus said, " What things? "

And they said unto him, " Concerning Jesus of Nazareth, which was a prophet, mighty in deed and word before God and all the people; and how the chief priests and our rulers delivered him to be condemned to death, and have crucified him. But we trusted that it had been he which should have redeemed Israel. And beside all this, today is the third day since these things were done. Yea, and certain women also of our company made us astonished, which were early at the sepulchre, and when they found not his body, they came, saying that they had also seen a vision of angels which said that he was alive. And certain of them which were with us went to the sepulchre, and found it even so as the women had said; but him they saw not."

Then Jesus said unto them, "O fools, and slow of heart to believe all that the prophets have spoken; ought not Christ to have suffered these things, and to enter into his glory?" And beginning at Moses and all the prophets, he expounded unto them in all the scriptures the things concerning himself.

And they drew nigh unto the village, whither they went; and Jesus made as though he would have gone further. But they constrained him, saying, "Abide with us, for it is toward evening, and the day is far spent." And he went in to tarry with them.

And it came to pass, as he sat at meat with them, he took bread, and blessed it, and brake, and gave to them. And their eyes were opened, and they knew him; and he vanished out of their sight. And they said one to another, "Did not our heart burn within us, while he talked with us by the way, and while he opened to us the scriptures?"

And they rose up the same hour, and returned to Jerusalem, and found the eleven gathered together, and them that were with them, saying, "The Lord is risen indeed, and hath appeared to Simon." And they told what things were done in the way, and how he was known of them in breaking of bread.

Then the eleven disciples went away into Galilee, into a mountain where Jesus had appointed them. The same day at evening, when the doors were shut where the disciples were assembled for fear of the Jews, came Jesus and stood in the midst, and said unto them, "Peace be unto you." But they were terrified and affrighted, and supposed that they had seen a spirit.

And Jesus said unto them, "Why are ye troubled? and why do thoughts arise in your hearts? Behold my hands and my feet, that it is I myself; handle me, and see, for a spirit hath not flesh and bones, as ye see me have." And when he had thus spoken, he showed them his hands and his feet. And while they yet believed not for joy, and wondered, he said unto them, "Have ye here any meat?" And they gave him a piece of broiled fish, and of an honeycomb, and he took it, and did eat before them. Then were the disciples glad when they saw the Lord.

Then opened he their understanding that they might understand the scriptures. And he said unto them, "These are the words which I spake unto you, while I was yet with you, that all things must be fulfilled, which were written in the law of Moses, and in the prophets, and in the psalms, concerning me. Thus it is written and thus it behooved Christ to suffer, and to rise from the dead the third day; and that repentance and remission of sins should be preached in his name among all nations, beginning at Jerusalem."

The disciples asked him, saying, "Lord, wilt thou at this time restore again the kingdom to Israel?"

And he said unto them, "It is not for you to know the times or the seasons which the Father hath put in his own power. But ye shall receive power after that the Holy Ghost is come upon you; and ye shall be witnesses unto me, both in Jerusalem, and in Samaria, and unto the uttermost part of the earth."

Then said Jesus to them again, "Peace be unto you; as my Father hath sent me, even so send I you." And when he had said this, he breathed on them, and saith, "Receive the Holy Ghost."

But Thomas, one of the twelve, was not with them when Jesus came. The other disciples therefore said unto him, "We have seen the Lord."

But Thomas said unto them, "Except I shall see in his hands the print of the nails, and put my finger into the print of the nails, and thrust my hand into his side, I will not believe."

And after eight days again his disciples were within, and Thomas with them. Then came Jesus, the doors being shut, and stood in the midst, and said, "Peace be unto you." Then said he to Thomas, "Reach hither thy finger, and behold my hands; and reach hither thy hand, and thrust it into my side; and be not faithless, but believing."

And Thomas answered and said unto him, "My Lord and my God."

Jesus saith unto him, "Thomas, because thou hast seen me, thou hast believed; blessed are they that have not seen, and yet have believed."

After that Jesus was seen of above five hundred brethren at once. And to the apostles whom he had chosen, he showed himself alive by many infallible proofs, being seen of them forty days, and speaking of the things pertaining to the kingdom of God.

After these things Jesus showed himself again to the disciples at the sea of Tiberias; and on this wise showed he himself. There were together Simon Peter, and Thomas called Didymus, and Nathanael of Cana in Galilee, and the sons of Zebedee, and two other of his disciples.

Simon Peter saith unto them, "I go a fishing."

They say unto him, "We also go with thee." They went forth, and entered into a ship immediately; and that night they caught nothing. But when the morning was now come, Jesus stood on the shore, but the disciples knew not that it was Jesus.

Then Jesus saith unto them, "Children, have ye any meat?"

They answered him, "No."

And he said unto them, "Cast the net on the right side of the ship, and ye shall find." They cast therefore, and now they were not able to draw it for the multitude of fishes.

Therefore, John, that disciple whom Jesus loved, saith unto Peter, " It is the Lord."

Now when Simon Peter heard that it was the Lord, he girt his fisher's coat unto him for he was naked, and did cast himself into the sea. And the other disciples came in a little ship, for they were not far from land, dragging the net with fishes. As soon then as they were come to land, they saw a fire of coals there, and fish laid thereon, and bread.

Jesus saith unto them, " Bring of the fish which ye have now caught." Simon Peter went up, and drew the net to land full of great fishes, an hundred and fifty and three; and for all there were so many, yet was not the net broken.

Jesus saith unto them, " Come and dine."

And none of the disciples durst ask him, " Who art thou? " knowing that it was the Lord.

Jesus then cometh, and taketh bread, and giveth them, and fish likewise. So when they had dined, Jesus saith to Simon Peter, " Simon, son of Jonas, lovest thou me more than these? "

He saith unto him, " Yea, Lord, thou knowest that I love thee."

Jesus saith unto him, " Feed my lambs."

Jesus saith to him again the second time, " Simon, son of Jonas, lovest thou me? "

He saith unto him, " Yea, Lord; thou knowest that I love thee."

He saith unto him, " Feed my sheep."

Jesus saith unto him the third time, " Simon, son of Jonas, lovest thou me? "

Peter was grieved because he said unto him the third time, " Lovest thou me? " And he said unto him, " Lord, thou knowest all things; Thou knowest that I love thee."

Jesus saith unto him, " Feed my sheep. Verily, verily, I say unto thee, when thou wast young, thou girdedst thyself, and walkedst whither thou wouldest; but when thou shalt be old, thou shalt stretch forth thy hands, and another shall gird thee, and carry thee whither thou wouldest not." And when he had spoken this, he saith unto Peter, "Follow me."

Then Peter, turning about, saw John, the disciple whom Jesus loved following; Peter seeing him saith to Jesus, "Lord, and what shall this man do?"

Jesus saith unto him, "If I will that he tarry till I come, what is that to thee? Follow thou me." Then went this saying abroad among the brethren, that that disciple should not die: yet Jesus said not unto him, "He shall not die;" but, "If I will that he tarry till I come, what is that to thee?"

And Jesus led the disciples out as far as to Bethany, and he lifted up his hands, and blessed them, and he said unto them, "Go ye into all the world, and preach the gospel to every creature. And these signs shall follow them that believe: in my name shall they cast out devils; they shall speak with new tongues: they shall take up serpents; and if they drink any deadly thing, it shall not hurt them; they shall lay hands on the sick, and they shall recover. Teach them to observe all things whatsoever I have commanded you. Ye are witnesses of these things. Go ye therefore, and teach all nations, baptizing them in the name of the Father, and of the Son, and of the Holy Ghost. But tarry ye in the city of Jerusalem, until ye be endued with power from on high. All power is given unto me in heaven and in earth. And, behold, I send the promise of my Father upon you, for John truly baptized with water, but ye shall be baptized with the Holy Ghost not many days hence. I ascend unto my Father, and your Father, and to my God, and your God; and lo, I am with you alway, even unto the end of the world. Amen."

And it came to pass, while he blessed them, he was parted from them, and carried up into heaven, and a cloud received him out of their sight. And while they looked steadfastly toward heaven as he went up, behold, two men stood by them in white apparel; which said, "Ye men of Galilee, why stand ye gazing up into heaven? this same Jesus which is taken up from you into heaven, shall so come in like manner as ye have seen him go into heaven." And they worshipped him, and returned to Jerusalem with great joy.

And there are also many other things which Jesus did, the which, if they should be written every one, I suppose that even the world itself could not contain the books that should be written. But these are written, that ye might believe that Jesus is the Christ, the Son of God; and that believing ye might have life through his name.

THE SPIRIT OF TRUTH

" When the Comforter is come,
Even the Spirit of Truth,
Which proceedeth from the Father,
He will guide you into all Truth.
I will not leave you comfortless,
I will come to you.
Peace I leave with you;
My peace I give unto you;
Not as the world giveth, give I unto you.
Let not your heart be troubled.
Neither let it be afraid."

Christ Jesus

"YE ARE ALL

CHILDREN OF LIGHT

Walk as Children of Light."

Paul

FOREWORD

Ye Are All Children of Light includes the rest of the books of the New Testament.

The Acts of the Apostles follows the spread of Christianity from Judea through Asia Minor and Greece and even to Rome. The dominating figure is Paul for it was mainly through his great work that we have the Christian religion as we know it. His letters or Epistles were written to specific congregations established by him to meet the particular need of that church, but they are of universal application.

In this Book, the narrative of the Book of Acts is interrupted to insert the Epistles at approximately the place where Paul wrote them; and then the narrative of the Acts is continued.

The letter to the Hebrews was attributed to Paul, but many scholars believe it to be the work of some other author.

In this Book, First, Second and Third John have been arranged by subject.

All references used from these books are shown in the List of References.

THE ACTS OF THE APOSTLES

THE LORD KNOWEST THE HEARTS OF ALL

Then returned the disciples unto Jerusalem. And when they were come in, they went up into an upper room, where abode Peter, and James, and John, and Andrew, Philip, and Thomas, Bartholomew, and Matthew, James the son of Alphaeus, and Simon Zelotes, and Judas the brother of James. These all continued with one accord in prayer and supplications, with the women, and Mary the mother of Jesus, and with his brethren.

And Peter stood up in the midst of the disciples, and said, (the number of names together were about an hundred and twenty) "Men and brethren, this scripture must needs have been fulfilled, which the Holy Ghost, by the mouth of David, spake before concerning Judas, which was guide to them that took Jesus. For he was numbered with us, and had obtained part of this ministry. Now Judas purchased a field with the reward of iniquity; and falling headlong, he burst asunder in the midst and all his bowels gushed out. And it was known unto all the dwellers at Jerusalem, so that field is called in their tongue, Aceldama, that is to say, 'The field of blood.' For it is written in the book of Psalms, 'Let his habitation be desolate, and let no man dwell therein; and his bishopric let another take.'

"Wherefore of these men which have companied with us all the time that the Lord Jesus went in and out among us, beginning from the baptism of John, unto the same day that he was taken up from us, must one be ordained to be a witness with us of his resurrection."

And they appointed two, Joseph called Barsabas, who was surnamed Justus, and Matthias. And they prayed, and said,

"Thou, Lord, which knowest the hearts of all men, show whether of these two thou hast chosen, that he may take part of this ministry and apostleship, from which Judas by transgression fell, that he might go to his own place."

And they gave forth their lots; and the lot fell upon Matthias; and he was numbered with the eleven apostles.

THE DAY OF PENTECOST

AND WHEN THE DAY of Pentecost was come, the disciples were all with one accord in one place. And suddenly there came a sound from heaven as of a rushing mighty wind, and it filled all the house where the disciples were sitting. And there appeared unto them cloven tongues like as of fire, and it sat upon each of them. And they were all filled with the Holy Ghost, and began to speak with other tongues, as the Spirit gave them utterance.

And there were dwelling at Jerusalem Jews, devout men, out of every nation under heaven. Now when this was noised abroad, the multitude came together, and were confounded, because that every man heard them speak in his own language. And they were all amazed and marvelled, saying one to another, "Behold, are not all these which speak Galilaeans? And how hear we every man in our own tongue, wherein we were born? We do hear them speak in our tongues the wonderful works of God." And they were all amazed, and were in doubt, saying one to another, "What meaneth this?"

Others mocking said, "These men are full of new wine."

But Peter, standing up with the eleven, lifted up his voice, and said unto them, "Ye men of Judaea, and all ye that dwell at Jerusalem, be this known unto you, and hearken to my words:

For these men are not drunken, as ye suppose, but this is that which was spoken by the prophet Joel:

"'And it shall come to pass in the last days,' saith God, 'I will pour out of my Spirit upon all flesh: and your sons and your daughters shall prophesy, and your young men shall see visions, and your old men shall dream dreams. And on my servants and on my handmaidens I will pour out my Spirit. And it shall come to pass, that whosoever shall call on the name of the Lord shall be saved.'

"Ye men of Israel, hear these words: Jesus of Nazareth, a man approved of God among you by miracles and wonders and signs, which God did by him in the midst of you, as ye yourselves also know; him, being delivered by the determinate counsel and foreknowledge of God, ye have taken and by wicked hands have crucified and slain; whom God hath raised up, having loosed the pains of death, because it was not possible that he should be holden of it.

"For David speaketh concerning him, 'I foresaw the Lord always before my face, for he is on my right hand, that I should not be moved. Therefore did my heart rejoice, and my tongue was glad; moreover also my flesh shall rest in hope, because thou wilt not leave my soul in hell, neither wilt thou suffer thine Holy One to see corruption. Thou hast made known to me the ways of life; thou shalt make me full of joy with thy countenance.'

"Men and brethren, let me freely speak unto you of the patriarch David, whose sepulcher is with us unto this day, who being a prophet, and seeing this before, spake of the resurrection of Christ. This Jesus hath God raised up, whereof we are all witnesses. Therefore let all the house of Israel know assuredly that God hath made that same Jesus, whom ye have crucified, both Lord and Christ."

Now when they heard this, they were pricked in their hearts, and said unto Peter and to the rest of the apostles, "Men and brethren, what shall we do?"

Then Peter said unto them, "Repent, and be baptized every one of you in the name of Jesus Christ for the remission of sins, and ye shall receive the gift of the Holy Ghost. For the promise is unto you, and to your children, and to all that are afar off, even as many as the Lord our God shall call." And with many other words did he testify and exhort, saying, "Save yourselves from this untoward generation."

Then they that gladly received his word were baptized. And the same day there were added unto them about three thousand souls. And they continued steadfastly in the apostles' doctrine and fellowship, and in breaking of bread, and in prayers. And fear came upon every soul; and many wonders and signs were done by the apostles.

And all that believed were together, and had all things in common. And they sold their possessions and goods, and parted them to all men, as every man had need. And they continuing daily with one accord in the temple, and breaking bread from house to house, did eat their meat with gladness and singleness of heart, praising God, and having favour with all the people. And the Lord added to the church daily such as should be saved.

IN THE NAME OF JESUS CHRIST, RISE UP AND WALK

Now Peter and John went up together into the temple at the hour of prayer, being the ninth hour. And a certain man, lame from his mother's womb was carried, whom they laid daily at the gate of the temple which is called Beautiful, to ask alms of them that entered into the temple. Who seeing Peter and John about to go into the temple, asked an alms.

And Peter fastening his eyes upon him with John, said,

"Look on us." And he gave heed unto them, expecting to receive something of them. Then Peter said, "Silver and gold have I none; but such as I have give I thee: In the name of Jesus Christ of Nazareth rise up and walk." And he took him by the right hand, and lifted him up: and immediately his feet and ankle bones received strength. And he leaping up, stood, and walked, and entered with them into the temple, walking, and leaping, and praising God.

And all the people saw him walking and praising God, and they knew that it was he which sat for alms at the Beautiful gate of the temple. And they were filled with wonder and amazement at that which had happened unto him. And as the lame man which was healed held Peter and John, all the people ran together unto them in the porch that is called Solomon's greatly wondering.

And when Peter saw it, he answered unto the people, "Ye men of Israel, why marvel ye at this? Or why look ye so earnestly on us, as though by our own power or holiness we had made this man to walk? The God of Abraham, and of Isaac, and of Jacob, the God of our fathers, hath glorified his Son Jesus; whom ye delivered up, and denied him in the presence of Pilate, when he was determined to let him go. But ye denied the Holy One and the Just, and desired a murderer to be granted unto you, and killed the Prince of Life, whom God hath raised from the dead, whereof we are witnesses. And his name, through faith in his name hath made this man strong, whom ye see and know. Yea, the faith which is by him hath given him this perfect soundness in the presence of you all.

"And now, brethren, I wot that through ignorance ye did it, as did also your rulers. But those things, which God before had showed by the mouth of all his prophets, that Christ should suffer, he hath so fulfilled. Repent ye therefore, and be converted, that your sins may be blotted out, when the times of refreshing shall come from the presence of the Lord.

"And he shall send Jesus Christ, which before was preached unto you; whom the heaven must receive until the times of restitution of all things, which God hath spoken by the mouth of all his holy prophets since the world began. For Moses truly said unto the fathers, 'A prophet shall the Lord your God raise up unto you of your brethren, like unto me; him shall ye hear in all things whatsoever he shall say unto you.'

"Ye are the children of the prophets, and of the covenant which God made with our fathers, saying unto Abraham, 'And in thy seed shall all the kindreds of the earth be blessed.' Unto you first; God, having raised up his Son Jesus, sent him to bless you, in turning away every one of you from your iniquities."

And as they spake unto the people, the priests, and the captains of the temple, and the Sadducees, came upon them, being grieved that they taught the people, and preached through Jesus the resurrection from the dead. And they laid hands on them, and put them in hold until the next day, for it was now eventide. Howbeit many of them which heard the word believed; and the number of the men was about five thousand.

And it came to pass on the morrow, that their rulers, and elders, and scribes, and Annas the high priest, and Caiaphas, and as many as were of the kindred of the high priest, were gathered together at Jerusalem. And when they had set the disciples in the midst, they asked, "By what power, or by what name, have ye done this?"

Then Peter, filled with the Holy Ghost, said unto them, "Ye rulers of the people, and elders of Israel, if we this day be examined of the good deed done to the impotent man, by what means he is made whole, be it known unto you all, and to all the people of Israel, that by the name of Jesus Christ of Nazareth, whom ye crucified, whom God raised from the dead, even by him doth this man stand here before you whole. This is the stone which was set at nought of you builders, which is become the head of the corner. Neither is there salvation in any other;

for there is none other name under heaven given among men, whereby we must be saved."

Now when they saw the boldness of Peter and John, and perceived that they were unlearned and ignorant men, they marvelled; and they took knowledge of them, that they had been with Jesus. And beholding the man which was healed standing with them, they could say nothing against it.

But when they had commanded the apostles to go aside out of the council, they conferred among themselves, saying, "What shall we do to these men? for that indeed a notable miracle hath been done by them is manifest to all that dwell in Jerusalem, and we cannot deny it. But that it spread no further among the people, let us straitly threaten them, that they speak henceforth to no man in this name." And they called the apostles, and commanded them not to speak at all nor teach in the name of Jesus.

But Peter and John answered and said unto them, "Whether it be right in the sight of God to hearken unto you more than unto God, judge ye. For we cannot but speak the things which we have seen and heard."

So when they had further threatened them, they let them go, finding not how they might punish them, because of the people: for all men glorified God for that which was done. For the man was above forty years old on whom this miracle of healing was shown.

And being let go, the disciples went to their own company, and reported all that the chief priests and elders had said unto them. And when they heard that, they lifted up their voice to God with one accord, and said, "Lord, thou art God, which hast made heaven, and earth, and the sea, and all that in them is. And now, Lord, behold their threatenings: and grant unto thy servants, that with all boldness they may speak thy word, by stretching forth thine hand to heal; and that signs and wonders may be done by the name of thy holy child Jesus." And when they had prayed, the place was shaken where they were assembled together; and they were all filled with the Holy Ghost, and they spake the word of God with boldness.

And the multitude of them that believed were of one heart and of one soul. Neither said any of them that ought of the things which he possessed was his own; but they had all things in common. Neither was there any among them that lacked: for as many as were possessors of lands or houses sold them, and brought the prices of the things that were sold, and laid them down at the apostles' feet; and distribution was made unto every man according as he had need.

THOU HAST NOT LIED UNTO MEN, BUT UNTO GOD

BUT A CERTAIN MAN named Ananias, with Sapphira his wife, sold a possession, and kept back part of the price, his wife also being privy to it, and brought a certain part, and laid it at the apostles' feet.

But Peter said, " Ananias, why hath Satan filled thine heart to lie to the Holy Ghost, and to keep back part of the price of the land? Whiles it remained, was it not thine own? and after it was sold, was it not in thine own power? Why hast thou conceived this thing in thine heart? Thou hast not lied unto men, but unto God."

And Ananias hearing these words fell down, and gave up the ghost. And great fear came on all them that heard these things. And the young men arose, wound him up, and carried him out, and buried him.

And it was about the space of three hours after, when his wife, not knowing what was done, came in. And Peter said unto her, "Tell me whether ye sold the land for so much?"

And she said, "Yea, for so much."

Then Peter said unto her, "How is it that ye have agreed together to tempt the Spirit of the Lord? Behold, the feet of them which have buried thy husband are at the door, and shall carry thee out."

Then she fell down straightway at his feet, and yielded up the ghost; and the young men came in, and found her dead, and, carrying her forth, buried her by her husband. And great fear came upon all the church, and upon as many as heard these things.

IF THIS WORK BE OF GOD, YE CANNOT OVERTHROW IT

AND BY THE HANDS of the apostles were many signs and wonders wrought among the people. And believers were the more added to the Lord, multitudes both of men and women, insomuch that they brought forth the sick into the streets, and laid them on beds and couches, that at the least the shadow of Peter passing by might overshadow some of them. There came also a multitude out of the cities round about, unto Jerusalem, bringing sick folks, and them which were vexed with unclean spirits; and they were healed every one.

Then the high priest rose up, and all they that were with him, which is of the sect of the Sadducees, and were filled with indignation, and laid their hands on the apostles, and put them in the common prison.

But the angel of the Lord by night opened the prison doors, and brought them forth, and said, " Go, stand and speak in the temple to the people all the words of this life." And when they heard that they entered into the temple early in the morning, and taught.

But the high priest came, and they that were with him, called the council together, and all the senate of the children of Israel, and sent to the prison to have the apostles brought.

But when the officers came, and found them not in the prison, they returned, and told, saying, " The prison truly found we shut with all safety, and the keepers standing without before the doors; but when we opened, we found no man within." Now when the high priest, and the captain of the temple, and the chief priests heard these things, they doubted them.

Then came one and told the high priest, saying, " Behold, the men whom ye put in prison are standing in the temple, and teaching the people."

Then went the captain with the officers, and brought the apostles, without violence for they feared the people, lest they should be stoned. And when they had brought the apostles, they set them before the council, and the high priest asked them, saying, " Did not we straitly command you, that ye should not teach in this name? and behold, ye have filled Jerusalem with your doctrine, and intend to bring this man's blood upon us."

Then Peter and the other apostles answered and said, " We ought to obey God rather than men. The God of our fathers raised up Jesus, whom ye slew and hanged on a tree. Him hath God exalted with his right hand to be a Prince and a Saviour, for to give repentance to Israel, and forgiveness of sins. And we are his witnesses of these things. And so is also the Holy Ghost, whom God hath given to them that obey him."

When the high priest and those that were with him heard that, they were cut to the heart, and took counsel to slay them.

Then stood up one in the council, a Pharisee, named Gamaliel, a doctor of the law, who had a good reputation among all the people, and commanded to put the apostles forth a little space. And he said, "Ye men of Israel, take heed to yourselves what ye intend to do as touching these men. Refrain from these men, and let them alone: for if this counsel or this work be of men, it will come to nought. But if it be of God, ye cannot overthrow it, lest haply ye be found even to fight against God."

And to him they agreed, and when they had called the apostles, and beaten them, they commanded that they should not speak in the name of Jesus, and let them go.

And the apostles departed from the presence of the council, rejoicing that they were counted worthy to suffer shame for his name. And daily in the temple, and in every house, they ceased not to teach and preach Jesus Christ.

THEY SAW THE FACE OF STEPHEN AS IF IT HAD BEEN THE FACE OF AN ANGEL

AND IN THOSE DAYS, when the number of the disciples was multiplied, there arose a murmuring of the Grecians against the Hebrews, because their widows were neglected in the daily ministration. Then the twelve apostles called the multitude unto them, and said, "It is not reasonable that we should leave the word of God, and serve tables. Wherefore, brethren, look ye out among you seven men of honest report, full of the Holy Ghost and wisdom, whom ye may appoint over this business. But we will give ourselves continually to prayer, and to the ministry of the word."

And the saying pleased the whole multitude: and they chose Stephen, a man full of faith and of the Holy Ghost, and Philip, and Prochorus, and Nicanor, and Timon, and Parmenas, and Nicolas, a proselyte of Antioch, whom they set before the apostles. And when they had prayed, they laid their hands on them. And the word of God increased; and the number of the disciples multiplied in Jerusalem greatly.

And Stephen, full of faith and power, did great wonders and miracles among the people. Then there arose certain of the synagogue, disputing with Stephen. And they were not able to resist the wisdom and the spirit by which he spake.

Then they bribed men to say, "We have heard him speak blasphemous words against Moses, and against God." And they stirred up the people, and the elders and the scribes, and came upon Stephen, and caught him and brought him to the council, and set up false witnesses, which said, "This man ceaseth not to speak blasphemous words against this holy place, and the law: For we have heard him say, that this Jesus of Nazareth shall destroy this place, and shall change the customs which Moses delivered us."

And all that sat in the council, looking steadfastly on Stephen, saw his face as it had been the face of an angel.

Then said the high priest, "Are these things so?"

And Stephen said, "Men, brethren, and fathers, hearken: The God of glory, the Most High, dwelleth not in temples made with hands; as saith the prophet, 'Heaven is my throne, and earth is my footstool: what house will ye build me? saith the Lord: or what is the place of my rest? Hath not my hand made all these things?' Ye stiff-necked and hard in heart, ye do always resist the Holy Ghost; as your fathers did, so do ye. Which of the prophets have not your fathers persecuted? And they have slain them which told of the coming of the Just One; of whom ye have been now the betrayers and murderers, who have received the law by the disposition of angels, and have not kept it." When they heard these things, they were cut to the heart, and they gnashed on him with their teeth.

But Stephen, being full of the Holy Ghost, looked up steadfastly into heaven, and saw the glory of God, and Jesus standing on the right hand of God. And he said, "Behold, I see the heavens opened, and the Son of man standing on the right hand of God."

Then they cried out with a loud voice, and stopped their ears, and ran upon him with one accord, and cast him out of the city, and stoned him. And the witnesses laid down their clothes at a young man's feet, whose name was Saul.

And they stoned Stephen, who called upon God, and said, "Lord Jesus, receive my spirit." And he kneeled down and cried with a loud voice, "Lord, lay not this sin to their charge." And when he had said this, he fell asleep.

And Saul was consenting unto his death.

And devout men carried Stephen to his burial, and made great lamentation over him.

BELIEVE WITH ALL THINE HEART

AND AT THAT TIME there was a great persecution against the church which was at Jerusalem; and they were all scattered abroad throughout the regions of Judea and Samaria, except the apostles. As for Saul, he made havoc of the church, entering into every house, and haling men and women, committed them to prison. Therefore they that were scattered abroad went every where preaching the word.

Then Philip went down to the city of Samaria, and preached Christ unto them. And the people with one accord gave heed unto those things which Philip spake, hearing and seeing the miracles which he did. For unclean spirits, crying with loud voice, came out of many that were possessed with them: and many taken with palsies, and that were lame, were healed. And there was great joy in that city.

But there was a certain man, called Simon, which beforetime in the same city used sorcery, and bewitched the people of Samaria, and gave out that he himself was some great one, to whom they all gave heed, from the least to the greatest, saying "This man is the great power of God." And to him they had regard, because that of long time he had bewitched them with sorceries.

But when they believed Philip, preaching the things concerning the kingdom of God, and the name of Jesus Christ, they were baptized, both men and women. Then Simon himself believed also; and when he was baptized, he continued with Philip, and wondered, beholding the miracles and signs that were done.

Now when the apostles which were at Jerusalem heard that Samaria had received the word of God, they sent unto them Peter and John, who, when they were come down, prayed for them that they might receive the Holy Ghost. Then they laid their hands on them, and they received the Holy Ghost.

And when Simon saw that through laying on of the apostles' hands the Holy Ghost was given, he offered them money, saying, "Give me also this power, that on whomsoever I lay hands, he may receive the Holy Ghost."

But Peter said unto him, "Thy money perish with thee, because thou hast thought that the gift of God may be purchased with money. Thou hast neither part nor lot in this matter, for thy heart is not right in the sight of God. Repent therefore of this thy wickedness, and pray God, if perhaps the thought of thine heart may be forgiven thee. For I perceive that thou art in the gall of bitterness, and in the bond of iniquity."

Then answered Simon, and said, "Pray ye to the Lord for me, that none of these things which ye have spoken come upon me."

And the apostles, when they had testified and preached the word of the Lord, returned to Jerusalem, and preached the gospel in many villages of the Samaritans.

And the angel of the Lord spake unto Philip, saying, "Arise, and go toward the south, unto the way that goeth down from Jerusalem unto Gaza, which is desert." And he arose and went.

And behold, a man of Ethiopia, an eunuch of great authority under Candace queen of the Ethiopians, who had the charge of all her treasures, and had come to Jerusalem for to worship, was returning, and was sitting in his chariot, reading Isaiah the prophet.

Then the Spirit said unto Philip, "Go near and join thyself to this chariot." And Philip ran thither to him, and heard him read the prophet Isaiah, and said, "Understandest thou what thou readest?"

And he said, "How can I, except some man should guide me?" And he desired Philip that he would come up, and sit with him. The place of the scripture which he read was this, "He was led as a sheep to the slaughter, and like a lamb dumb before his shearer, so opened he not his mouth. In his humiliation his judgment was taken away; and who shall declare his generation? for his life is taken from the earth."

And the eunuch said, "I pray thee, of whom speaketh the prophet this? of himself, or of some other man?"

Then Philip opened his mouth, and began at the same scripture, and preached unto him Jesus. And as they went on their way, they came to a certain water; and the eunuch said, "See, here is water; what doth hinder me to be baptized?"

And Philip said, "If thou believest with all thine heart, thou mayest."

And the eunuch answered, "I believe that Jesus Christ is the Son of God." And he commanded the chariot to stand still. And they went down into the water, both Philip and the eunuch, and Philip baptized him.

And when they were come up out of the water, the Spirit of the Lord caught away Philip, that the eunuch saw him no more. And the eunuch went on his way rejoicing.

But Philip was found at Azotus; and passing through, he preached in all the cities, till he came to Cesarea.

THERE SHINED ROUND ABOUT SAUL A LIGHT FROM HEAVEN

AND SAUL, yet breathing out threatenings and slaughter against the disciples of the Lord, went unto the high priest, and desired of him letters to Damascus to the synagogues, that if he found any of this way, whether they were men or women, he might bring them bound unto Jerusalem.

And as he journeyed, he came near Damascus; and suddenly there shined round about him a light from heaven. And he fell to the earth, and heard a voice saying unto him, "Saul, Saul, why persecutest thou me?"

And he said, "Who art thou, Lord?"

And the Lord said, "I am Jesus whom thou persecutest. It is hard for thee to kick against the pricks."

And he trembling, and astonished, said, "Lord, what wilt thou have me to do?"

And the Lord said unto him, "Arise, and go into the city, and it shall be told thee what thou must do."

And the men which journeyed with Saul stood speechless, hearing a voice, but seeing no man. And Saul arose from the earth; and when his eyes were opened, he saw no man; but they led him by the hand, and brought him into Damascus. And he was three days without sight, and neither did eat nor drink.

And there was a certain disciple at Damascus, named Ananias; and to him said the Lord in a vision, "Ananias."

And he said, "Behold, I am here, Lord."

And the Lord said unto him, "Arise, and go into the street which is called Straight, and inquire in the house of Judas for one called Saul of Tarsus: for behold, he prayeth, and hath seen in a vision a man named Ananias, coming in, and putting his hand on him, that he might receive his sight."

Then Ananias answered, " Lord, I have heard by many of this man, how much evil he hath done to thy saints at Jerusalem. And here he hath authority from the chief priests, to bind all that call on thy name."

But the Lord said unto him, " Go thy way: for he is a chosen vessel unto me, to bear my name before the Gentiles, and kings, and the children of Israel. For I will show him how great things he must suffer for my name's sake."

And Ananias went his way, and entered into the house; and putting his hands on him, said, " Brother Saul, the Lord, even Jesus that appeared unto thee in the way as thou camest, hath sent me, that thou mightest receive thy sight, and be filled with the Holy Ghost."

And immediately there fell from his eyes as it had been scales; and he received sight forthwith, and arose, and was baptized. And when he had received meat, he was strengthened.

Then was Saul certain days with the disciples which were at Damascus. And straightway he preached Christ in the synagogues, that he is the Son of God. But all that heard him were amazed, and said, " Is not this he that destroyed them which called on this name in Jerusalem, and came hither for the intent that he might bring them bound unto the chief priests? "

But Saul increased the more in strength, and confounded the Jews which dwelt at Damascus, proving that this is the very Christ. And after many days were fulfilled, the Jews took counsel to kill him. But their lying in wait was known to Saul, for they watched the gates day and night to kill him. Then the disciples took Saul by night, and let him down by the wall in a basket.

And when Saul was come to Jerusalem, he assayed to join himself to the disciples; but they were all afraid of him, and believed not that he was a disciple. But Barnabas took him, and brought him to the apostles, and declared unto them how Saul had seen the Lord in the way, and that he had spoken to him, and how he had preached boldly at Damascus in the name of Jesus.

And Saul was with them, coming in and going out at Jerusalem. And he spake boldly in the name of the Lord Jesus, and disputed against the Grecians: but they went about to slay him. Which when the brethren knew, they brought him down to Cesarea, and sent him forth to Tarsus.

Then had the churches rest throughout all Judea, and Galilee, and Samaria, and were edified; and walking in the fear of the Lord, and in the comfort of the Holy Ghost, were multiplied.

"TABITHA, ARISE"

AND IT CAME TO PASS, as Peter passed throughout all quarters, he came down also to the saints which dwelt at Lydda. And there he found a certain man named Eneas, which had kept his bed eight years, and was sick of the palsy.

And Peter said unto him "Eneas, Jesus Christ maketh thee whole: arise, and make thy bed." And he arose immediately. And all that dwelt at Lydda and Saron saw him, and turned to the Lord.

Now there was at Joppa a certain disciple named Tabitha, which by interpretation is called Dorcas. This woman was full of good works and alms-deeds which she did. And it came to pass in those days, that she was sick, and died: whom when they had washed, they laid her in an upper chamber.

And forasmuch as Lydda was nigh to Joppa, and the disciples

had heard that Peter was there, they sent unto him two men, desiring him that he would not delay to come to them. Then Peter arose, and went with them.

When Peter was come, they brought him into the upper chamber: and all the widows stood by him weeping, and showing the coats and garments which Dorcas made, while she was with them. But Peter put them all forth and kneeled down, and prayed. And turning him to the body said, "Tabitha, arise." And she opened her eyes: and when she saw Peter, she sat up. And he gave her his hand, and lifted her up; and when he had called the saints and widows, he presented her alive.

And it was known throughout all Joppa. And many believed in the Lord. And it came to pass that Peter tarried many days in Joppa with one Simon a tanner.

GOD IS NO RESPECTER OF PERSONS

THERE WAS a certain man in Cesarea, called Cornelius, a centurion of the band called the Italian band. He was a devout man, and one that feared God with all his house, and gave much alms to the people, and prayed to God always.

He saw in a vision, evidently about the ninth hour of the day, an angel of God coming in to him, and saying unto him, "Cornelius."

And when Cornelius looked on him, he was afraid, and said, "What is it, Lord?"

And he said unto him, "Thy prayers and thine alms are come up for a memorial before God. And now send men to

Joppa, and call for one Simon, whose surname is Peter. He lodgeth with one Simon a tanner, whose house is by the sea-side. He shall tell thee what thou oughtest to do."

And when the angel which spake unto Cornelius was departed, he called two of his household servants, and a devout soldier that waited on him continually; and when he had declared all these things unto them, he sent them to Joppa.

On the morrow, as they went on their journey, and drew nigh unto the city, Peter went up upon the house-top to pray, about the sixth hour. And he became very hungry, and would have eaten, but while they made ready, he fell into a trance: and he saw heaven opened, and a certain vessel descending unto him, as it had been a great sheet knit at the four corners, and let down to the earth, wherein were all manner of four-footed beasts of the earth, and wild beasts, and creeping things, and fowls of the air.

And there came a voice to him, saying, "Rise, Peter; kill, and eat."

But Peter said, "Not so, Lord, for I have never eaten any thing that is common or unclean."

And the voice spake unto him again the second time, "What God hath cleansed, that call not thou common." This was done thrice, and the vessel was received up again into heaven.

Now, while Peter doubted in himself what this vision which he had seen should mean, behold, the men which were sent from Cornelius had made inquiry for Simon's house, and stood before the gate, and called, and asked whether Simon, which was surnamed Peter, was lodged there.

While Peter thought on the vision, the Spirit said unto him, "Behold, three men seek thee. Arise therefore, and get thee down, and go with them, doubting nothing: for I have sent them."

Then Peter went down to the men which were sent from Cornelius, and said, "Behold, I am he whom ye seek: what is the cause wherefore ye are come? "

And they said, "Cornelius the centurion, a just man, and one that feareth God, and of good report among all the nation of the Jews, was warned from God by an holy angel to send for thee into his house, and to hear words of thee."

Then Peter called them in, and lodged them. And on the morrow he went away with them, and certain brethren from Joppa accompanied him.

And they entered into Cesarea. And Cornelius waited for them, and had called together his kinsmen and near friends.

And as Peter was coming in, Cornelius met him, and fell down at his feet, and worshipped him. But Peter took him up, saying, "Stand up: I myself also am a man."

And as Peter talked with him, he went in, and found many that were come together. And he said unto them, "Ye know how that it is an unlawful thing for a man that is a Jew to keep company, or come unto one of another nation. But God hath shown me that I should not call any man common or unclean. Therefore came I unto you without gainsaying, as soon as I was sent for: I ask therefore for what intent ye have sent for me?"

And Cornelius said, "Four days ago I was fasting until this hour; and at the ninth hour I prayed in my house, and behold, a man stood before me in bright clothing, and said, 'Cornelius, thy prayer is heard, and thine alms are had in remembrance in the sight of God. Send therefore to Joppa, and call hither Simon, whose surname is Peter; he is lodged in the house of one Simon a tanner, by the sea-side; who, when he cometh, shall speak unto thee.' Immediately therefore I sent to thee; and thou hast well done that thou art come. Now therefore are we all here present before God, to hear all things that are commanded thee of God."

Then Peter opened his mouth, and said, "Of a truth, I perceive that God is no respecter of persons, but in every nation, he that feareth him and worketh righteousness, is accepted with him.

"The word which God sent unto the children of Israel,

preaching peace by Jesus Christ, that word, I say, ye know, which was published throughout all Judea, and began from Galilee after the baptism which John preached. God anointed Jesus of Nazareth with the Holy Ghost and with power, and he went about doing good, and healing all that were oppressed of the devil, for God was with him. And we are witnesses of all things which he did, both in the land of the Jews, and in Jerusalem. Him they slew and hanged on a tree, whom God raised up the third day, and showed him openly, not to all the people, but unto witnesses chosen before of God, even to us, who did eat and drink with him after he rose from the dead. And he commanded us to preach unto the people, and to testify that it is he which was ordained of God to be the Judge of the quick and the dead. To him give all the prophets witness, that through his name whosoever believeth in him shall receive remission of sins."

While Peter yet spake these words, the Holy Ghost fell on all them which heard the word. And they of the circumcision which believed, were astonished, as many that came with Peter, because that on the Gentiles also was poured out the gift of the Holy Ghost. For they heard them speak with tongues, and magnify God.

Then said Peter, " Can any man forbid water, that these should not be baptized, which have received the Holy Ghost as well as we? " And he commanded them to be baptized in the name of the Lord. Then prayed they him to tarry certain days.

And the apostles and brethren that were in Judea, heard that the Gentiles had also received the word of God. And when Peter was come up to Jerusalem, they that were of the circumcision contended with him, saying, " Thou wentest in to men uncircumcised, and didst eat with them."

But Peter rehearsed the matter from the beginning, and expounded it by order unto them. Then he said, " And as I began to speak, the Holy Ghost fell on them, as on us at the beginning. Then I remembered the word of the Lord, how that he said, 'John indeed baptized with water, but ye shall be baptized with the Holy Ghost.' Forasmuch then as God gave them the like gift as he did unto us who believed on the Lord Jesus Christ, what was I, that I could withstand God?"

When they heard these things, they held their peace, and glorified God, saying, "Then hath God also granted to the Gentiles repentance unto life."

Now they which were scattered abroad because of the persecution that arose about Stephen, traveled as far as Phoenicia, and Cyprus, and Antioch, preaching the word to none but unto the Jews only. And the hand of the Lord was with them: and a great number believed, and turned unto the Lord.

Then tidings of these things came unto the ears of the church which was in Jerusalem, and they sent forth Barnabas, that he should go as far as Antioch. And when Barnabas came, and had seen the grace of God, he was glad, and exhorted them all that with purpose of heart they should cleave unto the Lord. For Barnabas was a good man, and full of the Holy Ghost, and of faith. And much people was added unto the Lord.

Then departed Barnabas to Tarsus, for to seek Saul. And when he found him, he brought him unto Antioch. And it came to pass, that a whole year they assembled themselves with the church, and taught much people. And the disciples were called Christians first at Antioch.

THE CHAINS FELL OFF PETER'S HANDS

NOW ABOUT that time, Herod the king stretched forth his hands to vex certain of the church. And he killed James the brother of John with the sword. And because he saw it pleased the Jews, he proceeded further to take Peter also. And when he had apprehended him, he put him in prison, and delivered him to four quaternions of soldiers to keep him. Then were the days of unleavened bread. And Herod intended after that to bring Peter forth to the people.

Peter therefore was kept in prison, and prayer was made without ceasing of the church unto God for him. And when Herod would have brought him forth, the same night, Peter was sleeping between two soldiers, bound with two chains; and the keepers before the door kept the prison.

And behold, the angel of the Lord came upon Peter, and a light shined in the prison. And the Angel smote Peter on the side, and raised him up, saying, "Arise up quickly." And his chains fell off from his hands.

And the angel said unto him, "Gird thyself, and bind on thy sandals," and so he did. And he saith unto Peter, "Cast thy garment about thee, and follow me." And Peter went out, and followed him, and wist not that it was true which was done by the angel; but thought he saw a vision.

When they were past the first and the second ward, they came unto the iron gate that leadeth unto the city, which opened to them of its own accord. And they went out, and passed on through one street, and forthwith the angel departed from him.

And when Peter was come to himself, he said, "Now I know of a surety, that the Lord hath sent his angel, and hath delivered me out of the hand of Herod, and from all the expectation of the people of the Jews." And when he had considered the thing, he came to the house of Mary the mother of John, where many were gathered together praying.

And as Peter knocked at the door of the gate, a damsel came to hearken, named Rhoda. And when she knew Peter's voice, she opened not the gate for gladness, but ran in, and told how Peter stood before the gate. And they said unto her, "Thou art mad." But she constantly affirmed that it was even so. Then said they, "It is his angel."

But Peter continued knocking. And when they had opened the door, and saw him, they were astonished. But he beckoning unto them with the hand to hold their peace, declared unto them how the Lord had brought him out of the prison. And he said, "Go show these things unto James, and to the brethren." And Peter departed, and went into another place.

Now as soon as it was day, there was no small stir among the soldiers, what was become of Peter. And when Herod sought for him, and found him not, he examined the keepers, and commanded that they should be put to death.

And Peter went down from Judea to Cesarea, and there abode. But the word of God grew and multiplied.

A LIGHT OF THE GENTILES

NOW THERE were in the church that was at Antioch, certain prophets and teachers. And as they ministered to the Lord, and fasted, the Holy Ghost said unto them, "Separate for me Barnabas and Saul for the work whereunto I have called them." And when they had fasted and prayed, and laid their hands on them, they sent them away.

So Barnabas and Saul (who is also called, Paul), being sent

forth by the Holy Ghost, departed and sailed to Cyprus. And when they had gone through the isle unto Paphos, they found a certain sorcerer, a false prophet, a Jew, whose name was Barjesus, who was with the deputy of the country, named Sergius Paulus. He was a prudent man, who called for Barnabas and Paul, and desired to hear the word of God. But Barjesus, the sorcerer, withstood them, seeking to turn away Sergius Paulus from the faith.

Then Paul set his eyes on Barjesus and said, "O full of subtility and all mischief, thou child of the devil, thou enemy of all righteousness, wilt thou not cease to pervert the right ways of the Lord? And now, behold, the hand of the Lord is upon thee, and thou shalt be blind, not seeing the sun for a season."

And immediately there fell on him a mist and a darkness, and he went about seeking some to lead him by the hand. Then Sergius Paulus, the deputy of the country, when he saw what was done, believed, being astonished at the doctrine of the Lord.

Now Paul and Barnabas left Paphos, and came to Antioch, and went into the synagogue on the sabbath day, and sat down. And after the reading of the law and the prophets, the rulers of the synagogue sent unto them, saying, "Ye men and brethren, if ye have any word of exhortation for the people, say on."

Then Paul stood up, and beckoning with his hand said, "Men of Israel, and ye that fear God, give audience. The God of this people of Israel chose our fathers, and exalted the people; and he raised up unto them David to be their king. Of this man's seed hath God, according to his promise, raised unto Israel a Saviour, Jesus. Men and brethren, children of the stock of Abraham, and whosoever among you feareth God, to you is the word of this salvation sent. For they that dwell at Jerusalem, and their rulers, because they knew him not, nor yet the voices of the prophets which are read every sabbath day, they have fulfilled them in condemning him. And though they found no cause of death in him, yet they demanded of Pilate that he should be slain. And when they had fulfilled all that was written of him, they took him down from the cross, and laid him in a sepulchre.

" But God raised him from the dead. And he was seen many days of them which came up with him from Galilee to Jerusalem, who are his witnesses unto the people. And we declare unto you glad tidings; How that the promise which was made unto the fathers, God hath fulfilled in that he hath raised up Jesus again. Be it known unto you therefore, men and brethren, that through this man is preached unto you the forgiveness of sins."

And when the Jews were gone out of the synagogue, the Gentiles besought that these words might be preached to them the next sabbath. And the next sabbath day came almost the whole city together to hear the word of God. But when the Jews saw the multitudes, they were filled with envy, and spake against those things which were spoken by Paul, contradicting and blaspheming.

Then Paul and Barnabas waxed bold, and said, " It was necessary that the word of God should first have been spoken to you: but seeing ye put it from you, and judge yourselves unworthy of everlasting life, lo, we turn to the Gentiles. For so hath the Lord commanded us, saying, 'I have set thee to be a light of the Gentiles, that thou shouldest be for salvation unto the ends of the earth.' "

And when the Gentiles heard this, they were glad, and glorified the word of the Lord; and as many as were ordained to eternal life, believed. And the word of the Lord was published throughout all the region.

But the Jews stirred up the devout and honourable women, and the chief men of the city, and raised persecution against Paul and Barnabas, and expelled them out of their coasts. But they shook off the dust of their feet against them, and came unto Iconium.

"STAND UPRIGHT ON THY FEET"

And it came to pass in Iconium, that Barnabas and Paul went together into the synagogue of the Jews, and so spake that a great multitude both of the Jews and also of the Greeks believed. But the unbelieving Jews stirred up the Gentiles, and made their minds evil affected against the brethren. But they abode there a long time, speaking boldly in the Lord, which gave testimony unto the word by signs and wonders done by their hands.

But the multitude of the city was divided: and part held with the Jews, and part with the apostles. And when there was an assault made both by the Gentiles, and also by the Jews with their rulers, to use the apostles despitefully, and to stone them, they became aware of it, and fled unto Lystra and Derbe, cities of Lycaonia, and unto the region that lieth round about. And there they preached the gospel.

And there sat a certain man at Lystra, impotent in his feet, being a cripple from his mother's womb, who never had walked. The same heard Paul speak. And Paul stedfastly beholding him, and perceiving that he had faith to be healed, said with a loud voice, "Stand upright on thy feet." And he leaped and walked.

And when the people saw what Paul had done, they lifted up their voices, saying in the speech of Lycaonia, "The gods are come down to us in the likeness of men." And they called Barnabas, Jupiter; and Paul, Mercurius, because he was the chief speaker.

Then the priest of Jupiter, which was before their city, brought oxen and garlands unto the gates, and would have done sacrifice with the people, but when the apostles, Barnabas and

Paul, heard of it, they rent their clothes, and ran in among the people, crying out and saying, "Sirs, why do ye these things? We also are men of like passions with you, and preach unto you that ye should turn from these vanities unto the living God, which made heaven, and earth, and the sea, and all that are therein. And he gave us rain from heaven, and fruitful seasons, filling our hearts with food and gladness." And with these sayings scarcely restrained they the people from doing sacrifice unto them.

And there came thither certain Jews from Antioch and Iconium, who persuaded the people, and having stoned Paul, they drew him out of the city, supposing he was dead.

Howbeit, as the disciples stood round about him, he rose up, and came into the city. And the next day he departed with Barnabas to Derbe. And he exhorted the disciples to continue in the faith, and that through much tribulation we enter into the kingdom of God.

And when they had preached the word in Perga, they went down into Attalia, and thence they sailed to Antioch, from whence they had been recommended to the grace of God for the work which they fulfilled. And when they were come, and had gathered the church together, they rehearsed all that God had done with them, and how he had opened the door of faith unto the Gentiles. And they abode there a long time with the disciples.

THROUGH THE GRACE OF THE LORD JESUS CHRIST WE SHALL BE SAVED

Certain men which came down from Judaea taught the brethren, and said, "Except ye be circumcised after the manner of Moses, ye cannot be saved." When therefore Paul and Barnabas had no small dissension and disputation with them, they determined that Paul and Barnabas, and certain other of them, should go up to Jerusalem unto the apostles and elders about this question.

And on their way they passed through Phoenicia and Samaria, declaring the conversion of the Gentiles. And they caused great joy unto all the brethren. And when they came to Jerusalem, they were received by the church, and by the apostles and elders, and they declared all things that God had done with them.

But there rose up certain of the sect of the Pharisees which believed, saying that it was needful to circumcise them, and to command them to keep the law of Moses. And the apostles and elders came together to consider this matter.

And when there had been much disputing, Peter rose up, and said, "Men and brethren, ye know that a good while ago God made choice among us, that the Gentiles should hear the word of the gospel, and believe. And God, which knoweth the hearts, bare them witness, giving them the Holy Ghost, even as he did unto us. And put no difference between us and them, purifying their hearts by faith. Now therefore why tempt ye God, to put a yoke upon the neck of the disciples, which neither our fathers nor we were able to bear? But we believe that through the grace of the Lord Jesus Christ we shall be saved, even as they."

Then all the multitude kept silence, and gave audience to Barnabas and Paul, declaring what miracles and wonders God had wrought among the Gentiles by them.

And after they had held their peace, James said, " Men and brethren, hearken unto me. Known unto God are all His works from the beginning of the world. Wherefore my sentence is, that we trouble not them who among the Gentiles have turned to God. But that we write unto them that they abstain from pollutions of idols, and from fornication."

Then it pleased the apostles and elders, and the whole church, to send chosen men of their own company to Antioch with Paul and Barnabas: namely, Judas surnamed Barsabas, and Silas, chief men among the brethren.

And they wrote letters to them after this manner: " The apostles and elders and brethren send greeting unto the brethren which are of the Gentiles in Antioch and Syria, and Cilicia. Forasmuch as we have heard that certain men which went out from us have troubled you with words, saying ' Ye must be circumcised, and keep the law,' to whom we gave no such commandment, it seemed good unto us, being assembled with one accord, to send chosen men unto you with our beloved Barnabas and Paul, men that have hazarded their lives for the name of our Lord Jesus Christ. We have sent therefore Judas and Silas, who shall also tell you the same things by mouth. For it seemed good to the Holy Ghost, and to us, to lay no greater burden upon you than these necessary things: That ye abstain from all evil, from which if ye keep yourselves, ye shall do well. Fare ye well."

So these men came to Antioch. And when they had gathered the multitude together, they delivered the epistle: which when they had read, they rejoiced for the consolation. And Judas and Silas, being prophets also, exhorted the brethren with many words, and confirmed them. And after they had tarried there a space, they were let go in peace unto the apostles. Notwithstanding it pleased Silas to abide there still. Also Paul and Barnabas continued in Antioch, teaching and preaching the word of the Lord.

And some days after, Paul said unto Barnabas, "Let us go again and visit our brethren in every city where we have preached the word of the Lord, and see how they do."

And Barnabas determined to take with them John, whose surname was Mark. But Paul thought it not good to take him with them who had departed and not gone with them to the work. And the contention was so sharp between them, that they parted asunder one from the other; and so Barnabas took Mark, and sailed unto Cyprus. And Paul chose Silas, and departed, being recommended by the brethren unto the grace of God.

And Paul went through Syria and Cilicia confirming the churches.

SUDDENLY THERE WAS A GREAT EARTHQUAKE, AND EVERY ONE'S BANDS WERE LOOSED

THEN PAUL and Silas came to Derbe and Lystra. And behold, a certain disciple was there named Timothy, the son of a woman which was a Jewess, but his father was a Greek. Timothy was well reported of by the brethren that were at Lystra and Iconium, and as Paul wanted Timothy to go with him, he took and circumcised him because of the Jews in those quarters, for they knew that his father was a Greek.

And as they went through the cities, they delivered them the decrees to keep that were ordained by the apostles and elders which were at Jerusalem. So the churches were established in the faith, and increased in number daily.

And they came down to Troas, and a vision appeared to Paul in the night: There stood a man of Macedonia, and prayed him saying, "Come over into Macedonia, and help us."

And after Paul had seen the vision, immediately they endeavored to go into Macedonia, assuredly gathering that the Lord had called them to preach the gospel unto them. Therefore leaving Troas they came to Neapolis, and from thence to Philippi which is the chief city of that part of Macedonia. And they remained in that city certain days.

On the sabbath they went out of the city by a river side where prayer was wont to be made. And they sat down and spake unto the women which resorted thither. And a certain woman named Lydia, a seller of purple of the city of Thyatira, who worshipped God, heard the things which were spoken by Paul, and when she was baptized, and her household, she besought Paul saying, "If ye have judged me to be faithful to the Lord, come into my house and abide there." And she constrained them.

And it came to pass that as they went to prayer, a certain damsel possessed with a spirit of divination, which brought her masters much gain by soothsaying, met them. And she followed Paul and the disciples, and cried, saying, "These men are the servants of the most high God, which show unto us the way of salvation." And this she did many days.

But Paul, being grieved, turned and said to the spirit, "I command thee in the name of Jesus Christ to come out of her." And he came out the same hour.

And when her masters saw that the hope of their gains was gone, they caught Paul and Silas, and drew them into the market place unto the rulers, and brought them to the magistrates, saying, "These men being Jews do exceedingly trouble our city; and teach customs which are not lawful for us to receive, neither to observe, being Romans."

And the multitude rose up together against them: and the magistrates rent off their clothes, and commanded to beat them. And when they had laid many stripes upon them, they cast them into prison, charging the jailor to keep them safely. The jailor having received such a charge, thrust them into the inner prison, and made their feet fast in the stocks.

And at midninght Paul and Silas prayed, and sang praises unto God: and the prisoners heard them. And suddenly there was a great earthquake, so that the foundations of the prison were shaken: and immediately all the doors were opened, and every one's bands were loosed.

And the keeper of the prison awaking out of his sleep, and seeing the prison doors open, he drew out his sword, and would have killed himself, supposing that the prisoners had fled. But Paul cried with a loud voice saying, "Do thyself no harm, for we are all here."

Then the keeper called for a light, and sprang in, and came trembling, and fell down before Paul and Silas, and brought them out, and said, "Sirs, what must I do to be saved?"

And they said, "Believe on the Lord Jesus Christ, and thou shalt be saved, and thy house." And they spake unto him the word of the Lord, and to all that were in his house.

And he took them the same hour of the night, and washed their stripes; and was baptized, he and all his, straightway. And when he had brought them into his house, he set meat before them, and rejoiced, believing in God with all his house.

And when it was day, the magistrates sent the serjeants, saying, "Let those men go."

And the keeper of the prison told this saying to Paul, "The magistrates have sent to let you go: now therefore depart, and go in peace."

But Paul said unto them, "They have beaten us openly uncondemned, being Romans, and have cast us into prison; now do they thrust us out privily? nay verily; but let them come themselves and fetch us out."

And the serjeants told these words unto the magistrates: and they feared, when they heard that they were Romans. And they came and besought them, and brought them out, and desired them to depart out of the city.

And they went out of the prison, and entered into the house of Lydia. And when they had seen the brethren, they comforted them, and departed.

WHOM YE IGNORANTLY WORSHIP, HIM DECLARE I UNTO YOU

Now Paul and Silas and Timothy came to Thessalonica, where there was a synagogue of the Jews. And Paul, as his manner was, went in unto them, and three sabbath days reasoned with them out of the scriptures, that Christ must needs have suffered, and risen again from the dead, and saying, "This Jesus, whom I preach unto you, is Christ." And some of them believed, and consorted with Paul and Silas, of the devout Greeks a great multitude, and of the chief women not a few.

But the Jews which believed not, moved with envy, and took certain lewd fellows of the baser sort, and gathered a company, and set all the city in an uproar, and assaulted the house of Jason, and sought to bring Paul and Silas out to the people. And when they found them not, they drew Jason and certain brethren unto the rulers of the city, crying, "These that have turned the world upside down are come hither also, whom Jason hath received. And these all do contrary to the decrees of Caesar, saying that there is another king, one Jesus."

And it troubled the people and the rulers of the city when they heard these things. And when they had taken security of Jason, and of the others, they let them go.

And the brethren immediately sent away Paul and Silas by night unto Berea. And when they came thither they went into the synagogue of the Jews. These were more noble than those in Thessalonica, in that they received the word with all readiness of mind, and searched the scriptures daily, whether those things were so. Therefore many of them believed, also honourable women which were Greeks, and of men, not a few.

But when the Jews of Thessalonica had knowledge that the word of God was preached by Paul at Berea, they came thither also, and stirred up the people. And immediately the brethren sent away Paul to go as it were to the sea, but Silas and Timothy abode there still. And they conducted Paul unto Athens, and receiving a commandment for Silas and Timothy to come to Paul with all speed, they departed.

Now while Paul waited for them at Athens, his spirit was stirred in him, when he saw the city wholly given to idolatry. Therefore he disputed in the synagogue with the Jews, and with the devout persons, and in the market daily with them that met with him.

Then certain philosophers of the Epicureans, and of the Stoicks, encountered him. And some said, "What will this babbler say?" and others, "He seemeth to be a setter forth of strange gods," because he preached unto them Jesus and the resurrection.

And they took him, and brought him unto Areopagus, saying, "May we know what this new doctrine, whereof thou speakest, is? For thou bringest strange things to our ears: we would know therefore what these things mean." For all of the Athenians and strangers which were there spent their time in nothing else, but either to tell, or to hear some new thing.

Then Paul stood in the midst of Mars' hill, and said, "Ye men of Athens I perceive that in all things ye are too superstitious. For as I passed by, and beheld your devotions, I found an altar with this inscription, TO THE UNKNOWN GOD. Whom therefore ye ignorantly worship, him declare I unto you.

"God that made the world and all things therein, seeing that he is Lord of heaven and earth, dwelleth not in temples made with hands, neither is worshipped with men's hands, as though he needed any thing, seeing he giveth to all life, and breath, and all things; and hath made of one blood all nations of men for to dwell on all the face of the earth, and hath determined the times before appointed, and the bounds of their habitation; that they should seek the Lord, if haply they might feel after him, and find him, though he be not far from every one of us. For in him we live, and move, and have our being; as certain also of your own poets have said, 'For we are also his offspring.'

"Forasmuch then as we are the offspring of God, we ought not to think that the Godhead is like unto gold, or silver, or stone, graven by art and man's device. And the times of this ignorance God winked at; but now commandeth all men every where to repent, because he hath appointed a day, in the which he will judge the world in righteousness by that man whom he hath ordained; whereof he hath given assurance unto all men, in that he hath raised him from the dead."

And when they heard of the resurrection of the dead, some mocked: and others said, "We will hear thee again of this matter." Howbeit certain men clave unto him and believed.

So Paul departed from among them.

BE NOT AFRAID, BUT SPEAK, HOLD NOT THY PEACE

AFTER THESE THINGS Paul departed from Athens, and came to Corinth, and found a certain Jew named Aquila, born in Pontus, who had lately come from Italy with his wife, Priscilla, because the emperor Claudius had commanded all Jews to depart from Rome. And because Paul was of the same craft, he abode with them and worked, for by their occupation they were tent makers.

And Paul reasoned in the synagogue every sabbath, and persuaded the Jews and the Greeks. And when Silas and Timothy had come from Macedonia, Paul was pressed in the spirit and testified to the Jews that Jesus was Christ. And when they opposed themselves, and blasphemed, he shook his raiment, and said unto them, "Your blood be upon your own heads; I am clean; from henceforth I will go unto the Gentiles."

And Paul entered into a certain man's house named Justus, one that worshipped God, whose house joined hard by the synagogue. And Caispus the chief ruler of the synagogue, believed on the Lord with all his house; and many of the Corinthians, hearing, believed, and were baptized.

Then spake the Lord to Paul in the night by a vision, "Be not afraid, but speak, and hold not thy peace: for I am with thee, and no man shall set on thee to hurt thee: for I have much people in this city."

And Paul continued there a year and six months, teaching the word of God among them.

(And during this time Paul and Silvanus and Timothy wrote letters to the church of the Thessalonians in Macedonia.)

Ye Are All Children of Light, and Children of Day

UNTO THE CHURCH OF THE THESSALONIANS:

GRACE BE UNTO YOU, and peace, from God our Father, and the Lord Jesus Christ:

We give thanks to God always for you all, making mention of you in our prayers; remembering your work of faith, and labour of love, and patience of hope in our Lord Jesus Christ, in the sight of God our Father. For our gospel came not unto you in word only, but in power, and in the Holy Ghost, and in much assurance, since ye knew what manner of men we were among you for your sake. And ye became followers of us, and of the Lord, having received the word in much affliction, with joy of the Holy Ghost, so that ye were ensamples to all that believe in Macedonia and Achaia. For they themselves show us how ye turned to God from idols to serve the living and true God, not as pleasing men, but God, which trieth our hearts.

And ye know how we exhorted and comforted and charged every one of you, as a father doth his children, that ye walk worthy of God, who hath called you unto his kingdom and glory. For this cause also thank we God without ceasing, because, when ye received the word of God which ye heard of us, ye received it not as the word of men, but as it is in truth, the word of God, which effectually worketh also in you that believe.

For ye, brethren, became followers of the churches of God, which in Judaea are in Christ Jesus. For ye also have suffered like things of your own countrymen, even as they have of the

Jews. Wherefore we thought it good to send Timothy, our brother and fellow labourer in the gospel of Christ, to establish you, and to comfort you concerning your faith. For verily, when we were with you, we told you before that we should suffer tribulation, even as it came to pass. And ye know, for this cause, when I could no longer forbear, I sent to know your faith, lest by some means the tempter may have tempted you, and our labour be in vain.

But now when Timothy came from you unto us, and brought us good tidings of your faith and charity, and that ye have good remembrance of us always, desiring greatly to see us, as we also to see you, therefore, brethren, we were comforted in all our affliction and distress by your faith, for now we live, if ye stand fast in the Lord. And the Lord make you to increase and abound in love one toward another, and toward all men, even as we do toward you.

Furthermore then we beseech you, brethren, and exhort you by the Lord Jesus, that as ye have received of us how ye ought to walk and to please God, that ye abound more and more. For this is the will of God, even your sanctification, that ye should abstain from fornication; that no man defraud his brother in any matter, because the Lord is the avenger of all such, for God hath not called us unto uncleanness, but unto holiness. He therefore that despiseth, despiseth not man, but God, who hath also given unto us his holy Spirit.

But touching brotherly love, ye need not that I write unto you, for ye yourselves are taught of God to love one another. And indeed ye do it toward all the brethren which are in all Macedonia. But we beseech you, brethren, that ye increase more and more. And that ye study to be quiet, and to do your own business, and to work with your own hands, as we commanded you; and that ye may walk honestly toward them that are without, that ye may lack nothing.

But of the times and the seasons, brethren, ye have no need

that I write unto you. For yourselves know perfectly that the day of the Lord so cometh as a thief in the night. For when they shall say, " Peace and safety; " then sudden destruction cometh upon them as travail upon a woman with child; and they shall not escape.

But ye, brethren, are not in darkness, that that day should overtake you as a thief. Ye are all the children of light, and the children of the day: we are not of the night, nor of darkness. Therefore let us not sleep, as do others; but let us watch and be sober. For they that sleep, sleep in the night; and they that be drunken are drunken in the night. But let us, who are of the day, be sober, putting on the breastplate of faith and love; and for an helmet, the hope of salvation. For God hath not appointed us to wrath, but to obtain salvation by our Lord Jesus Christ, who died for us, that, whether we wake or sleep, we should live together with him. Wherefore comfort yourselves together, and edify one another, even as also ye do.

And we beseech you, brethren, to know them which labour among you, and are over you in the Lord, and admonish you, and to esteem them very highly in love for their work's sake. And be at peace among yourselves.

Now we exhort you, brethren, warn them that are unruly, comfort the feebleminded, support the weak, be patient toward all men. See that none render evil for evil unto any man; but ever follow that which is good, both among yourselves, and to all men.

Rejoice evermore.

Pray without ceasing.

In everything give thanks: for this is the will of God in Christ Jesus concerning you.

Quench not the Spirit.

Despise not prophesyings.

Prove all things; hold fast that which is good.

Abstain from all appearance of evil.

And the very God of peace sanctify you wholly. And I pray God your whole spirit and soul and body be preserved blameless unto the coming of our Lord Jesus Christ. Faithful is he that calleth you, who also will do it.

Brethren, pray for us. Greet all the brethren. I charge you by the Lord that this epistle be read unto all the brethren.

The grace of our Lord Jesus Christ be with you. Amen.

Paul, Silas and Timothy

Be Not Weary in Well Doing

UNTO THE CHURCH OF THE THESSALONIANS:

GRACE UNTO YOU, and peace, from God our Father and the Lord Jesus Christ:

We are bound to thank God always for you, brethren, as it is meet, because that your faith groweth exceedingly, and the charity of every one of you all toward each other aboundeth; so that we ourselves glory in you in the churches of God for your patience and faith in all your persecutions and tribulations that ye endure. Wherefore also we pray always for you, that our God would count you worthy of this calling, and fulfil all the good pleasure of his goodness, and the work of faith with power: that the name of our Lord Jesus Christ may be glorified in you, and ye in him according to the grace of our God and the Lord Jesus Christ.

Now we beseech you, brethren, by the coming of our Lord Jesus Christ, and by our gathering together unto him, that ye be not soon shaken in mind, or be troubled, neither by spirit, nor by word, not by letter as from us, as that the day of Christ is at hand. Let no man deceive you by any means: for that day shall not come, except there come a falling away first, and that man of sin be revealed, the son of perdition; who opposeth and exalteth himself above all that is called God, or that is worshipped; so that he as God sitteth in the temple of God, showing himself that he is God. Remember ye not, that when I was yet with you, I told you these things? And now ye know what withholdeth that he might be revealed in his time. For the mystery of iniquity doth already work: only he who now letteth will let, until he be taken out of the way. And then shall that wicked be revealed, whom the Lord shall consume with the spirit of his mouth, and shall destroy with the brightness of his coming.

But we are bound to give thanks always to God for you, brethren, beloved of the Lord, because God hath from the beginning chosen you to salvation through sanctification of the Spirit and belief of the Truth. Therefore, brethren, stand fast, and hold the traditions which ye have been taught, whether by word, or our epistle. Now our Lord Jesus Christ himself, and God, even our Father, which hath loved us, and hath given us everlasting consolation and good hope through grace, comfort your hearts, and stablish you in every good word and work.

Finally, brethren, pray for us, that the word of the Lord may have free course, and be glorified, even as it is with you: and that we may be delivered from unreasonable and wicked men: for all men have one faith. But the Lord is faithful, who shall stablish you, and keep you from evil. And the Lord direct your hearts into the Love of God, and into the patient waiting for Christ.

Now we command you, brethren, in the name of our Lord Jesus Christ, that ye withdraw yourselves from every brother that walketh disorderly, and not after the tradition which he received of us. For yourselves know how ye ought to follow us: for we behaved not ourselves disorderly among you; neither did we eat any man's bread for nought; but wrought with labour and travail night and day, that we might not be chargeable to any of you; not because we have not power, but to make ourselves an ensample unto you to follow us. For even when we were with you, this we commanded you, that if any would not work, neither should he eat. For we hear that there are some which walk among you disorderly, working not at all, but are busybodies. Now them that are such we command and exhort by our Lord Jesus Christ, that with quietness they work, and eat their own bread. And if any man obey not, have no company with him, that he may be ashamed, yet count him not as an enemy, but admonish him as a brother. But ye, brethren, be not weary in well doing.

Now the Lord of peace himself give you peace always by all means. The Lord be with you all. Amen.

The salutation of Paul, with mine own hand. So write I.

THE ACTS OF THE APOSTLES
CONTINUED

I MUST KEEP THIS FEAST THAT COMETH IN JERUSALEM

Now when Gallio was proconsul of Achaia, the Jews with one accord rose up against Paul, and brought him to the judgment seat, saying, "This fellow persuadeth men to worship God contrary to the law."

But when Paul was about to open his mouth, Gallio said unto the Jews, "If it were a matter of wrong or wicked lewdness, O ye Jews, reason would that I should bear with you: but if it be a question of words and names, and of your law, look ye to it; for I will be no judge of such matters." And he drove them from the judgment seat.

Then all the Greeks took Sosthenes, the chief ruler of the synagogue, and beat him before the judgment seat. And Gallio cared for none of those things.

And Paul after this tarried there yet a good while, and then took his leave of the brethren, and sailed thence into Syria, and with him Priscilla and Aquila. And Paul came to Ephesus, and left them there, but he himself entered into the synagogue, and reasoned with the Jews.

When they desired him to tarry longer time with them, he consented not, but bade them farewell, saying, "I must by all means keep this feast that cometh in Jerusalem; but I will return again unto you, if God be willing." And he sailed from Ephesus.

And when Paul had landed at Caesarea, and gone up, and saluted the church (in Jerusalem), he went down to Antioch. And after he had spent some time there, he departed, and went over all the country of Galatia and Phrygia in order, strengthening all the disciples.

(And at this time he wrote the letter to the Galatians.)

If We Live in the Spirit, Let Us Also Walk in the Spirit

Unto the churches of galatia:

Grace be to you and peace from God the Father, and from our Lord Jesus Christ, to whom be glory for ever and ever. Amen.

I marvel that ye are so soon removed from him that called you into the grace of Christ unto another gospel; but there be some that trouble you, and would pervert the gospel of Christ. But though we, or an angel from heaven, preach any other gospel than that which we have preached unto you, let him be accursed. For do I now persuade men, or God? or do I seek to please men? for if I yet pleased men, I should not be the servant of Christ.

But I certify you, brethren, that the gospel which was preached by me is not after man. For I neither received it of man, neither was I taught it, but by the revelation of Jesus Christ. For ye have heard of my conversation in time past in the Jews' religion, how that beyond measure I persecuted the church of God, and wasted it; and profited in the Jews' religion above many my equals in mine own nation, being more exceedingly zealous of the traditions of my fathers.

But when it pleased God who called me by his grace, to reveal his Son in me, that I might preach him among the heathen, then immediately I conferred not with flesh and blood, neither went I up to Jerusalem to them which were apostles before me, but I went into Arabia, and returned again unto Damascus. Then after three years I went up to Jerusalem to see Peter, and abode with him fifteen days. But other of the apostles saw I none, save James, the Lord's brother.

Now the things which I write unto you, behold, before God, I lie not. Afterwards I came into the regions of Syria and Cilicia, and was unknown by face unto the churches of Judaea which were in Christ, but they had heard only that he which persecuted them in times past, now preached the faith which once he destroyed. And they glorified God in me.

Then fourteen years after, I went up again to Jerusalem with Barnabas, and took Titus with me also. And I went up by revelation, and communicated unto them that gospel which I preach among the Gentiles, but privately to them which were of reputation, lest by any means I should run, or had run, in vain. And when James, Cephas, and John, who seemed to be pillars, perceived the grace that was given unto me, they gave to me and Barnabas the right hands of fellowship; that we should go unto the Gentiles, and they unto the circumcision.

But when Peter was come to Antioch, I withstood him to the face, for before certain came from James, he did eat with the Gentiles: but when they were come, he withdrew and separated himself, fearing them which were of the circumcision. And the other Jews dissembled likewise with him; insomuch that Barnabas also was carried away with their dissimulation.

But when I saw that they walked not uprightly according to the truth of the gospel, I said unto Peter before them all, "If thou, being a Jew, livest after the manner of Gentiles, and not as do the Jews, why compellest thou the Gentiles to live as do the Jews? We who are Jews by nature, knowing that a man is not justified by the works of the law, but by the faith of Jesus Christ, even we have believed in Jesus Christ, that we might be justified by the faith of Christ, and not by the works of the law: for by the works of the law shall no flesh be justified. For I through the law am dead to the law, that I might live unto God. I live by the faith of the Son of God, who loved me, and gave himself for me."

O foolish Galatians, who hath bewitched you, that ye should not obey the Truth, before whose eyes Jesus Christ hath been evidently set forth, crucified among you? This only would I learn of you, Received ye the Spirit by the works of the law, or by the hearing of faith? Are ye so foolish? having begun in the Spirit, are ye now made perfect by the flesh? Have ye suffered so many things in vain? if it be in vain.

He therefore that ministereth to you the Spirit, and worketh miracles among you, doeth he it by the works of the law, or by the hearing of faith? Even as Abraham believed God, and it was accounted to him for righteousness, know ye therefore that they which are of faith, the same are the children of Abraham. And the scripture sayeth unto Abraham, "In thee shall all nations be blessed." So then they which be of faith are blessed with faithful Abraham, for the just shall live by faith.

For ye are all the children of God by faith in Christ Jesus. For as many of you as have been baptized into Christ have put on Christ. There is neither Jew nor Greek, there is neither bond nor free, there is neither male nor female: for ye are all one in Christ Jesus. And if ye be Christ's then are ye Abraham's seed, and heirs according to the promise.

Now I say, that the heir, as long as he is a child, differeth nothing from a servant, though he be lord of all, but is under tutors and governors until the time appointed of the father. Even so we, when we were children, were in bondage unto the elements of the world. But when the fulness of the time was come, God sent forth his Son, made of a woman, made under the law, to redeem them that were under the law, that we might receive the adoption of sons. And because ye are sons, God hath sent forth the Spirit of his Son into your hearts, crying, "Abba, Father." Wherefore thou art no more a servant, but a son; and if a son, then an heir of God through Christ.

Stand fast therefore in the liberty wherewith Christ hath made us free, and be not entangled again with the yoke of bondage. For we through the Spirit wait for the hope of righteousness by faith. For in Jesus Christ neither circumcision availeth anything, nor uncircumcision; but faith which worketh by love.

Ye did run well, who did hinder you that ye should not obey the Truth? For brethren, ye have been called unto liberty; only use not liberty for an occasion to the flesh, but by love serve one another. For all the law is fulfilled in one word, even in this: "Thou shalt love thy neighbour as thyself." But if ye bite and devour one another take heed that ye be not consumed one of another.

This I say then, Walk in the Spirit, and ye shall not fulfil the lust of the flesh. For the flesh lusteth against the Spirit, and the Spirit against the flesh: and these are contrary the one to the other; so that ye cannot do the things that ye would. But if ye be led of the Spirit, ye are not under the law.

Now the works of the flesh are manifest, which are these: Adultery, fornication, uncleanness, lasciviousness, idolatry, witchcraft, hatred, variance, emulations, wrath, strife, seditions, heresies, envyings, murders, drunkenness, revellings, and such like: of the which I tell you before, as I have also told you in time past, that they which do such things shall not inherit the kingdom of God.

But the fruit of the Spirit is love, joy, peace, longsuffering, gentleness, goodness, faith, meekness, temperance: against such there is no law. And they that are Christ's have crucified the flesh with the affections and lusts. If we live in the Spirit, let us also walk in the Spirit. Let us not be desirous of vain glory, provoking one another, envying one another.

Brethren, if a man be overtaken in a fault, ye which are spiritual, restore such an one in the spirit of meekness; considering thyself, lest thou also be tempted. Bear ye one another's burdens, and so fulfil the law of Christ. For if a man think himself to be something, when he is nothing, he deceiveth himself. But let every man prove his own work, and then shall he have rejoicing in himself alone, and not in another. For every man shall bear his own burden.

Be not deceived: God is not mocked; for whatsoever a man soweth, that shall he also reap. For he that soweth to his flesh shall of the flesh reap corruption: but he that soweth to the Spirit shall of the Spirit reap life everlasting. And let us not be weary in well doing: for in due season we shall reap, if we faint not. As we therefore have opportunity, let us do good unto all men, especially unto them who are of the household of faith.

God forbid that I should glory, save in the cross of our Lord Jesus Christ, by whom the world is crucified unto me, and I unto the world. For in Christ Jesus neither circumcision, availeth any thing, nor uncircumcision, but a new creature. And as many as walk according to this rule, peace be on them and mercy.

Ye see how large a letter I have written unto you with mine own hand. Brethren, the grace of our Lord Jesus Christ be with your spirit. Amen.

Paul the Apostle

THE ACTS OF THE APOSTLES
CONTINUED

AND GOD WROUGHT MIRACLES BY THE HANDS OF PAUL

NOW A CERTAIN Jew named Apollos, born at Alexandria, an eloquent man, and mighty in the scriptures, came to Ephesus. This man was instructed in the way of the Lord; and being fervent in spirit, he spake and taught diligently the things of the Lord, knowing only the baptism of John. And he began to speak boldly in the synagogue. But when Aquila and Priscilla heard him, they took him unto them, and expounded unto him the way of God more perfectly.

And when Apollos decided to pass into Achaia, the brethren wrote exhorting the disciples to receive him. And when he was come, he helped them much which had believed through grace, for he mightily convinced the Jews, and that publickly, showing by the scriptures that Jesus was Christ.

And it came to pass, that while Apollos was at Corinth, Paul having passed through the upper coasts came to Ephesus, and finding certain disciples, he said unto them, "Have ye received the Holy Ghost since ye believed?"

And they said unto him, "We have not so much as heard whether there be any Holy Ghost."

And he said unto them, "Into what then were ye baptized?"

And they said, "Into John's baptism."

Then said Paul, "John verily baptized with the baptism of repentance, saying unto the people, that they should believe on him which should come after him, that is, on Christ Jesus."

When they heard this, they were baptized in the name of the Lord Jesus. And when Paul had laid his hands upon them, the Holy Ghost came on them, and they spake with tongues, and prophesied. And they were in all about twelve men.

And Paul went into the synagogue, and spake boldly for the space of about three months, reasoning and persuading the things concerning the kingdom of God. But when some were hardened, and believed not, but spake evil of the Way before the multitude, Paul departed from them, and separated the disciples, reasoning daily in the school of one Tyrannus.

And this continued by the space of two years; so that all they which dwelt in Asia heard the word of the Lord Jesus, both Jews and Greeks.

And God wrought special miracles by the hands of Paul, so that handkerchiefs or aprons were brought from his body unto the sick and the diseases departed from them, and evil spirits went out of them.

Then certain of the vagabond Jews, exorcists, took upon them to call over them which had evil spirits the name of the Lord Jesus, saying, "We adjure you by Jesus whom Paul preacheth." And there were seven sons of one Sceva, a Jew, and chief of the priests, which did so.

And the evil spirit answered and said, "Jesus I know, and Paul I know; but who are ye?" And the man in whom the evil spirit was leaped on them, and overcame them, and prevailed against them, so that they fled out of that house naked and wounded.

And this was known to all the Jews and Greeks also dwelling at Ephesus; and fear fell on them all, and the name of the Lord Jesus was magnified. And many that believed came, and confessed, and showed their deeds. Many of them also which used curious arts brought their books together, and burned them before all men; and they counted the price of them, and found it fifty thousand pieces of silver. So mightily grew the word of God and prevailed.

(And during this time Paul wrote letters to the Corinthians, which follow.)

Ye Are the Temple of the Living God

O YE CORINTHIANS:

OUR MOUTH IS OPEN unto you, our heart is enlarged; I speak as unto my children, be ye also enlarged.

Be ye not unequally yoked together with unbelievers: for what fellowship hath righteousness with unrighteousness? and what communion hath light with darkness? and what concord hath Christ with Belial? or what part hath he that believeth with an infidel?

And what agreement hath the temple of God with idols? for ye are the temple of the living God; as God hath said, "I will dwell in them, and walk in them; and I will be their God, and they shall be my people. Wherefore come out from among them, and be ye separate," saith the Lord, "and touch not the unclean thing; and I will receive you. And I will be a Father unto you, and ye shall be my sons and daughters," saith the Lord Almighty.

Having therefore these promises, dearly beloved, let us cleanse ourselves from all filthiness of the flesh and spirit, perfecting holiness in the fear of God.

Receive us; we have wronged no man, we have corrupted no man, we have defrauded no man. I speak not this to condemn you: for I have said before, that ye are in our hearts to die and live with you.

Paul

(A fragment of a letter)

The Things of the Spirit of God Are Spiritually Discerned

UNTO THE CHURCH OF GOD WHICH IS AT CORINTH:

GRACE BE UNTO YOU, and peace, from God our Father, and from the Lord Jesus Christ. I thank my God always on your behalf, for the grace of God which is given you by Jesus Christ; that in every thing ye are enriched by him, in all utterance, and in all knowledge.

Now I beseech you, brethren, by the name of our Lord Jesus Christ, that ye all speak the same thing, and that there be no divisions among you; but that ye be perfectly joined together in the same mind and in the same judgment.

For it hath been declared unto me of you, my brethren, that there are contentions among you. Now this I say, that every one of you saith, "I am of Paul; and I of Apollos; and I of Cephas; and I of Christ." Is Christ divided? was Paul crucified for you? or were ye baptized in the name of Paul? I thank God that I baptized none of you. For Christ sent me not to baptize, but to preach the gospel: not with wisdom of words, lest the cross of Christ should be made of none effect.

For the preaching of the cross is to them that perish foolishness; but unto us which are saved it is the power of God. For it is written, "I will destroy the wisdom of the wise, and will bring to nothing the understanding of the prudent." Where is the wise? Where is the scribe? Where is the disputer of this world? hath not God made foolish the wisdom of this world?

For the Jews require a sign, and the Greeks seek after a wisdom: but we preach Christ crucified, unto the Jews a stumblingblock, and unto the Greeks foolishness; but unto them which are called, both Jews and Greeks, Christ the power of God, and the wisdom of God. Because the foolishness of God is wiser than men; and the weakness of God is stronger than men.

For ye see your calling, brethren, how that not many wise men after the flesh, not many mighty, not many noble, are called: but God hath chosen the foolish things of the world to confound the wise; and God hath chosen the weak things of the world to confound the things which are mighty; and base things of the world, and things which are despised, hath God chosen, yea, and things which are not, to bring to nought things that are, that no flesh should glory in his presence. But of him are ye in Christ Jesus, who of God is made unto us wisdom, and righteousness, and sanctification, and redemption: that according as it is written, "He that glorieth, let him glory in the Lord."

And I, brethren, when I came to you, came not with excellency of speech or of wisdom, declaring unto you the testimony of God. For I determined not to know any thing among you, save Jesus Christ, and him crucified. And I was with you in weakness, and in fear, and in much trembling. And my speech and my preaching was not with enticing words of man's wisdom, but in demonstration of the Spirit of power: that your faith should not stand in the wisdom of men, but in the power of God.

Howbeit we speak wisdom among them that are perfect: yet not the wisdom of this world, nor of the princes of this world, that come to nought: But we speak the wisdom of God in a mystery, even the hidden wisdom, which God ordained before the world unto our glory; which none of the princes of this world knew: for had they known it, they would not have crucified the Lord of glory.

But as it is written, " Eye hath not seen, nor ear heard, neither have entered into the heart of man, the things which God hath prepared for them that love him." But God hath revealed them unto us by his Spirit: for the Spirit searcheth all things, yea, the deep things of God. For what man knoweth the things of a man, save the spirit of man which is in him? Even so the things of God knoweth no man, but the Spirit of God.

Now we have received, not the spirit of the world, but the spirit which is of God; that we might know the things that are freely given to us of God. Which things also we speak, not in the words which man's wisdom teacheth, but which the Holy Ghost teacheth; comparing spiritual things with spiritual. But the natural man receiveth not the things of the Spirit of God: for they are foolishness unto him; neither can he know them, because they are spiritually discerned. But he that is spiritual judgeth all things, yet he himself is judged of no man. For who hath known the mind of the Lord, that he may instruct Him? But we have the mind of Christ.

And I, brethren, could not speak unto you as unto spiritual, but as unto carnal, even as unto babes in Christ. I have fed you with milk, and not with meat: for hitherto ye were not able to bear it, neither yet now are ye able. For ye are yet carnal: for whereas there is among you envying, and strife, and divisions, are ye not carnal, and walk as men? For while one saith, " I am of Paul;" and another, " I am of Apollos;" are ye not carnal? Who then is Paul, and who is Apollos, but ministers by whom ye believed, even as the Lord gave to every man? I have planted, Apollos watered: but God gave the increase. So then neither is he that planted anything, neither he that watereth, but God that giveth the increase.

Now he that planteth and he that watereth are one: and every man shall receive his own reward according to his own labour. For we are labourers together with God: ye are God's husbandry, ye are God's building. According to the grace of God which is given unto me, as a wise masterbuilder, I have laid the foundation, and another buildeth thereon. But let every man take heed how he buildeth thereupon. For other foundation can no man lay than that is laid, which is Jesus Christ.

Now if any man build upon this foundation, gold, silver, precious stones, wood, hay, stubble: every man's work shall be made manifest, for the day shall declare it, because it shall be revealed by fire; and the fire shall try every man's work of what sort it is. If any man's work abide which he hath built thereupon, he shall receive a reward. If any man's work shall be burned, he shall suffer loss: but he himself shall be saved; yet so as by fire.

Know ye not that ye are the temple of God, and that the Spirit of God dwelleth in you? If any man defile the temple of God, him shall God destroy; for the temple of God is holy, which temple ye are.

Let no man deceive himself. If any man among you seemeth to be wise, in this world, let him become a fool, that he may be wise. For the wisdom of this world is foolishness with God. For it is written, "He taketh the wise in their own craftiness." And again, "The Lord knoweth the thoughts of the wise, that they are vain." Therefore let no man glory in men. For all things are yours: whether of Paul, or Apollos, of Cephas, or the world, or life, or death, or things present, or things to come; all are yours; and ye are Christ's, and Christ is God's.

Let a man so account of us, as of the ministers of Christ, and stewards of the mysteries of God. Moreover it is required in stewards, that a man be found faithful. But with me it is a very small thing that I should be judged of you, or of man's judgment: yea, I judge not mine own self. For I know nothing by myself; yet am I not hereby justified: but he that judgeth me is the Lord. Therefore judge nothing before the time, until the Lord come, who both will bring to light the hidden things of darkness, and will make manifest the counsels of the hearts: and then shall every man have praise of God. And these things, brethren, I have in a figure transferred to myself and to Apollos for your sakes; that ye might learn in us not to think of men above that which is written, that no one of you be puffed up one against another.

We are fools for Christ's sake, but ye are wise in Christ; we are weak, but ye are strong; ye are honourable, but we are despised. Even unto this present hour we both hunger, and thirst, and are naked, and are buffeted, and have no certain dwellingplace; and labour, working with our own hands: being reviled, we bless; being persecuted, we suffer it; being defamed, we intreat; we are made as the filth of the world, and are the offscouring of all things unto this day. I write not these things to shame you, but as my beloved sons, I warn you.

Wherefore, I beseech you, be ye followers of me. For this cause have I sent unto you Timothy, who is my beloved son, and faithful in the Lord, who shall bring you into remembrance of my ways which be in Christ, as I teach every where in every church. Now some are puffed up, as though I would not come to you. But I will come to you shortly, if the Lord will, and will know, not the speech of them which are puffed up, but the power. For the kingdom of God is not in word, but in power.

Purge Out the Old Leaven, That Ye May Be a New Lump

It is reported commonly that there is fornication among you, and such fornication as is not so much as named among the Gentiles, that one should have his father's wife. And ye are puffed up, and have not rather mourned, that he that hath done this deed might be taken away from among you. For I verily, as absent in body, but present in spirit, have judged already, as though I were present, concerning him that hath done this deed.

Your glorying is not good. Know ye not that a little leaven leaveneth the whole lump? Purge out therefore the old leaven, that ye may be a new lump, as ye are unleavened. For even Christ our passover is sacrificed for us. Therefore let us keep the feast, not with old leaven, neither with the leaven of malice and wickedness; but with the unleavened bread of sincerity and truth.

I wrote you in an epistle not to company with fornicators. Yet not altogether with the fornicators of this world, or with the covetous, or extortioners, or with idolaters; for then must ye needs go out of this world. But now I have written unto you not to keep company, if any man that is called a brother be a fornicator, or covetous, or an idolater, or a railer, or a drunkard, or an extortioner; with such a one do not eat. For what have I to do to judge them also that are without? do not ye judge them that are within? But them that are without God judgeth. Therefore put away from among yourselves that wicked person.

Know ye not that the unrighteous shall not inherit the kingdom of God? Be not deceived: neither fornicators, nor idolaters, nor adulterers, nor effeminate, nor abusers of themselves with mankind, nor thieves, nor covetous, nor drunkards, nor revilers, nor extortioners, shall inherit the kingdom of God. And such were some of you, but ye are washed, and ye are sanctified, and ye are justified in the name of the Lord Jesus, and by the Spirit of God. And God hath both raised up the Lord, and will also raise up us by his own power.

He that is joined unto the Lord is one spirit. Flee fornication. Every sin that a man doeth is without the body; but he that committeth fornication sinneth against his own body.

What? know ye not that your body is the temple of the Holy Ghost which is in you, which ye have of God, and ye are not your own? For ye are bought with a price: therefore glorify God in your body, and in your spirit, which are God's.

As concerning therefore the eating of those things that are offered in sacrifice unto idols; we know that an idol is nothing in the world, and that there is none other God but one. For though there be that are called gods, whether in heaven or in earth (as there be gods many, and lords many), but to us there is but one God, the Father, of whom are all things, and we in him; and one Lord Jesus Christ, by whom are all things and we by him.

But meat commendeth us not to God: for neither, if we eat, are we the better; neither, if we eat not, are we the worse. But take heed lest by any means this liberty of yours become a stumblingblock to them that are weak. Wherefore, if meat make my brother to offend, I will eat no flesh while the world standeth, lest I make my brother to offend.

Know ye not that they which run in a race run all, but one receiveth the prize? So run, that ye may obtain. And every man that striveth for the mastery is temperate in all things. Now they do it to obtain a corruptible crown; but we an incorruptible. I therefore so run, not as uncertainly; so fight I, not as one that beateth the air; but I keep under my body, and bring it into subjection; lest that by any means, when I have preached to others, I myself should be a castaway.

Moreover, brethren, I would not that ye should be ignorant, how that all our fathers were under the cloud, and all passed through the sea; and were all baptized unto Moses in the cloud and in the sea; and did all eat the same spiritual meat; and did all drink the same spiritual drink: for they drank of that spiritual Rock that followed them, and that Rock was Christ.

But with many of them God was not well pleased; for they

were overthrown in the wilderness. Now these things were our examples, to the intent we should not lust after evil things, as they also lusted. Neither be ye idolaters, as were some of them, as it is written, "The people sat down to eat and drink, and rose up to play." Neither let us commit fornication, as some of them committed, and fell in one day three and twenty thousand. Neither let us tempt Christ, as some of them also tempted, and were destroyed of serpents. Neither murmur ye, as some of them also murmured, and were destroyed of the destroyer.

Now all these things happened unto them for examples: and they are written for our admonition, upon whom the ends of the world are come. Wherefore let him that thinketh he standeth take heed lest he fall. There hath no temptation taken you but such as is common to man: but God is faithful, who will not suffer you to be tempted above that ye are able; but will with the temptation also make a way to escape, that ye may be able to bear it.

Wherefore, my dearly beloved, flee from idolatry. I speak as to wise; judge ye what I say. The cup of blessing which we bless, is it not the communion of the blood of Christ? The bread which we break, is it not the communion of the body of Christ? For we being many are one bread, and one body: for we are all partakers of that one bread. Ye cannot drink the cup of the Lord, and the cup of devils: ye cannot be partakers of the Lord's table, and of the table of devils. Let no man seek his own, but every man another's good.

For I have received of the Lord that which also I delivered unto you: That the Lord Jesus the same night in which he was betrayed took bread, and when he had given thanks, he brake it, and said, "Take, eat; this is my body, which is broken for you; do this in remembrance of me." After the same manner also he took the cup, when he had supped, saying, "This cup is the new testament in my blood: this do ye, as oft as ye drink it in remembrance of me." For as often as ye eat this bread, and drink this cup, ye do show the Lord's death till he come. Wherefore whosoever shall eat this bread, and drink this cup of the Lord unworthily, shall be guilty of the body and blood of the Lord. But let a man examine himself, and so let him eat of that bread, and drink of that cup.

Spiritual Gifts

CONCERNING spiritual gifts, brethren, I would not have you ignorant. Now there are diversities of gifts, but the same Spirit. And there are differences of administration, but the same Lord. And there are diversities of operations, but it is the same God which worketh all in all.

But the manifestation of the Spirit is given to every man to profit withal. For to one is given by the Spirit the word of wisdom; to another the word of knowledge by the same Spirit; to another faith by the same Spirit; to another the gifts of healing by the same Spirit; to another the working of miracles; to another prophecy; to another discerning of spirits; to another divers kinds of tongues; to another the interpretation of tongues. But all these worketh that one and the selfsame Spirit, dividing to every man severally as he will.

For as the body is one, and hath many members, and all the members of that one body, being many, are one body, so also is Christ. For by one Spirit are we all baptized into one body, whether we be Jews or Gentiles, whether we be bond or free; and have been all made to drink into one Spirit.

For the body is not one member, but many. If the foot shall say, "Because I am not the hand, I am not of the body;" is it therefore not of the body? If the whole body were an eye, where were the hearing? If the whole were hearing, where were the smelling?

But now hath God set the members every one of them in the body, as it hath pleased him. And if they were all one member, where were the body? But now are they many members, yet but one body. And the eye cannot say unto the hand, "I have no need of thee;" nor again the head to the feet, "I have no need of you." Nay, much more those members of the body which seem to be more feeble, are necessary. And whether one member suffer, all the members suffer with it; or one member be honoured, all the members rejoice with it.

Now ye are the body of Christ, and members in particular. And God hath set some in the church, first apostles, secondarily prophets, thirdly teachers, after that miracles, then gifts of healing, helps, governments, diversities of tongues. Are all apostles? are all prophets? are all teachers? are all workers of miracles? Have all the gifts of healing? do all speak with tongues? do all interpret? But covet earnestly the best: and yet show I unto you a more excellent way.

Follow after charity, and desire spiritual gifts, so that ye may prophesy. For he that prophesieth speaketh unto men to edification, and exhortation, and comfort. He that speaketh in an unknown tongue edifieth himself; but he that prophesieth edifieth the church.

What is it then? I will pray with the spirit, and I will pray with the understanding also: I will sing with the spirit, and I will sing with the understanding also.

Yet in the church I had rather speak five words with my understanding, that by my voice I might teach others also, than ten thousand words in an unknown tongue. Brethren, be not children in understanding: howbeit in malice be ye children, but in understanding be men.

Now Abide Faith, Hope, Love, But the Greatest of These Is Love

THOUGH I speak with the tongues of men and of angels, and have not love, I am become as sounding brass, or a tinkling cymbal. And though I have the gift of prophecy, and understand all mysteries, and all knowledge; and though I have all faith, so that I could remove mountains, and have not love, I am nothing. And though I bestow all my goods to feed the poor, and though I give my body to be burned, and have not love, it profiteth me nothing.

Love suffereth long, and is kind.
Love envieth not.
Love vaunteth not itself;
is not puffed up,
doth not behave itself unseemly,
seeketh not her own,
is not easily provoked,
thinketh no evil,
rejoiceth not in iniquity, but rejoiceth in the Truth;
beareth all things,
believeth all things,
hopeth all things,
endureth all things.

Love never faileth: but whether there be prophecies, they shall fail; whether there be tongues, they shall cease; whether there be knowledge, it shall vanish away.

For we know in part, and we prophesy in part. But when that which is perfect is come, then that which is in part shall be done away. When I was a child, I spake as a child, I understood as a child, I thought as a child: but when I became a man, I put away childish things.

For now we see through a glass, darkly; but then face to face; now I know in part; but then shall I know even as also I am known. And now abideth faith, hope, love, these three; but the greatest of these is love.

O Death, Where Is Thy Sting? O Grave, Where Is Thy Victory?

BRETHREN, I declare unto you the gospel which I preached unto you, which also ye have received, and wherein ye stand; by which also ye are saved, if ye keep in memory what I preached unto you, unless ye have believed in vain.

For I delivered unto you first of all that which I also received, how that Christ died for our sins according to the scriptures; and that he was buried, and that he rose again the third day according to the scriptures; and that he was seen of Peter then of the twelve. After that, he was seen of above five hundred brethren at once; of whom the greater part remain unto this present, but some are fallen asleep.

After that, he was seen of James; then of all the apostles. And last of all he was seen of me also, as of one born out of due time. For I am the least of the apostles, that am not meet to be called an apostle, because I persecuted the church of God. But by the grace of God, I am what I am: and his grace which was bestowed upon me was not in vain; but I laboured more abundantly than they all: yet not I, but the grace of God which was with me.

Now if Christ be preached that he rose from the dead, how say some among you that there is no resurrection of the dead? But if there be no resurrection of the dead, then is Christ not risen: and if Christ be not risen, then is our preaching vain, and your faith is also vain. Yea, and we are found false witnesses of God: because we have testified of God that he raised up Christ: whom he raised not up, if so be that the dead rise not. For if the dead rise not, then is not Christ raised: and if Christ be not raised, your faith is vain; ye are yet in your sins. Then they also which are fallen asleep in Christ are perished.

If in this life only we have hope in Christ, we are of all men most miserable. But now is Christ risen from the dead, and become the firstfruits of them that slept. For since by man came death, by man came also the resurrection of the dead. For as in Adam all die, even so in Christ shall all be made alive. But every man in his own order: Christ the firstfruits; afterward they that are Christ's at his coming.

Then cometh the end, when he shall have delivered up the kingdom to God, even the Father; when he shall have put down all rule and all authority and power. For he must reign, till he hath put all enemies under his feet. The last enemy that shall be destroyed is death.

For he hath put all things under his feet. But when he saith all things are put under him, it is manifest that he is excepted, which did put all things under him. And when all things shall be subdued unto him, then shall the Son also himself be subject unto him that put all things under him, that God may be all in all.

Awake to righteousness, and sin not; for some have not the knowledge of God. I speak this to your shame.

But some man will say, "How are the dead raised up? and

with what body do they come? " Thou fool, that which thou sowest is not quickened, except it die; and that which thou sowest, thou sowest not that body that shall be, but bare grain, it may chance of wheat, or of some other grain. But God giveth it a body as it hath pleased him, to every seed his own body.

There are also celestial bodies, and bodies terrestrial: but the glory of the celestial is one, and the glory of the terrestrial is another. There is one glory of the sun, and another glory of the moon, and another glory of the stars: for one star differeth from another star in glory. So also is the resurrection of the dead. It is sown in corruption, it is raised in incorruption; it is sown in dishonour, it is raised in glory; it is sown in weakness, it is raised in power.

And so it is written, " The first man Adam was made a living soul; the last Adam was made a quickening spirit." The first man is of the earth, earthy; the second man is the Lord from heaven. As is the earthy, such are they also that are earthy: and as is the heavenly, such are they also that are heavenly. And as we have borne the image of the earthy, we shall also bear the image of the heavenly. Now this I say, brethren, that flesh and blood cannot inherit the kingdom of God; neither doth corruption inherit incorruption.

Behold, I show you a mystery: We shall not all sleep, but we shall all be changed. In a moment, in the twinkling of an eye, at the last trump; for the trumpet shall sound, and the dead shall be raised incorruptible, and we shall be changed. For this corruptible must put on incorruption, and this mortal must put on immortality. So when this corruptible shall have put on incorruption, and this mortal shall have put on immortality, then shall be brought to pass the saying that is written, " Death is swallowed up in victory."

O death, where is thy sting? O grave, where is thy victory? The sting of death is sin; and the strength of sin is the law. But thanks be to God, which giveth us the victory through our Lord Jesus Christ.

Therefore, my beloved brethren, be ye steadfast, unmoveable, always abounding in the work of the Lord, forasmuch as ye know that your labour is not in vain in the Lord.

Now I will come unto you, when I shall pass through Macedonia; for I do pass through Macedonia. And it may be that I will abide, yea, and winter with you, that ye may bring me on my journey whithersoever I go. But I will tarry at Ephesus until Pentecost. For a great door and effectual is opened unto me, and there are many adversaries.

Now if Timothy come, see that he may be with you without fear; for he worketh the work of the Lord as I also do. Let no man therefore despise him: but conduct him forth in peace, that he may come unto me; for I look for him with the brethren.

Watch ye, stand fast in the faith; quit you like men, be strong. Let all your things be done with charity.

The churches of Asia salute you. Aquila and Priscilla salute you, much in the Lord, with the church that is in their house. All the brethren greet you.

The grace of our Lord Jesus Christ be with you. My love be with you all in Christ Jesus.

The salutation of me, Paul, with mine own hand.

Where the Spirit of the Lord Is There Is Liberty

UNTO THE CHURCH OF GOD WHICH IS AT CORINTH,

GRACE BE TO YOU and peace from God our Father, and from the Lord Jesus Christ. Blessed be God, even the Father of our Lord Jesus Christ, the Father of mercies, and the God of all comfort, who comforteth us in all our tribulation, that we may be able to comfort them which are in any trouble, by the comfort wherewith we ourselves are comforted of God. For as the sufferings of Christ abound in us, so our consolation also aboundeth by Christ.

And our hope of you is stedfast, knowing, that as ye are partakers of the sufferings, so shall ye be also of the consolation. For we would not, brethren, have you ignorant of our trouble which came to us in Asia, that we were pressed out of measure, above strength, insomuch that we despaired even of life; but we had the sentence of death in ourselves, that we should not trust in ourselves, but in God which raiseth the dead, and who delivered us from so great a death, and doth deliver: in whom we trust that he will yet deliver us, ye also helping by prayer for us.

But I determined this with myself, that I would not come again to you in heaviness. For if I make you sorry, who is he then that maketh me glad, but the same which is made sorry by me? And I wrote this same unto you, lest, when I came, I should have sorrow from them of whom I ought to rejoice; having confidence in you all, that my joy is the joy of you all. For out of much affliction and anguish of heart I wrote unto you with many tears; not that ye should be grieved, but that ye might know the love which I have more abundantly unto you.

When I came to Troas to preach Christ's gospel, and a door was opened unto me of the Lord, I had no rest in my spirit, because I found not Titus my brother: but taking my leave of them, I went from thence into Macedonia. Now thanks be unto God, which always causeth us to triumph in Christ, and maketh manifest the savour of his knowledge by us in every place.

Ye are our epistle written in our hearts, known and read of all men. Forasmuch as ye are manifestly declared to be the epistle of Christ ministered by us, written not with ink, but with the Spirit of the living God; not in tables of stone, but in fleshy tables of the heart. And such trust have we through Christ to God-ward, not that we are sufficient of ourselves to think any thing as of ourselves; but our sufficiency is of God; who also hath made us able ministers of the new testament; not of the letter, but of the spirit, for the letter killeth, but the spirit giveth Life.

But if the ministration of death, written and engraven in stones, was glorious, so that the children of Israel could not stedfastly behold the face of Moses for the glory of his countenance, which glory was to be done away, how shall not the ministration of the Spirit be rather glorious? For if the ministration of condemnation be glory, much more doth the ministration of righteousness exceed in glory. For if that which is done away was glorious, much more that which remaineth is glorious.

Seeing then that we have such hope, we use great plainness of speech: and not as Moses, which put a veil over his face, that the children of Israel could not stedfastly look to the end of that which is abolished; but their minds were blinded; for until this day remaineth the same veil untaken away in the reading of the old testament, which veil is done away in Christ. For even unto this day, when Moses is read, the veil is upon their heart. Nevertheless when it shall turn to the Lord, the veil shall be taken away.

Now the Lord is that Spirit: and where the Spirit of the Lord is, there is liberty. But we all, with open face beholding as in a glass the glory of the Lord, are changed into the same image from glory to glory, even as by the Spirit of the Lord.

Therefore seeing we have this ministry, as we have received mercy, we faint not; but have renounced the hidden things of dishonesty, not walking in craftiness, nor handling the word of God deceitfully, but by manifestation of the Truth commending ourselves to every man's conscience in the sight of God.

But if our gospel be hid, it is hid to them that are lost; in whom the god of this world hath blinded the minds of them which believe not, lest the light of the glorious gospel of Christ, who is the image of God, should shine unto them. For we preach not ourselves, but Christ Jesus the Lord; and ourselves your servants for Jesus' sake. For God, who commanded the light to shine out of darkness, hath shined in our hearts, to give the light of the knowledge of the glory of God in the face of Jesus Christ.

But we have this treasure in earthen vessels, that the excellency of the power may be of God, and not of us. We are troubled on every side, yet not distressed; we are perplexed, but not in despair; persecuted, but not forsaken; cast down, but not destroyed; always bearing about in the body the dying of the Lord Jesus, that the life also of Jesus might be made manifest in our body. We having the same spirit of faith, according as it is written, I believed, and therefore have I spoken; we also believe, and therefore speak, knowing that he which raised up the Lord Jesus shall raise up us also by Jesus, and shall present us with you.

For all things are for your sakes, that the abundant grace might through the thanksgiving of many redound to the glory of God. For which cause we faint not; but though our outward man perish, yet the inward man is renewed day by day. For our light affliction, which is but for a moment, worketh for us a far more exceeding and eternal weight of glory, while we look not at the things which are seen, but at the things which are not seen: for the things which are seen are temporal, but the things which are not seen are eternal.

For we know that if our earthly house of this tabernacle were dissolved, we have a building of God, an house not made with hands, eternal in the heavens. For in this we groan, earnestly desiring to be clothed upon with our house which is from heaven, if so be that being clothed we shall not be found naked. For we that are in this tabernacle do groan, being burdened: not for that we would be unclothed, but clothed upon, that mortality might be swallowed up of life.

Now he that hath wrought us for the selfsame thing is God, who also hath given unto us the earnest of the Spirit. Therefore we are always confident, knowing that, whilst we are at home in the body, we are absent from the Lord, for we walk by faith, not by sight. We are confident, I say, and willing rather to be absent from the body, and to be present with the Lord.

For the love of Christ constraineth us; because we thus judge, that if one died for all, then were all dead: and that he died for all, that they which live should not henceforth live unto themselves, but unto him which died for them, and rose again. Wherefore henceforth know we no man after the flesh: yea, though we have known Christ after the flesh, yet now henceforth know we him no more. Therefore if any man be in Christ, he is a new creature; old things are passed away; behold, all things are become new.

All things are of God, who hath reconciled us to himself by Jesus Christ, and hath given to us the ministry of reconciliation: To wit, that God was in Christ, reconciling the world unto himself, not imputing their trespasses unto them; and hath committed unto us the word of reconciliation. Now then we are ambassadors for Christ, as though God did beseech you by us.

We pray you in Christ's stead, be ye reconciled to God.

We then, as workers together with him, beseech you also that ye receive not the grace of God in vain. (For he saith, "I have heard thee in a time accepted, and in the day of salvation have I succoured thee: behold, now is the accepted time; behold, now is the day of salvation:") giving no offence in any thing, that the ministry be not blamed, but in all things approving ourselves as the ministers of God, in much patience, in afflictions, in necessities, in distresses, in stripes, in imprisonments, in tumults, in labours, in watchings, in fastings; by pureness, by knowledge, by longsuffering, by kindness, by the Holy Ghost, by love unfeigned, by the word of Truth, by the power of God, by the armour of righteousness on the right hand and on the left, by honour and dishonour, by evil report and good report; as deceivers, and yet true; as unknown, and yet well known; as dying, and, behold, we live; as chastened, and not killed; as sorrowful, yet always rejoicing; as poor, yet making many rich; as having nothing, and yet possessing all things.

He That Soweth Bountifully Shall Reap Also Bountifully

When we were come into Macedonia, our flesh had no rest, but we were troubled on every side: without were fightings, within were fears. Nevertheless God, that comforteth those that are cast down, comforted us by the coming of Titus; not by his coming only, but by the consolation wherewith he was comforted in you, when he told us your earnest desire, your mourning, your fervent mind toward me;

so that I rejoiced the more. For though I made you sorry with a letter, I do not repent, though I did repent; for I perceive that the same letter hath made you sorry, though it were but for a season. For godly sorrow worketh repentance to salvation not to be repented of; but the sorrow of the world worketh death. I rejoice therefore that I have confidence in you in all things.

Moreover, brethren, we make known to you the grace of God bestowed on the churches of Macedonia; how that in a great trial of affliction the abundance of their joy and their deep poverty abounded unto the riches of their liberality. For according to their power, I bear record, yea, and beyond their power they gave willingly of themselves; praying us with much intreaty that we would receive the gift, and take upon us the fellowship of the ministering to the saints.

Therefore, as ye abound in every thing, in faith, and utterance, and knowledge, and in all diligence, and in your love to us, see that ye abound in this grace also. I speak not by commandment, but by occasion of the forwardness of others, and to prove the sincerity of your love. For ye know the grace of our Lord Jesus Christ, that, though he was rich, yet for your sakes he became poor, that ye through his poverty might be rich. And herein I give my advice; for this is expedient for you, who were the first to make a beginning a year ago, not only to will, but also to do. Now therefore perform the doing of it; that as there was a readiness to will, so there may be a performance also, out of that which ye have.

For if there be first a willing mind, it is accepted according to that a man hath, and not according to that he hath not. For I mean not that other men be eased, and ye burdened; but by an equality, that now at this time your abundance may be a supply for their want, that their abundance also may be a supply for your want; that there may be equality.

Therefore I thought it necessary to exhort the brethren, that they would go before unto you, and make up beforehand your bounty, whereof ye had notice before, that the same might be ready, as a matter of bounty, and not as of covetousness. But this I say, he which soweth sparingly shall reap also sparingly; and he which soweth bountifully shall reap also bountifully. Every man according as he purposeth in his heart, so let him give, not grudgingly, or of necessity: For God loveth a cheerful giver.

And God is able to make all grace abound toward you; that ye, always having all sufficiency in all things, may abound to every good work. Now he that ministereth seed to the sower both minister bread for your food, and multiply your seed sown, and increase the fruits of your righteousness, being enriched in every thing to all bountifulness, which causeth through us thanksgiving to God.

Thanks be to God for his unspeakable gift.

My Grace Is Sufficient for Thee

NOW BY THE meekness and gentleness of Christ, I Paul, who in presence am lowly among you, beseech you that I may be bold against some which think of us as if we walked according to the flesh. For though we walk in the flesh, we do not war after the flesh: for the weapons of our warfare are not carnal, but mighty through God to the pulling down of strong holds, casting down imaginations, and every high thing that exalteth itself against the knowledge of God, and bringing into captivity every thought to the obedience of Christ.

Do ye look on things after the outward appearance? If any man trust in himself that he is Christ's, let him of himself think this again, that as he is Christ's, even so are we Christ's. For though I should boast somewhat more of our authority, which the Lord hath given us for edification, and not for your destruction, I should not be ashamed. But he that glorieth, let him glory in the Lord. For not he that commendeth himself is approved, but whom the Lord commendeth.

Would to God ye could bear with me a little in my folly; and indeed bear with me. Though I be rude in speech, yet not in knowledge; but we have been throughly made manifest among you in all things. Have I committed an offence in abasing myself that ye might be exalted, because I have preached to you the gospel of God freely? I robbed other churches, taking wages of them to do you service. And when I was present with you, and wanted, I was chargeable to no man: for that which was lacking to me the brethren which came from Macedonia supplied; and in all things I have kept myself from being burdensome unto you, and so will I keep myself. But what I do, that I will do, that I may cut off occasion from them which desire occasion; that wherein they glory, they may be found even as we. For such men are false apostles, deceitful workers, transforming themselves into the apostles of Christ. And no marvel, for even Satan transformeth himself into an angel of light.

But I speak as concerning reproach, as though we had been weak. However whereinsoever any is bold, I am bold also. Are they Hebrews? so am I. Are they Israelites? so am I. Are they the seed of Abraham? so am I. Are they ministers of Christ? I am more; in labours more abundant, in stripes above measure, in prisons more frequent, in deaths oft. Of the Jews five times received I forty stripes save one. Thrice was I beaten with rods, once was I stoned, thrice I suffered shipwreck, a night and a day I have been in the deep; in journeyings often, in perils by mine own countrymen, in perils by the heathen, in perils in the city; in perils in the wilderness, in perils in the sea, in perils among false brethren; in weariness and painfulness, in watchings often, in hunger and thirst, in fastings often, in cold and nakedness. Beside those things that are without, that which cometh upon me daily, the care of all the churches. Who is weak, and I am not weak? who is offended, and I burn not? If I must needs glory, I will glory of the things which concern mine infirmities. The God and Father of our Lord Jesus Christ, which is blessed for evermore, knoweth that I lie not. In Damascus the governor under Aretas the king kept the city of the Damascenes with a garrison, in order to take me; and through a window in a basket was I let down by the wall, and escaped his hands.

It is not expedient for me to glory. For though I would desire to glory, I shall not be foolish, for I will say the truth, that now I forbear, lest any man should think of me above that which he seeth me to be, or that he heareth of me. And lest I should be exalted above measure through the abundance of the revelations, there was given to me a thorn in the flesh, the messenger of Satan to buffet me, lest I should be exalted above measure. For this thing I besought the Lord thrice, that it might depart from me. And he said unto me, "My grace is sufficient for thee;" for my strength is made perfect in weakness. Most gladly therefore will I rather glory in my infirmities, that the power of Christ may rest upon me. Therefore I take pleasure in infirmities, in reproaches, in necessities, in persecutions, in distresses for Christ's sake: for when I am weak, then am I strong.

Again, think ye, that we excuse ourselves unto you? we speak before God in Christ: but we do all things, dearly beloved, for your edification. For I fear, lest, when I come, I shall not find you such as I would, and that I shall be found unto you such as ye would not: lest there be debates, envyings, wraths, strifes, backbitings, whisperings, swellings, tumults: and lest, when I come again, my God will humble me among you, and that I shall bewail many which have sinned already, and have not repented of the uncleanness and fornication and lasciviousness which they have committed.

This third time I am coming to you. In the mouth of two or three witnesses shall every word be established. Examine yourselves, whether ye be in the faith; prove your own selves. Now I pray God that ye do no evil. For we can do nothing against the Truth, but for the Truth.

Finally, brethren, farewell. Be perfect, be of good comfort, be of one mind, live in peace; and the God of love and peace shall be with you. The grace of the Lord Jesus Christ, and the love of God, and communion of the Holy Ghost, be with you all. Amen.

Paul

THE ACTS OF THE APOSTLES
CONTINUED

AFTER I HAVE BEEN TO JERUSALEM, I MUST ALSO SEE ROME

Now after these things were ended, Paul purposed in the spirit, when he had passed through Macedonia and Achaia, to go to Jerusalem, saying, " After I have been there, I must also see Rome." So he sent into Macedonia two of them that ministered unto him, Timothy and Erastus, but he himself stayed in Asia for a season.

And about that time there arose no small stir about the Way. For a certain man named Demetrius, a silversmith, which made silver shrines for Diana, brought no small gain unto the craftsmen, whom he called together with the workmen of like occupation, and said, " Sirs, ye know that by this craft we have our wealth. Moreover ye see and hear that not alone at Ephesus, but almost throughout all Asia, this Paul hath persuaded, and turned away much people, saying that they be no gods which are made with hands. So not only this our craft is in danger to be set at nought, but also that the temple of the great goddess Diana should be despised, and her magnificence should be destroyed whom all Asia and the world worshippeth."

And when they heard these sayings, they were full of wrath, and cried out, saying, " Great is Diana of the Ephesians."

And the whole city was filled with confusion; and having caught Gaius and Aristarchus, men of Macedonia, Paul's companions in travel, they rushed with one accord into the theatre. And when Paul would have entered in unto the people, the disciples suffered him not. And certain of the chief of Asia, which were his friends, sent unto him, desiring him that he would not adventure himself into the theatre.

Some therefore cried one thing, and some another: for the assembly was confused; and many knew not wherefore they were come together. And they drew Alexander out of the multitude, the Jews putting him forward. And Alexander beckoned with his hand, and would have made his defence unto the people, but when they knew that he was a Jew, all with one voice cried out for the space of about two hours, "Great is Diana of the Ephesians."

And when the townclerk had quieted the multitude, he said, "Ye men of Ephesus, what man is there that knoweth not how that the city of the Ephesians is a worshipper of the great goddess Diana, and of the image which fell down from Jupiter? Seeing then that these things cannot be spoken against, ye ought to be quiet, and do nothing rashly. For ye have brought hither these men, which are neither robbers of churches, nor yet blasphemers of your goddess. Wherefore if Demetrius, and the craftsmen which are with him, have a matter against any man, the law is open, and there are deputies; let them implead one another. But if ye enquire any thing concerning other matters, it shall be determined in a lawful assembly. For we are in danger to be called in question for this day's uproar, there being no cause whereby we may give an account of this concourse." And when he had thus spoken, he dismissed the assembly.

And after the uproar was ceased, Paul called unto him the disciples and embraced them, and departed for to go into Macedonia. And when he had gone over those parts, and had given them much exhortation, he came into Greece, and there abode three months.

(And Paul lingering on his journey, sent forward a letter to Rome.)

Glory, Honour and Peace to Every Man That Doeth Good

TO ALL THAT BE IN ROME, BELOVED OF GOD:

GRACE TO YOU and peace from God our Father, and the Lord Jesus Christ.

First, I thank my God through Jesus Christ for you all, that your faith is spoken of throughout the whole world. For God is my witness, whom I serve with my spirit, that without ceasing I make mention of you always in my prayers; making request, if by any means I might have a prosperous journey by the will of God to come to you. For I long to see you, that I may impart unto you some spiritual gift, to the end ye may be established. That is, that I may be comforted with you by the mutual faith both of you and me.

Now I would not have you ignorant, brethren, that oftentimes I purposed to come unto you, but could not. So as much as in me is, I am ready to preach the gospel to you that are at Rome.

For I am not ashamed of the gospel of Christ: for it is the power of God unto salvation to every one that believeth; to the Jew first and also to the Greek. For therein is the righteousness of God revealed from faith to faith: as it is written, "The just shall live by faith."

For the wrath of God is revealed from heaven against all ungodliness and unrighteousness of men, who hold the truth in unrighteousness; because that which may be known of God is manifest in them, for God hath showed it unto them. For the invisible things of him from the creation of the world are clearly seen, being understood by the things that are made, even his eternal power and Godhead; so that they are without excuse, because when they knew God, they glorified him not as God, neither were thankful; but became vain in their imaginations, and their foolish heart was darkened. Professing themselves to be wise, they became fools, and changed the glory of the uncorruptible God into an image made like to corruptible man, and changed the Truth of God into a lie, and worshipped and served the creature more than the Creator.

And they did not like to retain God in their knowledge, being filled with all unrighteousness, fornication, wickedness, covetousness, maliciousness; full of envy, murder, debate, deceit, malignity, whisperers, backbiters, haters of God, despiteful, proud, boasters, inventers of evil things, disobedient to parents, without understanding, covenant breakers, without natural affection, implacable, unmerciful; knowing the judgment of God, that they which commit such things are worthy of death, and not only do them, but have pleasure in them that do them.

Therefore thou art inexcusable, O man, whosoever thou art that judgest: for wherein thou judgest another, thou condemnest thyself; for thou that judgest doest the same things. But we are sure that the judgment of God is according to Truth against them which commit such things.

And thinkest thou this, O man, that judgest them which do such things and doest the same, that thou shalt escape the judgment of God? Or despisest thou the riches of his goodness, and forbearance and longsuffering; not knowing that the goodness of God leadeth thee to repentance?

But after thy hardness, and impenitent heart, treasurest up unto thyself wrath against the day of wrath and revelation of the righteous judgment of God, who will render to every man according to his deeds: to them who by patient continuance in well doing, seek for glory and honour and immortality, eternal Life. But unto them that are contentious, and do not obey the Truth, but obey unrighteousness, indignation and wrath, tribulation and anguish upon every soul that doeth evil. But glory, honour, and peace, to every man that worketh good. For there is no respect of persons with God.

For as many as have sinned without law shall also perish without law; and as many as have sinned in the law shall be judged by the law; For not the hearers of the law are just before God, but the doers of the law shall be justified. For when the Gentiles, which have not the law, do by nature the things contained in the law, these, having not the law, are a law unto themselves. Which show the work of the law written in their hearts, their conscience also bearing witness, and their thoughts meanwhile accusing or else excusing one another, in the day when God shall judge the secrets of men by Jesus Christ according to my gospel.

Behold, thou art called a Jew, and restest in the law, and makest thy boast of God, and knowest his will, and approvest the things that are more excellent, being instructed out of the law; and art confident that thou thyself art a guide of the blind, a light of them which are in darkness, an instructor of the foolish, a teacher of babes, which hast the form of knowledge and of the truth in the law.

Thou therefore which teachest another, teachest thou not thyself? thou that preachest a man should not steal, dost thou steal? Thou that sayest a man should not commit adultery, dost thou commit adultery? thou that abhorrest idols, dost thou commit sacrilege? Thou that makest thy boast of the law, through breaking the law dishonourest thou God?

For the name of God is blasphemed among the Gentiles through you, as it is written, " For circumcision verily profiteth, if thou keep the law: but if thou be a breaker of the law, thy circumcision is made uncircumcision." Therefore if the uncircumcision keep the righteousness of the law, shall not his uncircumcision be counted for circumcision? And shall not uncircumcision which is by nature, if it fulfil the law, judge thee, who by the letter and circumcision dost transgress the law? For he is not a Jew which is one outwardly; neither is that circumcision, which is outward in the flesh. But he is a Jew, which is one inwardly; and circumcision is that of the heart, in the spirit, and not in the letter; whose praise is not of men, but of God.

What advantage then hath the Jew? or what profit is there of circumcision? Much every way: chiefly, because that unto the Jews were committed the oracles of God. For what if some did not believe? shall their unbelief make the faith of God without effect? God forbid: yea, let God be true, but every man a liar; as it is written, "That thou mightest be justified in thy sayings, and mightest overcome when thou art judged."

It is written, "There is none righteous, no, not one: there is none that understandeth, there is none that seeketh after God. They are all gone out of the way, they are together become unprofitable; there is none that doeth good, no, not one. Their throat is an open sepulchre, whose mouth is full of cursing and bitterness; their feet are swift to shed blood; destruction and misery are in their ways; and the way of peace have they not known; there is no fear of God before their eyes."

Now we know that what things soever the law saith, it saith to them who are under the law: that every mouth may be stopped, and all the world may become guilty before God. Therefore by the deeds of the law there shall no flesh be justified in his sight: for by the law is the knowledge of sin.

The Promise Came Through the Righteousness of Faith

NOW THE righteousness of God without the law is manifested, being witnessed by the law and the prophets; even the righteousness of God which is by faith of Jesus Christ unto all and upon all them that believe: for there is no difference. For all have sinned, and come short of the glory of God, being justified freely by his grace through the redemption that is in Christ Jesus.

Where is boasting then? It is excluded. By what law? of works? Nay; but by the law of faith. Therefore we conclude that a man is justified by faith without the deeds of the law. Is he the God of the Jews only? is he not also of the Gentiles? Yes, of the Gentiles also, seeing he is one God. Do we then make void the law through faith? God forbid: yea, we establish the law.

What shall we say then that Abraham our father, as pertaining to the flesh, hath found? For if Abraham were justified by works, he hath whereof to glory; but not before God. For what saith the scripture? Abraham believed God, and it was counted unto him for righteousness. For the promise, that he should be the heir of the world, was not to Abraham, or to his seed, through the law, but through the righteousness of faith.

For if they which are of the law be heirs, faith is made void, and the promise made of none effect: because the law worketh wrath. For where no law is, there is no transgression. Therefore it is of faith, that it might be by grace; to the end the promise might be sure to all the seed; not to that only which is of the law, but to that which is of the faith of Abraham; who is the father of us all.

Abraham staggered not at the promise of God through unbelief; but was strong in faith, giving glory to God; and being fully persuaded that what he had promised, he was able also to perform. And therefore it was imputed to him for righteousness.

Now it was not written for his sake alone, that it was imputed to him: but for us also, to whom it shall be imputed, if we believe on him that raised up Jesus our Lord from the dead; who was delivered for our offences, and was raised again for our justification.

The Gift of God Is Eternal Life

THEREFORE being justified by faith, we have peace with God through our Lord Jesus Christ: by whom also we have access by faith into this grace wherein we stand, and rejoice in hope of the glory of God. And not only so, but we glory in tribulation also: knowing that tribulation worketh patience; and patience, experience; and experience, hope; and hope maketh not ashamed, because the love of God is shed abroad in our hearts by the Holy Ghost which is given unto us.

For when we were yet without strength, in due time Christ died for the ungodly. For scarcely for a righteous man will one die; yet peradventure for a good man some would even dare to die. But God commendeth his love toward us, in that, while we were yet sinners, Christ died for us. Much more then, being now justified by his blood, we shall be saved from wrath through him. For if when we were enemies, we were reconciled to God by the death of his Son, much more, being reconciled, we shall be saved by his life.

And not only so, but we also joy in God through our Lord Jesus Christ, by whom we have now received the atonement. Wherefore, as by one man sin entered into the world, and death by sin; and so death passed upon all men, for that all have sinned; for until the law sin was not in the world; but sin is not imputed when there is no law. But not as the offence, so also is the free gift. For if through the offence of one many be dead, much more the grace of God, and the gift of grace, which is by one man, Jesus Christ, hath abounded unto many.

And not as it was by one that sinned, so is the gift: for the judgment was by one to condemnation, but the free gift is of many offences unto justification. For if by one man's offence death reigned by one; much more they which receive abundance of grace and of the gift of righteousness shall reign in life by one, Jesus Christ. Therefore as by the offence of one, judgment came upon all men to condemnation; even so by the righteousness of one the free gift came upon all men unto justification of life. For as by one man's disobedience many were made sinners so by the obedience of one shall many be made righteous.

Moreover the law entered, that the offence might abound. But where sin abounded, grace did much more abound. That as sin hath reigned unto death, even so might grace reign through righteousness unto eternal life by Jesus Christ our Lord.

What shall we say then? Shall we continue in sin, that grace may abound? God forbid. How shall we, that are dead to sin, live any longer therein? Know ye not, that so many of us were baptized into Jesus Christ were baptized into his death? Therefore we are buried with him by baptism into death: that like as Christ was raised up from the dead by the glory of the Father, even so we should walk in newness of life.

For if we have been planted together in the likeness of his death, we shall be also in the likeness of his resurrection, knowing this that we are crucified with him, that the body of sin might be destroyed, that henceforth we should not serve sin. For he that is dead is freed from sin. Now if we be dead with Christ, we believe that we shall also live with him: knowing that Christ being raised from the dead dieth no more, death hath no more dominion over him. For in that he died, he died unto sin once: but in that he liveth, he liveth unto God. Likewise reckon ye also yourselves to be dead indeed unto sin, but alive unto God through Jesus Christ our Lord.

Let not sin therefore reign in your mortal body, that ye should obey it in the lusts thereof. Neither yield ye your members as instruments of unrighteousness unto sin: but yield yourselves unto God, as those that are alive from the dead, and your members as instruments of righteousness unto God. For sin shall not have dominion over you: for ye are not under the law, but under grace.

What then? shall we sin, because we are not under the law, but under grace? God forbid. Know ye not, that to whom ye yield yourselves servants to obey, his servants ye are to whom ye obey; whether of sin unto death, or of obedience unto righteousness? But God be thanked that ye were the servants of sin, but ye have obeyed from the heart that form of doctrine which was delivered you. Being then made free from sin, ye became the servants of righteousness.

I speak after the manner of men because of the infirmity of your flesh; for as ye have yielded your members servants to uncleanness and to iniquity unto iniquity, even so now yield your members servants to righteousness unto holiness. For when ye were the servants of sin, ye were free from righteousness. What fruit had ye then in those things whereof ye are now ashamed? for the end of those things is death. But now being made free from sin, and become servants to God, ye have your fruit unto holiness, and the end everlasting life. For the wages of sin is death; but the gift of God is eternal Life through Jesus Christ our Lord.

Nothing Shall Be Able to Separate Us From the Love of God

THE LAW IS HOLY, and the commandment is holy, and just, and good. For we know that the law is spiritual: but I am carnal, sold under sin. For that which I do, I allow not: for what I would, that do I not; but what I hate, that do I. If then I do that which I would not, I consent unto the law that it is good. Now then it is no more I that do it, but sin that dwelleth in me. For I know that in me (that is, in my flesh), dwelleth no good thing: for to will is present with me; but how to perform that which is good I find not. For the good that I would, I do not: but the evil which I would not, that I do.

Now if I do that I would not, it is no more I that do it, but sin that dwelleth in me. I find then a law, that when I would do good, evil is present with me. For I delight in the law of God after the inward man: but I see another law in my members, warring against the law of my mind, and bringing me into captivity to the law of sin which is in my members. O wretched man that I am! who shall deliver me from the body of this death? I thank God through Jesus Christ our Lord.

There is therefore now no condemnation to them which are in Christ Jesus, who walk not after the flesh but after the Spirit. For the law of the Spirit of life in Christ Jesus hath made me free from the law of sin and death. For what the law could not do, in that it was weak through the flesh, God sending his own Son in the likeness of sinful flesh, and for sin, condemned sin in the flesh; that the righteousness of the law might be fulfilled in us, who walk not after the flesh, but after the Spirit. For they that are after the flesh do mind the things of the flesh; but they that are after the Spirit the things of the Spirit. For to be carnally minded is death; but to be spiritually minded is life and peace. Because the carnal mind is enmity against God: for it is not subject to the law of God, neither indeed can be. So then they that are in the flesh cannot please God. But ye are not in the flesh, but in the Spirit, if so be that the Spirit of God dwell in you. He that raised up Christ from the dead shall also quicken your mortal bodies by his Spirit that dwelleth in you.

Therefore brethren, we are debtors, not to the flesh, to live after the flesh. For if ye live after the flesh, ye shall die: but if ye through the Spirit do mortify the deeds of the body, ye shall live. For as many as are led by the Spirit of God, they are the sons of God. For ye have not received the spirit of bondage again to fear; but ye have received the Spirit of adoption, whereby we cry, "Abba, Father."

The Spirit itself beareth witness with our spirit, that we are the children of God: and if children, then heirs; heirs of God and joint heirs with Christ; if so be that we suffer with him, that we may be also glorified together. For I reckon that the sufferings of this present time are not worthy to be compared with the glory which shall be revealed in us. For the earnest expectation of the creature waiteth for the manifestation of the sons of God. For we are saved by hope: but hope that is seen is not hope, for what a man seeth, what doth he yet hope for? But if we hope for that we see not, then do we with patience wait for it.

And we know that all things work together for good to them that love God; to them who are the called according to his purpose. What shall we then say to these things? If God be for us, who can be against us?

Who shall separate us from the love of Christ? shall tribulation, or distress, or persecution, or famine, or nakedness, or peril, or sword? Nay, in all these things we are more than conquerors through him that loved us.

For I am persuaded, that neither death, nor life, nor angels, nor principalities, nor powers, nor things present, nor things to come, nor height, nor depth, nor any other creature, shall be able to separate us from the love of God, which is in Christ Jesus our Lord.

For Of Him, and Through Him, and To Him, Are All Things: to Whom Be Glory for Ever

I SAY THE TRUTH in Christ; I lie not, that I have great heaviness and continual sorrow in my heart, for I could wish that myself were accursed for my brethren, my kinsmen according to the flesh, who are Israelites to whom pertaineth the adoption, and the glory, and the covenants, and the giving of the law, and the service of God and the promises. Not as though the word of God hath taken none effect, for they are not all Israel which are of Israel. Neither because they are the seed of Abraham are they all children, but " In Isaac shall thy seed be called." That is they which are the children of the flesh, these are not the children of God: but the children of promise are counted for the seed.

What shall we say then? That the Gentiles, which followed not after righteousness, have attained to righteousness, even the righteousness which is of faith? But Israel, which followed after the law of righteousness, hath not attained to the law of righteousness. Wherefore? Because they sought it not by faith, but as it were by the works of the law. For they stumbled at that stumbling stone; as it is written, " Behold, I lay in Sion a stumblingstone and rock of offence: and whosoever believeth on him shall not be ashamed."

Brethren, my heart's desire and prayer to God for Israel is, that they might be saved. For I bear them record that they have a zeal of God, but not according to knowledge. For they being ignorant of God's righteousness, and going about to establish their own righteousness, have not submitted themselves unto the righteousness of God. For Christ is the end of the law for righteousness to every one that believeth.

For Moses describeth the righteousness which is of the law, "That the man which doeth those things shall live by them."

But the righteousness which is of faith speaketh, "The word is nigh thee, even in thy mouth, and in thy heart;" that is, the word of faith, which we preach; that if thou shalt confess with thy mouth the Lord Jesus, and shalt believe in thine heart that God hath raised him from the dead, thou shalt be saved. For with the heart man believeth unto righteousness; and with the mouth confession is made unto salvation. For whosoever shall call upon the name of the Lord shall be saved.

How then shall they call on him in whom they have not believed? and how shall they believe in him of whom they have not heard? and how shall they hear without a preacher? And how shall they preach, except they be sent?

It is written, "How beautiful are the feet of them that preach glad tidings of good things!" But they have not all obeyed the gospel. For Isaiah saith, "Lord, who hath believed our report?" So then faith cometh by hearing, and hearing by the word of God.

But I say, "Have they not heard?" Yes verily, their sound went into all the earth, and their words unto the ends of the world. Isaiah is very bold and saith, "I was found of them that sought not for me; I was made manifest unto them that asked not after me." But to Israel he saith, "All day long I have stretched forth my hands unto a disobedient and gainsaying people."

I say then, "Hath God cast away his people?" God forbid.

For I also am an Israelite, of the seed of Abraham, of the tribe of Benjamin. God hath not cast away his people which he foreknew.

I say then, "Have they stumbled that they should fall?" God forbid: but rather through their fall, salvation is come unto the Gentiles, for to provoke them to jealousy. Now if the fall of them be the riches of the world, and the diminishing of them the riches of the Gentiles, how much more their fulness?

For I speak to you Gentiles, inasmuch as I am the apostle of the Gentiles, I magnify mine office: if by any means I may provoke to emulation them which are my flesh, and might save some of them. For if the casting away of them be the reconciling of the world, what shall the receiving of them be, but life from the dead?

For if the firstfruit be holy, the lump is also holy: and if the root be holy, so are the branches. And if some of the branches be broken off, and thou, being a wild olive tree, wert grafted in among them, and with them partakest of the root and fatness of the olive tree, boast not against the branches, for if thou boast, thou barest not the root, but the root thee.

Thou wilt say then, "The branches were broken off, that I might be grafted in." Well, because of unbelief they were broken off, and thou standest by faith. Be not highminded, but fear. For if God spared not the natural branches, take heed lest he also spare not thee.

Behold therefore the goodness and severity of God: on them which fell, severity; but toward thee, goodness, if thou continue in his goodness: otherwise thou also shalt be cut off. And they also, if they abide not in unbelief, shall be grafted in; for God is able to graft them in again. For if thou wert cut out of the olive tree which is wild by nature, and wert grafted contrary to nature into a good olive tree; how much more shall these which be the natural branches be grafted into their own olive tree?

For I would not, brethren, that ye should be ignorant of this mystery, lest ye should be wise in your own conceits; that blindness in part has happened to Israel, until the fulness of the Gentiles be come in. And so all Israel shall be saved: as it is written, "There shall come out of Sion the Deliverer, and shall turn away ungodliness from Jacob: for this is my covenant unto them, when I shall take away their sins."

O the depth of the riches both of the wisdom and knowledge of God! how unsearchable are his judgments, and his ways past finding out! For who hath known the mind of the Lord? or who hath been his counsellor? Or who hath first given to him, and it shall be recompensed unto him again? For of him, and through him, and to him, are all things: to whom be glory for ever. Amen.

Love Is the Fulfilling of the Law

I BESEECH YOU therefore, brethren, by the mercies of God, that ye present your bodies a living sacrifice, holy, acceptable unto God, which is your reasonable service. And be not conformed to this world; but be ye transformed by the renewing of your mind, that ye may prove what is that good, and acceptable, and perfect, will of God.

For I say, through the grace given unto me, to every man that is among you, not to think of himself more highly than he ought to think; but to think soberly, according as God hath dealt to every man the measure of faith. For as we have many members in one body, and all members have not the same office, so we, being many, are one body in Christ, and every one, members one of another.

Having then gifts differing according to the grace that is given to us, whether prophecy, let us prophesy according to the proportion of faith; or ministry, let us wait on our ministering; or he that teacheth, on teaching; or he that exhorteth, on exhortation; he that giveth, let him do it with simplicity; he that ruleth, with diligence; he that showeth mercy, with cheerfulness.

Let love be without dissimulation.

Abhor that which is evil; cleave to that which is good.

Be kindly affectioned one to another with brotherly love; in honour preferring one another.

Not slothful in business.

Fervent in spirit, serving the Lord.

Rejoicing in hope;

Patient in tribulation.

Continuing instant in prayer.

Distributing to the necessity of saints; given to hospitality.

Bless them which persecute you; bless, and curse not.

Rejoice with them that do rejoice, and weep with them that weep.

Be of the same mind one toward another.

Mind not high things, but condescend to men of low estate.

Be not wise in your own conceits.

Recompense to no man evil for evil.

Provide things honest in the sight of all men.

If it be possible, as much as lieth in you, live peaceably with all men.

Dearly beloved, avenge not yourselves, but rather give place unto wrath; for it is written, " Vengeance is mine; I will repay, saith the Lord."

Therefore if thine enemy hunger, feed him; if he thirst, give him drink; for in so doing thou shalt heap coals of fire on his head.

Be not overcome of evil, but overcome evil with good.

Let every soul be subject unto the higher powers. For there is no power but of God; the powers that be are ordained of God. Whosoever therefore resisteth the power, resisteth the ordinance of God. Wilt thou then not be afraid of the power? do that which is good, and thou shalt have praise of the same. But if thou do that which is evil, be afraid. Render therefore to all their dues: tribute to whom tribute is due; custom to whom custom; fear to whom fear; honour to whom honour.

Owe no man anything, but to love one another: for he that loveth another hath fulfilled the law. For this, "Thou shalt not commit adultery, Thou shalt not kill, Thou shalt not steal, Thou shalt not bear false witness; Thou shalt not covet;" and if there be any other commandment, it is briefly comprehended in this saying, namely, "Thou shalt love thy neighbour as thyself." Love worketh no ill to his neighbour: therefore love is the fulfilling of the law.

It is high time to awake out of sleep. The night is far spent, the day is at hand: let us therefore cast off the works of darkness, and let us put on the armour of light. For whether we live, we live unto the Lord; whether we die, we die unto the Lord: whether we live therefore or die, we are the Lord's. For it is written, "As I live saith the Lord, every knee shall bow to me, and every tongue shall confess to God." So then every one shall give account of himself to God.

Whatsoever Things Were Written Aforetime Were Written for Our Learning

WE THAT ARE STRONG ought to bear the infirmities of the weak, and not to please ourselves. Let every one of us please his neighbour for his good to edification. For even Christ pleased not himself; but as it is written "The reproaches of them that reproached thee fell on me." For whatsoever things were written aforetime were written for our learning, that we through patience and comfort of the scriptures might have hope.

Now the God of patience and consolation grant you to be likeminded one toward another according to Christ Jesus; that ye may with one mind and one mouth glorify God, even the Father of our Lord Jesus Christ. Wherefore receive ye one another, as Christ also received us to the glory of God.

Now I say that Jesus Christ was a minister for the truth of God, to confirm the promises made unto the fathers: and that the Gentiles might glorify God for his mercy; as it is written, "For this cause I will confess to thee among the Gentiles, and sing unto thy name." And again he saith, "Rejoice, ye Gentiles, with his people." And again, "Praise the Lord, all ye Gentiles; and laud him all ye people." And again Isaiah saith, "There shall be a root of Jesse, and he that shall rise to reign over the Gentiles; in him shall the Gentiles trust."

Now the God of hope fill you with all joy and peace in believing that ye may abound in hope, through the power of the Holy Ghost. I myself am persuaded, my brethren, that ye also are full of goodness, filled with all knowledge, able also to admonish one another. Nevertheless, brethren, I have written the more boldly unto you, because of the grace that is given to me of God, that I should be the minister of Jesus Christ to the Gentiles, ministering the gospel of God. For which cause, also, I have been hindered from coming to you. But now having no more place in these parts, and having a great desire these many years to come unto you, whenever I take my journey into Spain, I will come to you: for I trust to see you in my journey.

But now I go unto Jerusalem to minister unto the saints. For it hath pleased them of Macedonia and Achaia to make a certain contribution for the poor saints which are at Jerusalem. It hath pleased them verily; and their debtors they are. For if the Gentiles have been made partakers of their spiritual things, their duty is also to minister unto them in carnal things. When therefore I have performed this, and have sealed to them this fruit, I will come by you into Spain.

Now I beseech you, brethren, for the Lord Jesus Christ's sake, and for the love of the Spirit, that ye pray for me: that I may be delivered from them that do not believe in Judaea; and that my service which I have for Jerusalem may be accepted; and that I may come unto you with joy by the will of God; and may, with you, be refreshed.

Now to him that is of power to stablish you according to my gospel, and the preaching of Jesus Christ, according to the revelation of the mystery, which was kept secret since the world began, but now is made manifest, and by the scriptures of the prophets, according to the commandment of the everlasting God, made known to all nations for the obedience of faith, To God, only wise, be glory through Jesus Christ for ever. Amen.

Paul

(Written from Corinth)

THE ACTS OF THE APOSTLES CONTINUED

TROUBLE NOT YOURSELVES, FOR HIS LIFE IS IN HIM

And after Paul had spent three months in Greece, and a plot had been laid against him by the Jews as he was about to sail into Syria, he decided to return through Macedonia. And there accompanied him Gaius, and Timothy and Tychicus and several others. And Paul sailed away from Philippi, after the days of unleavened bread, and came to Troas, and there remained seven days.

And upon the first day of the week, when the disciples came together to break bread, Paul preached unto them, ready to depart on the morrow, and continued his speech until midnight. And there were many lights in the upper chamber, where they were gathered together. And there sat in a window a certain young man named Eutychus, being fallen into a deep sleep; and as Paul was long preaching, he sunk down with sleep, and fell down from the third loft, and was taken up dead.

And Paul went down, and fell on him, and embracing him said, "Trouble not yourselves, for his life is in him."

And Paul came up again, and had eaten, and talked a long while, even till break of day, and so departed, and they brought the young man alive, and were not a little comforted.

And they left Troas and came to Miletus, and Paul sent to Ephesus and called the elders of the church, for he was hastening if it were possible for him to be in Jerusalem the day of Pentecost. And when they were come he said unto them, "Ye know, from the first day that I came into Asia, after what manner I have been with you at all seasons, serving the Lord with all humility of mind, and with many tears and trials which befell me by the plots of the Jews: how I shrank not from declaring unto you anything that was profitable, and teaching you publicly, and from house to house, testifying both to Jews and to Greeks repentance toward God and faith toward our Lord Jesus Christ.

"And now, behold, I go bound in the spirit unto Jerusalem, not knowing the things that shall befall me there, save that the Holy Ghost witnesseth in every city, saying that bonds and afflictions abide me. But none of these things move me, neither count I my life dear unto myself, so that I might finish my course with joy, and the ministry, which I have received of the Lord Jesus, to testify the gospel of the grace of God.

"And now, behold, I know that ye all, among whom I have gone preaching the kingdom of God, shall see my face no more. Wherefore I take you to record this day, that I am pure from the blood of all men. For I have not shunned to declare unto you all the counsel of God.

"Take heed therefore unto yourselves, and to all the flock over which the Holy Ghost hath made you overseers, to feed the church of God, which he hath purchased with his own blood. For I know that, after my departure shall grievous wolves enter in among you, not sparing the flock. Also of your own selves shall men arise, speaking perverse things, to draw away disciples after them. Therefore watch, and remember, that by the space of three years I ceased not to warn every one night and day with tears.

"And now, brethren, I commend you to God, and to the word of his grace, which is able to build you up, and to give you an inheritance among all them which are sanctified. I have coveted no man's silver, or gold, or apparel. Yea, ye yourselves know, that these hands have ministered unto my necessities, and to them that were with me. I have showed you all things, how that so labouring ye ought to support the weak, and to remember the words of the Lord Jesus, how he said, 'It is more blessed to give than to receive.'"

And when he had thus spoken, he kneeled down, and prayed with them all. And they all wept sore, and fell on Paul's neck, and kissed him, sorrowing most of all for the words which he spake, that they should see his face no more. And they accompanied him unto the ship.

THEY BESOUGHT PAUL NOT TO GO UP TO JERUSALEM

AND IT CAME TO PASS, that after Paul and his companions had parted from them, and had launched, they came with a straight course unto Coos, and the day following unto Rhodes, and from thence unto Patara; and finding a ship sailing over unto Phenicia, they went aboard, and set forth. And they passed Cyprus on the left and sailed into Syria, and landed at Tyre, for there the ship was to unlade her burden.

And finding disciples there, they tarried seven days, and the disciples warned Paul that he should not go up to Jerusalem. But when they had accomplished those days, they departed, and the disciples with wives and children, followed Paul out of the city, and they kneeled down on the shore and prayed.

And they of Paul's company departed, and came to Caesarea, and entered into the house of Philip, the evangelist, and abode with him. And as they tarried many days, there came down from Judaea a certain prophet named Agabus. And when he came in, he took Paul's girdle, and bound his hands and feet, and said, "So shall the Jews at Jerusalem bind the man that owneth this girdle, and shall deliver him into the hands of the Gentiles."

And when they heard these things, both his companions, and they of that place, besought Paul not to go up to Jerusalem.

Then Paul answered, "What mean ye to weep and to break

mine heart? for I am ready not to be bound only, but also to die at Jerusalem for the name of the Lord Jesus."

And when he would not be persuaded, they ceased, saying, "The will of the Lord be done."

BUT I WAS FREE BORN

AND AFTER THOSE DAYS, Paul and his companions took carriages and went up to Jerusalem. There went up with them also certain of the disciples of Caesarea, and brought with them one Mnason of Cyprus, an old disciple with whom they should lodge.

And when they were come to Jerusalem, the brethren received them gladly. And the day following, Paul went in with them unto James, and all the elders were present. And when Paul had saluted them, he declared particularly what things God had wrought among the Gentiles by his ministry.

And when they heard it, they glorified the Lord, and said unto him, "Thou seest, brother, how many thousands of Jews there are which believe; and they are all zealous of the law. And they are informed that thou teachest all the Jews which are among the Gentiles to forsake Moses, saying that they ought not to circumcise their children, neither to walk after the customs. What is it therefore? They will certainly hear that thou art come.

"Do therefore this that we say to thee: We have four men which have a vow on them; take them, and purify thyself with them, and be at charges with them, that they may shave their heads, and all may know that those things, whereof they were informed concerning thee, are not true, but that thou thyself also walkest orderly, and keepest the law. But as touching the Gentiles which believe, we have written and concluded that they observe no such thing, save only that they keep themselves from things offered to idols, and from blood, and from strangled, and from fornication."

Then Paul took the men, and the next day purifying himself with them entered into the temple, to signify the accomplishment of the days of purification, until an offering should be offered for every one of them.

And when the seven days were almost ended, the Jews of Asia, when they saw Paul in the temple, stirred up all the people, and laid hands on him, crying out, "Men of Israel, help: This is the man that teacheth all men everywhere against the people, and the law, and this place, and brought Greeks also into the temple, and hath polluted this holy place." (For they had seen an Ephesian, whom they supposed that Paul had brought into the temple.)

And all the city was moved, and the people ran together, and they took Paul, and drew him out of the temple; and forthwith the doors were shut. And as they went about to kill him, tidings came unto the chief captain of the band, that all Jerusalem was in an uproar. Who immediately took soldiers and centurions, and ran down upon them, and when they saw the chief captain and the soldiers, they left off beating Paul.

Then the chief captain came near, and took Paul, and commanded him to be bound with two chains, and inquired who he was, and what he had done. And some cried one thing, some another, among the multitude. And when he could not know the certainty for the tumult, he commanded him to be borne of the soldiers for the violence of the people. For the multitude followed after, crying, "Away with him."

And as Paul was to be led into the castle, he said unto the chief captain, "May I speak unto thee?"

And he said, "Canst thou speak Greek? Art not thou that Egyptian, which before these days madest an uproar, and leddest out into the wilderness four thousand men that were murderers?"

But Paul said, "I am a Jew of Tarsus, in Cilicia, a citizen of no mean city; and I beseech thee, allow me to speak unto the people." And when he had given him leave, Paul stood on the stairs, and beckoned with his hand unto the people. And when there was a great silence, he spoke unto them in the Hebrew tongue, saying,

"Men, brethren, and fathers, hear ye my defence which I make now unto you." (And when they heard that he spake in the Hebrew tongue, they were more silent:) and he saith: "I am a Jew, born in Tarsus, a city in Cilicia, yet brought up in this city at the feet of Gamaliel, and taught according to the perfect manner of the law of the fathers, and was zealous toward God, as ye all are this day. And I persecuted this Way unto the death, binding and delivering into prisons both men and women, as also the high priest and all of the elders bear witness. From them I received letters unto the brethren, and went to Damascus to bring them which were there bound unto Jerusalem to be punished.

"And it came to pass, that as I made my journey, and was come nigh unto Damascus about noon, suddenly there shone from heaven a great light round about me, and I fell unto the ground, and heard a voice saying unto me, 'Saul, Saul, why persecutest thou me?'

"And I answered, 'Who art thou Lord?'

"And he said unto me, 'I am Jesus of Nazareth, whom thou persecutest.'

"And they that were with me saw indeed the light, and were afraid, but they heard not the voice of him that spake to me. And I said, 'What shall I do, Lord?'

"And the Lord said unto me, 'Arise, and go into Damascus; and there it shall be told thee of all things which are appointed for thee to do.' And when I could not see for the glory of that light, being led by the hand of them that were with me, I came to Damascus.

"And one Ananias, a devout man according to the law, well reported of by all the Jews that dwelt there, came unto me, and stood, and said unto me, 'Brother Saul, receive thy sight.' And the same hour I looked up upon him. And he said, 'The God of our fathers hath chosen thee, that thou shouldest know his will, and see that Just One, and shouldest hear the voice of his mouth. And thou shalt be his witness unto all men of what thou hast seen and heard. And now why tarriest thou? arise, and be baptized, and wash away thy sins, calling on the name of the Lord.'

"And it came to pass, that when I was come again to Jerusalem, even while I prayed in the temple, I was in a trance; and saw him saying unto me, 'Make haste, and get thee quickly out of Jerusalem, for they will not receive thy testimony concerning me.'

"And I said, 'Lord, they know that I imprisoned and beat in every synagogue them that believe on thee. And when the blood of thy martyr Stephen was shed, I also was standing by, and consenting unto his death, and kept the raiment of them that slew him.'

"And he said unto me, 'Depart for I will send thee far hence unto the Gentiles.'"

And the people gave him audience unto this word, and then lifted up their voices, and said, "Away with such a fellow from the earth: for it is not fit that he should live." And as they cried out, and cast off their clothes, and threw dust into the air, the chief captain commanded that Paul be brought into the castle, and bade that he should be examined by scourging, that he might know wherefore they cried so against him.

And as they bound him with thongs, Paul said unto the centurion that stood by, "Is it lawful for you to scourge a man that is a Roman, and uncondemned?"

When the centurion heard that, he went and told the chief captain, saying, "Take heed what thou doest for this man is a Roman."

Then the chief captain came, and said unto Paul, "Tell me, art thou a Roman?"

He said, "Yes."

And the chief captain answered, "With a great sum obtained I this freedom."

And Paul said, "But I was free born."

Then they which should have examined him, departed from him, and the chief captain also was afraid, after he knew he was a Roman, and because he had bound him.

BE OF GOOD CHEER, PAUL, THOU MUST BEAR WITNESS ALSO IN ROME

On the morrow, because the chief captain would know the reason for the accusation by the Jews, he loosed Paul from his bands, and commanded the chief priests and all their council to appear, and brought Paul down, and set him before them.

And Paul, earnestly beholding the council, said, "Men and brethren, I have lived in all good conscience before God until this day." And the high priest Ananias commanded them that stood by Paul to smite him on the mouth. And Paul said unto him, "God shall smite thee, thou whited wall: for sittest thou to judge me after the law, and commandest me to be smitten contrary to the law?"

And they that stood by said, "Revilest thou God's high priest?"

Then said Paul, "I wist not, brethren, that he was the high priest; for it is written, 'Thou shalt not speak evil of the ruler of thy people.'"

But when Paul perceived that the one part were Sadducees, and the other Pharisees, he cried out in the council, " Men and brethren, I am a Pharisee, the son of a Pharisee; of the hope and resurrection of the dead I am called in question."

And when he had so said, there arose a dissension between the Pharisees and the Sadducees, and the multitude was divided. For the Sadducces say that there is no resurrection, neither angel, nor spirit, but the Pharisees confess both. And there arose a great cry; and the scribes that were of the Pharisees arose, and strove, saying, " We find no evil in this man; but if a spirit or an angel hath spoken to him, let us not fight against God."

And when there arose a great dissension, the chief captain, fearing lest Paul should be pulled in pieces by them, commanded the soldiers to go down, and to take him by force from among them, and to bring him into the castle.

And the night following, the Lord stood by Paul, and said, " Be of good cheer, Paul, for as thou hast testified of me in Jerusalem, so must thou bear witness also at Rome."

And when it was day, certain of the Jews banded together, and bound themselves under a curse, saying that they would neither eat nor drink till they had killed Paul. And there were more than forty which had made this conspiracy. And they came to the chief priests and elders, and said, " We have bound ourselves under a great curse that we will eat nothing until we have slain Paul. Now therefore ye with the council signify to the chief captain that he bring Paul down unto you tomorrow, as though ye would enquire something more concerning him; and we, when he come near, are ready to kill him."

And when Paul's sister's son heard of their lying in wait, he went and entered into the castle, and told Paul. Then Paul called one of the centurions unto him, and said, " Bring this young man unto the chief captain, for he hath a certain thing to tell him."

So the centurion took him, and brought him to the chief

captain, and said, "Paul the prisoner called me unto him, and prayed me to bring this young man unto thee, who hath something to say unto thee."

Then the chief captain took him by the hand, and went with him aside privately, and asked him, "What is that thou hast to tell me?"

And the young man said, "The Jews have agreed to desire that thou wouldest bring down Paul tomorrow into the council, as though they would enquire somewhat of him. But do not thou yield unto them, for there lie in wait for him more than forty men, which have bound themselves with an oath, that they will neither eat nor drink till they have killed Paul; and now are they ready, looking for a promise from thee."

So the chief captain let the young man depart, and charged him, "See thou tell no man that thou hast showed these things to me." And he called unto him two centurions, saying, "Make ready two hundred soldiers to go to Caesarea, and horsemen threescore and ten, and spearmen two hundred, at the third hour of the night. And provide them beasts, that they may set Paul on, and bring him safe unto Felix, the governor." And he wrote a letter after this manner:

"Claudius Lysias unto the most excellent governor Felix, sendeth greeting:

This man was taken of the Jews, and should have been killed by them, but I came with an army and rescued him, having understood that he was a Roman. And when I would have known whereof they accused him, I brought him forth into their council: whom I found to be accused of questions of their law, but to have nothing laid to his charge worthy of death or of bonds. And when it was told me how the Jews laid wait for the man, I sent straightway to thee, and gave commandment to his accusers also to say before thee what they had against him. Farewell."

Then the soldiers, as it was commanded them, took Paul, and brought him by night to Antipatris. But on the morrow they left the horsemen to go with him, and returned to the castle; and they, when they came to Caesarea, delivered the epistle to Felix the governor, and presented Paul also before him.

And when the governor had read the letter, he asked of what province Paul was. And when he understood that he was of Cilicia, he said, "I will hear thee when thine accusers are also come." And he commanded him to be kept in Herod's judgment hall.

And after five days Ananias the high priest, with the elders, and with a certain orator named Tertullus, came and informed the governor against Paul. And when Paul was called, Tertullus began to accuse him saying:

"Seeing that by thee we enjoy much peace, and that by thy providence worthy deeds are done unto our nation, we accept it always, and in all places, most noble Felix, with all thankfulness. But that I be not tedious unto thee, I pray that of thy clemency thou hear a few words of us. For we have found this man a pestilent fellow, and a mover of sedition among all the Jews throughout the world, and a ringleader of the sect of the Nazarenes: who also hath gone about to profane the temple: whom we took, and would have judged according to our law, but the chief captain Lysias came upon us, and with great violence took him away out of our hands, commanding his accusers to come unto thee. But by examining him thyself thou mayest take knowledge of all these things whereof we accuse him." And the Jews also assented, saying that these things were so.

Then Paul, after the governor had beckoned unto him to speak, answered, "Forasmuch as I know that thou hast been for many years a judge unto this nation, I do the more cheerfully answer for myself. It is not yet twelve days since I went up to Jerusalem to worship. They neither found me in the temple disputing with any man, neither raising up the people, neither in the synagogues, nor in the city, nor can they prove the things whereof they now accuse me. But this I confess unto thee, that after the way which they call heresy, so worship I the God of my fathers, believing all things which are written in the law and in the prophets: and have hope toward God, which they themselves also allow, that there shall be a resurrection of the dead, both of the just and unjust. And herein do I exercise myself, to have always a conscience void of offence toward God, and toward men.

"Now after many years I came to bring alms to my nation, and offerings. Whereupon certain Jews from Asia found me purified in the temple, neither with multitude nor with tumult. They ought to have been here before thee, and object, if they had anything against me, or else let these same here say, if they have found any evil doing in me, while I stood before the council, except for this one voice, that I cried standing among them, touching the resurrection of the dead, I am called in question by you this day."

And when Felix heard these things, having more exact knowledge of that Way, he deferred them, and said, "When Lysias the chief captain shall come down, I will know the uttermost of your matter." And he commanded a centurion to keep Paul, and to let him have liberty, and that he should forbid none of his acquaintance to minister or come unto him.

And after certain days, Felix came with his wife Drusilla who was a Jewess, and sent for Paul, and heard him concerning the faith in Christ. And as he reasoned of righteousness, temperance, and judgment to come, Felix trembled, and answered, "Go thy way for this time; when I have a convenient season, I will call for thee." He hoped that money would be given him of Paul, that he might loose him; whereupon he sent for him the oftener.

But after two years, Felix was succeeded by Procius Festus, and desiring to gain favor with the Jews, Felix left Paul in bonds.

I APPEAL TO CAESAR

Now when Festus came into the province, after three days he went from Caesarea up to Jerusalem. Then the high priest and the chief of the Jews informed him against Paul, and besought him that he would send Paul to Jerusalem, laying wait in the way to kill him.

But Festus answered that Paul should be kept at Caesarea, and that he himself would depart shortly thither. " Let them therefore," said he, " which among you are able, go down with me, and accuse this man, if there be any wickedness in him." And when he had tarried among them more than ten days, he went down unto Caesarea; and the next day sitting on the judgment seat commanded Paul to be brought.

And when Paul came in, the Jews which came down from Jerusalem stood round about, and laid many and grievous complaints against him, which they could not prove.

And Paul answered for himself, " Neither against the law of the Jews, neither against the temple, nor yet against Caesar, have I offended any thing at all."

But Festus, willing to do the Jews a pleasure, answered Paul, and said, " Wilt thou go up to Jerusalem, and there be judged of these things before me? "

Then said Paul, " I stand at Caesar's judgment seat, where I ought to be judged: to the Jews have I done no wrong, as thou very well knowest. For if I be an offender, or have committed any thing worthy of death, I refuse not to die: but if there be none of these things whereof these accuse me, no man may deliver me unto them. I appeal unto Caesar."

Then Festus, when he had conferred with the council, answered, "Thou hast appealed unto Caesar, unto Caesar shalt thou go."

And after certain days king Agrippa and Bernice came into Caesarea to salute Festus. And when they had been there many days, Festus declared Paul's cause unto the king, saying, "There is a certain man left in bonds by Felix, about whom, when I was at Jerusalem, the chief priests and the elders of the Jews informed me, desiring to have judgment against him. To whom I answered, 'It is not the manner of the Romans to deliver any man to die, before he which is accused have the accusers face to face, and have opportunity to answer for himself concerning the crime laid against him.' Therefore, when they were come hither, without any delay on the morrow, I sat on the judgment seat, and commanded the man to be brought forth. Against whom, when the accusers stood up, they brought no accusations of such things as I supposed, but had certain questions against him of their own superstition, and of one Jesus, which was dead, whom Paul affirmed to be alive. And because I doubted such questions, I asked him whether he would go to Jerusalem, and there be judged of these matters; but when Paul appealed to Caesar, I commanded him to be kept till I might send him to Caesar."

Then Agrippa said unto Festus, "I would also hear the man myself."

And he said, "Tomorrow thou shalt hear him."

And on the morrow, when Agrippa was come, and Bernice with great pomp, and was entered into the place of the hearing, with the chief captains and principal men of the city, at Festus' command Paul was brought forth.

And Festus said, "King Agrippa, and all men here present with us, ye see this man, about whom all the multitude of the Jews have dealt with me, both at Jerusalem, and also here, crying that he ought not to live any longer. But when I found that he had committed nothing worthy of death, and that he himself hath appealed to Caesar, I have determined to send him. Of him

I have no certain thing to write unto my lord. Wherefore I have brought him forth before you, and specially before thee, O king Agrippa, that, after examination, I might have somewhat to write. For it seemeth to me unreasonable to send a prisoner, and not signify the crimes laid against him."

Then Agrippa said unto Paul, "Thou art permitted to speak for thyself."

Then Paul stretched forth his hand, and answered for himself: "I think myself happy, king Agrippa, because I shall answer for myself this day before thee touching all the things whereof I am accused of the Jews, especially because I know thee to be expert in all customs and questions which are among the Jews, wherefore I beseech thee to hear me patiently.

"My manner of life from my youth, which was at first among mine own nation at Jerusalem, know all Jews, if they would testify, that after the most strict sect of our religion I lived a Pharisee. And now I stand and am judged for the hope of the promise made of God unto our fathers: unto which promise our twelve tribes, serving God day and night, hope to come. For which hope's sake, king Agrippa, I am accused of the Jews.

"Why should it be thought a thing incredible with you, that God should raise the dead? I thought myself, that I ought to do many things contrary to the name of Jesus of Nazareth. Which things I did in Jerusalem, and many of the saints did I shut up in prison, having received authority from the chief priests; and when they were put to death, I gave my voice against them. And I punished them oft in every synagogue, and compelled them to blaspheme; and being exceedingly mad against them, I persecuted them even unto strange cities.

"Whereupon as I went to Damascus with authority and commission from the chief priests, at midday, O king, I saw in the way a light from heaven, above the brightness of the sun, shining round about me and them which journeyed with me. And when we were all fallen to the earth, I heard a voice speaking unto me, and saying in the Hebrew tongue, ' Saul, Saul, why persecutest thou me? it is hard for thee to kick against the pricks.' And I said, ' Who art thou, Lord? ' And he said, ' I am Jesus whom thou persecutest. But rise and stand upon thy feet; for I have appeared unto thee for this purpose, to make thee a minister and a witness both of these things which thou hast seen, and of those things in the which I will appear unto thee; delivering thee from the people and from the Gentiles, unto whom now I send thee, to open their eyes, and to turn them from darkness to light, and from the power of Satan unto God, that they may receive forgiveness of sins, and inheritance among them which are sanctified by faith that is in me.'

" Whereupon, O king Agrippa, I was not disobedient unto the heavenly vision: but showed first unto them of Damascus, and at Jerusalem, and throughout all the coasts of Judaea, and then to the Gentiles, that they should repent and turn to God, and do works meet for repentance. For these causes the Jews caught me in the temple, and were about to kill me. Having therefore obtained help of God, I continue unto this day, witnessing both to small and great, saying none other things than those which the prophets and Moses did say should come: That Christ should suffer, and that he should be the first that should rise from the dead, and should show light unto the people, and to the Gentiles."

And as he thus spake for himself, Festus said, " Paul, thou art beside thyself; much learning doth make thee mad."

But Paul said, " I am not mad, most noble Festus; but speak forth the words of truth and soberness. For the king knoweth of these things, before whom also I speak freely: for I am persuaded that none of these things are hidden from him, for this thing was not done in a corner. King Agrippa, believest thou the prophets? I know that thou believest."

Then Agrippa said unto Paul, " Almost thou persuadest me to be a Christian."

And Paul said, "I would to God, that not only thou, but also all that hear me this day, were both almost, and altogether such as I am, except these bonds."

And when he had thus spoken, the king rose up, and the governor, and Bernice, and they that sat with them; and when they were gone aside, they talked between themselves, saying, "This man doeth nothing worthy of death or of bonds."

Then said Agrippa unto Festus, "This man might have been set at liberty, if he had not appealed unto Caesar."

PAUL SHOOK OFF THE VIPER INTO THE FIRE AND FELT NO HARM

AND WHEN it was determined that Paul should be sent into Italy, they delivered him and certain other prisoners unto one named Julius, a centurion of Augustus' band. And entering into a ship, they launched, meaning to sail by the coasts of Asia. And the next day they touched at Sidon. And Julius treated Paul courteously, and gave him liberty to go unto his friends to refresh himself.

And when they had launched from thence, they sailed under the lee of Cyprus, because the winds were contrary. And when they had sailed over the sea of Cilicia and Pamphylia, they came to Myra, a city of Lycia. And there the centurion found a ship of Alexandria sailing into Italy, and put Paul and the others therein. And when they had sailed slowly many days, the wind hindering them, they sailed under the lee of Crete, over against Salmone, and came unto a place which is called The fair havens, near the city of Lasea.

And when much time was spent, and the voyage was now

dangerous, because the Fast was now already past, Paul admonished them, and said, "Sirs, I perceive that this voyage will be with hurt and much damage, not only of the lading and ship, but also of our lives."

Nevertheless the centurion believed the master and the owner of the ship, more than those things spoken by Paul. And because the haven was not commodious to winter in, the majority advised to depart if by any means they might reach Phenice, and there to winter, which is a haven of Crete. And when the south wind blew softly, supposing that they had obtained their purpose, they weighed anchor, and sailed close by Crete. But not long after there arose a tempestuous wind, and when the ship was caught, and could not bear up into the wind, they let her drive, and they lowered the sail and so were driven. And being exceedingly tossed with the tempest, the next day they lightened the ship; and the third day they cast out with their own hands the tackling of the ship. And when neither sun nor stars in many days appeared, and no small tempest lay on them, all hope that they should be saved was then taken away.

And when they had been long without food, Paul stood forth in the midst, and said, "Sirs, ye should have hearkened unto me, and not have sailed from Crete. But now I exhort you to be of good cheer; for there shall be no loss of any man's life among you, but of the ship. For there stood by me this night the angel of God, whose I am, and whom I serve, saying, 'Fear not, Paul; thou must be brought before Caesar: and lo, God hath given thee all them that sail with thee.' Wherefore, sirs, be of good cheer; for I believe God, that it shall be even as it was told me. Howbeit we must be cast upon a certain island."

But when the fourteenth night was come, as they were being driven up and down in the sea of Adria, about midnight the shipmen thought that they drew near to some country, and they sounded and found it twenty fathoms; and when they had gone a little further they sounded again, and found it fifteen fathoms.

Then fearing lest they might come upon rocks, they cast four anchors out of the stern, and wished for the day.

And as the shipmen were about to flee out of the ship, when they had let down the boat into the sea, Paul said to the centurion and to the soldiers, "Except these abide in the ship, ye cannot be saved." Then the soldiers cut off the ropes of the boat, and let her fall off.

And while the day was coming on, Paul besought them all to take meat, saying, "This day is the fourteenth day that ye have tarried and continued fasting, having taken nothing. Wherefore I pray you to take some meat: for this is for your health: and there shall not an hair fall from the head of any of you." And when he had thus spoken, he took bread, and gave thanks to God in the presence of them all; and when he had broken it, he began to eat. Then were they all of good cheer, and they also took some meat. There were in the ship two hundred threescore and sixteen souls. And when they had eaten enough, they lightened the ship, and cast out the wheat into the sea.

And when it was day, they knew not the land, but they discovered a certain creek with a shore, into which they were minded, if it were possible, to thrust in the ship. And when they had taken up the anchors, they committed themselves unto the sea, and loosed the rudder bands, and hoisted up the mainsail to the wind, and made toward shore. And falling into a place where two seas met, they ran the ship aground, and the forepart stuck fast and remained unmoveable, but the hinder part was broken with the violence of the waves.

And the soldiers counselled to kill the prisoners, lest any of them should swim out, and escape. But the centurion, willing to save Paul, kept them from their purpose, and commanded that they which could swim should cast themselves first into the sea, and get to land, and the rest, some on boards, and some on broken pieces of the ship. And so it came to pass, that they escaped all safe to land.

And when they had escaped, then they knew that the island was called Melita. And the barbarous people showed them no little kindness, for they kindled a fire, and received every one, because of the present rain, and because of the cold.

And when Paul had gathered a bundle of sticks, and laid them on the fire, there came a viper out of the heat, and fastened on his hand. And when the barbarians saw the venomous beast hang on his hand, they said among themselves, "No doubt this man is a murderer, whom, though he hath escaped the sea, yet vengeance suffereth not to live."

But Paul shook off the beast into the fire, and felt no harm. Howbeit they looked when he should have swollen, or fallen down dead suddenly; but after they had looked a great while, and saw no harm come to him, they changed their minds, and said that he was a god.

In the same quarters were possessions of the chief man of the island, whose name was Publius; who received them and lodged them three days courteously. And it came to pass, that the father of Publius lay sick of a fever and of a bloody flux: to whom Paul entered in, and prayed, and laid his hands on him, and healed him. So when this was done, others also, which had diseases, in the island, came, and were healed. And the natives honoured them with many honours, and when they departed laded them with such things as were necessary.

After three months they departed in a ship of Alexandria, whose sign was Castor and Pollux. And when they came to Rome, the centurion delivered the prisoners to the captain of the guard; but Paul was allowed to dwell by himself with a soldier that kept him.

THE SALVATION OF GOD IS SENT UNTO THE GENTILES, AND THEY WILL HEAR IT

AND IT CAME TO PASS, after three days Paul called the chief of the Jews together. And when they were come, he said unto them, " Men and brethren, though I have committed nothing against the people, or customs of our fathers, yet was I delivered prisoner from Jerusalem into the hands of the Romans, who, when they had examined me, would have let me go, because there was no cause of death in me. But when the Jews spake against it, I was constrained to appeal unto Caesar; not that I had ought to accuse my nation of. For this cause therefore have I called for you, to see you, and to speak with you; because for the hope of Israel, I am bound with this chain."

And they said unto him, " We neither received letters out of Judaea concerning thee, neither any of the brethren that came showed or spake any harm of thee. But we desire to hear of thee what thou thinkest: for concerning this sect, we know that every where it is spoken against."

And when they had appointed him a day, there came many to him into his lodging; to whom he expounded and testified the kingdom of God, persuading them concerning Jesus both out of the law of Moses, and out of the prophets, from morning till evening. And some believed the things which were spoken, and some believed not.

And when they agreed not among themselves, they departed, after Paul had spoken this word, " Well spake the Holy Ghost by Isaiah the prophet unto our fathers, saying, ' Go unto this people, and say, " Hearing ye shall hear, and shall not understand; and seeing ye shall see, and not perceive; For the heart of this people is waxed gross, and their ears are dull of hearing, and their eyes have they closed; lest they should see with their eyes, and hear with their ears, and understand with their heart, and should be converted, and I should heal them." ' Be it known therefore unto you, that the salvation of God is sent unto the Gentiles, and that they will hear it."

And when he had said these words, the Jews departed, and had great reasoning among themselves.

And Paul dwelt two whole years in his own hired house, and received all that came in unto him, preaching the kingdom of God, and teaching those things which concern the Lord Jesus Christ, with all confidence, no man forbidding him.

(During this time Paul wrote letters to the churches, which are given on the following pages.)

Let This Mind Be in You, Which Was Also in Christ Jesus

TO ALL THE SAINTS IN CHRIST JESUS WHICH ARE AT PHILIPPI,

GRACE BE UNTO YOU, and peace, from God our Father, and from the Lord Jesus Christ. I thank my God upon every remembrance of you, always in every prayer of mine for you all, making request with joy, being confident that he which hath begun a good work in you will perform it until the day of Jesus Christ. It is meet for me to think this of you all, because I have you in my heart. For God is my record how greatly I long after you all.

And this I pray, that your love may abound yet more and more in knowledge and in all judgment; that ye may approve things that are excellent; that ye may be sincere and without offence till the day of Christ; and that ye be filled with the fruits of righteousness, which are by Jesus Christ, unto the glory and praise of God.

But I would have you understand, brethren, that the things which happened unto me have fallen out rather unto the futherance of the gospel. So that my bonds in Christ are manifest in all the palace, and in all other places. And many of the brethren in the Lord, waxing confident by my bonds, are much more bold to speak the word without fear. Some indeed preach Christ even of envy and strife; and some also of good will. The one preach Christ of contention, not sincerely, supposing to add affliction to my bonds. But the other of love, knowing that I am set for the defence of the gospel. What then? notwithstanding every way, whether in pretence, or in truth, Christ is preached; and I therein do rejoice, yea, and will rejoice.

For to me to live is Christ, and to die is gain. But if I live in the flesh, this is the fruit of my labour: yet what I shall choose, I wot not. For I am in a strait betwixt two, having a desire to depart, and to be with Christ; which is far better; nevertheless to abide in the flesh is more needful for you. And having this confidence, I know that I shall abide and continue with you all, for your furtherance and joy of faith, that your rejoicing may be more abundant, by my coming to you again.

If there be therefore any consolation in Christ, if any comfort of love, if any fellowship of the Spirit, if any bowels of mercies, fulfil ye my joy, that ye be likeminded, having the same love, being of one accord, of one mind. Let nothing be done through strife or vainglory; but in lowliness of mind let each esteem other better than themselves. Look not every man on his own things, but every man also on the things of others.

Let this mind be in you, which was also in Christ Jesus. Who being in the form of God, thought it not robbery to be equal with God, but made himself of no reputation, and took upon him the form of a servant, and was made in the likeness of men; and being found in fashion as a man, he humbled himself, and became obedient unto death, even the death of the cross. Wherefore God hath highly exalted him, and given him a name which is above every name: that at the name of Jesus every knee should bow, of things in heaven, and things in the earth, and things under the earth. And that every tongue should confess that Jesus Christ is Lord, to the glory of God the Father.

Wherefore, my beloved, as ye have always obeyed, not as in my presence only, but now much more in my absence, work out your own salvation with fear and trembling, for it is God which worketh in you both to will and to do of his good pleasure. Do all things without murmurings and disputings: that ye may be blameless and harmless, the sons of God, without rebuke, in the midst of a crooked and perverse nation, among whom ye shine as lights in the world, holding forth the word of life; that I may rejoice in the day of Christ, that I have not run in vain, neither laboured in vain.

I trust in the Lord Jesus to send Timothy shortly unto you, that I also may be of good comfort, when I know your state. For I have no man likeminded, who will naturally care for your state. For all seek their own, not the things which are Jesus Christ's. Therefore I hope to send presently, so soon as I shall see how it will go with me. But I trust in the Lord that I also shall come shortly.

Finally, my brethren, rejoice in the Lord. To write the same things to you, to me indeed is not grievous, but for you it is safe. Beware of dogs, beware of evil workers, beware of concision. For we are the circumcision, which worship God in the spirit, and rejoice in Christ Jesus, and have no confidence in the flesh.

Though I might also have confidence in the flesh. If any other man thinketh that he hath whereof he might trust in the flesh, I more: Circumcised the eighth day, of the stock of Israel, of the tribe of Benjamin, an Hebrew of the Hebrews; as touching the law, a Pharisee; concerning zeal, persecuting the church; touching the righteousness which is in the law, blameless.

But what things were gain to me, those I counted loss for Christ. Yea, doubtless, and I count all things but loss for the excellency of the knowledge of Christ Jesus my Lord: for whom I have suffered the loss of all things, and do count them but dung, that I may win Christ, and be found in him, not having mine own righteousness, which is of the law, but that which is through the faith of Christ, the righteousness which is of God by faith: that I may know him, and the power of his resurrection, and the fellowship of his sufferings, being made conformable unto his death, if by any means I might attain unto the resurrection of the dead.

Not as though I had already attained, either were already perfect: but I follow after, if that I may apprehend that for which also I am apprehended of Christ Jesus. Brethren, I count not myself to have apprehended, but this one thing I do, forgetting those things which are behind, and reaching forth unto those things which are before, I press toward the mark for the prize of the high calling of God in Christ Jesus.

Let us therefore, as many as be perfect, be thus minded; and if in any thing ye be otherwise minded, God shall reveal even this unto you. Nevertheless, whereto we have already attained, let us walk by the same rule, let us mind the same thing.

Brethren, be followers together of me, and mark them which walk so as ye have us for an example. For many walk, of whom I have told you often, and now tell you even weeping, that they are the enemies of the cross of Christ: whose end is destruction, whose God is their belly, and whose glory is in their shame, who mind earthly things.

For our conversation is in heaven; from whence also we look for the Saviour, the Lord Jesus Christ; who shall change our vile body, that it may be fashioned like unto his glorious body, according to the working whereby he is able even to subdue all things unto himself.

Therefore, my brethren, dearly beloved and longed for, my joy and crown, so stand fast in the Lord, my dearly beloved. Rejoice in the Lord alway: and again I say, rejoice. Let your moderation be known unto all men. Be careful for nothing, but in everything by prayer and supplication with thanksgiving, let your requests be made known unto God. And the peace of God, which passeth all understanding, shall keep your hearts and minds through Christ Jesus.

Finally, brethren:

whatsoever things are true,
whatsoever things are honest,
whatsoever things are just,
whatsoever things are pure,
whatsoever things are lovely,
whatsoever things are of good report,
if there be any virtue,
and if there be any praise,

THINK ON THESE THINGS.

Those things, which ye have both learned, and received, and heard, and seen in me, do: and the God of peace shall be with you.

I rejoiced in the Lord greatly, that now at the last your care of me flourished again; wherein ye were also careful, but ye lacked opportunity. Not that I speak in respect of want: for I have learned in whatsoever state I am, therewith to be content. I know both how to be abased, and I know how to abound: everywhere and in all things I am instructed both to be full and to be hungry, both to abound and to suffer need. I can do all things through Christ which strengtheneth me.

Notwithstanding ye have well done, that ye did communicate with my affliction. Now ye Philippians know also that in the beginning of the gospel when I departed from Macedonia, no church communicated with me as concerning giving and receiving, but ye only. For even in Thessalonica ye sent once and again unto my necessity. Not because I desire a gift, but I desire fruit that may abound to your account. But I have all, and abound: I am full, having received of Epaphroditus the things which were sent from you, a sacrifice acceptable, well pleasing to God.

My God shall supply all your need according to His riches in glory by Christ Jesus. Now unto God and our Father be glory for ever and ever. Amen.

Paul and Timothy

(Written to the Philippians from Rome.)

Set Your Affection on Things Above, Not on Things on the Earth

TO THE SAINTS AND FAITHFUL BRETHREN IN CHRIST WHICH ARE AT COLOSSE:

GRACE BE UNTO YOU, and peace, from God our Father and the Lord Jesus Christ. We give thanks to God and the Father of our Lord Jesus Christ, praying always for you, since we heard of your faith in Christ Jesus, and of the love which ye have to all the saints, for the hope which is laid up for you in heaven, whereof ye heard before in the word of the truth of the gospel, which is come unto you, as it is in all the world, and bringeth forth fruit, as it doth also in you, since the day ye heard of it, and knew the grace of God in Truth.

For this cause we also, since the day we heard it, do not cease to pray for you, and to desire that ye might be filled with the knowledge of his will in all wisdom and spiritual understanding. That ye might walk worthy of the Lord unto all pleasing, being fruitful in every good work, and increasing in the knowledge of God; strengthened with all might, according to his glorious power, unto all patience and longsuffering with joyfulness.

We give thanks unto the Father, which hath made us meet to be partakers of the inheritance of the saints in light. Who hath delivered us from the power of darkness, and hath translated us into the kingdom of his dear Son, in whom we have redemption through his blood, even the forgiveness of sins. Who is the image of the invisible God, the first-born of every creature, for by him were all things created that are in heaven, and that are in earth, visible and invisible, whether they be thrones, or dominions, or principalities, or powers; all things were created by him, and for him. For it pleased the Father that in Christ should all fulness dwell. And having made peace through the blood of his cross, by him to reconcile all things unto himself; by him, I say, whether they be things in earth, or things in heaven.

And you, that were sometimes alienated and enemies in your mind by wicked works, yet now hath he reconciled in the body of his flesh through death, to present you holy and unblameable and unreprovable in his sight. Continue ye in the faith grounded and settled, and be not moved away from the hope of the gospel, which ye have heard, and which was preached to every creature which is under heaven; whereof I Paul, am made a minister, according to the dispensation of God which is given to me for you, to fulfill the word of God; even the mystery which hath been hid from ages and from generations, but now is made manifest.

I would that ye knew what great conflict I have for you, and for them of Laodicea, and for as many as have not seen my face in the flesh; that their hearts might be comforted, being knit together in love, and unto all riches of the full assurance of understanding, to the acknowledgment of the mystery of God, the Father, and of Christ, in whom are hid all the treasures of wisdom and knowledge.

And this I say, lest any man should beguile you with enticing words. For though I be absent in the flesh, yet am I with you in the spirit, joying and beholding your order, and the steadfastness of your faith in Christ. As ye have therefore received Christ Jesus the Lord, so walk ye in him: rooted and built up in him, and stablished in the faith as ye have been taught, abounding therein with thanksgiving.

Beware lest any man spoil you through philosophy and vain deceit, after the tradition of men, after the rudiments of the world, and not after Christ, for in him dwelleth all the fulness of the Godhead bodily. And ye are complete in him which is the head of all principality and power. Let no man therefore judge you in meat, or in drink, or in respect of an holyday, or of the new moon, or of the sabbath days, which are a shadow of things to come. Let no man beguile you of your reward in a voluntary humility and worshipping of angels, intruding into those things which he hath not seen, vainly puffed up by his fleshly mind. Wherefore if ye be dead with Christ from the rudiments of the world, why are ye subject to ordinances: touch not, taste not; handle not; which are all to perish with the using, after the commandments and doctrines of men?

If ye then be risen with Christ, seek those things which are above, where Christ sitteth on the right hand of God. Set your affections on things above, not on things on the earth. For ye are dead, and your life is hid with Christ in God. When Christ, who is our life, shall appear, then shall ye also appear with him in glory.

Mortify therefore your members which are upon the earth: fornication, uncleanness, inordinate affection, evil concupiscence, and covetousness, which is idolatry: for which things sake the wrath of God cometh on the children of disobedience; in the which ye also walked sometime, when ye lived in them.

But now ye also put off all these: anger, wrath, malice, blasphemy, filthy communication, out of your mouth. Lie not one to another, seeing ye have put off the old man with his deeds; and have put on the new man, which is renewed in knowledge after the image of him that created him; where there is neither Greek nor Jew, circumcision nor uncircumcision, Barbarian, Scythian, bond nor free: but Christ is all, and in all.

Put on therefore, as the elect of God, holy and beloved, bowels of mercies, kindness, humbleness of mind, meekness, longsuffering; forbearing one another, and forgiving one another, if any man have a quarrel against any: even as Christ forgave you, so also do ye.

And above all these things put on charity, which is the bond of perfectness. And let the peace of God rule in your hearts, to the which also ye are called in one body; and be ye thankful. Let the word of Christ dwell in you richly in all wisdom: teaching and admonishing one another in psalms and hymns and spiritual songs, singing with grace in your hearts to the Lord. And whatsoever ye do in word or deed, do all in the name of the Lord Jesus, giving thanks to God the Father by him.

Wives, submit yourselves unto your own husbands, as it is fit in the Lord.

Husbands, love your wives, and be not bitter against them.

Children, obey your parents in all things: for this is well pleasing unto the Lord.

Fathers, provoke not your children to anger, lest they be discouraged.

Servants, obey in all things your masters according to the flesh; not with eyeservice, as men pleasers; but in singleness of heart, fearing God; and whatsoever ye do, do it heartily, as to the Lord, and not unto men; knowing that of the Lord, ye shall receive the reward of the inheritance, for ye serve the Lord Christ. But he that doeth wrong shall receive for the wrong which he hath done; and there is no respect of persons.

Masters, give unto your servants that which is just and equal; knowing that ye also have a Master in heaven.

Continue in prayer, and watch in the same with thanksgiving; withal praying also for us, that God would open unto us a door of utterance, to speak the mystery of Christ, for which I am also in bonds, that I may make it manifest, as I ought to speak. Walk in wisdom toward them that are without, redeeming the time.

Let your speech be alway with grace, seasoned with salt, that ye may know how ye ought to answer every man.

All my state shall Tychicus declare unto you, who is a beloved brother, and a faithful minister and fellowservant in the Lord, whom I have sent unto you for the same purpose, that he might know your estate, and comfort your hearts; with Onesimus, a faithful and beloved brother, who is one of you. They shall make known unto you all things which are done here.

Luke, the beloved physician, and Demas, greet you.

When this epistle is read among you, cause that it be read also in the church of the Laodiceans; and that ye likewise read the epistle from Laodicea. And say to Archippus, "Take heed to the ministry which thou hast received in the Lord, that thou fulfil it."

The salutation by the hand of me, Paul. Remember my bonds.

Grace be with you. Amen.

Paul

(Written from Rome to the Colossians.)

Receive Him as a Brother Beloved

UNTO PHILEMON, OUR DEARLY BELOVED, AND FELLOWLABOURER,

GRACE TO YOU, and peace, from God our Father, and the Lord Jesus Christ. I thank my God making mention of thee always in my prayers, hearing of thy love and faith, which thou hast toward the Lord Jesus, and toward all saints.

We have great joy and consolation in thy love. Yet for love's sake, I beseech thee as Paul the aged, and now also a prisoner of Jesus Christ, I beseech thee for my son Onesimus, whom I have begotten in my bonds, who in time past was to thee unprofitable, but now profitable to thee and to me. Whom I have sent again, thou therefore receive him, that is mine own son. I would have retained him with me, that in thy stead he might have ministered unto me in the bonds of the gospel. But without thy mind would I do nothing, that thy benefit should not be as it were of necessity, but willingly.

Perhaps he departed for a season, that thou shouldest receive him for ever, not now as a servant, but above a servant, a brother beloved, specially to me, but how much more unto thee, both in the flesh and in the Lord? If thou count me therefore a partner, receive him as myself.

If he hath wronged thee, or oweth thee ought, put that on mine account: I Paul have written it with mine own hand, I will repay it. Albeit I do not say to thee how thou owest unto me even thine own self.

Having confidence in thy obedience I wrote unto thee, knowing that thou wilt also do more than I say. But withal prepare me also a lodging, for I trust that through your prayers I shall be given unto you.

The grace of our Lord Jesus Christ be with your spirit.

Amen.

Paul the Apostle

(Written from Rome.)

A Pattern of Good Works

To Titus, mine own son after the common faith:

Grace, mercy, and peace, from God the Father and the Lord Jesus Christ our Saviour! I left thee in Crete, that thou shouldest set in order the things that are wanting, and ordain elders in every city, as I had appointed thee; if any be blameless, the husband of one wife, having faithful children, not accused of riot or unruly. For a bishop must be blameless, as the steward of God: not selfwilled, not soon angry, not given to wine, no striker, not given to filthy lucre, but a lover of hospitality, a lover of good men, sober, just, holy, temperate; holding fast the faithful word as he hath been taught, that he may be able by sound doctrine both to exhort and to convince the gainsayers.

For there are many unruly and vain talkers and deceivers, specially they of the circumcision, whose mouths must be stopped, who subvert whole houses, teaching things which they ought not for filthy lucre's sake. Even one of their own prophets said, " The Cretians are always liars, evil beasts." This witness is true. Wherefore rebuke them sharply, that they may be sound in the faith, not giving heed to Jewish fables, and commandments of men, that turn from the truth.

Unto the pure all things are pure; but unto them that are defiled and unbelieving is nothing pure; but even their mind and conscience is defiled. They profess that they know God; but in works they deny him, being abominable, and disobedient, and unto every good work reprobate.

But speak thou the things which become sound doctrine:

That the aged men be sober, grave, temperate, sound in faith, in charity, in patience.

The aged women likewise; that they be in behaviour as becometh holiness, not false accusers, not given to much wine, teachers of good things;

That they may teach the young women to be sober, to love their husbands, to love their children, to be discreet, chaste, keepers at home, good, obedient to their own husbands, that the word of God be not blasphemed.

Young men likewise exhort to be sober minded.

In all things showing thyself a pattern of good works: in doctrine showing uncorruptness, gravity, sincerity, sound speech, that cannot be condemned; that he that is of the contrary part may be ashamed, having no evil thing to say of you.

Exhort servants to be obedient unto their own masters, and to please them well in all things; not answering again; not purloining, but showing all good fidelity; that they may adorn the doctrine of God our Saviour in all things.

For the grace of God that bringeth salvation hath appeared to all men, teaching us that denying ungodliness and worldly lusts, we should live soberly, righteously, and godly, in this present world; looking for that blessed hope, and the glorious appearing of the great God and our Saviour Jesus Christ, who gave himself for us, that he might redeem us from all iniquity, and purify unto himself a peculiar people, zealous of good works. These things speak, and exhort, and rebuke with all authority. Let no man despise thee.

Put them in mind to be subject to principalities and powers, to obey magistrates, to be ready to every good work, to speak evil of no man, to be no brawlers, but gentile, showing all meekness unto all men.

For we ourselves also were sometimes foolish, disobedient, deceived, serving divers lusts and pleasures, living in malice and envy, hateful, and hating one another.

But after that, the kindness and love of God our Saviour toward man appeared. Not by works of righteousness which we have done, but according to his mercy he saved us, by the washing of regeneration, and renewing of the Holy Ghost, which he shed on us abundantly through Jesus Christ our Saviour. That being justified by his grace, we should be made heirs according to the hope of eternal life. This is a faithful saying, and these things I will that thou affirm constantly, that they which have believed in God might be careful to maintain good works. These things are good and profitable unto men.

But avoid foolish questions and genealogies, and contentions, and strivings about the law; for they are unprofitable and vain. A man that is an heretick after the first and second admonition reject: knowing that he that is such is subverted, and sinneth, being condemned of himself.

When I shall send Artemas unto thee, or Tychicus, be diligent to come unto me to Nicopolis: for I have determined there to winter. Bring Zenas the lawyer and Apollos on their journey diligently that nothing be wanting to them. And let ours also learn to maintain good works, for necessary uses, that they be not unfruitful.

All that are with me salute thee. Greet them that love us in the faith.

Grace be to you all. Amen.

Paul the Apostle

(Written from Nicopolis of Macedonia.)

Lay Hold On Eternal Life

TIMOTHY, MY OWN SON IN THE FAITH:

GRACE, MERCY, AND PEACE, from God our Father and Jesus Christ our Lord.

I exhort that, first of all, supplications, prayers, intercessions, and giving of thanks, be made for all men; for kings, and for all that are in authority; that we may lead a quiet and peaceable life in all godliness and honesty. For this is good and acceptable in the sight of God our Saviour; who will have all men to be saved, and to come unto the knowledge of the truth. For there is one God, and one mediator between God and men, the man Jesus Christ; who gave himself a ransom for all, to be testified in due time. I will therefore that men pray everywhere, lifting up holy hands, without wrath and doubting.

Now the Spirit speaketh expressly, that in the latter times some shall depart from the faith, giving heed to seducing spirits, and doctrines of devils; speaking lies in hypocrisy; having their conscience seared with a hot iron. But we know that the law is good, if a man use it lawfully. If any man teach otherwise, and consent not to wholesome words, even the words of our Lord Jesus Christ, and to the doctrine which is according to godliness, he is proud, knowing nothing, but doting about questions and strifes of words, whereof cometh envy, strife, railings, evil surmisings, perverse disputings of men of corrupt minds, and destitute of the truth, supposing that gain is godliness: from such withdraw thyself.

But godliness with contentment is great gain. For we brought nothing into this world, and it is certain we can carry nothing out. And having food and raiment let us be therewith content.

But they that will be rich fall into temptation and a snare, and into many foolish and hurtful lusts, which drown men in destruction and perdition. For the love of money is the root of all evil: which while some coveted after, they have erred from the faith, and pierced themselves through with many sorrows.

But thou, O man of God, flee these things; and follow after righteousness, godliness, faith, love, patience, meekness. Charge them that are rich in this world, that they be not highminded, nor trust in uncertain riches, but in the living God, who giveth us richly all things to enjoy; that they do good, that they be rich in good works, ready to distribute, willing to communicate; laying up in store for themselves a good foundation against the time to come, that they may lay hold on eternal life.

Fight the good fight of faith, lay hold on eternal life, whereunto thou art also called, and hast professed a good profession before many witnesses. I give thee charge in the sight of God, who quickeneth all things, and before Christ Jesus, who before Pontius Pilate witnessed a good confession; that thou keep this commandment without spot, unrebukeable, until the appearing of our Lord Jesus Christ: which in his times he shall show, who is the blessed and only Potentate, the King of kings, and Lord of lords; who only hath immortality, dwelling in the light which no man can approach unto; whom no man hath seen, nor can see: to whom be honour and power everlasting.

O Timothy, keep that which is committed to thy trust; avoiding profane and vain babblings, and oppositions of science falsely so called: which some professing have erred concerning the faith.

Now unto the King, eternal, immortal, invisible, the only wise God, be honour and glory for ever and ever. Amen.

Paul, an apostle of Jesus Christ

(Written from Laodicea)

God Hath Given Us the Spirit of Power, and of Love, and of a Sound Mind

TO TIMOTHY, MY DEARLY BELOVED SON:

GRACE, MERCY, AND PEACE, from God the Father and Christ Jesus our Lord.

God hath not given us the spirit of fear; but of power, and of love, and of a sound mind. Thou therefore, my son, be strong in the grace that is in Christ Jesus. And the things that thou hast heard of me among many witnesses, the same commit thou to faithful men, who shall be able to teach others also. Consider what I say; and the Lord give thee understanding in all things.

Study to show thyself approved unto God, a workman that needeth not to be ashamed, rightly dividing the word of truth. But shun profane and vain babblings: for they will increase unto more ungodliness. Nevertheless the foundation of God standeth sure, having this seal, The Lord knoweth them that are his. And, let every one that nameth the name of Christ depart from iniquity.

But in a great house there are not only vessels of gold and of silver, but also of wood and of earth; and some to honour, and some to dishonour. If a man therefore purge himself from these, he shall be a vessel unto honour, sanctified, and meet for the master's use, and prepared unto every good work.

Flee also youthful lusts: but follow righteousness, faith, charity, peace, with them that call on the Lord out of a pure heart. But foolish and unlearned questions avoid, knowing that they do gender strifes. And the servant of the Lord must not strive; but be gentle unto all men, apt to teach, patient; in meekness instructing those that oppose themselves; if God peradventure will give them repentance to the acknowledging of the truth.

This know also, that in the last days perilous times shall come. For men shall be lovers of their own selves, covetous, boasters, proud, blasphemers, disobedient to parents, unthankful, unholy, without natural affection, trucebreakers, false accusers, incontinent, fierce, despisers of those that are good, traitors, heady, highminded, lovers of pleasures more than lovers of God; having a form of godliness, but denying the power thereof: from such turn away. For of this sort are they which creep into houses, and lead captive silly women laden with sins, led away with divers lusts, ever learning, and never able to come to the knowledge of the truth. But they shall proceed no further: for their folly shall be manifest unto all men.

But thou hast fully known my doctrine, manner of life, purpose, faith, longsuffering, charity, patience, persecutions, afflictions, which came unto me at Antioch, at Iconium, at Lystra; what persecutions I endured: but out of them all the Lord delivered me. Yea, and all that will live godly in Christ Jesus shall suffer persecution. But evil men and seducers shall wax worse and worse, deceiving, and being deceived.

But continue thou in the things which thou hast learned and hast been assured of, knowing of whom thou hast learned them; and that from a child thou hast known the holy scriptures, which are able to make thee wise unto salvation through faith which is in Christ Jesus. All scripture is given by inspiration of God, and is profitable for doctrine, for reproof, for correction, for instruction in righteousness: that the man of God may be perfect, throughly furnished unto all good works.

I charge thee therefore before God, and the Lord Jesus Christ, who shall judge the quick and the dead at his appearing and his kingdom: preach the word; be instant in season, out of season;

reprove, rebuke, exhort with all longsuffering and doctrine. For the time will come when they will not endure sound doctrine; but after their own lusts shall they heap to themselves teachers, having itching ears; and they shall turn away their ears from the truth, and shall be turned unto fables.

But watch thou in all things, endure afflictions, do the work of an evangelist, make full proof of thy ministry. For I am now ready to be offered, and the time of my departure is at hand. I have fought a good fight, I have finished my course, I have kept the faith: henceforth there is laid up for me a crown of righteousness, which the Lord, the righteous judge, shall give me at that day: and not to me only, but unto all them also that love his appearing.

Do thy diligence to come shortly unto me: for Damas hath forsaken me, having loved this present world, and is departed unto Thessalonica. Only Luke is with me. Take Mark and bring him with thee: for he is profitable to me for the ministry.

At my first answer no man stood with me, but all men forsook me: I pray God that it may not be laid to their charge. Notwithstanding the Lord stood with me, and strengthened me; that by me the preaching might be fully known, and that all the Gentiles might hear: and I was delivered out of the mouth of the lion. And the Lord shall deliver me from every evil work, and will preserve me unto his heavenly kingdom: to whom be glory for ever and ever.

Do thy diligence to come before winter. The Lord Jesus Christ be with thy spirit.

Grace be unto you, Amen.

Paul, an apostle of Jesus Christ

(Written from Rome when Paul was brought before Nero the second time.)

Put on the Whole Armour of God That Ye May Be Able to Stand

TO THE SAINTS WHICH ARE AT EPHESUS,

GRACE BE TO YOU, and peace, from God our Father, and from the Lord Jesus Christ. Blessed be the God and Father of our Lord Jesus Christ, who hath blessed us with all spiritual blessings in heavenly places in Christ, according as he hath chosen us in him before the foundation of the world, that we should be holy and without blame before him in love; in whom we have redemption through his blood, and the forgiveness of sins, according to the riches of his grace, wherein he hath abounded toward us in all wisdom and prudence.

Wherefore I also, after I heard of your faith in the Lord Jesus, and love unto all the saints, cease not to give thanks for you, making mention of you in my prayers; that the God of our Lord Jesus Christ, the Father of glory, may give unto you the spirit of wisdom, and revelation in the knowledge of him. And the eyes of your understanding being enlightened, that ye may know the exceeding greatness of his power which he wrought in Christ when he raised him from the dead, and set him at his own right hand in heavenly places, far above all principality, and power, and might, and dominion, not only in this world but also in that which is to come, and hath put all things under his feet.

And you hath he quickened, who were dead in trespasses and sins, wherein in time past, ye walked according to the course of this world, according to the prince of the power of the air, the spirit that now worketh in the children of disobedience. Among whom also we all had our conversation in times past in the lusts of our flesh, fulfilling the desires of the flesh and of the mind; and by nature were the children of wrath, even as others.

But God, who is rich in mercy, for his great love wherewith he loved us, even when we were dead in sins, hath quickened us together with Christ (by grace ye are saved), and hath raised us up together, and made us sit together in heavenly places in Christ Jesus, that in the ages to come he might show the exceeding riches of his grace in his kindness toward us through Christ Jesus.

By grace are ye saved through faith, and that not of yourselves, it is the gift of God; not by works, lest any man should boast. For we are his workmanship, created in Christ Jesus unto good works, which God hath before ordained that we should walk in them. Wherefore remember that in time past, ye were without Christ, having no hope, and without God in the world.

But now in Christ Jesus, ye who sometimes were far off are made nigh by the blood of Christ, for through him we have access by one Spirit unto the Father. Now therefore ye are no more strangers and foreigners, but fellowcitizens with the saints, and of the household of God, and are built upon the foundation of the apostles and prophets, Jesus Christ himself being the chief corner stone, in whom all the building fitly framed together groweth unto an holy temple in the Lord; in whom we also are builded together for an habitation of God through the Spirit.

For this cause I, Paul, am the prisoner of Jesus Christ for you Gentiles. Ye have heard of the dispensation of the grace of God, how that by revelation he made known unto me the mystery, which in other ages was not made known unto the sons of men, that the Gentiles should be fellow heirs, and partakers of his promise in Christ, whereof I was made a minister. Unto me, who am less than the least of the saints, is this grace given, that I should preach among the Gentiles the unsearchable riches of Christ. For this cause I bow my knees unto the Father of our Lord Jesus Christ, that he would grant you to be strengethened by his Spirit in the inner man, that Christ may dwell in your hearts by faith; that ye, being rooted and grounded in Love, may be able to comprehend with all saints what is the breadth, and length, and depth, and height; and to know the love of Christ which passeth knowledge, that ye might be filled with all the fulness of God.

I therefore, the prisoner of the Lord, beseech you that ye walk worthy of the vocation wherewith ye are called, with all lowliness and meekness, with longsuffering, forbearing one another in love; endeavouring to keep the unity of the Spirit in the bond of peace. There is one body, and one Spirit, even as ye are called in one hope of your calling: One Lord, one faith, one baptism, One God and Father of all, who is above all, and through all, and in you all.

But unto every one of us is given grace according to the measure of the gift of Christ. Wherefore he saith, when he ascended up on high, he led captivity captive, and gave gifts unto men. And he gave some, apostles; and some, prophets; and some, evangelists; and some, pastors and teachers; for the perfecting of the saints, for the work of the ministry, for the edifying of the body of Christ: Till we all come in the unity of the faith, and of the knowledge of the Son of God, unto a perfect man, unto the measure of the stature of the fulness of Christ.

This I say therefore, and testify in the Lord, that ye henceforth walk not as other Gentiles walk, in the vanity of their mind, having the understanding darkened, being alienated from the life of God through the ignorance that is in them, because of the blindness of their heart; that ye put off concerning the former conversation the old man, which is corrupt according to the deceitful lusts; and be renewed in the spirit of your mind; and that ye put on the new man, which after God is created in righteousness and true holiness. Wherefore putting away lying, speak every man truth with his neighbour: for ye are members one of another.

If ye be angry, let not the sun go down upon your wrath. Neither give place to the devil. Let him that stole steal no more, but rather let him labour, working with his hands the thing which is good, that he may have to give to him that needeth. Let no corrupt communication proceed out of your mouth. Let all bitterness, and wrath, and anger, and clamour, and evil speaking, be put away from you, with all malice. And be ye kind one to another, tenderhearted, forgiving one another, even as God for Christ's sake hath forgiven you.

Be ye therefore followers of God, as dear children; and walk in love, as Christ also hath loved us. But fornication, and all uncleanness, or covetousness, let it not once be named among you, as becometh saints; neither filthiness, nor foolish talking, nor jesting, but rather giving of thanks. Let no man deceive you with vain words; for because of these things cometh the wrath of God upon the children of disobedience. Be not ye therefore partakers with them.

Ye were sometimes darkness, but now are ye light in the Lord: walk as children of light. For the fruit of the Spirit is in all goodness and righteousness and truth; proving what is acceptable unto the Lord. And have no fellowship with the unfruitful works of darkness, but rather reprove them. For it is a shame even to speak of those things which are done of them in secret. But all things that are reproved are made manifest by the light: for whatsoever doth make manifest is Light. Wherefore he saith, "Awake thou that sleepest, and arise from the dead, and Christ shall give thee Light."

See then that ye walk circumspectly, not as fools, but as wise, redeeming the time, because the days are evil. Wherefore be ye not unwise, but understanding what the will of the Lord is. And be not drunk with wine, wherein is excess; but be filled with the Spirit, giving thanks always for all things unto God and the Father in the name of our Lord Jesus Christ, submitting yourselves one to another in the fear of God.

Wives submit yourselves unto your own husbands, as unto the Lord. For the husband is the head of the wife, even as Christ is the head of the church.

Husbands, love your wives, even as Christ also loved the church, and gave himself for it, so ought men to love their wives. He that loveth his wife loveth himself. For no man ever yet hated his own flesh, but nourisheth and cherisheth it, even as the Lord the church. For this cause shall a man leave his father and mother, and shall be joined unto his wife, and they two shall be one flesh. This is a great mystery: but I speak concerning Christ and the church. Nevertheless, let every one of you in particular so love his wife even as himself. And the wife see that she reverence her husband.

Children, obey your parents in the Lord: for this is right, "Honour thy father and mother," which is the first commandment with promise, "that it may be well with thee, and thou mayest live long on the earth." And, ye fathers, provoke not your children to wrath: but bring them up in the nurture and admonition of the Lord.

Servants, be obedient to them that are your masters, not with eyeservice, as men pleasers; but as servants of Christ, doing the will of God from the heart; with good will doing service, as to the Lord, and not to men, knowing that whatsoever good thing any man doeth, the same shall he receive of the Lord, whether he be bond or free.

And ye masters, do the same things unto them, forbearing threatening, knowing that your Master also is in heaven; neither is there respect of persons with him.

Finally, my brethren, be strong in the Lord, and in the power of his might. Put on the whole armour of God, that ye may be able to stand against the wiles of the devil. For we wrestle not against flesh and blood, but against principalities, against powers, against the rulers of the darkness of this world, against spiritual wickedness in high places.

Wherefore take unto you the whole armour of God, that ye may be able to withstand in the evil day, and having done all, to stand. Stand therefore, having your loins girt about with Truth, and having on the breastplate of righteousness; and your feet shod with the preparation of the gospel of peace; above all, taking the shield of faith, wherewith ye shall be able to quench all the fiery darts of the wicked. And take the helmet of salvation, and the sword of the Spirit, which is the word of God. And pray always with all prayer and supplication in the Spirit.

And pray for me, that utterance may be given unto me, that I may open my mouth boldly, to make known the mystery of the gospel, for which I am an ambassador in bonds: that therein I may speak boldly as I ought to speak.

But that ye may know my affairs, and how I do, Tychicus, a beloved brother and faithful minister in the Lord, shall make known to you all things. Him have I sent unto you, that ye might know our affairs, and that he might comfort your hearts.

Peace be to the brethren, and grace be with all them that love our Lord Jesus Christ in sincerity.

Now unto him that is able to do exceeding abundantly above all that we ask or think, according to the power that worketh in us, unto him be glory in the church by Christ Jesus throughout all ages, world without end. Amen.

Paul, an apostle of Jesus Christ

(Written from Rome)

(This letter is thought to have been posthumously edited by one of Paul's students.)

HEBREWS

A letter written from Italy

THE NEW COVENANT

" I will put my laws into their mind,
And write them in their hearts;
And I will be to them a God,
And they shall be to me a people."

The Word of God Is Quick and Powerful, and Is a Discerner of the Thoughts and Intents of the Heart

GOD, WHO at sundry times and in divers manners spake in time past unto the fathers by the prophets, hath in these last days spoken unto us by his Son, whom he hath appointed heir of all things. Who, being the brightness of his glory, and the express image of his person, and upholding all things by the Word of his power, when he had by himself purged our sins, sat down on the right hand of the Majesty on high. For he hath by inheritance obtained a more excellent name than the angels, for unto which of the angels said God at any time, "Thou art my son, this day have I begotten thee"? And unto the Son, he saith, "Thou hast loved righteousness, and hated iniquity; therefore God, even thy God, hath anointed thee with the oil of gladness above thy fellows." And to which of the angels said he at any time, "Sit on my right hand, until I make thine enemies thy footstool"? Are they not all ministering spirits, sent forth to minister for them who shall be heirs of salvation?

Therefore we ought to give the more earnest heed to the things which we have heard, lest at any time we should let them slip. For if the word spoken by angels was stedfast, and every transgression and disobedience received a just recompence of reward, how shall we escape, if we neglect so great salvation; which at the first began to be spoken by the Lord, and was confirmed unto us by them that heard him? God also bore them witness, both with signs and wonders, and with divers miracles, and gifts of the Holy Ghost, according to his own will.

For it became him, for whom are all things, and by whom are all things, in bringing many sons unto glory, to make the Captain of their salvation perfect through sufferings. For both he that sanctifieth and they who are sanctified are all One; for which cause he is not ashamed to call them brethren, saying, "I will declare thy name unto my brethren."

Forasmuch then as the children are partakers of flesh and blood, he also took part of the same, that through death he might destroy him that had the power of death, that is the devil, and deliver them who through fear of death were all their lifetime subject to bondage. For verily he took not on him the nature of angels, but he took on the seed of Abraham. Wherefore in all things it behoved him to be made like unto his brethren, that he might be a merciful and faithful high priest in things pertaining to God, to make reconciliation for the sins of the people. For in that he himself hath suffered being tempted, he is able to succour them that are tempted.

Wherefore, holy brethren, partakers of the heavenly calling, consider the Apostle and High Priest of our profession, Christ Jesus, who was faithful to him that appointed him, as also Moses was faithful in all his house. For this man was counted worthy of more glory than Moses, inasmuch as he who hath builded the house hath more honour than the house. For every house is builded by some man; but he that built all things is God. And Moses verily was faithful in all his house, as a servant, for a testimony of those things which were to be spoken after; but Christ as a son over his own house, whose house are we, if we hold fast the confidence and the rejoicing of the hope firm unto the end. Wherefore, as the Holy Ghost saith, "Today, if ye will hear his voice, harden not your hearts, as in the provocation, in the day of temptation in the wilderness."

Take heed, brethren, lest there be in any of you an evil heart of unbelief, in departing from the living God. But exhort one another daily, while it is called Today, lest any of you be hardened through the deceitfulness of sin. For we are made partakers of Christ, if we hold the beginning of our confidence steadfast unto the en… while it is said, "Today if ye will hear his voice, harden …ur hearts as in the provocation, for some, when they had …did provoke." So we see that they could not enter in b… unbelief.

Let us th… ear, lest, a promise being left us of entering into his …f you should seem to come short of it. For unto …gospel preached, as well as unto them; but the wo… did not profit them, not being mixed with faith …ard it. For we which have believed do enter into …but they to whom it was first preached entered not …f unbelief. There remaineth therefore a rest to the …God.

…labour therefore to enter into that rest, lest any man …r the same example of unbelief. For the word of God is quick, and powerful, and sharper than any twoedged sword, piercing even to the dividing asunder of soul and spirit, and of the joints and marrow, and is a discerner of the thoughts and intents of the heart.

Christ, an High Priest of Good Things to Come

SEEING THEN that we have a great high priest, that is passed into the heavens, Jesus the Son of God, let us hold fast our profession. For we have not an high priest which cannot be touched with the feeling of our infirmities; but was in all points tempted like as we are, yet without sin. Let us therefore come boldly unto the throne of grace, that we may obtain mercy, and find grace to help in time of need.

For every high priest taken from among men is ordained for men in things pertaining to God, that he y offer both gifts and sacrifices for sins. And no man taketh thi Sour unto himself, but he that is called of God, as was Aaron. Christ glorified not himself to be made an high priest, but he unto him, "Thou art my Son, today have I begotten the he saith also in another place, "Thou art a priest for ever yder of Melchisedec."

Though he were a son, yet learned he obedience by which he suffered; and being made perfect, he be author of eternal salvation unto all them that obey him, c God an high priest after the order of Melchisedec. Of who have many things to say, and hard to understand, seeing ye dull of hearing. For when ye ought to be teachers, ye ha need that one teach you the first principles of the oracles of God, since you have become such as have need of milk, and not of strong meat. For everyone that useth milk is unskilful in the word of righteousness; for he is a babe. But strong meat belongeth to full grown men, even those who by reason of use have their senses exercised to discern both good and evil.

Wherefore leaving the principles of the doctrine of Christ, let us go on unto full growth, not laying again a foundation – of repentance from dead works, and of faith toward God, of the doctrine of baptisms, and of laying on of hands, and of resurrection of the dead, and of eternal judgment. And this we will do, if God permit. For it is impossible for those who were once enlightened, and have tasted of the heavenly gift, and were made partakers of the Holy Ghost, and have tasted the good word of God, and the powers of the world to come, if they shall fall away, to renew them again unto repentance, seeing they crucify to themselves the Son of God afresh, and put him to an open shame.

For the earth, which drinketh in the rain that cometh oft upon it, and bringeth forth herbs meet for them by whom it is dressed, receiveth blessing from God; but that which beareth thorns and briers is rejected, and is nigh unto cursing; whose end is to be burned. But, beloved, we are persuaded better things of you, and things that accompany salvation, though we thus speak. For God is not unrighteous to forget your work and labour of love, which ye have showed toward his name, in that ye have ministered to the saints, and do minister.

And we desire that every one of you do show the same diligence to the full assurance of hope unto the end: that ye be not slothful, but followers of them who through faith and patience inherit the promises. For in God we have a strong consolation, who have fled for refuge to lay hold upon the hope set before us: which hope we have as an anchor of the soul sure and stedfast, and which entereth into that within the veil; whither the forerunner is for us entered, even Jesus, made an high priest for ever after the order of Melchisedec.

For this Melchisedec, king of Salem, priest of the most high God, who met Abraham returning from the slaughter of the kings, and blessed him, to whom also Abraham gave a tenth part of all, first being by interpretation King of righteousness, and after that also King of Salem, which is King of peace, without father, without mother, without descent, having neither beginning of days, nor end of life, but made like unto the Son of God, abideth a priest continually. Now consider how great this man was, unto whom even the patriarch Abraham gave the tenth of the spoils. And verily they that are of the sons of Levi, who receive the office of the priesthood, have a commandment to take tithes of the people. But he whose descent is not counted from them received tithes of Abraham, and blessed him that had the promises.

If therefore perfection were by the Levitical priesthood, for under it the people received the law, what further need was there that another priest should rise after the order of Melchisdec, and not be called after the order of Aaron? For the priesthood being changed, there is made of necessity a change of the law. For he of whom these things are spoken pertaineth to another tribe, of which no man gave attendance at the altar. For it is evident that our Lord sprang out of Juda; of which tribe Moses spake nothing concerning priesthood. And it is yet far more evident for after the similitude of Melchisedec there ariseth another priest, who is made, not after the law of a carnal commandment, but after the power of an endless life. For he testifieth, "Thou art a priest for ever after the order of Melchisedec." For there is a disannulling of a foregoing commandment because of its weakness and unprofitableness, for the law made nothing perfect. But the bringing in of a better hope did, by the which we draw nigh unto God.

And by this was Jesus made a surety of a better testament, because he continueth ever, and hath an unchangeable priesthood. Wherefore he is able to save them to the uttermost that come unto God by him, seeing he ever liveth to make intercession for them. And such an high priest, who is holy, harmless, undefiled, separate from sinners, and made higher than the heavens, needeth not daily, as those high priests, to offer up sacrifice, first for his own sins, and then for the people's, for this he did once when he offered up himself. For the law maketh men high priests which have infirmity; but the word of the oath, which was after the law, appointeth a Son, perfected for evermore.

Now of the things which we have spoken this is the sum: We have an high priest, who is set on the right hand of the throne of the Majesty in the heavens: A minister of the sanctuary, and of the true tabernacle, which the Lord pitched, and not man. And he hath obtained a more excellent ministry, because he is the mediator of a better covenant, which was established upon better promises. For if that first covenant had been faultless, then should no place have been sought for the second.

For finding fault with them, he saith, "Behold, the days come, saith the Lord, when I will make a new covenant with the house of Israel, and with the house of Judah: not according to the covenant that I made with their fathers in the day when I took them by the hand to lead them out of the land of Egypt, because they continued not in my covenant, and I regarded them not, saith the Lord. For this is the covenant that I will make with the house of Israel after those days, saith the Lord; I will put my laws into their mind, and write them in their hearts; and I will be to them a God, and they shall be to me a people. And they shall not teach every man his neighbour, and every man his brother, saying, 'Know the Lord:' for they all shall know me, from the least to the greatest. For I will be merciful to their unrighteousness, and their sins and their iniquities will I remember no more." In saying, "A new covenant," he hath made the first old, and that which is old is ready to vanish away.

The first covenant had also ordinances of divine service, and a worldly sanctuary. But Christ being come an high priest of good things to come, by a greater and more perfect tabernacle, not made with hands, that is to say, not of this building, neither by the blood of goats and calves, but by his own blood, he entered in once into the holy place, having obtained eternal redemption for us. For if the blood of bulls and of goats, and the ashes of an heifer sprinkling the unclean, sanctifieth to the purifying of the flesh, how much more shall the blood of Christ, who through the eternal Spirit offered himself without spot to God, purge your conscience from dead works to serve the living God? and for this cause he is the mediator of the New Testament. For Christ is not entered into the holy places made with hands, but into heaven itself, now to appear in the presence of God for us. Not that he should offer himself often, as the high priest entereth into the holy place every year with blood of others, but once he appeared to put away sin by the sacrifice of himself; for Christ was offered once to bear the sins of many.

For the law having the shadow of good things to come, and not the very image of the things, can never with those sacrifices which they offered year by year continually, make the comers thereunto perfect. Because the worshippers once purged should have no more consciousness of sins. For in those sacrifices there is remembrance again made of sins every year. For it is not possible that the blood of bulls and of goats should take away sins. Wherefore, when Christ cometh into the world, he saith, "Sacrifice and offering thou wouldest not; in burnt offerings and sacrifices for sin, thou hast had no pleasure. Then said I, 'Lo, I come, (in the volume of the book it is written of me,) I come to do thy Will, O God.'"

By which Will we are sanctified through the offering of the body of Jesus Christ once for all. Every priest standeth daily ministering and offering oftentimes the same sacrifices, which can never take away sins. But this man, after he had offered one sacrifice for sins for ever, sat down on the right hand of God. Whereof the Holy Ghost also is a witness to us, for he said, "This is the covenant that I will make with them after those days," saith the Lord, "I will put my laws into their hearts, and in their minds will I write them; and their sins and their iniquities will I remember no more." Now where remission of these is, there is no more offering for sin.

Faith Is the Substance of Things Hoped for, the Evidence of Things Not Seen

HAVING THEREFORE, brethren, boldness to enter into the holiest by the blood of Jesus, by a new and living Way which he hath consecrated for us, through the veil, that is to say, his flesh, and having an high priest over the house of God, let us draw near with a true heart in full assurance of faith, having our hearts sprinkled from an evil conscience, and our bodies washed with pure water. Let us hold fast the profession of our faith without wavering, for he is faithful that promised.

Cast not away therefore your confidence, which hath great recompence of reward. For ye have need of patience, that, after ye have done the will of God, ye might receive the promise. For yet a little while, and he that shall come, will come, and will not tarry. Now the just shall live by faith: but if any man draw back, my soul shall have no pleasure in him. But we are not of them who draw back unto perdition; but of them that believe to the saving of the soul.

Now faith is the substance of things hoped for, the evidence of things not seen. For by it the elders obtained a good report. Through faith we understand that the worlds were framed by the word of God, so that things which are seen were not made of things which do appear.

By faith Abel offered unto God a more excellent sacrifice than Cain, by which he obtained witness that he was righteous, God testifying of his gifts.

By faith Enoch was translated that he should not see death; and was not found, because God had translated him: for before his translation he had this testimony, that he pleased God. But without faith it is impossible to please him: for he that cometh to God must believe that he is, and that he is a rewarder of them that diligently seek him.

By faith Noah, being warned of God of things not seen as yet, moved with fear, prepared an ark to the saving of his house; by which he condemned the world, and became heir of the righteousness which is by faith.

By faith Abraham, when he was called to go out into a place which he should after receive for an inheritance, obeyed; and he went out, not knowing whither he went. By faith he sojourned in the land of promise, as in a strange country, dwelling in tabernacles with Isaac and Jacob, the heirs with him of the same promise: for he looked for a city which hath foundations, whose builder and maker is God. Through faith also Sara herself received strength to conceive, and was delivered of a child when she was past age, because she judged him faithful who had promised. Therefore sprang of Abraham so many as the stars of the sky in multitude, and as the sand which is by the sea shore, innumerable. By faith Abraham, when he was tried, offered up Isaac: he that had received the promises offered up his only begotten son, of whom it was said, "In Isaac shall all thy seed be called," accounting that God was able to raise him up, even from the dead, from whence also he received him in a figure.

By faith Moses, when he was born, was hid three months by his parents, when they saw that he was a goodly child, and they were not afraid of the king's commandment. By faith Moses, when he was come to years, refused to be called the son of Pharaoh's daughter, choosing rather to suffer affliction with the people of God, than to enjoy the pleasures of sin for a season. Esteeming the reproach of Christ greater riches than the treasures of Egypt: for he had respect unto the recompence of the reward. By faith he forsook Egypt, not fearing the wrath of the king;

for he endured, as seeing him who is invisible. By faith they passed through the Red sea as on dry land, which the Egyptians attempting to do were drowned. By faith the walls of Jericho fell down after they were compassed about seven days.

And what shall I more say? for the time would fail to tell of Gideon, and of Barak, and of Samson, and of Jephtha; of David also, and Samuel, and of the prophets: who through faith subdued kingdoms, wrought righteousness, obtained promises, stopped the mouths of lions, quenched the violence of fire, escaped the edge of the sword, out of weakness were made strong, waxed valiant in fight, turned to flight the armies of the aliens. Women received their dead raised to life again; and others were tortured, not accepting deliverance, that they might obtain a better resurrection. And others had trial of cruel mockings and scourgings, yea, moreover of bonds and imprisonment. They were stoned, they were sawn asunder, were tempted, were slain with the sword; they wandered about in sheepskins and goatskins, being destitute, afflicted, tormented: of whom the world was not worthy.

Wherefore seeing we are compassed about with so great a cloud of witnesses, let us lay aside every weight, and the sin which doth so easily beset us, and let us run with patience the race that is set before us, looking unto Jesus the author and finisher of our faith: who for the joy that was set before him endured the cross, despising the shame, and is set down at the right hand of the throne of God. Consider him that endured such contradiction of sinners against himself, lest ye be wearied and faint in your minds. Ye have not resisted unto blood, striving against sin.

And ye have forgotten the exhortation which speaketh unto you as unto children, "My son, despise not thou the chastening of the Lord, nor faint when thou art rebuked of him: for whom the Lord loveth he chasteneth, and scourgeth every son whom he receiveth." If ye endure chastening, God dealeth with you as with sons; for what son is he whom the father chasteneth not? Furthermore we have had fathers of our flesh which corrected us, and we gave them reverence: shall we not much rather be in subjection unto the Father of spirits, and live? For they verily for a few days chastened us after their own pleasure; but he for our profit, that we might be partakers of his holiness. Now no chastening for the present seemeth to be joyous, but grievous: nevertheless afterward it yieldeth the peaceable fruit of righteousness unto them which are exercised thereby. And make straight paths for your feet, lest that which is lame be turned out of the way; but let it rather be healed. Follow peace with all men, and holiness, without which no man shall see the Lord, looking diligently lest any man fail of the grace of God; lest any root of bitterness springing up trouble you, and thereby many be defiled.

For ye are not come unto the mount that might be touched, and that burned with fire, nor unto blackness, and darkness, and tempest, and the sound of a trumpet, and the voice of words; which voice they that heard intreated that the word should not be spoken to them any more, for they could not endure that which was commanded. And so terrible was the sight that Moses said, "I exceedingly fear and quake." But ye are come unto mount Sion, and unto the city of the living God, the heavenly Jerusalem, and to an innumerable company of angels. And to Jesus the mediator of the new covenant. See that ye refuse not him that speaketh, for if we turn away from him that speaketh from heaven, whose voice then shook the earth, but now he hath promised, saying, "Yet once more I shake not the earth only, but also heaven." And this word, "Yet once more," signifieth the removing of those things that are shaken, as of things that are made, that those things which cannot be shaken may remain. Wherefore we receiving a kingdom which cannot be moved, let us have grace whereby we may serve God acceptably with reverence and godly fear: for our God is a consuming fire.

Let brotherly love continue. Be not forgetful to entertain strangers: for thereby some have entertained angels unaware. Remember them that are in bonds, and them which suffer adversity.

Let your conversation be without covetousness; and be content with such things as ye have: for he hath said, "I will never leave thee, nor forsake thee." So that we may boldly say, "The Lord is my helper, and I will not fear what man shall do unto me."

Be not carried about with divers and strange doctrines. For it is a good thing that the heart be established with grace.

Jesus Christ is the same yesterday, and today, and for ever. By him therefore let us offer the sacrifice of praise to God continually; that is, the fruit of our lips giving thanks to his name.

Now the God of peace, that brought again from the dead our Lord Jesus, that great shepherd of the sheep, through the blood of the everlasting covenant, make you perfect in every good work to do his will, working in you that which is wellpleasing in his sight, through Jesus Christ: to whom be glory for ever and ever.

Grace be with you all. Amen.

(Written to the Hebrews from Italy.)

(This letter was attributed to Paul, but many scholars believe it to be the work of some other author.)

LETTERS OF JAMES

A Servant of God and of the Lord
Jesus Christ

To the Twelve Tribes Which Are Scattered
Abroad, Greeting

Be Ye Doers of the Word

MY BRETHREN, count it all joy when ye fall into divers temptations, knowing this, that the trying of your faith worketh patience. But let patience have her perfect work, that ye may be perfect and entire, wanting nothing.

If any of you lack wisdom, let him ask of God, that giveth to all men liberally, and upbraideth not, and it shall be given him. But let him ask in faith, nothing wavering. For he that wavereth is like a wave of the sea driven with the wind and tossed. For let not that man think that he shall receive any thing of the Lord. A double-minded man is unstable in all his ways.

Blessed is the man that endureth temptation: for when he is tried, he shall receive the crown of life, which the Lord hath promised to them that love him. Let no man say when he is tempted, "I am tempted of God," for God cannot be tempted with evil, neither tempteth he any man. But every man is tempted, when he is drawn away of his own lust, and enticed. Then when lust hath conceived, it bringeth forth sin; and sin, when it is finished, bringeth forth death.

Do not err, my beloved brethren. Every good gift and every perfect gift is from above, and cometh down from the Father of lights, with whom is no variableness, neither shadow of turning. Wherefore, my beloved brethren, let every man be swift to hear, slow to speak, slow to wrath; for the wrath of man worketh not the righteousness of God. Wherefore lay apart all filthiness, and superfluity of naughtiness, and receive with meekness the ingrafted word, which is able to save your souls.

But be ye doers of the word, and not hearers only, deceiving your own selves. For if any be a hearer of the word, and not a doer, he is like unto a man beholding his natural face in a glass, for he beholdeth himself, and goeth his way, and straightway forgetteth what manner of man he was. But whoso looketh into the perfect law of liberty, and continueth therein, he being not a forgetful hearer, but a doer of the word, this man shall be blessed in his deed.

If any man among you seem to be religious, and bridleth not his tongue, but deceiveth his own heart, this man's religion is vain. Pure religion and undefiled before God and the Father is this: To visit the fatherless and widows in their affliction, and to keep himself unspotted from the world.

Respect of Persons

MY BRETHREN, have not the faith of our Lord Jesus Christ, the Lord of glory, with respect of persons. For if there come unto your assembly, a man with a gold ring, in goodly apparel, and there come in also a poor man in vile raiment, and ye have respect to him that weareth the gay clothing, and say unto him, "Sit thou here in a good place," and to the poor, "Stand thou there, or sit here under my footstool," are ye not then partial in yourselves, and are become judges of evil thoughts? Hearken, my beloved brethren, hath not God chosen the poor of this world, rich in faith, and heirs of the kingdom which he hath promised to them that love him? But ye have despised the poor.

If ye fulfil the royal law according to the scripture, "Thou shalt love thy neighbour as thyself," ye do well. But if ye have respect to persons, ye commit sin, and are convinced of the law as transgressors. For whosoever shall keep the whole law, and yet offend in one point, he is guilty of all. For he that said, "Do not commit adultery," said also, "Do not kill." Now if thou commit no adultery, yet if thou kill, thou art become a transgressor of the law. So speak ye and so do as they that shall be judged by the law of liberty. For he shall have judgment without mercy that hath showed no mercy.

Faith Without Works Is Dead

WHAT DOTH IT PROFIT, my brethren, though a man say he hath faith, and have not works? can faith save him? If a brother or sister be naked, and destitute of daily food, and one of you say unto them, "Depart in peace, be ye warmed and filled," notwithstanding ye give them not those things which are needful to the body, what doth it profit? Even so faith, if it hath not works, is dead, being alone.

Yea, a man may say, "Thou hast faith, and I have works; show me thy faith without thy works, and I will show thee my faith by my works." Thou believest that there is one God; thou doest well; the devils also believe, and tremble. But wilt thou know, O vain man, that faith without works is dead? Was not Abraham our father justified by works when he had offered Isaac his son upon the altar? Seest thou how faith wrought with his works, and by works was faith made perfect. And the scripture was fulfilled, which saith, "Abraham believed God, and it was imputed unto him for righteousness; and he was called the Friend of God."

Ye see then how that by works a man is justified, and not by faith only. For as the body without the spirit is dead, so faith without works is dead also.

Offend Not in Word

My Brethren,

If any man offend not in word, the same is a perfect man, and able also to bridle the whole body. Behold, we put bits in the horses' mouths, that they may obey us; and we turn about their whole body. Behold also the ships, which, though they be so great, and are driven of fierce winds, yet are they turned about with a very small helm whithersoever the governor listeth. Even so the tongue is a little member and boasteth great things. Behold, how great a matter a little fire kindleth!

And the tongue is a fire, a world of iniquity; so is the tongue among our members, that it defileth the whole body, and setteth on fire the course of nature. For every kind of beasts, and of birds, and of serpents, and of things in the sea, is tamed, and hath been tamed of mankind. But the tongue can no man tame; it is an unruly evil, full of deadly poison. Therewith bless we God, even the Father; and therewith curse we men, which are made after the similitude of God. Out of the same mouth proceedeth blessing and cursing. My brethren, these things ought not so to be. Doth a fountain send forth at the same place sweet water and bitter? Can the fig tree, my brethren, bear olive berries? either a vine, figs? so can no fountain both yield salt water and fresh.

Who is a wise man and endued with knowledge among you? Let him show out of a good conversation his works with meekness of wisdom. But if ye have bitter envying and strife in your hearts, glory not, and lie not against the truth. This wisdom descendeth not from above, but is earthly, sensual, devilish. For where envying and strife is, there is confusion and every evil work. But the wisdom that is from above is first pure, then peaceable, gentle, and easy to be entreated, full of mercy and good fruits, without partiality, and without hypocrisy. And the fruit of righteousness is sown in peace of them that make peace.

From Whence Come Wars?

FROM WHENCE come wars and fighting among you? come they not hence, even of your lusts that war in your members? Ye lust and have not; ye kill, and desire to have, and cannot obtain; ye fight and war, yet ye have not, because ye ask not. Ye ask and receive not, because ye ask amiss, that ye may consume it upon your lusts.

Ye adulterers and adulteresses know ye not that the friendship of the world is enmity with God? Whosoever therefore will be a friend of the world is the enemy of God. Do ye think that the scripture saith in vain, " The spirit that dwelleth in us lusteth to envy? " God resisteth the proud, but giveth grace unto the humble. Submit yourselves therefore to God. Resist the devil, and he will flee from you. Draw nigh to God, and he will draw nigh to you. Cleanse your hands, ye sinners, and purify your hearts, ye double-minded. Humble yourselves in the sight of the Lord, and he shall lift you up.

Speak not evil one of another, brethren. He that speaketh evil of his brother, and judgeth his brother, speaketh evil of the law, and judgeth the law; but if thou judge the law, thou art not a doer of the law, but a judge. There is one lawgiver, who is able to save, and to destroy; who art thou that judgest another? Grudge not one against another, brethren, lest ye be condemned. Behold, the Judge standeth before the door. Therefore to him that knoweth to do good, and doeth it not, to him it is sin.

Prayer Availeth Much

Is any among you afflicted? let him pray. Is any merry? let him sing psalms. Is any sick among you? let him call for the elders of the church, and let them pray over him, anointing him with oil in the name of the Lord. And the prayer of faith shall save the sick, and the Lord shall raise him up; and if he have committed sins, they shall be forgiven him. Confess your faults one to another, and pray one for another, that ye may be healed. The effectual fervent prayer of a righteous man availeth much. Elijah was a man subject to like passions as we are, and he prayed earnestly that it might not rain; and it rained not on the earth by the space of three years and six months. And he prayed again, and the heaven gave rain, and the earth brought forth her fruit.

Brethren, if any of you do err from the truth, and one convert him, let him know, that he which converteth the sinner from the error of his way shall save a soul from death, and shall hide a multitude of sins.

JUDE, THE SERVANT OF JESUS CHRIST,
AND THE BROTHER OF JAMES

To Them That Are Sanctified by God the Father,
And Preserved in Jesus Christ

Unto Him That Is Able to Keep You from Falling

UNTO THEM THAT ARE SANCTIFIED BY GOD THE FATHER:

MERCY UNTO YOU, and peace, and love be multiplied. Beloved, when I gave all diligence to write unto you of the common salvation, it was needful for me to write unto you, and exhort you that ye should earnestly contend for the faith which was once delivered unto the saints.

For there are certain men crept in unawares, ungodly men, turning the grace of our God into lasciviousness, and denying the only Lord God, and our Lord Jesus Christ. These speak evil of those things which they know not; but what they know naturally, as brute beasts, in those things they corrupt themselves. Woe unto them! For they have gone in the way of Cain, and ran greedily after the error of Balaam for reward. These are spots in your feasts of charity, when they feast with you, feeding themselves without fear: clouds they are without water carried about by winds; trees whose fruit withereth, without fruit, twice dead, plucked up by the roots; raging waves of the sea, foaming out their own shame; wandering stars, to whom is reserved the blackness of darkness for ever. These are murmurers, complainers, walking after their own lusts; and their mouth speaketh great swelling words, having men's persons in admiration because of advantage.

But, beloved, remember ye the words which were spoken before by the apostles of our Lord Jesus Christ, how that they told you there should be mockers in the last time, who should walk after their own ungodly lusts. These be they who are sensual, and separate themselves, having not the Spirit. But ye, beloved, build up yourselves on your most holy faith, praying in the Holy Ghost. Keep yourselves in the love of God, looking for the mercy of our Lord Jesus Christ unto eternal life.

And on some have compassion, making a difference; and others save with fear, pulling them out of the fire; hating even the garment spotted by the flesh.

Now unto him that is able to keep you from falling, and to present you faultless before the presence of his glory with exceeding joy, to the only wise God our Saviour, be glory and majesty, dominion and power, both now and ever. Amen.

Jude, the servant of Jesus Christ

LETTERS OF SIMON PETER

A Servant and Apostle of Jesus Christ

We, according to the promise,
look for new heavens, and a new earth
wherein dwelleth righteousness.

Be Ye Holy

GRACE UNTO YOU, AND PEACE BE MULTIPLIED:

BLESSED BE THE God and Father of our Lord Jesus Christ, which, according to his abundant mercy, hath begotten us again unto a lively hope by the resurrection of Jesus Christ from the dead, to an inheritance incorruptible, and undefiled, and that fadeth not away, reserved in heaven for you. Wherein ye greatly rejoice, though now for a season (if need be) ye are in heaviness through manifold temptations, that the trial of your faith, being much more precious than of gold that perisheth, though it be tried with fire, might be found unto praise, and honour, and glory, at the appearing of Jesus Christ; whom having not seen, ye love; in whom, though now ye see him not, yet believing, ye rejoice with joy unspeakable, and full of glory.

Wherefore gird up the loins of your mind, be sober, and hope to the end for the grace that is to be brought unto you at the revelation of Jesus Christ; as obedient children, not fashioning yourselves according to the former lusts in your ignorance, but as he which hath called you is holy, so be ye holy in all manner of conversation; because it is written, "Be ye holy; for I am holy."

And if ye call on the Father, who without respect of persons judgeth according to every man's work, pass the time of your sojourning here in fear. Forasmuch as ye know that ye were not redeemed with corruptible things, as silver and gold, from your vain conversation, received by tradition from your fathers, but with the precious blood of Christ, as of a lamb without blemish and without spot. Who verily was fore-ordained before the foundation of the world, but was manifest in these last times for you, who by him do believe in God, that raised him up from the dead, and gave him glory; that your faith and hope might be in God.

Seeing ye have purified your souls in obeying the truth through the Spirit unto unfeigned love of the brethren, see that ye love one another with a pure heart fervently; being born again, not of corruptible seed, but of incorruptible, by the word of God, which liveth and abideth for ever. For all flesh is as grass, and all the glory of man as the flower of grass. The grass withereth, and the flower thereof falleth away; but the word of the Lord endureth for ever. And this is the word which by the gospel is preached unto you. Wherefore, laying aside all malice, and all guile, and hypocrisies, and envies, and all evil-speakings, as new-born babes, desire the sincere milk of the word, that ye may grow thereby.

If so be ye have tasted that the Lord is gracious, to whom coming as unto a living stone, disallowed indeed of men, but chosen of God, and precious, ye also, as lively stones, are built up a spiritual house, an holy priesthood, to offer up spiritual sacrifices, acceptable to God by Jesus Christ.

By Your Good Works, Glorify God

YE ARE A chosen generation, an holy nation, a peculiar people; ye should show forth the praises of him who hath called you out of darkness into his marvellous light. Dearly beloved, I beseech you, as strangers and pilgrims, abstain from fleshly lusts, which war against the soul; having your conversation honest among the Gentiles, that, whereas they speak against you as evildoers, they may by your good works, which they shall behold, glorify God in the day of visitation. For so is the will of God, that with well-doing ye may put to silence the ignorance of foolish men.

Servants, be subject to your masters with all fear; not only to the good and gentle, but also to the froward. For this is thankworthy, if a man for conscience toward God endure grief, suffering wrongfully. For what glory is it, if, when ye be buffeted for your faults, ye shall take it patiently? but if, when ye do well, and suffer for it, ye take it patiently, this is acceptable with God. For even hereunto were ye called: because Christ also suffered for us, leaving us an example, that ye should follow his steps; who did no sin, neither was guile found in his mouth; who, when he was reviled, reviled not again; when he suffered, he threatened not; but committed himself to him that judgeth righteously; who his own self bare our sins, that we being dead to sins, should live unto righteousness; by whose stripes ye were healed. For ye were as sheep going astray; but are now returned unto the Shepherd.

Be ye all of one mind, having compassion one of another; love as brethren, be pitiful, be courteous; not rendering evil for evil, or railing for railing; but contrariwise, blessing; knowing that ye are thereunto called, that ye should inherit a blessing. For he that will love life, and see good days, let him refrain his tongue from evil, and his lips that they speak no guile; let him eschew evil and do good; let him seek peace, and ensue it. For the eyes of the Lord are over the righteous, and his ears are open unto their prayers; but the face of the Lord is against them that do evil.

And who is he that will harm you, if ye be followers of that which is good? But if ye suffer for righteousness' sake, happy are ye; and be not afraid of their terror, neither be troubled; but sanctify the Lord God in your hearts; and be ready always to give an answer to every man that asketh you a reason of the hope that is in you, with meekness and fear. Having a good conscience, that, whereas they speak evil of you, as of evildoers, they may be ashamed that falsely accuse your good conversation in Christ. For it is better, if the will of God be so, that ye suffer for well-doing, than for evil-doing. For Christ also hath once suffered for sins, the just for the unjust, that he might bring us to God, being put to death in the flesh, but quickened by the Spirit. Forasmuch then as Christ hath suffered for us in the flesh, arm yourselves likewise with the same mind.

But the end of all things is at hand; be ye therefore sober, and watch unto prayer. And above all things have fervent charity among yourselves. Use hospitality one to another without grudging. As every man hath received the gift, even so minister the same one to another, as good stewards of the manifold grace of God. If any man speak, let him speak as the oracles of God; if any man minister, let him do it as of the ability which God giveth; that God in all things may be glorified through Jesus Christ; to whom be praise and dominion for ever and ever.

Beloved, think it not strange, concerning the fiery trial which is to try you, as though some strange thing happened unto you; but rejoice, inasmuch as ye are partakers of Christ's sufferings; that, when his glory shall be revealed, ye may be glad also with exceeding joy. If ye be reproached for the name of Christ, happy are ye; for the Spirit of glory and of God resteth upon you. Wherefore, let them that suffer according to the will of God, commit the keeping of their souls to him in well-doing, as unto a faithful Creator.

Feed the flock of God which is among you, taking the oversight thereof, not by constraint, but willingly; not for filthy lucre, but of a ready mind; neither as being lords over God's heritage, but being ensamples to the flock. And when the chief Shepherd shall appear, ye shall receive a crown of glory that fadeth not away. Humble yourselves therefore under the mighty hand of God, that he may exalt you in due time; casting all your care upon him, for he careth for you.

Be sober, be vigilant; because your adversary the devil, as a roaring lion, walketh about, seeking whom he may devour; whom resist steadfast in the faith, knowing that the same afflictions are accomplished in your brethren that are in the world. But the God of all grace, who hath called us unto his eternal glory by Christ Jesus, after that ye have suffered awhile, make you perfect, stablish, strengthen, settle you. To him be glory and dominion for ever and ever. Amen.

Be Partakers of the Divine Nature

GRACE AND PEACE be multiplied unto you through the knowledge of God, and of Jesus our Lord, according as his divine power hath given unto us all things that pertain unto life and godliness, through the knowledge of him that hath called us to glory and virtue. Whereby are given unto us exceeding great and precious promises; that by these ye might be partakers of the divine nature, having escaped the corruption that is in the world through lust.

And beside this giving all diligence, add to your faith, virtue; and to virtue, knowledge; and to knowledge, temperance; and to temperance, patience; and to patience, godliness; and to godliness, brotherly kindness; and to brotherly kindness charity. For if these things be in you, and abound, they make you that ye shall neither be barren nor unfruitful in the knowledge of our Lord Jesus Christ. But he that lacketh these things is blind, and cannot see afar off, and hath forgotten that he was purged from his old sins. Wherefore the rather, brethren, give diligence to make your calling and election sure; for if ye do these things, ye shall never fall; for so an entrance shall be ministered unto you abundantly into the everlasting kingdom of our Lord and Saviour Jesus Christ.

For we have not followed cunningly devised fables, when we made known unto you the power and coming of our Lord Jesus Christ, but were eye-witnesses of his majesty. For he received from God the Father honour and glory, when there came such a voice to him from the excellent glory, "This is my beloved Son, in whom I am well pleased." And this voice which came from heaven we heard, when we were with him in the holy mount.

We have also a more sure word of prophecy; whereunto ye do well that ye take heed, as unto a light that shineth in a dark place, until the day dawn, and the day-star arise in your hearts; knowing this first, that no prophecy of the scripture is of any private interpretation. For the prophecy came not in old time by the will of man; but holy men of God spake as they were moved by the Holy Ghost.

But there were false prophets also among the people, even as there shall be false teachers among you, who privily shall bring in damnable heresies, even denying the Lord that bought them, and bring upon themselves swift destruction. And many shall follow their pernicious ways; by reason of whom the way of truth shall be evil spoken of. And through covetousness shall they with feigned words make merchandise of you. These are wells without water, clouds that are carried with a tempest; to whom the mist of darkness is reserved for ever. For it had been better for them not to have known the way of righteousness, than, after they have known it, to turn from the holy commandment delivered unto them.

Beloved, I now write unto you, that ye may be mindful of the words which were spoken before by the holy prophets, and of the commandment of us the apostles of the Lord and Saviour; knowing this first, that there shall come in the last days scoffers, walking after their own lusts, and saying, "Where is the promise of his coming? for since the fathers fell asleep, all things continue as they were from the beginning of the creation." But, beloved, be not ignorant of this one thing, that one day is with the Lord as a thousand years, and a thousand years as one day. The Lord is not slack concerning his promise, as some men count slackness; but is long-suffering to us-ward, not willing that any should perish, but that all should come to repentance. But the day of the Lord will come as a thief in the night; in the which the heavens shall pass away with a great noise, and the elements shall melt with fervent heat, the earth also and the works that are therein shall be burned up.

Seeing then that all these things shall be dissolved, what manner of persons ought ye to be in all holy conversation and godliness, looking for and hasting unto the coming of the day of God, wherein the heavens being on fire shall be dissolved, and the elements shall melt with fervent heat? Nevertheless we, according to his promise, look for new heavens, and a new earth, wherein dwelleth righteousness. Wherefore, beloved, seeing that ye look for such things, be diligent that ye may be found of him in peace, without spot, and blameless.

Ye therefore, beloved, seeing ye know these things before, beware lest ye also, being led away with the error of the wicked, fall from your own steadfastness. But grow in grace, and in the knowledge of our Lord and Saviour Jesus Christ. To him be glory both now and for ever. Amen.

LETTERS OF JOHN

The Beloved Disciple

I write unto you, fathers, because ye have known
Him that is from the beginning;

I write unto you, young men, because ye are strong,
and the word of God abideth in you;

I write unto you, little children, because ye have
known the Father;

And these things write we unto you that your joy
may be full.

LIGHT

GOD IS LIGHT, and in him is no darkness at all. This is the message which we have heard of him and declare unto you.

If we say that we have fellowship with him, and walk in darkness, we lie, and do not the truth; but if we walk in the light, as he is in the light, we have fellowship one with another.

A new commandment I write unto you, which thing is true in him and in you: because the darkness is past, and the true light now shineth.

He that saith he is in the light, and hateth his brother, is in darkness even until now. He that loveth his brother abideth in the light, and there is none occasion of stumbling in him. But he that hateth his brother is in darkness, and walketh in darkness, and knoweth not whither he goeth, because that darkness hath blinded his eyes.

SPIRIT

BELOVED, believe not every spirit, but try the spirits whether they are of God, because many false prophets are gone out into the world. Hereby know ye the Spirit of God: every spirit that confesseth that Jesus Christ is come in the flesh is of God. And every spirit that confesseth not that Jesus Christ is come in the flesh is not of God; and this is that spirit of antichrist, whereof ye have heard that it should come; and even now already is it in the world.

Ye are of God, little children, and have overcome them; because greater is he that is in you, than he that is in the world. They are of the world; therefore speak they of the world, and the world heareth them.

We are of God; hereby know we that we dwell in him, and he in us because he hath given us of his Spirit. And it is the Spirit that beareth witness, because the Spirit is truth.

LIFE

THAT WHICH WAS from the beginning, which we have heard, which we have seen with our eyes, which we have looked upon, and our hands have handled of the Word of life, that which we have seen and heard declare we unto you, that ye also may have fellowship with us: and truly our fellowship is with the Father, and with his Son Jesus Christ. For the life was manifested, and we have seen it, and bear witness, and show unto you that eternal life which was with the Father, and was manifested unto us.

And this is the record, that God hath given to us eternal life, and this life is in his Son. He that hath the Son hath life; and he that hath not the Son of God hath not life.

These things have I written unto you that believe on the name of the Son of God; that ye may know that ye have eternal life, and that ye may believe on the name of the Son of God. And we know that the Son of God is come, and hath given us an understanding, that we may know him that is true, and we are in him that is true, even in his Son Jesus Christ. This is the true God, and eternal life. And this is the promise that he hath promised us, even eternal life.

TRUTH

WE HAVE AN UNCTION from the Holy One, and understand all things. I have not written unto you because ye know not the truth, but because ye know it, and that no lie is of the truth.

Brethren, I write no new commandment unto you, but an old commandment which ye had from the beginning. The old commandment is the word which ye had from the beginning. And hereby we do know that we know him if we keep his commandments. He that saith, "I know him," and keepeth not his commandments is a liar, and the truth is not in him. But whoso keepeth his word in him verily is the love of God perfected. And hereby we know that we are of the truth, and shall assure our hearts before him. And whatsoever we ask, we receive of him, because we keep his commandments and do those things that are pleasing in his sight.

We are of God: he that knoweth God heareth us; he that is not of God heareth not us. Hereby know we the spirit of truth and the spirit of error. And it is the Spirit that beareth witness, because the Spirit is truth.

LOVE

BELOVED,

LET US LOVE one another, for love is of God, and every one that loveth is born of God, and knoweth God. He that loveth not, knoweth not God, for God is love.

In this was manifested the love of God toward us, because God sent his only begotten Son into the world, that we might live through him. Herein is love, not that we loved God, but that he loved us, and sent his son to be the propitiation for our sins.

Hereby know we that we dwell in him, and he in us because he hath given us of his Spirit. And we have known and believed the love that God hath to us. God is love: and he that dwelleth in love dwelleth in God, and God in him. Herein is our love made perfect, that we may have boldness in the day of judgment: because as he is, so are we in this world.

There is no fear in love, but perfect love casteth out fear, because fear hath torment. He that feareth is not made perfect in love.

We love him because he first loved us. And this is love, that we walk after his commandment. This is the commandment, that, as ye have heard from the beginning, ye should walk in it.

LOVE ONE ANOTHER

BELOVED,

IF GOD so loved us, we ought also to love one another. No man hath seen God at any time. If we love one another, God dwelleth in us, and his love is perfected in us. If a man say, " I love God," and hateth his brother, he is a liar; for he that loveth not his brother whom he hath seen, how can he love God whom he hath not seen?

Whosoever hateth his brother, is a murderer. For he that hateth his brother is in darkness, and walketh in darkness, and knoweth not whither he goeth, because that darkness hath blinded his eyes. For this is the message that ye heard from the beginning, that we should love one another. And whoso hath this world's good, and seeth his brother have need, and shutteth up his bowels of compassion from him, how dwelleth the love of God in him?

And this commandment have we from him: That he who loveth God, love his brother also. By this we know that we love the children of God, when we love God, and keep his commandments. For this is the love of God, that we keep his commandments, and his commandments are not grievous.

My little children, let us not love in word, neither in tongue, but in deed, and in truth.

LOVE NOT THE WORLD

LOVE NOT the world, neither the things that are in the world. If any man love the world, the love of Father is not in him. For all that is in the world, the lust of the flesh, and the lust of the eyes, and the pride of life, is not of the Father, but is of the world.

And the world passeth away, and the lust thereof; but he that doeth the will of God abideth for ever.

HE THAT DOETH GOOD IS OF GOD

MY LITTLE CHILDREN,

THESE THINGS write I unto you, that ye sin not. And if any man sin, we have an advocate with the Father, Jesus Christ the righteous. And he is the propitiation for our sins; and not for ours only, but also for the sins of the whole world. And hereby we know that we know him, if we keep his commandments.

Little children, let no man deceive you; he that doeth righteousness is righteous, even as he is righteous. Whosoever is born of God doth not commit sin; and he cannot sin, because he is born of God. In this the children of God are manifest; whosoever doeth not righteousness is not of God, neither he that loveth not his brother.

All unrighteousness is sin. Whosoever committeth sin transgresseth also the law; for sin is the trangression of the law. He that saith, " I know him," and keepeth not his commandments, is a liar, and the truth is not in him. He that saith he abideth in him ought himself also so to walk, even as he walked. Whosoever abideth in him sinneth not; whosoever sinneth hath not seen him neither known him.

Beloved, follow not that which is evil, but that which is good. He that doeth good is of God; but he that doeth evil hath not seen God. And now, little children, abide in him. And whatsoever we ask, we receive of him because we keep his commandments, and do those things that are pleasing in his sight.

JESUS CHRIST, THE SON OF GOD

WE HAVE SEEN and do testify that the Father sent the Son to be the Saviour of the world. Whosoever shall confess that Jesus is the Son of God, God dwelleth in him, and he in God. Whosoever believeth that Jesus is the Christ is born of God.

For whatsoever is born of God overcometh the world; and this is the victory that overcometh the world, even our faith. Who is he that overcometh the world, but he that believeth that Jesus is the Son of God?

He that believeth on the Son of God hath the witness in himself; he that believeth not God, hath made him a liar, because he believeth not the record that God gave of his Son. Who is a liar but he that denieth that Jesus is the Christ? He is antichrist, that denieth the Father and the Son. Whosoever denieth the Son, the same hath not the Father: but he that acknowledgeth the Son hath the Father also.

We know that the Son of God is come, and hath given us an understanding, that we may know him that is true, and we are in him that is true, even in his Son Jesus Christ. This is the true God, and eternal life.

Whosoever transgresseth, and abideth not in the doctrine of Christ, hath not God. He that abideth in the doctrine of Christ, he hath both the Father and the Son.

Let that therefore abide in you which ye have heard from the beginning. If that which ye have heard from the beginning shall remain in you, ye also shall continue in the Son and in the Father.

NOW ARE WE THE SONS OF GOD

BEHOLD, what manner of love the Father hath bestowed upon us, that we should be called the sons of God; therefore the world knoweth us not, because it knew him not.

Beloved, now are we the sons of God, and it doth not yet appear what we shall be; but we know that, when he shall appear, we shall be like him, for we shall see him as he is. And every man that hath this hope in him purifieth himself, even as he is pure.

THE BOOK OF REVELATION

THE REVELATION

of

JESUS CHRIST

Which God gave Him, and He sent
by His Angel unto His Servant

JOHN

Blessed is he that readeth,

And they that hear

The words of the prophecy,

And keep the things which are written therein:

FOR THE TIME IS AT HAND!

He That Hath an Ear, Let Him Hear What the Spirit Saith unto the Churches

JOHN TO THE SEVEN CHURCHES WHICH ARE IN ASIA:

GRACE BE UNTO YOU and peace, from him which is, and which was, and which is to come; and from the seven Spirits which are before the throne; and from Jesus Christ who is the faithful witness, and the first begotten of the dead, and the prince of the kings of the earth. Unto him that loved us, and washed us from our sins in his own blood, and hath made us kings and priests unto God and his Father: To him be glory and dominion forever and ever.

Behold, he cometh with clouds; and every eye shall see him, and they also which pierced him; and all kindreds of the earth, shall wail because of him. "I am Alpha and Omega, the beginning and the ending," saith the Lord, which is, and which was, and which is to come, the Almighty.

I, John, who am your brother, and companion in tribulation, and in the kingdom, and patience of Jesus Christ, was in the isle of Patmos, for the word of God, and for the testimony of Jesus Christ.

I was in the spirit on the Lord's day, and I heard behind me a great voice, as of a trumpet, saying, "I am Alpha and Omega, the first and the last; and what thou seest, write in a book, and send it unto the seven churches which are in Asia."

And I turned to see the voice that spake with me. And being turned, I saw seven golden candlesticks; and in the midst of the seven candlesticks one like unto the Son of man, clothed with a garment down to the foot, and girt about the paps with a golden girdle. His head and his hairs were white like wool, as white as snow; and his eyes were as a flame of fire; and his feet like unto fine brass, as if they burned in a furnace; and his voice as the sound of many waters. And he had in his right hand seven stars; and out of his mouth went a sharp twoedged sword; and his countenance was as the sun shineth in his strength.

And when I saw him I fell at his feet as dead, and he laid his right hand upon me saying unto me, "Fear not. I am he that liveth, and was dead; and, behold, I am alive for ever more, and have the keys of hell and of death. Write the things which thou hast seen, and the things which are, and the things which shall be hereafter: the mystery of the seven stars which thou sawest in my right hand, and the seven golden candlesticks. The seven stars are the angels of the seven churches; and the seven candlesticks which thou sawest are the seven churches.

I

"Unto the angel of the church of Ephesus write: 'These things saith he that holdeth the seven stars in his right hand, who walketh in the midst of the seven golden candlesticks, I know thy works, and thy labour, and thy patience, and how thou canst not bear them which are evil; and thou hast tried them which say they are apostles, and are not, and hast found them liars; and hast borne, and hast patience, and for my name's sake hast laboured, and hast not fainted.

"'Nevertheless, I have somewhat against thee, because thou hast left thy first love. Remember therefore from whence thou art fallen, and repent, and do the first works; or else I will come unto thee quickly, and will remove thy candlestick out of his place, except thou repent. But this thou hast, that thou hatest the deeds of the Nicolaitanes, which I also hate.

" 'He that hath an ear, let him hear what the Spirit saith unto the churches: To him that overcometh will I give to eat of the tree of life, which is in the midst of the paradise of God.' "

II

"And unto the angel of the church in Smyrna write: 'These things saith the first and the last, which was dead, and is alive;

" 'I know thy works, and tribulation, and poverty; (but thou art rich) and I know the blasphemy of them which say they are Jews, and are not, but are the synagogue of Satan. Fear none of those things which thou shalt suffer: behold, the devil shall cast some of you into prison, that ye may be tried; and ye shall have tribulation ten days: be thou faithful unto death, and I will give thee a crown of life.

" 'He that hath an ear, let him hear what the Spirit saith unto the churches: He that overcometh shall not be hurt of the second death.' "

III

"And to the angel of the church in Pergamos write: 'These things saith he which hath the sharp sword with two edges: I know thy works, and where thou dwellest, even where Satan's seat is, and thou holdest fast my name, and hast not denied my faith, even in those days wherein Antipas was my faithful martyr, who was slain among you where Satan dwelleth.

" 'But I have a few things against thee, because thou hast there them that hold the doctrine of Balaam, who taught Balac to cast a stumblingblock before the children of Israel, to eat things sacrificed unto idols, and to commit fornication. So hast thou also them that hold the doctrine of the Nicolaitanes, which thing I hate. Repent! or else I will come unto thee quickly, and will fight against them with the sword of my mouth.

" 'He that hath an ear, let him hear what the Spirit saith unto the churches: To him that overcometh will I give to eat of the hidden manna, and will give him a white stone, and in the stone a new name written, which no man knoweth saving he that receiveth it.' "

IV

"And unto the angel of the church in Thyatira write: 'These things saith the Son of God, who hath his eyes like unto a flame of fire, and his feet are like fine brass; I know thy works, and charity, and service, and faith, and thy patience, and thy works, and the last to be more than the first.

" 'Notwithstanding I have a few things against thee, because thou sufferest that woman Jezebel, which calleth herself a prophetess, to teach and to seduce my servants to commit fornication, and to eat things sacrificed unto idols. And I gave her space to repent of her fornication, and she repented not. Behold, I will cast her into a bed, and them that commit adultery with her into great tribulation, except they repent of their deeds. And I will kill her children with death; and all churches shall know that I am he which searcheth the reins and hearts: and I will give unto every one of you according to your works. But unto you I say, and unto the rest in Thyatira, as many as have not this doctrine, and which have not known the depths of Satan as they speak, I will put upon you none other burden. But that which ye have already hold fast till I come.

" 'And he that overcometh, and keepeth my works unto the end, to him will I give power over the nations: And he shall rule them with a rod of iron, as the vessels of a potter shall they be broken to shivers, even as I received of my Father. And I will give him the morning star. He that hath an ear, let him hear what the Spirit saith unto the churches.' "

V

"And unto the angel of the church in Sardis write: 'These things saith he that hath the seven Spirits of God, and the Seven Stars: I know thy works, that thou hast a name that thou livest, and art dead.

"'Be watchful, and strengthen the things which remain, that are ready to die; for I have not found thy works perfect before God. Remember therefore how thou hast received and heard, and hold fast, and repent. If therefore thou shalt not watch, I will come on thee as a thief, and thou shalt not know what hour I will come upon thee. Thou hast a few names even in Sardis which have not defiled their garments; and they shall walk with me in white: for they are worthy.

"'He that overcometh, the same shall be clothed in white raiment; and I will not blot out his name out of the book of life, but I will confess his name before my Father, and before his angels. He that hath an ear, let him hear what the Spirit saith unto the churches.'"

VI

"And to the angel of the church in Philadelphia write: 'These things saith he that is holy, he that is true, he that hath the key of David, he that openeth, and no man shutteth, and shutteth, and no man openeth:

"'I know thy works: behold, I have set before thee an open door, and no man can shut it; for thou hast a little strength, and hast kept my word, and hast not denied my name. Behold, I will make them of the synagogue of Satan which say they are Jews, and are not, but do lie; behold, I will make them to come and worship before thy feet, and to know that I have loved thee. Because thou hast kept the word of my patience, I also will keep thee from the hour of temptation, which shall come upon all the world, to try them that dwell upon the earth. Behold, I come quickly: hold that fast which thou hast, that no man take thy crown.

"'Him that overcometh will I make a pillar in the temple of my God, and he shall go no more out: and I will write upon him the name of my God, and the name of the city of my God, which is new Jerusalem, which cometh down out of heaven from my God: and I will write upon him my new name. He that hath an ear, let him hear what the Spirit saith unto the churches.' "

VII

"And unto the angel of the church of the Laodiceans write: 'These things saith the Amen, the faithful and true witness, the beginning of the creation of God:

" 'I know thy works, that thou art neither cold nor hot; I would thou wert cold or hot. So then because thou art lukewarm, and neither cold nor hot, I will spue thee out of my mouth. Because thou sayest, "I am rich, and increased with goods, and have need of nothing;" and knowest not that thou art wretched, and miserable, and poor, and blind, and naked. I counsel thee to buy of me gold tried in the fire, that thou mayest be rich; and white raiment that thou mayest be clothed, and that the shame of thy nakedness do not appear; and anoint thine eyes with eyesalve, that thou mayest see. As many as I love, I rebuke and chasten: be zealous therefore and repent. Behold, I stand at the door and knock: if any man hear my voice, and open the door, I will come in to him, and will sup with him, and he with me.

" 'To him that overcometh will I grant to sit with me in my throne, even as I also overcame, and am set down with my Father in his throne. He that hath an ear, let him hear what the Spirit saith unto the churches.' "

HOLY, HOLY, HOLY, LORD GOD ALMIGHTY WHICH WAS, AND IS, AND IS TO COME

AFTER THIS I looked, and behold, a door was opened in heaven: and the first voice which I heard was as it were of a trumpet talking with me, which said, "Come up hither, and I will show thee things which must be hereafter."

And immediately I was in the spirit: and behold, a throne was set in heaven, and One sat on the throne. And he that sat was to look upon like a jasper and a sardus stone; and there was a rainbow round about the throne, in sight like unto an emerald.

And round about the throne were four and twenty seats; and upon the seats I saw four and twenty elders sitting, clothed in white raiment; and they had on their heads crowns of gold.

And out of the throne proceeded lightnings and thunderings and voices: and there were seven lamps of fire burning before the throne, which are the seven Spirits of God.

And before the throne there was a sea of glass like unto crystal; and in the midst of the throne, and round about the throne were four beasts. And the first beast was like a lion, and the second beast was like a calf, and the third beast had a face as a man, and the fourth beast was like a flying eagle. And the four beasts had each of them six wings about him; and they were full of eyes within: and they rest not day and night, saying, "Holy, holy, holy, Lord God Almighty, which was, and is, and is to come."

And when those beasts give glory and honour and thanks to him that sat on the throne, who liveth forever and ever, the four and twenty elders fall down before him that sat on the throne, and worship him that liveth for ever and ever, and cast their crowns before the throne, saying, "Thou art worthy, O Lord, to receive glory and honour and power: for thou hast created all things, and for thy pleasure they are and were created."

And I saw in the right hand of him that sat on the throne a book written within and on the backside, sealed with seven seals. And I saw a strong angel proclaiming with a loud voice, "Who is worthy to open the book, and to loose the seals thereof?"

And no man in heaven, nor in earth, neither under the earth, was able to open the book, neither to look thereon. And I wept much, because no man was found worthy to open and to read the book, neither to look thereon. And one of the elders saith unto me, "Weep not: behold, the Lion of the tribe of Juda, the Root of David, hath prevailed to open the book, and to loose the seven seals thereof."

And I beheld, and, lo, in the midst of the throne and of the four beasts, and in the midst of the elders, stood a Lamb as it had been slain, having seven horns and seven eyes, which are seven Spirits of God sent forth into all the earth. And he came and took the book out of the right hand of him that sat upon the throne. And when he had taken the book, the four beasts and the four and twenty elders fell down before the Lamb, having every one of them harps, and golden vials full of odours, which are the prayers of saints. And they sang a new song, saying, "Thou art worthy to take the book, and to open the seals thereof: for thou wast slain, and hast redeemed us to God by thy blood out of every kindred, and tongue, and people, and nation; and hast made us unto our God kings and priests: and we shall reign on the earth."

THE LAMB IS WORTHY TO OPEN THE SEVEN SEALS

AND I BEHELD, and I heard the voice of many angels round about the throne, and the beasts, and the elders: and the number of them was ten thousand times ten thousand, and thousands of thousands, saying with a loud voice, "Worthy is the Lamb that was slain to receive power, and riches, and wisdom, and strength, and honour, and glory and blessing."

And every creature which is in heaven, and on the earth, and under the earth, and such as are in the sea, and all that are in them, heard I saying, "Blessing, and honour, and glory, and power, be unto him that sitteth upon the throne, and unto the Lamb for ever and ever." And the beasts said, "Amen." And the four and twenty elders fell down and worshipped him that liveth for ever and ever.

And I saw when the Lamb opened one of the seals, and I heard, as it were the noise of thunder, one of the beasts saying, "Come and see." And I saw, and behold a white horse: and he that sat on him had a bow; and a crown was given unto him: and he went forth conquering, and to conquer.

And when he had opened the second seal, I heard the second beast say, "Come and see." And there went out another horse that was red: and power was given to him that sat thereon to take peace from the earth, and that they should kill one another: and there was given unto him a great sword.

And when he had opened the third seal, I heard the third beast say, " Come and see." And I beheld, and lo, a black horse and he that sat on him had a pair of balances in his hand. And I heard a voice in the midst of the four beasts say, "A measure of wheat for a penny, and three measures of barley for a penny; and see thou hurt not the oil and the wine."

And when he had opened the fourth seal, I heard the voice of the fourth beast say, " Come and see." And I looked, and behold a pale horse: and his name that sat on him was Death, and Hell followed with him. And power was given them over the fourth part of the earth, to kill with sword, and with hunger, and with death, and with the beasts of the earth.

And when he had opened the fifth seal, I saw under the altar the souls of them that were slain for the word of God, and for the testimony which they held. And they cried with a loud voice, saying, " How long, O Lord, holy and true, dost thou not judge and avenge our blood on them that dwell on the earth? " And white robes were given unto every one of them; and it was said unto them, that they should rest yet a little season, until their fellow-servants also and their brethren, that should be killed as they were should be fulfilled.

And I beheld when he had opened the sixth seal, and lo, there was a great earthquake; and the sun became black as sackcloth of hair, and the moon became as blood; and the stars of heaven fell unto the earth, even as a fig tree casteth her untimely figs, when she is shaken of a mighty wind. And the heaven departed as a scroll when it is rolled together; and every mountain and island were moved out of their places. And the kings of the earth, and the great men, and the rich men, and the chief captains, and the mighty men, and every bondman, and every free man, hid themselves in the dens and in the rocks of the mountains; and said to the mountains and rocks, " Fall on us, and hide us from the face of him that sitteth on the throne, and from the wrath of the Lamb; for the great day of his wrath is come, and who shall be able to stand? "

And after these things I saw four angels standing on the four corners of the earth, holding the four winds of the earth, that the wind should not blow on the earth, nor on the sea, nor on any tree.

And I saw another angel ascending from the east, having the seal of the living God: and he cried with a loud voice to the four angels to whom it was given to hurt the earth and the sea, saying, " Hurt not the earth neither the sea, nor the trees, till we have sealed the servants of our God in their foreheads."

And I heard the number of them which were sealed: and there were sealed an hundred and forty and four thousand of all the children of Israel.

After this I beheld, and, lo, a great multitude, which no man could number, of all nations, and kindreds, and people, and tongues, stood before the throne, and before the Lamb, clothed with white robes, and palms in their hands, and cried with a loud voice, saying, " Salvation to our God which sitteth upon the throne, and unto the Lamb."

And all the angels stood round about the throne, and about the elders and the four beasts, and fell before the throne on their faces, and worshipped God, saying, "Amen! Blessing and glory, and wisdom, and thanksgiving, and honour, and power, and might, be unto our God for ever and ever. Amen."

And one of the elders answered, saying unto me, " What are these which are arrayed in white robes, and whence came they? "

And I said unto him, " Sir, thou knowest."

And he said unto me, " These are they which came out of great tribulation, and have washed their robes, and made them white in the blood of the Lamb. Therefore are they before the throne of God, and serve him day and night in his temple; and he that sitteth on the throne shall dwell among them. They shall hunger no more, neither thirst any more, neither shall the sun strike upon them, for the Lamb shall be their Shepherd, and shall lead them unto living fountains of waters; and God shall wipe all tears from their eyes."

And when he had opened the seventh seal, there was silence in heaven about the space of half an hour.

SEVEN TRUMPETS SOUND

And I saw the seven angels which stood before God; and to them were given seven trumpets.

And another angel came and stood at the altar, having a golden censer; and there was given unto him much incense, that he should offer it with the prayers of all saints upon the golden altar which was before the throne. And the smoke of the incense, which came with the prayers of the saints, ascended up before God out of the angel's hand.

And the angel took the censer, and filled it with fire of the altar, and cast it into the earth: and there were voices, and thunderings, and lightnings, and an earthquake. And the seven angels which had the seven trumpets prepared themselves to sound.

The first angel sounded, and there followed hail and fire mingled with blood, and they were cast upon the earth: and the third part of trees was burnt up, and all the green grass was burnt up.

And the second angel sounded, and as it were a great mountain burning with fire was cast into the sea: and the third part of the sea became blood; and the third part of the creatures which were in the sea, and had life, died; and the third part of the ships were destroyed.

And the third angel sounded, and there fell a great star from heaven, burning as it were a lamp, and it fell upon the third part of the rivers, and upon the fountains of waters; and the name of the star is called wormwood: and the third part of the waters became wormwood; and many died of the waters, because they were made bitter.

And the fourth angel sounded, and the third part of the sun was smitten, and the third part of the moon, and the third part of the stars; so the third part of them was darkened, and the day shone not for a third part of it, and the night likewise.

And I beheld, and heard an eagle flying through the midst of heaven, saying with a loud voice, "Woe, Woe, Woe, to the inhabitants of the earth by reason of the other voices of the trumpet of the three angels, which are yet to sound!"

And the fifth angel sounded, and I saw a star fall from heaven unto the earth: and to him was given the key to the bottomless pit. And he opened the bottomless pit, and there arose a smoke out of the pit, as the smoke of a great furnace; and the sun and the air were darkened by reason of the smoke of the pit. And there came out of the smoke locusts upon the earth: and unto them was given power, as the scorpions of the earth have power. And it was commanded them that they should not hurt the grass of the earth, neither any green thing, neither any tree; but only those men which have not the seal of God in their foreheads. And to them it was given that they should not kill them, but that they should be tormented five months; and their torment was as the torment of a scorpion, when he striketh a man. And in those days shall men seek death, and shall not find it; and shall desire to die, and death shall flee from them.

One woe is past; and, behold there come two woes more hereafter.

And the sixth angel sounded, and I heard a voice from the four horns of the golden altar which is before God, saying to the sixth angel which had the trumpet, "Loose the four angels which are bound in the great river Euphrates." And the four angels were loosed which were prepared for an hour, and a day, and a month, and a year, for to slay the third part of men.

And I saw in the vision, an army of horsemen and them that sat on them having breastplates of fire, and of jacinth, and brimstone; and the heads of the horses were as the heads of lions; and out of their mouths issued fire and smoke and brimstone. By these was the third part of men killed, by the fire, and by the smoke, and by the brimstone which issued out of their mouths. For their power is in their mouth, and in their tails: for their tails were like unto serpents, and had heads, and with them they do hurt.

And the rest of the men which were not killed by these plagues yet repented not of the works of their hands, that they should not worship devils, and idols of gold, and silver, and brass, and stone, and wood, which neither can see, nor hear, nor walk. Neither repented they of their murders, nor of their sorceries, nor of their fornications, nor of their thefts.

The Little Book

And I saw another mighty angel come down from heaven, clothed with a cloud: and a rainbow was upon his head, and his face was as it were the sun, and his feet as pillars of fire. And he had in his hand a little book open; and he set his right foot upon the sea, and his left foot upon the earth. And he cried with a loud voice, as when a lion roareth; and when he had cried, seven thunders uttered their voices. And when the seven thunders had uttered their voices, I was about to write: and I heard a voice from heaven saying unto me, "Seal up those things which the seven thunders uttered, and write them not."

And the angel which I saw stand upon the sea and upon the earth lifted up his hand to heaven, and sware by him that liveth for ever and ever, who created Heaven, and the things that therein are, and the earth, and the things that therein are, and the sea, and the things which are therein, that there should be time no longer. But in the days of the voice of the seventh angel, when he shall begin to sound, the mystery of God should be finished, as he hath declared to his servants the prophets.

And the voice which I heard from heaven spake unto me again, and said, "Go and take the little book which is open in the hand of the angel which standeth upon the sea and upon the earth."

And I went unto the angel, and said unto him, "Give me the little book."

And he said unto me, "Take it, and eat it up; and it shall make thy belly bitter, but it shall be in thy mouth sweet as honey." And I took the little book out of the angel's hand, and ate it up; and it was in my mouth sweet as honey: and as soon as I had eaten it, my belly was bitter.

And he said unto me, "Thou must prophesy again before many peoples, and nations, and tongues, and kings."

The Reed Like a Rod

And there was given me a reed like unto a rod: and the angel stood, saying, "Rise and measure the temple of God, and the altar, and them that worship therein. But the court which is without the temple leave out, and measure it not; for it is given unto the Gentiles; and the holy city shall they tread under foot forty and two months.

"And I will give power unto my two witnesses, and they shall prophesy a thousand two hundred and threescore days, clothed in sackcloth. These are the two olive trees, and the two candlesticks standing before the God of the earth. And if any man will hurt them, fire proceedeth out of their mouth, and devoureth their enemies: and if any man will hurt them, he must in this manner be killed. These have power to shut heaven, that it rain not in the days of their prophecy, and have power over the waters to turn them to blood, and to smite the earth with all plagues, as often as they will.

"And when they shall have finished their testimony, the beast that ascendeth out of the bottomless pit shall make war against them, and shall overcome them, and kill them. And their dead bodies shall lie in the street of the great city which is called Sodom and Egypt, where also our Lord was crucified. And they of the people and kindreds and tongues and nations shall see their dead bodies three days and a half, and shall not suffer their dead bodies to be put in graves. And they that dwell upon the earth shall rejoice over them, and make merry, and shall send gifts one to another; because these two prophets tormented them that dwell on the earth.

"And after three days and a half the Spirit of Life from God entered into them, and they stood upon their feet; and great fear fell upon them which saw them. And they heard a great voice from heaven saying unto them, 'Come up hither.' And they ascended up to heaven in a cloud; and their enemies beheld them. And the same hour was there a great earthquake, and the tenth part of the city fell, and in the earthquake were slain of men seven thousand; and the remnant were affrighted, and gave glory to the God of heaven."

The second woe is past; and behold, the third woe cometh quickly.

And the seventh angel sounded; and there were great voices in heaven, saying, "The kingdoms of this world are become the kingdoms of our Lord, and of his Christ; and he shall reign for ever and ever."

And the four and twenty elders which sat before God on their seats, fell upon their faces, and worshipped God, saying,

"We give thee thanks, O Lord God Almighty, which art, and wast, and art to come: because thou hast taken to thee thy great power, and hast reigned."

And the nations were angry, and thy wrath is come, and the time of the dead, that they should be judged, and that thou shouldest give reward unto thy servants the prophets, and to the saints, and them that fear thy name, small and great; and shouldest destroy them which destroy the earth.

THE POWER OF HIS CHRIST

AND THE TEMPLE of God was opened in heaven, and there was seen in his temple the ark of his testament: and there were lightnings, and voices, and thunderings, and an earthquake, and great hail.

And there appeared a great wonder in heaven: a woman clothed with the sun, and the moon under her feet, and upon her head a crown of twelve stars. And she being with child cried, travailing in birth, and pained to be delivered.

And there appeared another wonder in heaven: and behold, a great red dragon, having seven heads and ten horns, and seven crowns upon his heads. And his tail drew the third part of the stars of heaven and did cast them to the earth. And the dragon stood before the woman which was ready to be delivered, for to devour her child as soon as it was born.

And she brought forth a man child who was to rule all nations with a rod of iron: and her child was caught up unto God, and to his throne. And the woman fled into the wilderness, where she hath a place prepared of God, that they should feed her there a thousand two hundred and threescore days.

And there was war in heaven: Michael and his angels fought against the dragon; and the dragon fought and his angels, and prevailed not; neither was their place found any more in heaven. And the great dragon was cast out, that old serpent, called the Devil, and Satan, which deceiveth the whole world: he was cast out into the earth, and his angels were cast out with him.

And I heard a loud voice saying in heaven, "Now is come

salvation, and strength, and the kingdom of our God, and the power of his Christ: for the accuser of our brethren is cast down, which accused them before our God day and night. And they overcame him by the blood of the Lamb, and by the word of their testimony; and they loved not their lives unto the death. Therefore rejoice, ye heavens, and ye that dwell in them. Woe to the inhabiters of the earth and of the sea? for the devil is come down unto you, having great wrath, because he knoweth that he hath but a short time.

And when the dragon saw that he was cast unto the earth, he persecuted the woman which brought forth the man child. And to the woman were given two wings of a great eagle, that she might fly into the wilderness, into her place, where she is nourished for a time, and times, and half a time, from the face of the serpent.

And the serpent cast out of his mouth water as a flood after the woman, that he might cause her to be carried away by the flood. And the earth helped the woman, and the earth opened her mouth, and swallowed up the flood which the dragon cast out of his mouth. And the dragon was wroth with the woman, and went to make war with the remnant of her seed, which keep the commandments of God, and have the testimony of Jesus Christ.

And I stood upon the sand of the sea, and saw a beast rise up out of the sea, having seven heads and ten horns, and upon his horns ten crowns, and upon his heads the name of blasphemy. And the beast which I saw was like unto a leopard, and his feet were as the feet of a bear, and his mouth as the mouth of a lion: and the dragon gave him his power, and his seat, and great authority.

And I saw one of his heads as it were wounded to death: and his deadly wound was healed; and all the world wondered after the beast. And they worshipped the dragon which gave power unto the beast: and they worshipped the beast, saying, "Who is like unto the beast? who is able to make war with him?"

And there was given unto him a mouth speaking great things and blasphemies; and power was given unto him to continue forty and two months. And he opened his mouth in blasphemy against God, to blaspheme his name, and his tabernacle, and them that dwell in heaven. And it was given unto him to make war with the saints, to overcome them; and power was given him over all kindreds, and tongues, and nations. And all that dwell upon the earth shall worship him, whose names are not written in the book of life of the Lamb slain from the foundation of the world.

If any man have an ear, let him hear! He that leadeth into captivity shall go into captivity: he that killeth with the sword must be killed with the sword. Here is the patience and the faith of the saints.

And I beheld another beast coming up out of the earth; and he had two horns like a lamb, and he spake as a dragon. And he exercised all the power of the first beast before him, and causeth the earth and them which dwell therein to worship the first beast, whose deadly wound was healed. And he doeth great wonders, so that he maketh fire come down from heaven on the earth in the sight of men. And he deceived them that dwell on the earth by means of those miracles which he had power to do in the sight of the beast; saying to them that dwell on the earth, that they should make an image to the beast, which had the wound by a sword, and did live. And he had power to give life unto the image of the beast, that the image of the beast should both speak, and cause that as many as would not worship the image of the beast should be killed. And he caused all, both small and great, rich and poor, free and bond, to receive a mark in their right hand, or in their foreheads. And that no man might buy or sell, save he that had the mark, or the name of the beast, or the number of his name.

Here is wisdom! Let him that hath understanding count the number of the beast: for it is the number of a man; and his number is six hundred threescore and six.

And I looked, and, lo, a Lamb stood on the mount Sion, and with him an hundred and forty and four thousand, having his Father's name written in their foreheads. And I heard a voice from heaven, as the voice of many waters, and as the voice of a great thunder; and I heard the voice of harpers harping with their harps.

And they sang as it were a new song before the throne, and before the beasts and the elders: and no man could learn that song but the forty and four thousand, which were redeemed from the earth. These are they which were not defiled with women; for they are virgins. These are they which follow the Lamb withersoever he goeth. These were redeemed from among men, being the first fruits unto God and to the Lamb. And in their mouth was found no guile: for they are without fault before the throne of God.

And I saw another angel fly in the midst of heaven, having the everlasting gospel to preach unto them that dwell on the earth, and to every nation, and kindred, and tongue, and people; saying with a loud voice, "Fear God, and give glory to him; for the hour of his judgment is come; and worship him that made heaven, and earth, and the sea, and the fountains of waters."

And there followed another angel, saying, "Babylon is fallen, is fallen, that great city, because she made all nations drink of the wine of the wrath of her fornications."

And the third angel followed them, saying with a loud voice, "If any man worship the beast and his image, and receive his mark on his forehead, or in his hand, the same shall drink of the wine of the wrath of God which is poured out without mixture into the cup of his indignation; and he shall be tormented with fire and brimstone, in the presence of the holy angels, and in the presence of the Lamb. And the smoke of their torment ascendeth up forever and ever: and they have no rest day nor night, they who worship the beast and his image, and whosoever receiveth the mark of his name."

Here is the patience of the saints: here are they that keep the commandments of God, and the faith of Jesus. And I heard a voice from heaven saying unto me, "Write, blessed are the dead which die in the Lord from henceforth: Yea," saith the Spirit, "that they may rest from their labours and their works do follow them."

And I looked, and behold a white cloud, and upon the cloud one sat like unto the Son of man, having on his head a golden crown, and in his hand a sharp sickle.

And another angel came out of the temple, crying with a loud voice to him that sat on the cloud, "Thrust in thy sickle, and reap; for the time is come for thee to reap; for the harvest of the earth is ripe." And he that sat on the cloud thrust in his sickle on the earth; and the earth was reaped.

And another angel came out of the temple which is in heaven, he also having a sharp sickle.

And another angel came out from the altar which had power over fire: and cried with a loud cry to him that had the sharp sickle, saying, "Thrust in thy sharp sickle, and gather the clusters of the vine of the earth; for her grapes are fully ripe."

And the angel thrust in his sickle into the earth, and gathered the vine of the earth, and cast it into the great winepress of the wrath of God. And the winepress was trodden without the city, and blood came out of the winepress even unto the horse bridles, by the space of a thousand and six hundred furlongs.

THE SEVEN VIALS POURED OUT

And I saw another sign in heaven, great and marvelous, seven angels having the seven last plagues, for in them is filled up the wrath of God.

And I saw as it were a sea of glass mingled with fire: and them that had gotten the victory over the beast, and over his image, and over his mark, and over the number of his name, stand on the sea of glass, having the harps of God. And they sing the song of Moses, the servant of God, and the song of the Lamb, saying,

" Great and marvellous are thy works,
Lord God Almighty;
Just and true are thy ways,
Thou King of saints.
Who shall not fear thee, O Lord,
And glorify thy name?
For thou only art holy:
For all nations shall come and worship before thee;
For thy judgments are made manifest."

And after that I looked, and behold, the temple of the tabernacle of the testimony in heaven was opened: and the seven angels came out of the temple, having the seven last plagues, clothed in pure and white linen, and having their breasts girded with golden girdles.

And one of the four beasts gave unto the seven angels seven golden vials full of the wrath of God, who liveth for ever and ever. And the temple was filled with smoke from the glory of

God, and from his power; and no man was able to enter into the temple, till the seven plagues of the seven angels were fulfilled.

And I heard a great voice out of the temple saying to the seven angels, "Go your ways, and pour out the vials of the wrath of God upon the earth." And the first went and poured out his vial upon the earth; and there fell a noisome and grievous sore upon the men which had the mark of the beast, and upon them which worshipped his image.

And the second angel poured out his vial upon the sea; and it became as the blood of a dead man: and every living soul died in the sea.

And the third angel poured out his vial upon the rivers and fountains of waters; and they became blood. And I heard the angel of the waters say, "Thou art righteous, O Lord, which art, and wast, and shall be, because thou hast judged thus. For they have shed the blood of saints and prophets, and thou hast given them blood to drink; for they are worthy."

And I heard another out of the altar say, "Even so, Lord God Almighty, true and righteous are thy judgments."

And the fourth angel poured out his vial upon the sun; and power was given unto him to scorch men with fire. And men were scorched with great heat, and blasphemed the name of God, which hath power over these plagues: and they repented not to give him glory.

And the fifth angel poured out his vial upon the seat of the beast; and his kingdom was full of darkness; and they gnawed their tongues for pain, and blasphemed the God of heaven because of their pains and their sores, and repented not of their deeds.

And the sixth angel poured out his vial upon the great river Euphrates; and the water thereof was dried up, that the way of the kings of the east might be prepared. And I saw three unclean spirits like frogs come out of the mouth of the dragon, and out of the mouth of the beast, and out of the mouth of the false prophet. For they are the spirits of devils, working miracles, which go forth unto the kings of the earth and of the whole world, to gather them to the battle of that great day of God Almighty.

Blessed is He that Watcheth

"Behold, I come as a thief. Blessed is he that watcheth, and keepeth his garments, lest he walk naked, and they see his shame." And he gathered them together into a place called in the Hebrew tongue Armageddon.

And the seventh angel poured out his vial into the air, and there came a great voice out of the temple of heaven, from the throne, saying, "It is done." And there were voices, and thunders, and lightnings; and there was a great earthquake, such as was not seen since men were upon the earth, so mighty an earthquake, and so great. And the great city was divided into three parts, and the cities of the nations fell: and great Babylon came in remembrance before God, to give unto her the cup of the wine of the fierceness of his wrath.

And every island fled away, and the mountains were not found. And there fell upon men a great hail out of heaven, every stone about the weight of a talent: and men blasphemed God because of the plague of the hail; for the plague thereof was exceeding great.

And there came one of the seven angels which had the seven vials, and talked with me, saying unto me, "Come hither; I will show unto thee the judgment of the great whore that sitteth upon many waters; with whom the kings of the earth have committed fornication, and the inhabitants of the earth have been made drunk with the wine of her fornication."

So he carried me away in the spirit into the wilderness; and I saw a woman sit upon a scarlet coloured beast, full of names of blasphemy, having seven heads and ten horns. And the woman was arrayed in purple and scarlet colour, and decked with gold and precious stones and pearls, and having a golden cup in her hand full of abominations and filthiness of her fornication. And upon her forehead was a name written, MYSTERY, BABYLON THE GREAT, THE MOTHER OF HARLOTS AND ABOMINATIONS OF THE EARTH. And I saw the woman drunken with the blood of the saints, and with the blood of the martyrs of Jesus: and when I saw her, I wondered with great admiration. *(Amazement.)*

And the angel said unto me, "Wherefore didst thou marvel? I will tell thee the mystery of the woman, and of the beast that carried her, which hath the seven heads and ten horns. The beast that thou sawest was, and is not; and shall ascend out of the bottomless pit, and go into perdition. And they that dwell on the earth shall wonder, whose names were not written in the book of Life from the foundation of the world, when they behold the beast that was, and is not, and yet is.

"And here is the mind which hath wisdom. The seven heads are seven mountains on which the woman sitteth. And there are seven kings. These shall make war with the Lamb, and the Lamb shall overcome them: for he is Lord of lords, and King of kings: and they that are with him are called, and chosen and faithful."

And he saith unto me, "The waters which thou sawest, where the whore sitteth, are peoples, and multitudes, and nations and tongues. And the ten horns which thou sawest upon the beast, these shall hate the whore, and shall make her desolate and naked, and shall eat her flesh, and burn her with fire. For God hath put in their hearts to fulfill his will, and to agree, and give their kingdom unto the beast until the words of God shall be fulfilled. And the woman which thou sawest is that great city which reigneth over the kings of the earth."

And after these things I saw another angel come down from heaven, having great power; and the earth was lightened with his glory. And he cried mightily with a strong voice, saying, "Babylon the great is fallen, is fallen, and is become the habitation of devils, and the hold of every foul spirit, and a cage of every unclean and hateful bird. For all nations have drunk of the wine of the wrath of her fornication, and the kings of the earth have committed fornication with her, and the merchants of the earth are waxed rich through the abundance of her delicacies."

And I heard another voice from heaven, saying, "Come out of her, my people, that ye be not partakers of her sins, and that ye receive not of her plagues. For her sins have reached unto heaven, and God hath remembered her iniquities. Reward her even as she rewarded you, and double unto her double according to her works: in the cup which she hath filled, fill to her double. How much she hath glorified herself, and lived deliciously, so much torment and sorrow give her: for she saith in her heart, 'I sit a queen, and am no widow, and shall see no sorrow.' Therefore shall her plagues come in one day, death, and mourning, and famine; and she shall be utterly burned with fire: for strong is the Lord God who judgeth her.

"And the kings of the earth, who have committed fornication and lived deliciously with her, shall bewail her, and lament for her, when they shall see the smoke of her burning, standing afar off for the fear of her torment, saying, 'Alas, alas that great city Babylon, that mighty city! for in one hour is thy judgment come.'

"And the merchants of the earth shall weep and mourn over her; for no man buyeth their merchandise any more: the merchandise of gold, and silver, and precious stones, and of pearls, and fine linen, and purple, and silk, and scarlet, and all thyine wood, and all manner vessels of ivory, and all manner vessels of most precious wood, and of brass, and iron, and marble, and cinnamon, and odours, and ointments, and frankincense, and wine, and oil, and fine flour, and wheat, and beasts, and sheep, and horses, and chariots, and slaves, and souls of men. And the fruits that thy soul lusted after are departed from thee, and all things which were dainty and goodly are departed from thee, and thou shalt find them no more at all.

"And the merchants of these things, which were made rich by her, shall stand afar off for the fear of her torment, weeping and wailing, saying, 'Alas, alas that great city, that was clothed in fine linen, and purple, and scarlet, and decked with gold, and precious stones, and pearls! For in one hour so great riches is come to nought.'

"And every ship-master, and all the company in ships, and sailors, and as many as trade by sea, stood afar off, and cried when they saw the smoke of her burning, saying, 'What city is like unto this great city!' And they cast dust on their heads, and cried, weeping and wailing, saying, 'Alas, alas that great city, wherein were made rich all that had ships in the sea by reason of her costliness! for in one hour is she made desolate.'

"Rejoice over her, thou heaven, and ye holy apostles and prophets, for God hath avenged you on her."

And a mighty angel took up a stone like a great millstone and cast it into the sea, saying, "Thus with violence shall that great city, Babylon be thrown down, and shall be found no more at all. And the voice of harpers, and musicians, and pipers and trumpeters, shall be heard no more at all in thee; and no craftsman, of whatsoever craft he be, shall be found any more in thee; and the sound of a millstone shall be heard no more at all in thee; and the light of a candle shall shine no more at all in thee; and the voice of the bridegroom and of the bride shall be heard no more at all in thee: for thy merchants were the great men of the earth; for by thy sorceries were all nations deceived. And in her was found the blood of prophets, and of saints, and of all that were slain upon the earth."

"THE LORD GOD OMNIPOTENT REIGNETH"

AND AFTER these things I heard a great voice of much people in heaven, saying, "Alleluia: Salvation, and glory, and honour, and power unto the Lord our God: for true and righteous are his judgments; for he hath judged the great whore, which did corrupt the earth with her fornication, and hath avenged the blood of his servants at her hand." And again they said, "Alleluia! " And her smoke rose up for ever and ever.

And the four and twenty elders and the four beasts fell down and worshipped God that sat on the throne, saying, "Amen: Alleluia."

And a voice came out of the throne, saying, " Praise our God, all ye his servants, and ye that fear him, both small and great."

And I heard as it were the voice of a great multitude, and as the voice of many waters, and as the voice of mighty thunderings, saying, "Alleluia, for the Lord God Omnipotent reigneth. Let us be glad and rejoice, and give honour to him: for the marriage of the Lamb is come, and his wife hath made herself ready."

And to her was granted that she should be arrayed in fine linen, clean and white: for the fine linen is the righteousness of saints. And he saith unto me, "Write, blessed are they which are called unto the marriage supper of the Lamb." And he saith unto me, "These are the true sayings of God."

And I fell at his feet to worship him. And he said unto me, " See thou do it not: I am thy fellowservant, and of thy brethren that have the testimony of Jesus: WORSHIP GOD: for the testimony of Jesus is the spirit of prophecy."

And I saw heaven opened, and behold a white horse; and he that sat upon him was called Faithful and True, and in righteousness he doth judge and make war. His eyes were as a flame of fire, and on his head were many crowns; and he had a name written that no man knew, but he himself. And he was clothed with a vesture dipped in blood: and his name is called The Word of God.

And the armies which were in heaven followed him upon white horses, clothed in fine linen, white and clean. And out of his mouth goeth a sharp sword, that with it he should smite the nations: and he shall rule them with a rod of iron: and he treadeth the winepress of the fierceness and wrath of Almighty God. And he hath on his vesture and on his thigh a name written, KING OF KINGS, AND LORD OF LORDS.

And I saw an angel standing in the sun: and he cried with a loud voice, saying to all the fowls that fly in the midst of heaven, "Come and gather yourselves together unto the supper of the great God; that ye may eat the flesh of kings, and the flesh of captains, and the flesh of mighty men, and the flesh of horses, and of them that sit on them, and the flesh of all men, both free and bond, both small and great."

And I saw the beast, and the kings of the earth, and their armies, gathered together to make war against him that sat on the horse, and against his army. And the beast was taken, and with him the false prophet that wrought miracles before him, with which he deceived them that had received the mark of the beast, and them that worshipped his image. These both were cast alive into a lake of fire burning with brimstone. And the remnant were slain with the sword of him that sat upon the horse, which sword proceeded out of his mouth: and all the fowls were filled with their flesh.

And I saw an angel come down from heaven having the key of the bottomless pit and a great chain in his hand. And he laid hold on the dragon, that old serpent, which is the devil, and Satan, and bound him a thousand years, and cast him into the bottomless pit, and shut him up, and set a seal upon him, that he should deceive the nations no more, till the thousand years should be fulfilled: and after that he must be loosed a little season.

And I saw thrones, and they that sat upon them, and judgment was given unto them: and I saw the souls of them that were beheaded for the witness of Jesus, and for the word of God, and which had not worshipped the beast, neither his image, neither had received his mark upon their foreheads, or in their hands; and they lived and reigned with Christ a thousand years. But the rest of the dead lived not again until the thousand years were finished. This is the first resurrection: Blessed and holy is he that hath part in the first resurrection: on such the second death hath no power, but they shall be priests of God and of Christ, and shall reign with him a thousand years.

And when the thousand years are expired, Satan shall be loosed out of his prison. And shall go out to deceive the nations which are in the four quarters of the earth, Gog and Magog, to gather them together to battle: the number of whom is as the sand of the sea. And they went up on the breadth of the earth, and compassed the camp of the saints about, and the beloved city: and fire came down from God out of heaven, and devoured them. And the devil that deceived them was cast into the lake of fire and brimstone, where the beast and the false prophet are, and shall be tormented day and night for ever and ever.

And I saw a great white throne, and him that sat on it, from whose face the earth and the heaven fled away; and there was found no place for them. And I saw the dead, small and great, stand before God; and the books were opened: and another book was opened, which is the book of Life: and the dead were judged out of those things which were written in the books, according to their works. And the sea gave up the dead which were in it; and death and hell delivered up the dead which were in them: and they were judged every man according to their works. And death and hell were cast into the lake of fire. This is the second death. And whosoever was not found written in the Book of Life was cast into the lake of fire.

THE HOLY CITY, NEW JERUSALEM

AND I SAW a new heaven and a new earth: for the first heaven and the first earth were passed away; and there was no more sea. And I, John, saw the holy city, New Jerusalem, coming down from God out of heaven, prepared as a bride adorned for her husband.

And I heard a great voice out of heaven saying, "Behold, the tabernacle of God is with men, and he will dwell with them, and they shall be his people, and God himself shall be with them, and be their God. And God shall wipe away all tears from their eyes; and there shall be no more death, neither sorrow, nor crying, neither shall there be any more pain: for the former things are passed away."

And he that sat upon the throne said, "Behold, I make all things new." And he said unto me, "Write: for these words are true and faithful."

And he said unto me, "It is done. I am Alpha and Omega, the beginning and the end. I will give unto him that is athirst of the fountain of the water of Life freely. He that overcometh shall inherit all things; and I will be his God, and he shall be my son. But the fearful, and unbelieving, and the abominable, and the murderers, and whoremongers, and sorcerers, and idolaters, and all liars, shall have their part in the lake which burneth with fire and brimstone: which is the second death."

And there came unto me one of the seven angels which had the seven vials full of the seven last plagues, and talked with me, saying, "Come hither, I will show thee the bride, the Lamb's wife." And he carried me away in the spirit to a great and high mountain, and showed me that great city, the holy Jerusalem, descending out of heaven from God, having the glory of God.

And her light was like unto a stone most precious, even like a jasper stone, clear as crystal. And had a wall great and high. And had twelve gates, and at the gates twelve angels, and names written thereon, which are the names of the twelve tribes of the children of Israel: on the east three gates; on the north three gates; on the south three gates; and on the west three gates. And the wall of the city had twelve foundations, and in them the names of the twelve apostles of the Lamb.

And he that talked with me had a golden reed to measure the city, and the gates thereof, and the wall thereof. And the city lieth four square, and the length is as large as the breadth: and he measured the city with the reed, twelve thousand furlongs. The length and the breadth and the height of it are equal. And he measured the wall thereof, an hundred and forty and four cubits, according to the measure of a man, that is, of an angel.

And the building of the wall of it was of jasper: and the city was pure gold, like unto clear glass. And the foundations of the wall of the city were garnished with all manner of precious stones. The first foundation was jasper; the second, sapphire; the third, chalcedony; the fourth, emerald; the fifth, sardonyx; the sixth, sardius; the seventh, chrysolite; the eighth, beryl; the ninth, a topaz; the tenth, a chrysoprasus; the eleventh, a jacinth; the twelfth, an amethyst. And the twelve gates were twelve pearls; every several gate was of one pearl.

And the street of the city was pure gold, as it were transparent glass.

And I saw no temple therein: for the Lord God Almighty and the Lamb are the temple of it.

And the city had no need of the sun, neither of the moon to shine in it: for the glory of God did lighten it, and the Lamb is the light thereof. And the nations of them which are saved shall walk in the light of it; and the kings of the earth do bring their glory and honour into it. And the gates of it shall not be shut at all by day: for there shall be no night there. And they shall bring the glory and honour of the nations into it. And there shall in no wise enter into it anything that defileth, neither whatsoever worketh abomination, or maketh a lie: but they which are written in the Lamb's book of Life.

And he showed me a pure river of water of life, clear as crystal, proceeding out of the throne of God and of the Lamb. In the midst of the street of it, and on either side of the river, was there the tree of Life, which bare twelve manner of fruits, and yielded her fruit every month: and the leaves of the tree were for the healing of the nations.

And there shall be no more curse: but the throne of God and of the Lamb shall be in it; and his servants shall serve him: and they shall see his face; and his name shall be in their foreheads.

And there shall be no night there; and they need no candle, neither light of the sun; for the Lord God giveth them light; and they shall reign for ever and ever.

And he said unto me, "These sayings are faithful and true; and the Lord God of the holy prophets sent his angel to show unto his servants the things which must shortly be done. Behold, I come quickly: blessed is he that keepeth the sayings of the prophecy of this book."

And I, John, saw these things, and heard them. And when I had heard and seen, I fell down to worship before the feet of the angel which showed me these things. Then saith he unto me, "See thou do it not: for I am thy fellowservant, and of thy brethren the prophets, and of them which keep the sayings of this book: WORSHIP GOD."

And he saith unto me, " Seal not the sayings of the prophecy of this book: for the time is at hand. He that is unjust, let him be unjust still; and he which is filthy, let him be filthy still; and he that is righteous, let him be righteous still; and he that is holy, let him be holy still. And behold, I come quickly; and my reward is with me, to give every man according as his work shall be.

" I am Alpha and Omega, the beginning and the end, the first and the last.

" Blessed are they that do his commandments, that they may have right to the tree of Life, and may enter in through the gates into the city. For without are dogs, and sorcerers, and whoremongers, and murderers, and idolaters, and whosoever loveth and maketh a lie.

" I Jesus have sent mine angel to testify unto you these things in the churches. I am the root and the offspring of David, and the bright, and morning star.

"And the Spirit and the bride say, 'Come.' And let him that heareth, say, 'Come.' And let him that is athirst come. And whosoever will, let him take the water of Life freely.

" For I testify unto every man that heareth the words of the prophecy of this book, 'If any man shall add unto these things, God shall add unto him the plagues that are written in this book: and if any man shall take away from the words of the book of this prophecy, God shall take away his part out of the book of Life, and out of the holy city, and from the things which are written in this book."

He which testifieth these things saith, " Surely I come quickly. Amen."

" Even so, come, Lord Jesus."

The grace of our Lord Jesus Christ be with you all. Amen.

Now unto Him that is able to keep you from falling, and to present you faultless before the presence of His glory with exceeding joy, to the only wise God our Saviour, be glory and majesty, dominion and power, both now and ever. Amen.

Jude 1:25

GLOSSARY

This Glossary, based on the books listed in the Bibliography, is of necessity very restricted. It is also a limited Index with only one page reference given where people and places are first mentioned. The abbreviation O.T. is used for the Old Testament, and N.T. for the New Testament.

— A —

Aaron - was interpreter for his brother Moses, and was consecrated as the first high priest. Page 80

Abaddon - the place of destruction; the angel of the bottomless pit. Rev. 9:11.

Abednego - an Israelite youth cast into the fiery furnace with Shadrach and Meshach by Nebuchadnezzar. Page 573

Abel - second son of Adam and Eve, slain by Cain. Page 8

Abigail - wife of Nabal, later David's wife. Page 280

Abner - Saul's cousin and commander in chief of his army. Page 283

Abominable - hateful, detestable, or shamefully vile.

Abomination - abhorrence, disgust and loathing; detestation.

Abram or Abraham - father of a multitude; the first of the patriarchs, and founder of the Hebrew nation. Page 14

Absalom - third son of king David who revolted against David; his head was caught in the branches of a tree and he was killed by Joab, general of David's army. Page 321

Aceldama - field near Jerusalem where Judas committed suicide; translated " Field of Blood."

Achish - a Philistine king of Gath; David found refuge with him when Saul sought his life. Page 285

Adam - the first man; human frailty. Page 6

Adulterate - to corrupt; debase or make impure; to defile by adultery.

Adultery - lewdness or unchastity of thought as well as of act; faithlessness; idolatry; corruption; degradation. Page 119

Advice - recommendation regarding course of conduct.

Ahab - wicked king of Israel; was married to Jezebel who spurred him on to have Naboth killed; persecuted Elijah. Page 380

Ahaz - a weak idolatrous king of Judah; he was warned by Isaiah but did not listen. He introduced the sundial. Page 446

Ai - a city lying east of Bethel. Page 181

Aijalon - a broad beautiful valley where Joshua commanded the sun and the moon to stand still. Page 188

Amaziah - king of Judah, son of Joash. Page 429

Amiable - lovely; admirable.

Amman - capital of Trans-Jordan; formerly called Rabbath Amon or Philadelphia.

Amnon - David's eldest son; killed by Absalom for treachery to their sister Tamar. Page 321

Amos - a Hebrew prophet of the 8th century B.C. He was called the "Shepherd of Tekoa." A book of the O.T. Page 433

Anak - long-necked men; a race of giants of southern Canaan. Page 139

Ananias - a follower of the Apostles; he lied to Peter and died. Page 1024

Ananias of Damascus - a disciple who came to Saul and restored his sight. Page 1033

Andrew - a disciple of Jesus; brother of Peter. Page 847

Angel - thoughts of God ministering to man's needs, with inspiration, encouragement, enlightenment; spiritual intuitions.

Annas - a high priest in Jerusalem at the time of Jesus.

Antioch - a town in Syria where Paul preached; here the disciples were first called Christians. Page 1040

Apocrypha - fourteen books of the O.T. in the Vulgate, but not found in Hebrew; now excluded from the Authorized Version.

Apocalypse - to uncover; to disclose; a kind of literature designed to give hope and courage in times of persecution; always written in code.

Apostle - a disciple; an advocate of a great moral reform; one of twelve disciples of Jesus, chosen and sent forth to preach the gospel.

Aquila - a tentmaker who with his wife Priscilla aided Paul. Page 1055

Ararat - mountain district of Asia; the resting place of Noah's ark after the deluge. Page 12

Ark - place of safety; refuge; the vessel in which Noah and his family and all variety of animals were preserved during the Deluge. Page 10

Ark of the Covenant - the oblong chest of acacia wood, overlaid with gold which supported the Mercy Seat with its golden cherubs, and occupied the most sacred place in the sanctuary. In it Moses placed the Ten Commandments written on tables of stone, and known as the Covenant with God, or the Covenant of Love. Page 128

Armageddon - protected hilltop city of Megiddo in Israel; thus a place of protection, and a call to alertness in daily individual experience. The great final conflict between good and evil. Page 1254

Artaxerxes - king of Persia who allowed the rebuilding of the wall of Jerusalem. Page 613

Asa - a king of Judah in O.T. history; means physician. Page 374

Ascension - a rising; an exaltation; the visible ascending of Jesus on the fortieth day after his resurrection. Page 1007

Askelon - a city of the Philistines. Page 215

Asher - a son of Jacob. Page 69

Astonied - amazed; perplexed; dismayed; dazed.

Athaliah - an impious and murderous queen of Judah, daughter of Ahab and Jezebel of Israel, and wife of Jehoram of Judah. Page 423

— B —

Baal - an ancient deity, especially of Syria and Phoenicia; a false god; an idol. Baalim - another name for Baal. Page 150

Baal-peor - an O.T. deity; hence an evil spirit; a devil. Page 155

Babbler - in old English, one who had much of interest to say; in modern English, one who talks idly or chatters. Acts 17:18.

Babel - a structure impossibly lofty; a visionary scheme; a place of noise and confusion; town where confusion of languages occurred. Page 14

Babylon - a great city in the Euphrates valley; center of world commerce and marked by luxury and magnificence; the Jews were carried captive to Babylon. In Revelation Babylon stands for carnal mind. Page 462

Balaam - a prophet whom Balak, king of Moab, induced to curse Israel; he could not curse them, but suggested that the Moabites seduce them to commit fornication causing a plague in their camp. Page 150

Balak - king of Moab who hired Balaam to curse the Israelites. Page 149

Baptism - a religious ablution signifying purification or consecration; closer communion with God; any purifying experience.

Barak - a Jewish captain who was incited by Deborah to deliver Israel. Page 201

Barnabas - an early disciple and companion of Paul on his first missionary trip. Page 1040

Bartholomew - one of Jesus' twelve disciples, also called Nathanael. Page 857

Baruch - a faithful attendant and scribe of Jeremiah. Page 495

Bath-sheba - wife of Uriah the Hittite, and later wife of David and mother of Solomon. Page 315

Beast - In Revelation 4:7, the four beasts before the throne were like a lion, a calf or young ox, the face of a man, and a flying eagle, and correspond to the four living creatures of Ezekiel 1:10; see Glossary for each.
In Revelation 13 and 17, the blasphemous beast with seven heads and ten horns symbolizes the Antichrist, and the number of the beast 666 is symbolical in falling short of the holy, or whole number 7. He is totally unlike the four beasts mentioned above.

Beatitude - consummate bliss; blessedness. Page 858

Beelzebub - O.T. deity; prince of demons; hence a devil; later a false god.

Beersheba - an old place in Palestine which formed the southern limits of the country. Page 26

Bel - the chief god of Babylon; see also Baal.

Beginning - first cause; origin; source. Page 1

Being - life; conscious existence; essence; infinite Being, God.

Believe - to hold as true; to have faith or confidence in.

Belshazzar - the last king of Babylonia whose doom was foretold by Daniel. Page 583

Belteshazzar - Daniel's Babylonian name. Page 573

Benjamin - Jacob's youngest son; his mother Rachel died at his birth. Page 49

Bethany - a village about 2 miles from Jerusalem; was the home of Mary, Martha, and Lazarus. Page 919

Bethesda - flowing water; pool inside the east wall of Jerusalem. Page 882

Bethlehem - one of the oldest towns in Palestine; early name Ephratah; birthplace of Jesus. Pages 445 and 835

Bible - a book of writings accepted by Christians as inspired by God and of divine authority.

Blood - a vital principle of life; hence life; purification by suffering and tribulation; sacrifice.

Blessed - hallowed; holy; spiritual happiness.

Boaz - kinsman of Naomi who married Ruth; mentioned in genealogy of Jesus. Page 232

Body - a kind or form of matter. The bread in the sacrament of the Lord's last supper. "This is my body which is given for you," Luke 22:19; symbolizes sacrifice.

Bread - food; sustenance. "I am the living bread," John 6:51; spiritual sustenance.

Bread of Life - spiritual sustenance; the Word.

Breath - power of respiration, hence life, spirit, strength; that which is produced by breath – word, inspiration, soul, spirit.

—C—

Caesarea Philippi - a city at the base of Mt. Hermon, north of the Sea of Galilee. Page 922

Caiaphas - high priest of the Jews under Tiberius; presided at Jesus' Trial. Page 989

Cain - eldest son of Adam and Eve; murdered his brother Abel. Page 8

Caleb - one of twelve spies sent by Moses to view the land of Canaan; with Joshua brought a favorable report, and later was allowed to enter the Promised Land. Page 139

Calf or young ox - symbol of the All-intelligence of God, in apocalyptic literature; in Ezekiel one of the four living creatures; and in Revelation one of the four beasts before the throne. Pages 521 and 1235

Calvary - the place outside of the ancient city of Jerusalem, where Jesus was crucified. Page 996

Cana of Galilee - the village where Jesus changed the water to wine. Page 849

Canaan, Land of - country west of the Jordan and the Dead Sea, given by God to Abraham's posterity, the children of Israel. Page 15

Capernaum - a village on the western shore of the Sea of Galilee. Page 847

Carchemish - here Nebuchadnezzar defeated the Egyptians. They did not rise again as a great nation until modern times. Page 504

Carmel - a mountain ridge which forms the southern boundary of Palestine.

Carnal - fleshly; corporeal; sensual; sexual; lacking spirituality.

Chaldean - pertaining to Chaldea or its people; hence pertaining to astrology, magic or occult learning. Page 574

Chalice - a drinking cup; cup used in the sacrament of the Lord's Supper.

Character - a graphic symbol, hence appearance or outward trait viewed as a token of the real nature; characteristic serving as an index to inner nature; that which a person or thing really is.

Cherubim - represent Wisdom and Understanding. Cherubim were made of gold and placed at the two ends of the mercy seat upon the Ark. Page 128

Chide - to rebuke; to find fault; to contend angrily.

Children of Israel - descendants of Jacob or Israel, children of spiritual victory; God's chosen people; the elect; namely: Asher, Benjamin, Dan, Gad, Issachar, Joseph, Judah, Levi, Naphtali, Reuben, Simeon, and Zebulun. Page 69

Children of Light - Christians having received the divine Light, or being enlightened by it.

Christ - the Messiah or Lord's anointed; Jesus called the Christ as the person who fulfilled this prophecy or expectation. Page 834

Christian - one who believes in Jesus the Christ and the Truth as taught by him; one who follows Christ's precepts and example.

Church - divine worship; a place of worship or religious service.

Clouts - rags.

Commandment - order; charge; behest; one of the Ten Commandments given to Moses by God. Page 110

Communion - act of sharing; intimate or spiritual interchange of thought; the act of partaking of the sacrament.

Communism - any system of social organization in which goods are held in common; was tried by early apostles. Page 1024

Corinth - an ancient and celebrated city of Greece; Paul preached there and two of his Epistles were written to the Corinthians. Page 1075

Covenant - an agreement between persons or parties; a solemn compact; an undertaking or promise of legal validity.

Covet - to desire possession of; to long inordinately for something that is another's; to desire sensuously. Page 111

Create - to bring into being; to cause to exist.

Creator - one who creates, produces or constitutes; the Supreme Being, "God the creator of the ends of the earth." Isa. 40:28. Page 3

Crucify - to put to death by nailing or binding the hands and feet to a cross; to subdue completely; to mortify; to torment.

Curse - a pronouncement of doom; harassment.

Cursed - imperfect; tormented.

Cyrus - founder of the Persian empire; he helped the Jews return to Jerusalem from Babylon to rebuild the temple. Page 597

– D –

DAGON - the national god of the Philistines. Page 248

DAMASCUS - one of the most ancient and most important cities of Syria; a great trade center; Paul was converted on his way to Damascus. Page 17

DAN - a son of Jacob; one of the twelve tribes, replaced by Manasseh. Page 69

DANIEL - a great Hebrew prophet who was a captive in Babylon. Book of Daniel, O. T., attributed to him. Page 573

DARK - not receiving, reflecting, transmitting or radiating light; destitute of moral or spiritual light; in spiritual or intellectual darkness.

DARKNESS - absence of light; state of ignorance or error; deprived of spiritual light. Page 3

DAVID - beloved; youngest son of Jesse of Bethlehem and later king of Israel. Page 263

DAWN - to begin to appear; to begin to be perceived or understood; expand; develop or give promise.

DAY - the time of light; a space of time; a period of grace; sunshine. Page 3

DEAD - deprived of life or opposed to life; bereft or devoid of intellectual or spiritual powers.

DEAD SEA - or Salt Sea into which the Jordan river runs. The sea has no outlet and so is salt or bitter.

DEADLY - aiming or willing to destroy; excessive; terrible.

DEARTH - famine.

DEBORAH - a Hebrew prophetess and judge of Israel who helped free the Israelites from the Canaanites. Page 201

DECALOGUE - the Ten Commandments given by God to Moses on Mount Sinai; originally written on two tables of stone. Page 109

DELILAH - a woman of the Philistines who betrayed Samson. Page 217

DEMONSTRATE - to prove; to establish beyond possibility of doubt; manifest; to show or prove to the mind or understanding; to prove by reasoning.

DEMONSTRATION - proof; a piece of indubitable evidence; a course of reasoning showing that a certain result is a necessary consequence of assumed premises.

DEUTERONOMY - a restatement of the law; the fifth Book of Moses. A Book of the O.T. Page 160

Devil - the tempter and spiritual enemy of mankind; evil.

Dialectic - the science or art of discriminating Truth from error.

Disannul - to annul completely.

Disciple - one who receives instruction from another; a learner; a follower of Christ.

Disease - lack of ease; discomfort; trouble; derangement or disorder of the mind, moral character, or habits.

Distress - oppressed; suffering; " pressed on every side."

Domination - the act of dominating and controlling; absolute ownership; arbitrary insolent sway.

Dominion - control; sovereignty; supremacy. God gave man dominion. Gen. 2:28 Page 4

Dorcas - a Christian disciple who was raised from the dead by Peter, also called Tabitha. Page 1035

Dragon - in Revelation a symbol of resistance to Truth. ". . . that old serpent, called the devil, and satan, which deceiveth the whole world." Rev. 12:9.

Dream - a state of mind marked by confusion of the sense of reality; a fanciful creation of the imagination.

Drink - to take in; to hear; to receive within one through the senses.

Dust - nothingness; " cloud of dust " turmoil or confusion; something worthless; earth. Page 5

— E —

Eagle - a bird noted for strength, size, keenness of vision and powers of flight. One of the four living creatures in Ezekiel, and one of the four beasts of Revelation; symbolizes the All-Activity of God, in apocalyptic literature.

Earth - the planet on which man dwells; materialism; dust; nothingness; worldly things as opposed to spiritual.

Ecclesiastes - a book of the O.T. containing maxims for the cultivation of wisdom. Page 811

Eden - the place where Adam and Eve first dwelt; pleasure; delight. Page 5

Edify - to build up.

EDOM - Esau and his descendants. Page 34

EGLON - a very fat king of Moab; was killed by Ehud to deliver Israel. Page 199

EGYPT - a powerful empire of antiquity where the Israelites were in bondage. Page 73

EHUD - a judge of Israel who slew Eglon, king of Moab. Page 199

ELEAZAR - Aaron's son and his successor in office of high priest. Page 148

ELI - high priest of Israel in whose care the child Samuel was placed. Page 241

ELIAB - eldest son of Jesse the Bethlehemite. Page 262

ELIAKIM - was chief embassy to Rabshakeh for Hezekiah. Page 467

ELIAS - is the Greek form of the Hebrew word Elijah. Elias is the form used in the N.T., but in this book the Hebrew name Elijah has been used in both Old and New Testaments.

ELIJAH - a great Hebrew prophet of the 9th century B.C. Page 380

ELISHA - a Hebrew prophet; the disciple and successor of Elijah. Page 388

ELIZABETH - mother of John the Baptist. Page 831

ELKANAH - husband of Hannah and father of Samuel. Page 241

ELOHIM - a term used in Hebrew scripture for God.

EMMAUS - a village north of Jerusalem. Page 1002

ENCHANT - to act on by charms or sorcery; to lay under a spell, hence to delude; to spellbind.

ENCHANTER - one who enchants; sorcerer, magician or a wizard.

ENCHANTMENT - necromancy; magic; witchcraft; that which enchants or charms the heart or senses.

ENOCH - early patriarch said to have walked with God. Page 10

EPHESUS - an ancient Ionian city; Paul wrote an epistle to the Ephesians. Page 1168

The seat of one of the Seven Churches of Asia Minor. Page 1230

EPHOD - an official garment for the high priest.

EPHRAIM - younger son of Joseph. Page 58

EPISTLE - a letter; a formal or elegant letter.

ERROR - belief in what is untrue; a departure from truth or accuracy.

Esaias - the Greek form of the name which in Hebrew is Isaiah. In this book Isaiah is used in both the Old and the New Testaments.

Esau - Isaac's son and brother of Jacob; sold his birthright for a mess of pottage. Page 34

Essence - substance; existence; being or entity; fundamental intrinsic being; prime character, or intrinsic nature.

Esther - a beautiful Jewess who became queen of king Ahasuerus when queen Vashti was dismissed. Book of Esther, O.T. Page 637

Euphrates - one of the four rivers of Paradise.

Eve - the first woman and wife of Adam, and mother of Cain, Abel, and Seth. Page 8

Evil - not good; worthless; defective; unsound; unwholesome; diseased.

Exodus - The second Book of Moses; a going or a marching out. Page 73

Ezekiel - a Hebrew prophet of the 6th century B.C.; he collected manuscripts and established synagogues in captivity. A book of the O.T. Page 519

Ezra - a Hebrew priest and scribe of the 5th century B.C. Returned to Jerusalem from captivity; was proscriptive and dogmatic. Page 595

— F —

Fact - a thing done; actuality; actual existence rather than hypothesis.

Faith - belief or trust in God; complete confidence.

False - not true; erroneous; incorrect; not genuine or real; supposititious.

Fear - apprehension of evil; dread; disquiet; awe or awareness of a superior power or force. Profound reverence for the Supreme Being.

Felix - governor of Judea who questioned Paul. Page 1134

Festus - governor of Judea who found Paul innocent. Page 1136

Fire - combustion; burning heat; severe trial; ardor of spirit or temperament; to cauterize; to purify.

Forgive - to give; to give up; to pardon; to absolve; to cease to feel resentment.

Fornication - adultery; idolatry; harlotry; unlawful lust.

Foursquare - square; unshakable firmness; perfection.

Heaven - completeness, wholeness; celestial abode of bliss; place of supreme happiness; the spiritual realm of the real.

Heavy - not easy to bear; burdened; sad.

Hebrew - a group of northern Semitic tribes, including the Israelites.

Hebrews - Epistle to the Hebrews, a N.T. Book. Page 1175

Hebron - a town of great antiquity near Jerusalem. Page 193

Hell - corruption; misery, place of punishment.

Hermon - a mountain in northern Palestine; the mount of transfiguration.

Hezekiah - a good king of Judah at the time of Isaiah, the prophet; destroyed Sennacherib's army. Page 463

Hiddekel - one of the four rivers flowing out of Eden.

Hilkiah - high priest of Israel in the reign of king Josiah; found the Book of the Law of Moses in the temple. Page 484

Hiram - king of Tyre and friend of David and Solomon. Page 305

Holiness - spiritual purity; state of being holy; freedom from sin.

Holy - spiritually whole, sound or perfect; pure in heart; acceptable to God. Page 114

Holy Ghost - spiritually whole; perfect; pure; entirely Spirit; the Comforter.

Holy of Holies - the place in the temple where the Ark of the Covenant of Moses was kept; the symbol of God's presence in the temple.

Horeb - mountain where Moses saw the burning bush. Page 78

Horses - usually stand for dependence on material power, or symbol of aggressive thought.

Hosea - a prophet of the 8th century B.C.; O.T. Book of that name ascribed to him. Page 437

Host - a great multitude or throng; one who provides food or lodging for another.

Humble - not proud or assertive in spirit; unpretending; modest; meek; mild.

Humility - freedom from pride and arrogance; a modest estimate of one's own worth.

Hunger - strong desire; craving.

Hypnosis - a state resembling sleep, but is induced by suggestions of the hypnotizer with whom the hypnotized subject remains in rapport and responsive to his suggestions even after awakening.

Hypnotize - to induce hypnosis; to entrance, dazzle or overcome by suggestion.

Hypothesis - a tentative theory or supposition provisionally adopted to explain certain facts and to guide in the investigation of others.

—I—

Idea - an image in mind; the immediate object of understanding; an ideal.

Identity - oneness; self-sameness; sameness of essential character.

Idol - an image or representation of a deity used as an object of worship; a false god; a graven image. Page 115

Illuminate - to enlighten; to throw light on; to elucidate.

Illusion - a deception by false appearance; an unreal or misleading image presented to vision; a misconception.

Image - a visible presentation or similitude; a reproduction; a likeness; "God created man in his own image." Gen. 1:27 Page 4

Immanuel - "God is with us."

Immortal - not mortal; imperishable; pertaining to immortality.

Incense - fumes of spices burnt as an act of worship and of gratitude. Aaron burned incense every morning and evening upon the golden altar in gratitude to God. Page 130

Infinite - without limits of any kind, especially of God the Absolute; boundless; immeasurable; illimitable.

Iniquity - gross injustice; wickedness; sin.

Integrity - moral soundness; honesty; purity.

Isaac - son of Abraham and Sarah; the "Child of promise." Page 26

Isaiah I - a great Hebrew prophet in Judah about 740 B.C. Page 439

Isaiah II - a great Hebrew prophet in captivity about 670 B.C. The writings of both of these prophets are included in the Book of Isaiah in the O.T. Isaiah I is now considered to have written chapters 1 to 39, and Isaiah II chapters 40 to 66. Page 539

Ishbosheth - the son of Saul. Page 299

Ishmael - the son of Abraham and Hagar. Page 19

Israel - the name given to Jacob after he wrestled with the angel; hence "one who wins spiritual victory." Children of Israel, "Children of spiritual victory" or the chosen people of God. Page 47

Israel - the ten tribes that composed the kingdom of Israel. Page 366

– J –

Jacob - son of Isaac and Rebekah; his name was changed to Israel when he wrestled with the angel and means "spiritual victory." He was the ancestor of the children of Israel. Page 34

Jael - wife of Heber; killed Sisera to help free the Israelites. Page 202

James - the brother of Jesus and probably wrote the Book of James in the N. T. Page 846

James - son of Alphaeus; one of Jesus' twelve disciples. Page 857

James - son of Zebedee and brother of John; one of Jesus' twelve disciples. Page 848

Japheth - one of the sons of Noah. Page 13

Jehoiachin - king of Judah; carried into captivity by Nebuchadnezzar. Page 497

Jehoiada - a priest who revolted against Athaliah and made Joash king of Judah. Page 423

Jehoiakim - king of Judah; rebelled against Nebuchadnezzar. Page 489

Jehoram or Joram - king of Israel and second son of Ahab. Page 400

Jehoram - king of Judah and son of Jehoshaphat. Page 400

Jehoshaphat - king of Judah and son of Asa. Page 378

Jehovah - the Supreme Being; God; The Almighty.

Jehu - an officer in Israel who rebelled against Ahab and all of his house. Page 419

Jeptha - a judge in Israel who sacrificed his daughter because of his vow. Page 211

Jeremiah - will rise; a prophet in Jerusalem at the time of Nebuchadnezzar's conquest. The book of Jeremiah and the book of Lamentations are attributed to him. Page 483

Jericho - a city in Palestine north of the Dead Sea. Page 174

Jeroboam - revolted against Solomon's son Rehoboam, and set up the kingdom of Israel with ten tribes of the children of Israel, leaving two tribes in the kingdom of Judah under Rehoboam. Later kings of Israel were also named Jeroboam. Page 364

Jerusalem - the chief city of Palestine, sometimes called the Holy City, or the city of David. The capital of Judah in O.T. Page 187

Jesse - the father of David Page 262

Jesus - the son of Mary and the source of the Christian religion, and Saviour in the Christian faith. "Jesus Christ the anointed." See also "Christ." Page 834

Jethro - father-in-law of Moses, and priest of Midian. Page 77

Jew - one belonging to the tribe of Judah; later, any member of the Hebrew race.

Jezebel - stands for hypnotism; mesmerism; lust for power; domination; the wife of king Ahab. Page 380

Joab - captain in David's army. Page 301

Joash - a king of Judah, saved by the priest, Jehoiada. Page 423

Joash - a king of Israel. Page 427

Job - O.T. patriarch who undergoes afflictions with fortitude and faith. Book of the O.T. Page 649

Joel - a prophet in Judah. Book of the O.T. Page 627

John - one of Jesus' twelve disciples; son of Zebedee and brother of James. The fourth Gospel, three Epistles, and the Book of Revelation are attributed to him. Page 848

John the Baptist - forerunner of the Christ, who prepared the way for him. Page 831

Jonah - a Hebrew prophet sent to warn Nineveh. O.T. Book. Page 621

Jonathan - son of Saul and beloved friend of David. Page 269

Joppa - a seaport town in southern Palestine. Page 355

Jordan - an important river in Palestine through which Joshua led the children of Israel on dry ground, and in which John baptized Jesus. Page 16

Joseph - son of Jacob whom his brothers sold into Egypt. Page 50

Joseph - husband of the Virgin Mary. Page 834

Joseph of Arimathea - a wealthy Jew who asked Pilate's permission to take the body of Jesus and place it in his own new tomb. Page 999

Joshua - the successor to Moses who led the children of Israel into the Promised Land. A book of the O.T. Page 159

Josiah - a king of Judah who made a great effort to reform his people with the aid of Zephaniah and Jeremiah. Was killed at Megiddo. Page 483

Judah - a son of Jacob, and ancestor of the tribe of Judah. An ancient kingdom in Palestine. Page 69

Judas the brother of James - one of Jesus' twelve disciples. Page 857

Judas Iscariot - one of Jesus' twelve disciples and the one who betrayed him. Page 857

Justice - the principle of rectitude; integrity; conformity to truth, fact or right reasoning; one of the cardinal virtues.

Justification - defence, vindication.

– K –

Key - dominion; spiritual understanding; that which affords or prevents entrance; that which serves to reveal, discover, or solve something unknown or difficult.

Kidron - a brook near Jerusalem crossed by David in his flight from Absalom. Page 328

Kill - to deprive of life; to destroy; to defeat; to destroy vitality. "Thou shalt not kill." Page 111

Kingdom of God - the spiritual realm of the real. Paul says, "The kingdom of God is righteousness, and peace, and joy." Rom. 14:17.

Kish - Saul's father. Page 253

Know - to be convinced of the truth; to perceive with understanding and conviction.

Knowledge - clear perception of fact, truth or duty; enlightenment; learning; wisdom; science; the act of knowing.

Korah - a Levite who led a rebellion against Moses. Page 142

– L –

Laban - brother of Rebekah and father of Leah and Rachel. Page 31

Lamech - the father of Noah. Page 10

Laodicea - one of the Seven Churches of Asia Minor. Page 1234

Latent - not visible or apparent; hidden; concealed; dormant.

Law - the will of God whether expressed in Scripture, implanted in instinct, or deduced by reason; the whole body of God's commandments or revelation; a specific or general rule of right living. Page 105

Lazarus - brother of Mary and Martha and raised from the dead by Jesus. Page 919

Lazarus - a beggar in Jesus' parable of the rich man and the beggar. Page 932

Leah - the daughter of Laban given to Jacob as his wife when he expected Rachel. Page 40

Leaven - that which rises and expands; used to produce fermentation.

Lebanon - mountain range north of Palestine famous for cedar trees. Page 159

Levi - one of Jacob's sons whose descendants were chosen for the priesthood. Page 69

Leviticus - the law; the third Book of Moses, O.T. Page 114

Life - conscious existence conceived as a quality of the soul or as the soul's nature and being; spiritual Life; the fact of being. "I AM GOD." Is. 45:22.

Light - mental or spiritual illumination or enlightenment or its source; that which illumines or makes clear to the mind. "God is light." I John 1:5.

Lion - a large animal known as the king of beasts because of its size and courage. One of the four living creatures of Ezekiel and one of the four beasts before the throne in Revelation, and symbolizes the All-Power of God, in apocalyptic literature.

Living creatures - see Ezekiel 1:10, and in the Glossary see Ox or Calf, Eagle, Lion, Man. These living creatures correspond to the four beasts of Revelation 4:7.

Locust - insect of the grasshopper family which commits terrible ravage on vegetation. Locust thought, confusion and destruction, all phases of lack and limitation.

Lofty - exalted; haughty; arrogant.

Logic - sound reasoning.

Logos - the word or form which expresses a thought; also the thought; the rational principle in the universe.

Lost - ruined or destroyed physically or morally; having wandered from or unable to find the way; bewildered; perplexed.

Lot - son of Haran and nephew of Abraham who went with Abraham to Canaan. Page 14

LOT'S WIFE - became a "pillar of salt" from looking back. Page 25

LOVE - the most profound word in the English language for "God is Love." I John 4:8.

LUKE - a physician and fellow worker with Paul. The N.T. Book of Luke attributed to him. Page 825

LUST - sensuous desire; bodily appetite; sexual desire or violent degrading passion.

LYDDA - scene of one of Peter's miracles. Page 1035

LYSTRA - here Paul cured a cripple. Page 1045

– M –

MACEDONIA - a Roman province and scene of some of Paul's labors.

MACHPELAH - a field and cave near Hebron where Abraham, Sarah and many descendants were buried. Page 28

MAGNETISM - power to attract as a magnet attracts; power to charm or captivate.

MAGNIFY - to laud or extol; to increase the importance of; to praise highly.

MALACHI - a Book of the O.T. ascribed to an unknown Hebrew prophet, about 450 B.C. Page 633

MALPRACTICE - treatment contrary to accepted rules with injurious results; infidelity.

MAMMON - personification of riches; luxury.

MAN - a person; an individual; "The image and likeness of God." Gen. 1:27. Page 4
In apocalyptic literature man symbolizes the All-Mind of God. In Ezekiel man is one of the four living creatures, in Revelation he is one of the four beasts before the throne.

MANASSEH - eldest son of Joseph. Page 58

MANIFEST - to reveal; prove; to show plainly beyond the question of a doubt; to make clear to the understanding.

MANIFESTATION - discovery to the eye or to the understanding; revelation; disclosure; display of power and purpose.

MANIPULATE - to treat, work or operate with the mind or intellect; to manage or treat artfully or fraudulently.

MANNA - the food God sent to the children of Israel in the wilderness; hence divinely supplied spiritual nourishment. Page 101

MARK - author of the second Gospel, and assisted Paul in his labors. Page 825

MARS HILL - in Athens where Paul preached to the Athenians. Page 1054

MARTHA - sister of Mary and Lazarus and friend of Jesus. Page 887

MARTYR - a witness; one who sacrifices his life, station, etc. for the sake of principle.

MARVEL - that which causes wonder and astonishment.

MARY - (1) The Virgin Mary, mother of Jesus. Page 834
(2) The sister of Martha and Lazarus. Page 887
(3) The wife of Cleophas. Page 997
(4) Mary Magdalene whom Jesus forgave. Page 936
(5) Mary the mother of James. Page 999

MATERIAL - of or pertaining to matter, not spiritual.

MATTER - that which is considered to constitute the physical universe, but the nature of matter is unknown.

MATTHEW - a tax gatherer and one of Jesus' twelve disciples. Author of the first Gospel, N.T. Pages 825 and 853

MEDES - a people of Persia. Page 586

MEEK - gentle; not easily provoked or irritated; patient, not haughty or resentful.

MEGIDDO - a battlefield on the border of Samaria and Galilee. Here king Josiah was slain. Page 488

MELCHIZEDEK - "king of Salem, and priest of the most high God" to whom Abraham paid tithes; by interpretation, "King of righteousness, and also King of peace." Page 17
See Hebrews 7:2, 3 Page 1181

MELITA - the island where Paul was shipwrecked. Page 1144

MEPHIBOSHETH - son of Jonathan. Page 312

MERCY - compassionate forgiveness; willingness to spare; compassionate treatment.

MERCY SEAT - the gold plate resting on the Ark of the Covenant, on which the blood of sacrificial animals was sprinkled, in the tent of meeting in propitiation for sins. Page 128

Meshach - a Hebrew youth cast into the fiery furnace by Nebuchadnezzar along with Shadrach and Abednego. Page 573

Mesmerize - to hypnotize; to overcome by suggestion.

Messiah - the Anointed One, title of Jesus the Christ; the expected deliverer of the Hebrews.

Methuselah - the father of Lamech; said to have lived the longest of any man. Page 10

Micah - Hebrew prophet of the 8th century B.C. Wrote the Book of Micah, O.T. Page 441

Michael - one of the archangels; Power. Page 593

Michal - daughter of Saul given in marriage to David. Page 269

Mind - the conscious element or factor in the universe; Spirit; intelligence.

Miracle - an event transcending our knowledge of the laws of nature; a wonder; a marvel.

Miriam - sister of Moses. Page 99

Mist - dimness; obscurity; uncertainty; state of doubt; anything which darkens or obscures. Page 5

Moab - grandson of Lot; descendants lived east of the Dead Sea. Page 149

Mordecai - the cousin of Queen Esther who saved the Jews from destruction. Page 640

Moses - considered the greatest O.T. figure who led the children of Israel out of bondage in Egypt, and gave them the Ten Commandments. Page 75

Mystery - a profound secret; beyond ordinary comprehension.

– N –

Naaman - a Syrian noble whom Elisha cured of leprosy. Page 409

Nabal - a surly sheep owner whose wife, Abigail, later became David's wife. Page 279

Naboth - a rich Jezreelite whom Jezebel had slain to give his vineyard to Ahab. Page 389

Nahum - a prophet in Israel about 612 B.C. A Book of the O.T. not included in this book.

Nain - a village in Palestine where Jesus raised the widow's son from the dead. Page 865

NAME - nature; character or reputation; title by which any person is known.

NAOMI - the mother-in-law of Ruth the Moabitess. Page 231

NAPHTALI - son of Jacob, and one of the twelve tribes of Israel. Page 69

NATHAN - the prophet who rebuked David for his adultery and treachery. Page 317

NATHANAEL - one of Jesus' twelve disciples; sometimes called Bartholomew. Page 848

NATURE - the essential character or constitution of a thing; one's real being or self; quality of mind or character.

NAZARETH - the town in Galilee where Jesus was brought up. Page 834

NEBO - the mountain in Moab from which Moses saw the Promised Land. Page 168

NEBUCHADNEZZAR - king of Babylon who carried Israel away captive, and burned Jerusalem. Page 493

NEBUZARADAN - captain of Nebuchadnezzar's guard, who showed kindness to Jeremiah. Page 506

NECHO - called Pharaoh Necho, king of Egypt who was defeated by Nebuchadnezzar at Carchemish. Page 488

NECROMANCY - the device for revealing the future by pretended communication with the dead; magic in general; conjuration; enchantment.

NEHEMIAH - cupbearer to king Artaxerxes; he returned to Jerusalem to rebuild the wall. A book of the O.T. Page 611

NEW TESTAMENT - the covenant of God with man embodied in the coming of the Christ and the teachings of Christ and his followers as set forth in the Bible: hence, usually that portion of the Bible in which this covenant is contained. Page 823

NICODEMUS - a Pharisee and ruler of the Jews who came to talk to Jesus by night. Later assisted with the burial. Page 867

NOAH - built the Ark at the warning of God and saved his family and all variety of animals from the flood. Page 10

NOD - the land to which Cain fled. Page 9

NUN - the father of Joshua. Page 159

–O–

OBED - the son of Ruth, and the father of Jesse, who was the father of David. Page 237

Obey - to be ruled by; to be obedient; to comply with a command or request.

Offend - to cause to stumble; to transgress or violate.

Og - king of Bashan who was overcome by Moses. Page 149

Old Testament - the covenant of God with the Hebrews as set forth in the Bible; also the books of the Bible in which this covenant is given, the canonical books including the Law, Prophets, and Hagiographa.

Omri - king of Israel and father of Ahab. Page 380

Onesimus - the slave for whom Paul pleaded in the letter to Philemon. Page 1158

Overcome - to surmount; to go beyond.

Ox - the animal on whose patient labor depended all the ordinary operations of farming in the old days. In apocalyptic literature the ox or calf symbolizes the All-intelligence of God. In Ezekiel the ox is one of the four living creatures, and in Revelation the calf is one of the four beasts before the throne Pages 521 and 1235

—P—

Palestine - the land of Canaan; the Promised Land.

Panacea - all healing; a remedy for all ills.

Parable - a short fictitious narrative from which a moral or spiritual truth is drawn, as the parables of Jesus.

Paran, Wilderness of - " Ishmael grew . . . and dwelt in the wilderness of Paran." Page 27
Part of the Sinai Peninsula where the children of Israel wandered. Page 135

Passover - an annual feast of the Jews commemorating the sparing of the Israelites in Egypt whose houses were marked by the blood of the lamb. Page 94

Patience - cheerful or hopeful endurance; enduring; patient continuance; constancy.

Patmos - the island on which John lived as an exile, and where he received the Revelation. Page 1229

Paul - originally called Saul of Tarsus; his conversion changed his ways and he became the Apostle to the Gentiles; he was most instrumental in establishing Christianity as it is today. Page 1042

Peace - harmony, tranquility of mind or conscience; freedom from fears; quiet.

PENIEL - spiritual struggle; an allusion to Jacob's spiritual victory when he wrestled with the angel at Peniel. Page 48

PENTATEUCH - the first five books of the Bible collectively; also called the the Law of Moses; the five Books of Moses. Pages 3 to 169

PENTECOST - a solemn festival of the Jews celebrated fifty days after the Passover.

PERFECT - complete; flawless; pure. "Thou shalt be perfect with the Lord thy God." Deut. 18:13.

PERGAMOS - seat of one of the Seven Churches of Asia Minor. Page 1231

PERPLEXITY - bewilderment; distracting uncertainty; "no way out."

PERSIA - an ancient empire which once held the Holy Land tributary.

PETER - original name was Simon; a fisherman; one of the twelve disciples of Jesus, and later a leader of the Apostles. Page 847
He wrote I and II Peter, books of the N.T. Page 1203

PHARAOH - the title of the sovereigns of ancient Egypt. Page 55

PHARISAICAL - outwardly but not inwardly religious; hypocritical; self-righteous.

PHARISEES - a sect who strictly observed written law and ceremonies.

PHILADELPHIA - brotherly love; seat of one of the Seven Churches of Asia Minor. Page 1233

PHILEMON - Paul's letter to Philemon is a Book of the N.T. Page 1158

PHILIP - one of Jesus' twelve disciples. Page 848

PHILIPPI - a city of Macedonia; Paul addressed an epistle to the Philippians, N.T. Page 1147

PHILISTINES - a warlike race who occupied the coastland of Palestine and harassed the Israelites for centuries. Page 246

PHINEAS - son of Eleazar the high priest of Israel. Page 155
One of the two sons of Eli. Page 243

PHOENICIA - land along the Palestinean seacoast including Tyre and Sidon.

PILATE - or Pontius Pilate who was the Roman governor of Judea who gave Jesus up to be crucified. Page 991

POOR - destitute of such qualities as are desirable; barren; insufficient.

POOR IN SPIRIT - humble in spirit; devoid of pride or arrogancy.

POSTULATE - a proposition claimed or assumed to be true.

Potiphar - an Egyptian noble to whom Joseph was sold by the Midianites who had bought him of his brothers. Page 52

Power - force or energy; " There is no power but of God." Rom. 13:1.

Priscilla - wife of Aquila and friend of Paul. Page 1055

Practice - application of knowledge.

Prayer - an earnest entreaty; the offering of supplication, adoration, or thanksgiving to God.

Priest - one set aside to perform sacred duties.

Prick - to spur; to goad.

Principle - a source or origin; primordial element; ultimate basis or cause; a fundamental truth.

Prophet - one inspired or instructed by God; an inspired revealer, hence one more than humanly wise; a seer.

Proverb - a general truth which has gained credit by long use.

Proverbs - a book of the O.T. containing a variety of profound maxims. Page 759

Prudent - capable of directing oneself wisely and judiciously; highly sensible

Psalm - a sacred song or poem. Psalms, a book of the O. T. Page 671

Publican - a collector of public revenues who paid a fixed sum for the privilege.

Pure - without stain or taint; faultless; innocent; chaste.

— Q —

Quaternion - a set of four things or persons.

Quick - alive.

Quiet - still; hushed; gentle; mild; not turbulent.

— R —

Rabbi - a Jewish teacher or doctor of the law.

Rab-shaketh - an Assyrian officer who attempted to persuade Judah to rebel against Hezekiah. Page 467

Rachel - Jacob's wife; mother of Joseph and Benjamin. Page 40

RAHAB - the harlot of Jericho who hid the Israelite spies. Page 174

RAMAH - a village in Israel where Samuel lived. Page 251

REBEKAH - wife of Isaac and mother of Jacob and Esau. Page 30

RECOMMEND - to advise; counsel; to attract favor to.

RED SEA - a body of water between Egypt and Arabia; formerly the reed sea. Moses led the children of Israel across the Red Sea on dry land. Page 96

REDEMPTION - rescue; restoration; deliverance; release.

REED - a variety of tall grass; an ancient Jewish standard of measurement; in religion that standard is the Oneness of Deity.

REFLECTION - the production of an image as by a mirror. "God created man in his own image." Gen. 1:27.

REHOBOAM - son of Solomon; ten tribes of Israel rebelled and followed Jeroboam, and Rehoboam was left as king of two tribes, Judah and Benjamin. Page 366

REPENT - to amend; to change one's mind; to have a new mind.

REUBEN - Jacob's eldest son; one of the twelve tribes of Israel. Page 69

REVEAL - to make known; to unveil; disclose; make clear.

REVELATION - the act of revealing or communicating divine Truth; God's disclosure of Himself or His will to man through signs, laws, or inspiration. The last book of the N.T., an apocalypse. Page 1225

REVILE - to regard as vile; to debase; to reproach; to rail at.

RICH - having abundance; abounding in superior pleasing or effective qualities.

RIGHTEOUS - wise; having wisdom; a right thinker; doing that which is right.

RIGHTEOUSNESS - the state of acceptance with God or good; godliness; equity; right thinking.

RUTH - a Moabitish woman; the daughter-in-law of Naomi. A Book of the O.T. Page 229

—S—

SABBATH - the seventh day; a season or day of rest. Page 110

SACKBUT - early form of slide trombone.

SACKCLOTH - coarse cloth, probably goat's or camel's hair, worn as a sign of mourning or distress; a sign of penitence, "sackcloth and ashes."

Sacrament - an oath or solemn covenant; a sacred ceremony used to impress an obligation; a seal or bond as between God and man.

Sadducee - one of a sect among the ancient Jews that denied the resurrection, personal immortality, future retribution, fate, the existence of angels and postulated the freedom of the will.

Salem - the place where Melchizedek was king. Page 18

Salome - the daughter of Herodias who asked from Herod the head of John the Baptist. Page 871

Salome - the mother of James and John and wife of Zebedeee. Page 1000

Salt - that which preserves or purifies; a corrective; bitterness.

Salvation - the saving of man from the spiritual consequences of sin; redemption; preservation from destruction, failure or other evil; deliverance through the atonement of Christ.

Samaria - an ancient city and area in Palestine. Page 383

Samaritan - an inhabitant of Samaria.

Samson - a judge of Israel; enticed by Delilah to his undoing. Page 213

Samuel - a famous Hebrew judge and prophet; established the monarchy with Saul as king; later anointed David. Page 241

Sanctification - the act or process of God's grace by which the affections of men are purified.

Sanctuary - a place of refuge; the most sacred part of any religious building, especially the vicinity of the altar. The part of the temple at Jerusalem called the Holy of Holies in which was kept the Ark of the Covenant, and into which no person was allowed to enter except the high priest and he only once a year.

Sanhedrin - assembly; the supreme council and tribunal of the Jews.

Sarah - wife of Abraham and mother of Isaac. She was first called Sarai. Page 15

Sardis - seat of one of the Seven Churches of Asia Minor. Page 1232

Satan - an adversary; a fiend; one of diabolical wickedness.

Saul - son of Kish and crowned by Samuel as the first king of Israel. Page 253

Saul of Tarsus - the name of the Apostle Paul before his conversion. Page 1029

Science - knowledge systematized and formulated with reference to the discovery of general truths or the operation of general law.

SCORPION - an insect with a venomous sting at the end of its tail. In apocalyptic literature the scorpion represents indecision, confusion, destructive thinking.

SEA - a vast expanse of water; an overwhelming flood; without landmarks or guidance; lost; bewildered. In vision literature the sea stands for hidden erroneous conditions.

SELF - a being in relation to his own identity.
SELFISH - caring unduly or supremely for one's self.
SELF-RIGHTEOUS - righteous in one's own esteem.
SELF-CENTERED - all interest centered on self, etc.

SENNACHERIB - an Assyrian king whose army was mysteriously destroyed during his campaign against Hezekiah, king of Judah. Page 466

SERPENT - a deceiver; a snake. "There are several words in the Bible for various sorts of serpents, and it is not always certain which kind is referred to. Satan is called a serpent partly because of various qualities of the serpent which seem similar to his, and partly because the serpent was a common symbol of evil." Cruden's Concordance.

SETH - son of Adam and Eve. Page 9

SHADRACH - a Hebrew youth who with Meshach and Abednego was cast into a fiery furnace by Nebuchadnezzar. Page 573

SHARON - a land of great richness in western Palestine.

SHEBA - a district in southern Arabia, whose Queen came to the court of Solomon to ask many questions. Page 361

SHEKINAH - the divine manifestation through which God's presence is felt by man.

SHEM - the eldest son of Noah Page 13

SHILOH - an early Hebrew sanctuary where the Ark of the Covenant was kept in the days of the Judges. Page 192

SHIMEI - a Benjamite of the house of Saul who cursed David as he fled from Absalom. Page 330

SHITTIM WOOD - a variety of acacia of which the ark and altars of the Jewish tabernacle were made.

SHUNAMMITE - a woman of Shunem whose son Elisha raised from the dead. Page 405

SICK - imperfect.

SIDON - a seaport town of Phoenicia.

SILAS - an apostle from Jerusalem who worked with Paul. Page 1048

Siloam - a spring and pool of water where Jesus sent the blind man to wash. Page 913

Simeon - one of Jacob's twelve sons. Page 69

Simon Peter - see Peter

Simon Zelotes - one of Jesus' twelve disciples. Page 857

Sin - "all unrighteousness is sin." I John 5:17

Sinai - a mountain in the Sinai Peninsula where Moses was given the Ten Commandments. Page 109

Sisera - Captain of the army of Jabin, king of Canaan, killed by Jael. Page 201

Sleep - to lie dormant; a temporary diminution of feeling and thought. Page 6

Smyrna - the seat of one of the Seven Churches of Asia Minor. Page 1231

Sodom - a city on the Dead Sea destroyed because of its wickedness. Page 23

Solomon - son of David and king after him. Noted for his wisdom. The Books of Proverbs and Song of Solomon, O.T., attributed to him. Page 320

Soul - essence; substance; animating principle; or actuating cause of life; the repository of imperishable Truth; the seat of real life.

Space - that which is characterized by extension in all directions; boundlessness; duration.

Spikenard - a fragrant ointment of the ancients.

Spirit - the breath of life or life principle; hence the agent for vital and conscious functions in man; the manifestation of the divine nature; soul. " God is Spirit." John 4:24.

Spiritual - controlled and inspired by Spirit; proceeding from the Holy Spirit; pure; holy; divine; heavenly minded; opposed to carnal.

Stand - to hold a place; to be fixed or steadfast; to endure.

Steal - to take or appropriate without right or leave; to get by unfair means; to practice or be guilty of theft.

Stephen - the first Christian martyr accused of blasphemy and stoned to death. Page 1027

Strawed - spread.

Substance - that which is real; the real essence or nature of a thing; the abiding part of any existence.

SUGGESTION - the uncritical acceptance of an idea or proposal made by a person to whom the subject is submissive.

SUPERSTITION - unreasoning fear of the unknown.

SWORD - a symbol of power; a piercing means or agency of attack or defense, as some words are swords: ". . . take the sword of the Spirit which is the word of God." Eph. 6:17.

— T —

TABITHA - also called Dorcas, was a woman disciple of Joppa "full of good works"; when she died the disciples called Peter, who raised her from the dead. Page 1035

TARSUS - a city in Cilicia; birthplace of Paul who was first called Saul of Tarsus. Page 1033

TEKOA - a village north of Jerusalem; birthplace of the prophet Amos. Page 433

TEMPTATION - a test.

TEMPTER - one who tempts or entices; the great enticer of evil.

TERAH - the father of Abraham, Nahor and Haran, and through them the ancestor of the Israelites, Ishmaelites, Midianites, Moabites and Ammonites. Page 14

THESSALONICA - a town of Macedonia where Paul and Silas worked; two of Paul's epistles are to the Thessalonians, N.T. Page 1056

THOMAS - one of the twelve Disciples of Jesus. Doubted the resurrection until he inspected Jesus' hands. Page 857

THYATIRA - seat of one of the Seven Churches of Asia Minor. Page 1232

TIBERIAS - a city on the Sea of Galilee which is sometimes called the Lake of Tiberias.

TIME - beginning and enduring; the measured aspect of duration; "Of time as of space we cannot assert a real existence; it is not in things but in our mode of perceiving them." Karl Pearson.

TIMOTHY - a disciple of Paul, sometimes called Timotheus; Page 1049
Two of Paul's epistles were addressed to him, N.T. Page 1163

TRUTH - quality or state of being true; spiritual reality; real state of things; fact; reality; actual being or nature; actual existence; an established principle; fixed law. "Spirit is Truth." I John 5:6.

TYRE - an ancient city of Phoenicia; Hiram king of Tyre was a friend of David and Solomon. Page 353

— U —

Understand - to apprehend the meaning of; to grasp the idea; to have received knowledge.

Understanding - the power to distinguish truth from error or falsehood; the power of perception; comprehension of the divine, in apocalyptic literature symbolized by burnished feet.

Universe - all created things viewed as constituting one system or whole; the creation.

Upright - morally correct; honest; just.

Ur - of the Chaldees was the early home of Abraham; from here he journeyed to the land of Canaan. Page 14

Uriah - captain of David's army and husband of Bathsheba. Page 315

Urim and Thummin — light; perfection; the urim and thummin were given to the high priest as a symbol of spiritual clearness and justice, and of spiritual activity and decision. Page 129

Uzziah - king of Judah who was struck with leprosy because of sacrilegious action in the temple. Page 431

— V —

Vanity - emptiness, idleness; falsity; devoid of use, truth or worth; self-glorification.

Vashti - queen of king Ahasuerus who was replaced by Esther. Page 639

Veil - a fabric hung up to intercept the view; a curtain hung before the sanctuary. " Within the Veil," within the holy of holies; concealed by the veil in the temple; beyond the veil of sense perception. Page 128

Viper - a venomous snake; a dangerous, treacherous, or malignant person.

Vow - a solemn promise made before God.

— W —

Watch - to be awake; to keep guard; to attend with alert vigilance.

Water - the liquid which descends from the clouds in rain and which forms rivers, lakes and seas.

Water, flowing - true teachings.

Water of Life - spiritual understanding; spiritual refreshment.

Wealth - a comparative abundance of things which are objects of human desire; good; well-being; happiness.

Wealthy - characterized by abundance; enjoying a condition of well-being.

White - free from spot or blemish; innocent; pure.

Whoredom - adultery; fornication; idolatry; infidelity.

Wine - many different words meaning various kinds of fresh grape juice, sweet wine, and fermented wine, were all translated " wine " by Bible translators. The word also means inspiration.

Wisdom - knowledge with the capacity to use it; discernment and judgment; ability to judge soundly.

Wise - righteous; judging soundly what is true and false; guided by wisdom; enlightened.

Witch - one given to mischief; one who practices enchantment.

Witchcraft - the practices or art of enchantment, or irresistible influence, as hypnotism.

Witness - testimony; that which serves as evidence of proof.

Wizard - conjurer; a clever or skillful person; an enchanter.

Word - the symbol of an idea; thought expressed. " The Word " is the divine wisdom finding manifestation in the world of men, and above all in Christ Jesus. Page 829

Work - n. anything accomplished; achievement; that which is produced by mental labor.
v.t. to bring to pass; produce; accomplish; to solve as a problem.

Worship - n. adoration, reverence.
v.t. reverence with supreme respect and veneration; to honor with love.

World - the creation; the system of created things; the universe; the earth and its inhabitants; the sum of human affairs and interests.

" **Wrath of God** " - the love of God correcting and purifying.

—Z—

Zacchaeus - a tax-collector of Jericho who climbed into a sycamore tree to see Jesus as he passed by. Page 952

Zacharias - father of John the Baptist. Page 831

Zebedee - the father of Jesus' disciples, James and John. Page 848

Zebulun - one of the twelve sons of Jacob. Page 69

Zechariah - a prophet who aided Zerubbabel in rebuilding the temple in Jerusalem; author of O.T. Book. Page 601

Zedekiah - the last king of Judah who rebelled against Nebuchadnezzar and brought on the captivity of the Jews and the destruction of Jerusalem. Page 497

Zephaniah - a prophet in the time of king Josiah, and his uncle; wrote O.T. book of that name. Page 485

Zerubbabel - leader of the Jews in their return from Babylon, and in rebuilding the temple in Jerusalem. Page 597

Zion - a hill in Jerusalem where David built his palace and later the place of the temple; figuratively the heavenly city of God. Page 304

Zipporah - wife of Moses, and daughter of Jethro, the priest of Midian. Page 77

LIST OF REFERENCES

THE OLD TESTAMENT

The Everlasting Light. Isaiah 60:19.

The Things of the Spirit . . . I Corinthians 2:14.

Thou Shalt Have No Other Gods Before Me. Exodus 20:3.

In the Beginning God. Genesis 1:1.

GENESIS

God Will Provide Himself a Lamb. Gen. 22:8. Page 27
Gen. 22:1-8, 9p., 11, 12, 13p. 23:2p., 1p., 2p., 19p.

The Lord Shall Send His Angel Before Thee. Gen. 24:7. Page 29
Gen. 24:1-6, 7p., 8, 9, 10p., 11-15, 16p., 17-24, 25p., 26-28, 29p., 30p., 29p., 30p., 31-33, 34 (reworded), 35-38, 40p., 41p., 42-46, 47p., 48-58, 60p., 61p., 63, 64, 65p., 66, 67. 25:7, 8p., 9p., 10p.

Two Nations, and Two Manner of People. Gen. 25:23. Page 34
Gen. 25:20p., 21, 22, 23p. (*shall be separated from thy bowels* to *shalt thou bear*), 24p. (*there were twins in her womb* to *Rebekah bare twins*), 25, 26p. 26:13, 14p.

What Profit Shall This Birthright Do Me? Gen. 25:32. Page 34
Gen. 25:27-29, 30p., 31-34.

Bless Me, Even Me Also, O My Father! Gen. 27:34. Page 35
Gen. 27:1-4, 5p. (reworded), 6p., 7-22, 23p., 24, 25, 26p., 27-31, 32p., 33-36, 37p., 38, 39p., 40, 41p.

God Is In This Place, and I Knew It Not. Gen. 28:16. Page 38
Gen. 27:41p., 42, 43, 44p., 45p., 46. 28:1p., 2p., 3p., 4, 5p., 10-18, 19p., 20-22. 29:1p.

I Will Serve Thee Seven Years for Rachel. Gen. 29:18. Page 40
Gen. 29:1p., 2-4, 5p., 6, 9p., 10p., 11, 12p., 13p., 14-20, 21p., 22, 23p., 25p., 26-28, 30p., 32p., 33p. (29:34, 35 and 30:6-21, summarized in one sentence), 29:31p. 30:1, 22p., 23p., 24p.

The Lord Watch Between Me and Thee. Gen. 31:49. Page 42
Gen. 30:25-27, 28p., 29p., 30-32, 33p., 34-37, 38p., 39, 41p., 42, 40p., 43. 31:1-9, 11p., 13p., 14-17, 18p., 20p., 21p., 19p., 22, 23p., 24p., 25p., 26-30, 31p., 32p., 33, 34p., 35p., 34p., 36p., 37, 38p., 41p., 42p., 43-46, 48p., 49p., 52, 53p., 54, 55.

I Will Not Let Thee Go, Except Thou Bless Me. Gen. 32:26. Page 46
Gen. 32:1p., 3-9, 10p., 11, 12, 13 (14 and 15 summarized), 16-18, 19p., 20p., 21p., 22p., 23p., 24-30, 31p.

I Saw Thy Face, As Though It Were the Face of God. Gen 33:10. Page 48
Gen. 33:1-5, 7-11, 16, 17p. 35:16 (*Rachel travailed* to *bare Jacob another son*), 18, 19p., 20p., 27p., 28, 29p.

Hear This Dream Which I Have Dreamed. Gen. 37:6. Page 50
Gen. 37:1p., 2p., 3-12, 13p., 14p., 17p., 18-20, 21p., 22p., 23, 24, 25p., 26, 27, 28p., 29-31, 32p., 33-35.

Do Not Interpretations Belong to God? Gen. 40:8. Page 52
Gen. 39:1p., 2p., 3, 4, 5p., 6, 7, 8p., 9, 10p., 11p., 12, 16, 17p., 18, 19p., 20p., 21, 22p., 23p. 40:1p., 2p., 3p., 4p., 5p., 6, 7p., 8-23.

God Shall Give Pharaoh an Answer of Peace. Gen. 41:16. Page 55
Gen. 41:1-9, 10 (*ward* to *prison*), 11p., 12p., 13-27, 28p., 29-43, 45p., 46-49, 50p., 51-57.

EXODUS

THE LAW

The Ten Commandments. Ex. 34:28. Page 109
Ex. 19:1p., 2p., 3-8, 9p., 10p., 11, 14, 15p., 16-19, 20p. Ex. 20:1-24. 23:20, 25, 27, 31p., 32, 33p., 24, 33p. 24: 3-5, 7, 12, 13p., 14-17, 18p.

The Law Is Holy, and the Commandment Is Holy, and Just and Good. Rom. 7:12. Page 114
Ex. 24:18p. Lev. 19:1, 2. 11:45. 20:22p., 24p., 26p. 11:44p. Deut. 6:5.

I. Ex. 20:3. Deut. 28:14. 13:1-3, 6, 8, 4. Ex. 23:13.

II. Ex. 20:4p. Lev. 19:4. 26:1. Deut. 4:15p., 16-18, 19p., 23, 24. Ex. 20:5p., 6. Lev. 19:18.

III. Ex. 20:7p. Lev. 22:32. Ex. 20:7p.

IV. Ex. 20:8. 31:13p., 16p., 17, 14p. Deut. 5:12. Ex. 31:15p. 23:12. Lev. 25:3p., 4, 5, 20-22. Deut. 15:1, 2, 3p., 12-15, 18. Lev. 25:8, 9p., 10-14, 17p., 18, 19. 26:2.

V. Ex. 20:12p. Deut. 5:16.

VI. Ex. 20:13. Lev. 24:17-20. Ex. 23:7p. Deut. 24:16p. Lev. 24:22. Ex. 23:19p. Lev. 19:33, 34p. Deut. 24:14. 15:7, 8. Lev. 25:35p., 36. Deut. 15:10, 11. Lev. 19:9. Deut. 24:19p. Lev. 19:17, 18.

VII. Ex. 20:14. Lev. 20:10p., 12p., 17p. 19:19p. 18:24p. Lev. 19:31p. 20:6. Deut. 18:10, 11, 12p. Lev. 18:24p., 25, 26p., 28, 30p. Deut. 18:13. Lev. 20:7.

VIII. Ex. 20:15. Lev. 19:11, 13p. Deut. 22:1, 3p., 4. Lev. 19:35, 36. Deut. 16:18, 19. 25:1. 1:17p. 16:20.

IX. Ex. 20:16. 23:1p. Deut. 5:20. Ex. 23:1p., 2. Deut. 19:16-20. Lev. 19:16p. Ex. 27:7p. Deut. 32:4p.

X. Ex. 20:17p. Deut. 5:21. 16:15p. Lev. 19:18p. 26:3-5, 10. Ex. 23:25p. Lev. 26:6, 11, 12. 19:2p. 27:34. Ex. 31:18.

Who Is on The Lord's Side? Ex. 32:26. Page 123
Ex. 32:1-4, 6-8, 15, 16, 19-24, 26p., 29p., 30-33, 34p. 33:1p., 2p. 32:34p. 33:5p., 3p., 6p., 7-10. 34:1-3.

Moses' Face Shone. Ex. 34:35. Page 126
Ex. 34:4-6, 7p., 8. 33:11p. 34:9. 33:12p., 13, 14, 18, 19p., 21p., 22. 34:8, 27, 28, 29p., 30, 31p., 33p., 32p., 31p., 32p., 33, 35p.

Make Me a Sanctuary. Ex. 25:8. Page 127
Ex. 25:1, 2, 8, 9, 10p., 11p., 12p., 13, 14p., 16p. 31:18p. 25:17p., 18p., 20p., 21p., 22p. 26:31p., 32p., 33p., 34p., 1p. 27:9p., 18p., 17p. 25:23p., 24p., 26p., 28p., 29p., 30, 31, 32p., 37p. 27:20p. 26:35p. 30:1, 2p., 3p., 4p., 5. 28:1p., 2p., 29p., 30p. 30:25p., 30, 31p., 32p., 7p., 8, 10p. 27:1p., 2p., 6, 7p., 3. 29:36p., 37p., 38p., 39p., 41, 42p., 45, 46p. 30:18p., 19, 20p., 21p. 25:40p., 9. 35:1p., 5p., 20, 22p., 24p., 25, 27, 28p., 29p. 36:2p., 3p., 4, 5, 6p., 7. 39:32p., 33p., 43p. 40:1, 12, 13p., 14p., 15p. Num. 6:23-27. Ex. 40:16, 33p., 34. Num. 9:16, 17, 18p.

NUMBERS

Num. 1:1p., 2p., 3, 4p., 16p., 17p., 18p. 19p., 44p., 20p. (12 tribes named), 45p., 46p., 47, 48, 49p., 50p., 51p., 52. 2:2p. 1:53p. Deut. 18:9p., 1p., 2p., 3p., 5. Num. 1:54.

Thou Shalt See My Word Come to Pass. Num. 11:23. Page 135
Num. 10:11p., 12p., 33p., 12p. 11:4p., 5-9, 10p., 11, 12p., 13, 14, 16-19, 20p., 21-25, 28p., 29-32.

My Servant Moses Is Faithful in All My House. Num. 12:7. Page 137
Num. 12:1p., 2-11, 12p., 13, 14p., 15.

We Were in Our Own Sight as Grasshoppers. Num. 13:33. Page 138
Num. 13:1, 2p., 3p., 17-20, 21p., 22p., 23p., 25, 26p., 27p., 28-31, 32p., 33. 14:1, 2p., 3, 4. Deut. 1:29, 30, 31. Num. 14:6, 7p., 8-11, 13p., 19-24, 25p., 26-28, 29p., 30p., 31, 32p., 33p., 34p., 35p., 39, 40p., 41, 42p., 43p., 44, 45p. Deut. 1:44, 45.

The Lord Will Show Whom He Hath Chosen. Num. 16:5. Page 142
Num. 16:1p., 2-4, 5p., 6. 7p., 8-13, 14p., 15, 16, 17p., 18-21, 25-28, 29p., 30-33, 35, 34, 41-44, 45p., 46-49.

The Rod of Aaron Budded and Bloomed. Num. 17:8. Page 145
Num. 17:1, 2p., 3-5, 6p., 7-11.

Speak Ye to the Rock. Num. 20:8. Page 146
Num. 20:1p., 2, 3p., 4-13.

All the Congregation Mourned for Aaron. Num. 20:29. Page 147
Num. 20:14-19, 21-27, 28p. 33:38p., 39. 20:28p., 29.

Moses Made a Serpent of Brass. Num. 21:9. Page 148
Num. 21:4-9.

What The Lord Saith, That Will I Speak. Num. 24:13. Page 149
Num. 21:10p., 11p., 21, 22, 23p., 24p., 25p., 33, 34p., 35. 22:1, 2p., 4p., 2p., 3p., 4p., 5p., 6-8, 9p., 12p., 13-21, 22p., 23-34, 35p., 36p., 37, 38, 39p., 41p. 23:1, 2p., 3, 4p., 5, 6p., 7p., 8, 9, 10p., 11, 12p., 13p., 14p., 15, 16, 17-19, 20p., 21, 23p., 25, 26p., 27p., 28p., 29,30. 24:1, 2, 3p., 4p., 5, 6p., 7p., 8, 9p., 10p., 11, 12p., 13, 17p., 19p., 14p., 25. 25:1, 2p., 3p., 5, 6, 7p., 8p., 9. 31:6p., 7p., 8p., 9, 10p., 12p., 14p., 15-17, 19p., 28p., 48p., 50p., 54p.

Inheritance Law of the Children of Israel. Page 156
Num. 26:1p., 2, 63p., 51p., 65, 52, 53, 54p., 55, 56p. 27:1p., 2p., 3p., 4-8, 11p. 32:1, 2p., 4p., 5p., 6p., 7-9, 13p., 14-18, 19p., 20p., 21p., 22, 23, 33p.

A Man in Whom Is the Spirit. Num. 27:8. Page 159
Num. 27:12 (*Abarim* to *Nebo*), 13, 14p., 15. Deut. 3:24, 25, 26p., 27p., 26p. Num. 27:15p., 16p., 17p., 18, 19p., 20, 19p. Deut. 3:28p. Num. 27:22, 23p.

DEUTERONOMY

Thou Shalt Be Perfect With the Lord Thy God. Deut. 18:13. Page 160
Deut. 1:3p., 1p. 9:1. 1:10. 29:5. 2:7. 4:1. 2:21p. 9:1p., 2p., 3p. 31:3p., 2p., 7, 8. 3:18p. 23:9, 14p. 20:1-4, 5p., 8p. 11:22-25. 12:2, 3. 31:6. 17:14p. 9:4p., 5p. 8:2-10. 12:12p. 8:11p., 12-17, 18p., 19p., 20p., 19p. 28:15p., 49, 50, 52p., 53p., 54p., 55p., 56p., 64-67. 4:28-31, 1p., 5p., 6-8, 39. 6:4, 5, 6p., 7, 8, 18p. 18:13. 7:7, 8p., 12, 13. 28:8p. 7:15p. 18:13, 15, 17p., 18. 29:10. 30:10-20. 31:30. 32:1-4, 9-12, 39p., 43p.

The Eternal God Is Thy Refuge. Deut. 33:27. Page 168
Deut. 32:48, 49p., 50p., 52. 33:1p., 2p., 27, 28p., 29. 34:1p., 2-7, 8p., 10.

THE BOOK OF JOSHUA

Joshua. All Good Things Have Come Upon You. Jos. 23:15. Page 171

Joshua Shall Go Before His People. Deut. 31:28. Page 173
Jos. 1:1-11, 16, 17.

Two Men Sent to Jericho. Jos. 2:1. Page 174
Jos. 2:1p., 4p., 2p., 3p., 4p., 5p., 7p., 6, 8p., 9, 10p., 11, 12p., 13p., 14p., 15p., 16-18, 19p., 20-23, 24p.

Ye Shall Know That The Living God Is Among You. Jos. 3:10 Page 176
Jos. 3:1p., 2p., 7-11, 13p., 14p., 15p., 16p., 17. 4:1-6, 7p., 22-24, 7p., 8p., 9p., 15-18. 5:10-12.

Captain of the Host of the Lord. Jos. 5:14. Page 178
Jos. 5:13-15.

Shout! For the Lord Hath Given You the City. Jos. 6:16. Page 179
Jos. 6:1-12, 13p., 14-16, 17p., 18, 19, 20p., 21-24, 25p., 27.

Get Up! Wherefore Liest Thou Upon Thy Face? Jos. 7:10. Page 181
Jos. 7:1p., 2p., 3-16, 17p., 18p., 19, 20p., 21-24, 25p., 26p.

Fear Not, Arise, Go Up to Ai. Jos. 8:1. Page 183
Jos. 8:1, 2p., 3p., 4p., 5p., 6p., 7-10, 11p., 14p., 15-19, 20p., 21, 28, 30p., 31p., 32, 34p., 35p.

Gibeon Made Peace with Israel. Jos. 10:1. Page 185
Jos. 9:3, 4, 5p., 6, 7p., 8, 9, 10p., 11-20, 21p., 22-26, 27p.

The Sun Stood Still in the Midst of Heaven. Jos. 10:13. Page 187
Jos. 10:1p., 2, 3p., 4-8, 9p., 10p., 11p., 12-19, 20-25, 26p., 27p., 40, 42, 43.

So Joshua Took the Whole Land. Jos. 11:23 Page 190
Jos. 11:1p., 2-9 (*houghed* to *killed*), 12, 15p., 16, 17p., 18, 19p., 23.

THE BOOK OF JUDGES

DAN

BENJAMIN Page 224

Judg. 19:1p., 2p., 3p., 4p., 10p., 11, 12p., 14, 15p., 16p., 17, 18p., 19-21, 22p., 23p., 25p. (26-29 reworded), 30. 20:1p., 3p., 4p., 5p., 6p., 7-9, 11p., 12, 13p., 14p., 18p., 19p., 34p., 31p., 34p., 35p., 36p., 45p., 48p. 21:1, 6 (*repented* to *grieved*), 3, 7, 16p., 17, 19p., 20-23, 24, 25p.

THE BOOK OF RUTH

Thou Hast Shown Kindness. Ruth 3:10 Page 229
Ruth 1:1, 2p., 3-5, 6p., 7-10, 11p., 12p., 14-20, 21p., 22p. 2:1, 2p., 3p., 4, 5, 6p., 7p., 9, 10, 11p., 12, 13p., 14-17, 18p., 19p., 20p., 21p., 22p., 23. 3:1p., 2-18. 4:1-10, 11p., 13p., 14-16, 17p., 22.

I SAMUEL

Behold, To Obey Is Better Than Sacrifice. I Sam. 15:22 Page 239

For This Child I Prayed. I Sam 1:27 Page 241
I Sam. 1:1p., 2-4, 5p., 6p., 2p., 6p. (*adversary* to *Penninah*), 7p., 8, 9p., 10, 11, 9p., 12-16, 17p., 18, 19p., 20p., 21p., 22-23, 24, 25p., 26-28.

Eli Heard All That His Sons Did. I Sam. 2:22 Page 243
I Sam. 1:3p 2:12, 17p., 22p., 23, 24, 25p., 27p., 30p., 31p., 33p., 34, 35.

Speak Lord, For Thy Servant Heareth. I Sam. 3:9. Page 244
I Sam. 2:26, 18-21. 3:1-10, 11p., 12p., 13-18, 19p., 21p. 4:1p. 5:20.

The Ark of God Was Taken. I Sam. 4:11. Page 246
I Sam. 4:1p., 2p., 3p., 4p., 5-13, 14p., 15-18.

Send Away the Ark of The God of Israel. I Sam. 5:11. Page 248
I Sam. 5:1, 2p., 3, 4, 6p., 7-10, 11p., 12p. 6:1, 2, 3p., 4, 5, 7-13, 14p., 15p., 21p., 16.

Hitherto Hath The Lord Helped Us. I Sam. 7:12. Page 250
I Sam. 7:3p., 4-7, 8p., 9p., 10, 11p., 12p., 13-17.

Give Us a King . . . I Sam. 8:6p., 20p. Page 252
I Sam. 8:1, 3-22.

Behold The King Whom Ye Have Chosen. I Sam. 12:13. Page 253
I Sam. 9:1p., 2-20, 21p., 22, 24p., 25p., 27p. 10:1, 2p., 3, 4, 5p., 6, 7, 17, 18p., 19p., 20-25p. 11:14, 15p. 12:1, 2p., 3-5, 6p., 7, 12p., 13-19, 20p., 21p., 20p., 22p., 23p., 24. 14:47p., 48p., 52.

Behold, To Obey Is Better Than Sacrifice . . . I Sam. 15:22. Page 259
I Sam. 13:1. 15:1p., 2-5, 7p., 8-11, 12p., 13-15, 16p., 17-23. 13:13p., 14. 15:24-28.

The Lord Seeth Not as Man Seeth. I Sam. 16:7. Page 262
I Sam. 16:1-13.

David Took an Harp, and Played, and Saul Was Refreshed. I Sam. 16:23. Page 263
I Sam. 16:14p., 15p., 16p., 17-22, 23p. Psalm 23. I Sam. 16:23p.

The Lord Saveth Not With Sword and Spear. I Sam. 17:47. Page 265
I Sam. 17:1p., 2-11, 16, 12p., 14, 15 (reworded), 17, 18, 20-24, 25p., 26p., 27p., 25p., 28, 29, 30p., 26p., 31 (reworded), 32-35, 36p., 37-50, 51p., 52, 53p.

Jonathan Loved David as His Own Soul. I Sam. 18:1 Page 269
I Sam. 17:57p. 18:2. 14:49. 18:1p., 3-9, 10p., 11-20, 21p., 22-24, 25p., 26, 27p., 28, 29. 19:1, 2p., 3-8, 9p., 10-18. 20:1-3, 4p., 5p., 6-9, 10p., 11p., 12p., 13, 14p., 15p., 16p., 18-25, 26p., 27p., 28, 29p., 30p., 31-42.

Thou Hast Rewarded Me Good For Evil. I Sam. 24:17. Page 276
I Sam. 21:1-3, 4p., 6p., 8, 9. 22:1-4, 6p. 23:14-18. 24:2-22.

Thy Advice Hath Kept Me From Avenging Myself. I Sam. 25:33 Page 279
I Sam. 25:1-12, 21, 13-20, 23, 24p., 25, 26p., 27, 28p., 30-33, 35-37, 38p., 39p., 40, 41p., 42-44.

The Lord Delivered Thee Into Mine Hand. I Sam. 26:23. Page 282
I Sam. 26:1p., 2-5, 6p., 7-9, 10p., 11-17, 18p., 19p., 20p., 21-25. 27:1-3, 5, 6, 4. Psalm 18:1-3, 20-22, 24-26, 28, 30-32.

A Woman at Endor That Hath a Familiar Spirit. I Sam. 28:7. Page 286
I Sam. 28:3-15, 16p., 17p., 18p., 19, 20p., 21-25.

But David Encouraged Himself in The Lord His God. I Sam. 30:6. Page 289
I Sam. 29:1, 2, 3p., 4p., 5-11. 30:1p., 2-19, 20p., 21p., 22p., 23-26. Psalm 18:46-49.

The Battle Went Sore Against Saul. I Sam. 31:3. Page 293
I Sam. 31:1-3, 4 (*uncircumcised* to *Philistines*), 5-13. I Chron. 10:13, 14p.

How Are the Mighty Fallen! II Sam. 1:19. Page 294
II Sam. 1:1p., 2p., 3p., 4p., 5p., 6p., 7-14, 16p., 15, 17, 19, 20p., 21, 23, 25-27.

THE SECOND BOOK OF SAMUEL, AND THE FIRST BOOK OF CHRONICLES

Thy Gentleness Hath Made Me Great. II Sam. 22:36p. Page 297

They Anointed David King Over Judah. II Sam. 2:3p. Page 299
II Sam. 2:1 (*after this* to *after the death of Saul*), 2p., 3-7, 8p., 9, 10.

David Lamented Over Abner. II Sam. 3:33. Page 300
II Sam. 3:1, 6, (7 and 8 reworded), 9, 10, 11p., 12p., 13-21, 22p., 23p., 24, 25p., 26p., 27p., 30p., 28p., 29p., 31, 32, 35, 36, 37p., 38, 39p. 4:1, 2p., 5p., 6p., 7p., 8, 9p., 10p., 11, 12p.

Thou Shalt Be Ruler Over My People Israel. I Chron. 11:2. Page 303
II Sam. 5:1. I Chron. 11:2 3. 12:16p., 17p., 18, 38p., 40p., 39, 40p., 22. 11:9p., 4p., 5. II Sam. 5:7p., 9p. (*fort* to *Zion*). I Chron. 11:8p. II Sam. 5:10. Psalm 48:1-3, 11-13, 14p. 147:12.

They Brought the Ark of God to the City of David. II Sam. 6:12. Page 305
I Chron. 14:1, 2, 17. II Sam. 6:1p. I Chron. 13:1p., 2p., 3, 4, 6p. II Sam. 6:3p., 6-8, 10p., 11. I Chron. 15:1p., 2, 3, 11p., 12-15, 25, 27p. II Sam. 6:14p., 16, 23. I Chron. 16:1-4, 7-12, 23, 25p., 27-29, 31, 36p., 37, 40.

Thy Kingdom Shall Be Established For Ever. II Sam. 7:16p. Page 308
I Chron. 15:1p. II Sam. 5:13p. (order changed). I Chron. 17:1. II Sam. 7:3. I Chron. 17:3, 4. II Sam. 7:6, 8p., 9. I Chron. 17:11, 12p., 13p., 14p. II Sam. 7:16p. I Chron. 17:16, 19, 20. II Sam. 7:28p.

David Dedicated Unto The Lord the Silver and Gold. I Chron. 18:11. Page 310
I Chron. 14:8-10, 11p., 13-16. 18:1p., 2, 3p., 4p., 5, 6. II Sam. 8:7, 8p., 9, 10p. I Chron. 18:11p., 14.

I Show Thee Kindness for Jonathan's Sake. II Sam. 9:7. Page 311
II Sam. 9:1-3, 4p., 5p., 6p., 7-9, 10p., 11p., 12p., 13p.

David Sent to Comfort Hunan. II Sam. 10:2. Page 313
II Sam. 10:1, 2p., 3-5. I Chron. 19:6p., 7. II Sam. 10:8p., 9-11. I Chron. 19:13, 14, 15, 16p., 17p. II Sam. 10:18p., 19p.

Why Hast Thou Despised the Commandment of The Lord? II Sam. 12:9. Page 315
II Sam. 11:1-3, 4p., 5-20, 21p., 22-27. 12:1p., 2-7, 8p., 9, 10, 11p., 12, 13p., 14, 15p., 16, 17. (*David mourned*, added). Psalms 38:1-6, 9, 10, 17, 18, 21, 22. II Sam. 12:18, 19, 20p. Psalms 51:1-3, 9, 10, 16, 17. II Sam. 12:20p., 21-23, 24p., 26-30, 31p.

The King's Heart Was Toward Absalom. II Sam. 14:1. Page 321
II Sam. 13:1, 2p., 3-6, 7p., 8-17, 18p., 19p., 18p., 19p., 20-25, 26p., 27-31, 32p., 33p., 34p., 35, 36p., 37p., 38p., 39. 14:1p., 2-6, 7p., 8, 11p., 12-14, 15p., 16, 17p., 18p., 19p., 20p., 21-24, 27-30, 31p., 32, 33.

O Absalom, My Son, My Son. II Sam. 18:33. Page 326
II Sam. 14:25, 26p. (*polled* to *shaved*). 15:1p., 2p., 3, 4, 5p., 6, 7p., 8p., 9, 10, 11p., 12p., 13, 14, 15p., 16p., 17, 18p., 20-22, 23p., 24p., 25-30. Psalms 3:1-6, 7p., 8. II Sam. 15:31-37. 16:1, 2, 3p., 4, 5p., 6-10, 11p., 12-14, 15p., 16-18, 19p., 20, 21, 22p. 17:1-29 (parts of some verses omitted). 18:1, 2p., 3-10, 11p., 12p., 13-17, 21, 24, 25, 31-33. 19:1, 2p., 3, 4, 5p., 6p., 7, 8p., 11p., 12, 14, 15, 18p., 16p., 17p., 18p., 19, 20, 21p., 22p., 23p., 24, 25p., 26, 27, 28p., 29, 30. 20:3p. 22:1p., 2, 3, 5-7, 17-19, 32, 33, 36.

God Save King Solomon. I Kings. 1:34. Page 340
I Kings 1:1p., 5-53 (parts of some verses omitted).

Thine, O Lord, Is the Greatness, and the Power, and the Glory, and the Victory, and the Majesty. I Chron. 29:11. Page 343
I Chron. 28:1p., 2-7, 9p., 10p., 20p., 11p., 19. 29:1p., 2p., 3p., 4p., 5p. 22:14p., 15p. 29:5p. 22:16p. 29:6, 7p., 9p., 10-14, 16-20, 21p., 22-25, 26, 27p. I Kings 2:1-3, 10. I Sam. 23:1p., 2, 3p., 4. I Chron. 29:28.

Behold, Heaven and the Heaven of Heavens Cannot Contain Thee. II Chron. 6:18 Page 349

FIRST AND SECOND KINGS, AND SECOND CHRONICLES, AND SOME PROPHETS

Behold, I Have Given Thee a Wise and an Understanding Heart. I Kings 3:12. Page 351
II Chron. 1:1. I Kings 3:3p. II Chron. 1:2p., 3p., 6, 7p. I Kings 3:5p., 6-14, 15p. II Chron. 1:13p. I Kings 1:15p., 16-28 (parts of some verses omitted).

The House Which I Build Is Great: for Great Is Our God. II Chron. 2:5. Page 353
I Kings 5:1 (with greetings, added), 2, 4, 5. II Chron. 2, 3p., 4p., 5-10. I Kings 5:7. II Chron. 2:11, 12p. I Kings 5:8p. II Chron. 2:13p., 14p. I Kings 5:8p. II Chron. 2:16. I Kings 5:9p. II Chron. 2:15. II Kings 5:11, 12p. II Chron. 2:17p., 18. I Kings 5:17, 18 (order changed). II Chron. 3:1p. I Kings 6:1p., 2, 7, (15, 16 reworded), 20p. II Chron. 3:14. I Kings 6:23p., 27p., 28, 29p., 30. II Chron. 3:17p. 4:9. I Kings 7:23p., 25p., 26p. II Chron. 4:6p., 10. I Kings 7:48p. II Chron. 4:7p. I Kings 7:48p., 50p., 47. II Chron. 4:1p. I Kings 7:45p. II Chron. 4:6. 5:1. I Kings 6:38p. 7:1p., 9p., 7p. 3:1. 7:8p., 51p.

The Heavens Cannot Contain Thee, How Much Less This House Which I Have Built. II Chron. 6:18. Page 358
II Chron. 5: 2, 4p., 5p., 6p., 7p., 8p., 10. Ex. 40:21. II Chron. 5:11p., 12p., 13p., 14. 6:3, 12, 13p., 14, 18, 19, 20p., 21. I Kings 8:33-40. II Chron. 6:40, 41. I Kings 8:54p., 55p., 56-58, 60-63. II Chron. 7-11.

The Queen of Sheba Heard of the Fame of Solomon. II Chron. 9:11. Page 361
I Kings 4:1p., 21p., 24p., 25, 29, 30, 34. II Chron. 9:24, 14p., 17, 18p., 19, 20p., 21p., 22, 1-8. I Kings 10:10, 13.

The Proverbs of Solomon, King of Israel. Page 363
II Chron. 9:23. I Kings 4:32, 33, 31. Proverbs 1:5p.

But When Solomon Was Old, He Loved Many Strange Women. I Kings 11:4p. 1p. Page 363
Better a poor and wise child . . . Ecl. 4:13p. I Kings 11:1p., 4p., 6p., 7p. (reworded), 9, 10p., 11-13, 26p., 28p., 29-31, 33 (reworded), 34p., 32, 34p., 35-38, 40p., 42,43.

Israel Rebelled Against the House of David. I Kings 12:19. Page 366
II Chron. 10:1, 2p., 3, 4. I Kings 12:5, 6. II Chron. 10:7-9, 10p., 11, 12p., (13 and 14 rearranged), 15p. I Kings 12:16, 18, 19, 17, 20-23, 24p.

MICAH

ISAIAH I

ISAIAH I

O Jerusalem, Wash Thine Heart From Wickedness. Jeremiah 4:14. Page 483
II Chron. 34:1, 2p., 3p. Jer. 1:2p., 4p., 1p., 5p., 6-14, 15p., 16p., 17, 18p. 19. II Chron. 34:8p. (*Others*, added), 9p., (10, 11, reworded), 14p., 16p., 18p., 19, 20p., 21, 22p., 23p., 24, 25p., 26p., 27p., 28, 29, 30p. Zephaniah 1: (*Explanation*, added), 1p., 2, 4p., 5p., 6, 7p., 15, 17p., 18. 2:1-3. Jer. 2:1p., 2p., 5, 11-13, 19p. 4:1, 14. II Chron. 34:31p. II Kings 23:3p. II Chron. 34:33p. II Kings 23:24, 21p. II Chron. 35:10, 17p., 20p. II Kings 23:29p. II Chron. 35:21p., 22p., 23, 24p., 25p., 24p., 25p. 36:1p.

Let Not the Wise Man Glory in His Wisdom. Jer. 9:23p. Page 489
II Kings 23:31p., 33p., 34p., 35p., 37p. Jer. 26:1p., 2p. 7:2p., 3p., 4p., 5p., 7, 9, 10p., 11p., 13p., 14p., 15p., 28p., 34. 26:8, 9, 11, 12p. 5:21, 25. 26:12p., 13-15, 16p., 17-19. 9:23.

O Earth, Earth, Earth, Hear the Word of The Lord. Jer. 22:29. Page 491
Jer. 18:1-8. 22:1. 5:11, 12, 13p. 22:2p., 3p., 5. 16:13p. 5:15, 17p. 22:25. 6:19p. 9:16p. 11:12, 13p. 16:20. 10:10p., 12. 17:7, 8, 13p. 18:12, 18, 19 (*Jeremiah said*, added), 20, 23p. 20:1p., 2, 3p., 4-6. 22:18p., 17p., 18p., 19, 21, 22, 25, 26p. 13:15, 16, 17, 18p. 22:29.

The Roll of a Book. Jer. 36:2. Page 495
Jer. 36: (*Jeremiah was shut up in prison*, added), 1p., 2p., 4p. (*scribe*, added) 5p., 6, 7p., 8p., 11p., 12p., 13p., 14p., 16p., 17p. (18-20 reworded), 21p., 22p., 23p., 24, 26p., 29p., 26p. (*so they could not be found*, added) 27p., 28p., 32p.

Two Baskets of Figs. Jer. 24:1. Page 497
II Chron. 36:5p., 7p., 6, 8p., 9p., 10p. II Kings 24:11p., 12p. (*king of Babylon* to *Nebuchadnezzar*) 15p., 13. II Chron. 36:10p. Jer. 37:2. 24:1 (written in third person), 2-7, 8p., 9p.

Ye Shall Seek Me, and Find Me . . . Jer. 31:3. Page 499
Jer. 29:1, 4-7, 8p., 9, 10p., 11-14, (24, 25 reworded), 27p., 28p., 29, 30, 31p. 32.

Obey, I Beseech Thee, the Voice of The Lord. Jer. 38:20. Page 500
Jer. 37: (3 and 5 reworded), 6, 7p., 8-12, 13p., 14p. 38:4p., 2p., 3p., 4p., 5, 6p., 7p., 8p., 9p., 10p., 11p., 12p., 13, (14-21 parts used), 23p., 24, 27p., 26p., 28p. Lamentations 3:52-55, 56p., 57, 58.

The Punishment of Thine Iniquity Is Accomplished, O Jerusalem. (*Daughter of Zion, to Jerusalem.*) Lam. 4:22. Page 504
Jer. 46:2 (reworded). II Kings 24:7. Jer. 52:3p., 4p., 6p. 32:17, 19p. 38:2p. 52:6p. Lam. 4:1, 2, 5, 8, 9, 22p. Jer. 14:17p., 18p. 52: (5 reworded), (7-12 parts used), 13, 17p. (18-23 condensed), 14, 15p., 16p., 26p., 27p., 39:11p., 12, 14p. 40:4p., 5p., 4p., 6p. 52: (15, 16 reworded). 40:6p.

Jerusalem Hath Grievously Sinned. Lam. 1:1-3, 6-8, 16, 18. Page 507

Oh, Remnant of Judah, Go Ye Not into Egypt. Jer. 42:19p. Page 508
Jer. 41: (1-3, 11-13, parts used). 42:1p., 2p., 3p., 6p., 7, 9p., 10p., 11p., 12p., 15p., 16, 19p. 43:1p., 2p., 4p., 6p., 7p., 8p., 9p., 10p., 11p., 12p. 44:27p., 28p., 26p.

HABAKKUK

EZEKIEL

ISAIAH II

DANIEL

The Wise shall understand. Dan. 12:10. Page 591

Dan. 10:1p., 2-7, 8p., 9-12, 14-16, 17p., 18, 19, 20p., 21p. 11:2p., 3, 4p. 12:1-13.

EZRA

God Hath Charged Me to Build Him a Temple in Jerusalem. Ezra 1:2. Page 595

Ezra 1: (1 reworded), 2, 3p., (5 reworded), 7, 8p., 11p. 2:64p., 65p., 70p. Page 597

Haggai 1: (1 reworded), 2, 4p., 5-8, 9p., 10, 11p., 12p.

Ezra 3:1p., 2p. (*others,* added), 3p., 4p., 7p. (8p. reworded), (10-13 parts only.)

Haggai 2:1p., 2p., 3, 4p., 8p., 9p.

Ezra 4:1, (2-5 parts only), 11p., 12p., 13, 14p., 15p., 16, 17p., 18-24. 5:1p.

Zech. 4:6p., 9.

Ezra 5:(2-4 parts), 7p., 8, 9p., 11p., 13, 17p. 6:(1-11 parts), 13p., 14p., 16.

Zech 8: (words added), 7, 8p., 3p., 5, 9p., 10p., 11p., 12, 13, 16, 17p., 20p., 21p., 22, 23p. Ezra 6:21p., 22p.

Rejoice Greatly, O Daughter of Zion. Zech. 9:9. Page 604

Zech. 9:9, 10, 14p., 16, 17p.

The Two Anointed Ones. Zechariah 4:14p. Page 605

Zech. 1:1p. 4: (1 words added), 2-5, 6p., 11p., 12p., 13, 14.

Ezra, the Scribe, Came to Jerusalem. Ezra 7:8. Page 606

Ezra 7:1p., 7p., 10, (11-19 parts only), 25p., 27 (*Ezra said,* added), 28p. 8 (written in 3rd person): 15p., 1p., 15p., 21p., 22, 23, 24p., 25p., 26p., 28p., 29p., 32, 33p., 35p. 9 (1-6 parts only), 15p. 10 (1-3 parts), 4, 6p., 7, 9p., (10-14 parts), 16p., 17, 44p.

NEHEMIAH

Arise, and Build the Wall. (Written in 3rd person.) Nehemiah 2:18p. Page 611

Neh. 1: (1-4 parts). 2: (1-9 parts), 10, 11 (12-20 parts). 4:1-3, 6, 7p., 8, 9p., 11, 13p., 14p., 16p., 17p., 18-20, 22p., 21, 23p. 6:1p., 2p., 3, 4, 5p., 6p., 7, 8, 10p., 11p., 12p., 15p., 16. 7:4, 3p., 2p., 73p. 8:1, 4p., 5p., 6p., 8. 9:5p., 6. 8:6p., 8, 3p., 8p., 9p., 10p. 12:27p., 43p. 11:1, 2. 13: (6p. reworded), 7p., 23, 24, 25p., 27p., 3p., 15p., 19p., 20p., 21p., 14p., 31p.

JONAH

I Will Pay That That I Have Vowed. Jonah 2:9 Page 621
Jonah – Chapters 1-3. 4:1-6 (7 reworded), 8p., 9-11.

JOEL

I Will Pour Out My Spirit. Joel 2:28. Page 627

Joel 1:1, 2p., 4, 5p., 6p., 7, 19p., 11p., 12p., 14p., 15, 16, 19, 20. 2:1, 2p., 6p., 9, 10, 11p., 13p., 15, 16p., 17p., 19, 21, 23, 25p., 26p., 27p., 28, 32p. 3:1, 2p., 9p., 11p., 13p., 14, 15, 16p., 18p., 21p.

MALACHI

I Will Open the Windows of Heaven . . . Malachi 3:10p. Page 633
Mal. 2:10p. 3:1-5, 6p., 7p., 10, 16, 17, 18. 4:1p., 2p., 4, 5, 6p.

ESTHER

Who Knoweth Whether Thou Art Come . . . Esther 4:14 Page 637

Est. 1:1p., 2p., 1p., 3p., 4, 5p., 9p., 7p. (10-13 parts), 15p., 16, 17p., (19-22 parts). 2:1p., 2p., 4 (5-7 reworded), 8p., 9p., 10, 11, 13p., 17p., 18p., 21p., 22p. (23 reworded). 3:1p., 2p., 5, 6p., 4p., 8p., 9p., 10p., 11, 12p., 13p., 15. 4:1, 3, 4p., 5p., 7p., 8p., 9 (10 reworded), 11p., 12, 13p., 14p., 15-17. 5:(1-3 parts), 4, 5, 6p., 7p., 8-10, 11p., 12p., 13, 14. 6:(1-5 parts), 6, 7p., 8, 9p., 10-12, 13p., 14. 7:1 (2-10 parts). 8:1p., 2, 3p., 5p., 6, 7p., 8, 9p., 10p., 11, 14p., 17p. 9:(20-22 parts), 29p., 32p.

JOB

Job. I Have Heard of Thee by the Hearing of the Ear: But Now Mine Eye Seeth Thee. Job 42:5 Page 649

Job 1:1-3, 6-22. 2:1-13. 3:1p., 2, 3p., 4, 20, 25, 26. 4:1, 2, 7, 8, 12, 13, 15p., 16, 17. 5:1, 2, 6, 7, 8, 9, 17, 19. 6:1-3, 24. 7:6, 7, 11, 17, 21. 8:1, 2, 5, 6, 20. 9:1, 2, 13, 20, 22. 10:15, 20, 21. 11:1, 2, 4, 5, 6p., 7, 8, 14p., 15-17, 19p., 20p. 12:1, 2p. 13:1-3. 14:1-4. 15:1, 2, 9, 12, 20, 24, 25. 16:1, 2, 4, 6, 20, 21. 17:10. 18:1, 2p., 3, 5, 6, 21. 19:1-4, 6, 7-10, 13, 14, 20, 21, 23, 25p., 27p. 20:1, 4-6, 7p., 8, 27-29. 21:1, 3, 4, 7, 9, 14, 15, 16, 22, 23, 25, 26, 27, 34. 22:1, 5, 7, 9, 12, 21-23. 23:1, 3-5, 8, 10-12. 27:3, 4. 28:1, 2, 12-14, 15, 20, 23, 28. 29:2-5, 14-16, 18. 30:1p., 15, 16, 20, 26. 31:4-6, 40p. 32:1, 2p., 3-5, 6p., 7-9. 33:1, 4, 14, 23, 26. 34:4, 5, 10-12, 35. 35:5. 36:4p., 5, 22, 24. 37:14p., 16p., 23. 38:1-4, 6, 7, 8p., 11, 12, 16, 18, 19, 22, 24-28, 31-36, 40:2. 42:1-3, 5, 10, 12, 13, 16.

O worship the Lord
In the beauty of holiness

THE BOOK OF PSALMS

O Worship the Lord in the beauty of holiness. 96:9. Page 671

Psalm Group Title References Page

1. Guidance. Blessed is the man. Ps. 1:1-6. 673

3. Protection. I will not be afraid. Ps. 3:1-6, 8. 720

5. Rejoicing. In the morning, I will look up. Ps. 5:8, 11p., 12. 683

8. Humility. What is man that thou art mindful of him? Ps. 8:1, 3-6, 9. 705

9. Praise. The Lord shall endure forever. Ps. 9:1, 2, 7-11, 16. 744

11. Protection. The righteous Lord loveth righteousness. Ps. 11:1, 2, 4, 5p., 7. 721

15. Guidance. Who shall abide in thy tabernacle. Ps. 15:1-3, 4p., 5p. 674

16. Sustenance. Thou maintainest my lot. Ps. 16:1, 5, 6, 8, 9p., 11. 690

17. Humility. When I awake with thy likeness. Ps. 17:6, 7p., 8p., 15. 705

18. Protection. God girdeth me with strength. Ps. 18:1-4, 6, 16, 19-22, 25-28, 30-32, 46. 722

19. Humility Cleanse thou me from secret faults. Ps. 19:1-3, 4p., 7-9, 10p., 11p., 12, 14. 706

22. Forgiveness. Thou art holy. Ps. 22:1, 2, 3p., 4, 5, 7, 27, 28, 31. 737

23. Sustenance. I shall not want. Ps. 23:1-6. 689

24. Guidance. Who shall ascend into the hill of the Lord. Ps. 24:3-5. 679
Protection. The earth is the Lord's. Ps. 24:1, 2, 9, 10. 731

25. Forgiveness. According to thy mercy remember thou me. Ps. 25:1, 2p., 4-9, 10, 11, 15, 21. 733

27. Protection. My heart shall not fear. Ps. 27:1, 3-5, 6p., 8, 13, 14. 724

Psalm	Group	Title	References	Page
28.	Rejoicing.	My heart greatly rejoiceth.	Ps. 28:7, 9.	684
29.	Praise.	Worship the Lord in the beauty of holiness.	Ps. 29:1, 2, 11.	743
30.	Gratitude.	Joy cometh in the morning.	Ps. 30:1p., 2-4, 5p., 7p., 11, 12.	699
31.	Gratitude.	O how great is thy goodness.	Ps. 31:19, 21p.	699
32.	Forgiveness.	Thou forgavest my sin.	Ps. 32:1, 2, 5, 7, 9p., 10, 11.	734
33.	Rejoicing.	Blessed is the nation.	Ps. 33:4-9, 11, 12.	684
34.	Guidance.	The Love of the Lord. (*Fear* to *Love*)	Ps. 34:11-15.	674
	Protection.	The Lord delivereth out of all troubles.	Ps. 34:17-22.	721
	Sustenance.	Magnify the Lord.	Ps. 34:1, 3, 4, 6, 7-10.	691
36.	Sustenance.	They shall be abundantly satisfied.	Ps. 36:6p., 7-10.	690
37.	*Guidance.*	*Fret not thyself.*	Ps. 37:1-11, 14, 15, 23-25, 27, 29, 31, 34p., 35-37.	675
39.	Guidance.	I will keep my mouth with a bridle.	Ps. 39:1p., 4-7, 8p.	676
40.	Gratitude.	The Lord hath put a new song in my mouth.	Ps. 40:1-3, 5-8.	700
	...iveness.	Hope thou in God.	Ps. 42:1-3, 7, 8, 11.	736
		...O send out thy light.	Ps. 43:3-5.	677
		...ery present help.	Ps. 46:1-11.	719
			Ps. 48:1-3, 9, 10, 14p.	743
		...raise glorifieth me.		745
		...God are a broken and a	...12, 15-17.	735
		...nischief.	Ps. 52:1-7.	678
				678
				692
		...e.	Ps. 56:1-4.	725
		... refuge.		738

Psalm Group Title References Page

60. Protection. God hath spoken in his holiness. 727
Ps. 60:6p., 10p., 11, 12p.

61. Protection. Thou has been a shelter for us. Ps. 61:1-4, 8p. 728

62. Sustenance. The Lord renders to every man according to his 693
work. Ps. 62:5-8, 11, 12.

63. Rejoicing. In the shadow of thy wings will I rejoice. Ps. 63:1-7. 687

64. Protection. Hide me from the secret counsel of the wicked. 728
Ps. 64:1-6, 8-10.

65. Sustenance. We shall be satisfied with the goodness of thy house. 694
Ps. 65:2, 4, 9, 10, 11p., 12p., 13.

66. Rejoicing. Make a joyful noise. Ps. 66:1, 2, 4, 5p., 7p., 8, 9. 683

67. Praise. Cause thy face to shine upon us. Ps. 67:1-6. 746

68. Rejoicing. Blessed be the Lord. Ps. 68: 6p., 19p., 20, 32. 685

69. Forgiveness. In the multitude of thy mercy hear me. 739
Ps. 69:1-3, 5, 13-17, 29p., 30.

71. Sustenance. I will go in the strength of the Lord. 695
Ps. 71:1, 2p., 3, 5, 9, 16-18, 23p., 24p.

72. Praise. Let the whole earth be filled with his glory.
Ps. 72:18, 19.

73. Humility. It is good for me to draw near to God.
Ps. 73:1-3, 7p., 21p., 22p., 23, 24p., 25, 26, 28.

75. Thanksgiving. God is the judge. Ps. 75:1, 6, 7.

84. Humility. The Lord will give grace and glor
Ps. 84:1-4, 5p., 10-12.

85. Sustenance. The Lord shall give that wh
Ps. 85:8-13.

86. Humility. Teach me thy way. Ps

89. Rejoicing. In thy name shall the
Ps. 89:8, 9, 11, 14-16, 52.

90. Humility. Let the beauty of
Ps. 90:1, 2, 4, 16, 17.

91. Protection. There sh

92. Thanksgiving. I

93. Protection.
of the sea

THE PROVERBS OF SOLOMON, THE SON OF DAVID, KING OF ISRAEL

SELECTIONS

ECCLESIASTES

THE SONG OF SOLOMON

LIST OF REFERENCES FOR

THE LIGHT SHINETH

The Word was made flesh and dwelt among us. – John 1:14.

Do Good on the Sabbath Days. Luke 6:9p. Page 854
Luke 6:1p. Matt. 12:1p. Luke 6:1p., 2, 3p. Matt. 12:3p., 4, 7. Mark 2:27p., 28. Matt. 12:9p., 10p. Mark 3:1p., 2p. (*they* to *scribes and Pharisees*). Matt. 12:10p. Luke 6:8, 9. Matt. 12:11p., 12. Mark 3:5p. Matt. 12:13p. Luke 6:11. Matt. 12:15, 22-27. Luke 11:20-26. Matt. 12:31-33. Luke 6:43, 44. Matt. 12:34-37. Mark 3:22p., 30p., 21. Luke 8:19. Mark 3:31p. Luke 8:20p., 21. Matt. 12:50. Mark 3:7p. Luke 6:12p., 13p. Mark 3:14p. Luke 6:14 (*sometimes called Nathanael,* added), 15, 16.

Blessed Are Ye. Luke 6:21p. Page 858
Luke 6:17p., 19. Matt. 5:1-28, 29p. Mark 9:47p. Matt. 5:30. Mark 9:45. Matt. 5:31, 32p. Mark 10:11, 12. Matt. 5:33-41. Luke 6:30. Matt. 5:42p. Luke 6:31. Matt. 5:43, 44. Luke 6:36p., 32-34, 35p. Matt. 5:45p. Luke 6:35p. Matt. 5:45p., 48. 6:1-4. Luke 6:38. Matt. 6:5-13, 16-18. 7:1, 2. Luke 6:37, 39p., 41, 42, 40. 11:34. Matt. 6:23p. Luke 11:35, 36. Matt. 7:6, 15-20. Luke 6:46. Matt. 7:21, 13, 14, 22, 23, 24p. Luke 6:47p., 48p. Matt. 7:25, 26p. Luke 6:49p. Matt. 7:26p., 27-29.

Speak the Word Only. Matt. 8:8p. Page 865
Matt 8:1, 5p. Luke 7:2, 3p. Matt. 8: 5p., 6-8. Luke 7:8, 9. Matt. 8:13. Luke 7:11-17.

That Which Is Born of the Spirit Is Spirit. John 3:6. Page 866
John 2:13-25. 3:1-21.

God Giveth Not the Spirit by Measure. John 3:34 (*The Father* to *God*). Page 868
John 3:35, 22. 4:2. 3:23p., 25-35, 36p. 4:1p., 3p. Luke 3:19p. (*tetrarch* to *king, him* to *John*), 20. Matt. 4:12, 23, 24. Luke 7:18, 19, 21-23, 24-27. Matt. 11:11p., 13, 14 (Elias to Elijah). Luke 7:31p., 32-35. Matt. 11:15. Luke 9:7p. (tetrarch to king). Mark 6:20p., 17p., 18, 19, 21p. (*was come* to *came*), 22p., 23, 24, 25p. Matt. 14:8p. Mark 6:26p. Matt. 14:9p. Mark 6:26p., 27p., 28, 29 (*his corpse* to *John*). Matt. 14:12p., 13p.

Worship the Father in Spirit and in Truth. John 4:23p. Page 871
John 4:3p., 4-43.

Go Thy Way, Thy Son Liveth. John 4:50p. Page 874
John 4:45-54.

The Seed Is the Word of God. Luke 8:11p. Page 875
Mark 4:1p. Matt. 13:2. Mark 4:2p., 3p. Luke 8:5p. Mark 4:4-7. Matt. 13: 8, 9. Mark 4:10p. Matt. 13:10p., 11-16. Luke 8:9. Mark 4:13. Matt. 13:18. Luke 8:11p. Matt. 13:19p. Luke 8:12p. Matt. 13:19-21 parts. Mark 4:17p. Matt. 13:21p., 22p. Mark 4:19p. Luke 8:14p. Mark 4:19p. Matt. 13:23p. Luke 8:15p. Matt. 13:23p. Mark 4:21p. Luke 8:16p. Mark 4:21p. Luke 8:16p. Mark 4:22. Luke 8:18p. Mark 4:24p. Luke 8:18p. Matt. 13:31p. Mark 4:26p., 27-29. Matt. 13:24-30. Mark 4:33, 34p. Matt. 13:35, 36p., 37p., 38-43.

Peace Be Still. Mark 4:39p. Page 879
Mark 4:35. Luke 8:22p. (*lake* to *sea*), 23p. Mark 4:37p. Luke 8:23p. Mark 4:38p. Luke 8:24p. Mark 4:38p., 39p. Luke 8:24p. Mark 4:39p. Luke 8:24p. Mark 4:39p. Matt. 8:27.

They Found the Man Clothed and in His Right Mind. Luke 8:35. Page 879
Mark 5:1p. Luke 8:26p. Mark 5:2p. Luke 8:27p. Mark 5:3-5. Luke 8:28. Mark 5:8. Luke 8:30p. Mark 5:9p. Luke 8:30p., 32p. Mark 5:12, 13, 14p. Matt. 8:34p. Luke 8:35p., 37p. Mark 5:18. Luke 8:38p. Mark 5:19p., 20.

The Damsel Is Not Dead. Mark 5:39p. Page 881
Mark 5:21p. Luke 8:40p. Mark 5:22, 23. Luke 8:42p. Mark 5:24-26, 27p. Matt. 9:20p., 21. Luke 8:44p. Mark 5:29p., 30p. Luke 8:45p., 46p. Mark 5:32, 33. Luke 8:48, 49. Mark 5:36. Luke 8:50p. Matt. 9:23p. Mark 5:38p., 39p. Luke 8:53. Mark 5:40p. Luke 8:51p. Mark 5:40p. Luke 8:54p., 55p. Mark 5:43p. Luke 8:56.

Wilt Thou Be Made Whole? John 5:6p. Page 882
John 5:1-47. 6:1.

Heal the Sick, Cleanse the Lepers, Raise the Dead . . . Matt. 10:8p. Page 885
Matt. 10:1. Luke 9:2. Matt. 10:2p., 3p., 4p., 5-8. Luke 9:3p. Matt. 10:9-20, 22, 24-26, 32, 33, 40-42, 27, 28p. Luke 12:6, 7. 9:6.

But One Thing Is Needful. Luke 10:42p. Page 887
Matt. 11:1p. Luke 10:38-42.

How Many Loaves Have Ye? Mark 6:38. Page 888
Luke 9:10p. Mark 6:30p., 31, 32p., 33p. Matt. 14:13p. John 6:5p. (*company* to *multitude*). Mark 6:34p. Luke 9:11p. Matt. 14:15p. Mark 6:35p., 36. Matt. 14:16. Mark 6:37p. John 6:7p. Mark 6:40. Matt. 14:19p. (*Jesus*, added), 20p. John 6:12. Matt. 14:20p., 21. John 6:14, 15p. Matt. 14:22p. John 6:17p. Matt. 14:22p., 23.

Jesus Came Unto Them Walking on the Sea. Matt. 14:25p. Page 890
John 6:16p., 17, 18. Matt. 14:24, 25p. John 6:19p. Matt. 14:26-32. John 6:21p. Matt. 14:33p. Mark 6:51p. Matt. 14:33p. Mark 6:54-56.

I Am the Living Bread. John 6:51p. Page 891
John 6:22p. (24-26 parts), 27, 28p., 29p., 30-33, 34p., 35-58, 60-63, 64p., 65p., 64p., 66-69.

The Things Which Defile. Matt. 15:20p. Page 894
Matt. 15:1p. Mark 7:2, 3, 4p., 5p. Matt. 15:2-5, 6p. Mark 7:12. Matt. 15:6p. Mark 7:13p., 9p. Luke 11:39p., 40. Matt. 15:7p., 8, 9. Mark 7:14p., 15. Matt. 15:12-14. Luke 11:45p., 46, 52-54. Mark 7:17. Matt. 15:16. Mark 7:18p., 19p. Matt. 15:17p., 18. Mark 7:21, 22, 23p. Matt. 15:20.

Be It Unto Thee Even As Thou Wilt. Matt. 15:28. Page 896
Matt. 15:21. Mark 7:24p. Matt. 15:22p. Mark 7:25p. Matt. 15:22p., 23-28. Mark 7:31p., 32-37. Matt. 15:29p., 30, 31. Mark 8:1p., 2. Matt. 15:32p., 33-39.

Beware of Hypocrisy. Luke 12:1. Page 898
Matt. 16:1, 2, 3p. Luke 12:54p., 55. Matt. 16:3p., 4p. 12:40-42. Mark 8:13. Matt. 16:6. Mark 8:14. Matt. 16:7, 8. Mark 8:17p., 18-20. Matt. 16:11p. Luke 12:1p., 2, 4, 5. Matt. 16:12. Mark 8:22-26.

Behold, I Give Unto You Power. Luke 10:19. Page 900
Luke 10:1-11. Matt. 10:15. Luke 10:13, 14. Matt. 11:23, 24. Luke 10:16-22. Matt. 11:28-30. Luke 10:23, 24. 17:22p., 23-25.

Lord, Teach Us to Pray. Luke 11:1p. Page 902
Luke 11:1, 2p. Matt. 6:10-13. Mark 11:25. Matt. 6:14. Mark 11:26. Matt. 6:5-8. 18:19, 20. Luke 11:5p., 6-11. Matt. 7:11, 12. Luke 17:5p., 6 (*Lord* to *Jesus*). Mark 11:24. Matt. 6:24, 25p. Luke 12:23. Matt. 6:26, 27. Luke 12:26. Matt. 6:28-31. Luke 12:30p. Matt. 6:32p., 33. Luke 12:32. Matt. 6:19-21. Luke 12:33p.

How Oft Shall I Forgive My Brother? Matt. 18:21p. Page 905
I John 2:11. Luke 17:1p., 3, 4. Matt. 18:15-18, 21-35.

Judge Righteous Judgment. John 7:24p. Page 906
John 7:1p. Mark 6:1 (*Nazareth,* added), 2, 3p. Luke 4:23. Mark 6:4p. Matt. 13:58. Mark 6:5p., 6. John 7:2-21, 23p., 24-38, 39p., 40-53. 8:1.

Ye Shall Know the Truth. John 8:32p. Page 910
John 8:2-13, 14p., 15-19, 23p., 24-26, 28p., 29-40, 41p., 42-59.

I Am Come That They Which See Not Might See. John 9:39. Page 913
John 9:1-13, 15, 14, 16, 17p., 18-38, 39p., 40p., 41. 10:1-21, 24-42.

I Am the Resurrection, and the Life. John 11:25. Page 919
John 11:1, 3-6, 7, 8, 16p., 9-15, 17-29, 31-50, 51p., 52, 53, 54p.

Whom Say Ye That I Am? Mark 8:29. Page 922
Mark 8:27p. Matt. 16:13-16, 17p., 18, 20. Mark 8:31. Matt. 16:22p., 23p. Mark 8:33p. Matt. 16:24p. Mark 8:34p. Luke 9:23p. Matt. 16:25, 26. Luke 9:26. Matt. 16:27. Luke 9:27. Mark 9:1p.

The Christ, the Son of the Living God. Matt. 16:16. Page 923
John 1:14p. Mark 9:2p. Luke 9:28p., 29p. Mark 9:2. Luke 9:29p. Mark 9:3p. Matt. 17:2p. Luke 9:29p., 30-32, 33p. Mark 9:6. Matt. 17:5p., 6, 7, 8p. Mark 9:8p. Matt. 17:9. Mark 9:10. Matt. 17:10-13. Luke 9:36p.

All Things Are Possible to Him That Believeth. Mark 9:23. Page 925
Matt. 17:20p. Luke 9:37p. Mark 9:14p., 15, 16, 17p. Matt, 17:14p. Luke 9:38p. Matt. 17:15p., 16, 17. Mark 9:20p., 21, 18p., 22p., 23, 24, 25p., 26, 27p. Matt. 17:18p. Luke 9:42p., 43-45. Matt. 17:19-21. Mark 9:38, 39. Luke 9:50p. Mark 9:41, 30.

Of Such Is the Kingdom of Heaven. Matt. 19:14p. Page 927
Matt. 17:24-27. Mark 9:33p., 34. Luke 9:47p. Mark 9:35p. Luke 22:25p., 26, 27; 17:7-10. Matt. 19:13. Mark 10:14-16; 9:36. Matt. 18:3p., 4. Mark 9:37. Luke 17:1p. Matt. 18:6, 10.

Forsake All, and Follow Me. From Luke 14:33 (reworded). Page 929
Mark 10:17. Matt. 19:17, 18p. Mark 10:19p. Matt. 19: 18p., 19, 20p. Mark 10:20p. Matt. 19:20p. Mark 10:21p. Matt. 19:21p. Mark 10:21p. Matt. 19:22p. Luke 18:23p. Matt. 19:22p. Mark 10:22p., 23, 24p., 25, 26. Luke 18:27. Mark 10:27p. Luke 18:28, 29. Matt. 10:37-39. Luke 18:29p., 30p. Mark 10:30p. Luke 18:30p. Matt. 19:28p., 29. Luke 14:27-33. Luke 9:57p. Matt. 8:19p., 20. Luke 9:59-62.

Beware of Covetousness. Luke 12:15p. Page 931
Mark 10:1. Luke 12:1p., 13-21; 16:14-17, 19, 20, 21p., 22-31, 1-13; 12:41, 42-48.

Thy Sins Are Forgiven. Luke 7:48. Page 935
Luke 7:36-50; 8:1-3.

Thou Art Loosed from Thine Infirmity. Luke 13:12. Page 936
Luke 13:10-17.

The Great Supper. Luke 14:16p. Page 937
Luke 14:1p., 2, 3p., 4-15, 16p. Matt. 22:2p. Luke 14:16p., 17-24. Matt. 22:8p.

The Son of Man Came to Save That Which Was Lost. Matt. 18:11. Page 939
Luke 15:1, 2. Matt. 18:11 (*And Jesus said*, added). Luke 15:3. Matt. 18:12. Luke 15:4p., 5p. Matt. 18:13p. Luke 15:6, 7. Matt. 18:14p. Luke 15:8-32.

The Kingdom of God Is Within You. Luke 17:21. Page 941
Luke 17:20, 21. 13:18, 19p. Matt. 13:32p. Luke 13:19p., 20, 21. Matt. 13:44-46. 20:1-16. 25:1-13. 13:47-49, 50p. Luke 13:23-30. Matt. 13:51, 52.

How Often Would I Have Gathered Thy Children Together. Luke 13:34. Page 945
Luke 13:31. 9.7 (*tetrarch* to *king*). Mark 6:14p. Luke 9:7p., 8p. Mark 6:16, 14p. Luke 13:32-35.

Love Is The Fulfilling of the Law. Rom. 13:10p. Page 947
John 18:37p.

On the Way Going Up to Jerusalem. Mark 10:32p. Page 949
John 11:55, 56p. Mark 14:1p., 2. John 13:1. Luke 9:51p. 13:22. Mark 10:32p. Matt. 20:17p. Mark 10:32p., 33p. Luke 18:31p. Matt. 20:18p., 19p. Luke 18:32p., 33. Mark 9:32. 10:35p., 37p., 38, 39p. Matt. 20:23p., 24-28. Luke 22:28-30. Mark 10:32p. Luke 17:11p. 9:52p., 53-56. 17:12-19; 18:35p. Mark 10:46p. Luke 18:36-39. Mark 10:49-52. Luke 18:43p. 19:1p., 2-12, 13p. Matt. 25:15-25, 26p. Luke 19:22p. Matt. 25:26p. Luke 10:23. Matt. 25:28, 30p., 29. Luke 19:28.

Mary Anointed the Feet of Jesus. John 12:3p. Page 954
John 11:18. 12:1, 2, 3p. Mark 14:3p. John 12:3p. Mark 14:4. John 12:4p., 5, 6. Mark 14: 6-9. John 12:9-11.

Hosanna in the Highest. Mark 11:10p. Page 955
John 12:12p. Luke 19:29p., 30p., 31. Matt. 21:3p. Luke 19:32-34. Mark 11:6p. Luke 19:35. Mark 21:4p., 5p. Luke 19:36-44. John 12:12p., 13. Mark 11:8-10. Matt. 21:10, 11. John 12:19-32 (some parts omitted), 34, 35, 36p. Matt. 21:12p. Mark 11:11p., 15p., 17p. Matt. 21:14-16, 23p., 24-33, 34p. Mark 12:2p., 3-5. Luke 20:13. Matt. 21:38, 39. Luke 20:15p., 16. Matt. 21:42-44. Mark 12:12p. 11:11p. Matt. 21:17p.

Which Is the Great Commandment? Matt. 22:36p. Page 960
Mark 11:12. Matt. 21:19p. Mark 11:14p., 15p. Luke 20:19p., 20p. Matt. 22: 15p. Luke 20:21. Matt. 22:17-22. Mark 12:18. Matt. 22:24. Mark 12:20-23. Matt. 22:29p. Luke 20:34p., 35, 36. Matt. 22:31p., 32. Luke 20:38p. Matt. 22:33, 34. Mark 10:2p., 3p., 4, 5p. Matt. 19:8p. Mark 10:6-9, 11p., 12. Luke 16:18p. Matt. 19:10, 11, 12p. 22:35p. Mark 12:28p. Matt. 22:35p., 36, 37p. Mark 12:29p., 30p. Matt. 22:38, 39p. Mark 12:31p. Matt. 22:40. Mark 12:31p. Luke 10:29-37. Mark 12:32, 33, 34p. John 12:37, 38, 42, 43. Mark 11:19. Matt. 21:17p.

His Commandment Is Life Everlasting. John 12:50. Page 964
Matt. 21:18p. Mark 11:20p., 21p., 22p. Matt. 21:21p. Mark 11:23p., 24, 27p. Luke 19:47p., 48p. 13:1p., 2p., 3-5. 18:1-5, 6p., 7, 8. 13:6-9. 18:9-14. 21:1-4. 20:1p. Matt. 22:41p., 42p. Luke 20:41-43. Matt. 22:45, 46. John 12:44-50. Luke 12:49-51p. Matt. 10:34p., 35. Luke 12:52. Matt. 10:36. John 12:36p. Mark 13:1p.

Watch and Pray. Mark 13:33p. Page 968
Mark 13:1p. Matt. 24:1p. Mark 13:1p. Luke 21:5p. Mark 13:1p., 2p. Luke 21:6p., 37p. Matt. 24:3p. Luke 21:7p. Matt. 24:4, 5. Mark 13:7p. Matt. 24:7. Mark 13:8p., 9p. Matt. 24:9. Matt. 13:9p. Luke 21:14. Mark 13:11p. Luke 21:15. Matt. 24:10. Mark 13:12. Luke 21:16p. Mark 13: 13p. Matt. 24:12, 13. Luke 21:19. Matt. 24:14, 15p. Mark 13:14p. Matt. 24: 17, 18. Luke 21:23p., 24p. Mark 13:18, 19. Luke 21:22. Mark 13:20-23. Matt. 24:29p. Mark 13:25. Luke 21:25p., 26. Mark 13:26, 27. Luke 21:28. Mark 13:28. Luke 21:31. Mark 13:29p., 31-33. Luke 17:26. Matt. 24:38p. Luke 17:27-30, 34-36. Matt. 24:42-44. Luke 12:35, 37, 38. 21:34-36. Mark 13:33, 35p., 36, 37.

For One Is Your Father Which Is in Heaven. Matt. 23:9p. Page 972
Luke 21:38. Matt. 23:1-9, 11-13, 16p., 14p., 23p. Luke 11:42p. Matt. 23:23p., 24p., 25p., 26, 27p., 28-36. 25:31-46. John 12:36p. Luke 22:39p. Matt. 26:3, 4. 21:46p. John 11:57. Luke 22:3, 4. Matt. 26:15p. Luke 22:5p. Matt. 26:15p. Luke 22:6.

I Am the Way, the Truth, and the Life. John 14:6. Page 976
Isaiah 35:8. Luke 22:7p., 1p. Matt. 26:17p. Luke 22:8, 10p., 11. Mark 14:15-17. Luke 22:14-16. Mark 14:22p. Luke 22:19p. Mark 14:23p. Matt. 26:27p., 28. Mark 14:25, 23p. John 13:2p., 3-9, 10p., 12-19, 21p., 22p. Matt. 26:22. John 13:26p., 27p., 28-30, 31p., 33-36. 14:1-26. 15:1-27. 16:1-4, 5p. 14:28-30, 31p., 27. 16:6-22, 23p., 24-33. 17:1-26. Mark 14:16p., 27-29p. Matt. 26:33p. Luke 22:33p. John 13:37p., 38p. Luke 22:34p. Mark 14:30p. Luke 22:34p. Mark 14:31p. Matt. 26:35p. Luke 22:31p., 32, 35, 36-38. John 14:31p.

Not My Will, But Thine, Be Done. Luke 22:42p. Page 987
John 18:1p. Matt. 26:36p. John 18:1p. Luke 22:39p. John 18:2. Luke 22:40. Matt. 26:36p., 37, 38, 39p. Mark 14:36p. Matt. 26:39p. Luke 22:42p., 45, 46p. Mark 14:37p. Matt. 26:40p., 41-43, 44p. Luke 22:44, 43. Matt. 26:45p. Mark 14:41p., 42, 43p. John 18:3p., 4, 5p., 6, 7. Matt. 26:48p. Mark 14:44p., 45. Luke 22:48. Matt. 26:50p. Luke 22:49p. (*they which were about him,* to *the disciples*). John 18:10p., 11p. Matt. 26: 52p., 53, 54p. John 18:11p. Matt. 26:54p. Luke 22:51p., 52, 53. John 18:8p., 12p. Matt. 26:57p., 56p. Mark 14:54, 55. Luke 22:56, 57, 58p. John 18:26, 25p. Luke 22:59p. Mark 14:70p. Matt. 26:73p., 74. Luke 22: 61, 62.

I Bear Witness Unto the Truth. John 18:37p. Page 990
Luke 22:66p. Matt. 26:59p., 60p. Mark 14:56p. John 18:19-23. Mark 14:60p. Luke 22:67p. Matt. 26:63, 64p. Luke 22:67p., 68-70. Matt. 26:64p., 65-68. 27:2-6, 7p., 9p., 7p., 8, 11p. (*Pilate,* added). John 18:28p., 29-31, 33-38. Matt. 27:18. Luke 23:5-10, 11p. John 19:1, 2, 3p. Matt. 27:30. John 19:4-11. Matt. 27:19. John 19:12p. Luke 23:13p., 14-19. Matt. 27:24, 25. Mark 15:12. Luke 23:21-25.

Truly This Is the Son of God. Matt. 27:54p. Page 996
John 19:16p., 17p. (*Golgotha,* inserted). Luke 23:27-31, 26, 32p., 33 (*malefactors* to *thieves*). Mark 15:28. Luke 23:34p. Matt. 27:37, 39-43. Mark 15:32p. Luke 23:39, 40p., 41-43. John 19:23, 24p., 25p., 26-28 (*Disciple* to *John*). Mark 15:36. John 19:30p. Luke 23:46p. John 19:30p. Luke 23:45p. Matt. 27:51, 45p., 54. John 19:32 (*thief,* inserted), 33, 34, 36, 37. Luke 23:48, 49. John 19:38p. Matt. 27:57p. John 19:38p. Matt. 27:60p. John 19:41p., 39, 40p. Luke 23:53p. John 19:41. Matt. 27:60p. Luke 23:54, 55p. Matt. 27:56 (*Zebedee's children* to *James and John*). Luke 23:55p., 56. Matt. 27:62p., 63-66.

I Ascend Unto My Father, and Your Father, My God, and Your God. John 20:17p. Page 1000
Matt. 28:1p., 2p., 3, 4. Luke 24:1p. Mark 16:1p., 2p., 3, 4 (order changed). Luke 24:3, 4, 5p. Mark 16:6p. Matt. 28:5p. Luke 24:5p. Matt. 28:6p. Luke 24:6p., 7. Mark 19:6p., 7, 8p. John 20:2-7, 11-17. Matt. 28:8p. Mark 16:10p. John 20:18p. Luke 24:11, 12p. John 20:3p. Luke 24:12p. John 20:4p. (*that other disciple* to *John*). Luke 24:12p. John 20:4p., 5, 6p., 7. Luke 24:12p. (*they,* added). Matt. 28:11p., 12-14, 15p. Luke 24:13-17, 18p., 19-35. Matt. 28:16. John 20:19p. Luke 24:37-43. John 20:20p. Luke 24:45, 44, 46p., 47. Acts 1:6p., 7, 8. John 20:21, 24p., 25-29. I Cor. 15:6p. Acts 1:2p., 3p. John 21:1-7, 8p., 9-13, 15-18, 19p., 20p., 21-23. Luke 24:50. Mark 16:15, 17, 18. Matt. 28:20p. Luke 24:48. Matt. 28:19. Luke 24:49p. Matt. 28:18p. Luke 24:49p. Acts 1:5. John 20:17p. Matt. 28:20p. Luke 24:51. Acts 1:9p., 10, 11. Luke 24:52, 53p. John 21:25. John 20:31.

The Spirit of Truth. John 15:26p. Page 1009
John 15:26p. 16:13p. 14:18, 27.

ACTS

THE ACTS OF THE APOSTLES

I THESSALONIANS

II THESSALONIANS

THE ACTS OF THE APOSTLES (*Continued*)

GALATIANS

THE ACTS OF THE APOSTLES (*Continued*)

FIRST CORINTHIANS

SECOND CORINTHIANS

THE ACTS OF THE APOSTLES (*Continued*) Page 1101

ROMANS

THE ACTS OF THE APOSTLES (*Continued*)

PHILIPPIANS

Let This Mind Be in You Which Was Also in Christ Jesus. Page 1147
Phil. 1:1p., 2-4, 6, 7p., 8p., 9-18, 21-25, 26p. 2:1-16, 19-21, 23, 24p. 3:1-21. 4:1, 4, 5p., 6-20.

COLOSSIANS

Set Your Affections on Things Above, Not on Things on the Earth. Col. 3:2. Page 1153
Col. 1:2-6, 9-16, 19, 21, 22, 23p., 25, 26. 2:1-10, 16, 17p., 18, 20p., 21, 22. 3:1-25. 4:1-9, 14, 16-18.

PHILEMON

Receive Him As a Brother Beloved. Phile. 1:16p. Page 1158
Phile. 1:1p., 3-5, 7p., 9-11, 12p., 13p., 14, 15p., 16-19, 21, 22, 25.

TITUS

A Pattern of Good Works. Titus 2:7. Page 1160
Titus 1:4, 5p., 6-11, 12p., 13-16. 2:1-15. 3:1-15.

I TIMOTHY

Lay Hold on Eternal Life. I Tim. 6:12. Page 1163
I Tim. 1:1p., 2. 2:1p., 2-6, 8. 4:1, 2. 1:8. 6:3-11, 17-19, 12-16, 20, 21p., 1:17.

II TIMOTHY

God Hath Given Us the Spirit of Power, And of Love, And of a Sound Mind. II Tim. 1:7. Page 1165
II Tim. 1:2, 7. 2:1, 2, 7, 15, 16, 19-25. 3:1-7, 9p., 10-17. 4:1-9, 10p., 11, 16-18, 21p., 22.

EPHESIANS

Put On the Whole Armour of God, That Ye May Be Able to Stand. Eph. 6:11. Page 1168
Eph. 1:1p., 2-4, 7, 8, 15-17, 18p., 19p., 20, 21p., 22p. 2:1-10, 11p., 12p., 13, 18-22. 3:1, 2p., 3p., 5p., 6p., 7p., 8, 14, 16p., 17-19. 4:1-8, 11-13, 17, 18, 22-25, 26p., 27, 28, 29p., 31, 32. 5:1, 2p., 3, 4p., 6-18, 20-22, 23p., 25, 28p., 29, 31-33. 6:1-4, 5p., 6-17, (18, 19 reworded), 20, 21, 22p., 23p., 24. 3:20, 21.

HEBREWS

The New Covenant. Heb. 8:10. Page 1175

The Word of God Is Quick and Powerful, and Is a Discerner of the Thoughts and Intents of the Heart. Heb. 4:12. Page 1177
Heb. 1:1, 2p., 3, 4p., 5p., 8p., 9, 13, 14. 2:1-4, 10, 11, 12p., 14p., 15-18. 3:1-8, 12-15, 16p., 19. 4:1, 2, 3p., 6p., 9, 11, 12.

Christ, an High Priest of Good Things to Come. Heb. 9:11. Page 1179
Heb. 4:14-16. 5:1, 4-6, 8-10, 11 (*uttered* to *understand*), 12p., (*since,* added), 13, 14p. (*full of age* to *full grown men*). 6:1p., 2-12, 18p., 19, 20. 7:1-4, 5p., 6, 11-17, 18 (reworded), 19, 22, 24p., 25, 26p., 27p., 28p. (*consecrated* to *perfected*). 8:1, 2, 6p., 7-12, 13p. 9:1p., 11-14, 15p., 24p., 25, 26p., 28p. 10:1, 2p., 3-6, 7p., 9p., 10-12, 15p., 16-18.

Now Faith Is the Substance of Things Hoped for, the Evidence of Things Not Seen. Heb. 11:1. Page 1185
Heb. 10:19-23, 35-39. 11:1-3, 4p., 5-11, 12p., 17-19, 23-27, 29, 30, 32-37, 38p. 12:1-7, 9p., 10, 11, 13-15, 18, 19, 20p., 21, 22, 24p., 25p., 26-29. 13:1, 2, 3p., 5, 6, 9p., 8 (*is,* added), 15, 20, 21, 25.

LETTERS OF JAMES Page 1191

Be Ye Doers of the Word. James 1:22. Page 1193
James 1:2-8, 12-17, 19-27.

Respect of Persons. James 2:1. Page 1194
James 2:1-5, 6p., 8-12, 13p.

Faith Without Works Is Dead. James 2:26. Page 1195
James 2:14-24, 26.

Offend Not in Word. James 3:2. Page 1196
James 3:2p., 3-18.

From Whence Come Wars? James 4:1. Page 1197
James 4:1-5, 6p., 7-12. 5:9. 4:17.

Prayer Availeth Much. James 5:16. Page 1198
James 5:13-20.

JUDE, THE SERVANT OF JESUS CHRIST AND BROTHER OF JAMES Page 1199

Unto Him That Is Able to Keep You From Falling. Jude 1:24 Page 1201
Jude 1:1-3, 4p., 10, 11p., 12, 13, 16-18, 19 (reworded), 20p., 21-25.

LETTERS OF SIMON PETER. I, II Peter. Page 1203

Be Ye Holy. I Peter 1:16. Page 1205
I Peter 1:2p., 3, 4, 6-8, 13-19, 22-25. 2:1-5.

By Your Good Works, Glorify God. I Peter 2:12. Page 1206
I Peter 2:9p., 11, 12, 15, 18-23, 24p., 25p. 3:8p., 9-18. 4:1p., 7, 8p., 9-13, 14p.
5:2-4, 6-11.

Be Partakers of the Divine Nature. II Peter 1:4. Page 1209
II Peter 1:2-11, 16-21. 2:1, 2, 3p., 17, 21. 3:1p., 2-4, 8-14, 17, 18.

LETTERS OF JOHN, THE BELOVED DISCIPLE. I, II, III John. Page 1213

I Write Unto You . . . I John 2:13p., 14p., 13p., 1:4.

Light. I John 1:5p. Page 1215
I John 1:5 (order changed), 6, 7p. 2:8-11.

Spirit. I John 4:2. Page 1216
I John 4:1-5, 6p., 13. 5:6p.

Life. I John 1:1. Page 1217
I John 1:1, 3, 2. 5:11-13, 20. 2:25.

Truth. I John 5:6. Page 1218
I John 2:20, 21, 7, 3, 4, 5p. 3:19, 22. 4:6. 5:6p.

Love. I John 4:8. Page 1219
I John 4:7-10, 13, 16-19. II John 6.

Love one Another. I John 4:7. Page 1220
I John 4:11, 12, 20. 3:15p. 2:11. 3:11, 17. 4:21. 5:2, 3. 3:18.

Love Not the World. I John 2:15. Page 1221
I John 2:15-17.

He That Doeth Good Is of God. III John 1:11p. Page 1222
I John 2:1-3. 3:7, 9p., 10p. 5:17p. 3:4. 2:4, 6. 3:6. III John 1:11.
I John 2:28p. 3:22.

Jesus Christ, the Son of God. I John 5:20. Page 1223
I John 4:14, 15. 5:1p., 4, 5, 10. 2:22, 23. 5:20. 2:24.

Now Are We the Sons of God. I John 3:2. Page 1224
I John 3:1-3.

REVELATION

BOOKS OF THE BIBLE

THE OLD TESTAMENT

THE NEW TESTAMENT

*See Isaiah in Glossary.

BIBLIOGRAPHY

King James Version. The Holy Bible, containing the Old and the New Testaments. Thomas Nelson and Sons. No date.

Cruden, Alexander. Cruden's Complete Concordance to the Old and New Testaments. The John Winston Co., Philadelphia, Pa. c. 1930.

Strong, James. Exhaustive Concordance of the Bible. Abingdon-Cokesbury Press. New York – Nashville. c. 1890. Fourteenth printing 1943.

Peloubet, F. N. Peloubet's Bible Dictionary. John Winston Co., Philadelphia, Pa. c. 1947.

Webster's New International Dictionary of the English Language. Second Edition. Unabridged. G. & C. Merriam Company, Publishers, Springfield, Mass. 1950.